KT-522-650

THE
BIG
BASICS
BOOK OF

Bexley Library Service
Reference Library

BEXLEY LIBRARY SERVICE		
LOC CR	Cl. No. 004.16 BUC	
PRICE 18.40	ACC DATE 18.1.99	BKS DW
COLL CODE REF	ITEM LOAN TYPE REF	
KEYER YC	LANG	CH	PR

25/1/99

WITHDRAWN
FROM
STOCK

Second Editon

by Lisa A. Bucki, Jennifer Fulton,
and Ed Guilford

30109 0 14428935

©1997 QUE® Corporation

All rights reserved. No part of this book shall be reproduced, stored in a retrieval system, or transmitted by any means, electronic, mechanical, photocopying, recording, or otherwise, without written permission from the publisher. No patent liability is assumed with respect to the use of the information contained herein. While every precaution has been taken in the preparation of this book, the publisher and author assume no responsibility for errors or omissions. Neither is any liability assumed for damages resulting from the use of the information contained herein. For information, address Que Corporation, 201 West 103rd Street, Indianapolis, IN 46290. You can reach Que's direct sales line by calling 1-800-428-5331.

Library of Congress Catalog Card Number: 97-68092

International Standard Book Number: 0-7897-1339-X

99   98   97   8   7   6   5   4   3   2

Interpretation of the printing code: the rightmost double-digit number is the year of the book's first printing; the rightmost single-digit number is the number of the book's printing. For example, a printing code of 97-1 shows that this copy of the book was printed during the first printing of the book in 1997.

Screen reproductions in this book were created by means of the program Collage Complete from Inner Media, Inc, Hollis, NH.

Printed in the United States of America

President
Roland Elgey

Senior Vice President/Publishing
Don Fowley

Publisher
Joseph B. Wikert

Publishing Director
Brad R. Koch

General Manager
Joe Muldoon

Editorial Services Director
Elizabeth Keaffaber

Managing Editor
Thomas F. Hayes

Acquisitions Editors
Jill Byus
Nancy Maragioglio
Martha O'Sullivan

Senior Product Director
Lisa D. Wagner

Product Development Specialist
Melanie Palaisa

Production Editor
Audra Gable

Web Master
Thomas H. Bennett

Product Marketing Manager
Kourtnaye Sturgeon

Product Marketing Manager
Grechen Schlesinger

Technical Editors
Rick Brown
Nadeem Muhammed
Coletta Witherspoon

Media Development Specialist
David Garratt

Technical Support Specialist
Nadeem Muhammed

Acquisitions Coordinator
Michelle R. Newcomb

Software Relations Coordinator
Susan D. Gallagher

Editorial Assistants
Jeff Chandler
Virginia Stoller
Jennifer L. Chisholm

Book Designer
Barb Kordesh

Cover Designer
Jay Corpus

Production Team
Trey Frank
Heather Howell
Anjy Perry
Nicole Ruessler
Julie Searls
Sossity Smith
Lisa Stumpf

Indexer
Greg Pearson

We'd Like to Hear from You!

QUE Corporation has a long-standing reputation for high-quality books and products. To ensure your continued satisfaction, we also understand the importance of customer service and support.

Tech Support

If you need assistance with the information in this book or with a CD or disk accompanying the book, please access Macmillan Computer Publishing's online Knowledge Base at:

http://www.superlibrary.com/general/support

Our most Frequently Asked Questions are answered there. If you do not find the answer to your questions on our Web site, you may contact Macmillan Technical Support by phone at **317/581-3833** or via e-mail at **support@mcp.com**.

Also be sure to visit QUE's Desktop Applications and Operating Systems team Web resource center for all the latest information, enhancements, errata, downloads, and more:

http://www.quecorp.com/desktop_os/

Orders, Catalogs, and Customer Service

To order other QUE or Macmillan Computer Publishing books, catalogs, or products, please contact our Customer Service Department:

Phone: 800/428-5331
Fax: 800/835-3202
International Fax: 317/228-4400

Or visit our online bookstore at **http://www.mcp.com/**.

Comments and Suggestions

We want you to let us know what you like or dislike most about this book or other QUE products. Your comments will help us to continue publishing the best books available on computer topics in today's market.

Lisa Wagner, Senior Product Director
QUE Corporation
201 West 103rd Street, 4B
Indianapolis, Indiana 46290 USA
Fax: 317/581-4663
E-mail: **lwagner@que.mcp.com**

Please be sure to include the book's title and author as well as your name and your phone or fax number.

We will carefully review your comments and share them with the author. Please note that due to the high volume of mail we receive, we may not be able to reply to every message.

Thank you for choosing QUE!

Contents

Part 1   How to...

Part 2   Do It Yourself...   271

Make Your Computer Work Faster and Better   337

Install New Hardware   365

Keep Your Data Safe   399

Work on the Internet   423

Part 3   101 Quick Fixes

Part 4   Buyers Guide...   519

Software Buyer's Guide   521

Introduction

You've avoided it whenever you could. You've dreaded it and tried to fake it. You've pretended that your kids and acquaintances aren't a little bit ahead of you. But you've finally accepted it. The computer age is here, and it's knocking at your door.

Welcome to *The Big Basics Book of PCs, Second Edition*. This book gives a gentle, thorough introduction to personal computers (PCs). It doesn't try to teach you a little bit about a lot of topics. It doesn't try to make you an expert in the span of 400 pages. It doesn't try to teach about things you'll use once in a computing lifetime (such as how to create a spreadsheet program for calculating the circumference of a circle).

Instead, *The Big Basics Book of PCs, Second Edition* provides complete information on all the features and tasks that you need and want to know. It zeroes in on the tasks that are essential for your computer survival, and teaches each one in simple, picture-by-picture steps. Like the visual books you've used to learn how to cook or how to add a deck to your house, this book offers concise, informal steps highlighted by clear illustrations that show you exactly what to do next. You'll learn how to do all of these things—and more!

- Buy the computer that's right for you, and how to set it up. You'll conquer your anxiety about dealing with the hardware, and your computer will enjoy a long, useful life, because you'll clean it like a pro and add new upgrades whenever they hit the market.

- Conquer Windows, the best thing to ever happen to PCs. Although the little pictures in Windows may seem obscure and confusing, you'll soon be navigating Windows with no problem.

- Make peace with DOS, your computer's Disk Operating System. Even though you may not have to use it often, you'll benefit by knowing the tricks of the trade for communicating in DOS's secret code.

- Communicate with the outside world. Send and receive mail electronically. Get the latest news and stock quotes. Search for facts or shop. Take advantage of popular online services like America Online and CompuServe. And, jump onto the biggest part of the Information Superhighway, commonly called the Internet.

- Choose the programs you need and see how to get them up and running on your system.

- Find out the best way to fix common problems when they crop up.

What's New in This Edition?

The computing world evolves at light speed, so a lot has changed since we published the first edition of this book. We've covered the major new developments for you in the pages that follow.

Most significantly, Microsoft released an update to its blockbuster Windows 95 software. This update, called OEM Service Release 2 (OSR 2) or Windows 95B, has been shipping (installed) on new computers since the fall of 1996. OSR 2 contains many new feautures, and we've highlighted the key ones for you.

Unless you've been living under a rock, you know that Internet connections have become a significant part of home computing in the last two years. OSR 2 offers some new features to reduce the hassle of setting up your Internet connection, and we teach you about them in the last section of Part 1. We've also greatly expanded other Internet coverage. You'll see here how to browse the Web and manage your e-mail with the top Internet software products.

How Can I Find What I Need in This Book?

To make it easy to use, we've divided The Big Basics Book of PCs into four distinct parts. Each part keys in on a particular type of information and presents that information in the best format for beginners. You don't need to read the book from cover to cover if you don't want to. You can just skip to whichever section you need.

Part 1: How To covers all the skills that a new or casual computer user needs. It only takes a few pages to explain each operation, but you get all the facts and advice you need. A clear illustration accompanies almost every step, and you're told when another part of the book offers even more information about a topic.

Part 2: Do It Yourself also offers illustrated steps for particular operations. This part, however, covers practical projects you can use to hone your skills and get more productive with your computer.

Part 3: 101 Quick Fixes anticipates the inevitable, identifying the problems every computer user will encounter and offering the simplest and most durable solutions for those problems. Scan the Quick Finder Table to find your problem quickly.

Part 4: Buyer's Guide highlights a sampling of the thousands of computer programs that are now available. This part focuses in on the most popular and useful programs, giving you the lowdown on each so you can see if it's for you—before spending any money for it. The Buyer's Guide also provides information about hardware manufacturers and Web sites, to give you leads in shopping for hardware.

Conventions, Conventions, Conventions

This book was specially designed to make it easy to use. Each task has a title that tells you what you'll be doing. Immediately following the title is text that tells you why you might want to perform the task and provides additional details on what to do. Each task then provides at least one *Guided Tour*, which shows you step-by-step how to perform the task. The following figure shows you the format of the book.

Tips provide shortcuts or reference other useful information. Additional information answers all your questions. Running heads help you find what you want to learn. The *Guided Tour* shows you how to complete a computer task step-by-step.

The following special conventions were used to make the book easier to use:

Text you are supposed to type appears bold. For example, if the step says, type **win** and press **Enter**, type the command "win" and press the **Enter**, key on your keyboard.

Keys you are supposed to press are bold, too, to make them easier to spot.

Key+Key combinations are used when you have to press two or more keys to enter a command. When you encounter one of these combinations, hold down the first key and press the second key.

Menu names and **commands** you need to choose are also bold. When you're told to open a menu and select a command, move the mouse pointer over it, and press and release the left mouse button.

Running heads help you find what you want to learn.

Tips provide shortcuts or reference other useful information.

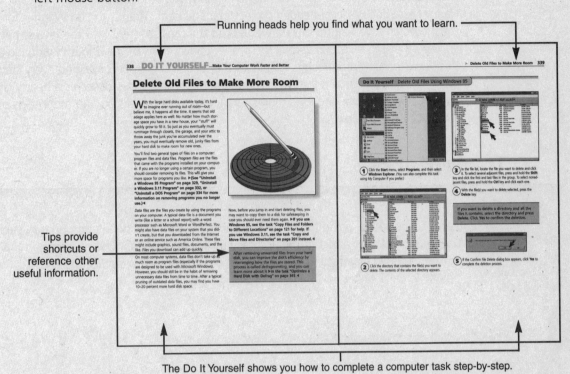

The Do It Yourself shows you how to complete a computer task step-by-step.

Look for these sidebars for tips, hints, and shortcuts.

In Conclusion...

Even if you think using a computer is as fun as having your toenails pulled out, you can learn something from this book. It makes the computer learning curve as painless as possible, so you can become as confident as the next person (or your kid) when you use your computer. And so, on to the action!

Acknowledgments

No book is an individual project. Special thanks to the many people who initiated the project—Martha O'Sullivan, Angie Wethington, Jill Byus, Henly Wolin, and Melanie Palaisa. Several people rolled up their sleeves to hone this material, and we're indebted to them, as well. We appreciate Nancy Maragioglio's level-headed project management. Thanks to Lisa Wagner for pulling together the pieces and working to ensure we packed the most content into the fewest pages. Audra Gable ensured that the text followed all the proper conventions of the English language and shepherded this book through production. Thanks to the technical editors for testing every step and checking every screen shot. Finally, the Que Production department also deserves a hearty cheer (and a caffeine subsidy) for working long nights to transform stacks of text and mountains of figures into an attractive bound book.

Trademarks

Terms suspected of being trademarks or service marks have been appropriately capitalized. Que Corporation cannot attest to the accuracy of this information. Use of a term in this book should not be regarded as affecting the validity of any trademark or service mark.

PART 1

How To...

Have you ever tried to pound in a nail with a screwdriver? If you have, you know that it usually doesn't work out very well. (And you know that screwdriver handles are not shatterproof.) You have to choose the right tool and use it correctly to get the job done.

This part of *The Big Basics Book of PCs, Second Edition* introduces you to what could become one of the most important tools in your life: your computer. You'll learn how to buy the computer that's right for your needs and how to set it up. After that, this part explains how to take command of your computer, from handling the hardware to developing good computing habits (like saving your work so you can change it later or use it again). Finally, you can take a crack at exploring the Information Superhighway. You'll see how you can connect with other computers all over the world.

Even if you've never been able to pound in a nail without bending it, the computer is one tool you'll soon master. With this part of the book (and a little practice to build your confidence), you'll be ready to tackle any computing project.

What You Will Find in This Part

HOW TO...

Buy and Set Up a Computer

These days, it's as convenient to buy a computer as it is to buy a pair of jeans. You can walk into any one of hundreds of office, computer, appliance, or department stores; plunk down a credit card; and walk out with a couple of boxes of computer equipment.

Even though it's convenient, buying and setting up a computer isn't always easy. You may not know what size you need or what to do to make your computer as comfortable as a second skin.

The first few tasks in this book will help you with the process. You'll learn what you can do with a computer, how to select a computer that meets your needs, and how to set it up so it not only works correctly but is also convenient and comfortable to use.

What You Will Find in This Section

Decide What You Want to Use the Computer For

Before you buy a computer, you need to ask yourself the same kinds of basic questions you'd ask before buying a car or house. Consider this question first: "What am I going to use it for?"

If you're buying a computer for your home and family, you can use it for entertainment, education, keeping track of personal finances, and more. You can also use your computer to work at home, write letters, do your taxes, or run a small business.

When you're thinking about what you want to do with the computer you're about to buy, take a look at different *software programs*. Each type of program gives your computer the instructions to get a particular job done. You'll find programs you want to start using right away and others you may want to experiment with in a few months or when the need arises. Either way, knowing what types of programs you want to use will help you decide what kind of computer to buy. Each piece of software requires particular pieces of computer hardware (*components*). Deciding on the software first can help you make a list of just the components you'll need and how powerful they need to be.

If you want to check out some different programs without schlepping to your local computer store, ▶see the "Software Buyer's Guide" beginning on page 521.◀

Guided Tour Types of Programs

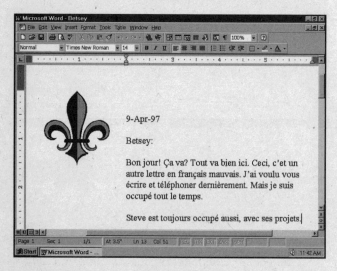

Process words. Use a *word processing* program to type, edit, and apply attractive formatting to text.

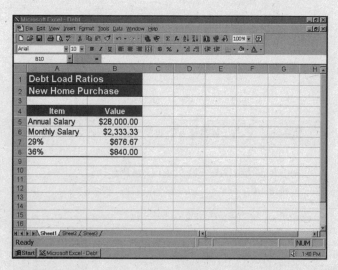

Crunch numbers. Use a *spreadsheet* program to organize numbers in a grid and use formulas to perform calculations.

Guided Tour Types of Programs

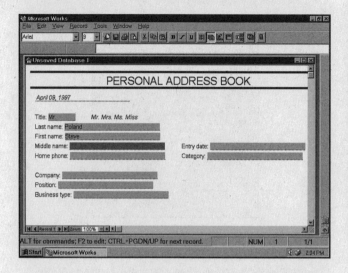

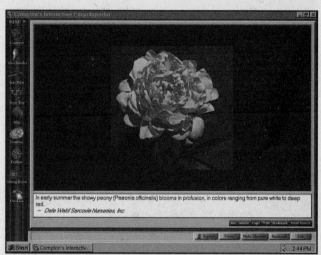

Manage data. Use a *database* to store and sort lists of information, such as phone lists and home inventories.

Educate and entertain. Have fun (mindless or otherwise) searching for treasure, learning from an illustrated online encyclopedia, and more. Today's more powerful computers have led to elaborate computer games, educational programs, and entertainment resources that use pictures, animation, and sound.

Multimedia programs combine text, pictures, sound, full-motion video, and animation.

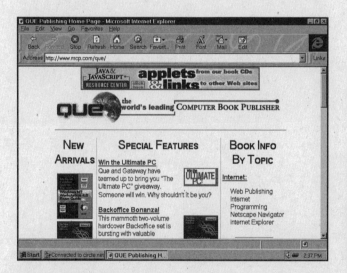

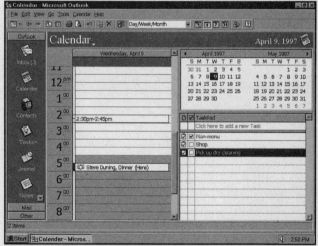

Communicate. Use a piece of hardware called a *modem* with your computer to transmit data over phone lines. You can send and receive faxes and electronic mail (*e-mail*), chat with other users, or access a wealth of data available through online services and the Internet.

Manage time, money, and more. Use computer programs to organize your time, manage your contacts with others, or even write checks and budget your money. Specialized programs can help you track your diet or fitness level and even plan landscaping and home renovation projects.

(continues)

Guided Tour Types of Programs   (continued)

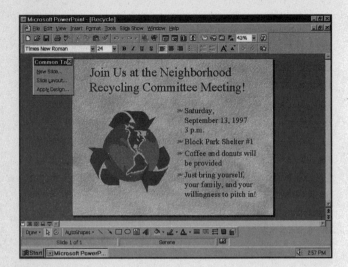

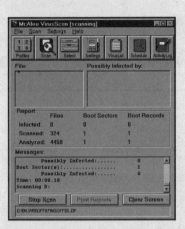

Present and publish information.   Use a *presentation graphics* program to create presentations and pages that convey a message with style or grab attention. Use a *desktop publishing* program to create newsletters, flyers, and other publications. Other programs let you create and work with drawings and *fonts* (fancy lettering). You can even capture, edit, and print digital photos and video.

Maintain your computer and its files.   Use utility programs to back up files, check for *viruses* (data-destroying programs that can infect your computer anonymously), compress or zip files so they take up less disk space, and perform more disk-management activities to keep your computer healthy.

Look at Software Requirements

After you've chosen the software programs you want to use, you'll need to figure out how powerful your computer has to be to run them. The programs you want to run may also require you to have certain other kinds of software on your computer. Fortunately, software publishers give you a hand with figuring out what your program needs by providing you with a list like the one shown here.

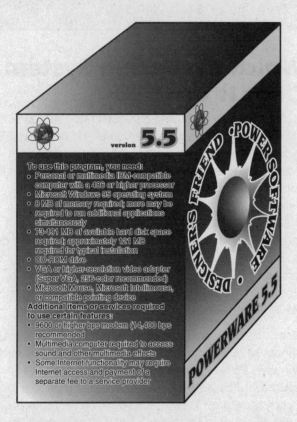

Check the software product box for a section labeled something like "Recommended Hardware and Software Requirements" or "To use this program, you need…" This section usually appears on the side or back of the box, and it tells you several important things (such as whether the program requires Microsoft Windows 95). Don't worry if you don't understand some of the techie terms you find on the box (or, for that matter, in this task). You'll learn more about Windows 95 later in this part of the book, and you'll learn more about *hardware*—the actual computer components—in the next task, "Decide What Kind of Computer You Want."

The system you buy should be able to run the software you choose and meet its most demanding minimum requirements for hardware and software. You can't take the requirements for all the software programs and somehow "average" them.

> More and more often, computers are coming packaged with a wealth of software (you'll learn more about this in the task "Decide Where to Buy It," later in this section). If the software program you want to use comes with the computer, rest assured that the computer can run it.

Here are the requirements you need to consider; they're outlined on the package for each software program you purchase.

What Type of Computer Do You Need?

To run software created for a Macintosh computer, you must have a Macintosh, commonly called a "Mac." To run software created for an IBM-compatible (Windows-compatible) computer, you need that kind of computer. IBM- or Windows-compatible computers are generally called PCs.

How Powerful Must the Computer Be?

Usually the box will tell you what kind of *central processing unit* (the *CPU* or "brain") your computer needs to have. This is designated by a number for the CPU such as "386" or "486." In general, a higher number indicates a more powerful processor, but different CPU manufacturers use slightly different numbering systems (such as the Cyrix 6x86). The leading CPU manufacturer, Intel, calls its most common desktop processor the *Pentium* rather than referring to it by number (although you'll sometimes see the Pentium called a "586"). Intel also offers two even more powerful CPUs: the Pentium Pro and Pentium II. So far, these two CPUs are sold mostly in high-end business systems, but Pentium Pro or Pentium II systems may eventually become the most common systems offered at your local computer store. If you're buying a system with a CPU made by AMD, Cyrix, or IBM/Cyrix, the CPU will usually be compared with a Pentium or Pentium Pro.

Your computer's CPU must be *at least* as powerful as the one required. If you have any doubts about how the processor will work, ask the retailer to show you how the software you want runs on a system with a processor like the one you're considering buying. A number such as "133MHz" or "160MHz" indicates how fast the processor is. Higher numbers designate faster processors. Many PCs have the processor type and speed stamped on the front.

Do You Need a Multimedia or Business System?

Most PC manufacturers give you the choice between two broad categories of IBM-compatible systems. The first category, *business* or *workstation* systems, includes systems that are very powerful and may be set up to connect to a network of other computers. The other, *multimedia* or *home* systems, include special components for handling sound and more intensive video (features of many home-oriented programs such as games or educational software).

Oddly enough, a few years ago, the typical business system had more bells and whistles than most home systems. Today, the reverse is often true. Businesses seek more cost-effective, straightforward systems because business users don't necessarily need to run multimedia components included in business software. So some business systems may come without certain multimedia components or may have less powerful multimedia components. In contrast, home consumers seek a system that can handle a wide range of software and serve family educational and entertainment needs for several years. So home-oriented systems do include multimedia and communications capabilities.

Some CPUs now offer *MMX technology*. CPUs with MMX are optimized for running multimedia applications and, therefore, offering faster multimedia playback than standard CPUs. However, when manufacturers introduce any new hardware technology, the software makers need to catch up. At the time of this writing, most applications can't yet take advantage of MMX capabilities. So before you pay the extra $200 or so for an MMX system, make sure the software you want to run requires it or that there's a good chance you'll need the MMX capabilities later.

Which Operating System Does It Use?

Most of you will be buying computers that run under the operating system called *Windows 95*. Windows 95 includes an underlying version of MS-DOS, the *Disk Operating System* from Microsoft that provides basic control of your computer. If your computer uses Windows 95, don't buy programs made for the OS/2, UNIX, or System 7.6 (Macintosh) operating systems. If you have a computer that's running an older version of DOS and Windows 3.11, make sure you have the right version of DOS to run the program. For example, if a program requires MS-DOS 5.0 to run, you must have MS-DOS with version number 5.0 *or higher*.

Many newer programs need to be run under Microsoft Windows 95. In addition to the Disk Operating System, Windows 95 is a *graphical user interface (GUI)*. It's called a GUI because you use a mouse and on-screen *graphics* (pictures) known as *icons* to control your computer, as opposed to a simple blank screen where you type arcane commands.

New systems shipping from manufacturers today have a more recent version of Windows 95 called OEM Service Release 2 (OSR 2), or Windows 95 B. This update of Windows 95 better manages large hard disk drives (where files are stored), power management features, and more. If you buy a new system, make sure it has OSR 2 installed. If the system you're considering has an older version of Windows and DOS installed along with Windows 95, the Windows 95 version may not be OSR 2, so you might want to reconsider the purchase decision.

How Much Memory and Storage Should the Computer Have?

Random-Access Memory, or *RAM*, holds the instructions and data you're working with while your computer is turned on. When you install a program and save your work, both are stored on the computer's *hard drive*, a semipermanent storage area that lets you access the program or data later. Programs require a minimum amount of RAM to run correctly. They also take up a certain amount of storage space on the hard drive; make sure you have enough hard drive space available to install the program.

What Kind of Input Device and Monitor Are Needed?

Some programs require a mouse for selecting commands; you can work better with many game programs using an alternative device called a joystick. The

software box will say which is best. Monitors (and the internal *video cards* they connect to) come in several flavors, depending on the *resolution* each provides. The two types of monitors sold with most new systems today, from lowest to highest resolution, are VGA (Video Graphics Array) and SVGA (Super VGA). Programs with generous graphics generally require better-resolution monitors such as Super VGA.

Are There Optional Programs or Equipment that Can or Should Be Used?

Some programs may require a sound card and speakers to take full advantage of the program's features. Most communications programs require a modem or fax/modem; if any special equipment is required or recommended, the software box will usually say so. Some programs also require that you have a particular Windows 95 component (such as Windows networking capabilities) or some other type of software (like a page layout program) installed.

If your computer doesn't meet the minimum requirements, the software may run unreliably or may not run at all. Even if your computer meets the minimum, the program may not run to your satisfaction. Often the system that runs the program best has requirements that exceed those on the software box. The next task, "Decide What Kind of Computer You Want," gives guidelines for selecting a system that will run most software—and run it well.

Guided Tour How to Read a Software Product Box

To use this program, you need:
- Personal or multimedia IBM-compatible computer with a 486 or higher processor
- Microsoft Windows 95 operating system

1 What type of computer do you need?

2 How powerful must the computer be?

3 Which operating system does it use?

- 8 MB of memory required; more may be required to run additional applications simultaneously
- 73-191 MB of available hard disk space required; approximately 121 MB required for typical installation
- CD-ROM drive

4 How much memory and storage should the computer have?

5 What kind of disk drive is needed for the setup disk(s)?

- VGA or higher-resolution video adapter (Super VGA, 256-color recommended)
- Microsoft Mouse, Microsoft Intellimouse, or compatible pointing device

6 What kind of mouse and monitor (video capabilities) are needed?

Additional items or services required to use certain features:
- 9600 or higher bps modem (14,400 bps recommended)
- Multimedia computer required to access sound and other multimedia effects
- Some Internet functionality may require Internet access and payment of a separate fee to a service provider

7 Are there optional programs or equipment that can or should be used?

Decide What Kind of Computer You Want

Once you've chosen the software you want to use (and know its hardware and software requirements), you should have a good starting point for choosing a computer. Before you go shopping, make a list of the minimum requirements you want your computer system to have. Today, most manufacturers offer fully equipped home multimedia systems, each of which has most of the components described next. These packages are very comparable in price and performance, so your decision may come down to being based on one or two minimum requirements from your list.

Your budget also has an impact on your computer purchase decisions. Obviously, there's no need to mortgage your house to buy a top-of-the-line setup, but you also don't want to buy a system that'll be obsolete as soon as you bring it home. Allow yourself room to grow with your computer. As a rule of thumb, decide what system you need now, add $500 to your budget, and then buy a system that's faster than the one you need now and has more memory and storage space.

This task reviews the components you need to make decisions about selecting the computer system you want. The *Recommendations* you find here are designed to give you a system that will serve you well through the next few years.

If you travel for business, consider a notebook (sometimes called *laptop*) computer that's compact and folds open like a notebook. Convenience comes at a price, though. Notebooks cost at least $1,000 more than comparable desktop systems.

System unit: All instructions flow through the components in this box. The system unit of a traditional desktop PC has a fairly large *footprint*, which means it takes up a lot of desk space. *Tower* units stand vertically and can be tucked away under a desk. Many manufacturers are moving toward selling tower units or slightly shorter *minitower* units only.

Central processing unit (CPU): This chip executes commands and controls the flow of data. A two-part name like "Pentium, 133MHz" identifies most CPUs. The first part ("Pentium") indicates the type of CPU the system has. The second part in the processor's name (such as "133MHz") indicates the CPU's speed; higher is better. *Recommendation*: Pentium 166MHz, with MMX if you plan to run a lot of games or multimedia CD-ROMs.

Most systems feature CPUs made by the market leader, Intel. However, two rival companies offer CPUs designed to compete with the Pentium. AMD offers the K5 and K6 CPUs, and Cyrix offers the 5×86 and 6x86 CPUs (sometimes along with IBM). These companies claim their CPUs actually run faster than Pentium chips with a comparable speed. (Several computer magazines use special testing software to compare CPU speeds.) That may be true, but don't base your purchase decision on CPU speed and power alone. Consider the full system package and the reputation of the manufacturer. The AMD and Cyrix chips often power systems offered by less-established, smaller manufacturers.

Random-access memory (RAM): A computer's RAM consists of a bank of chips that act as "working memory," holding program instructions and data only while your computer's on. Unless the instructions and data are saved to a disk, RAM forgets them when you turn your computer off. RAM is measured in *megabytes* (*M*). Each M represents over one million characters of data. Most computers today come with 16M of RAM. There are a few different flavors and speeds of RAM, as well. One of the most prominent today is Extended Data Output (EDO) RAM, but an even faster type of RAM that has just hit the market is called SyncDRAM. You also will hear about what's called a *cache* when you hear about RAM. A cache is an extra holding area for program instructions that need to be frequently swapped in and out of RAM; your system can access those instructions from the cache more quickly than it could from a hard disk, so a cache helps RAM work more effectively. The smallest cache size used is 256K. *Recommendation*: 32M EDO RAM, 512K cache.

Hard disk drive: Your computer stores information semipermanently on the *hard disk* (also called the *hard disk drive* or *hard drive)*, which consists of several metal disks in an airtight case. You can save programs and data on the hard disk and then later delete them to reuse the space they occupied. Hard disk capacities are measured in megabytes (1,000M equals a *gigabyte*, or *1G)*. A too-small hard drive limits the number of programs you can install; these days the minimum is usually 1.2G. You also want to consider a hard drive's *access time*. A slow hard drive can slow down your whole system, no matter how fast the processor is. A lower access time indicates a faster drive (10ms is faster than 12ms). Most drives available today are Enhanced IDE (which are faster than the older IDE drives), but some systems come with faster SCSI hard drives. *Recommendation*: 2.5G, with 12ms access time or better.

Floppy disks and other removable disk drives: Like a hard drive, any removable disk lets you store data and program instructions semipermanently. The difference: *Floppy disks* or *removable disks* store data on portable disks or cartridges you can slide in and out of a slot in the system unit or the drive unit. Older floppy disk drives used flexible 5.25-inch disks, which are now almost obsolete. Recent floppy drives use 3.5-inch HD (high-density) disks that hold 1.44M of data; these have hard plastic shells that protect your data better. Other types of removable disk drives include the 100M Zip drive and 1G Jaz drive (created by Iomega) and 230M EZFlyer and SyJet 1.5G (from SyQuest). At this point, you have to add most of these removable disk alternatives after you purchase a system, but some systems now include a Zip drive for extra removable storage. *Recommendation*: One 3.5-inch high-capacity drive.

CD-ROM drive: This drive uses lasers to read a *CD-ROM* (*Compact Disc Read-Only Memory*). Like audio CDs, CD-ROMs are 4.5-inch metallic-looking platters. Each disc can hold more than 650M of data. Most new systems come with an internal CD-ROM drive, and they are also optional on most laptop models. The effectiveness of a CD-ROM drive depends on its access *time* and *transfer rate*—how fast it can get and deliver information. Look for a high transfer rate (in kilobytes per second) and a small access time (in milliseconds). Relative drive speed is generally referred to in shorthand, with "Single-speed" or "1X" representing the speed of the original drives on the market. *Six-speed* (6X) CD-ROM drives (which are about six times as fast as 1X drives) are common now, and the fastest drives are 16X. Recommendation: 8X or faster.

Monitor: The monitor displays your program and data visually (like a TV screen) and connects to a graphics card inside your computer. The monitor's *resolution* must match that of the card. New monitors sold today use VGA (Video Graphics Array) and SVGA (Super VGA). Also consider some basic numbers: Most monitors can display in several *dots-per-inch* (*dpi*) modes, from 640×480 up to 1280×1024 or more; *dot pitch* (the distance between dots) should be as small as possible. Also, the graphics card contains its own RAM (which may be described as VRAM, DRAM, or EDO RAM); make sure you have enough, particularly if you plan to run multimedia applications. A graphics card also displays images more quickly using what's called 64-bit PCI local bus video, and will handle multimedia better if it supports 3-D graphics. Most new systems now adhere to this minimum standard. *Recommendation*: Monitor: 15-inch color SVGA(1024 x 768 dpi),.28mm dot pitch, non-interlaced. Graphics card: 3-D graphics, 64-bit PCI local bus, 2M RAM.

Keyboard/mouse/joystick: These devices let you control the computer by giving your input. Enter characters with the keyboard; use the mouse to point to things on-screen, click to make selections, and drag items from place to place; use a joystick to control computer games. Choose a device that operates smoothly and feels comfortable. If you have wrist and hand problems, consider a trackball (which looks like an upside-down mouse and is less fatiguing) or an ergonomic keyboard; several manufacturers offer these products for your comfort. *Recommendation:* Keyboard with numeric keypad, Microsoft-compatible mouse, joystick only for game use.

Expansion slots: These slots within the system unit enable you to plug in additional circuit boards (expansion boards or expansion cards) for new devices, such as a scanner, that you add to your computer. You'll need these to add components to or upgrade your computer, especially if you don't buy a computer that's multimedia-equipped. *Recommendation:* At least five expansion slots (two ISA slots for older expansion boards and three PCI slots for current and future technology).

Ports: Use these receptacles (on the back of your system unit) to plug in equipment like printers. Most computers now come with separate mouse, keyboard, and monitor ports. *Parallel* ports are usually for plugging in printers; *serial* ports connect a mouse, an external modem, or a printer designed to be used with them. Some computers also provide special game ports for plugging in joysticks. *Recommendation:* One port each for keyboard, mouse, and monitor, plus one parallel and one serial.

Bus type: Data travels in a computer along circuits called *buses* on the computer's main circuit board (the *motherboard*). Although three main buses (data bus, address bus, and control bus) manage the computer's operation, often these are collectively called *the bus*. The now-standard *PCI Local Bus* carries data along at least 32 lines, that is, 32 bits at a time. *Local bus* computer designs add more buses so the system can communicate directly with components like the monitor, resulting in much better performance. New systems also should support Universal Serial Bus (USB), a new type of bus for connecting peripheral devices to the system. *Recommendation:* PCI Local Bus, USB-enabled, with enhanced IDE interface (used for the hard disk drive).

Printers: Printers make *hard copies* (printouts) of your work in black and white or color. *Inkjet* or *bubblejet* printers blow liquid ink at the page in precise patterns, creating characters on single sheets of paper. *Laser* printers, generally more expensive, use an electrically charged drum to transfer *toner* (dry ink) onto paper. Inkjet printers offer lower resolution (dpi), and laser printers offer the best (up to 1200 dpi). But entry-level prices for inkjet printers are attractive, at around $200 for black and white and $300 for color, which makes them economical and versatile

printers. *Recommendation:* Color inkjet printer with 720×720 dpi.

Modems: These devices let computers communicate and transfer data over phone lines. With a modem, you can exchange electronic mail and files with other computer users, send and receive faxes (if you have a fax/modem), talk with others over the phone (for voice-capable modems) or use the (voice-capable) modem as a phone messaging system, and connect to online services or the Internet to gather information. Modems can be *internal* (on a card inside the system unit) or *external* (a box connecting to an expansion card). Modems transfer data at a rate measured in *bits per second* (*bps*); higher numbers mean a faster modem. Features that help a modem work faster include data compression and error correction (indicated with "V." plus a number and perhaps "*bis*"). Modems that have *data compression* make the data more compact before sending it (so they can send more of it), and they *decompress* data when they receive it. *Error correction* means your modem automatically senses mistakes in data and retransmits it as needed. *Recommendation:* 33,600bps internal data/voice/fax modem.

You may see or hear two new modem buzz words as you shop. The first is "x2." This is a standard from U.S. Robotics that makes modems capable of downloading at about 56,000 bps. A couple of cautions are in order, though. First, not all online services and Internet connections let you take advantage of this technology. So make sure you need and can use the faster download speed before you pay for it. Second, some modems actually need to be upgraded to the x2 standard, which right now costs about $60.

The other new modem buzz word is "VoiceView." This technology lets a modem handle regular voice calls, for hands-free phone conversations. It also enables the modem to do two things at once, like show video while you talk so you can video conference. VoiceView is a nice feature for home office systems and is now included in many system packages without a significant price difference when compared to systems without a VoiceView-capable modem.

Sound cards, speakers, and microphones:
These enable your computer to play and record
sound. The *sound card* plugs into a slot in the system unit; it runs speakers, a microphone, and
even specialized music equipment that uses MIDI
(Musical Instrument Digital Interface). Most sound
cards offer 16-bit sound quality and provide a
kind of output called *wavetable*. The more
wavetable "voices" the card offers, the higher its
quality. Cards with 32 and 64 voices are now on
the market. In addition to a MIDI/game port, the
card should offer 3-D Surround Sound. For
smooth operation, a sound card also should offer
its own RAM module. Your card should be compatible with the popular Sound Blaster card.
Recommendation: 32-voice wavetable, 3-D surround Sound-Blaster-compatible sound card with
MIDI/game port and 512K RAM module; 10-watt
speakers.

Scanners: Scanners use light to convert an optical
image to a digital image you can view or save
using your computer. You can choose either a
hand-held scanner (which you drag over the
image much like a mouse) or a *flatbed* model that
looks and works much like a photocopier. Color
and *grayscale* (black-and-white) models are available; higher resolution (more dots per inch—higher dpi) produces crisper images. Special scanner
models are designed specifically for scanning color
photos into your system; some of these are
installed right in the system unit or on the system
monitor. *Recommendation:* Optional. Home users
can get away with a hand-held 400-dpi color
scanner or photo scanner; professional publishers
should choose color flatbed units with 1000-dpi
resolution.

Digital cameras and video cameras: The next
part of our home lives that's "going digital" is
photography and video recording. Starting at

about $500, you can add a digital camera to your
system. These cameras look and snap photos
much like familiar 35mm cameras; instead of storing the images on film, however, they store the
digital images in memory cards in the camera until
you download them to your computer via a connection to a special card you install. Once you
copy a digital photo to your system, you can edit
and print it just as you would any graphic image.
These cameras capture in varying resolutions and
color depths, and they can hold varying numbers
of images—all depending on how much memory
the camera has.

Digital video cameras are still a bit primitive. While
these aren't yet suited for capturing home movies,
you can use them to make video conference calls
(if your system also has a voice-capable modem)
or to grab still images. These small cameras cost a
few hundred dollars and connect to a video capture card installed in your system; they can be
mounted on top of the monitor. For video confer-
encing, other users must have a camera and software that's compatible with yours. However,
there's not much variation between models at
this point. *Recommendation (Digital camera):*
640×480 resolution or better, 24-bit color (16.7
million colors), stores 60 images at standard resolution, expandable storage.

Surge suppressors and UPSs: *Surge suppressors*
protect against sudden spikes in power, which can
zap your computer and data. They also give you a
strip of additional plugs for your computer's components. (Be careful: Not *all* plug-in strips are
surge suppressors.) A UPS (*uninterruptible power
supply*) feeds electrical current to your computer
in the event of a power loss (commonly called a
brownout) that could cause data in RAM to be
lost. *Recommendation:* Surge suppressor.

Guided Tour   Computer Components

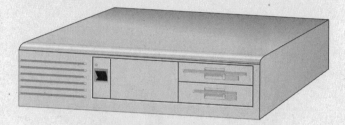

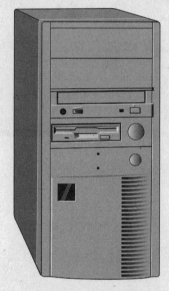

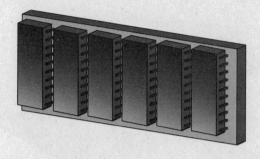

Random-access memory (RAM): A computer's RAM consists of a bank of chips that act as "working memory," holding program instructions and data only while your computer's on.

System unit: All instructions flow through the components in this box. (The lower picture shows a tower unit.)

Hard disk drive: Your computer stores information semipermanently on the *hard disk drive*—several metal disks in an airtight case.

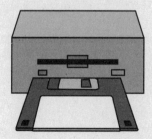

Central processing unit (CPU): This chip executes commands and controls the flow of data.

Floppy disk and other removable disk drives: Like a hard disk drive, this drive lets you store data and program instructions semipermanently. The difference: Floppy disk and other removable drives store data on portable *floppy disks* or cartridges you can slide in and out of a slot in the system unit.

(continues)

Guided Tour Computer Components *(continued)*

CD-ROM drive: This drive uses lasers to read a *CD-ROM* (*Compact Disc Read-Only Memory*). Each disc can hold more than 650M of data.

Keyboard/mouse/joystick: These devices let you control the computer by giving your input.

Monitor: The monitor displays your program and data and connects to a graphics card inside your computer.

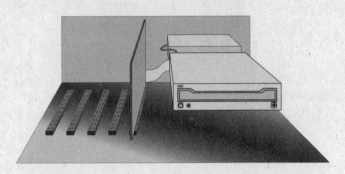

Expansion slots: These slots within the system unit enable you to plug in additional circuit boards (expansion boards or expansion cards) for new devices, such as a scanner, that you add to your computer.

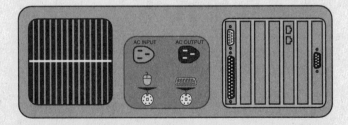

Ports: Use these receptacles (on the back of your system unit) to plug in equipment like printers.

Bus type: Data travels in a computer along circuits called *buses* on the computer's main circuit board (the *motherboard*).

Guided Tour Computer Components

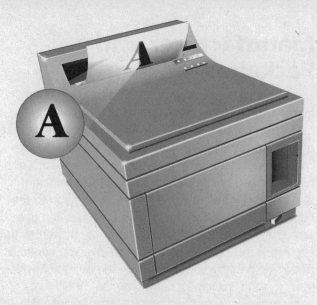

Printers: Printers make *hard copies* (printouts) of your work in black and white or color.

Modems: These devices let computers communicate and transfer data over phone lines.

Sound cards, speakers, and microphones: These enable your computer to play and record sound.

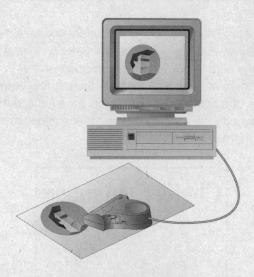

Scanners: Scanners use light to convert an optical image to a digital image you can view or save using your computer.

Digital cameras and video cameras: Digital cameras capture photos as graphic images that you can store, edit, and print with your computer. Video cameras enable you to capture still shots, too, or even hold a video conference (along with a voice-capable modem).

Surge suppressors and UPSs: Surge suppressors protect against sudden spikes in power, which can zap your computer and data. They also give you a strip of additional plugs for your computer's components. A UPS (uninterruptible power supply) is a battery that provides a current flow of electricity to your computer, even when there's a power outage.

Decide Where to Buy It

One final decision awaits you before you take the plunge and buy your new computer. You have to choose where to buy it, and this decision isn't as straightforward as it may seem. In the last few years, dozens of manufacturers and sellers have jumped into the fray, offering a variety of computer components through retail and mail outlets.

Chet's Computers

6 Months Same As Cash!

✓ **Complete Pentium systems**
✓ **Prices start at $1,499**
✓ **One year on-site warranty on parts and service**
✓ **We repair and upgrade systems**

12 E. 10th, 555-4321

Where you decide to buy your computer depends not only on the kind of computer you want to buy, but also on your computing confidence and what you expect to happen after the sale. Computer magazines and your local newspaper offer advertisements for a variety of computer sellers. While the ads may look the same, there are great differences in what you get from various computer sellers.

When you choose where to buy your computer, compare factors like price, service, and warranty. Be sure you're comparing apples to apples where possible— compare prices on systems from the same manufacturer with the same features, or on comparable services. Here are the primary factors to consider.

Manufacturer and Packages

Make sure you're buying a computer from a reputable manufacturer. Go to the library and check computer magazines such as *PC World* to find the top brands that offer the most reliable products. Most sellers offer *preconfigured* systems with everything you need (such as a fully equipped multimedia package). Also compare the free software offered with a system. In addition to the basic operating system, many manufacturers and dealers include hundreds of dollars' worth of software with every new system. This software can save you hundreds of dollars (because you won't have to purchase it yourself), so shop around for a package that offers the applications you want and need. Most packages also include a starter membership with one or more online services or *Internet service providers* (ISPs), companies that provide access to the Internet. However, you can usually get free membership startup deals directly from online service or ISPs, even if they don't come with your computer.

Pricing

In the last two years, computer pricing has become much more comparable between the various computer sellers; catalogs and manufacturers don't necessarily offer the best prices. Sometimes, you can get the best deal when an appliance store puts a model on sale or offers a rebate. Compare prices from a few sources and make sure you're getting the best deal. Verify whether certain extras and necessities are included in the price; sometimes shipping, printer cables, or even the monitor will cost extra.

Financing

Department stores, appliance stores, and computer discount stores frequently offer financing or special deals like "six months same as cash" (in addition to credit card purchasing). Be careful with store financing: interest rates can be as high as credit card rates—or higher. Mail-order catalog companies, manufacturers, and VARs typically let you use a credit card to purchase your computer.

Where You Can Buy Your Computer

Seller	Description
Catalog companies	Sell equipment and software from a variety of manufacturers. Offer convenience but minimum of service or technical support (for the catalog brands). Purchase with credit card. For more experienced users.
Manufacturer direct	Manufacturer sells its own equipment by phone, mail, or the World Wide Web. Convenient, with competitive pricing and warranty. Purchase with credit card. Knowledgeable sales staff. For experienced users or those who want to purchase a particular brand.
Appliance/department store	Offer computers alongside other electronic equipment. Typically, selection, service, and the salesperson's knowledge are limited, although financing may be offered. For moderately experienced users.
Computer discount stores	These computer superstores offer the broadest selection and best pricing available from retailers. Knowledgeable sales force and financing help smooth the sale. Most offer carry-in repair and upgrade service. Inexperienced users can comfortably buy a computer here.
Value-added resellers (VARs)	These sellers include small retail computer stores and companies that sell computers direct to businesses. Typically, their salespeople are most knowledgeable, and they offer the highest level of after-sale service. Many perform warranty work for computer manufacturers. All this service costs more, though. For very inexperienced users, businesses, or those who want to purchase a high level of after-sale support.

Warranty and Return Policy

Most manufacturers offer a warranty (one year minimum) on parts and labor. Generally, the warranty covers *on-site* repairs—a repair representative will come to you to fix your system. However, in some cases, you'll need to transport the system to the store where you purchased it (or to an authorized dealer), or you might have to ship it (or a component) back to the manufacturer for repair. Appliance and department stores, computer superstores, and VARs all let you buy an extended warranty that covers the system up to three years, starting when the manufacturer's warranty expires. Most warranties require that repairs or upgrades be performed by an authorized dealer; using any other repair service (or doing it yourself) voids the warranty.

If you decide that a computer doesn't meet all your needs or that you don't need the system for some reason, most sellers offer some type of return policy. Usually, you can return the entire system within 30 days of purchasing it. You'll be required to return the system in its original packaging in most instances. If you purchased the system from a manufacturer or mail order catalog, you may need to pay to return the system. Be sure you understand the seller's return policy.

Service

You can purchase additional computer services (for example, upgrading your system) from computer superstores, VARs, and computer repair companies. In general, a computer superstore's fees will be much lower than a VAR's or repair company's.

The superstore requires you to carry your system in, while a VAR or repair company will come to you (for a fee, of course). Superstores offer some services (such as adding a modem to your system) at a flat rate rather than an hourly fee. And if the technician encounters a problem while performing the service, you don't have to pay for extra time used to fix the problem. Be sure to have an authorized dealer perform repairs and upgrades to your system if it's still under warranty.

Guided Tour   Things to Look for When Buying a Computer

Chet's Computers

6 Months Same As Cash!

✓ **Complete Pentium systems**
✓ **Prices start at $1,499**

Manufacturer and packages: Make sure you're buying a computer from a reputable manufacturer.

Pricing: Compare prices from a few sources; make sure you're getting the best deal.

Financing: Be careful with store financing; interest rates can be as high as credit card rates—or higher.

✓ **One year on-site warranty on parts and service**
✓ **We repair and upgrade systems**

Warranty and return policy: Most manufacturers offer a warranty (one year minimum) on parts and labor; the maximum is three years.

Service: You can purchase additional computer services (for example, upgrading your system) from computer superstores and VARs.

Decide Where to Put a New Computer

Like any tool, your computer requires that you observe a few guidelines to use it comfortably and safely. Following these rules will prolong the life of your computer by protecting it from damage.

You should be particularly careful about where you place a computer within your home. Let common sense guide you. If the computer is for your whole family, put it in a room where you can easily supervise the kids while they use it. Make sure the kids can seat themselves at it comfortably without grabbing or leaning on any of the components. If you'll be using your home computer for business, put it in a more secluded spot (such as a den or home office) where you can have solitude while you work.

Likewise, you should use common sense with regard to what you place on and around your computer. Avoid bringing beverages around your computer; a spilled drink can fry a keyboard or burn up a CPU. You don't want to pile a ton of books on your system unit or get crumbs in a disk drive. You should also avoid smoking around your computer; smoke residue can clog and gunk up your disk drives. (If the keyboard keys get coated with dirt, you can unplug the keyboard from the system and clean it with a sparing application of distilled water.)

Following are the common-sense guidelines you need to follow in deciding where to put your computer:

> Use a computer desk and comfy chair. You need a wide, stable surface for your system unit, monitor, and printer. And make sure you have a comfortable chair with good support and adjustable height. Computer desks or workstations can be an economical solution. Prices range from around a hundred dollars to a couple thousand for decorator-style units. Your best bet is to visit an office, computer, or furniture store (instead of shopping from a catalog) and try out several computer desk and chair models before you buy. The extra comfort will be well worth the extra shopping time. Also, keep in mind how much equipment you have. If you've added a scanner or have a large printer, some workstations and computer desks won't offer enough surface space.

Keep it cool and dry. Excessive heat can damage your computer, particularly the hard drive. Likewise, humidity (or worse, dripping water) can zap your computer or make it behave erratically. Avoid placing your computer in damp areas like basements, hot rooms like attics, or other areas that aren't air-conditioned. Don't place the computer in front of a window that receives heavy direct sunlight, which can overheat the system and cause uncomfortable glare. Also, make sure there are several inches of clearance behind the system unit so its exhaust fan can draw in fresh air to cool the computer when it runs.

Avoid dust and pet hair. The system unit's fan tends to suck in dust along with fresh air; sliding a disk into a drive can push in dirt and hair as well. Keep the area around your computer free from dust, hair, or equipment that attracts either of these (like a clothes dryer). If you can't avoid dust, consider buying plastic dust covers for your system components.

Provide proper lighting. Place your computer so the room's light source is above and slightly behind the monitor. Improper lighting that falls on the monitor from the front or sides causes glare and reflections on the monitor, which can strain your eyes and make the screen hard to read.

Use a stable electrical outlet. Never plug your computer into an outlet that's on a household circuit used by other appliances—even small ones like a toaster or blow-dryer. These can suck current away from the computer, causing power drops that will make the system lose data.

Put a modem-equipped computer near a phone line. If your computer system has a modem, be sure to put the system near a phone jack or a location where one can be installed.

Keep it away from family traffic. Use common sense. Don't place the computer where anyone can trip over the power or mouse cords, put the groceries down on the keyboard accidentally, throw things at the monitor, or the like.

Guided Tour Set Up Your Work Environment

① **Use a computer desk and comfy chair.** Make sure the chair gives you adequate back support and height, so that your hands reach the keyboard at a comfortable angle. Also be sure the computer desk or workstation offers a shelf for the keyboard and ample space for all your hardware.

② **Keep it cool and dry.** Excessive heat can damage your computer, particularly the hard disk drive. Likewise, humidity (or worse, dripping water) can zap your computer or make it behave erratically.

③ **Avoid dust and pet hair.** The system unit's fan tends to suck in dust along with fresh air; sliding a disk into a drive can push in dirt and hair as well.

④ **Provide proper lighting.** Place your computer so the room's light source is above and slightly behind the monitor.

⑤ **Use a stable electrical outlet.** Never plug your computer into an outlet that's on a household circuit used by other appliances.

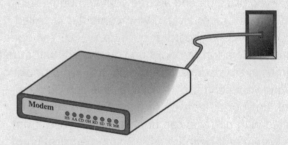

⑥ **Put a modem-equipped computer near a phone line.** If you'll be a heavy modem user, you may want to have a second phone line installed with a jack (plug) for it near your computer. As an alternative, you can buy an inexpensive device that enables you to plug both a phone and a modem into a single jack so you can use each one as needed; keep in mind, however, that you can't use the phone and modem simultaneously under this arrangement.

⑦ **Keep it away from family traffic.** Use common sense. You know where your home's traffic areas are.

Because computers use a lot of electricity, they tend to attract a lot of dust and pet hair. These can cause wear on your computer's parts—or even errors—if they get sucked into a disk drive. ▶**For information on keeping your computer happy and dust-free, see "Keep Your Computer Clean and Healthy" on page 273.**◀

Unpack and Check a New Computer

Bringing home a new computer can be like getting a much-anticipated gift. You're tempted to just rip into the package and whoop it up. While there's no need to be a total party-pooper, resist the temptation to rip into your computer packages and burn the refuse.

Use a reasonable amount of care when unpacking your system to avoid damaging any of the components. Also, take the time to do things that will ensure you can take advantage of your computer's warranty: Register the system and (horrors) keep a few things you would normally throw out. The *Guided Tour* explains the process.

> The advice in this task also applies when you purchase upgrades or replacements for individual pieces of hardware. ▶**Take the steps recommended here before performing any of the operations described in the section "Install New Hardware" on page 365.◀**

Guided Tour   Inspect Your New Computer

1 Carefully open the boxes containing the computer components by pulling the outside tape. Avoid slitting the box with scissors or a knife, which can scratch the components.

2 Remove each component from its box, placing it carefully on a computer desk or other flat, secure surface. Place any paperwork from the boxes in a handy location nearby. Also remove any cardboard protectors from the floppy disk drives. Check the box carefully for all cables, manuals, screws, and other vital items from the manufacturer. You don't want to pack away or accidentally discard anything you might need to properly set up and run your computer.

3 Return all cardboard, Styrofoam, and plastic packing materials to the boxes, including the floppy disk protectors. Store the boxes in a safe, dry place. You'll use these if you ever need to transport the computer. (Also, some companies will not allow returns unless the computer is packed in its original boxes.)

Chet's Computers
Packing Slip

Order #	Order Date	Ship Date	P.O. Number
123-777	6/6/97	6/10/97	784-335

Quantity	Description	Price
1	Pentium 133 with 2.5G hard drive, 16M RAM	$1,499.00
1	15" SVGA monitor	499.00
1	InkJet Printer	399.00
Tax and shipping:		139.85
Total:		$2,536.85

4 Take the packing slip or receipt from the pile of papers you put aside and check it to make sure you received all the pieces you paid for. Review the setup instructions quickly.

Have you received all the connectors you need? If something's missing, contact the seller immediately.

5 Inspect all components for damage. If you find problems, call the seller immediately.

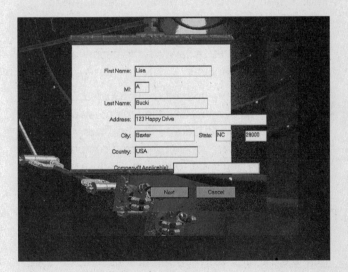

6 Fill out and mail your Registration Card. Alternatively, some manufacturers provide an online registration process that begins automatically when you start the computer the first time. If you want to get technical support from the manufacturer or seller, you must follow its registration process.

7 Take all the paperwork that came with your computer—packing slip, invoices, receipts, and warranty information—and file it with your other important personal papers.

Connect the Components

If you can plug in an electrical cord, you can connect a computer system's components. It's all a matter of plugging the right connector into the right socket. The sockets and connectors have similar shapes (and corresponding numbers of holes and pins), so matching them up is easy. Some computer manufacturers even label the various sockets on the back of the system unit for you.

Just remember, if you feel you're having to force a connector into position, back off. You may be trying to plug it into the wrong socket, and you may risk breaking pins off the connector if you force it. One more tip: Avoid getting magnetic or electrical fields too close to the computer (don't even use magnetic-head screwdrivers), and *don't turn on any component until you have the whole system assembled and you have plugged the system into a surge protector.*

You may need a few tools to assemble your computer. These are primarily used to tighten connectors into place. So before you start, gather up a medium-sized Phillips-head screwdriver, a medium-sized flat-head screwdriver, and a small flat-head screwdriver. Also grab a small envelope or plastic baggie for leftover screws and the like; file these away with the paperwork that came with your computer.

One last thing before you follow the *Guided Tour* for assembling your system: Take the time to lay out all the parts where you want them so that you won't have to untangle cables after you've connected components. For example, if you want to place the mouse to the right of the keyboard and the printer somewhere to the left (or the reverse if you're left handed and want your mouse on your left), arrange them that way before making the connections.

Here are the basic assembly instructions:

1. **Connect the keyboard.** Find a round socket on the back of the computer that accommodates a connector with five or six pins and a square. The socket also will have a slot at the top or bottom. Align the keyboard plug's pins with the holes in the socket; this should also line up the ridge on the keyboard plug with the slot in the socket. Press the plug gently into place.

2. **Connect the mouse.** The connector will look like the round keyboard plug or will be an oblong shape (with 15 or fewer pins). Align the mouse plug's pins with the holes in the socket; press the plug gently into place. If you have an oblong connector with screws, gently tighten the screws.

3. **Connect the monitor.** It has two cords: one has an oblong plug with 15 or fewer pins, and the other plugs into a source of power (on the back of the system unit or on a surge suppressor). Plug in the oblong connector and the power cord; *do not* turn on the monitor yet.

4. **Connect the printer.** Most likely, its cord will have a *parallel* connector with 25 pins that plugs into a socket with 25 holes on the system unit. Printers using serial ports have 9- or 25-pin connections; in this case, the system unit has the pins and the connecting end of the cable has the holes. Check your printer's cable: Which connection do you have? Ease the plug into place, by tightening the screws or clicking the metal clips. Plug your printer's power cord into the surge suppressor, but *do not* turn on the printer yet.

5. **Set up your modem.** You may need to make several connections if the modem is external. Using a cord that ends in plastic clips like those on a phone cord (*RJ-11 connections*), plug one end into the Line jack on the back of the modem; plug the other end into your home's phone-line jack. Take the serial cable that comes with the modem. Plug one end into the serial port on the back of the modem, and plug the other into the corresponding 25-pin socket on the back of your computer. Finally, plug the modem power cord (if any) into the surge suppressor. For internal modems, use an RJ-11 cord to connect the Line jack on the back of the system unit to the wall phone jack. If your modem has an extra jack labeled "Phone," you can plug your phone into it.

6. **Plug in the speakers and microphone.** Connect them to the sound card at the back of the system unit. Plug the microphone into the "Mic In" jack, and plug the speakers into the "Spk Out" jack. If you're not using batteries for the speakers, you'll need a power adapter unit;

plug one end into the power jack on the back of one of the speakers and the other end into the surge suppressor (*don't* turn on the speakers yet)!

The plug for some power adapters is a large square box. When you plug it into a surge suppressor, it can cover other receptacles on the adapter. To avoid this, try plugging the big adapter plug into one end of the suppressor strip or the other.

7. **Finally, plug the system unit itself into your surge-suppressor power source.** The cable for the system unit has one end with prongs and one with slots. Plug the end with slots into the receptacle with prongs (sometimes labeled "AC Input"). Plug the normal end of the cable into the surge suppressor.

8. ▶**See "Start Up Your Computer and Windows 95" on page 30 to learn how to power up your system.**◀

Most computer manufacturers provide documentation identifying the various sockets and connectors on the back of the system unit. If you have any doubts about where things go for your computer, specifically, check the documentation.

Guided Tour   Plug It All In

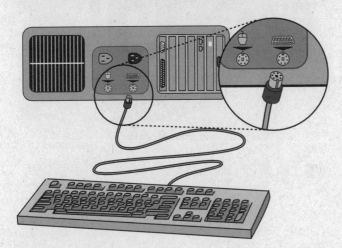

1 Connect the keyboard.

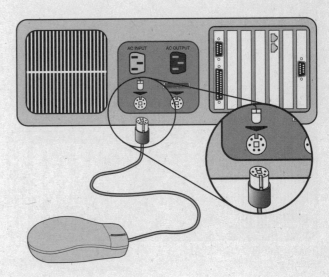

2 Connect the mouse.

(continues)

Guided Tour   Plug It All In   (continued)

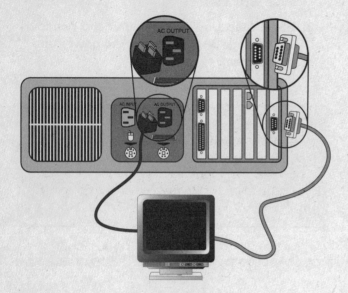

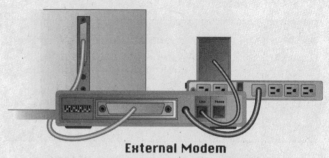

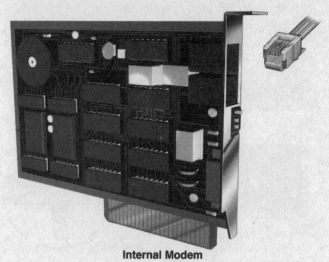

External Modem

Internal Modem

3 Connect the monitor.

5 Set up your modem connections.

4 Connect the printer.

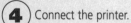

Guided Tour Plug It All In

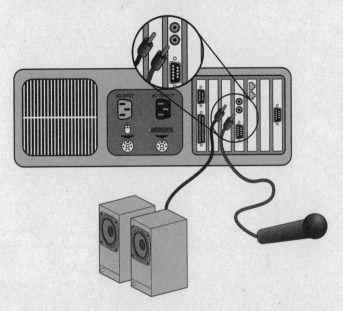

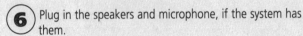

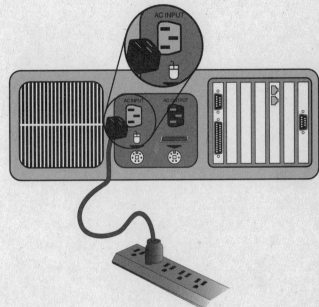

6 Plug in the speakers and microphone, if the system has them.

7 Finally, plug the system unit itself into your surge-suppressor power source.

HOW TO...

Operate Your Computer

Remember the footage of NASA from the late '60s and early '70s showing rows of people with monitors and huge, beastly computers that filled entire rooms? Back then, you literally had to be a rocket scientist to operate a computer.

Today's computers not only pack much more power into much smaller spaces, but also offer features to make them easier and more natural to use. Anyone can sit down and operate a computer by flipping a few switches, pecking at a keyboard, or using a mouse.

This section takes you quickly through the basics of using your computer hardware. (The software's another story, and you'll learn about that soon.)

What You Will Find in This Section

Start Up Your Computer and Windows 95

As with any electronic device, you have to turn on your computer to get it to work. This simple process involves several steps you should practice religiously. Although you might not damage your computer if you do it differently, turning on the system components in the right order can help prolong the life of your system.

Starting your computer is also called *booting up* (because your system "pulls itself up by its boot-straps"). The computer reads built-in startup instructions from the operating system and some special chips, and then it performs a Power-On Self-Test (POST) to check its ability to "talk" to the system components.

Many users and experts debate when you should turn your computer on and off. Some insist that we all should conserve energy, turning a computer off every time we've finished using it. At the other extreme, some people think computers should never be shut down; they think all this powering up and down wears out the computer's components faster. For best results, use the following *Guided Tour* to start off your computing day.

> Most new systems offer power management features and can go into "sleep" mode to save power if the computer sits idle for several minutes. Sleep mode enables you to conserve power while leaving your system on—reducing wear from powering up the system and leaving it on to receive faxes and voice mail messages.

When you start a newer system, the Windows 95 operating system loads, and you'll see the Windows desktop on-screen. (If you have an older system, you may see the DOS prompt or the Windows Program Manager screen.) ▶For help with using Windows 95, see "Get Around in Windows 95 Programs" on page 65.◀ ▶To get started with Windows 3.11, see "Work in Windows 3.11" on page 181.◀ Other systems may display a special menu or screen installed by the manufacturer. In still other instances, the manufacturer may have installed a multimedia presentation that runs the first time you start the computer. After you view this information the first time, the computer will start normally, skipping the presentation.

> Some users like to plug all their computer components into the surge suppressor and leave all the power switches on so they can turn on the whole system just by flipping the surge suppressor switch. This is a *bad* idea because it sends a power surge into the individual components, zapping them slightly and causing excess wear. For safety, follow the steps here for powering up.

Fix Startup Problems

If you use the steps for starting your computer system and nothing happens—or you get an error—don't worry! Here's how you can fix common startup problems. ▶If none of these solutions work, see the "101 Quick Fixes" section on page 459.◀

- If the monitor is completely dark, try turning up its brightness or contrast settings. ▶For more about this, see "Adjust a Monitor for Viewing Comfort," later in this section on page 41.◀

- If the monitor is dark or you don't hear a particular component whir to life, something isn't plugged together properly. Turn off the power for all the components and the surge suppressor. Make sure all the computer cables are firmly connected, and make sure all the pieces are plugged into the surge suppressor. Then retry the startup process.

- If you see a message on-screen saying **Non-system disk or disk error**, you probably have a disk in the floppy drive. Remove the disk and press any key to continue the startup process.

Make sure the floppy disk drive is empty. Otherwise, the computer will try to start itself from any floppy disk it finds in drive A

Guided Tour Start Your Computer

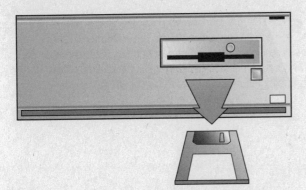

1 (most of which will not have any system-startup instructions).

Make sure the surge-suppressor strip is plugged into the wall

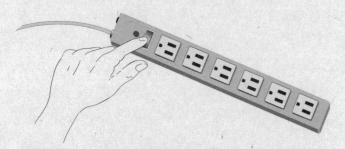

2 socket and that all system components are plugged into the surge suppressor. Turn on the surge suppressor.

Turn on the monitor's power. If the power switch is on the back

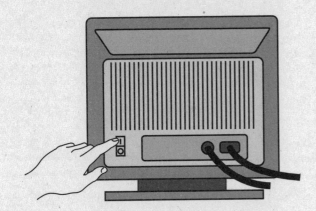

3 of the monitor, it will probably have a **I** (vertical hash mark) on the top half and an **O** (circle) on the bottom half. To turn the monitor on, press down the half with the **I** mark. Other monitors have a knob or button on the front that you can simply press.

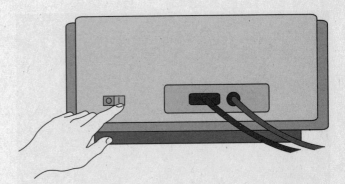

4 If you have a printer that you need to turn on manually (these days, some power up on their own when you print a document), turn it on next; the power switch is usually on the back or right side. The **Online** indicator for the printer should light up, indicating that it's ready to go. Also turn on other devices attached to your system (such as scanners and Zip drives) before continuing.

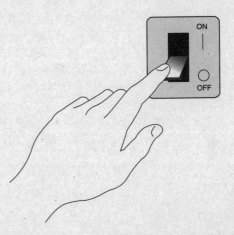

5 Time to turn on the system unit. Find the On/Off switch on the back, right, or front side of the system unit; turn it to **On** or press it to the "on" position.

(continues)

Guided Tour   Start Your Computer   *(continued)*

6 Watch the monitor; you may see several self-test messages flash on the screen. When the computer finishes its self-test, you'll see the Welcome to Windows 95 screen with the Windows 95 desktop beneath it. Simply click the **Close** button to display the desktop by itself (as shown here).

Shut Down Windows 95 and Your System at the End of the Day

When you shut down your computer, resist the temptation to just turn off the components' power switches because you could lose work if you haven't saved properly. For the greatest safety, make sure you save all your work first—and then exit all programs—before shutting down your computer.

To make sure you don't lose any work you're creating with a particular software application, save it to a file on the hard disk so you can work with it later. Otherwise, when you shut down the system, your work will be cleared out of Random-Access Memory (RAM) and lost forever.

Also, it's important to shut down your applications before quitting. Quitting with an application running also can leave temporary (.tmp) files on your hard disk. These files can be large, and your system can accumulate a number of them. These files needlessly decrease available hard disk space and could even cause the Windows 95 operating system to have performance problems. The *Guided Tour* here outlines the cleanest and safest way to shut down Windows 95 and your system.

> To exit Windows 3.11, click the Program Manager **File** menu in the upper-right corner of the screen and then click **Exit Windows**. A dialog box appears, asking you to confirm. Click the **Yes** button. When the DOS prompt (C:\>) appears, you can turn off the system. ▶**For more information about starting and exiting Windows 3.11, see "Start and Exit Windows 3.11" on page 182.**◀

Guided Tour Shut Down Your Computer

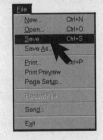

1 Save your files by opening the application's **File** menu and choosing **Save**. The program will ask you to specify a name and location for the file holding your work. ▶**For more information, see "Save Your Work in a Windows Program" on page 94.**◀

2 Quit (exit) any programs you're using by opening the **File** menu and choosing **Exit** or **Quit**. Your computer closes the program and removes it from your screen. ▶**See "Exit a Windows Program" on page 100 and "Exit a DOS Program" on page 226.**◀

(continues)

Guided Tour Shut Down Your Computer *(continued)*

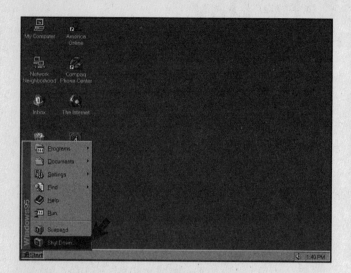

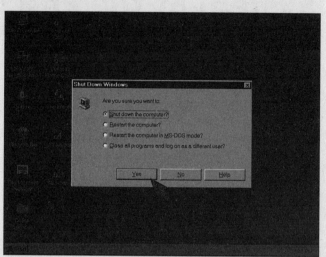

3 To exit Windows 95, click the **Start** button in the lower-left corner of the screen to open the Start menu, and then choose **Shut Down**.

4 The Shut Down Windows dialog box appears, asking you to confirm that you really want to shut down. Make sure **Shut down the computer?** is selected, and then click the **Yes** button.

5 After a few seconds, an on-screen message tells you it's safe to turn off your computer. Turn off the power switch on the system unit first. Then turn off the power switches on the monitor, printer, and other devices.

6 Turn off the surge suppressor's power switch.

Insert and Remove Floppy and Removable Disks

Computers let you work smarter because you can share information between them. If two similar computers have the same program installed, you can create work on one of the computers, save the work, transport it to the other computer, and then resume your work. In fact, your reason for buying a home computer might be to bring work home from the office so you can complete it at home in privacy and comfort (or to meet a looming deadline). One method of transferring data between computers is to use a floppy disk.

Most new computers sold today have only a single floppy disk drive that holds 3.5-inch floppy disks. (The older style, 5.25-inch floppy disks, actually held less data than the smaller 3.5-inch disks and were more easily damaged because they were truly "floppy" or flexible.)

A 3.5-inch floppy disk has a hard plastic shell encasing the magnetic storage material, which provides physical protection for your valuable magnetic data. The small size makes a 3.5-inch floppy easier to store and more convenient to carry. Note that a 3.5-inch floppy disk drive is so small that it can be positioned vertically in the system unit.

Some new computers are shipping with a Zip drive, a drive that uses 100M removable disks that are slightly larger than but look similar to 3.5-inch disks. You insert and remove a Zip disk just as you insert and remove the standard 3.5-inch floppy.

Guided Tour Insert and Remove Floppy Disks

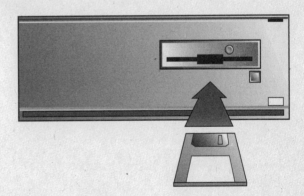

1 Turn your 3.5-inch disk label-side-up. Grip the edge opposite the edge covered by the sliding door. (If you were inserting a 5.25-inch disk, you would need to hold it label up, with the square notch to the right and the side with two smaller notches facing the drive slot.)

2 Insert the leading edge of the disk (it's covered by the metal sliding door on a 3.5-inch floppy) into the drive slot. Push it (gently) all the way into the drive. When the disk seats, the drive's eject button pops out. (For a 5.25-inch disk, you have to press the drive lever down until it clicks in place in front of the slot.)

3 When you finish using the disk, save your work on it. After the drive's indicator light goes out, you can remove the disk (which you should do before you use another one or shut down your computer).

(continues)

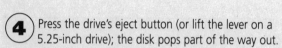

Guided Tour   Insert and Remove Floppy Disks   (continued)

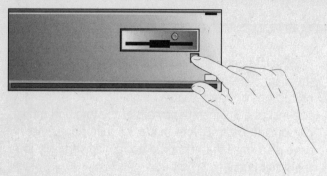 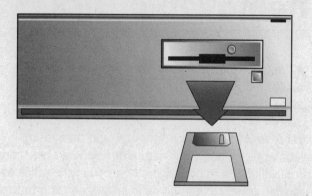

4 Press the drive's eject button (or lift the lever on a 5.25-inch drive); the disk pops part of the way out.

5 Pull the disk the rest of the way out.

Never remove a floppy disk from the drive when the drive indicator light is still on. Doing so usually damages your files, and you could lose the data permanently.

Understand Floppy Disk Capacity

You may have noticed that your floppy disks or disk labels have "HD" or something similar on them. These hieroglyphics refer to the disk's *density* or *capacity*, which is as important as the floppy's size. Both affect how much data a floppy disk can hold.

Manufacturers indicate this amount in *kilobytes* (each K is just over 1,000 characters) and *megabytes* (each M is more than one million characters). All floppy disks sold today are *double-sided* (DS); they store data on both sides (many early floppies were single-sided).

The disk's capacity depends on how efficient its magnetic storage material is. The newer *high-density* (HD) disks hold more data than *double-density* (DD) disks of the same size. For a comparison of various disk capacities, see the table at the bottom of the page.

> Software companies publish installation disks in 3.5-inch HD and CD-ROM format only. However, some 3.5-inch installation disks come in a special HD (DMF) format that lends even greater capacity than the standard HD format. Although your 3.5-inch floppy drive can read the HD (DMF) disks to install the program, it can't copy the disks or format other 3.5-inch floppies with the HD (DMF) format.

Take Care of Your Floppy Disks

While floppy disks aren't as fragile as they used to be, they aren't indestructible, either. Use a reasonable amount of care and caution when handling floppy disks. Here are some guidelines.

- Avoid touching the magnetic disk surface when it's exposed. Skin oil and other substances can damage the disk's magnetic properties.

- Avoid placing the disk anywhere near dust, dirt, or liquid; these can damage magnetic material. If you insert a dirty disk into a disk drive, the gunk on the disk can damage the drive.

- Keep the disk well away from magnets, electrical wires, electronic appliances, computer components, or anything that might be magnetized—like paper clips. That's right—never clip a disk to your paperwork. Electric power generates a magnetic field that can affect the disk's magnetic material. It also is a safe practice to keep your telephone away from your disks and the computer, as telephones also have magnets.

- Keep disks away from heat sources (like photocopiers) that can warp them.

- For 5.25-inch disks, make sure you write on the label with a felt-tip pen before sticking it on the disk. A sharp pencil or ballpoint could dent a disk's magnetic surface.

- *Write-protect* your disks to preserve data. This procedure lets the disk drive read what's on a disk, but prevents the drive from altering the data in any way. You write-protect a 3.5-inch disk by sliding a small tab (you'll see this if you look at the back of the disk) to open the little tab window. To write-protect a 5.25-inch disk, bend a piece of tape (or a write-protect tab) over the rectangular notch near one corner of the disk.

Floppy Disk Capacities

Size	Type	Capacity
3.5-inch	DSDD, double-sided double-density	720K
3.5-inch	DSHD, double-sided high-density	1.44M
3.5-inch	ED, extra-high-density	2.88M
5.25-inch	DSDD, double-sided double-density	360K
5.25-inch	DSHD, double-sided high-density	1.2M

Insert and Remove CD-ROMs

Many computer users experience a thrill the first time they play an audio CD—or a multimedia CD-ROM computer program—from their PC's CD-ROM drive. The CD-ROM drive revolutionized personal computers, giving them the capability of handling text, graphics, video, animation, and sound—making the PC a true multimedia machine. The CD-ROM drive reads the data on the disc by spinning it and bouncing a laser off the surface.

Previously, multimedia escaped the reach of most computers because video, animation, and sound take huge amounts of storage space. Each reflective CD-ROM holds over 650M, room for quite a bit of sound and video. CD-ROM drives that can write as well as read data have become widely available (as an add-on for your system) and relatively affordable, although not as affordable as a drive that reads or plays only. The next generation of CD media will be the DVD (digital versatile disc). This format will have four or more times the density of today's CD-ROMs—enough to hold a full motion picture, with the soundtrack in four different languages. DVD players that attach to televisions are now available; as the format gains acceptance, look for DVD players to begin appearing in PCs. DVD players can play conventional CD-ROMs in addition to the DVD.

Some CD-ROM drives use a *disk caddy*; you have to put the disc in a caddy before you put it in the drive. Drives without a caddy have a drawer that slides in and out for the disc. A brand new type of CD-ROM drive on the market doesn't have such a drawer; you simply insert the disc directly into a slot in the drive, much like a floppy disk drive. You'll learn how to insert and remove a CD-ROM disk in a drive with a drawer in the following *Guided Tour*.

CD-ROM drives spin the disc so fast that your computer can grab data from any spot on the disc almost immediately. Data CDs organize information in drives and directories, just like hard and floppy disks. ►**For more information, see "Understand How the Computer Stores Files" on page 51.**◄

Use a Program's Controls to Open and Close the CD-ROM Drive

In life, you can count on the fact that mechanical parts wear out and break. Your CD-ROM drive has several mechanical parts, especially if it uses a drawer rather than a caddy. For example, buttons like the eject button on audio equipment and computers are notorious for wearing out. Similarly, too much downward pressure on a drive drawer can move it out of alignment or break it.

To prevent such disasters, some publishers of software for use with CDs provide ways to use the software to open and close the drive door. Here's how the basic process works:

1. If the program requires it, insert the CD manually into the drive. If you try to run the program and there's no disc in the drive, you'll see an error message.

2. Make sure you're finished using the disc. If it's an audio CD, stop playing it. If you're running a program from the CD, use the **File**, **Exit** command to close the program.

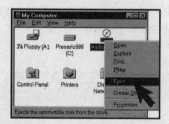

3. Open the drive or eject the caddy by clicking in the appropriate place or by choosing the appropriate menu command. For example, you may

have to click an eject icon (a symbol or picture), as shown here. (You can click the eject icon again to close the drawer in such a case.) To eject a program CD-ROM, double-click the **My Computer** icon on the desktop. In the My Computer window

that opens, right-click the CD-ROM drive icon with the mouse (➤**see "Operate a Mouse" on page 44 of this section to learn more about right-clicking**◄), and then choose **Eject** from the menu that appears.

Guided Tour Work with CD-ROMs

1 Check the shiny side of the CD for fingerprints, clinging hairs, or other debris. If you find any, wipe the CD gently with a soft cloth. Wipe from the center hole to the outside edges; do *not* wipe in a circular motion.

2 Open the CD-ROM drive by pressing its eject button; if your drive uses a caddy, flip open the CD-ROM caddy.

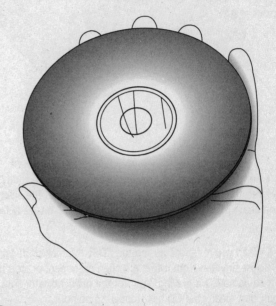

3 Grip the CD lightly (with your fingertips around its edge) and pick it up; the printed side should face your palm.

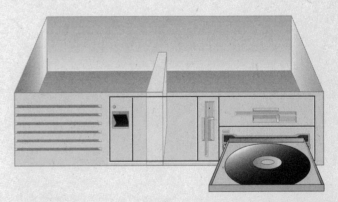

4 With your palm (and therefore the shiny side of the CD) pointing down, carefully center the CD and place it in the drive drawer or the CD caddy. You should be able to see the printed side of the CD facing up. If you're using a caddy, close its lid and insert it into the slot in the drive.

(continues)

Guided Tour Work with CD-ROMs   *(continued)*

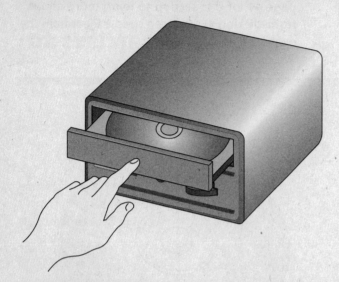

5 Gently push the drive drawer closed, or push the caddy into the drive slot. (Alternatively, you can press the eject button again.) The drive will close and the disc will be ready to use.

6 When you're finished using the CD-ROM, make sure you close any files from it that are open on-screen, or stop the disc if an audio CD is playing. Wait for the drive indicator light to go out; that means the CD has stopped spinning.

7 Press the CD-ROM drive's eject button. The drawer or caddy will slide out. Remove the CD or caddy from the drive. If the CD has a drawer, press it gently so it retracts into the drive, or press the eject button again to close it.

Adjust a Monitor for Viewing Comfort

Today's monitor manufacturers realize how fatiguing it can be to work with a bad monitor. In fact, eye-strain and neck strain still bother most computer users at one time or another. And because people are spending more and more time with computers every day, comfort is becoming an important issue.

Buy a quality monitor that's *non-interlaced* (interlaced monitors flash in subtle ways that cause eye discomfort); it should also have a low dot pitch (.28mm or less) for a sharp image. In addition, your monitor's controls can help you use your monitor more safely and comfortably. ▶**For more on purchasing a monitor, see "Decide What Kind of Computer You Want" on page 11.**◀

Even though you can adjust your monitor, you still may encounter screen glare. This is often a problem when you place your computer near a window. The changing daylight can cause a glare at particular times or during certain outdoor conditions.

Of course, you can do the obvious: close the curtains or blinds to adjust the daylight coming in. Most people, however, find natural daylight restful—especially if the interior is lighted by fluorescent fixtures.

Don't worry. You can try a couple of tricks to get the best of both worlds.

> Most monitors can display in several resolutions, depending on which display driver file you install and use. ▶**To learn how to change your monitor's resolution in Windows 95, see "Change the Desktop Display" on page 162.**◀

A Few Quick Exercises to Help Your Eyes

No matter how expensive your monitor was or how you adjust it, you should still pay attention to your physical comfort when you use your computer. Before you realize it's happening, you can develop a headache, burning eyes, or a stiff neck.

The best defense is to take a break after every half-hour to hour of work (or play). Get up from the computer and walk around the office a bit. Take that coffee or restroom break.

In addition, you can do some simple exercises to release stress and rest your muscles—even your eye muscles. Push yourself away from the computer for a moment to take a break and try it.

- Release the tension in your neck by moving your head gently. In a seated position, place your hands in your lap and relax your shoulders. Slowly drop your chin to your chest, and then raise it back up until you're looking to the joint where the wall meets the ceiling. Drop your head back down, and then look slowly to the left and right, past each of your shoulders. Repeat as needed.

- Squint your eyes hard and hold for a few seconds. Release and repeat as needed.

- Make a fist and point your index finger toward the ceiling. Hold the finger about four inches from your eyes; focus on the finger until you can see it clearly. Slowly move your hand away from your face, keeping your eyes focused on your finger, until you've fully extended your arm. Then slowly bring your hand back to its original position, keeping your eyes focused on your finger. Repeat as needed.

Guided Tour Adjust Your Monitor

1 Place the monitor at the appropriate height and distance in relation to where you sit. The monitor should be about two feet from your eyes, at eye level or slightly below. If necessary, use a monitor stand or a few books to raise the monitor to eye level.

2 Most monitors have a tilt-and-swivel base. If necessary, use it to adjust the screen even if you can't place it exactly at eye level.

5 If the screen image is cut off or fuzzy on one side, you need to adjust the H-phase (horizontal control). Look for a knob and turn it to center the image on-screen. Some systems have two knobs: one that controls the horizontal width of the image and one that controls the horizontal position of the image.

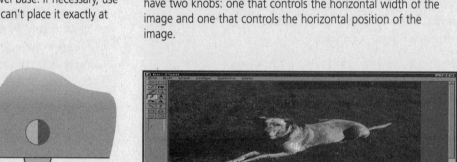

3 To adjust the brightness, look for the knob labeled **Bright** or indicated with a "sun" icon.

4 To adjust the contrast (the difference between light and dark), look for the knob labeled **Contrast** or indicated with a half-dark and half-light icon.

6 If the screen image appears smashed or stretched vertically, you need to adjust the V-size (vertical control). Look for a knob and turn it to adjust the height of the image on-screen; you may need to turn a second knob to adjust the vertical position of the image.

Guided Tour   Reduce Screen Glare

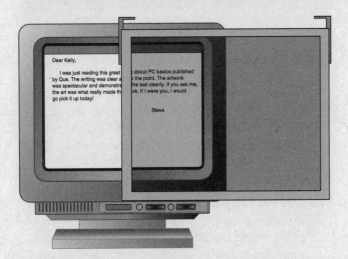

1 For around $30, you can buy an anti-glare screen that you can affix to the front of your monitor. More expensive filters also offer radiation protection and privacy protection (making it impossible to read your screen unless you're facing it head-on).

2 For a more down-and-dirty solution, you can use an ordinary manila file folder to cut glare. Simply put it on top of the monitor, fold it down both sides, and then tape it in place so it protrudes a few inches past the front of the monitor, shading the monitor to prevent any glare.

Operate a Mouse

Computers do so much these days—in terms of graphics, games, music, and so on—that the keyboard alone doesn't cut it as the only input device. The *mouse* makes it easier to work in most programs, saving you the trouble of remembering arcane commands or keystroke combinations.

As you move the mouse around on your desk, a smooth ball within it rolls and transmits your movements to a pointer on-screen (an upside-down version of a mouse called a *trackball* lets you roll a ball to move the pointer); the pointer mirrors the way you move the mouse. You can move the pointer smoothly from one edge of the screen to the other instead of wearing out your finger pressing the arrow keys. Depending on the program you're using, the pointer can take various shapes, including an arrow, a box, a vertical hash mark, an hourglass, and a *crosshair* (crossed lines resembling a plus sign).

For best results, you should have a *mouse pad* (purchased separately) under your mouse. The mouse's roller ball easily grips the pad's rubberized surface, which helps keep mouse movement smooth and even.

Master Common Mouse Techniques

Basic mouse techniques are fairly easy—both to learn and to get used to in real-life situations. For the most part, software publishers design their products to let you use the mouse in a consistent way. If one publisher develops a new way of using the mouse, other publishers tend to use it in their programs as well. The result: Once you learn a new technique, you can use it over and over.

You'll learn more about using a mouse with Windows programs later, in the sections called ►"Get Around in Windows 95 Programs" (on page 65) and "Work in Windows 3.11" (on page 181).◄

1. **Choosing menus, commands, and dialog box options.** Instead of using awkward or mysterious keystrokes, you can click or double-click to tell the computer what to do.

2. **Starting and exiting programs in Windows.** To start a program in Windows 95 with the mouse, you click the **Start** button, move the mouse pointer over **Programs**, and then click the name of the program you want to run (►see "Start Programs with the Start Button" on page 69◄). In Windows 3.11, you generally double-click the program's on-screen icon (a small picture that represents the program).

3. **Making selections to edit, copy, move, or cut.** With the mouse, you can select a drawn object or block of text, and then quickly perform a command on the entire selection. Drag over text or click an on-screen object to select it. To move the selected text, open the **Edit** menu and select **Cut**; reposition the insertion point by clicking; then open the **Edit** menu and select **Copy**. To insert the selected text, open the **Edit** menu and select **Copy**; reposition the insertion point by clicking; then open the **Edit** menu and select **Copy**.

4. **Drawing and painting.** With your mouse and one of today's drawing or painting programs, you can create realistic, attractive drawings on-screen. Using a mouse to generate computer art takes some practice, just like learning to use a pencil or paintbrush.

5. **Dragging to manage files in Windows.** To copy files at the DOS prompt, you have to remember and type the exact file name to copy and the exact name of the directory to copy it to. Now, however, you can use your mouse to move and copy files in Windows by dragging the file icons. ►**You'll learn more about this in the section called "Organize Files and Folders with Windows 95" on page 101.**◄

6. **Moving and copying data with drag-and-drop.** In most newer Windows programs, you can simply drag a selected item to a new location (which moves it), or you can press the **Ctrl** key and drag to copy it to another spot.

7. **Right-click to display shortcut menus.** In some Windows 3.11 applications and in Windows 95, you can right-click a selected object (a file icon, text, graphic, the desktop, etc.) to display a shortcut menu holding options only for that object. Then select an option from the shortcut menu.

Guided Tour   Work with a Mouse

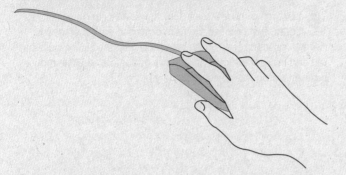

1 To use the mouse, rest the tip of your index finger on or near the left mouse button; your palm should cup gently over the body of the mouse.

2 Move the mouse by pushing and pulling it around on the mouse pad. As you do, the mouse pointer moves on-screen in the same direction. Lifting the mouse prevents its roller ball from moving.

3 *Pointing* is the basic mouse movement. To point at something on-screen, move the mouse until the pointer rests on it.

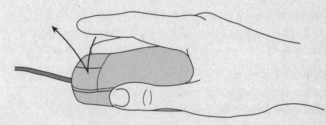

4 *Clicking* selects whatever the mouse pointer rests on. To click an on-screen item, first you point to it. Then you press and release the LEFT mouse button once. To *right-click*, point with the mouse, and then press and release the RIGHT mouse button once.

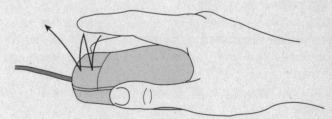

5 *Double-clicking* enters the command or activates the item the pointer rests on. To double-click an on-screen item, first point to it with the mouse. Then, without moving the mouse, quickly press and release the LEFT mouse button *twice*.

(continues)

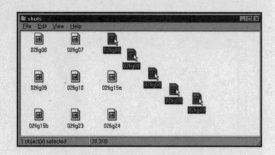

6 *Dragging* moves, selects, or draws an item on-screen. To drag, first point to the item or to one end of what you want to select or draw. Then press and *hold* the LEFT mouse button and move the mouse to a new position. Release the mouse button to drop the object in its new position.

Reset (Warm-Boot) a Locked-Up Computer

You can be working happily along on your computer system, and it can lock up or suddenly stop working. Your computer can lock up for a variety of reasons, although it's less common under Windows 95 than under DOS and Windows 3.11. It usually happens because software instructions conflict, and your computer can't decide what to do—or because too many instructions come flying at your computer at once, and it just gets paralyzed.

When your computer locks up, your only option is to *reset* or *reboot* it. Rebooting the system clears out whatever was jamming the computer and takes the computer back through the operating system startup instructions. Unfortunately, if your computer locks up and you haven't saved what you're working on, that work is lost. Therefore, save your work often—every 10 minutes or after making any major changes to an important piece of work.

Most often, you will reboot by *warm-booting* your system. It's called a warm-boot because the computer's already warmed up; you just use some keystrokes to reset the system without cutting the power flow to the computer. If this process doesn't work, jump to the *Guided Tour* for "cold-booting" later in this task. You should warm-boot rather than cold-boot whenever possible. Before you reboot your system, however, you should try a few tests to find out whether the computer's really locked up:

- Wait about 15 seconds and try resuming your work. You might be typing or entering commands faster than your computer can interpret them; if so, wait for it to catch up. You also need to make sure the computer isn't saving data while you reboot. Waiting a bit and checking to make sure none of the drive lights are on are good safety measures.

- Press **F1** for Help. If you're trying to perform an operation that's impossible, Help will explain what's going on.

- Sometimes you can select something with the mouse without realizing it, which might keep you from performing a later operation. Try clicking in various places on-screen.

- Press the **Spacebar** or try some other keystrokes to see whether the keyboard simply has a stuck key.

Several things can cause your computer to lock up, including problems with the computer's memory or video, or with a program. ▶To help diagnose some of these problems, check out Part 3, "101 Quick Fixes," starting on page 459.◀

In Windows 95, you can press **Ctrl+Alt+Del** (press and hold the Ctrl key, the Alt key, and the Del key simultaneously) to cancel a program that's giving you trouble. In the Close Program dialog box that appears, you'll see **[Not Responding]** beside the name of the program if it's irretrievably stalled. In that case, click the program's name and click **End Task**; otherwise, click **Cancel** and wait a few moments for the program to respond. Whenever possible, you should use the Shut Down command on the Start menu to close Windows. If the mouse locks up or you otherwise can't click the Start button to display its menu, press **Ctrl+Alt+Del** and then click **Shut Down**.

To reboot from an older version of DOS, remove all floppy disks from their drives, and then press **Ctrl+Alt+Del**. The computer goes through its startup routine. When it finishes, you can restart any DOS programs that were running.

Restart Windows 95 in Safe Mode

If you install a new program or a hardware device (such as a new video card), and you have problems starting Windows 95, you can start it in *safe mode*. Windows often gives you the option of starting in safe mode whenever you restart after the system locks up or when you don't shut down correctly. When Windows starts in safe mode, it runs with a plain-vanilla setup that's almost sure to prod Windows into action. In safe mode, Windows 95 will not load any fancy display programs, and you won't be able to use your CD-ROM drive or printer. The purpose of safe mode is to get Windows up and running so you can correct any problems that are preventing it from starting in its usual way. Here's what you do to start Windows 95 in safe mode:

1. Turn on your monitor and then your system unit.

2. When you see the message **Starting Windows 95**, press and release the **F8** key. A list of startup options appears.

3. Press **3** to select safe mode, and then press **Enter**. Windows starts in safe mode, and a dialog box appears telling you that.

4. Click the **OK** button to close the dialog box. The Welcome to Windows 95 screen appears.

To *restart* Windows in safe mode, open the **Start** menu, select **Shut Down**, click **Restart the computer?**, and click **Yes**. When you see the Starting Windows 95 message, press and release the **F8** key.

Guided Tour   Warm-Boot from Windows 95

1 Remove any disks that are in floppy disk drives. If you don't, your computer will try to read from the floppy disk instead of your hard drive when it restarts.

2 Click the **Start** button and click **Shut Down**.

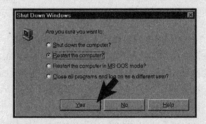

3 In the dialog box that appears, click **Restart the Computer?**, and then click **Yes**. (If you click **Restart the Computer?**, press and hold the **Shift** key, and then click **Yes**, Windows will restart without restarting the computer, which can save a little time.) Whatever was on-screen will be wiped off. The computer will go through its startup process all over.

4 Restart any programs you had open before you warm-booted. If the system locks up every time you perform a particular operation, it has some kind of conflict. ▶**See "101 Quick Fixes" (starting on page 459) for clues to what the problem is.**◀

Guided Tour Warm-Boot from Windows 3.11

1 Press and hold the **Ctrl** key, the **Alt** key, and the **Delete** key simultaneously.

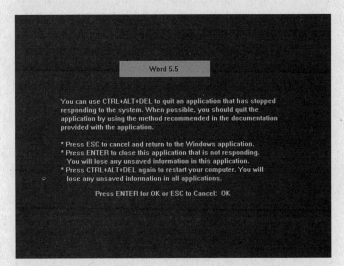

Word 5.5

You can use CTRL+ALT+DEL to quit an application that has stopped responding to the system. When possible, you should quit the application by using the method recommended in the documentation provided with the application.

* Press ESC to cancel and return to the Windows application.
* Press ENTER to close this application that is not responding. You will lose any unsaved information in this application.
* Press CTRL+ALT+DEL again to restart your computer. You will lose any unsaved information in all applications.

Press ENTER for OK or ESC to Cancel: OK

2 Your computer displays a screen naming the application that's locked up in Windows. Read this screen carefully to know exactly which program has locked up and what your options are.

3 To shut down only the application that's locked up (but leave Windows running), press the **Enter** key. The application closes, and Windows reappears on-screen. You should save your work in any other applications you're running because Windows still may be unstable.

4 If you want to do more than just shut down the locked-up application, you can continue the process and reboot the whole system. (WARNING: This is dangerous to do, because it can cause you to lose data and mess up your programs.) Start by removing any disks from the floppy disk drives.

5 Press and hold the **Ctrl** key, the **Alt** key, and the **Delete** key simultaneously.

6 You'll need to restart Windows and restart any programs you had open before you warm-booted.

Cold-Boot Your System

Sometimes warm-booting your system doesn't work. You press Ctrl+Alt+Delete and nothing happens. The mouse stops working, so you can't click the Start button to choose the Shut Down command. This usually means your computer has locked up in such a way that it can't accept keyboard and mouse commands.

When warm-booting doesn't work, you have to *cold-boot* your system. Cold-booting means you use the hardware to reset the computer, depriving it of power

or making it "cold." There are two different ways to cold-boot. One involves your system's Reset button (if it has one). The second method greatly resembles restarting your system, which was described in an earlier task (▶**"Start Up Your Computer and Windows 95" on page 30**◀). Don't use the second method unless the Reset button doesn't work or your system doesn't have a Reset button.

Guided Tour   Cold-Boot with the Reset Button

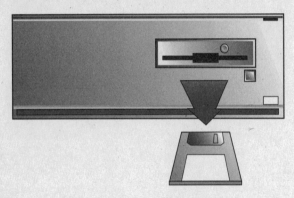

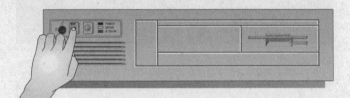

2 Press the **Reset** button on the front or side of the computer. Your computer will beep at you, and whatever was on-screen will be wiped off. The computer will go through its startup process all over.

1 Remove any disks that are in floppy disk drives. If you don't, your computer will try to read from the floppy disk instead of your hard drive when it restarts.

Guided Tour   Cold-Boot with the Power Switch

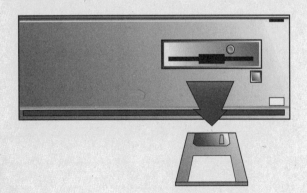

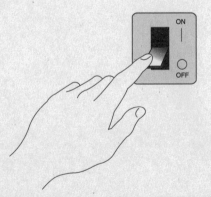

1 Remove any disks that are in floppy disk drives. If you don't, your computer will try to read from the floppy disk instead of your hard drive when it restarts.

2 Turn the system unit's power switch to the **Off** position. Listen to your computer, so you can hear it power down. When it's silent (the power-down process has finished), wait about two minutes and turn the power switch back to the **On** position.

HOW TO...
Understand How the Computer Stores Files

magine the ideal home or business office. You've got a nice, orderly desk. Your favorite framed lithograph hangs just above it. Sunlight streams in through the window. And you've got 50,000 pages of information stacked all around.

"Hey," you might think, "that last part doesn't sound so great." And it wouldn't be, because the average office isn't designed to hold 50,000 pages of information. But the average computer can hold that much and more!

The way the computer converts characters, sound, and pictures to an electrical state fascinates new and experienced users alike. But the computer's capability to condense great mounds of information and store it on a few magnetic disks not only fascinates, it serves an important purpose: It enables your office to absorb some of today's information overload.

The next few tasks explain how a computer stores and organizes files so you can make the best use of this resource. You'll also find tips here to help you make smarter use of the disk space you have.

What You Will Find in This Section

Understand Disks and Drives

A task earlier in this book explained the basics for working with floppy and removable disks, but it didn't give you the lowdown on how the disks store information or how your computer can work with that information. When you're working with your computer and it's powered up, your data exists only in the computer's *Random-Access Memory* (RAM). RAM holds the data and program instructions your computer is working with while the computer is turned on. Turn the computer off, and RAM's contents are lost.

To store that data so you can work with it again, you need to save the data in a more permanent way; you put it in *storage*. Disks are your computer's storage area. They hold your data for you until you delete it or move it. When you save information, your computer takes what's in RAM and writes it onto a disk. When you want to use stored data again, your computer looks at that data on the hard disk drive and reads a copy of it back into RAM. If you change your data, you'll need to save it to the hard disk drive again to preserve your changes, and so on.

New users frequently use the terms "floppy disk" and "hard drive" to refer to the two main storage tools of the computer. A "disk" and a "drive," however, are not the same thing.

The *disk* is the spinning platter of magnetic material that holds the stored data. The hard "drive" within your computer actually holds a stack of these magnetic disk platters—that's how it holds so much data.

The actual collection of mechanisms that spins the disk, writes information on the disk, and reads information from the disk is the *disk drive*. The hard disk drive in your computer has a sealed case that holds both the drive and the stack of disks. As you've already learned, you can insert and remove disks from floppy disk drives and other removable drives through a slot on the front of the drive.

> ▶To learn how to save your work (store it on a disk), see "Save Your Work in a Windows Program" on page 94.◀

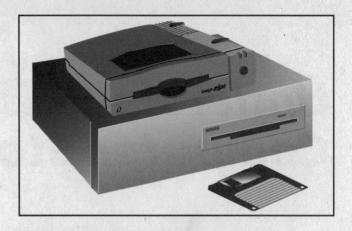

Working by Bits and Bytes

Your computer isn't as smart as it might first seem. At its most basic level, it can only understand two digits: 0 and 1. The computer combines 0s and 1s to create unique characters, and then those characters are combined to form words, values, commands, and so on.

Whether hard or floppy, your disks are coated with tiny magnetic particles, each of which can be magnetized by an electrical charge. Each of these particles is known as a *bit*—short for *BInary digiT*. The binary language a computer uses has only two characters: 0 and 1. When a bit has a high charge or is magnetized (the "on" state), the computer reads it as a 1. When a bit has a low charge or is not magnetized (the "off" state), the computer reads it as a 0.

A combination of eight bits forms a *byte*, which is one character of data. There is a unique set of bits for each letter of the alphabet, for every single-digit number, and for many special characters (like $). For example, the two *bytes* (combinations of eight on/off bits) shown here represent the number 53.

0	0	1	1	0	1	0	1

The capacity of every disk and memory chip can be measured in bytes. A *kilobyte* is just over 1,000 bytes. A *megabyte* is just over 1,000,000 bytes, and a *gigabyte* is roughly a thousand megabytes (a billion bytes).

To translate the capacity of any disk into real-world terms, think of each byte as a character. A 3.5-inch HD (high-density) disk holds 1.44 megabytes, which is roughly 1.4 million characters. So if the average page of data has 35 lines of 65 characters each (2,275 characters), a single 1.44-megabyte disk can hold more than 600 pages of data (2,275 characters times 600 pages equals 1,365,000 characters), which is about as many pages as there are in this book—if the data doesn't have a lot of fancy formatting.

Tracks, Sectors, Clusters, and Formatting

These magnetic bits aren't just floating around on the disk's surface. They're actually arranged in a very specific pattern to make it easy for the disk drive to store and find data. Each disk has concentric rings called *tracks* dividing it. To further organize the data, the disk has *sectors*, pie-shaped wedges separated by imaginary lines radiating from the center of the disk (as shown in the following illustration).

Tiny magnetic codes on the disk identify the tracks and sectors that store every group of bits. Your system manages data in units called *clusters* or *allocation units*. Each cluster might hold one or more sectors. Under older versions of DOS and Windows, the smallest cluster size possible for hard disks over 256M was 8K (8,000 bytes or characters). Because all your files won't necessarily contain even multiples of 8,000 characters, some space is wasted. For example, a file with 8,001 bytes would occupy two full clusters, even though most of the second cluster was wasted. Windows 95 OEM Service Release 2 (OSR 2), which has shipped on new computers since the fall of 1996, uses the more efficient FAT32 system with smaller 4K clusters. With 4K clusters, you can pack 10–15 percent more information on the same drive. This is yet another reason to ensure that the computer you buy uses OSR 2, not the original release of Windows 95. As a bonus, the new FAT32 system supports much larger hard disks than earlier file systems. **▶To learn more about what a FAT does, see the task later in this section called "Understand Files" (on page 57).◀**

Before your computer can write any information on a disk, the disk must be *formatted*—that is, the magnetic bits must be arranged into tracks and sectors. Usually your hard drive is already formatted when you get your computer. On the other hand, you may need to format a floppy disk before using it. **▶To learn how to do this, see "Format Disks" on page 151.◀**

Understand How the Drive Reads and Writes

When a drive *writes to* a disk, it's actually magnetizing selected bits to create bytes, or characters. When the drive *reads from* a disk, it reads the bits comprising each byte and places a copy of that information in RAM. A mechanical part called the *read/write head* floats over the disk surface, magnetizing bits or reading their magnetic charges.

The drive's read head is smart and fast. It knows exactly where the different parts of a file are stored and finds them all to load them into RAM. Similarly, it's adept at finding available space on a disk to copy a file to. A disk drive's speed is called its *access time*. Smaller access times indicate faster drives. For example, you should look for a hard drive with an access time of 12 ms (milliseconds) or less. Otherwise, you'll find yourself tapping your toe while you're waiting for your drive to perform various operations.

The *Guided Tour* that follows will explain how the drive works with the disk.

> You've got to keep dust out of your disk drive to keep it in good working order. ▶**To learn more about disk drive care and feeding, see "Clean the Disk Drives" on page 301.**◀

Name that Drive

As you've already noticed, your computer probably has at least two drives. Your computer uses a simple system to tell them apart: the ABCs. You'll need to know your computer's naming system when you want to save, retrieve, or otherwise work with data (operations covered in the sections called "Get Around in Windows 95 Programs," "Organize Files and Folders with Windows 95," and "Work with DOS").

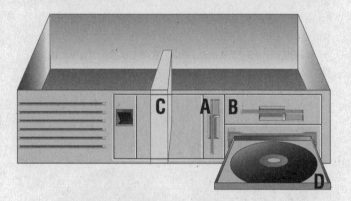

- If your computer has only one floppy disk drive, it's drive *A*. If your system has two floppy disk drives, the one that's to the left or on top is usually drive *A* (although this may not be true if the leftmost floppy drive is oriented vertically).

- On a system with two floppy disk drives, the bottom or right one is usually drive *B*.

- Generally, the hard disk drive inside your computer is drive *C*. If you have multiple hard disk drives, the first will be *C*, the second will be *D*, and so on. Hard disks are assigned drive letters before CD-ROM drives, removable disk drives, and any network drives your system can access.

- Your CD-ROM drive, if you have one, is usually drive *D*. However, if you have multiple hard disks or removable drives attached to your system, the CD-ROM drive will usually be bumped to a later letter. For example, one of my systems has three hard disks, a Syquest removable disk drive, and a CD-ROM drive. The three hard disk drives are *C*, *D*, and *E*; the Syquest is *F*; and the CD-ROM is *G*. Network drives your system can access normally are assigned a much higher letter, like *I* or *H*.

Guided Tour Write to a Disk

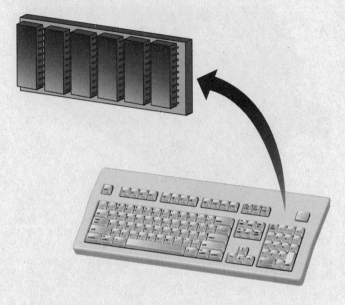

1 As you enter data or work with your computer, the computer holds that data with its RAM chips.

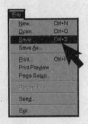

2 When you issue a Save command from the program you're working in, you must tell the computer which drive holds the disk you want to save the information to, and you must enter a name for that data.

3 The disk drive motor starts spinning the disk, and the disk drive indicator light comes on.

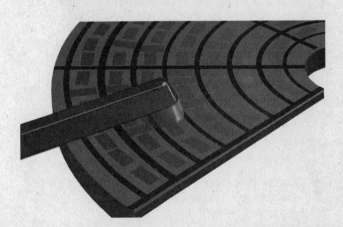

4 The read/write head moves over the disk, looking for tracks and sectors that are empty. When it finds an available byte, it magnetizes the appropriate bits to form a combination of eight bits that represent a character, or byte, on the disk.

5 The read/write head continues moving over the disk and writing new bytes until it has written all the data from RAM on the disk. When the drive head finishes writing, the drive motor stops, and the drive indicator light goes off.

Guided Tour Read from a Disk

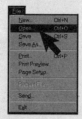

1 Choose the **Open** command in the application program you're using. A dialog box appears, letting you choose the file you want to open. ▶**You'll find more on files in the next task and more on opening files in the section "Open a File in a Windows Program" on page 91.◀**

3 The read/write head moves over the disk, looking for the bytes (characters) that make up the file. When it finds a byte, it reads the combination of the bits and transmits the combination to RAM.

2 The disk drive motor starts spinning the disk, and the disk drive indicator light comes on.

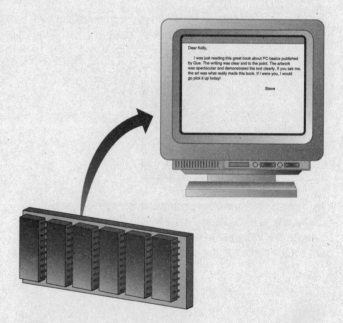

4 The RAM interprets each byte and displays the character it represents on-screen.

5 The read/write head continues moving over the disk and reading until it has read all the file's data from the disk to RAM.

6 When the drive head finishes reading, the drive motor stops, and the drive indicator light goes off.

Understand Files

When you're working with a pile of papers that are all part of a single project, you generally don't just leave them lying around haphazardly. Instead, you put them all in a manila file folder and write a name for that collection of papers on the tab of the folder.

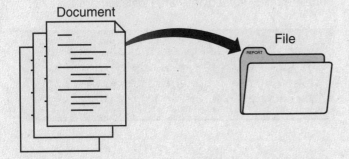

In the same way, your computer programs let you collect data that goes together—such as all the words that make up a document or all the instructions for a program—and save them in a file with a unique name. When you create and name a file, you simultaneously tell your computer what disk to store it on. In general, computers have two kinds of files. *Program files* (which you usually purchase from a software publisher) hold program instructions that you install on your computer. *Data files* hold the work you create on your computer when you use the various programs.

When you want to work with a program, you *activate* or start the program file. When you want to work again with the information in a data file, you use your program to open the file and read it into RAM. The mechanical steps for how this process works are basically the same as the writing-and-reading steps covered in the previous task, "Understand Disks and Drives." The one exception, however, occurs because of the FAT.

➤**See "Save Your Work in a Windows Program" on page 94 for more about this process called *saving*.**◄

What's a FAT?

FAT stands for *File Allocation Table*. Every formatted disk has specialized hidden files holding the FAT. So what does the FAT do, you ask? The FAT keeps track of where all the bytes for each file are physically stored on the disk. Let's look at this in more detail.

As you learned in the task titled "Understand Disks and Drives," the surface of a disk is divided into tracks (concentric circles) and sectors (each of these is shaped like a wedge of pie). Adjacent sectors on a track form a *cluster*. The smallest space that a file can occupy is a cluster. Depending on the size of the file, it can take up one cluster or many clusters. The FAT keeps track of the clusters that hold the contents of each file.

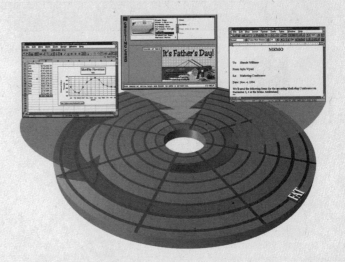

To make the situation even more complicated, suppose there's no empty group of clusters large enough to hold a particular file. Then the file has to be split up and stored on non-adjacent clusters (clusters that aren't *contiguous*). When this happens, the file is said to be *fragmented*. In fact, this is the most typical situation, especially on hard disks. As you save and delete files on the disk, clusters break up into smaller and smaller groups. When a file is fragmented, the FAT becomes even more important if you're going to keep track of the file's pieces.

The *Guided Tour* that follows will give you an example of how the FAT helps work with the clusters of a file stored on a disk.

A disk with fragmented files takes more time to use because the drive's read/write head has to skip around a lot to find information. ▶**For instructions on correcting this problem, see "Optimize a Hard Disk with Defrag" on page [p2s12 TBD].**◀

Where Files Go When You Delete Them

Deleting a file means you erase its contents so you can't use them anymore, which sounds like it wipes the data from the disk immediately. Well, that's not completely true. When you delete a file, its contents remain on the disk. In the FAT, the file's *location* is deleted, so that the FAT *thinks* there isn't anything in that spot on

the disk. Later, when you save another file, the computer writes its contents on the clusters that are marked available, wiping out each cluster's previous contents.

With Windows 95, deleted files are tracked in the Recycle Bin. As long as a file appears in the Recycle Bin, you can restore it if you later decide you want to use it again. Under an older version of MS-DOS (version 5.0 or later), you can restore a file only if you have a utility program for undeleting files. You have to use an undelete utility *immediately* after deleting a file.

▶**See "Delete and Restore Files and Folders" on page 130 for the steps on removing files to free up disk space and restoring files from the Recycle Bin.**◀

Guided Tour How the FAT Tracks Files

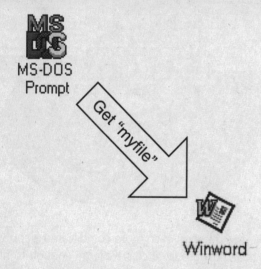

1 Suppose you're working with a program and you use its Open command to open a file. The program starts by talking with the Disk Operating System (DOS), telling DOS to get the file. (The Windows 95 operating system includes an underlying version of DOS.)

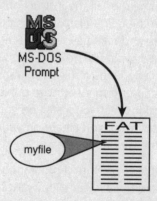

2 DOS looks at the FAT file and finds out the locations of all the clusters that make up the file.

3 The program starts to read the file: A signal tells the read/write head of the drive where to find the first cluster, and the drive reads the cluster's contents into RAM. A signal then directs the head to the next cluster, and so on, until the entire file is in RAM.

Name Files and Decode File Names

File names must be unique in order for your computer to be able to tell them apart. Under Windows 3.11 or an earlier version of DOS, certain *conventions* govern file naming. When you name a file, you give it a base name of up to eight characters and an optional three-character extension (which tells what kind of file it is), creating what's called an "8.3" file name. You can't use spaces or some characters in a file name's base name or extension. These forbidden characters are reserved for the system and commands:

" . / \ [ ] : * < > | + ; . ? space

With Windows 95, you can ignore most of the old file name rules. It lets you use long file names (up to 255 characters). Folder names also can be long and can include special characters. In addition, you can use spaces, but you can't use any of the following characters: \ ? : * " < > |. Windows 95 (but not its DOS) recognizes upper- and lowercase letters in file names. So with Windows 95, you can use file names like "Letter to Mortgage Company 09/05/96" and "Phone List for Little League." Even though you don't usually see file name extensions in Windows 95, it does use them behind the scenes to identify each file's type.

The file name extension can give you a clue about what a file is used for or what program it comes from. This table lists a few of the common file extensions.

File Name Extensions for Common File Types

Extension	File Type/Program It Comes From
.AVI	Video for Windows video file
.BAK	Backup file
.BAT	Batch file (a collection of commands)
.BMP	Windows bitmap graphic file
.COM	Program command file
.DAT	Data file
.DOC	Document file from Microsoft Word or another word processor
.DOT	Microsoft Word template file
.EXE	Executable program file
.GIF	Graphics Interchange Format graphics file
.HLP	Help file
.HTM	Hypertext Markup Language (HTML) Web page file
.JPG	JPEG graphic file
.MDB	Database file from the Microsoft Access program
.MID	MIDI music file
.PPT	Microsoft PowerPoint presentation file
.PCX	PC Paintbrush or Windows Paint file
.TXT	Plain text (ASCII) file
.WAV	Sound file

(continues)

File Name Extensions for Common File Types   Continued

Extension	File Type/Program It Comes From
.WKS, .WK1, .WK2, or .WK3	Lotus 1-2-3 file
.WP or .WPF	Document file from WordPerfect
.XLS	Spreadsheet file from Microsoft Excel
.ZIP	A file containing one or more files compressed with the PKZIP file-compression program

The file name may also include the *path* for the file. The path includes the letter for the drive where a file is stored, followed by a colon, followed by the folders and subfolders (called directories and subdirectories under Windows 3.11 and older versions of DOS) leading to the one holding the file. Folder and subfolder names are separated with backslashes (\). If, for example, a file were on drive C: in the \TEMP subfolder within the \WINDOWS folder, the full path would be **C:\WINDOWS\TEMP**.

If you go to the DOS prompt from Windows 95, you have to use 8.3 file names to refer to files. This becomes a problem when you want to refer to a file with a Windows 95 long file name. At the Windows 95 DOS prompt, a file name like "My Glossary.doc" is abbreviated to "myglos~1.doc." If you have multiple file names that are similar, you'll have trouble distinguishing them under DOS; DOS will abbreviate and sequentially number the files, as in "myglos~1.doc," "myglos~2.doc," and so on. There's really no easy way to work around this issue. If you'll need to work frequently at the Windows 95 DOS prompt, your best bet is to conform to the old 8.3 file name convention when working with Windows 95 programs so you'll be able to tell your files apart at the DOS prompt.

Guided Tour Parts of a File Name

```
C:\work\memos\maysales.doc
```

1 A file name consists of several parts. You will need to specify each of these parts when you name a file and when you open it; they tell your system how to find the file. From left to right, a file name goes from general to specific as it identifies the file.

```
C:
```

2 First, you indicate the drive letter for the drive holding the disk on which you want to store the file (or where the file is already stored). In Windows 95 programs, you can choose the drive to which you want to save from a drop-down list.

```
C:\work\memos
```

3 The next part of the file name is the rest of its path: the route to the folder you want to store the file in (or retrieve it from). Again, Windows 95 programs let you choose the folder from a list instead of typing it in. (You'll learn more about folders in the next task.)

```
C:\work\memos\maysales
```

4 Next comes the *base name* for the file. Specify up to 255 characters. Make it unique, and choose a name that reflects what's in the file.

```
C:\work\memos\maysales.doc
```

5 A *period* ends the base name and is followed by the file's three-letter *extension* (which typically identifies the file type). When you save a file, Windows 95 and Windows 95 programs add the correct extension automatically. When you open a file, most programs filter the list of files in a directory to show only those files that have extensions indicating a kind of file the program can use.

Understand Folders (Directories)

Y ou learned in an earlier task that even a small hard disk can hold 50,000 pages of data. If each of these pages were stored in a separate file, you'd have 50,000 names to keep track of on that drive. Even Einstein couldn't remember all that!

Think of how you would solve this problem with paper files: You'd get a file cabinet with drawers and put files relating to the same project (or same client) in the same drawer. This technique cuts down drastically on the number of names you have to remember.

You can use a similar technique to organize files on the hard and floppy disks you use with your computer. For example, you would want to store all the files running the Excel spreadsheet program in the same "file drawer."

In computing, these electronic file drawers are called *folders* (or *directories* under earlier versions of DOS and Windows 3.11). When you install a program, the process creates folders for its program files. In addition, you can create a nearly unlimited number of folders on any disk—hard or floppy. In file names, you separate folders with the backslash character (\), which is often located just to the left of or below the Backspace key (at the right end of your keyboard's second row of keys).

You arrange folders according to a hierarchical structure that has a root and branches; it's usually called the *folder tree* or *directory tree*. When you start the Windows 95 Explorer, which you use to manage files, you literally see a tree of file folders on-screen. Other programs let you choose from folder lists that also are presented in a tree structure. At the DOS prompt, you have to be able to remember and type in folder names.

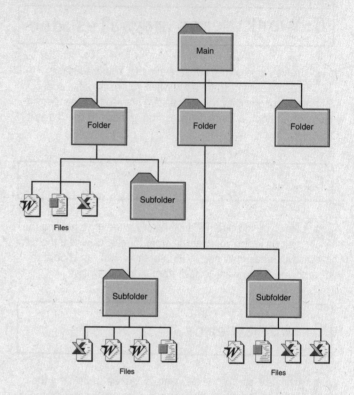

The base folder for every disk is called the *main folder* (or the *root directory* under older versions of DOS and Windows 3.11). All the remaining folders on the disk branch out from the main. When you store a file in the main folder, you use a single backslash to identify the folder. You can have a virtually unlimited number of folders and subfolders. However, adding too many is overkill and could slow you down if you have to search through a lot of folders to find what you need. As always, use moderation and common sense when you create folders.

Creating folders is as easy as picking a name and location. ►To learn how to do it, read "Create New Folders" on page 135.◄

Guided Tour Understand Folders (Directories)

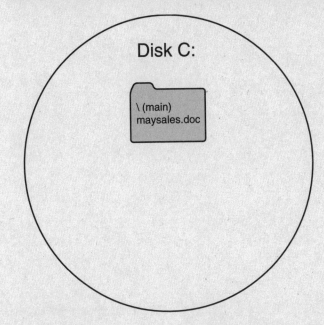

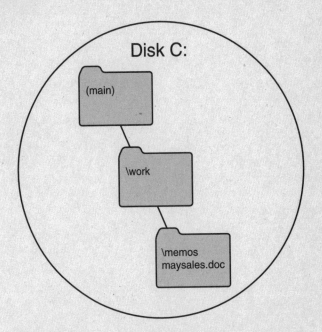

1 For example, the file name **c:\maysales.doc** signifies a file stored in the main folder, which you know because there's only a backslash between the drive letter (**c:**) and the file name (**maysales.doc**).

3 A *subfolder* (or *subdirectory*) branches from a folder. In the file name **c:\work\memos\maysales.doc**, **memos** is a subfolder within the **\work** folder.

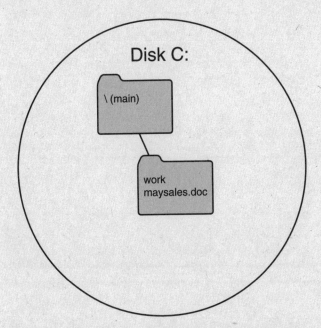

2 Any folder that branches directly from the main is just called a *folder* (or *directory*), or *first-level folder*. For example, in the file name **c:\work\maysales.doc**, **work** is a folder. It follows the first \ for the main folder, which means that it branches off the main folder. The file **maysales.doc** is in the **\work** folder.

HOW TO...

Get Around in Windows 95 Programs

I n an attempt to make your PC as easy to use (yet more powerful) as a Macintosh, in 1995 Microsoft Corporation developed a new version of Windows named Windows 95. Like its predecessor Windows 3.11, Windows 95 provides a graphical user interface (GUI) that enables you to control your computer through icons (pictures) on-screen. Each application or document you open on-screen appears in its own window—hence the name of the product.

The Windows 95 screen (like that of its predecessor) still makes use of windows, icons, and your mouse to help you point and click your way to success. However, Windows 95 has improved on those basic features and has added several new features that can help you take control of your computer and improve its efficiency. In fact, this book focuses on Windows 95 OEM Service Release 2 (OSR 2), also called Windows 95 B, which offers further improvements over the original Windows 95 release.

What You Will Find in This Section

Understand the Windows 95 Desktop

The Windows 95 desktop contains only a few icons, a Start button, a bar at the bottom, and a great expanse of open space. Before you start running programs and getting into the inner workings of Windows 95, take a look at the various elements that make up the desktop. Then take the *Guided Tour* for some hands-on experience.

> PCs typically come with a wealth of software packages preinstalled by the manufacturer. So your desktop and Start menu may include different, more, or fewer icons than the desktop pictured throughout this book.

- The *desktop* is the "great expanse of space" mentioned earlier. Whenever you run a program, that program opens in a window on the desktop. In addition, you can place icons on the desktop for quick access to the programs you use most often.

- The *Start button* opens a menu that lets you run your Windows program and shut down your computer.

- The *taskbar* (where the Start button is located) shows the names of all the programs you're currently running. You can quickly switch to a program by clicking its name in the taskbar. At the right end of the taskbar, Windows displays the time, as well as icons for certain pieces of hardware (like your speakers or printer) when they're active or icons for some programs (like Lotus 97 SmartSuite).

- *My Computer* is a *shortcut* icon that opens a window showing all the disk drives on your computer. Double-click this icon to open its window, and then double-click a drive icon to see what's on the drive.

- The *Recycle Bin* allows you to quickly clean files, folders, and icons off your system.

- If Windows 95 networking features are installed on your system, you'll have a *Network Neighborhood* icon.

- The Windows 95 OEM Service Release 2 (OSR 2) desktop offers you the Internet Setup Wizard, which you start using the icon labeled *The Internet*. The first time you use this icon, it sets up your system to connect to the Internet. Thereafter, the icon starts the Internet Explorer 3.0 Web browser program that's also included in OSR 2.

- Your desktop may include other icons for connecting to online services, launching other programs, or storing files

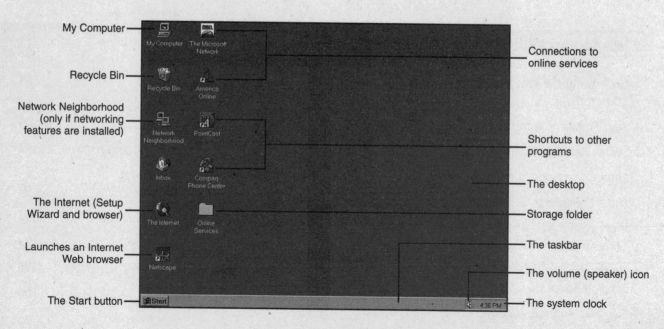

Guided Tour Tour Windows 95

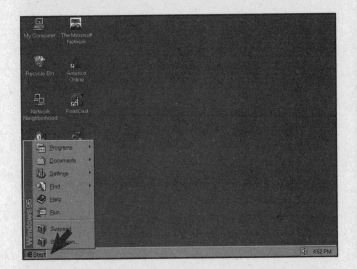

1 In the lower-left corner of the Windows screen is a Start button. Click the **Start** button for a menu that leads to Windows 95 features and other menus offering commands for all the programs you can run.

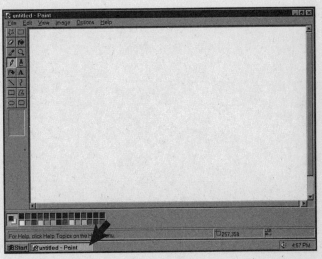

3 When you run a program, it appears in a window. Its name also appears on the taskbar at the bottom of the screen. You can click the program's name at any time to go to it. **▶See "Switch Between Running Programs" on page 71 for details.◄**

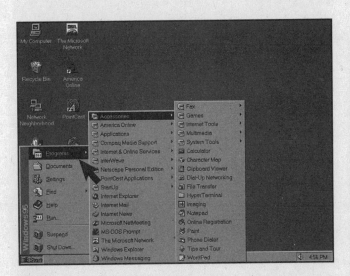

2 Some of the options on the Start menu are followed by an arrow. If you rest the mouse pointer on one of these items, a submenu opens, showing additional items. When you see the program you want, click it to run the program. **▶To learn more about running programs, see "Start Programs with the Start Button" on page 69.◄**

4 At the right end of the taskbar, a clock shows the current time. To see today's date, rest the mouse pointer on the time.

(continues)

Guided Tour Tour Windows 95 *(continued)*

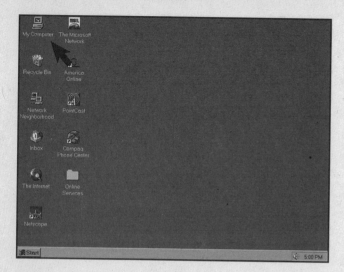

5 In the upper-left corner of the Windows desktop is the My Computer icon. Double-click this icon to view a window that shows icons for all the disk drives on your computer.
▶**For specifics on using My Computer, see the next section, "Organize Files and Folders with Windows 95," on page 101.◀**

6 To see what's on a disk, double-click the disk's icon in the My Computer window to open another window. Each window shows the files and folders (directories) on the disk it represents.

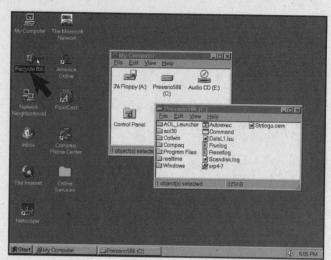

7 The Recycle Bin icon allows you to quickly remove a file, folder, or icon from your computer. Simply drag the icon that you want to remove from its folder window until it is over the **Recycle Bin** icon. Then release the mouse button.

8 To see what's in the Recycle Bin, double-click the **Recycle Bin** icon. A window opens, showing the Recycle Bin's contents and allowing you to restore the items or delete them.
▶**See "Delete and Restore Files and Folders" on page 130 for complete instructions.◀**

Start Programs with the Start Button

In Windows 3.11, you had to navigate the Program Manager, program group windows, and program icons. Windows 95 neatly tucks away all programs in the Start menu. To start any program, you click the **Start** button and then weave your way through a series of menus and submenus with your mouse. When you see the program you want, you draw a bead on it and fire (click). The program starts, and you're ready to work.

How do programs get their names listed on the Start menu? Well, if you installed Windows 95 over your old version of Windows, or if your computer came with Windows 95 installed, the installation program added the program names automatically. The programs that are built into Windows 95 are also listed on one of the Start menu's submenus already. In addition, whenever you install a new program (▶see **"Install a Program in Windows 95" on page 312◀**), Windows adds the program's name to the Start menu or one of its submenus. You also can manually add a program to the Start menu, ▶as described in the section **"Add a New Program to the Windows 95 Start Menu" on page 314.◀**

When you start a program, it opens in its own window in Windows 95. You can control each window's size and position on-screen. ▶See **"Size and Arrange Windows" later in this section (on page 81) for more details.◀** For hands-on experience starting a program in Windows 95, take the *Guided Tour*.

To run a program that isn't on the Programs menu or a submenu, click the **Start** button and click **Run**. Type the command required to start the program, and then click **OK**. If you don't know the command required to start the program, click the **Browse** button in the Run dialog box and use the Browse dialog box to find the startup command. ▶See **"Work with Folder and File Lists in Dialog Boxes" (on page 79) later in this section to learn how to browse for files.◀**

Start a Program with a Desktop Shortcut Icon

The last task gave you a snapshot of the Windows 95 desktop. There you saw that the desktop includes icons called *shortcuts*. Shortcut icons point to specific programs and documents. Each shortcut icon has a small arrow in its lower-left corner. A shortcut isn't an actual program startup file or document file. Rather, it's a link to another file that lets you launch or open the file. So even though you have a single copy of the actual program startup file or document file on your hard disk, you can create multiple shortcuts to it. As a result, you can start a program from the desktop or any other folder that contains a shortcut to it.

▶**You'll learn to create your own shortcuts in the later task called "Save Time with Shortcuts" on page 159.◀** For now, all you need to know is that you can double-click any program's shortcut icon on the desktop to start the program the shortcut points to. As you learned in the last task, you also can double-click any other icon on the desktop to access a Windows 95 feature, folder, or file that the icon represents.

Guided Tour Start Programs

1 Click the **Start** button in the lower-left corner of the screen. The Start menu pops up out of the taskbar, providing options for shutting down your computer, changing settings, and more.

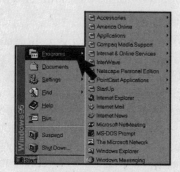

2 To see a list of available programs, rest the mouse pointer on (point to) **Programs** at the top of the Start menu. The Programs submenu shoots out from the Start menu. The items at the bottom of the list are programs you can run. At the top of the list are program groups (you can tell this because each item is followed by an arrow). If you move the mouse pointer over a program group, a submenu appears showing the names of the programs in that group.

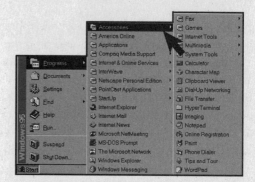

3 Rest the mouse pointer on (point to) one of the program groups at the top of the list. Each program group name is followed by an arrow, which indicates that this item opens a submenu. For example, point to **Accessories**, and the Accessories group opens, showing the names of the programs that come with Windows 95 (and from our PC manufacturer).

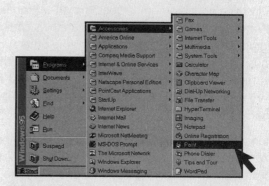

4 To run a program, click it. The program opens in its own window.

Switch Between Running Programs

Do you like to watch television while you work out? Talk on a cellular phone while driving? Do two or more things at once at all possible times? If you like to juggle a lot of tasks—and if you have a powerful enough computer system with enough RAM— Windows 95 can run more than one program at once. To take advantage of that capability, you can start as many programs as your computer's RAM can hold and then switch between them to perform various operations.

As you run programs and open documents, however, the Windows desktop can become so cluttered that you might never find what you need. You can use the

Windows 95 *taskbar* to dig your way out of the deepest stack of program windows.

Whenever you start a program in Windows 95, a button with the program's name is added to the taskbar at the bottom of the screen. Whenever you want to return to a program, click the program's button in the taskbar, and the program immediately jumps to the front of the stack.

As in Windows 3.11, you also can use the **Alt+Tab** key combination to switch among running applications.

The following *Guided Tour* helps you explore both of these methods for switching between programs.

Guided Tour   Switch Between Programs

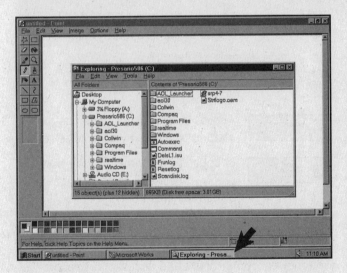

1 Run the programs you want to use. When you run a program, its name is added to the taskbar.

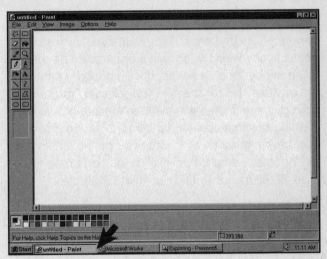

2 To switch to a program, click its name in the taskbar. Whether the program window was minimized or behind a stack of other windows, it is moved to the front of the stack and activated.

3 To use the keyboard to switch to another program, press and hold the **Alt** key, and then press **Tab** without releasing the Alt key. A small window displays an icon for each running application. While still holding down the **Alt** key, press **Tab** repeatedly until the square outline surrounds the icon for the program you want. When that program is selected, release both keys.

Enter Commands in Windows 95

You may remember that Ali Baba said "Open Sesame!" and a secret passageway opened magically before him. He gave a command, and the secret door performed an action. Similarly, you issue a command to Windows 95 (or a Windows 95 application), and the program performs an action.

Near the top of the screen in every Windows 95 program component (such as the Windows 95 Explorer, which you use to work with files ►**as described in the next section of this book on page 101◄**) or Windows 95 application, you'll find a *menu bar*. It lists the available *pull-down menus*, each of which offers a group of related commands.

To tell an application what to do, you open a pull-down menu and choose a command from that menu. To close a menu without selecting a command from it, press **Esc** or click outside the menu.

Windows 95 offers an even more accessible command feature: shortcut menus. If you right-click any icon or object in any window (or even a blank space on the Windows desktop), a menu pops up displaying the options available for the item you selected. You can then click the desired command to execute it or to see a dialog box that asks for additional input. So if you ever have a question as to what you can do with a particular object, simply right-click it; you don't have to scan all the menus to find out what's available.

Skip the Menu

Consistent with the promise that Windows 95 programs are easy to use, many programs offer *buttons* (icons) you can click instead of choosing a command from a menu. Often, you'll find these in a row called a *toolbar*. Each button performs exactly the same action as a particular typed command or a menu selection; it's just simpler and faster to use. Some toolbar buttons even let you skip a few steps (dialog boxes, for example). Each button has a picture that suggests what its command does. For example, the button for printing shows (surprise!) a printer. The following table shows some common buttons you might see in Microsoft applications; toolbar buttons from other software publishers will look and function much like these.

 Starts a new document or opens an existing document.

 Saves the current document to disk.

 Prints the current document.

 Lets you preview what the current document will look like when you print it.

 Cuts out the text or data you've selected and puts it in the Windows Clipboard (a temporary storage location).

 Copies the selected text or data and puts the copy in the Windows Clipboard.

 Pastes what's in the Clipboard onto the screen at the location of the insertion point.

 Undoes the previous command or action.

 Applies bold, italic, or underline formatting to the text you've selected.

 Changes the alignment of the paragraph you've selected to left-, center-, or right-alignment.

Speak in Command Code

You may encounter books and tech support people who use what sounds like a secret code when they discuss choosing a menu and a command. For example, you may read or hear something like "Choose File, Exit."

Breaking the code is easy. The first word after "Choose" is usually a menu name. The next word is the name of a command on that menu. So "Choose **File, Exit**" translates to "Open the **File** menu and choose the **Exit** command."

Valuable Menu Command Secrets

Most software publishing companies have agreed to use *common user access* standards, which means they design their Windows 95 applications to be easy to use and to work like other Windows 95 applications. All Windows 95 applications offer a *graphical user interface* (GUI) just like Windows 95. Familiar visual cues help you get around in the program.

Whenever possible, Windows 95 applications put their menus in much the same place on-screen and offer similar commands. The File menu tends to be first on the menu bar, for example, and it usually offers New, Open, Save, and Exit commands—no matter which Windows 95 application you're using. Normally, you'll also find a Window menu that lists the names of open documents; to switch to the document you want to work on, choose it. Most applications also provide a

Help menu at the far right end of the menu bar. Once you're familiar with where commands are in one program, it'll be fairly easy to find them in another program.

Similarly, when you see certain symbols next to command names on menus, they will mean the same thing from program to program: what will happen after you choose a command. For example, an ellipsis (...) after any command name means that when you select that command, a dialog box will appear, requesting more information.

> Menus provide *shortcut key combinations* next to some commands. Once you learn these shortcut keys, you can press a key combination to execute the associated command without ever opening the menu.

Guided Tour   Choose a Menu Command

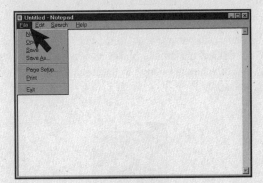

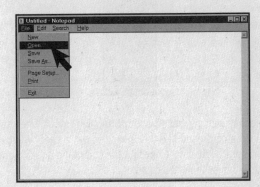

1 To open a pull-down menu, click its name in the menu bar (or press and hold the **Alt** key and then press the underlined *selection letter* in the menu's name; for example, press **Alt+F** to open the File menu as shown).

2 If you want to close a menu without choosing a command from it, click another menu name, click outside the menu, or press **Esc**.

3 To choose a command from a menu, click it. (To use keys, simply press the selection letter, or press the **down arrow** until the command name you want is highlighted and then press **Enter**.)

Guided Tour Learn the Parts of a Menu

When a command doesn't have any symbol beside it, it simply runs when you choose it. For example, choosing the **Exit** command would prompt you to save any unsaved work and then exit (close) the program.

Commands that have an ellipsis (...) beside them open a dialog box that requests more information from you so the command can run. (▶See the task "Use a Dialog Box" on page 76.◀)

Some commands *toggle* on and off (turn on or off) when selected. When a command like this is toggled on, a check mark appears to the left of it. Choosing the command again toggles it off and removes the check mark.

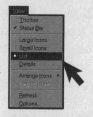

Sometimes horizontal divider lines separate commands into groups. If you see a round dot to the left of a command in a group, that means only one command in the group can be selected (toggled on). The **List** command shown here is the command that's currently selected in the second group. If you choose a different command, the dot appears next to that command and not the List command.

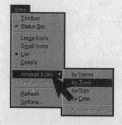

When a command has a triangle to the right of it, choosing that command displays a *submenu* (sometimes called a *cascading* menu) that offers more options. In that submenu, click the option you want.

You can't choose commands that appear dim or *grayed out*, like the first several commands on this Edit menu. Dimmed commands are unavailable because you need to perform some other action to activate the command. For example, you need to select something in the document to activate the Cut and Copy commands on the Edit menu in most programs.

Guided Tour   Right-Click for Shortcut Menus

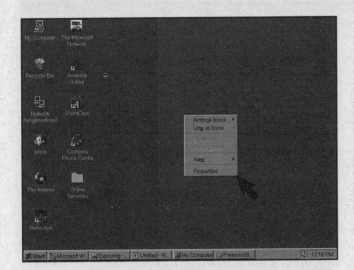

1 To enter a command for an icon, an area of the screen, or any other object, right-click the object and a shortcut menu appears. The shortcut menu shown here appears if you right-click a blank area of the Windows 95 desktop.

2 Click the command you want to enter. What happens next depends on the command you select.

Use a Dialog Box

In novels and short stories, any interaction between characters that has them talk to each other is called *dialog*. When you interact with Windows 95 or an application, the program may "ask" you to provide information or a choice so it can do what you want. It "asks" you by displaying a *dialog box*, a special window that lets you tell it exactly what to do. When you tell the program to proceed, it does what you told it to do when you filled in the dialog box.

Dialog boxes appear after you choose a menu or shortcut menu command that's followed by an *ellipsis* (...). The box may ask you to perform precise actions like these:

- Choose which file to open from a particular drive and folder.

- Specify whether you want your text to appear bold, italicized, or underlined.

- Select a particular clip art (picture) file to insert into a document.

- Tell an application whether to ignore or change a word during a spelling check.

Dialog boxes offer different *controls* for choosing options. In some cases, you simply choose all the options that apply. In other cases, you have to select a single option from a group of several. Dialog boxes usually group related options in a box with a title. In a dialog box you use to format text, for example, you may find effects like bold, italic, and underline grouped in an area called "Style." Many dialog boxes offer preview areas to show you what the options you selected would do if you approved them. This task presents the different kinds of controls and explains how to use each one.

Command buttons run a command or display another dialog box when the button name is followed by an ellipsis (...). Simply click a command button with the mouse to select it. The most common command buttons are OK, Cancel, and Apply. Choosing OK accepts the options you selected and closes the dialog box. Choosing Cancel closes the dialog box without running a command. Choosing Apply accepts your dialog box

options without closing the dialog box, so you can view on-screen changes and make additional selections if necessary.

Check boxes toggle an option on and off (a check mark or an **X** appears in the box when the option is turned on). To select or deselect a check box, click it. Even though check boxes may be grouped, you can select all the options in the group, none of them, or any combination of them.

Option buttons (sometimes called radio buttons) always appear in groups because they are mutually exclusive; you can select only one button at a time from each group. To select the one you want, click it.

When you have to enter a *value* (such as the number of copies you want to print of a document) or a *name* (like a new file name), the place you enter it is a *text box*. To use one, click in the box to place the *insertion point* (a vertical cursor) in it, and then type in your selection.

List boxes let you choose from a list of choices for an option. To make a choice, click it. In many cases, double-clicking a choice in the list selects that choice and closes the dialog box, accepting any other options you've selected. (Sometimes a text box appears above the list box, giving you the option of typing a choice or choosing it from the list.)

Drop-down lists hide all but the currently selected option until you display the list. Click the **drop-down arrow** beside the list to display the choices, and then click the new choice.

Tabs enable a dialog box to hold multiple groups of options. To select a tab to see the options it holds, click the tab.

Increment or spinner buttons let you increase or decrease a value. Click and hold on the **up arrow** to increase the value. Click and hold on the **down arrow** to decrease the value. You also may see a *slider*, on which you drag a bar to increase or decrease a value.

For some dialog box options, the dialog box displays an *icon* for each choice or a graphic or palette showing a variety of choices. Simply click the choice you want.

To move between dialog box controls with the keyboard, you can press the **Tab** key repeatedly until a dotted-line highlight surrounds the option you want to work with. If the option has a *selection letter* (underlined letter), you can move to it by pressing and holding the **Alt** key and pressing the selection letter.

Get Help in Dialog Boxes

Windows 95 dialog boxes look a little more like windows than their Windows 3.11 counterparts did. In the upper-right corner of most dialog boxes, you'll see a Close button (which contains an X) and a question mark button. The question mark button is an ingenious tool for providing information about the options you have. When you click the question mark button, the mouse pointer grows a question mark. When you click an option with that question mark pointer, a small box

appears explaining what the option does (as shown in this figure).

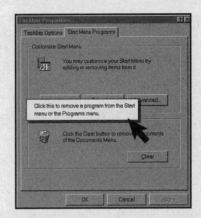

Another way to view information about a dialog box option is to right-click the option and then click **What's This?**.

Guided Tour　Parts of a Dialog Box

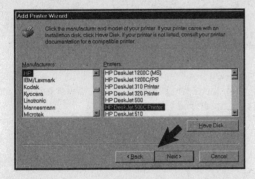

Command buttons run a command or display another dialog box when the button name is followed by an ellipsis (...).

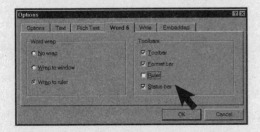

Check boxes toggle an option on and off (a check mark or an **X** appears in the box when the option is turned on).

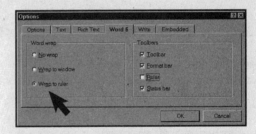

Option buttons always appear in groups. To select the one you want, click it.

You enter a value or a name (like a new file name) in a *text box* or *edit box*.

(continues)

Guided Tour Parts of a Dialog Box *(continued)*

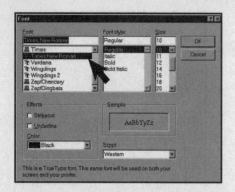

List boxes let you choose from a list of choices for an option.

Increment or *spinner buttons* let you increase or decrease a value. Click and hold an arrow to change the displayed value.

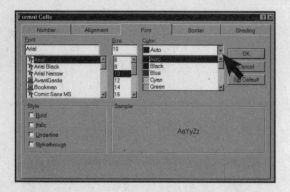

Drop-down lists open to display a list of choices. Click the **drop-down arrow** beside the list to display the choices, and then click the new choice.

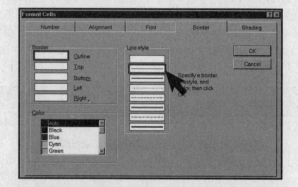

For some dialog box options (such as the Line Style choices shown here), the dialog box displays an *icon* for each choice. Simply click the choice you want.

Tabs enable a dialog box to hold multiple groups of options. Click a tab to choose it.

Work with Folder and File Lists in Dialog Boxes

Whenever you issue a command to perform a *file operation* (such as the Open or Save command on the File menu), the dialog box that appears usually includes a Look In drop-down list box, with another list box below it.

The Look In list enables you to navigate a folder tree for all the disk drives attached to your system, with the Desktop being the topmost level (because you can store files and folders on the Windows 95 desktop). A small icon identifies each disk drive, folder, and subfolder. An open-file icon indicates which folder you're currently viewing. Closed-file icons identify other folders. The

files and subfolders in the currently selected folder generally appear in the list below the Look In list. The following *Guided Tour* shows you how to navigate through the various levels of a Look In drop-down list box.

> Within a file handling dialog box, you can right-click any file or folder icon in the list below the Look In list for a shortcut menu that lets you work with the folder or file—deleting it, renaming it, and more.

Guided Tour Use a Look In List

1 Click the **drop-down arrow** to open the Look In list.

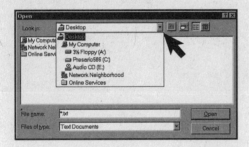

2 To go to the main folder (root directory) of a drive, click its drive icon in the tree. The Look In list closes, and the first-level folders and files in the selected folder appear in the list below.

3 To move "down" one level in the tree (display the files in a subfolder of the current folder), double-click the folder or subfolder in the list of files and folders.

4 To move "up" one level in the tree, click the **Up One Level** button at the top of the dialog box. To jump up by more than one level, open the **Look In** list and click any higher-level folder on the same disk (which would have an open-file icon beside it) or another disk drive icon.

5 When the file you want appears in the list below the Look In list, double-click the file to open it.

Work with Scroll Bars in Dialog Boxes

When it holds a particularly long list or more contents than it can show at once, a dialog box may display only part of a list or other type of content. This problem also can occur when a My Computer or Explorer window is too small to display icons for all the programs, folders, files, shortcuts, and other items it holds.

Whenever a dialog box or program can't display all the available choices in a list or window, it displays one or more *scroll bars*. You use the scroll bars to move through the list or window to see the rest of the choices. Vertical scroll bars run down the right side of a list or window; horizontal scroll bars run along the bottom edge.

To work with scroll bars, you must use a mouse. You can choose from several techniques, which you'll learn in the following *Guided Tour*.

Guided Tour   Use Scroll Bars

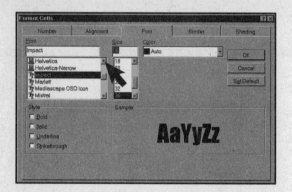

1 To display one more item at the top or bottom of the list (or to move through a window by a small increment), click the arrow at either end of the scroll bar. You can click and hold on the arrow to scroll steadily; release the mouse button to stop.

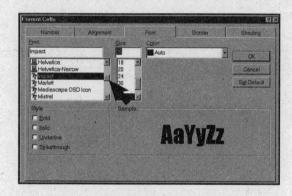

3 To move really fast, drag the scroll box along the scroll bar.

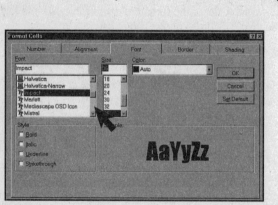

2 To move in larger increments, click the scroll bar itself. Click toward the arrow that indicates the direction in which you want to move.

Size and Arrange Windows

Windows is called Windows for a couple of reasons. First, "Cool Interface with Little Pictures and Boxes" was just too long. Second, Windows uses *windows* on-screen to organize information and commands, as described here:

- Program icons and choices on the Start menu open windows that hold documents.

- Dialog boxes are windows; you can move them around on-screen.

- A window opens when you start My Computer or the Explorer to manage files and disks or when you start any other application from Windows. You'll learn more about managing files with My Computer and the Explorer in the next section of this book.

- Each file you open within an application opens in its own document window.

Windows let you have several things going on at once. You can arrange and size multiple program windows or document windows within a program so you can see them all on-screen. This is useful when you want to copy or move information from window to window. For example, with My Computer or Explorer, you can copy and move files from one disk to another by dragging their file names from one disk's window to another. Windows offers two shortcut options for arranging all the windows you've opened on-screen. *Tiling* reduces the size of all the open windows and arranges them so you can see all of them at once. *Cascading* gives all the open windows an identical size, and then stacks them on-screen like overlapping cards.

Select a Window

To work in or with an open window, you have to select it first; then it becomes the *active window*. The title bar of the active window always appears in a color different from those of other open windows. If it's visible, click the window you want to select. When you select a new window, the one you choose typically jumps in front of all other open windows.

To move from one open application window to another, click the window you want (if you can see it on-screen), or click the application's name in the taskbar, or press **Alt+Tab** until the application you want appears.

To select a document window within an application, use the application's Window menu. The names of open document windows typically appear at the bottom of this menu. Click the **Window** menu, and then click the name of the window you want to select.

Control Windows

You can make a window any size you want or move it anywhere on-screen by dragging with the mouse. The window parts described next enable you to control a window.

The *Maximize button* shows a picture of a big window. Clicking it maximizes the window, increasing a program window to full-screen size or increasing a document window to the largest size available within the program window. When you maximize a window, the Maximize button changes to a *Restore button*, which looks like two overlapping windows. Clicking the Restore button returns the window to the size it was before you maximized it, which is called restoring the window.

The *Minimize button* (which showed a down arrow in Windows 3.11) now shows what looks like a pancake—or the window as it would be if flattened. Minimizing a program window displays it as a button on the taskbar; minimizing a document window within a program flattens the document to a narrow slice of the title bar that contains the Control-menu box, the file's name, and Restore, Maximize, and Close buttons.

The *Close button* (the button with the X on it) has no counterpart in Windows 3.11. You can quickly close a window by clicking this button. When you close a program window, the program shuts down. Closing a document window closes that file only, leaving the application open so you can work on other things.

The *Control-menu box* takes on various forms depending on the program you're running. You can click this button to display a menu for sizing, moving, and closing the window.

The *title bar* shows the program name and the name of the current document file (or "Untitled" if you haven't named the file). You can drag a window's title bar to move the window, or you can drag a window's border to resize the window, as long as the window isn't maximized. The lower-right corner of each window that's not maximized has a *resize area* which you can drag to quickly change the size and dimensions of the window. The window *border* is the boundary of the window; you can drag the border to resize the window in most cases.

Display the Control Menu for a Window

Every window has a small icon in the upper-left corner: the *Control-menu box*. When you select this icon, it displays the Control menu, which in turn offers commands you can use to manipulate or work within the document or program window. For example, a Close command on this menu closes the document or application. There's a Control menu for every application window, folder window, and document window you open in an application.

To display a Control menu, click the window's **Control-menu box** or right-click the window's title bar. When the Control menu appears, select commands from it as you would from any other menu. To close a window, you can double-click the **Control-menu box**.

Control-menu boxes   Minimize button   Maximize button   Restore button   Close button

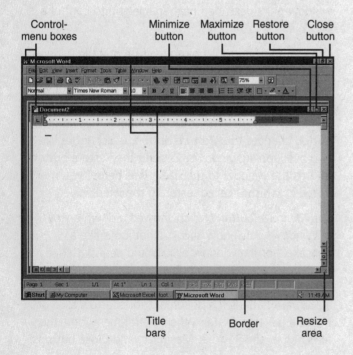

Title bars   Border   Resize area

Guided Tour Move and Resize a Window

To move a window, click the window's title bar and drag it in the direction you want. When the gray shadow outline of the window is where you want it, release the mouse button.

To resize a window's height or width, position the mouse pointer over the side, top, or bottom border until it turns into a double-headed arrow. Then click and drag the window's border outward or inward until it's the size you want (indicated with a gray shadow outline). To resize both the height and width, drag the resize area in the lower-right corner and release the mouse when the window reaches the size you want (indicated with a gray shadow outline).

Guided Tour Minimize, Maximize, Restore, and Close Windows

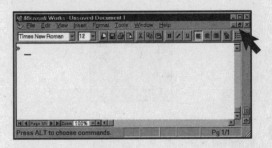

To minimize a program window or a document window, click the **Minimize** button.

To restore a maximized window to its previous size, click the **Restore** button.

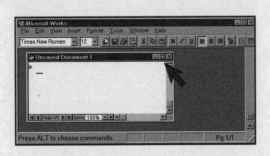

To maximize a window, click the **Maximize** button.

To close any window, click its **Close** button. Using the keyboard, you can press **Ctrl+F4** to close a document window or program-group window, and you can press **Alt+F4** to close an application window.

Guided Tour   Tile and Cascade Windows

1 To *tile* windows (arrange them side by side) within an application, open the **Window** menu and click **Tile**.

2 Windows resizes all the open windows, and then arranges them so you can see them all (and some of their contents) on-screen.

3 To *cascade* windows (overlap them in order), open the **Window** menu and click **Cascade**.

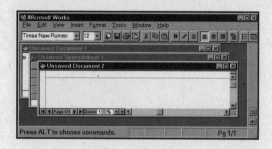

4 Windows resizes all the open windows and arranges them so they overlap in a neat stack on-screen. Only the contents of the top window are visible on-screen.

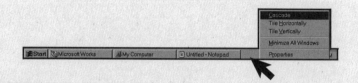

5 You can use the taskbar to quickly arrange open program windows. Right-click a blank area of the taskbar and choose **Cascade**, **Tile Horizontally**, **Tile Vertically**, or **Minimize All Windows** from the shortcut menu.

Get On-Screen Help

Have you ever wished you had an experienced Windows tutor sitting next to you, offering helpful comments, tips, and explanations? Windows 95 offers such an aide in the form of its Help system. The Windows 95 Help system includes step-by-step instructions and animations of the basic tasks you might perform.

You simply open the **Start** menu and click **Help**. A Help window appears, showing tabs for a table of contents of Help topics, a searchable index, and a Find feature for searching out specific Help topics. The Contents tab is useful for finding out how to perform a specific task (such as running a program or maintaining your computer). Think of Contents as an on-screen book. The Index tab shows an alphabetical listing of topics, tasks, and anything else you might find in a typical index. The index is good if you already know what you're looking for. The Find tab gives you a tool for searching for specific information when you're not quite sure what information you need.

Select the type of information you want, and then double-click a topic to learn how to perform any task in Windows. The next *Guided Tours* lead you through the process of taking a Windows 95 tour and searching for specific help.

Use Other Help Buttons

Some windows in the Help system offer a row of command buttons below the title bar. These buttons perform operations that let you navigate and perform other special operations in Help. Here's what each button does:

 Click the **Help Topics** button to display the main Help Topics window (the one you see immediately after clicking the Start button and clicking Help).

Click the **Back** button to return to the previous Help screen.

 Click the **Options** button to display a menu of commands for working with the current Help screen, such as printing or copying it.

 Click one of the double-arrow buttons to move to the previous or next Help topic.

Get Help from the Office 97 Office Assistant

Quite a few manufacturers offer the Microsoft Office 97 Small Business Edition (SBE) preinstalled on new systems. If your system comes with SBE, you'll soon find another type of help in the Office applications: the Office Assistant. The Office Assistant is an animated character that appears in a small window on-screen. As you work, it may offer hints or ask if you need help with a particular feature. You also can ask the Office Assistant a question, in your own words, at any time. Here's how:

1. If the Office Assistant isn't currently on-screen, click the **Office Assistant** button at the far right end of the Standard toolbar (which is usually by default the top toolbar in an Office application). If the Assistant is on-screen, just click within the Assistant window.

2. In the yellow thought balloon that appears above the Assistant, simply type your question in the **What would you like to do?** text box, and then click **Search**.

3. The Assistant displays a list of topics that might answer your question. Click the button or icon to the left of the topic that appears to be the best match to display a Help window for that topic.

When you finish working in the Help window, click its **Close** (X) button. You can click the Close (X) button on the Office Assistant window to put the Office Assistant away when you don't need it.

Guided Tour Have Windows Show You How to Perform a Task

1 No matter which type of help you need, you must open the Help system by clicking the **Start** button and then clicking **Help**.

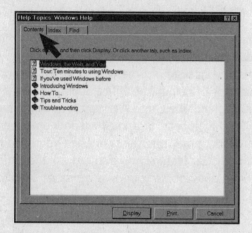

2 Windows displays a dialog box that provides a table of contents list, a searchable index tab, and a tab for finding help topics. Click the **Contents** tab if it is not in front.

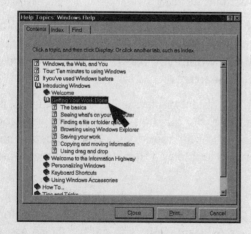

3 The Contents tab lists several "books" full of Help topics. You can double-click a book to view the topics in it. For example, to display the screen shown in the figure above, double-click **Introducing Windows** and then **Getting Your Work Done**.

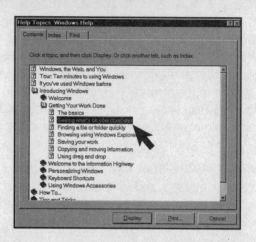

4 Double-click one of the Help topics, which are denoted by page icons instead of book icons.

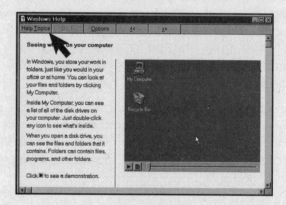

5 The Help topic may appear as a screen with an explanation (left) and an animation (right), as shown here. Click the **Play** button below the animation to start playing it. Other Help topic windows might give a list of numbered steps to follow, a static graphic with a description, or a list of information.

6 When you're finished working in the Help topic window, you can go back to the list of Help topics by clicking the **Help Topics** button at the top of the Help window.

Guided Tour Have Windows Show You How to Perform a Task

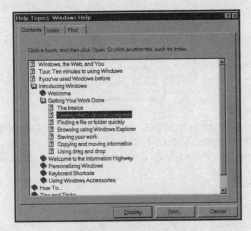

8 When you are done with the Help system, click the **Close** button (the button with the X in the upper-right corner of the window).

> At the top of the Contents list is an icon labeled **Tour: Ten Minutes to Using Windows.** Double-click this icon to view a multimedia tour that explains the Windows 95 basics. If you do not see this icon, you may not have installed the complete Windows 95 Help system.

7 When you are returned to the Contents list, you can double-click another topic, double-click an open book to close it, or double-click a closed book to see the topics in that book.

Guided Tour Search the Index for Specific Help

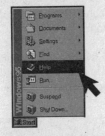

1 To display the Windows Help system, click the **Start** button and click **Help**.

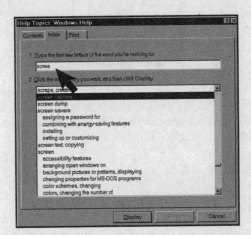

3 The index is set up like the index of a book. You can drag the scroll box to view additional entries and then click the desired entry, or you can start typing the entry in the text box. As you type, Windows highlights the first index entry that matches what you've typed.

(continues)

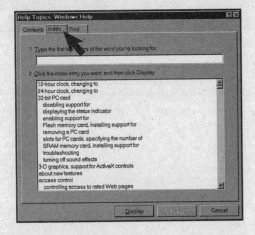

2 Unless you clicked a different tab, the Contents tab is up front. Click the **Index** tab to display a complete index of entries in the Help system.

Guided Tour   Search the Index for Specific Help   *(continued)*

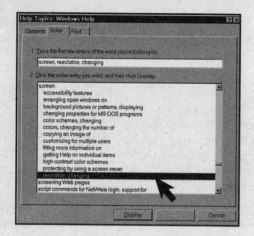

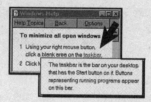

4 When the desired index entry appears, double-click it. Or highlight the entry and click the **Display** button at the bottom of the window.

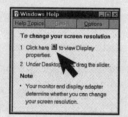

6 In some Help windows, you'll come across green underlined words. If you click one of those words, a box pops up, providing a definition or additional information about the word.

7 At the bottom of many Help windows are buttons for obtaining additional help. Click a button to view more information about a topic.

5 The Help Topics window disappears, and a new window appears, showing an explanation for the selected topic. If you see a button like the one shown here, you can click it to start performing the task.

8 You can always get back to the index by clicking the **Help Topics** button. To exit the Help system, click the **Close** button in the upper-right corner of the window.

The Find tab is similar to the Index tab, though more complex. It allows you to perform a thorough search of Help topics. (Personally, I have more luck finding information in the index.)

Start a New File in a Windows Program

When you start a Windows 95 application, usually it will open a blank new document on the screen. You can work with that document, or you can open a different file and work with that one instead. Chances are, however, that you will create more than one new document per work session. You might write a letter, create a report, and then put together a to-do list. Every time you want to start another document, you'll need to open a new file in the program.

In most programs, starting a new file takes no more than a simple menu command or the clicking of a button. You issue the command, and a new document window appears on-screen. (In *integrated software* programs that combine several applications—for example, Microsoft Works for Windows—you also have to tell the program what *kind* of file to open.)

Be aware that some programs can have only one document open at a time. (When you start a new document in the Windows 95 WordPad accessory program, for example, it closes any document that's already open on-screen.) So make sure you save your work in the open document before you start a new file (▶**see "Save Your Work in a Windows Program" on page 94**◀).

> A *document* is a file you create in any Windows program. Documents can be (for example) spreadsheet, plain text, word processing, graphics, or database files.

Jump-Start a File

Many programs offer automated features that help you develop new files. These helpers display dialog boxes that ask you for information and give you choices for putting a document together. In a presentation graphics (slide show) program, for example, you could choose a look for your slide show, screen colors, and a topic (see the following figure). The program would then set the whole thing up and suggest an outline for you.

In Microsoft products, these automated helpers are called *Wizards*. In Corel WordPerfect products, they're called *Experts*. Lotus products offer some automated help called SmartAssistants. Look for the command to start one of these helpers on the File menu in your application; alternatively, some applications offer the startup command in a New File dialog box. Then you follow the on-screen prompts to set up your document.

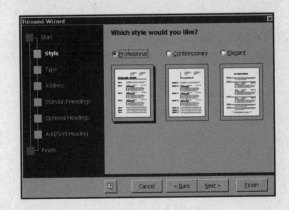

Guided Tour Start a New File

1 Open the **File** menu and click the **New** command. If your program offers a toolbar, it may have a New button you can click to start a new file.

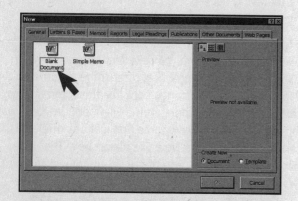

2 If the program asks you to choose a template (as shown here), specify a file type. If it asks for some other information, make your selections.

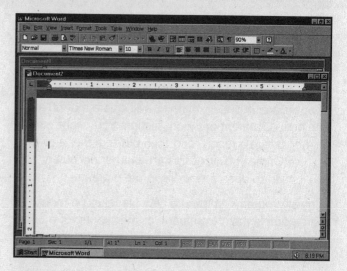

3 The new (blank) document window appears on-screen.

Open a File in a Windows Program

Going to the movie theater gives you a one-time thrill. You watch the movie once in sequence, and that's it. Renting a movie and watching it on a VCR is a different story. Once you load it into the VCR, you can watch it over and over, pause it, watch parts in slow motion, and otherwise have more fun.

Opening a file in a Windows 95 application program is similar. To work on a file you previously saved to disk (which you'll learn to do in the next task), first you need to open it. This procedure loads the file from the disk where it's stored into your computer's RAM (random-access memory). With the file in RAM, you can print it, add to it, change or delete the information in it, or update it in any way you see fit.

To open a particular file, you have to know which disk and folder it's stored on and what the file's name is.

►To learn how to save a file, see "Save Your Work in a Windows Program" on page 94.◄

Open a File of Another Type

Often you may have to take a file you've created in one program and open it in a different program. For example, let's say you use one word processing program at work. You create a file there and you want to bring it home to finish it up, but you use a different word processing program on your home computer.

Many Windows applications enable you to open files that were created in various formats. In Microsoft Works for Windows 95 (for example), you can open files from several different word processors: Microsoft Word for Windows and DOS, WordPerfect for DOS and Windows, Windows Write, and even Works files for the Macintosh.

This *file exchange* capability makes it easy for many users to share work. The quality of the file exchange varies, however, depending on how sophisticated the program is. Some exchanges let you open only the file's basic data. Other programs preserve graphics and formatting when you open a file from another application.

If the Open dialog box in your application has a "Files of Type" or similar option, that means you can open files in other formats. If your program doesn't have this option in the Open dialog box, look for an Import command on the File menu; it will do the same thing. The following steps describe how you would open a file created in Microsoft Word 97.

1. If your program closes the currently open file when you open a new file (as do the Windows 95 WordPad and Notepad accessory programs), be sure to save your work.

2. If the file you want to open is on a floppy disk, insert the floppy disk in the appropriate floppy disk drive.

3. Open the **File** menu and click the **Open** command. (If your program offers a toolbar, it may have an Open button that you can click.)

4. Click the **Files of Type** drop-down arrow to display its choices. Use the scroll bar to display the type of file you want to open, and then click that file type.

5. Choose the drive and folder in which the file is stored and select the file name. Then click the **Open** or **OK** button.

6. If the program displays a dialog box that asks you to confirm that you're opening a file and transferring formats, click the **Yes** button or the **OK** button to continue.

Understand Wild Card Characters

You may have noticed that the Open dialog box doesn't always spell out the full file name or file name extension. (►**For more on file names and extensions, see "Understand Files" on page 57.**◄) The dialog box replaces part of the file name with an asterisk *wild card character*.

You use wild card characters to search for groups of files with similar names. The * (asterisk) wild card takes the place of a group of *contiguous* characters, such as the three-letter extension in a file name. The

? (question mark) wild card stands for a single charac- ter. Suppose, for example, you entered a file name in the File Name text box of the Open dialog box and included a wild card character in the file name. The File

Name list would then display all the files in the current folder that matched what you typed.

This table shows some examples of how wild card char- acters work.

Example Entry	Description
client?.doc	Matching files have names that begin with **client**, followed by one more character, and then the **.doc** extension.
cl*.doc	Matching files have names that begin with **cl**, followed by a group of up to 253 more characters and spaces, and then the **.doc** extension.
*.xls	Matching files have any base name, plus the **.xls** extension; all files of the type indicated by the extension match.
.	Indicates all files in the current directory of the current disk.

Guided Tour   Open a File

1 If the file you want to open is on a floppy disk, insert the floppy disk in the appropriate floppy disk drive.

2 Open the **File** menu and click the **Open** command. (In some programs, the command might be different—such as **Open Existing File**). If your program offers a toolbar, it may have an Open icon you can click to start a new file.

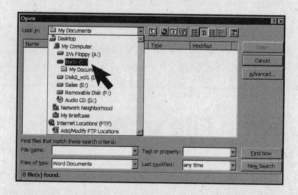

3 In the Open dialog box, click the **Look In** drop-down arrow to display the list, and then click the icon to select the disk drive holding the file you want to open. ▶**See "Work with Folder and File Lists in Dialog Boxes" on page 79 (ear- lier in this section) for more about working with the Look In list.◀**

Guided Tour Open a File

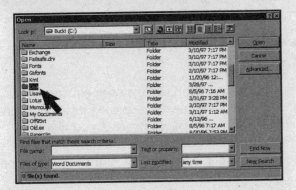

4 In the list of folders and files that appears, scroll (if necessary) to display the folder that holds the file you want to open. Double-click the folder icon to select it.

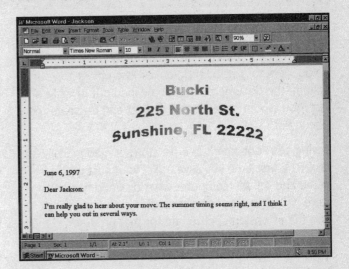

6 The file opens on-screen so you can work with it.

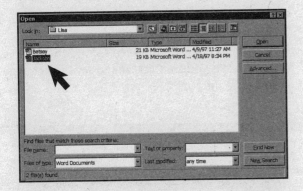

5 Click the icon beside the name of the file you want to open in the list of files below the Look In list. Then click the **Open** or **OK** button. (To open a file quickly, simply double-click it.)

7 Some programs offer a shortcut for opening files you've worked with recently. These files are listed at the bottom of the File menu. If you know you've worked with a file recently, simply open the **File** menu and click the name of the file you want to open.

Save Your Work in a Windows Program

While you're creating a document, it exists first in your computer's RAM (Random-Access Memory). If you were to exit the program or lose power to your system, the document would be wiped out of RAM and lost. You would have to start all over and re-create the document.

Saving your document in a file stores it magnetically on disk. The first time you save a file, you must give it a name and tell the computer what disk and folder to store it in. The program automatically adds a period and the extension appropriate for that program to the end of the file name. You won't have to specify the file's name again to save it; subsequent saves update the file that's already on disk.

As a rule, you should try to save your work every five to ten minutes to protect against data loss.

Close Your File After Saving

When you save a file, it remains open on-screen in its window. If you're working on several files at once and want to "clean up" your work area by putting away some of those files, simply close the current file once you've saved your work. Use one of these two methods to close a file:

- Open the **File** menu and click **Close**. If you've made changes to the file that haven't been saved, a dialog box will tell you so. Click **Yes** to save the changes and close the file.

- Click the **Close** button of the window holding the document you want to close. If you've made changes to the file and haven't saved them, a dialog box tells you so. Click **Yes** to save the changes and close the file.

Guided Tour　Save a File

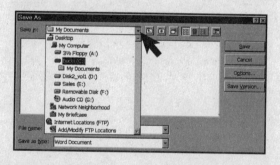

1 Open the **File** menu and click the **Save** command (or simply press **Ctrl+S**). If your program offers a Save button on a toolbar, click it to save the file.

2 In the Save As dialog box, click the **Save In** drop-down arrow to display the list, and then click the drive icon for the disk drive where you want to save the file. The Save In list works like the Look In list (▶**which you learned about in the earlier task titled "Work with Folder and File Lists in Dialog Boxes" on page 79◀**).

Guided Tour Save a File

3 In the list of files and folders that appears, scroll if necessary and then double-click the folder icon for the folder where you want to save the file.

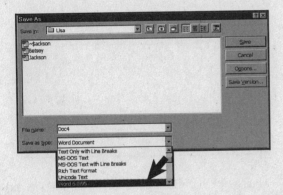

4 To save your file in another format, click the **Save As Type** drop-down arrow to display its choices. Scroll to the format you want, and then click your choice.

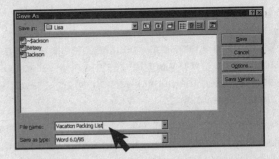

5 Double-click in the **File Name** text box to highlight its contents. Then type a name for the new file. (You don't have to add the file name extension.)

6 If the application offers a *create backup copy* option (which will create a backup file during subsequent saves), click to select that option. Then click the **Save** button.

7 If you continue working on the file, be sure to save it again before you close it or exit the program. To do so, open the **File** menu and click **Save** again.

Save Your File Under a New Name

After you save a file the first time, using the Save command again simply updates the file under its existing name. If you want to create a new version of a file and still keep the original version on disk, save the file under a new name.

For example, let's say you develop a January sales report that's really effective. You want to use the same format for February, but you still need to keep the January

report on disk. You can open the January file (let's say it's called January Report.xls) and save it as another file, February Report.xls. Then you could edit February Report.xls as needed.

It's important to save the file under the new name first, and then edit it. Otherwise, you risk saving your new changes in the original file, where you don't want them to be.

Guided Tour   Save with a New Name

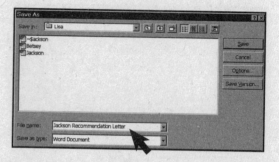

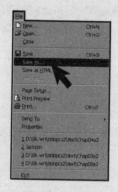

1 Click the **File** menu to open it, and then click the **Save As** command. (You can't click the Save button in this case.)

3 Double-click in the **File Name** text box to select its contents. Type a new name for the file. (You don't have to add the file name extension.) Click **Save** to finish the Save As process.

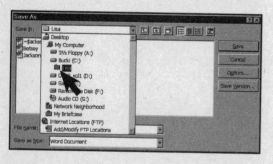

2 If you want to save the new version of the file to a new drive and folder, specify them.

Save Your Files Automatically

For safety's sake, you should save your files every five to ten minutes. This will prevent you from losing your changes if your computer loses power or locks up, forcing you to reboot. Some programs offer autosave protection; when you turn on this feature, the program saves all open files at an interval you specify. The *Guided Tour* here shows how to turn on the AutoSave feature in Word 97, the latest version for Windows 95. (The steps may be different for you, depending on the program you are working in.)

Guided Tour   Save Files Automatically

1 Open the **Tools** menu and click the **Options** command.

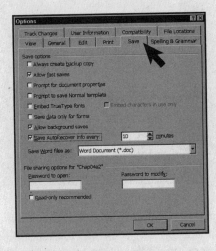

2 Click the **Save** tab of the Options dialog box, and then click to select the check box beside the **Save AutoRecover Info Every** option.

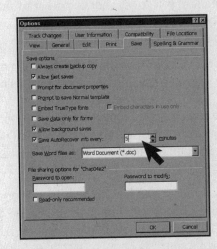

3 Double-click the entry in the **Minutes** text box and type a new value (or you can click the **down arrow** or the **up arrow** beside the text box to adjust the value).

4 Click the **OK** button to close the dialog box and activate the AutoSave feature. When the interval you've set has passed, the program will pause and save your file (and may tell you about it at the bottom of the screen).

Print in a Windows Program

Documents exist to be looked at. They carry a message from you to a friend, colleague, boss, client, student, or teacher—or anyone you want to communicate with or persuade. The reality is that you can't call every one of these people to come look at your computer screen or e-mail a document to them in all instances.

Instead, you'll need to print out your document. This process requires you to tell your computer to send the information you've created and saved to your system's printer so it can be put on paper.

Windows 95 includes built-in printer management features that control every print job and help eliminate problems. It acts as a go-between to let your Windows 95 application programs communicate with your printer. Once your printer is set up to work correctly with Windows 95, printing from any Windows application should be easy.

This *Guided Tour* shows how to print from Word 97. The available options vary from one application to the next (depending on your application's features), but generally you can specify how many copies to print and whether you want to print all or part of a document. ►A later task called "Control Your Printer" (on page [p1s6 TBD]) explains how to set up a printer in Windows 95 and how to manage print jobs.◄

> A lot of problems can crop up when you try to print a document. ►If you run into trouble, see "Printing Problems" on page [p3 TBD], in the "101 Quick Fixes" part of the book.◄

Preview the Printed Document

If you create a document, often you do a lot of *formatting*, which can include adjusting major settings like the page margins and page breaks; at some point you could lose sight of what the final document will look like. In the old days, you had to print out a preliminary copy of the file and then go back to fix the formatting (either to fit the page or to look more attractive on the page).

Today, most software publishers have built a feature into their products that shows you what the printed document will look like. In some applications, you can even print (or make changes to margins and the like) while a document is in this *Print Preview mode* (shown here).

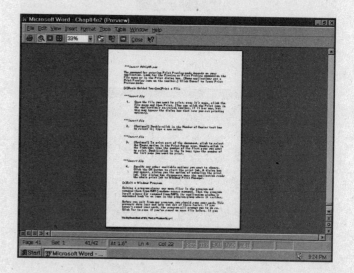

The command for entering Print Preview mode depends on your application. Look for the Preview or Print Preview command on the File menu or in the Print dialog box. (Some applications also put a Print Preview button on the toolbar.) Click Close or a similar command to leave Print Preview mode.

Guided Tour Print a File

1 Open the file you want to print. Then open the **File** menu and click **Print**. (You can click the **Print** button in the application's on-screen toolbar, if it has one, but that may bypass the dialog box in which you can set printing options.)

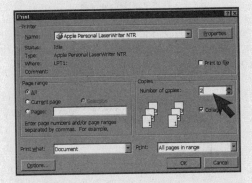

2 (Optional) Double-click in the **Number of Copies** text box to select it, and then type a new value.

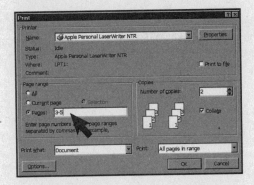

3 (Optional) To print only a part of the document, click to select the **Pages** option in the Page Range area. Then click in the **Pages** text box and type the range of pages you want to print. You can separate contiguous pages to print with a colon or hyphen, as in 3:5 or 3–5. To enter noncontiguous pages to print, separate the page numbers with commas, as in 3,5.

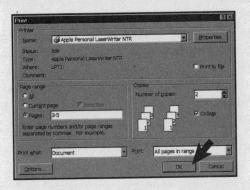

4 Specify any other available options you want to choose. Then click the **OK** button to start the print job. A dialog box may appear, giving you the option of canceling the print job. This dialog box disappears once the application sends the whole print job to the Windows 95 print management application.

If you've set up multiple printers or fax modems (you have to "print" to a fax modem to send a fax) under Windows 95, most applications will usually let you select the printer to use in the Print dialog box. In the Print dialog box for Word 97, shown in the steps above, you use the **Name** drop-down list to select the printer you want. The **Properties** button lets you control the various settings offered by the selected printer, such as the paper size and graphics resolution. ▶**To learn more about printer properties and how to set up a printer under Windows 95, see "Control Your Printer" on page 168.**◀

Exit a Windows Program

Exiting a program closes any open files in the program and removes them from RAM (Random Access Memory). Then the program itself closes (is removed from RAM), and its application window is minimized back to an icon in the program group where it resides.

Before you exit from any program, you should save your work. This prevents data loss and gets you out of there faster. If you haven't saved your work, the program will prompt you to do so. Click **Yes** to save if you've saved an open file before. If you haven't saved the open file, the Save As dialog box will appear. Name the file and specify a location for it.

When you've saved your work, you have several ways to exit a file; this *Guided Tour* shows you those options.

Guided Tour Exit a Program

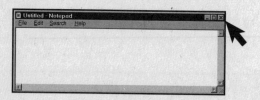

Click the application window's **Close** button, or double-click the application window's **Control-menu box**.

If the program is minimized to a button on the taskbar, right-click the button to display its shortcut menu, and then click the **Close** command.

Click the **File** menu to open it, and then click the program's **Exit** command.

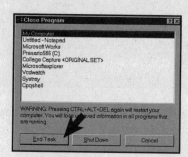

If the application you want to exit from seems to be stalled or hung up, press **Ctrl+Alt+Delete** to display the Close Program dialog box. Click the name of the application you want to exit, and then click the **End Task** button.

HOW TO...

Organize Files and Folders with Windows 95

Windows 95 provides easy tools for managing your files and folders—in the Windows Explorer. Explorer provides a graphical view of the folder tree and the files in a folder, so you can move around or select a file with a simple mouse click. This approach not only offers common-sense menu commands to get the job done, it also enables you to handle some operations with the mouse alone!

This section covers Windows Explorer basics and some tricks to make you more effective! Although most of the file management techniques in Windows 95 are similar to those in Windows 3.11, there are some major differences. ▶**To learn about file management in Windows 3.11, see the section "Work in Windows 3.11" on page 181.**◀

What You Will Find in This Section

Manage Disks, Folders, and Files

If you learned to manage files with the Windows 3.11 File Manager, you'll have to erase your memory. Windows 95 has replaced File Manager with two new folder and file management tools: Windows Explorer and My Computer. Both of these Windows 95 components display the contents of each disk drive and folder in windows on-screen. You see not only file and folder names, but also icons for those files and folders. You can handle some operations simply by dragging files around or by double-clicking a file icon.

Windows Explorer is considered to be File Manager's replacement. Like File Manager, it includes a folder tree on the left and a file list on the right. You can still copy and move files from one folder to another by dragging them, as you may have done in File Manager. My Computer takes a slightly different, more Macintosh-like, approach to file management. Each My Computer window contains icons that represent folders and files.

As with other Windows 95 applications, both Windows Explorer and My Computer open in their own windows on-screen. You can maximize the windows to full-screen size, resize them and move them around, or minimize them to a button on the taskbar for temporary storage. When you finish working with either Explorer or My Computer, you can close them to free up RAM (Random-Access Memory) for other programs.

The *Guided Tour* shows you how to run both Windows Explorer and My Computer. Later tours in this chapter explain how to select files; copy, move, and delete selected files; create new folders; rename folders and files; and so on.

After this task, the rest of the tasks in this section illustrate how to manage files using the Windows Explorer. Most of the techniques you use in My Computer are identical, but significant differences will be pointed out for you along the way.

Guided Tour   Run Windows Explorer

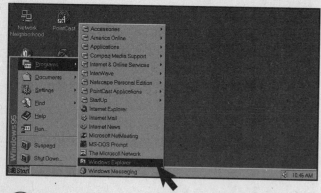

1 Windows Explorer lets you copy, move, and delete files and folders. To start it, click the **Start** button, point to the **Programs** choice, and click **Windows Explorer**.

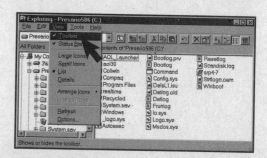

2 The toolbar at the top of the screen is very helpful. If it does not appear on your screen, open the **View** menu and select **Toolbar**.

Guided Tour   Run Windows Explorer

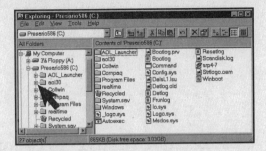

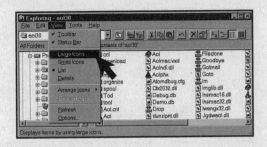

3 The folder tree on the left shows the names of all the drives and folders. A plus sign next to a drive or folder means that there are more items inside. Click the plus sign to see those items in the folder tree. The plus sign changes to a minus sign that you can click to collapse (hide) the folder's contents in the tree.

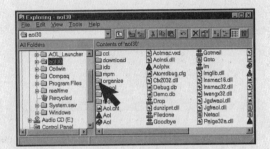

4 The file list on the right shows the names of the folders and files that are in the selected folder. Click a folder icon in the folder tree at the left (changing its icon to an open folder), or double-click a folder in the file list to see its contents.

5 The View menu lets you change the size and arrangement of the icons. ▶**See "Rearrange the List of Files or Icons" on page 138 for details.**◀

6 When you finish with Windows Explorer, you can exit by clicking the window's **Close** button or by choosing **Close** from the **File** menu.

> If you see a program icon in Explorer or My Computer, you can double-click it to run the program.

Guided Tour   Run My Computer

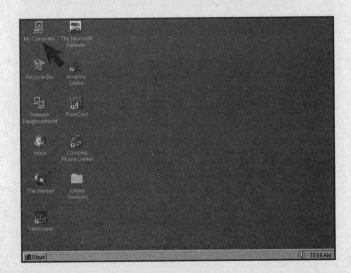

1 My Computer takes a different approach to file and folder management. To run it, double-click the **My Computer** icon on the Windows desktop.

(continues)

Guided Tour Run My Computer   (continued)

2 My Computer initially shows you icons for all your drives, for the Control Panel, and for your printers. Double-click a drive icon to view its contents.

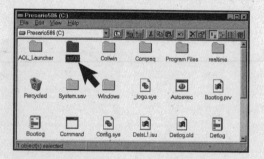

3 You can see the contents of a folder by double-clicking it. This opens a new window that shows the folder's files and subfolders (if there are any).

> My Computer opens a window for each drive or folder you double-click. If you want to display only one window whose contents change with each selection, open the **View** menu and select **Options**. Click **Browse Folders By Using a Single Window That Changes As You Open Each Folder**, and then click **OK**.

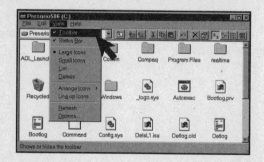

4 If you don't see a toolbar at the top of your window, you can turn it on by opening the **View** menu and selecting **Toolbar**.

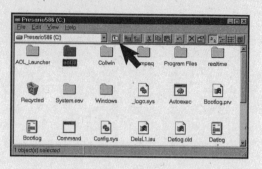

5 The Up One Level button is especially useful. You can click it to move to a higher level folder (or to the previous window). You can do the same thing by pressing the Backspace key.

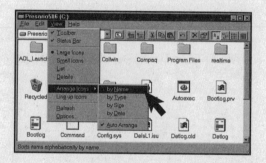

6 The View menu lets you change the size and arrangement of the icons. ▶**See "Rearrange the List of Files or Icons" on page 138 for details.**◀

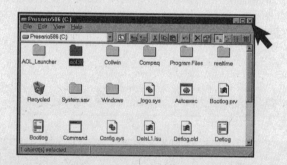

7 If your screen becomes too cluttered, you can close any open My Computer window by clicking its **Close** button or by choosing **Close** from the **File** menu.

View Different Disks (Drives)

The last task briefly introduced you to the Windows Explorer, the main tool you'll use for managing files in Windows 95. The Explorer window is divided into two parts. The left side shows the *folder tree* for all the disks installed on your system, starting with the Windows 95 desktop, which can also hold files and folders. The right side of the window displays the *file list* for the drive or folder you've selected in the folder tree on the left. The file list displays both folders and files contained within the drive or folder selected in the folder tree.

When you initially start the Windows Explorer, it displays the contents of the drive where Windows 95 is installed—usually the C drive. When you view the contents of a different disk drive, Explorer changes the current folder tree and the file list to show the contents of the drive you've selected. With Windows Explorer, you can display only the contents of a single disk drive at a time. To view the contents of more than one disk at a time, you can use My Computer. The *Guided Tour* describes a few ways to see what's stored on a particular disk.

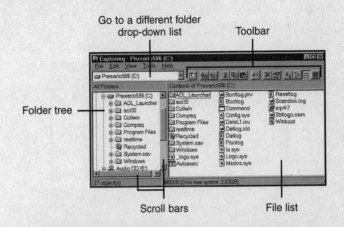

Go to a different folder drop-down list

Toolbar

Folder tree

Scroll bars

File list

➤To learn more about displaying specific folder contents, see "View Different Folders" on page 108.◄

Guided Tour   View a Disk with the Folder Drop-Down List

1 If you want to view the contents of a floppy disk, insert that disk in its disk drive.

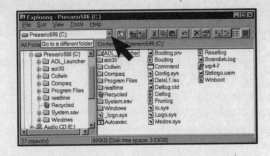

2 Click the drop-down arrow to open the **Go to a Different Folder** drop-down list.

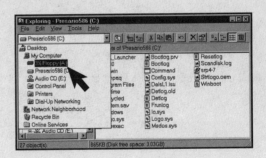

3 In the open drop-down list, click the drive holding the disk you want to view. Its files and folders appear in the file list.

Guided Tour View a Disk with the Folder Tree

1 If you want to view the contents of a floppy disk, insert that disk in the disk drive.

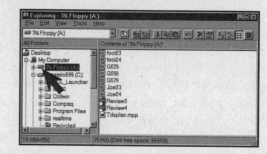

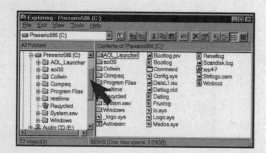

3 Click the disk icon. Its files and folders appear in the file list on the right.

2 Use the scroll bar to scroll through the folder tree until you see the icon for the disk you want to view.

Guided Tour View Multiple Disks with My Computer

1 If you want to view the contents of a floppy disk, insert that disk in the disk drive.

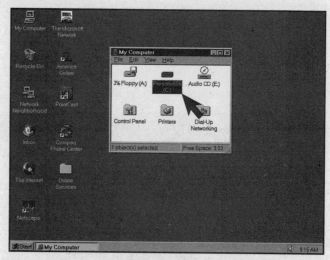

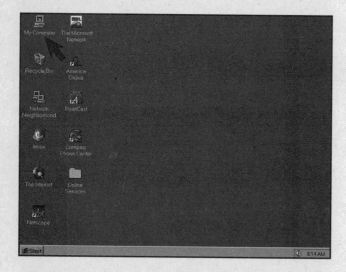

3 Double-click the icon for the first disk drive to open a window displaying its contents.

2 Open My Computer by double-clicking its icon on the desktop.

Guided Tour View Multiple Disks with My Computer

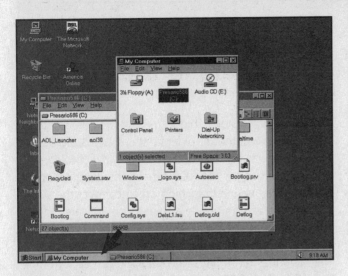

4 If the My Computer window isn't fully visible on-screen, click the **My Computer** button on the taskbar.

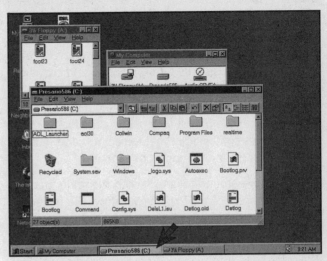

6 To view the contents of any open drive window, either click part of the window to make it the active window, or click the button for the drive on the taskbar.

You can always view drives and folders in a single My Computer window whose contents change with each selection. To do so, open the **View** menu and select **Options**. Click **Browse Folders By Using a Single Window That Changes As You Open Each Folder**, and then click **OK**.

You can manipulate the open Explorer window or any open My Computer window just as you would any other program window. ▶**For a refresher on working with windows, see "Size and Arrange Windows" on page 81.**◀

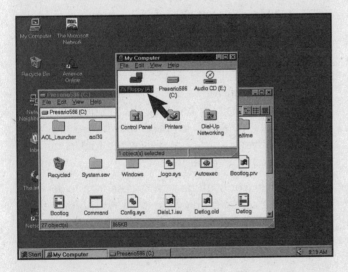

5 Double-click the icon for another disk drive to open a new window displaying its contents.

View Different Folders

Like the Windows 3.11 File Manager, the Windows Explorer makes it easy to browse around to look at the contents of a disk. By simply pointing and clicking icons, you can select any folder or file on the disk shown in the Explorer window. Selecting a different folder changes the file list so it displays the files and subdirectories contained in that folder. You also must select a folder to move, copy, or delete it.

You can move around folders in both the folder tree and file list areas of the Explorer window. The folder tree gives a more graphical picture of which folders contain subfolders.

The folder tree display starts from the desktop, which appears at the top of the directory tree window (but may not be visible in the file list). You can scroll through the list (using the scroll bars), and then select a drive and folder to move *down* a level in the tree, displaying its subfolders (in both the folder tree and file list) and files (in the file list only).

Explorer displays icons to represent folders and subfolders in the directory tree. You'll see these two icons:

 The open file icon represents the currently selected folder; the contents of that folder appear in the file list.

 Closed file icons represent other folders and subfolders; subfolders are indented under the folder that holds them.

It pays to know how to navigate folders both in the folder tree and file list. This task gives you the techniques for both.

> **This task focuses on selecting folders. ▶To learn more about selecting files in the file list, see "Select Files and Folders" on page 116.◀**

View and Hide Subfolders in the Folder Tree

The Windows Explorer folder tree can provide greater detail about whether a folder contains any subfolders. A line connects folders on the same level; subfolders are indented below the folder that contains them and have a separate line branching off to connect the subfolders. A plus sign beside a folder icon indicates that the folder contains subfolders; click the plus sign to display the subfolders at the lower level. The plus sign then changes to a minus sign that you can click to hide the subfolders. Drive icons also offer plus or minus signs with which you can control which drive's folders appear in the folder tree.

 A file icon with a minus sign represents a folder that holds subfolders you can hide (collapse). You can also click the minus sign to hide the folders contained on a disk.

 A file icon with a plus sign represents a folder that contains subfolders you can display (expand). A disk icon also may have a plus sign that you can click to display the folders on the disk in the folder tree.

 A file icon with no sign represents a folder that contains only files; it has no subfolders to display.

> **Guided Tour** Use the Folder Tree to View a Folder's Contents

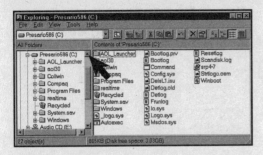

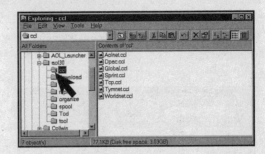

1 Use the scroll bar, if necessary, to display the folder you want in the folder tree.

4 To move to the first subfolder in a folder, click it or press the **down arrow** key.

5 Use the **up** and **down arrow** keys or click to move among the subfolders or to move back up to the folder holding the subfolders.

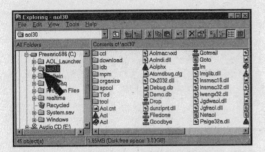

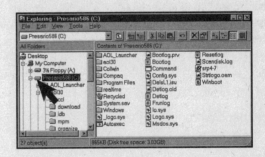

2 Click a folder to select it. To select with the keyboard, press **Tab** to move the highlight to the folder tree, and then use the **up** and **down arrow** keys to select a folder.

6 To return to the main folder for the drive, scroll up to display the drive icon, and then click it. With the keyboard, press the **up** and **down arrow** keys until you highlight the drive icon.

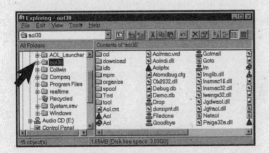

3 To display (or hide) a folder's subfolders in the tree, double-click the folder name or icon. You can click the plus sign beside an icon to display its subfolders, or you can click the minus sign to hide the subfolders. With the keyboard, select the folder using the **arrow keys**, and then press the + or – on the numeric keypad.

Guided Tour Display a Folder's Contents in the File List

1 In the folder tree, select the disk drive holding the folder you want to view, or select a folder in the tree to view one of its subfolders.

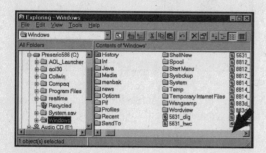

2 Use the scroll bar below the file list, if necessary, to display the folder whose contents you want to view. With the keyboard, press **Tab** to move through the file list, and then use the **up** and **down arrow** keys to highlight the folder you want to view.

3 Double-click the folder to list its contents. With the keyboard, if you've highlighted the folder name, press **Enter** to display its contents. Repeat this step to display a subfolder's contents.

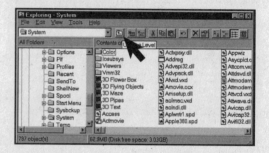

4 To move back up one folder level, click the **Up One Level** button on the Explorer toolbar. With the keyboard, press **Shift+Tab** to return the highlight to the folder tree, use the **up arrow** key to highlight the folder to move back to, and press **Enter**.

Guided Tour View Multiple Folders with My Computer

1 If you want to view the contents of a floppy disk, insert that disk in the disk drive.

2 Open My Computer by double-clicking its icon on the desktop.

3 Double-click the icon for the disk drive holding the folder(s) you want to view. A window opens, displaying its contents.

Guided Tour View Multiple Folders with My Computer

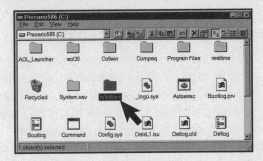

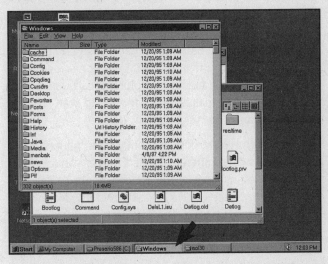

④ If necessary, scroll to display the icon for the folder with the contents you want to view. Then double-click the folder's icon.

⑦ To view the contents of any open folder window, either click part of the window to make it the active window or click the button for the folder window on the taskbar.

> To arrange the open My Computer windows on-screen, right-click the taskbar and click **Cascade, Tile Horizontally** or **Cascade, Tile Vertically.**

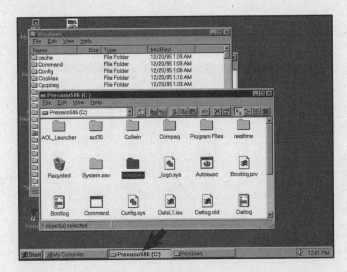

⑤ If the disk drive window you opened in step 3 isn't fully visible on-screen, click its button on the taskbar.

> To reduce all the open windows down to taskbar buttons, choose **Minimize All Windows** from the shortcut menu. ▶**For more details, see "Size and Arrange Windows" on page 81.◀**

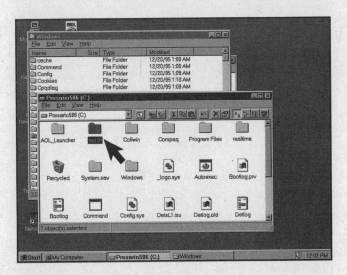

⑥ Double-click the icon for another folder to open a window displaying its contents.

Change the Explorer Window View

Normally the Windows Explorer window has a very distinctive look that enables you to view numerous folders and files in a relatively small area on-screen. The default view for the file list in Explorer is called *list view*. In theory, list view makes it easy for you to scan for and find the folder or file you want.

Yet, you might work more efficiently if the folders and files looked a little different in the Explorer window. For example, the tiny icons in the list view might be too difficult for you to see or click. Or, you might want to see more details about a file. There are actually four views available in the Windows Explorer: *large icons*, *small icons*, *list*, and *details*. You can use a menu choice or a button on the Explorer toolbar to switch between views. The table below shows the button for each view and includes a description of the view.

The *Guided Tour* that follows explains how to use the Windows Explorer's View menu to change how folders and files are displayed in the Explorer window. You can use the same steps to change the view in any My Computer window.

> You also can change the order in which folders and files are listed in the Explorer window or any My Computer window. ▶**To learn how, see "Rearrange the List of Files or Icons" on page 138.**◀

Change the Options

You can control a few additional aspects of the Explorer display. For example, you can hide certain system files such as .sys files that Windows needs to operate or .dll files that programs need to run correctly. Hiding those files makes it more difficult for you to accidentally delete them. In addition, you can control whether or not certain information appears in the Explorer window. The *Guided Tour* explains how to make these changes, which are illustrated in this figure:

Hide or show the full DOS path for the selected folder.

Hide or show these description bars.

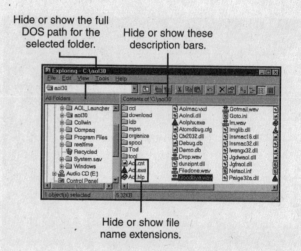

Hide or show file name extensions.

Explorer's View Icons

Icon	Description of the View
	Large icons view shows each folder and file with a very large icon and the folder or file name below the icon.
	Small icons view resembles the list view. Small icons identify folders and files, but they're alphabetically arranged from left to right.
	List view uses small icons and arranges folders and files alphabetically in columns. Therefore, you see the folders first at the left side of the file list, with files following at the bottom of the column and in subsequent columns.
	Details view lists folders and then files in one long column in the file list, giving the size, type, and last modification date for each folder or file. This information is particularly useful when you're working with files; you can compare a file's modified date and time to see which version of a file you worked on most recently.

To determine whether or not a status bar appears on the Explorer window or any My Computer window, open the **View** menu, select the **Status Bar** command, and click to place a check mark next to the status bar. Click the command again to remove the check and hide the status bar.

Change the Split View

Ever mindful that you want to be efficient, Windows' creators always give you the option of arranging your window space the way you want. In the Windows Explorer, this means you can decide just how much space the folder tree and the file list take up.

Most often, you'll want to make the folder tree's portion narrower so you can see more of the folder's contents. This eliminates a lot of white space that otherwise may appear with the folder tree. Use the *split bar* (the vertical bar that appears just to the right of the folder tree scroll bar) and the mouse to make this adjustment.

Guided Tour Adjust the Split View

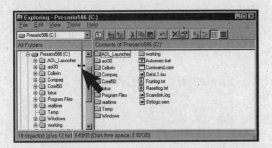

1 Point to the split bar with the mouse until you see the split pointer, which has left- and right-pointing arrows.

2 Press and hold the left mouse button; drag the split bar as shown in this figure. Release the mouse button when both sides of the Explorer window are the size you want.

Guided Tour Change How Files and Folders Are Displayed

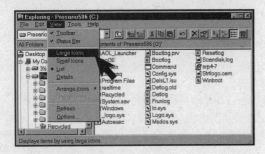

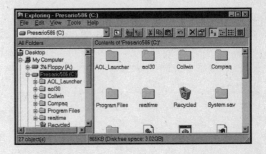

1 Open the **View** menu and click the command for the view you want. Or click the toolbar button for the view you want to select. Or right-click the file list to display its short-cut menu, point to **View**, and then click the command to select the view.

2 The window immediately adjusts to display the selected view. Repeat step 1 as often as necessary to find the view you prefer.

Guided Tour Change the View Options

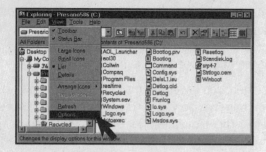

1 Open the Explorer window's **View** menu and click **Options**. The Options dialog box opens, with the View tab selected. (If you display the Options dialog box for a My Computer window, you must actually click the **View** tab to select it.)

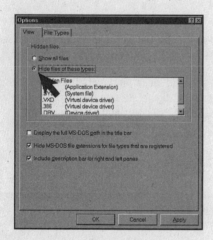

2 To hide system files to protect against deleting them, select the **Hide Files of These Types** option button. Click the other option (Show All Files) to redisplay files that are hidden.

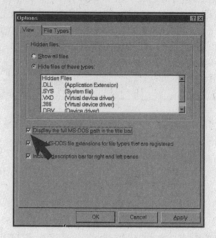

3 If you want the title bar of the Explorer window to show the path for the selected folder or subfolder, click to place a check beside **Display the Full MS-DOS Path in the Title Bar**. If you remove the check from this check box, Windows displays only the name of the current folder or subfolder in the title bar.

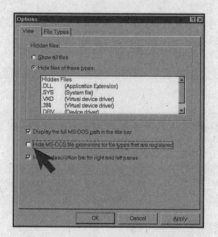

4 If you want to see all file name extensions in the file list, click to remove the check mark from beside **Hide MS-DOS File Extensions for File Types That Are Registered**. When that check box is checked, you won't see extensions for most file types.

Guided Tour   Change the View Options

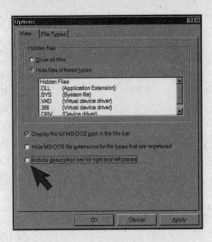

5 To remove the description bars above the folder tree and file list panes inside the Explorer window so there's more room to display folders and files, click to remove the check mark from beside **Include Description Bar for Right and Left Panes**. (Anytime you want to see those bars again, display the Options dialog box and click to place a check mark in this box.)

6 Click **OK** to finish adjusting the display and close the Options dialog box.

Select Files and Folders

Windows Explorer lets you manage files and folders, and you probably can guess what the first step to managing them is: You have to *select* files and folders before you can do anything with them. When you select files or folders, you highlight them so you can do something to them (such as move them or copy them to another disk).

You don't need step-by-step instructions for selecting a single file or folder. Just find the file or subfolder you want in the file list (or find the first-level folder in the folder tree), and click its icon to highlight it. With the keyboard, press **Tab** to move the highlight to the file list and then use the **arrow keys** to move the highlight to the file you want. To learn how to select more than one file or folder at a time, see the *Guided Tour* for this task.

There's a shortcut for selecting all the files and folders currently displayed in the current directory of the directory window. Display the files and subfolders you want to select in the file list, and then press **Ctrl+A** or open the **Edit** menu and choose **Select All**.

Icons: What They Represent

As you look at the icons and file names in a list, you'll notice that unless you display them as described in the last task, the file name extensions don't appear. For example, you won't see .DOC for documents or .EXE for executable program files. Instead, Windows 95 relies heavily on the appearance of each icon to convey the function of the file. Looking at the file list in Explorer or in a My Computer folder window, use the following guide to identify file types:

Command

DOS program icons look like tiny windows. You can usually double-click one of these icons to run a DOS program.

Calc

Windows program icons are usually colorful and look like pictures that represent the programs.

Bubbles

Document icons usually look like a piece of paper with one corner folded over. You can't "run" a document, but if you double-click a document icon that's associated with a program, Windows will run the program and open the document in it. Many document icons include a picture of the program that opens the document in the foreground. This usually shows that the document is associated with a specific program.

Mcenu

Help file icons look like a book with a question mark. Double-clicking one of these files displays its contents in a Help window on-screen.

Extra

Some icons indicate specialized types of files. This one is a document associated with the Windows 95 Notepad accessory program. Other icons represent special system files or specialized files from other programs.

Before you delete or move a file with an icon you don't recognize, make sure you find out what the file does, or keep a copy of the file so you can replace it if needed.

If you want to see the file name extensions for your files, open the **View** menu and select **Options**. Click the **View** tab, and then click **Hide MS-DOS File Extensions for File Types That Are Registered** to remove the check mark from the box. Click the **OK** button to put the change into effect.

Associate Files with an Application

Windows 95 keeps track of the applications used to create document files (and other files that aren't system or program files). It tracks the association between file name extensions (which indicate a particular kind of file) and the applications that can create or open files of that type. Why would Windows care which application created a particular file? Because if a file is associated with that application, you can open the file in Windows

Explorer or a My Computer window; doing so starts the application and opens the file in it.

Windows 95 sets up automatic associations between Windows applications and the files they create. For example, Windows assumes any files with the .TXT extension were created in the Windows Notepad accessory program. So if you open a file with the .TXT extension from Explorer or My Computer, Windows opens the Notepad application and then the .TXT file.

When you install a new application in Windows 95 (▶see **"Install a Program in Windows 95," page 312**◀), the installation process automatically associates the application with files created in the application. You can change any existing association in Explorer, or you can create a new association. You might need to do this if, for example, an application program comes with a READ.ME file that tells you about the program. To open and read this file, you could associate the .ME file name extension with the Windows Notepad accessory program. Note, however, that you should only associate a file type with an application that *can* open files of that type; otherwise, it won't work the way you expect it to.

See the *Guided Tour* to learn how to set up or change a file association.

Open or Start Files

You highlight a file or folder when you select it in the file list; then you can move it, copy it, and so on. Opening (starting) a file in Explorer or a My Computer

window runs a program file or opens a data file. The result of opening a file depends on the kind of file you open, as explained here:

- Opening an executable file with an .EXE, .COM, .PIF, or .BAT extension runs the program that the file is supposed to start. If you open a file called **msworks.exe**, for example, Windows runs Microsoft Works for Windows.

- Opening a document file associated with an application starts the application and then loads the document file.

Windows 95 offers a few different ways to open a file in the file list of Explorer or in a My Computer window:

- Double-click the file.

- In Explorer, press **Tab** to move the highlight to the file list, use the **arrow keys** to highlight the file you want to open, and then press **Enter**.

- When you see the file you want to open, click it to select (highlight) it. Then click the **File**, **Open** command, or right-click the selected file to display its shortcut menu and click **Open**.

If you want to open an application and load a particular file in it, you can do it in Explorer or My Computer. Drag the document's file name and drop it on top of the executable file's name. If, for example, you dragged a file named **notes.txt** until it was over the file **notepad.exe**, Windows would start the Notepad accessory and load **notes.txt**.

Guided Tour Select Adjacent Files and Folders

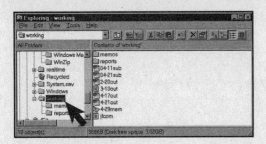

1 Use the folder tree to select the folder holding the files and subfolders you want to select.

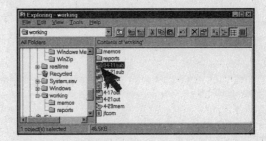

2 Click the icon for the first (top) file or subfolder in the group you want to select.

(continues)

Guided Tour Select Adjacent Files and Folders *(continued)*

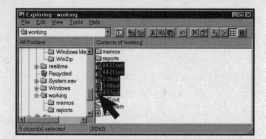

3 Press and hold **Shift**, and then click the icon for the last file or subfolder in the group you want to select.

To select adjacent files and folders in a My Computer window, you can drag to create a box around them. As you drag, all the files and folders are highlighted.

Guided Tour Select Nonadjacent Files and Folders

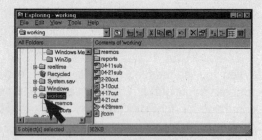

1 Use the folder tree to select the folder holding the files and subfolders you want to select.

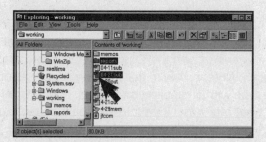

3 Press and hold **Ctrl**, and then click the icon for the next file or subfolder you want to select.

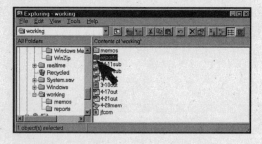

2 Click the icon for the first file or subfolder that you want to select.

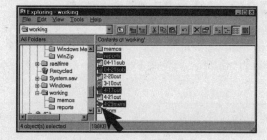

4 Continue to hold **Ctrl** while clicking to select any additional files and subfolders.

Guided Tour Associate a File Type with an Application

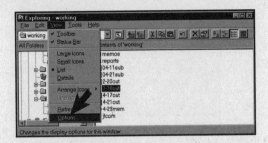

1 In the Explorer or My Computer window, open the **View** menu and click **Options**.

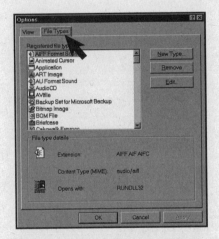

2 Click the **File Types** tab to display its options.

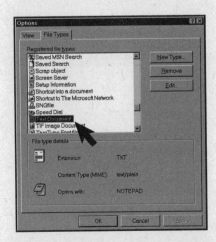

3 Scroll through the **Registered File Types** list to display the name of the file type you want to associate with a new application. Click the file type's name to select it, and then click **Edit**.

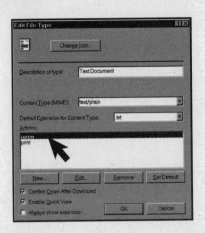

4 In the **Actions** list of the Edit File Type dialog box, click **open** to change the application that will open when you double-click files of the selected type. Then click **Edit**.

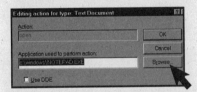

5 In the Editing Action for Type: *XX* dialog box, click the **Browse** button.

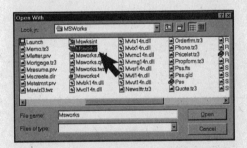

6 In the Open With dialog box, navigate to and select the startup file for the application that you want to associate with the file type you selected in step 3. Click that program file name, and then click **Open**.

7 Click **OK** to close the Editing Action for Type: *XX* dialog box.

(continues)

Guided Tour Associate a File Type with an Application *(continued)*

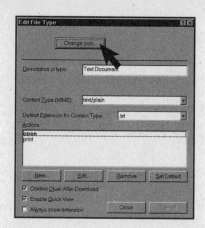

8 Back in the Edit File Type dialog box, click the **Change Icon** button.

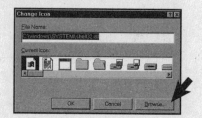

9 In the Change Icon dialog box, click the **Browse** button.

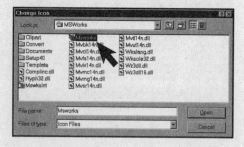

10 In the second Change Icon dialog box that appears, navigate to and select the same program startup file that you selected in step 6. Select it again and click **Open**.

If you've forgotten how to select files and folders in dialog boxes (such as the Open With dialog box in step 6), ▶refer to the task "Work with Folder and File Lists in Dialog Boxes" on page 79.◀

11 Back in the first Change Icon dialog box, you may see multiple icons. If you do, scroll to review the icons and click the one you want to use for the associated type of file. When you've selected the icon you want, click **OK** to close the Change Icon dialog box.

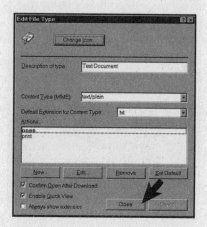

12 Click **Close** to close the Edit File Type dialog box.

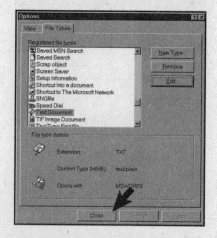

13 Click **Close** again to close the Options dialog box and complete the association.

Copy Files and Folders to Different Locations

Copying a file or folder creates an exact copy of the file's or folder's contents and places it in the folder on the disk you specify, leaving the original intact. Copying is one of the computer's great convenience features. Not only does it save you work, but it enables you to move your work from one computer to another (or share it) even if those computers aren't connected. For example, you might copy files in any of the following situations:

- You wrote a great recruiting letter to a prospective school volunteer, and you want to reuse most of the letter's contents for additional letters.

- You created an effective monthly budget spreadsheet, and you want to use a copy of it for the current month.

- You slaved all day on a report without finishing it, and you want to take a copy of it home to wrap it up over the weekend on your home computer.

- You have filled up your computer's hard drive, and you want to move some files to floppy or other removable disks by copying them to the floppy or removable disks first and then deleting them from the hard disk.

If you're a mouse fan, you're in luck when copying files. Instead of going through complicated typing routines, you can copy a file to a new location simply by dragging it into the directory you want to copy it to.

There are some tricks to doing this, depending on whether you're copying a file to another disk or to a folder on the same disk as the original file. The *Guided Tour* here leads you through the steps and gives you the details.

> To copy files, you need to understand how to select folders, subfolders, and files. ▶See these earlier tasks: "View Different Disks (Drives)" on page 105, "View Different Folders" on page 108, and "Select Files and Folders" on page 116.◀

Understand Dragging Within and Between Disks

The easiest technique for copying and moving files and folders is to drag the selection from one disk or folder icon to another. You need to know some simple rules when dragging your selections in Windows Explorer or between My Computer windows:

- Whenever you drag between two folders on the *same* disk drive, Windows assumes you want to *move* the selection unless you tell it otherwise. Windows helps prevent you from cluttering up a disk with multiple copies of the same file(s) or folder(s).

- Whenever you drag between locations on *different* disk drives, Windows assumes you want to *copy* the selection unless you tell it otherwise. In this instance, Windows helps ensure the integrity of your files, as moving between drives can result in data loss; if you copy instead, your original file(s) and folder(s) remain intact.

This task and the next provide very specific steps for performing copy and move operations between locations on the same disk drive and between different disk drives. You'll also learn how to override Windows' natural tendencies so you can copy a selection between folders on the same disk or move a selection from one disk to another.

Use Toolbar Buttons and Shortcut Menus to Work with Files and Folders

When displayed, the toolbar of the Explorer window or any My Computer window offers buttons that you can use to quickly work with selected files and folders. These buttons resemble some you see in other Windows applications for copying and moving text and data. The following table shows you the buttons.

Helpful Toolbar Buttons

Button	Description for Use
	Click the *Cut* button to remove the selected file(s) and folder(s) from their current location and place them on the Windows Clipboard, a temporary storage area. Then you can paste the selection to a new location (▶see **"Move Files and Folders" on page 126**◀).
	Click the *Copy* button to place a copy of the selection on the Windows Clipboard so you can paste a copy of the selection to a new location.
	Use the *Paste* button after you've cut or copied files and folders and selected a new location for them. Pasting then places them in the new location. (The Paste button won't have any effect if you haven't previously cut or copied a selection.)
	Click the *Undo* button when you realize your prior action was a mistake. (You'll learn more about undoing an action shortly.)
	Click the *Delete* button to move selected files and folders to the Recycle Bin. A later task, "Delete and Restore Files and Folders" (▶**on page 130**◀), provides more details about removing information from a disk.

In addition to using toolbar buttons to work with selected files and folders, you can right-click any selected file or folder to display a shortcut menu of commands for working with that selection. The shortcut menu typically offers Cut, Copy, and Delete commands that are the equivalent of the toolbar buttons with the same names. After you've copied or cut a selection, you can right-click a disk or folder icon and use the Paste command on the shortcut menu that appears.

▶As you learned in the task "Work with Folder and File Lists in Dialog Boxes" (on page 79)◀, many dialog boxes in Windows 95 applications list files and folders. You can right-click a file or folder icon *within* such a dialog box listing to display a shortcut menu with choices for copying and renaming files and more. In most cases, those shortcut menu choices work just like the ones in Explorer. In addition, many file dialog boxes include toolbar buttons you can use to change the file listing (such as for changing to Details view or List view).

Undo a File or Folder Action

The Undo feature lets you undo an action such as copying or moving a file. Note that some Windows 95 applications let you undo multiple previous actions. However, in Windows Explorer, you can undo only the single most recent action you've performed. Say you copied two files to a new folder and then moved another file to the same folder. You could undo the move operation but not the copy operation.

To undo an action, immediately click the **Undo** button, or open the **Edit** menu and select the **Undo** command. Note that the Undo command changes slightly depending on the last action you performed: Sometimes it's called Undo Copy, Undo Move, and so on.

Guided Tour Drag to Copy to a Folder on Another Disk

1 If you're copying the file(s) or folder(s) to a folder on a floppy or removable disk, insert the disk in the drive.

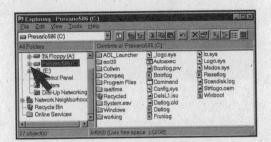

2 In the folder tree, click the plus sign beside the icon for the disk drive to copy to, and Windows displays the folders on the disk. If you want to copy to a subfolder of a folder on the disk, you need to click the plus sign to display the icon for that subfolder, too.

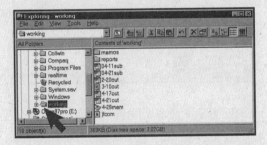

3 If necessary, scroll through the folder tree and select the folder or subfolder holding the file(s) or folder(s) you want to copy, so that they appear in the file list.

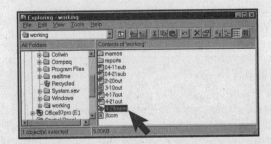

4 In the file list, select the file(s) and folder(s) you want to copy.

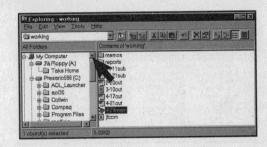

5 Use the scroll bar beside the folder tree to display the disk drive and folder icons for the disk and folder to which you want to copy the selection.

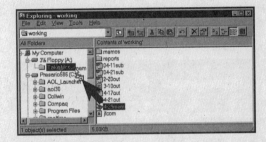

6 Point to the selected file(s) and folder(s) in the file list. Press and hold the left mouse button and drag the selection to the folder or subfolder you want to copy to in the folder tree. A plus sign appears beside the mouse pointer to indicate the selection will be copied to the disk.

7 With the pointer over the folder or subfolder you want to copy to, release the mouse button. Windows tells you it's copying the selected file(s) and folder(s). When it finishes, you can verify the copy by selecting the disk and folder you copied to in the folder tree and checking its contents in the file list.

Guided Tour Drag to Copy to a Folder on the Same Disk

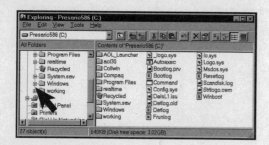

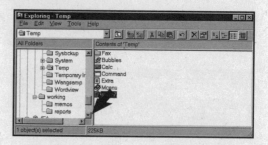

1 If you want to copy to a subfolder of one of the first-level folders on the disk, in the folder tree, click the plus sign beside the icon for the folder holding the subfolder to which you want to copy. If you want to copy to a subfolder of a subfolder, you need to click the appropriate subfolder's plus sign to display the icon for the lower-level subfolder.

4 Use the scroll bar beside the folder tree to display the folder or subfolder to which you want to copy the selection.

5 Point to the selected file(s). Press and hold **Ctrl**, and then press and hold the left mouse button.

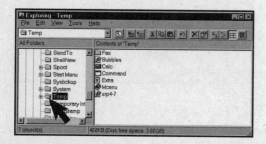

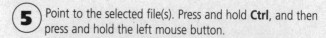

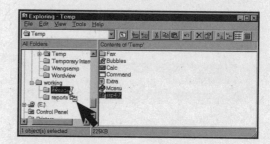

2 Scroll through the folder tree (if necessary) and select the folder or subfolder holding the file(s) or folder(s) you want to copy. They will then appear in the file list.

6 Begin dragging toward the folder tree. When you move the file over the folder tree, a plus sign (+) appears beside the pointer. In the folder tree, drag the file(s) to the icon for the folder or subfolder to which you want to copy.

7 Release the mouse button, and then release the Ctrl key. Windows tells you it's copying the selected file(s) and folder(s). When it finishes, you can verify the copy by selecting the disk and folder you copied to in the folder tree and checking its contents in the file list.

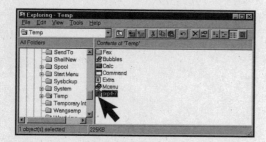

3 In the file list, select the file(s) and folder(s) you want to copy.

Instead of pressing Ctrl while dragging, you can press and hold the right mouse button while dragging a selection to copy between folders on the same disk or to copy between different disks. When you release the right mouse button, a brief shortcut menu appears. Click the **Copy Here** choice to complete the copy operation.

Guided Tour　Copy Using Edit Copy

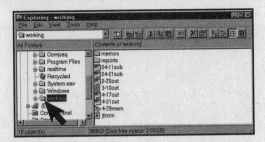

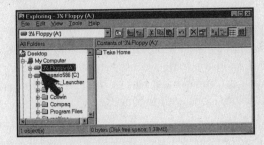

1 Use the folder tree to select the disk drive, folder, or sub-folder that holds the file(s) or folder(s) you want to copy so they appear in the file list.

4 Use the folder tree to select to the disk and folder to which you want to copy the files.

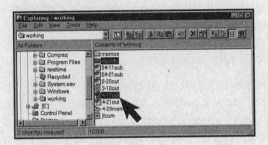

2 In the file list, select the file(s) or folder(s) you want to copy.

5 Open the **Edit** menu and select **Paste**, or right-click the file list and choose **Paste** from the shortcut menu. Alternatively, you can press **Ctrl+V** or click the **Paste** button on the toolbar. Windows pastes a copy of the selection into the folder you specified.

3 Open the **Edit** menu and select **Copy**, or right-click the selection and choose **Copy** from the shortcut menu. Alternatively, you can press **Ctrl+C** or click the **Copy** button on the toolbar.

If you open two My Computer windows for folders on the same disk drive, you can press and hold **Ctrl** and drag the files between windows to copy from one folder to the other. If you open My Computer Windows for folders on different disk drives, you can simply drag files and folder icons between the windows to copy.

Move Files and Folders

Moving a file or folder removes it from the disk and folder where it's presently stored and places it on a new disk in the folder you specify. As with copying files, you can move most files by dragging them to different folder icons with the mouse.

Knowing how to move files gives you a lot of control over the contents of your hard disk. It's also a more efficient method of repositioning a file than is copying and then deleting the original. Consider moving a file when you're in any of the following situations:

- You haven't opened a file or any of a group of files in six months or more. Old files can clutter your hard disk; move them to floppy disks or another removable disk and store them in a cool, dry place.

- You brought a file home to work on it, but you don't really need to keep a copy on your home computer. Move it back to a floppy and take it back to work.

- You had a very cluttered folder, so you created some subfolders in it to organize its files. Move the files to the appropriate subfolders.

One caveat: Be careful when moving certain files (or avoid moving them entirely). If you move a file that a program needs—such as a specialized data file, a template or style sheet file, or the startup file—you'll get error messages when the program tries to access the file and can't find it where it's supposed to be.

> To move files, you need to understand how to select folders, subfolders, and files. ▶See these earlier tasks: "View Different Disks (Drives)" on page 105, "View Different Folders" on page 108, and "Select Files and Folders" on page 116.◀

Move Folders

When you create a folder or subfolder, it's not set in stone on the folder tree. You can move it to a new location, and you can even move a folder to where it's contained within another folder (*demote* the original folder to a subfolder).

When you move a bag of groceries from your car trunk to your kitchen, all the contents travel with the bag. (You don't end up with your ice cream and oranges in the trunk and an empty bag in your hand.) Similarly, when you move a folder, you move its total contents—not only its files, but also its subfolders (along with any files and subfolders they contain).

You use the same techniques to move folders or files: You drag the folder's icon to a new location on the folder tree. If you press **Shift** while dragging, you can move a folder to another disk in the folder tree. The *Guided Tour* describes this process in detail.

Guided Tour Drag to Move a Selection to Another Disk

1 If you want to move the file(s) or folder(s) to a folder on a floppy or removable disk, insert the disk in the drive.

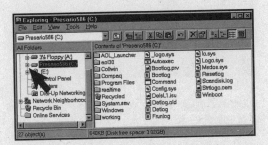

2 In the folder tree, click the plus sign beside the icon for the disk drive to which you want to move the selection; the contents of the disk appear. If you want to move the selection to a subfolder of a folder on the disk, click the plus sign to display the icon for that subfolder, too.

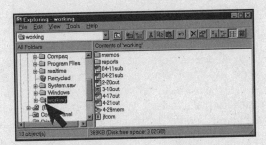

3 Scroll through the folder tree (if necessary) and select the folder or subfolder holding the file(s) or folder(s) you want to move. They will then appear in the file list.

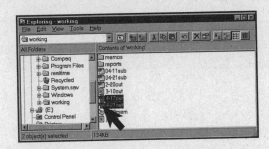

4 In the file list, select the file(s) and folder(s) you want to move.

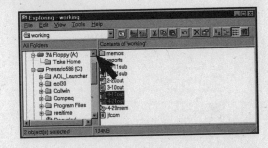

5 Use the scroll bar beside the folder tree to display the disk drive and folder icons for the disk and folder to which you want to move the selection.

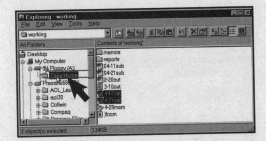

6 Point to the selected file(s) and folder(s) in the file list. Then press and hold the left mouse button, press and hold **Shift**, and drag the selection over the disk drive icon or folder you want to move to in the folder tree.

7 Release the mouse button, and then release the Shift key. Windows tells you it's moving the selected file(s) and folder(s). When it finishes, you can verify the move by selecting the disk and folder you moved to in the folder tree and checking its contents in the file list.

If you selected multiple contiguous (adjoining) files or folders, be careful to point to the last file in the selection when you press **Shift** and then press the mouse button. Otherwise, you risk deselecting some of the files.

Guided Tour Drag to Move a Selection on the Same Disk

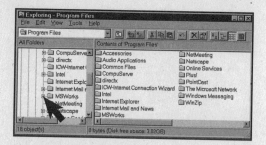

1 To move the selection to a subfolder of one of the first-level folders on the disk, in the folder tree, click the plus sign beside the icon for the folder holding the subfolder to which you want to move. If you're moving to a subfolder of a subfolder, you need to click the appropriate subfolder's plus sign to display the icon for the lower-level subfolder, too.

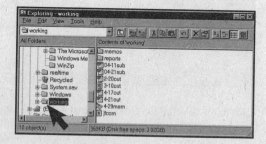

2 Scroll through the folder tree (if necessary) and select the folder or subfolder holding the file(s) or folder(s) you want to move so they appear in the file list.

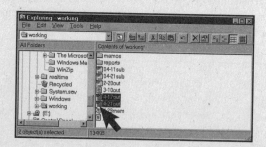

3 In the file list, select the file(s) and folder(s) you want to move.

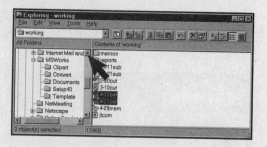

4 Use the scroll bar beside the folder tree to display the folder or subfolder to which you want to move the selection.

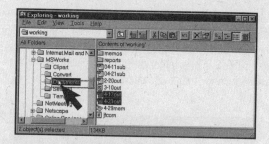

5 Drag the selection over the folder you want to move it to in the folder tree. When the pointer is over the proper folder, release the mouse button. Windows tells you it's moving the selected file(s) and folder(s). When it finishes, you can verify the move by selecting the disk and folder you moved to in the folder tree and checking its contents in the file list.

You can press and hold the right mouse button while dragging a selection to move between folders on the same disk or different disks. When you release the right mouse button, a shortcut menu appears. Click the **Move Here** choice to complete the move.

Guided Tour Move Files with Edit Cut

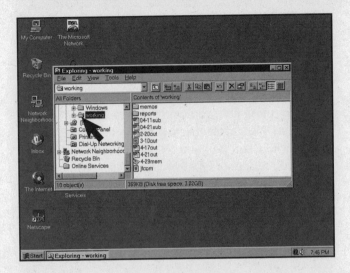

3 Open the **Edit** menu and choose **Cut**, or right-click the selection and choose **Cut** from the shortcut menu. Alternatively, press **Ctrl+X** or click the **Cut** button on the toolbar.

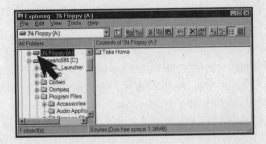

1 Use the folder tree to select the disk drive, folder, or sub-folder that holds the file(s) or folder(s) you want to move so they appear in the file list.

4 Use the folder tree to select the disk and folder to which you want to move the files.

5 Open the **Edit** menu and choose **Paste**, or right-click the file list and choose **Paste** from the shortcut menu. Alternatively, press **Ctrl+V** or click the **Paste** button on the toolbar. Windows pastes the selection into the folder you specified, removing the selection from its original location.

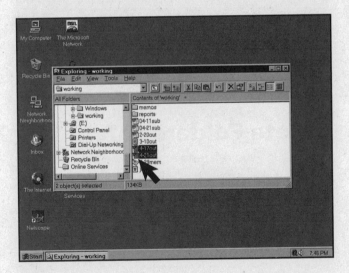

2 In the file list, select the file(s) or folder(s) you want to move.

If you've opened two My Computer windows for folders on different disk drives, you can press and hold **Shift** and drag the files between windows to move from one folder to the other. If you've opened My Computer windows for folders on the same disk drive, you can simply drag files and folder icons between the windows to move them.

Delete and Restore Files and Folders

It's true: There's no such thing as a big enough hard drive, and every once in a while, you'll have to "clean house." Most hard disks seem infested with tiny pixies who go around at night copying files until every nook and cranny on the disk is completely full. Here are just a few instances of when you'll need to delete files:

- When the information in the files is so outdated you'll never need it again. For example, you may not need to keep a complaint letter from 1985 on disk.

- When your system's accumulated a lot of .TMP files (files Windows temporarily creates for data files) in the \WINDOWS\TEMP directory or a program directory. Your system normally deletes these files when you shut it down, but if your system locks up and you have to reboot, these files may not be deleted correctly.

- When an application has created a lot of .BAK files (document backup files) that you don't think you need.

- When you are out of space on your hard disk and something has to go!

As you work, your hard disk becomes cluttered with files that you never use or even look at. Your windows become cluttered with file and folder names you don't recognize. And, more importantly, these files and folders start to take up precious disk space that you need for storing more useful items.

To delete useless items, you can use either My Computer or Windows Explorer. You can drag files over the **Recycle Bin** on the Windows desktop, or you can open the **File** menu and select **Delete**. Either way, the files are dumped in the Recycle Bin and stored there until you decide you'll never need them again.

The *Guided Tour* leads you through the process of deleting files and folders—and restoring them (just in case you deleted them accidentally).

Delete Files Safely

Don't delete a file unless you know what kind of file it is and you are sure you want to delete it. Although Windows has built-in safeguards to prevent you from deleting program and system files, you should still be careful.

Never delete the following files from your hard disk: COMMAND.COM, AUTOEXEC.BAT, CONFIG.SYS. If you get rid of these files, you won't be able to boot your computer! Also, avoid deleting files with .BAT, .EXE, .COM, .PIF, .DLL, .DAT, and .INI file name extensions, unless you're sure of what you're doing. These files execute programs or give them instructions that enable them to work properly; without one of these files, your applications may not work.

Caution! When you delete files or folders from a floppy disk or some types of removable disks, Windows *does not* place the files in the Recycle Bin. In fact, unless you have a special utility to restore deleted files, you will not be able to get them back. So before you delete a crucial file or folder from a floppy or removable disk, make sure you have a current copy of the file on another floppy or your hard disk.

Delete Folders Safely

Even though you can restore deleted files and folders, you should still keep a few safety guidelines in mind when you're deleting folders:

- Avoid deleting program folders or subfolders, unless you're sure of what you're doing or want to delete the program altogether.

- Before you delete a folder, check to see whether it contains any system or hidden files that you may want to preserve or move elsewhere.

- **BEWARE:** Deleting a folder deletes everything it contains: all its files, any subfolders, and all *their* files. Make sure you check through a folder's contents before you delete it.

If you don't want to delete all the files in a folder or subfolder, move those files out first. ▶For guidance on moving files, see "Move Files and Folders" on page 126.◀

Guided Tour Delete Files and Folders

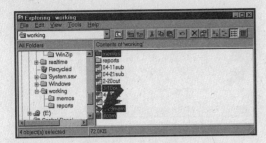

1 Before you can delete files and folders, you must select the ones you want to delete. ▶**See "Select Files and Folders" on page 116 for instructions.**◀

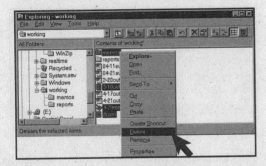

2 You have several options for deleting selected files. You can right-click a selected file and click **Delete**; you can open the **File** menu and select **Delete**; or you can press the **Delete** key.

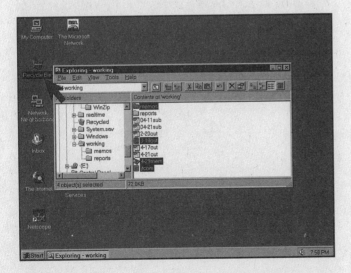

3 Another way to delete files is to drag any one of the selected files over the **Recycle Bin** icon on the desktop and release the mouse button.

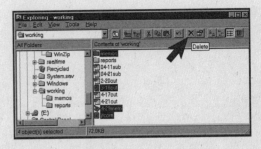

4 If the toolbar is displayed in My Computer or Windows Explorer, you can click the **Delete** button to quickly delete the selected files.

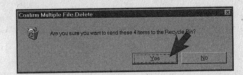

5 Regardless of which deletion method you choose, a dialog box appears, asking you to confirm the deletion. Click **Yes**.

Guided Tour Restore Accidentally Deleted Items

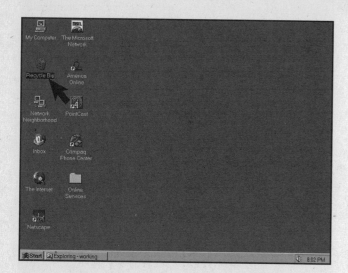

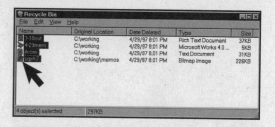

(2) The Recycle Bin shows the names of all the items you've deleted. To restore one or more items to their original locations, select the items just as you would in My Computer or Windows Explorer.

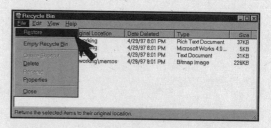

(1) Whenever you delete a file or folder, it is moved to the Recycle Bin until you choose to empty the bin. As long as a deleted item remains in the Recycle Bin, you can still restore it at any time. To display the contents of the Recycle Bin, double-click its icon.

The Recycle Bin icon on the desktop changes to reflect whether or not you've deleted files. When the Recycle Bin is completely empty, the icon is an empty wastebasket. When the Recycle Bin holds files you can restore, its wastebasket icon holds wadded-up paper.

(3) Open the **File** menu and select **Restore**. The selected files are moved from the Recycle Bin to their original folders.

The Recycle Bin stores deleted items on your hard disk, consuming valuable space. You should check the Bin regularly and empty it if it contains items you know you won't want to restore. Open the **File** menu and select **Empty Recycle Bin**.

Rename Files or Folders

Good file and folder names should be descriptive. The name of the file should give you some idea of its contents. Similarly, a good folder name should jog your memory about what kinds of files you've stored in the folder.

You could certainly choose a better file name than "stuff.doc" or a better folder name than "files." You should choose accurate file names such as "B Braun 9-9" for a letter to Bob Braun dated 9-9. Use clear folder names, too. For example, you might use "Braun Letters" for a folder that holds all your correspondence files with Bob Braun.

If you fall prey to lazy file-naming tendencies, you may find yourself with a disk full of files and folders you can't tell apart based on their names alone. Take the time to do some renaming; use the upcoming *Guided Tour* to learn how.

If you keep all your personal and business records in manila folders, you probably are used to the idea of pasting one label over another to rename the folder or use it for some other records. You can do the same thing more easily in Windows 95 by simply editing the file or folder name in the file list. And because Windows 95 allows for long file names (up to 255 characters), you can even give some of your old data files more descriptive names. File names can include spaces and special capitalization; just keep in mind that you cannot use any of the following characters:

$$\setminus ? : * ? " < > |$$

Although Windows 95 lets you use long file names, your old DOS and Windows 3.11 programs cannot recognize these long file names (they simply abbreviate the name and crop off any characters beyond the standard eight). If you continue to use old programs, you might want to keep the original file names you gave to your data files when you created them or stick with file names that are no more than eight characters long.

Guided Tour   Rename Files and Folders

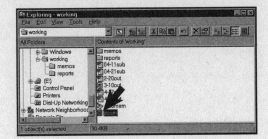

1 To rename a file or folder, it must be displayed in My Computer or Windows Explorer. Click the name or icon of the file or folder you want to rename. When you click a file or folder icon, it becomes highlighted.

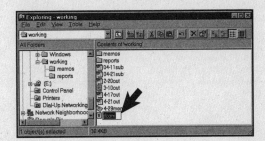

2 Pause, and then click the name of the file or folder again or press **F2**. Alternatively, right-click the file or folder and choose **Rename** from the shortcut menu. No matter which method you use, the name appears highlighted in a box.

(continues)

Guided Tour Rename Files and Folders *(continued)*

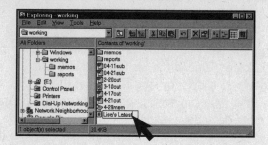 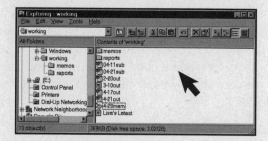

3 You can now type a new name for the file or folder to completely replace its current name. Or, click the name again to position the insertion point for editing, use the arrow keys to move the insertion point, and press **Backspace** or **Delete** to delete characters. You can then type your change.

4 Click anywhere outside the file or folder icon to make your change permanent, or simply press the **Enter** key.

Rename only files and folders you have created. Do *not* rename any Windows 95 files or program files or folders.

Create New Folders

As you rearrange files and folders on your hard disk, you will occasionally need to create new folders in which to stick files and subfolders. Windows 95 allows you to create folders on any disk or inside any folder that's displayed. You can even create folders and sub-folders on floppy disks, although most users aren't aware of this capability. The Explorer folder tree uses a file folder icon along with a name to represent each folder.

When you create a new folder, you not only specify where on the disk you want it located, but you also assign it a name. As for files, you can use long names for your folders, and folder names can include spaces and special capitalization. Just make sure you give descriptive names to your new directories.

When creating subfolders inside folders, try not to embed folders any more than three deep. For example, you don't want a Data folder containing a Letters folder, containing a My Letters folder, containing a My Letters in 1996 folder, containing a My Letters in June folder, containing...well, you get the idea. If you go too deep, you'll have to open all those folders each time you want to load one of your files. Just a word of advice.

> A quick way to create a folder is to right-click a blank area inside the window in which you want the new folder to appear. Point to **New**, and then click **Folder**. A folder icon named **New Folder** appears. You can type a new name for the folder.

Guided Tour Add a New Folder

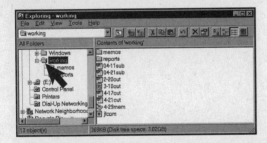

1 Any folder you create will be placed inside the active folder. Select the folder in which you want the new folder placed.

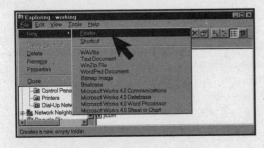

2 Open the **File** menu, point to **New**, and then click **Folder**.

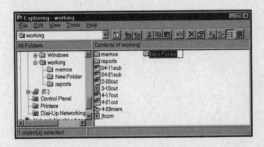

3 Windows plops a new folder, cleverly called New Folder, at the end of the file list.

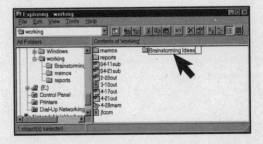

4 Type a new, more descriptive name for the folder, and then press **Enter**. When you start typing, the name you type replaces "New Folder."

HOW TO
Take More Control over Windows 95

A s people use computers more and more for both personal and professional tasks, computers have grown into much more than clunky,
oversized calculators that let you store and work with data.
Computers increasingly offer you choices in how to work and a
greater variety of ways to control the operations that you do perform.

This section helps you discover features that help you work more efficiently, and it also helps you adjust certain aspects of Windows 95
OEM Service Release 2 (OSR 2) to make your computing work more
enjoyable and comfortable. Some of the tasks here enable you to
adjust how you work with files and your mouse; others help you tackle other mission-critical functions. Whether or not you use the techniques covered in other tasks is a matter of preference. If you like the
default look and feel of Windows 95, leave it as is. Otherwise, you
can have as much fun as you want making the types of changes dis-
cussed in some tasks here.

What You Will Find in This Section

Rearrange the List of Files or Icons

As you work with your files and folders in the Windows Explorer or a My Computer window, you may find that the folder and file icons or names are not arranged efficiently. For example, you might want to view a list of the files grouped by date so you can see which files you changed most recently, or by type so you can more easily select all your document files.

You can easily change the order in which the Explorer displays folders and files in its file list or the order in which any My Computer window displays icons and names. (Note that the settings you choose apply to the current My Computer window only, not all open My Computer windows.)

> ▶The preceding section, "Organize Files and Folders with Windows 95" (page 101)◀ explained how to use Windows Explorer and My Computer to manage your files on disk.
> ▶The task called "Change the Explorer Window View" on page 112◀ showed how to choose a display format for files and folders: with large icons or small icons, in a list, or with details.

To change the order in which folders and files are listed, you open the **View** menu, point to **Arrange Icons** to display its submenu, and select any of the following options:

- **by Name** displays the folders and then files in ascending (A–Z or 0 and up) alphanumeric order according to the file name. This is the default arrangement.

- **by Type** lists folders first and then lists files by file type, using the often-hidden file name extensions to group the files. Windows sorts the groups of similar files alphabetically (ascending order) by file name extension. That is, .bak files are listed before .dat files, and so on. Within each group, files are alphabetized by file name.

- **by Size** leaves the folders at the start of the list but sorts the files according to how large each one is (how much storage space it takes on disk). Files are sorted from the smallest to the largest.

- **by Date** sorts and lists folders and then files according to the dates on which each was most recently changed. Often for folders, this is simply the date the folder was created. Each time you edit and save a file, Windows tracks the date and time that you saved the modification. So, by Date lists the folders and files by date in descending order, from most recently modified to least recently modified.

The *Guided Tour* in this task shows you how to choose the order in which you'd like to display files.

> The initial My Computer window (the one that appears when you double-click the My Computer icon on the desktop) offers slightly different commands on the Arrange Icons submenu of the View menu: by Drive Letter, by Type, by Size, and by Free Space. These commands, obviously, let you choose how the disk drive icons are arranged in the window. The default is by Drive Letter.

Work with File Details

Sometimes it may be difficult to see the impact of your selection in the Arrange Icons submenu, particularly if you've previously chosen to display large icons for files and folders with the Large Icons choice on the View menu. Even if you've selected the Small Icons or the List choice from the View menu, it still might be hard to see the impact of changing the arrangement, because those views show you only a file or folder name—and no other information.

To get the most clear idea of how an Arrange Icons submenu choice rearranges folders and files in either Explorer or the current My Computer window, first choose the **Details** choice from the **View** menu. This view provides four types of information, in columns, with the following headings: *Name*, *Size* (for files only), *Type*, and *Modified* (file modification date).

When file details appear on-screen, you get more visual feedback about the changes each time you rearrange the order of files and folders using a choice from the

Arrange Icons submenu of the View menu. However, the Details view provides an additional capability that the other views don't: You can quickly re-sort files using the Name, Size, Type, and Modified column headings that appear, as demonstrated by the examples in the *Guided Tour*. Simply double-click one of the column headings to sort the folders and files by that column (folders will always stay grouped together, either first or last). For example, click the **Name** column head to sort files and folders by name in ascending (A–Z) alphanumeric order, with folders first. Click the **Name** column head again to sort in descending (Z–A) order, with files first and then folders.

Tidy Up Icons and Refresh the Window

There are a few more actions that may come in handy when you want to clean up the Explorer file list or an open My Computer window:

- **Automatically arranging icons.** This feature is available after you choose Large Icons or Small Icons from the View menu. Windows can clean up the icons in the file list and place them back in orderly rows and columns any time you delete, add, or drag around a file or folder icon. You can turn this Auto Arrange feature on and off as you want, as described in the *Guided Tour*.

- **Lining up icons.** Another option for lining up large icons or small icons after you move them or

make another change is to manually line up the icons using the Line Up Icons command. This command arranges icons on an invisible grid so they don't overlap, but it usually does not arrange them to make the best use of screen space. See the *Guided Tour* for a review of this command.

- **Refreshing a window.** At times, changes you make may not appear immediately on-screen. For example, if you swap floppy disks, the files on the new disk won't appear automatically. Or, if you delete numerous files from a hard disk, neither the My Computer window nor the Explorer window status bar will update its display to show you how much space is now free on the disk. In cases like these, you need to refresh the window. To do so, press **F5**, or open the **View** menu and click **Refresh**.

The commands described in this task apply to the icons on the Windows 95 desktop, too. If you right-click any area of the desktop, you'll get a shortcut menu. The shortcut menu has a Line Up Icons choice, an Arrange Icons command that displays a submenu with choices for sorting the icons, and an Auto Arrange command. Press **F5** at the desktop to refresh it so you can see changes you may have made to the Windows Registry. ▶**(See the task called "Manage Windows 95 System Registry File" on page 359.)**◀

Guided Tour Reorder the File List or Icons

1 To more easily see how the order of files changes in the Explorer, for this example, open the **View** menu and select **Details**. The file list displays the Name, Size, Type, and Modified date for the files in the current folder.

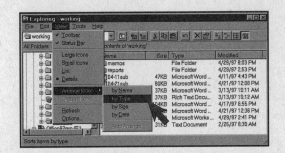

2 By default, folders and files are listed by name. To reorder them by type, open the **View** menu, point to **Arrange Icons**, and select **by Type** in the submenu.

(continues)

Guided Tour Reorder the File List or Icons *(continued)*

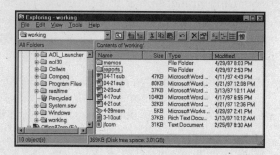

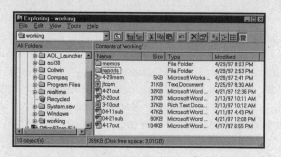

3 Items are listed alphabetically according to their type (the Type column). As you can see in the Type column of the file list shown here, Windows groups all the Microsoft Word document (.doc) files and then lists a Works (.wps) file, a Rich Text Format (.rtf) file, and a text (.txt) file.

> You can display the file name extensions in Explorer. ►To learn how, see "Change the Explorer Window View" on page 112.◄

5 The Size list in this figure shows that the files are sorted from smallest to largest.

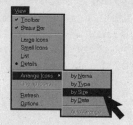

4 To sort files according to their relative size (from smallest to largest), open the **View** menu, point to **Arrange Icons**, and select the **by Size** command.

6 To change the order once again, this time so that the files are sorted according to the date in the Modified column (the date the file was last modified), open the **View** menu, point to **Arrange Icons**, and select the **by Date** command. The files are rearranged so that the ones with the most recent dates appear at the top of the list.

7 To list files in the original order (by name) again, open the **View** menu, point to **Arrange Icons**, and select **by Name**.

Guided Tour Sort by File Details

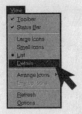

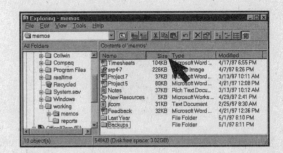

1 To use the techniques covered here, you must be viewing file details. To do so, open the **View** menu and select **Details**. The file list displays the Name, Size, Type, and Modified date for the files in the current folder.

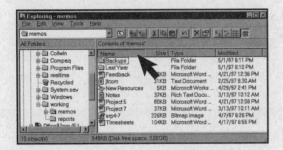

2 As shown above, files are initially sorted by name in ascending (A–Z or 0 and up) alphanumeric order. To sort in descending alphanumeric order, click the **Name** column heading in the file list.

3 Windows sorts the files, placing the folders last as shown here. To sort by size instead, click the **Size** column heading.

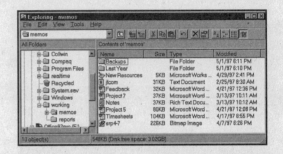

4 As shown in this figure, the files are re-sorted with folders first and then files, from smallest to largest.

5 Click the **Size** column heading again to list the files from largest to smallest, or click any of the other column heads to sort and re-sort as needed.

Guided Tour Line Up Icons

1 To work with icons, open the **View** menu and select either **Large Icons** or **Small Icons**.

2 Copy, cut, drag, and otherwise work with the icons as needed.

(continues)

Guided Tour Line Up Icons *(continued)*

3 When the icons become too messy or are stacked up and overlapping, you can line them up. Open the **View** menu and select **Line Up Icons**.

4 Windows lines up the icons to an invisible grid, as shown here. The icons "snap" to the closest grid location instead of aligning to fill contiguous rows and columns. To make the icons neater still, use the Auto Arrange command, covered in the next set of steps.

Guided Tour Auto Arrange Icons

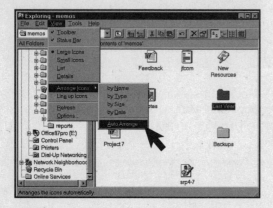

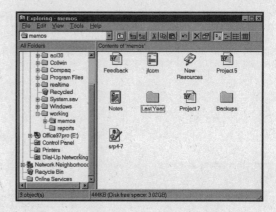

1 When you're working with icons and want to align them automatically in a neat, condensed order, open the **View** menu, point to **Arrange Icons**, and select **Auto Arrange** in the submenu that appears.

2 As shown above, the icons snap into place, filling consecutive positions in the invisible grid that Windows uses to position icons.

3 To turn off auto arranging of icons, repeat step 1.

Work with Properties for a Disk or File

Windows 95 did bring a few new terms to computing lingo, including *properties*. Properties are characteristics and other information specifying how and why a file, disk, hardware device (such as your monitor), or other item in Windows looks and behaves the way it does.

In some instances, you can view only particular properties to see what they are. For example, you can only view information telling you how much of a disk's space is currently used or full; you *can't* change the amount of free or used disk space. You can change other properties, though. For example, you can add or change the label for any disk. (A label is just a name for the disk; for hard disks, that label appears in Explorer or My Computer. You may want to label your floppy disks by date, for example, and then add the date on each disk's external sticky label to keep them organized.)

For files and folders, you can view properties such as the size and creation date, but you can modify these other properties called *attributes*:

- *Read-Only.* When you open a file marked as read-only, the application won't let you edit the file. If you need to make a change to the file, remove this attribute and then reopen it.

- *Archive.* When this attribute is turned on, it cues some programs to create a backup copy of the file.

- *Hidden.* If you've selected this attribute, the file or folder will not appear in Explorer or My Computer windows. (You can display hidden files. ▶**See "Change the Explorer Window View" on page 112 to review how.◀**)

- *System.* This attribute is assigned to vital files that Windows needs to run. Like hidden files, these files don't appear on-screen unless you specify that they should. Windows hides system files to prevent you from deleting them.

If you try to delete a file or folder that has the read-only, hidden, or system attribute turned on, the message box that asks you to verify the deletion reminds you of the file's special attribute(s). This extra warning should help prevent you from sending a vital file to the Recycle Bin. (If you do accidentally send a file to the Recycle Bin, you can restore it, ▶**as described in the earlier task "Delete and Restore Files and Folders" on page 130.◀**)

Some types of files, particularly those from word processors and other applications, offer additional properties that you can view and in some cases edit. The *Guided Tour* shows you how to access all the properties for a disk, folder, or file.

Windows 95 displays properties in a dialog box that's sometimes called a *properties sheet*. Don't let the name throw you. They work just like other dialog boxes.

Guided Tour Change a Disk's Properties

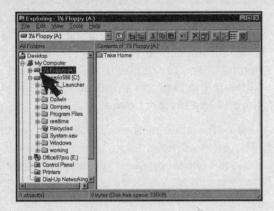

1 In the Explorer folder tree or in the initial My Computer window, select the drive for which you want to review attributes.

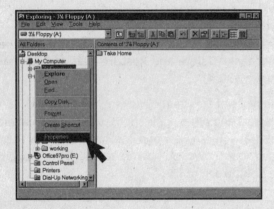

2 Right-click the disk to display its shortcut menu (or open the **File** menu) and select **Properties**. The Properties dialog box for the disk appears on-screen, with its General tab displayed by default.

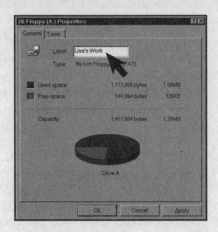

3 By default, an insertion point appears in the Label text box if the disk has no label. If there is a label, it's selected. Simply type a new label for the disk.

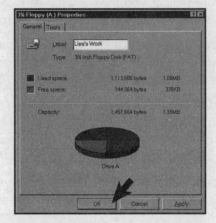

4 Review other attributes, such as the disk type (which will be FAT32 for hard disks under Windows 95 OEM Service Release 2), used space, free space for more files, and total capacity. When you finish, click **OK** to close the Properties dialog box.

Each disk's Properties dialog box has a second tab named Tools. ▶You'll learn to use those tools to care for your disks in the later section "Keep Your Data Safe" on page 399.◀

Guided Tour   Change a File or Folder's Properties

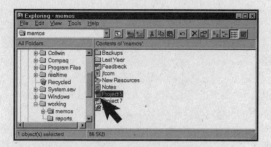

1 In the Explorer file list or a My Computer window, select the file(s) and/or folder(s) for which you want to review attributes.

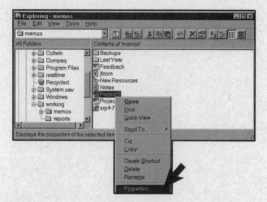

2 Right-click the selection to display a shortcut menu (or open the **File** menu) and select **Properties**. The Properties dialog box for the selection appears on-screen, with its General tab displayed by default.

3 You can review such information as the document type, size, and creation date. You also can add or remove attributes. To turn on an attribute for the file, click its check box to check it. To remove any attribute, click its check box to remove the check.

4 If the Properties dialog box has additional tabs, click each one to work with the information it offers. In this example, click the **Summary** tab to display it. This tab offers some of the Properties information entered for the file in Microsoft Word. You can't edit the information here.

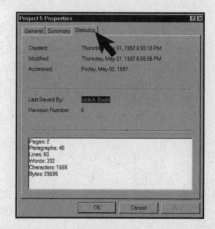

5 This dialog box has an additional tab. Click the **Statistics** tab to view its contents. In this case, the tab shows file statistics tracked by Word. You can view, but cannot edit, this information.

(continues)

Guided Tour Change a File or Folder's Properties *(continued)*

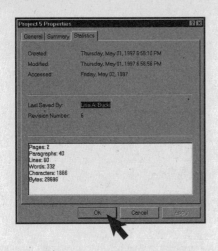

If you select multiple files or folders and then display the Properties dialog box, one or more of the Attributes check boxes on the General tab may be filled with gray shading. This means that some of the selected files and folders have that attribute assigned, but others don't. Click the check box to clear that attribute for all files and folders, and then click again to turn on the attribute for the whole selection.

6 Click to move among the tabs to change or review attributes as needed. When you finish, click **OK** to close the dialog box and accept any changes you've made.

Search for Files

Over time, you'll accumulate hundreds of files on your hard disk, plus uncounted dozens on floppy disks. That's a lot of files. Chances are, you won't remember each one in great detail. And even if you do, it's easy to forget which directory on your hard disk you saved a file to.

Windows 95 releases you from the burden of remembering where every file is by giving you the ability to search for files. You can use the Windows search capability to:

- **Search for a folder.** To do so, you specify the folder's name.

- **Search for a single file.** In this case, you specify the exact file name.

- **Search for files with similar name characteristics.** Using wild-card characters, you can find files with similar names. For example, enter ***.txt** to find all files with the **.TXT** file name extension, or type **braun*.*** to find all files beginning with BRAUN. ▶**(For a review of using wild cards like the asterisk to specify file names, see "Open a File in a Windows Program" on page 91.)**◀

Before you start the search, you select the disk and folder you want to start the search from; Windows searches down the folder tree from there. If you want to search an entire disk, for example, start the search from the disk itself. If you start the search from another folder, such as \WINDOWS, Windows searches only the \WINDOWS folder and its subfolders, ignoring what's on the rest of the hard disk.

Also, you can determine whether or not Windows searches subfolders at all. Turning off this option makes the search go faster, although it means you might not find all the matching files on a disk (or find any files at all).

Use Your Search Results

After you perform a search, Windows displays the search results, a list of the file(s) matching the criteria for your search. This list isn't just for show. You can perform certain file operations within it, which can save you from having to open a new window for a file that's been found. You can do any of these things with found file(s) in the list:

- Select one or more files (as you would in any other window) to perform file-related operations.

- Right-click the selected file(s) to display a shortcut menu of commands you can use to work with the file.

- Use the **Cut** command on the shortcut menu to move the file(s) elsewhere.

- Use the **Copy** command to copy the file(s) elsewhere.

- Use the **Delete** command to remove the file(s) from your disk.

- Rename the file(s) using **Rename**.

- View file details using the **Properties** command.

Save Searches for Later Use

As you'll see in the *Guided Tour* in this task, specifying a search is straightforward, but if you specify several criteria, it could take a few minutes. Windows 95 enables you to save the criteria you create for a search so that you can later run the same search with only a couple of simple steps. When you save a search, Windows adds an icon for the search to the desktop. (Of course, you can move the icon to another location if you prefer.) To restart the search, all you have to do is double-click the icon.

Guided Tour Look for Files

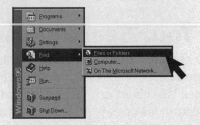

1 Click the **Start** button on the taskbar, point to **Find**, and select **Files or Folders**. The Find window appears.

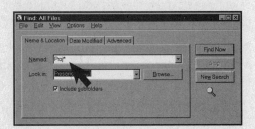

2 In the **Named** text box, enter the name of the file or folder (or the file specification with wild cards for a group of files) you want to search for. The example entry here searches for any file with a name starting with *Proj*.

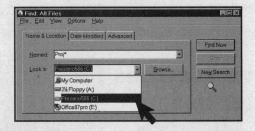

3 Change the **Look In** selection, if necessary, to indicate what disk and folder to start the search from. You can use the **Look In** drop-down list to choose a different disk, or you can click the **Browse** button to display a Browse for Folder dialog box to select a specific folder in its folder tree.

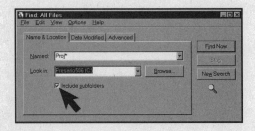

4 If you want to prevent a subfolder search (which speeds up the search), deselect the **Include Subfolders** check box.

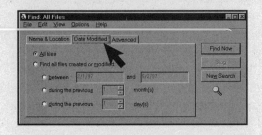

5 Click the **Date Modified** tab to display its options.

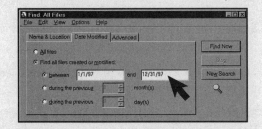

6 To limit the search to files created and modified within certain dates, click **Find All Files Created or Modified**, and then specify the date range using one of the three option buttons. For example, to find files in the current year, click **between**, and then enter **1/1/97** and **12/31/97** in the accompanying text boxes.

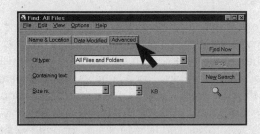

7 Click the **Advanced** tab to display its options.

Guided Tour Look for Files

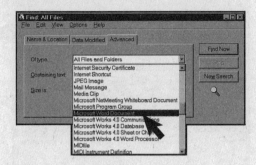

8 Use the **Of Type** drop-down list to search for files of a particular type (these are installed programs that Windows recognizes). The choice you make here works in conjunction with the name entered in step 2 (so it would find, for example, only Microsoft Word files with names starting with *Proj*).

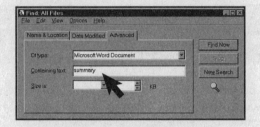

9 In the **Containing Text** text box, enter key words that appear in the file to further limit the search.

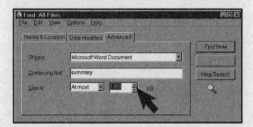

10 To limit the search by the size of the file, make a choice from the **Size Is** drop-down list, and then use the **KB** spinner to specify a file size. For example, you might want to search for files smaller than 1,000KB (1M) to ensure that each will fit on a floppy disk.

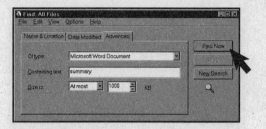

11 Click **Find Now** to start the search.

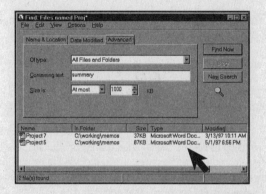

12 Windows searches the disk from the folder you specified and displays the search results in a list at the bottom of the Find dialog box. You can work with the files from this list and then close the Find window when you finish.

If you've already chosen a disk or folder in the Explorer, you can start a search in that disk or folder. Open the **Tools** menu, point to **Find**, and click **Files or Folders**. The Find window appears, with the disk or folder you chose earlier already specified in the Look In list. Proceed as described in steps 4–12 to finish the search.

Guided Tour Save and Rerun a Search

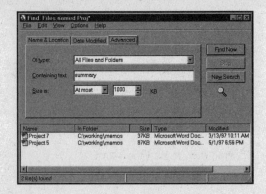

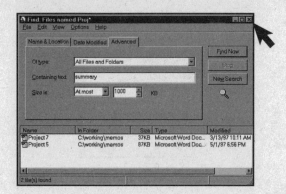

1 Set up all your criteria and run the search (as described in the previous *Guided Tour* steps).

2 You can save the search criteria only, or you can save the search criteria and the results. To include the results in the saved search, open the **Options** menu in the Find window and select **Save Results** to toggle that command on.

3 To save only the search, open the **File** menu in the Find window and select **Save Search**.

4 Click the **Close** button to close the Find window. You'll see the icon for the saved search on the Windows desktop.

5 Double-click the icon for the search, and the Find window opens. If you saved the search criteria only, click the **Find Now** button to rerun the search. If you saved the search results, they automatically appear. Work with the listed files, and then close the Find window when you finish.

Format Disks

➤**You'll recall from the task called "Understand Disks and Drives" (on page [p1s3 TBD])**◄ that all disks are covered with a magnetic material. Your computer's disk drive gives an "on" or "off" state to tiny pieces of this material to create readable characters of information. To enable your drive to handle such a delicate operation, the magnetic material needs to be precisely arranged on the disk's surface. *Formatting* is the process of arranging the magnetic material on the disk so it can store information.

Formatting not only organizes the magnetic storage information on a disk, it also sets up the *File Allocation Table (FAT)* that your computer uses to keep track of which parts of which files are stored on specific parts of the disk. ➤**(For more on the FAT, see "Understand Files" on page 57.)**◄ Each disk has a specific capacity of storage space based on the density of the magnetic material. Different floppy drives are specifically geared to handle disks of a particular density. (More on this in a moment.) After you format a disk, you can save and copy files on it.

You can format disks that already have information on them to "freshen" them up and deal with minor errors on the disk's surface. Use caution when reformatting floppies and removable disks, however. *Formatting wipes out any information that exists on the disk and clears out the contents of the FAT*. You don't want to format a disk that holds data you need, which means you almost never want to format a hard disk, especially drive C.

> If you accidentally format a disk that has data you need, that data is lost forever. There's no way to restore the data, and it's not put in the Recycle Bin so that you can retrieve it. Always double- or even triple-check to make sure that you're not formatting a floppy disk that you need or a hard disk drive (especially drive C) that has important data and programs.

Explorer and My Computer let you format any floppy disk that matches the size and capacity of your floppy disk drive. You also can set a few other disk options. You can format many removable disks, too, but sometimes the removable drive manufacturer provides a utility program that does the job better. When the manufacturer provides one, be sure to use that utility program.

> Because formatting is a tedious operation, you can buy preformatted disks. However, if you don't want to spend a few extra cents for this convenience, you can format your own disks.

Choose Format Options

The Format dialog box offers three choices in the Format Type area that enable you to control how the format operation is performed:

You can choose **Quick (erase)** to reformat a disk that's been formatted before. Quick formatting is faster because it cleans up the disk storage and clears out the FAT, but it doesn't scan for bad sectors (information) on the disk. If you think a disk has bad sectors, perform a full format.

Perform a **Full** format if a disk hasn't previously been formatted or has been formatted for a Macintosh. This is also the best option to choose if you suspect other problems with the disk, such as if you think the disk's files may be infected with a virus. This formatting prepares the disk's surface for file storage and then scans the disk for bad sectors.

If you've already formatted a disk and just want to copy system files to it, choose **Copy System Files Only**. Windows copies the system files to the disk without deleting any existing files from the disk. This option makes the disk *bootable*; that is, if you insert the disk in drive A and start your computer, it reads the floppy disk for startup information.

The Other Options area at the bottom of the dialog box offers choices that aren't crucial to the format operation. However, those options (described here) can help you catalog and work with formatted disks.

Label You can enter a label for the disk (which is also called a *volume label* in old DOS lingo). To add a label, first clear the check beside the **No Label** check box (if necessary), and then make your entry in the **Label** text box. Your label can have up to 11 characters including spaces, but it *cannot* include tabs or these characters:

    * / \ | . , ; : + = [ ] ( ) & ^ < > "

Display Summary When Finished Check this option if you want to see a report when the formatting is finished. The report tells you the disk's available space, the space occupied by the system files if you copied them to the disk, and space taken up by bad sectors. The latter tidbit is good to know; if a disk has a lot of bad sectors, its magnetic media may be going bad, so you should consider discarding it. ▶**For information about correcting errors on disks, see "Check a Disk for Errors with ScanDisk" on page 407.◀**

Copy System Files Select this to have Windows both format the disk and copy system startup files to the disk instead of simply copying the system files.

Name That Capacity

You may have noticed that your floppy disks or disk labels have "HD" or "DD" or something similar on them. These hieroglyphics refer to the disk's *density* (capacity), which is as important as the floppy's size. Disks of differing capacity and size combinations hold differing amounts of data. ▶**(See "Insert and Remove Floppy and Removable Disks" on page 35 to learn more about different floppy disk capacities.)◀**

The disk's capacity depends on how efficient its magnetic storage material is. High-density (HD) disks hold more data than do double-density (DD) disks of the same size. Older disk drives can only work with DD disks. Computers built in the last few years, however, have high-density floppy disk drives that can work with both HD and DD disks of the right size (5.25" or 3.5"). One caution: Unless you tell Windows otherwise, it will try to format a DD disk as high-density. If you format a disk this way, it might work okay for a while, but eventually it'll cause you to lose data. Play it safe and format DD disks as DD disks and HD disks as HD disks.

> Formatting a DD disk as HD can slow down the formatting process drastically toward the end, which may clue you in to the fact that you've specified the wrong disk capacity for formatting.

Floppy Disk Capacities

Disk Size	Type	Capacity
3.5-inch	DSHD, double-sided high-density	1.44M
3.5-inch	DSDD, double-sided double-density	720K
5.25-inch	DSHD, double-sided high-density	1.2M
5.25-inch	DSDD, double-sided double-density	360K

Guided Tour Format a Disk in Windows

1 If you're formatting a disk you've used before, double-check to make sure you've copied any files you might need from that disk. Insert the floppy disk in the appropriate drive.

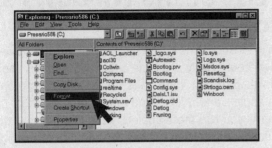

2 In the Explorer folder tree or in the initial My Computer window, right-click the disk and click **Format**. (In My Computer only, you can alternatively click the disk icon once, open the **File** menu, and select **Format**.)

3 Use the **Capacity** drop-down list to specify the correct capacity of the floppy disk you're formatting.

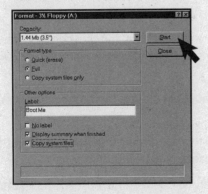

4 Specify any formatting options you desire (they're described in detail above), and then click **Start** to begin the format.

5 Windows shows you the formatting progress. If necessary, click **Cancel** to stop formatting.

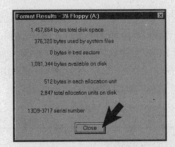

6 When it's finished formatting the disk, Windows displays the Format Results summary (if you specified that a summary should be displayed). Click **Close** to close the summary after reviewing it.

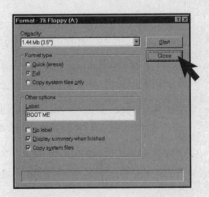

7 Click **Close** again to close the Format dialog box.

In either Explorer or My Computer, if you try to select a disk that isn't formatted, Windows displays a message telling you that the disk isn't formatted and asking whether you want to format it. Click **Yes**.

Use Built-In Windows Programs

Windows 95 comes with a host of free programs, commonly called *applets* (small application programs), which you can use to do real work in Windows. Although some of these programs are not state-of-the-art and won't provide you with the advanced options you'll find in other commercial programs, they do give you the power to do basic jobs in Windows, such as writing letters, drawing pictures, and dialing your phone. The latest release of Windows that ships on new PCs, OEM Service Release 2 (OSR 2), offers a few new applets that didn't appear in the original Windows 95 release, helping you tackle more tasks than ever before.

Windows also includes a set of *utilities* to help you properly maintain your computer. For instance, ScanDisk can help restore data from damaged disks, and Disk Defragmenter can reduce file fragmentation and speed up your hard disk.

The *Guided Tour* shows you where to look for and how to run these Windows applets.

A List of the Windows 95 Programs

Detailed instructions on how to use all the Windows 95 applets could easily consume another 600-page book. So, instead of that, here's a list of the most commonly used applets and utilities and a brief description of each. As you run these applets, keep in mind that the Windows Help system is close at hand. For instructions on how to use any of these applets, simply open the **Help** menu and click a topic.

If you don't find some of the applets listed below on your system, that means they haven't been installed. Use the Windows Help system to learn more about installing other Windows components.

Icon	Applet Name and Description
	Calculator is just like a hand-held calculator.
	Character Map lets you copy and insert special characters that do not appear on your keyboard.
	Clipboard Viewer displays the contents of the data that you cut or copy from a document. (The Clipboard stores data temporarily so you can paste it into another location.)
	Dial-Up Networking is a *remote-computing* program, which lets you connect two computers (for example, your home and office computers) over the phone line. Each computer must have a modem.
	File Transfer enables you to send files while simultaneously talking to someone on the phone by using your voice-enabled modem. This applet is new to OSR 2.
	Direct Cable Connection lets you connect two computers with a cable and transfer files between the two computers. This is especially useful if you have to transfer files between a laptop and desktop computer.
	HyperTerminal is a modem communications program that connects you to another computer or to online services.
	Wang **Imaging** for Windows, new to OSR 2, enables you to view graphics files in a variety of formats such as JPG, XIF, TIFF, BMP, and FAX. You also can scan images directly into this applet.
	Notepad lets you create and edit plain text files, which can be opened in almost any program.
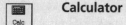	**Paint** offers a complete set of tools for drawing and painting pictures on your screen. You can also use Paint to create your own background designs for the Windows desktop.

Icon	Applet Name and Description
	Phone Dialer is a programmable phone keyboard. You can use it (along with a modem) to dial phone numbers for you. After Dialer places the call, you can pick up the receiver and start talking.
	WordPad is a more sophisticated word-processing program than Notepad. It allows you to style text to make your documents more attractive.
	Fax is a new program that can transform your computer (equipped with a fax modem) into a fax machine. You can then receive faxes and send the documents you type to other fax machines.
	Games is a group of computer games including FreeCell, Hearts, Minesweeper, and Solitaire. Most of these games are very addictive, but they do help hone your mouse skills.
	The **Get on the Internet** choice runs the Internet Connection Wizard, which helps you set up your computer to connect to an Internet service provider. These and the next three Internet features are only bundled in OSR 2.
	The desktop icon labeled **The Internet** launches the Internet Connection Wizard the first time you select it, and thereafter launches Internet Explorer, a Web browser program.
	Internet Mail is an easy e-mail program for use with an Internet e-mail account.
	Internet News enables you to browse Internet newsgroups, online "bulletin boards" where users can post and read messages.
	Microsoft NetMeeting, new in OSR 2, enables multiple users to hold an online conference by typing using an on-screen Whiteboard where users can draw and type text.
	Multimedia consists of several programs that control your sound card and CD-ROM drive. CD Player lets you play audio CDs. Media Player plays computerized movie clips and sound recordings. Sound Recorder lets you plug a microphone into your sound card and record voices and other sounds. And Volume Control allows you to crank up the volume of your sound card or CD player.
	Backup is a utility that copies the files on your hard disk, compresses them (so they take up less space), and places the compressed files on a set of floppy disks or a backup tape. If anything happens to your files, you can use Backup to restore the backed up files to your hard disk.
	Disk Defragmenter rearranges the parts of each file on your hard disk so your disk drive doesn't have to hunt all over for them. This increases the speed of your drive and the overall speed of your computer. Run this monthly.
	DriveSpace compresses files on your hard disk, so they take up less space and decompresses the files automatically when you need them. If you're running out of hard disk space, back up all your files and run DriveSpace.
	ScanDisk looks for lost pieces of files on a disk and for bad spots on the disk itself. It can help you recover lost data, repair floppy disks, and reduce future data loss by preventing Windows from storing data on any bad areas of the disk.
	Windows Messaging (formerly Microsoft Exchange) is a one-stop electronic mailbox for all your network e-mail and e-mail that you receive from online services.
	The Microsoft Network is an online service offered by Microsoft Corporation. If you have a modem, you can subscribe to the service and use it to connect to other computer users, do research, shop, send and receive mail, and much more.

Guided Tour Use Windows Programs

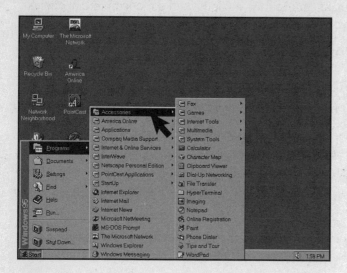

1 You can get to all Windows applets via the Start button. Click the **Start** button, point to **Programs**, and then point to **Accessories**.

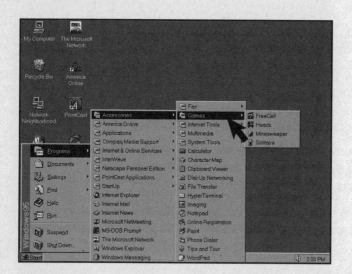

2 At the bottom of the Programs menu are a couple of applets, but the Accessories menu is the place where most applets hang out. At the top of the Accessories menu are the names of additional submenus. If the applet you want is on a submenu, point to the submenu name to display its applets.

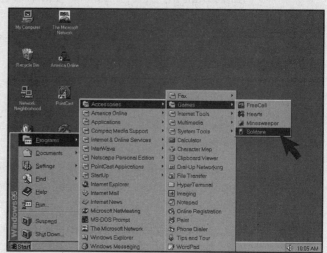

3 When you see the name of the applet you want to run (either in the Accessories menu or one of its submenus), click it.

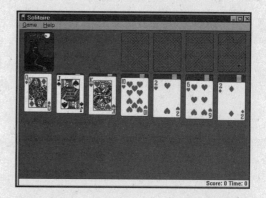

4 Windows runs the applet and automatically closes the Start menu. The applet displays its own window, complete with title bar and menu bar, so you can start performing a task.

Drag and Drop

One of the fundamental benefits of Windows 95 is that you can use the mouse to speed up many operations. You've already seen throughout the book how you can use a mouse to drag icons and files around, either on the desktop or within a window.

There's an even more useful way to exploit the mouse—a capability called *drag and drop*. Drag and drop capabilities began showing up in applications late in the life of Windows 3.11. Windows 95 now offers some drag and drop capabilities, as do most

Windows 95 applications (see the instructions that came with your program to learn more).

While dragging and dropping isn't rocket science, it's important that you be familiar with the basic technique. It's a technique that's used in a variety of applications and ways, and it can expedite your work. The *Guided Tour* demonstrates an example of using drag and drop to move text. Instead of having to click a couple of toolbar buttons or select a couple of commands, you can accomplish the edit with one fluid motion.

Guided Tour Move Text with Drag and Drop

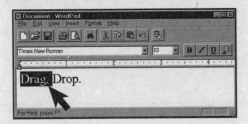

1 Select the text you want to move.

3 Release the mouse button, and the text drops into place.

If you want to drag and drop a selection to the end of a document, click to place the insertion point at the end of the last paragraph (and to make sure no other text is highlighted) and then press **Enter** to add a blank line before dragging. Otherwise, the selection will be appended to (run into) the last paragraph in the document.

2 Point to the selection, press and hold the left mouse button, and drag until the mouse pointer points to the new location you want. You'll see a vertical insertion point, and the mouse pointer will have a gray box representing the selection you're dragging.

Create Scraps

As advertised in the last task, dragging and dropping comes into play in a variety of ways in Windows 95 and its applications. You can put drag and drop to use in creating *scraps* on the desktop. Scraps are portions of a file that you copy and store in an icon on the desktop.

A scrap works like those familiar sticky notes you probably have stuck to your papers or monitor. But scraps are even better because you can open them up in an instant and copy their contents. Here are just a few ideas for using scraps:

- Suppose you have a lengthy to-do list typed into a WordPad document. At the start of each workday, create a desktop scrap holding the current day's tasks. Then it'll be easy to open your list frequently and review it.

- You have lengthy signature and address information that you want to include at the bottom of many of your documents, no matter what application you create each document in. Keep the information in a scrap so you can copy and paste the information as needed.

- You have certain information that you need to reference frequently as you create a number of flyers or reports. Use a scrap as an easy holding area from which you can copy the information over and over.

You can create scraps from just about any Windows 95 application. However, you might want to stick with applications that are small and load quickly (like the Windows 95 WordPad applet) so you don't have to wait for a large, slow application to load just to see a 10-word or 10-number scrap. The *Guided Tour* explains how to drag and drop to create a scrap.

Guided Tour   Make and Use a Scrap

1 Open the document that you want to create the scrap from, and size the document window so that the desktop is visible.

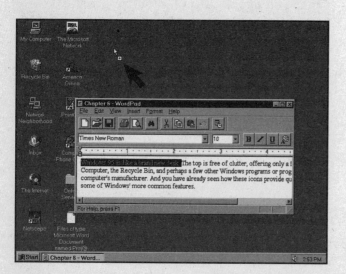

2 Select the information that you want to use as the scrap, drag it over the desktop, and drop it into place. As you drag, the mouse pointer displays a plus sign and a gray box representing the selection. When you drop the selection, Windows creates the scrap icon on the desktop.

3 You can close the document and application holding the original material and continue working.

4 When you need to view or copy the scrap's contents, double-click the scrap icon on the desktop. The scrap opens in its original application.

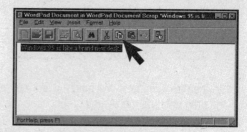

5 If you need to reuse the scrap text, select it and copy it by clicking the **Copy** button on the toolbar, or by opening the **Edit** menu and choosing **Copy**.

6 Start or switch to the application where you'd like to use the scrap, position the insertion point, and click the **Paste** button or use the **Edit**, **Paste** command to paste it.

Save Time with Shortcuts

Windows 95 is like a brand new desk. The top is free of clutter, offering only a few icons for running My Computer, the Recycle Bin, and perhaps a few other programs. And you have already seen how these icons provide quick access for getting at some of the more common Windows features. Wouldn't it be nice if you could add some icons for the programs you use most often so you don't have to weave your way through the Start/Programs menu? Well, you can—by adding shortcuts to the desktop. *Shortcuts* are icons

that point to specific programs and documents. When you double-click the icon, Windows opens the corresponding program or document.

Windows provides two ways to add shortcuts to the desktop. The easiest way is to drag an icon from My Computer or Windows Explorer onto the desktop. Another way is to right-click the desktop, select **New**, select **Shortcut**, and then follow the on-screen instructions to complete the task.

Guided Tour   Create a Shortcut

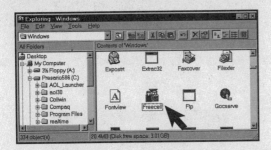

1 You can create shortcuts for quick access to files and programs. First, run Explorer or My Computer and display the icon for which you want to create a shortcut.

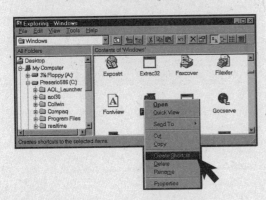

2 Right-click the icon for which you want to create a shortcut, and then click **Create Shortcut**.

An even quicker way to create a shortcut on the desktop is to hold down the **Ctrl** key and drag the original icon from Explorer or My Computer onto the desktop.

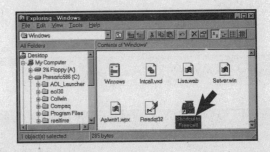

3 Windows creates a clone of the selected icon and places it in the same window that contains the original icon. Drag the shortcut icon onto the Windows desktop to move it there.

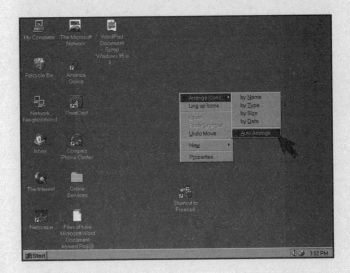

4 You can have Windows rearrange the shortcut icons on the desktop. Right-click a blank area of the desktop, move the mouse pointer over **Arrange Icons**, and click the desired arrangement.

Change an Object's Properties

Your desktop consists of a collection of *objects*, each of which is controlled by its own settings. The taskbar is one object, file and folder icons are objects, each window is an object, and even the desktop itself is treated as an object. You can control these objects by changing their *properties*. For example, you can change the display properties to turn on a screen saver program or adjust the color of the Windows background.

The procedure for changing an object's properties is fairly simple. You right-click the object to view its short-cut menu, and then you click **Properties**. This brings up a dialog box that allows you to change the object's properties. This dialog box varies according to the object you selected. You enter your preferences, and then click **OK**.

Because there are so many different objects in Windows, and because their properties vary so greatly, the *Guided Tour* walks you through the process of changing a specific object (the Recycle Bin) in order to illustrate the process of changing any object's properties. ▶**(To change the display properties for your monitor, see "Change the Desktop Display" on page 162.)◀**

To try changing the properties of other items, right-click the item: the taskbar, My Computer, a file icon, or a folder icon, for example. Most Properties dialog boxes have a question mark button in the upper-right corner, which you can click for help with specific options.

Guided Tour   Change Properties

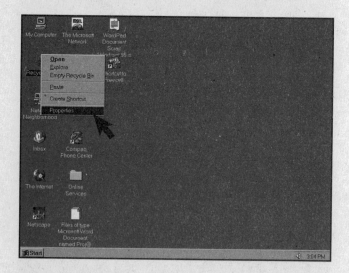

1 You can change the properties of almost any object in Windows. Right-click the object whose properties you want to change and click **Properties**.

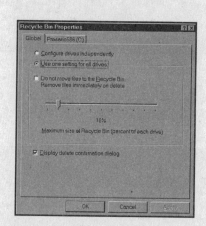

2 If, for example, you choose to change the properties of the Recycle Bin, Windows shows you the Recycle Bin Properties dialog box.

Guided Tour   Change Properties

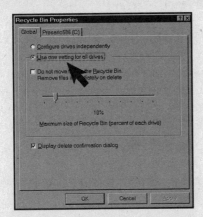

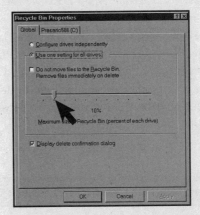

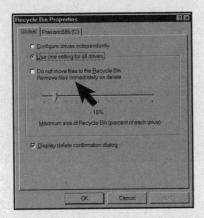

3 You can change the Recycle Bin properties for each hard drive, or you can use the same settings on all the drives on your system. For now, select **Use One Setting for All Drives**.

4 The Recycle Bin is used as a buffer to help you restore accidentally deleted files. If you want to turn this buffer off (a dangerous thing to do), click **Do Not Move Files to the Recycle Bin**. Turning this option on tells Windows to immediately remove files from your hard disk when you delete them. I *strongly* recommend that you not do this.

5 The Recycle Bin is set up to use 10% of your disk space for storing deleted files. After the 10% is used up, Recycle Bin automatically deletes older files. You can drag the slider to the left or right to have Windows use more or less space for Recycle Bin.

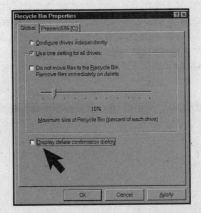

6 Whenever you delete a file, a dialog box appears asking if you're sure. To prevent this dialog box from appearing, click **Display Delete Confirmation Dialog** to remove the check from the box.

7 Click **OK** to save your changes.

Change the Desktop Display

If you work in a large office, you probably walk past computers every day and see some sort of funky color scheme or design on the monitor. Maybe you've wondered how your colleague has managed to decorate his or her screen so expertly, and you have a secret desire to give your monitor a custom look.

Windows 95 provides an easy way for you to change the look of your Windows desktop. You can change the color of the desktop, add a design, change the resolution (so more information is displayed), and even turn on a screensaver, which displays moving pictures on the screen. The *Guided Tour* shows just how easy it is to customize your desktop.

Guided Tour Change the Background Color and Design

1 To change any of the display properties, right-click a blank area of the Windows desktop and click **Properties**. (Another way to change display properties is to click the **Start** button, point to **Settings**, click **Control Panel**, and then double-click the **Display** icon.)

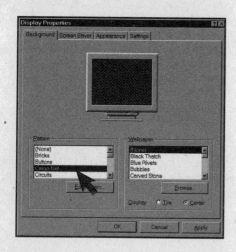

2 The Background tab appears up front. From the **Pattern** list, click the desired background pattern. A pattern gives some texture to the background, such as bricks or pillars.

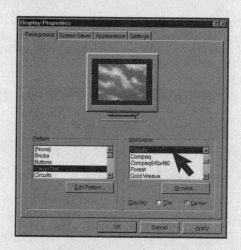

3 From the **Wallpaper** list, click the desired wallpaper design. Wallpaper is any graphic that lays on top of the desktop. Windows comes with several wallpaper designs from which you can select. As you can see, wallpaper covers a pattern, so you don't need to select both.

You can create your own wallpaper by using the Paint program that comes with Windows (**Start, Programs, Accessories, Paint**). After creating your picture, open the **File** menu and select one of the **Set As Wallpaper** options.

Guided Tour Change the Background Color and Design

4 Select **Tile** to have the wallpaper design fill the screen, or select **Center** to have one section of the design placed in the middle of the screen.

5 The preview area shows how the screen will look with the new settings. Click **Apply** if you want to see how the desktop looks and think you might want to pick another design (repeat steps 2–4). To finish, click **OK** to save your changes.

Guided Tour Turn on a Screen Saver

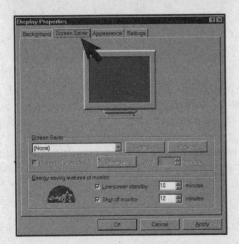

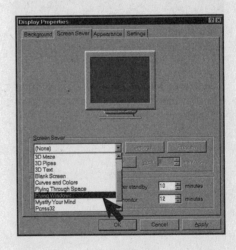

1 A screen saver displays moving pictures that can prevent a stagnant image from burning into your screen. To turn on a Windows screen saver, right-click a blank area of the Windows desktop and click **Properties**. Click the **Screen Saver** tab to display its options. If you have a monitor that offers power-saving features, such as reduced power use, you can enter the power saving settings here.

2 Windows comes with several basic screen savers. Open the **Screen Saver** drop-down list and click the desired screen saver.

(continues)

Guided Tour Turn on a Screen Saver   *(continued)*
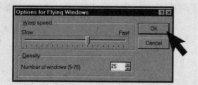

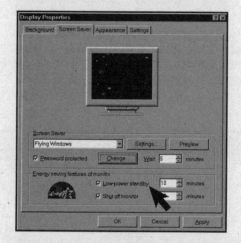

3 To change the settings for the selected screen saver, click the **Settings** button, enter your preferences, and click **OK**. (Preferences vary depending on the screen saver; for example, if you turn on Flying Windows, you can specify the number of flying windows and the speed at which they fly.)

5 To use the screen saver to protect your computer from unauthorized use, click the **Password Protected** option. Then click the **Change** button, type your password in the **New Password** and **Confirm New Password** text boxes, and click **OK**. (Whatever you type appears as asterisks so nobody can read the password over your shoulder as you type it.)

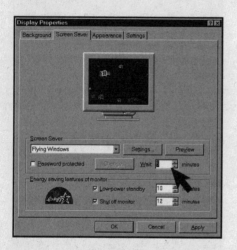

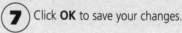

4 Click the arrows next to the **Wait ____ Minutes** spin box to specify how long your computer should be inactive before the screen saver kicks in.

6 If you have an energy smart monitor, you can pick one of the following options to have Windows power down the monitor during periods of inactivity: **Low-Power Standby** triggers the monitor's power-saving feature. The monitor remains on. Use the **Minutes** spin box to specify how long the computer must remain inactive before the power saver kicks in. **Shut Off Monitor** turns the monitor off after the number of minutes you specify in the **Minutes** spin box.

7 Click **OK** to save your changes.

Guided Tour   Change the Appearance of Windows

1 You can change the color of title bars, the thickness of window borders, and the size of text. Right-click a blank area of the Windows desktop and click **Properties**. To change the look of your windows, click the **Appearance** tab.

3 You can also change the look of individual objects. Click the object in the preview area. The **Item** drop-down list shows the name of the selected item, allowing you to change its look.

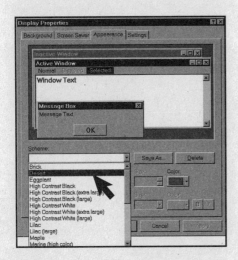

2 Windows comes with several predesigned color schemes. To use one of these schemes, open the **Scheme** drop-down list and click the desired color scheme.

4 To change the size of the selected item, click the arrows to the right of the **Size** spin box.

(continues)

Guided Tour Change the Appearance of Windows *(continued)*

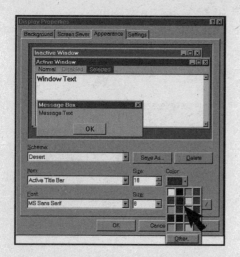

(7) To save your settings as a new color scheme, click the **Save As** button, type a name for the new color scheme, and click **OK**.

(8) Click **Apply** if you want to see how Windows looks and think you might want to make more changes (repeat steps 2–7). To put your changes into effect, click **OK**.

(5) To change the color of the selected item, open the **Color** drop-down list and click the desired color.

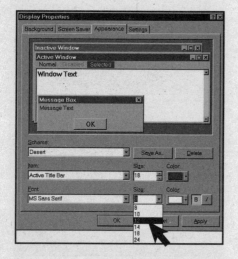

(6) If the selected item has text in it (as in a title bar or menu), you can use the **Font**, **Size**, and **Color** drop-down lists to control the appearance of the text.

Guided Tour   Change the Display Resolution

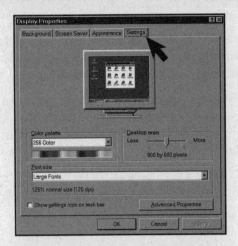

1 Display resolution controls the quality of the display. Right-click a blank area of the Windows desktop and click **Properties**. Click the **Settings** tab to view the current resolution settings. You can set the number of colors used in the display and the amount of information displayed on the desktop.

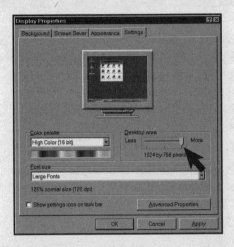

3 Drag the slider under **Desktop Area** to the right to increase the screen resolution, or drag it to the left to decrease resolution. Higher resolutions (for example, 1024-by-768) display more information on the screen but display smaller objects than do lower resolutions (such as 640-by-480).

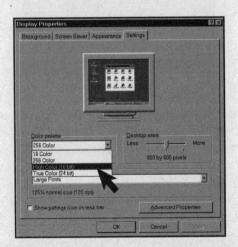

2 Open the **Color Palette** drop-down list and select the number of colors you want your monitor to display. For routine work in your applications, 256 colors will do. To play video clips and view pictures, pick **High Color** or **True Color**, if available. (When you pick more colors, more memory is required to display those colors.)

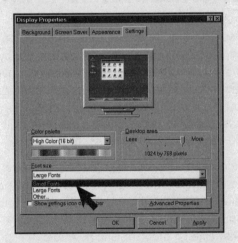

4 If you picked a higher resolution, you can use the **Font Size** drop-down list to select a large or small font for the display. (You might want to pick a larger font size so you can read the type.) Or, click the **Other** choice in the Font Size drop-down list, specify a **Scale** percentage for the fonts, and click **OK**.

5 Click **OK** to save your settings. Windows might tell you that you have to restart Windows to put your changes into effect. Click **Yes** to restart.

Control Your Printer

Unless you've made a complete transition to paper-less publishing, chances are that you have some sort of printer connected to your computer. If you already set it up to work in Windows 95 and the printer is working flawlessly, you can safely skip this task and move on to more interesting material.

However, if you haven't set up your printer yet, or if the printer is printing strange symbols, or if you simply can't get the printer to start (or stop) printing, this *Guided Tour* can help.

The first part of the *Guided Tour* leads you through the process of setting up your printer for the first time in Windows 95. If you just connected a new printer or if you picked the wrong printer during the Windows installation, this section will help you get started.

How Windows 95 Prints

Windows allows you to print documents (from Windows programs) in the background while you are working in other programs. Windows does this by print-ing the documents to a temporary file on your hard disk and then *spooling* the documents to your printer. When you print a document from a Windows program, Windows stores the document in a queue (a waiting line) and then feeds the document to the printer.

The second part of the *Guided Tour* explains how to manage the documents that Windows is in the process of printing. You'll learn how to start and stop your printer (in the event of a mishap), how to resume after you've corrected a problem, and how to cancel printing altogether.

Change Print Quality and Other Settings

Most printers are set up to print on 8.5-by-11-inch paper in portrait orientation (length-wise, as opposed to sideways), using a certain print quality for text and graphics. Windows gives you a great deal of control over these settings—even more control than you can take by pressing the buttons on your printer. To change the print settings in Windows, take the following steps (you may have different settings available, depending on what type of printer you use):

1. Double-click **My Computer**, and double-click the **Printers** icon. Or, click the **Start** button, point to **Settings**, and then click **Printers**.

2. Right-click the icon for the printer whose settings you want to change and click **Properties**. The Properties dialog box for the selected printer appears. Each tab lets you control a different aspect of printing.

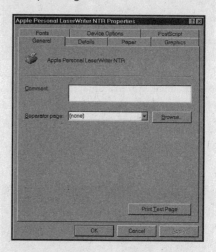

3. Click the **General** tab if it doesn't appear at the front. If you share this printer with other users, you can type a note in the **Comment** text box to let other users know of printer settings or prob-lems. To insert a page between documents (so you know where a document begins and ends), select an option from the **Separator Page** drop-down list.

4. Click the **Details** tab, and then choose any of the options described here:

   If you installed a printer and it doesn't respond, try selecting a different port from the **Print to the Following Port** drop-down list. (LPT1 is the most common port setting.)

   You can choose a different printer driver for this printer from the **Print Using the Following Driver** drop-down list, but you're better off installing the new driver. ▶**For more on installing hardware and drivers, see "Install New Hardware" on page 365.**◀

The **Capture Printer Port** and **End Capture** buttons allow you to map the printer port to a network drive (if your computer is on a network) and to disconnect the printer from the network drive.

The **Timeout Settings** specify how long Windows should wait before reporting a printer error (for example, if you forgot to turn on the printer or it ran out of paper). If you have trouble printing large documents, you might want to increase the time in the **Transmission Retry** text box to 90.

The **Spool Settings** button opens a dialog box that allows you to turn on print spooling (for faster printing) or to print directly to the printer. You should usually use print spooling unless you have trouble with a particular print job.

The **Port Settings** button lets you turn print spooling for DOS programs on or off.

5. Click the **Paper** tab, and do any of the following:

   In the **Paper Size** list, click the desired paper or envelope size on which you want to print.

   Under **Orientation**, select **Portrait** to print text across the page as in a personal or business letter, or click **Landscape** to print text sideways on a page (so the page is wider than it is tall).

   Open the **Paper Source** drop-down list, and click the type of paper feed you intend to use. For example, if you have a printer with two or more paper trays, you can select a specific tray.

6. Click the **Graphics** tab to change the following options for printing pictures:

   From the **Resolution** drop-down list, select the desired print quality for pictures. Print

quality is measured in dots per inch. The more dots, the higher the quality, but it takes longer to print. This does not affect text quality unless you choose to print text as graphics.

Under **Dithering**, select **None** for black-and-white graphics (no gray shading), **Coarse** if you selected a resolution of 300 dots per inch or more, **Fine** if you selected a resolution of 200 dots per inch or less, or **Line art** if you want clearly defined lines to appear between shaded areas. Error diffusion makes the picture look fuzzy.

Drag the **Intensity** slider to control the lightness or darkness of graphic images.

7. If you purchased a font cartridge for your printer, you can click the **Fonts** tab to install the cartridge.

8. Click the **Device Options** tab to change the following options:

   Print quality lets you specify the print quality for text. If you select a high quality, the print will look nice, but the printer will use more ink and take more time to print a document.

   Available printer memory lets you select the amount of memory installed in the printer. Some printers let you plug in a cartridge or add memory chips to increase the amount of information the printer can process. Don't change this setting unless you've added memory to your printer.

9. Click OK to save your changes.

If you have a question about any option in the dialog box, right-click the option's name, and then click **What's This?**.

Guided Tour   Set Up a Printer for Windows

1 In addition to providing access to your disk drives, My Computer lets you manage your printers. Double-click the **My Computer** icon.

2 Double-click the **Printers** icon.

In place of steps 1 and 2, you can click the **Start** button, point to **Settings**, and click **Printers**.

3 The Printers window appears, showing icons for all the printers installed on your computer. Double-click the **Add Printer** button.

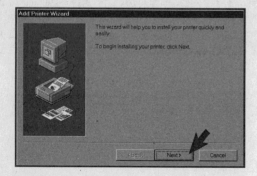

4 The Add Printer Wizard appears, which will lead you through the process of installing a printer driver. Click the **Next** button.

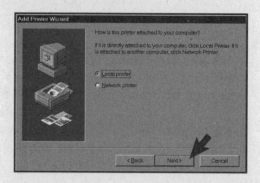

5 The wizard asks if you want to install a local printer (connected directly to your system) or a network printer (which will be available to other computers on the network). Make sure **Local Printer** is selected, and then click the **Next** button.

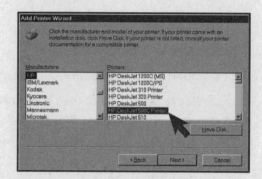

6 The wizard now asks you to specify the manufacturer and model of your printer. Click the brand name of the printer in the **Manufacturers** list, and then click the make and model of your printer in the **Printers** list. Click the **Next** button.

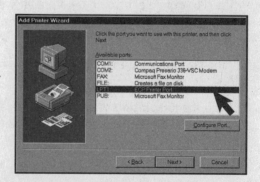

7 A list of printer ports appears. Most printers connect to the parallel printer port (LPT1). If in doubt, pick **LPT1**. Click the **Next** button.

Guided Tour   Set Up a Printer for Windows

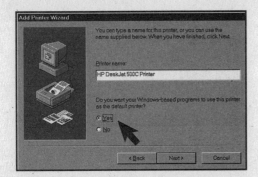

10 If prompted to insert a disk, insert the disk and click **OK**.

To pick a different printer as the default, right-click its icon and click **Set As Default**.

8 The wizard asks if you want to use this printer as the default printer for your Windows programs. To have this printer act as your full-time printer for all your Windows programs, click **Yes** and click the **Next** button. If you select **No**, you'll have to select this printer in your program's printer setup each time you want to use it.

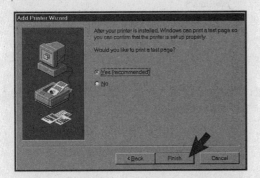

9 Click the **Finish** button. If the files for the selected printer are on your hard disk, the wizard installs the printer and adds an icon for it in the Printers window. If the files are not available, the wizard prompts you to insert a Windows disk or the manufacturer's disk.

Guided Tour Pause, Resume, and Cancel Printing

1 When you start printing, a printer icon appears next to the time in the taskbar. Double-click the printer icon to view a list of documents in the print queue.

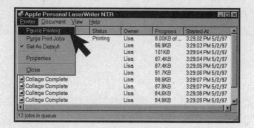

2 The print queue window appears, showing the status of the documents in the print queue. You can stop all printing by opening the **Printer** menu and clicking **Pause Printing**.

3 To pause the printing of a single document select the document, open the **Document** menu, and click **Pause Printing**. (Your printer may continue printing one or two pages, because Windows cannot control what is stored in your printer's memory.)

4 To continue printing, open the **Printer** or **Document** menu and click **Pause Printing** again to remove the check mark.

5 You can cancel all print jobs (and stop printing) by opening the **Printer** menu and selecting **Purge Print Jobs**. This removes all documents from the print queue.

6 To remove one or more particular documents from the print queue, click the first document, press and hold **Ctrl**, and click additional documents. Then open the **Document** menu and select **Cancel Printing**.

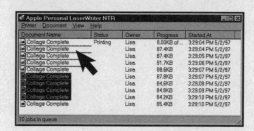

7 You can rearrange documents in the print queue by dragging the document names up or down in the list.

You can create a shortcut icon for your printer on the desktop by dragging your printer icon onto the desktop. To print a file, simply drag it from My Computer or Windows Explorer over the printer icon and release the mouse button.

Take Control of Your Keyboard and Mouse

Chances are that your keyboard and mouse behave pretty much as you want them to. The mouse pointer looks okay, it travels across the screen at a good clip, and (if you're right-handed) you don't have trouble left- and right-clicking. Likewise with the keyboard: If you hold down a key, it starts to repeat, and it repeats at a rate that is comfortable.

However, Windows does let you control the behavior of the keyboard and mouse. You can change the look of the mouse pointer, change the speed at which it travels across the screen, and even switch the functions of the left and right mouse buttons for all you lefties. You can also change the length of time you have to hold down a key before it starts to repeat, as well as the speed at which the key repeats. The *Guided Tour* leads you through changing these configuration options.

Guided Tour Change Your Mouse Settings

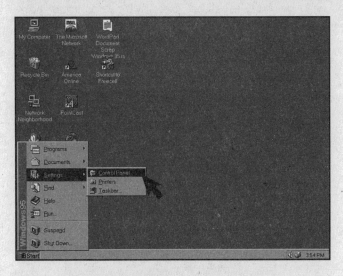

1 You change your mouse settings by using an icon in the Control Panel. To display the Control Panel, click the **Start** button, point to **Settings**, and click **Control Panel**.

2 Double-click the **Mouse** icon.

(continues)

Guided Tour Change Your Mouse Settings *(continued)*

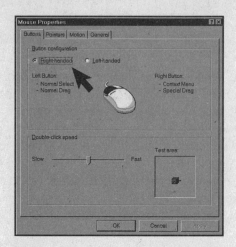

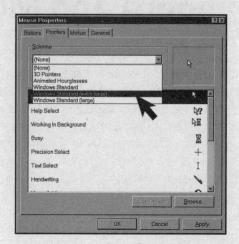

3 The Buttons tab appears in front. Under **Button Configuration**, click **Right-Handed** or **Left-Handed**. Left-handed swaps the functions of the left and right mouse buttons so that the left button brings up shortcut menus and the right button selects items.

5 Click the **Pointers** tab. Then open the **Scheme** drop-down list and click the desired mouse pointer scheme. The list of mouse pointers change to display the various mouse pointers in this scheme. (You can change the look of an individual pointer by clicking it, clicking the **Browse** button, and selecting a different pointer.)

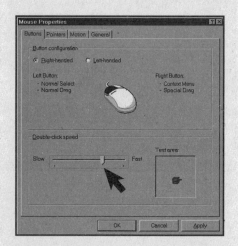

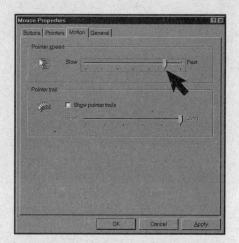

4 To change the speed at which you must click twice for Windows to acknowledge a double-click, drag the **Double-Click Speed** slider to the left or right. (You can double-click the jack-in-the box animation to test the speed.)

6 Click the **Motion** tab to set the speed at which the mouse pointer travels across the screen. Drag the **Pointer Speed** slider to the left or right to change the speed of the pointer.

Guided Tour Change Your Mouse Settings

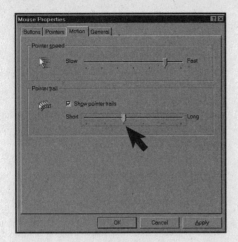

7 To have the mouse leave a trail as it travels across the screen, click **Show Pointer Trails**, and then use the slider to set the length of the pointer tail. (Roll your mouse around to test the effects of your change.)

8 Click the **OK** button to save your new mouse settings.

The General tab lets you pick a different mouse driver (the program that tells Windows how to control the mouse). If your mouse is working okay, avoid this option. If your mouse seems to freeze your computer, try selecting a different mouse driver.

Guided Tour Change Your Keyboard Settings

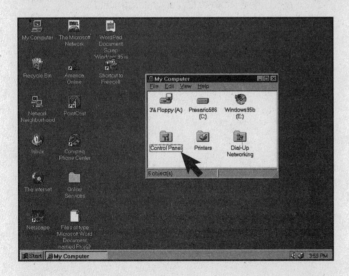

2 Double-click the **Keyboard** icon.

1 You change your keyboard settings by using an icon in the Control Panel. To try another way to display the Control Panel, double-click **My Computer**, and then double-click the **Control Panel** icon.

Guided Tour   Change Your Keyboard Settings   *(continued)*

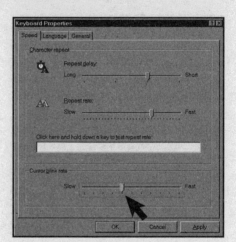

(**3**) To change how long you have to hold down a key before it starts repeating, drag the **Repeat Delay** slider to the left (so you have to hold down the key longer) or to the right (so the character will start repeating more quickly).

(**5**) To change the speed at which the insertion point blinks, drag the **Cursor Blink Rate** slider to the left or right.

(**6**) Click the **OK** button. Your changes are saved, and your keyboard will start acting as you instructed.

(**4**) To change how fast the character repeats when it starts repeating, drag the **Repeat Rate** slider to the left (to repeat slowly) or to the right (for a quicker pace).

Work with Sounds

Most computers now come with sound cards, and the first time you power up your system, you may find the sound blaringly loud. Before you go deaf or blow your brand-spanking-new speakers, you may need to turn down the volume.

In addition, your computer's manufacturer may or may not have set up your system with a particular *sound scheme*. Just as a color scheme applies specific colors and other settings to the different parts of a window, a sound scheme assigns a particular sound to an action you perform in Windows. Each time you repeat that action, Windows repeats the sound.

The *Guided Tour* shows you how to tackle both of these easy jobs.

> Windows comes with several sound schemes, but they may not all be installed on your system. Consult Windows Help to learn how to add sound schemes.

Guided Tour Adjust the Volume

1. Click the speaker icon at the far right end of the taskbar.

2. A volume slider appears. Drag the slider to decrease or increase the volume. Or, to turn off sound altogether, click to check the **Mute** check box.

3. Click outside the slider to close it and accept your changes.

> If you don't see the speaker volume icon on the taskbar, click the **Start** button, point to **Settings**, and click **Control Panel**. Double-click the **Multimedia** icon, click the **Audio** tab to display it (if necessary), and then click to check the **Show Volume Control on the Taskbar** check box. Click **OK**.

Guided Tour   Choose a Sound Scheme

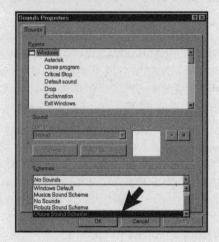

1 To display the Control Panel, click the **Start** button, point to **Settings**, and click **Control Panel.**

3 Open the **Schemes** drop-down list and choose a sound scheme.

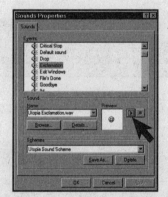

2 Double-click the **Sounds** icon.

4 To test a particular sound in the scheme, click one of the choices with a speaker beside it in the **Events** list, and then click the button with the right-pointing arrow just to the right of the Preview box (in the Sound area of the dialog box).

5 Click **OK** to finish choosing the new scheme.

Use a Few Taskbar Tricks

Notice that the right end of the taskbar displays the current time and a small icon of a speaker (if you have a sound card). When you see an icon or item in this area of the taskbar, take one of the following steps to control it:

- Point to the time display to view the current date.

- Double-click the time to view a dialog box that lets you set the time and date on your computer.

- Click the speaker icon for a simple volume slider, or double-click the icon to change the volume and balance for individual items like your sound card, microphone, and CD-ROM drive.

- If you see a printer icon, you are currently printing one or more documents. To see which documents are printing, double-click the printer icon. ▶**For more details, see "Control Your Printer" on page 168.**◀

In addition, you do have some control over the look and feel of the taskbar itself. The *Guided Tour* that follows walks you through setting your taskbar options.

Guided Tour   Adjust the Taskbar

1 You can move the taskbar to a different place on the desktop. Point to a blank space on the taskbar (not to a program name or the time), hold down the left mouse button, and drag the taskbar to the left, top, right, or bottom of the desktop.

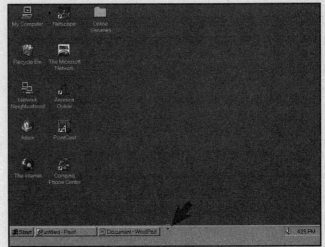

2 You can resize the taskbar to give more room to the program names. Drag an edge of the taskbar up or down to make it fatter or skinnier.

(continues)

Guided Tour   Adjust the Taskbar   *(continued)*

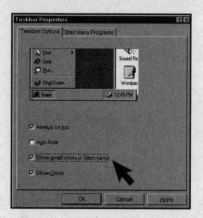

3 You can change other properties of the taskbar, to hide the time or keep the taskbar on top, for example. Right-click a blank area of the taskbar and click **Properties**.

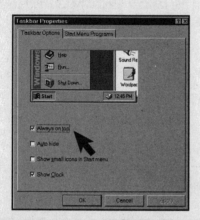

5 Enter your preferences and click **OK**.

4 You can now change the way the taskbar is displayed. **Always on Top** keeps the taskbar in the front of all windows. **Auto Hide** shrinks the taskbar so you have to move the mouse pointer to the bottom of the screen to bring it into view. **Show Small Icons in Start Menu** controls the size of icons on the Start menu. **Show Clock** turns the time display on or off. (A check mark indicates an option is turned on.)

HOW TO...

Work in Windows 3.11

Despite the wide acceptance of Windows 95, you still may encounter computer systems using Windows 3.11 from time to time. For example, for some time after Windows 95 was introduced, many new notebook computers still came with Windows 3.11, either alone or along with Windows 95. The laptop you may bring home from your company may have Windows 3.11. Or you might even buy a used computer for the kids that has the older version of Windows. When you find Windows 3.11 on a computer, turn here to learn the basics. This section explains how to start and exit Windows 3.11, navigate in Windows 3.11 programs, and work with files in the File Manager.

There are a few different flavors of the older Windows in existence. Windows 3.1 was the original, plain-vanilla version. The slightly improved 3.11 version came later. And Microsoft designed Windows for Workgroups 3.11 for systems connected to a network, although it worked just fine on standalone systems. The screens shown in this section are from Windows for Workgroups 3.11. Your screens may look a little different, but the steps for each task will be the same.

What You Will Find in This Section

Start and Exit Windows 3.11

Windows 3.11 loads automatically when you start up some systems. In other cases, you'll need to launch Windows 3.11 on your own. If you do have to start Windows manually, you do so by typing a command at the DOS prompt, which will appear when you start up the system. When Windows starts, the Windows Program Manager appears on your screen.

Windows can run in two different modes (*Standard* and *386 Enhanced*), depending on how capable your hardware is. Normally, Windows chooses the appropriate startup mode. If you get a lot of error messages, or have problems getting certain pieces of hardware (such as a sound card) to work correctly in 386 Enhanced mode, you can choose a different mode when you type in the Windows startup command. You simply add a *switch* (extra characters that modify a DOS command). The **/s** switch specifies Standard mode; the **/3** switch specifies 386 Enhanced mode. For example, you might type **WIN /s**.

When you finish working with Windows 3.11, you should exit Windows and return to the DOS prompt before turning off your computer. The *Guided Tour* covers how to both start Windows 3.11 and shut down at the end of the day.

> ▶**For more on using switches with DOS commands, see "Enter Commands in DOS" on page 215.**◀

Boot Windows 3.11 If You Also Have Windows 95

If you know that your system has Windows 3.11 installed but Windows 95 loads automatically when you turn on your computer, you may have what's called a *dual-boot* setup. If this is the case, you'll have to take special action when your computer starts so you can access your old version of DOS (any version before Windows 95 DOS), from which you can start Windows 3.11. Windows 3.11 will not start from the Windows 95 DOS prompt.

To access your old version of DOS, press **F8** while your computer is starting up. You'll see the Windows 95 Startup Menu, which presents various options for booting your computer. Press **8** to select 8 Previous Version of MS-DOS (or use the appropriate number if this choice has a different number on your system's Startup Menu). Then press **Enter**. Your computer loads your old DOS version. You can then follow the steps in the *Guided Tour* for starting Windows 3.11.

Check Your Mode

When Windows 3.11 is running, it can tell you what mode it's running in. As a bonus, you'll also see what version of Windows you have, and how much memory's available on your system.

To check your mode, click the **Help** menu at the far right end of the menu bar in Program Manager. Then click **About Program Manager**. Look near the bottom of the About Program Manager dialog box. You'll see the mode Windows is running in. Click the **OK** button in the upper-right corner of the dialog box to close it.

Guided Tour   Start Up Windows 3.11

```
C:\>cd windows
```

1 Type **cd windows** and press **Enter**. If the directory that holds your Windows files is named something other than "windows," type that directory name instead. Skip this step if you let Setup add Windows to your PATH statement when you installed Windows.

```
C:\WINDOWS>win /3
```

2 Type **win** at the **c:\windows>** prompt. If you want to start in a particular mode, press the **Spacebar**, and then add the **/s** or **/3** switch to choose Standard or 386 Enhanced mode, respectively.

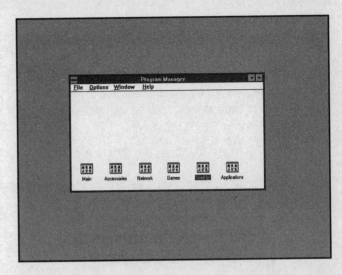

3 Press **Enter** to load Windows. After an introductory screen flashes on-screen, the Windows Program Manager window appears on the *desktop* (the background area on which all open windows sit).

Guided Tour   Exit Windows 3.11 and Shut Down Your Computer

1 Save any open files by opening the application's **File** menu and choosing **Save**. If you need to specify a name for a particular file, do so.

2 Quit (exit) any DOS- or Windows-based programs you're using by opening the **File** menu and choosing **Exit** or **Quit**. Your computer removes the program from your screen.

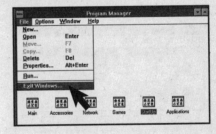

3 To exit Windows, open the Program Manager **File** menu and click **Exit** (or press **Alt+F4**). Select **OK** in the dialog box that appears, and your system displays the DOS prompt. (**▶ For more on Program Manager, see the next task, "Understand Program Manager" on page 184. ◀**)

4 Now you can turn off the power switch on the system unit. Turn off the power switches on the monitor and printer; then turn off the surge suppressor's power switch.

Understand Program Manager

The task called "Operate a Mouse" (▶on page 44◀) explained how to perform basic mouse techniques. You use the same techniques described there to work with the Windows 3.11 Program Manager. The trick is to know which mouse technique to use with which part of the Program Manager screen.

The *Guided Tour* here identifies the different parts of

Program Manager for you and explains how to use each one to perform particular operations. Most of the window parts identified here also appear in windows for most other Windows applications. Once you've mastered moving around in Program Manager, you can survive in most other Windows programs.

Guided Tour   The Program Manager

Program group icons hold programs. Double-click a group icon to open its window and display its programs.

Program-item icons represent application programs. Double-click a program-item icon to open it (start the application in its own window).

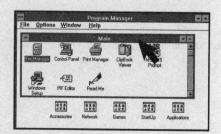

The *title bar* identifies a window. To move a window, point to its title bar and drag.

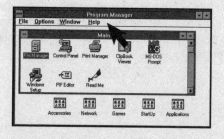

The *menu bar* lists the menus available in Program Manager (or your application program). Click a menu's name to open it and list its commands.

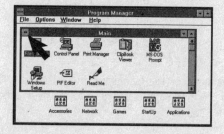

Click the *Control-menu box* to display a list of commands you can perform on a window. Double-click a Control-menu box to close an application.

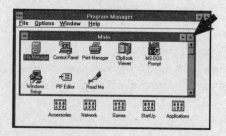

Click the *Maximize* button (when it appears in a window) to enlarge the window to full-screen size.

Guided Tour   The Program Manager

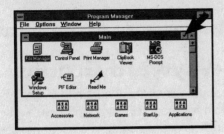

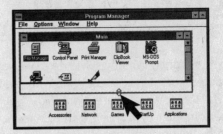

Click the *Minimize* button to shrink a window to an icon. Double-click the icon for the minimized window to open it back up.

Drag a *window border* to resize the window. As you drag, the mouse pointer changes to a double-headed arrow. Release the mouse button when the gray border reaches the new window size you want.

Open and Close a Windows 3.11 Program Group

Microsoft designed Windows 3.11 to make your computer much easier to use than with the DOS interface. The Windows interface is *graphical*; you operate the computer by working with pictures (icons) rather than by typing commands that look like secret code. This interface makes programs and commands easier to get to by grouping them together—in windows and on menus—so you don't have to wind your way through the directory tree to perform an operation.

A *program group* in the Windows Program Manager holds icons that represent all the program files and data files for every application. In the Program Manager window, a *program-group icon* represents each program group. Although the icons for program groups look identical, each one has its own label so you can tell them apart.

Before you start a program in Windows, you must open the program group containing the icons for that program. A *program-group window* appears on-screen; you start your program by double-clicking the program's icon in this window.

Find Wayward Groups

If you reduce the size of the Program Manager window to make room for other windows (and have a lot of Windows applications installed), you might not see the icon for the program group you want to open. In this case, you can use the mouse to scroll the contents of the window so you can see the icon to open, or you can use the Windows menu.

- Click and hold an arrow at one end of the vertical or horizontal scroll bar until the group icon becomes visible.

- Click the **Window** menu in the menu bar, and then click the name of the group you want to open. If you have more groups than the menu can display, click the **More Windows** choice at the bottom of the window. The Select Window dialog box lists other groups; click the one you want.

Guided Tour Open and Close a Windows Program Group

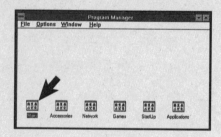

1 The simplest way to open a group is to double-click the group icon.

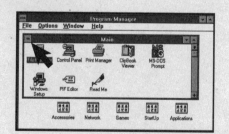

2 To close the group window, double-click the **Control-menu box** (in the upper-left corner of the window).

Start and Exit a Windows 3.11 Program

Program Manager organizes programs in groups. To work with a program or group, you use the icon for that group and individual program. While the group icons look identical (except for the name that appears with each one), the program-item icons are more unique, offering you a quick way to identify visually the program you want to use.

Most often, you'll use your mouse to start Windows programs: You select the program's icon from its program group. The overall process is to double-click the group icon for the group that holds the program, and then double-click to select a program.

If a program doesn't have an icon, don't worry; you can still run it. When you finish working with a program, you need to exit it. You'll learn all these techniques in this task.

Start a Program Without an Icon

You may use certain application programs so infrequently that you haven't set up an icon for them.

Program Manager doesn't have to have a program item icon for a program you want to run; you can run the program from the Program Manager or File Manager with the Run command instead (more on File Manager in the next section). To do so:

1. Click the **File** menu in either Program Manager or File Manager, and then click the **Run** command. The Run dialog box appears, with a blinking insertion point in the Command Line text box.

2. You can type the full path and startup command for the file in the **Command Line** text box, or you can click the **Browse** button and use the Browse dialog box that appears to find the file. **(▶See "Use Windows 3.11 Menus and Dialog Boxes" on page 189 for more information.◀)**

3. Click the **OK** button to close the Run dialog box and run the application program. The application appears on-screen.

Guided Tour Start a Program with an Icon

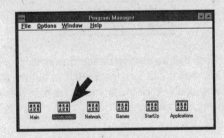

1 Double-click the icon for the program group that holds the program you want to start.

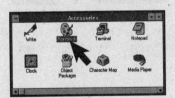

2 When the icon for the program you want to start appears on-screen, double-click it. To start other programs, follow these same steps.

Switch Between Open Programs

Windows 3.11 was a great improvement over DOS in that it enabled you to work more effectively with multiple programs. On systems with enough power (an 80386 or better with more than 4M of RAM), Windows 3.11 could run more than one program at once. Taking advantage of that capability, you can start as many programs as your computer can handle and then switch between them to perform various operations.

When you start one Windows application, Windows is really running two programs: the application *and*

Windows Program Manager. You can switch between these two programs as you work, and you can even open additional applications. There are two ways to make this miracle happen. You can use a keyboard shortcut or the Windows Task List.

Use either method to return to the Program Manager. When the Program Manager is the program you're working with, other programs appear as minimized icons along the bottom of the screen. From the Program Manager, you can start additional Windows applications.

Guided Tour　Switch Programs Using the Keyboard

1 Press and hold the **Alt** key. Press **Tab** repeatedly until the name of the program you want to switch to appears at the top of the screen. Then release both keys, and the program appears.

Guided Tour　Switch Programs Using the Task List

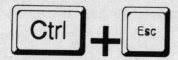

1 Press and hold the **Ctrl** key, and then press the **Esc** key. Release both keys, and the Windows Task List appears.

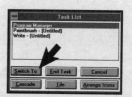

2 To choose the program you want to work in, click its name in the list and click the **Switch To** button. (Another method: Simply double-click the program's name in the list, and the program appears on-screen.)

Use Windows 3.11 Menus and Dialog Boxes

Windows 3.11 established many of the tools for entering commands that still appear in Windows 95, such as the standard menu bars at the top of each window. If you click a command followed by an ellipsis (…), a dialog box appears asking for additional input. And many Windows 3.11 programs contain toolbars of buttons that let you bypass the menus.

Windows 3.11 dialog boxes don't differ much from the dialog boxes you see in Windows 95. You'll see list boxes, check boxes, option buttons, command buttons, and other standard dialog box features. To get help about the features of a particular dialog box, click the **Help** button in the dialog box.

> ▶Two earlier tasks covered working with Windows 95 commands and dialog boxes in greater detail: "Enter Commands in Windows 95" (page [p1s4 TBD]) and "Use a Dialog Box" (page [p1s4 TBD]).◀ Many of the techniques described in those tasks apply in Windows 3.11, too.

Key Commands in Windows 3.11 Programs

Because most Windows 95 programs are based on their Windows 3.11 predecessors, the applications share common features and commands. ▶**Several tasks in the earlier section called "Get Around in Windows 95 Programs" (page 65)◀** describe how to perform key operations in Windows 95 programs. Most of those commands appear in Windows 3.11 applications, too. The File menu in most Windows 3.11 (and Windows 95) applications offers these key commands:

- *New* opens a new blank document on-screen.
- *Open* enables you to choose an existing file to open on-screen.
- *Save* and *Save As* allow you to save and name your files.
- *Exit* closes the program.

Guided Tour Enter a Menu Command from a Pull-Down Menu

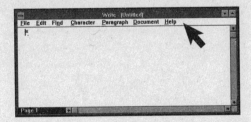

① As in Windows 95, most program windows contain a menu bar, located below the title bar.

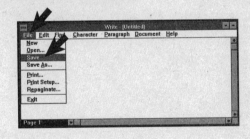

② Click the name of a menu to open it.

③ To enter a command, click the menu option.

Guided Tour   Work in a Dialog Box

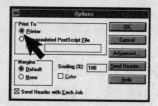

Commands followed by an ellipsis display a dialog box. You click buttons, check boxes, and option buttons to select them.

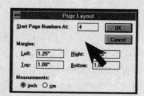

To change a text box entry, double-click the entry and type a new entry. If the text box has spinner buttons beside it, click the **up** and **down arrows** to change the entry.

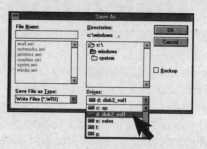

For a drop-down list like the Drives list shown here, click the **drop-down arrow** beside the list, and then click the choice you want in the list.

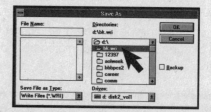

In a list, you generally click your choice. The only difference is for directory lists like the one shown here. To move "down" one level in the tree, double-click the folder icon for the subdirectory you want; it should be indented to the right slightly. To move "up" one level, double-click its folder icon, which should be further to the left in the tree.

Click the **OK** button to accept your choices and close the dialog box.

Get Help in Windows 3.11

Some people can drive through a new city once and remember it perfectly. The next time, they don't even need a map to figure out where they're going. Most of us need a little more repetition to remember how to navigate a new area—or a new program. Even experienced computer users can't remember every feature of every program they use.

As for Windows 95, Windows 3.11 and its applications programs offer help on program features. Usually you can find this help on a Help menu located to the right of all other choices on the menu bar.

Windows Help uses a system of *hypertext links* to get you to the topic you need to read. In this system, you click a highlighted (or different-colored) topic you want to learn more about; this is the link that jumps you to another document that covers the topic. The Help window offers a row of command buttons below the menu bar; simply click these buttons to navigate: Click **Contents** to return to the Contents screen, or click **Back** to go back to the previous Help information, for example.

In many Windows 3.11 programs, you can click a Help icon in the toolbar (or press **F1**) to access the Help system. Some software also gives you *context-sensitive help*, which tells you about what you're doing at that particular time. You press **Shift+F1** and then click part of the screen to get context-sensitive help.

Sometimes the most direct route to the help you need is to perform a search for a *key word*. You can enter a term to search for, or you can choose a search topic from a list. The Help system shows you a list of specific help topics related to the word you searched for. You select the topic.

> Learning to work with the Windows Help system's *hypertext links* prepares you to surf the Net. Browser programs for the Internet's World Wide Web sites use a similar system of linked topics.

Guided Tour Use the Help Menu

1 From the Windows Program Manager or File Manager (or any other Windows application, for that matter), click the **Help** menu and select **Contents**.

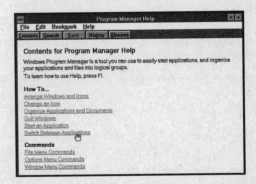

2 Selecting a topic that appears in green with a solid underline takes you to a Help screen with more information about that topic. Move the mouse pointer over the topic you want until you see the hand pointer, and then click.

(continues)

Guided Tour Use the Help Menu *(continued)*

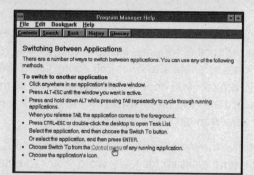

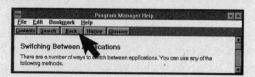

5 To move to the previous Help screen, click the **Back** button in the row of buttons below the menu bar in the Help window.

3 Help displays the related screen with more information. It may offer steps, additional links, or *glossary topics* (which are green and have a dashed underline). To select one of these, move the mouse pointer over it until you see the hand pointer, and then click.

6 To leave Help and close the Help window, click **File** and then **Exit**. (For a quick exit, double-click the Help window's **Control-menu box**.)

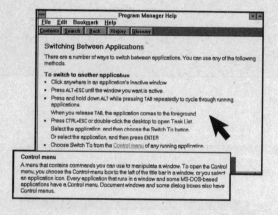

4 To close a glossary topic like the one shown here, click outside it or press **Esc**.

Guided Tour   Search for Help About a Specific Topic

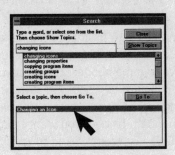

1 From the Program Manager or File Manager window, click the **Help** menu and select **Search for Help on**. (If you've already started Help, you can click the **Search** command button.)

3 One or more topics appear in the list at the bottom of the dialog box. To view a topic, click it and click the **Go To** button (or simply double-click the topic).

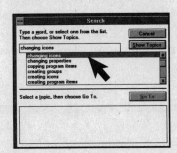

2 In the text box at the top of the dialog box, type the word you want to search for; the most similar topic will be highlighted in the list automatically. Alternatively, scroll down through the list and click a search word. Click the **Show Topics** button to display related topics (or double-click a word from the search list to see its topics).

Start and Exit File Manager

Before Windows 3.11 hit the scene, managing your files through DOS could give you a headache. In DOS, you have to remember exactly what you named a file—and the full path to where you saved it—in order to do anything with it. Even worse, you have to remember another full path name if you want to copy a file somewhere. DOS just wasn't made to save you time and effort.

Luckily, Windows File Manager is. File Manager displays the contents of each drive and directory in windows on-screen. You see not only file names, but also the

icons for files; you can handle some operations simply by dragging files around or by double-clicking a file name. File Manager makes it much easier to work with the files on your hard disk and floppy disks.

As with other applications, you can maximize the File Manager window to full-screen size, resize it and move it around, or minimize it to an icon to put it away temporarily. When you finish working with File Manager, you should exit it to free up RAM (Random-Access Memory) for the other applications you're working in.

Guided Tour   Start File Manager

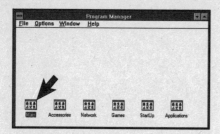

1 Double-click the **Main** program group icon to open its window.

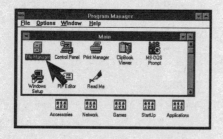

2 Double-click the **File Manager** icon to start File Manager.

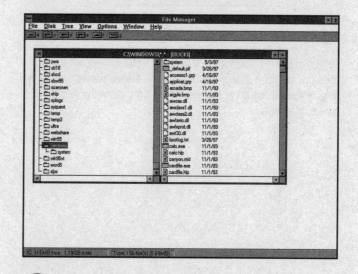

3 File Manager opens in its own window on-screen. You can work in File Manager and resize or move its window as you see fit.

Guided Tour   Exit File Manager

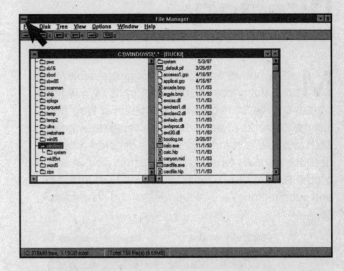

1 To exit File Manager, open the **File** menu and click **Exit**.

2 For a quick exit, you can double-click the File Manager's **Control-menu box** to close File Manager.

View the Contents of a Disk or Directory

Most Windows application programs enable you to open many documents, each in its own window on-screen. File Manager works in a similar way, displaying the contents of each drive in a separate window. Each window is commonly called a *directory window* because it shows what's in the directory you've selected on the current disk. (Under Windows 95, directories and subdirectories are called *folders* and *subfolders*.)

Normally, File Manager divides each directory window into two parts. The left side shows the *directory tree* for the current disk, starting with the root (main) directory. The right side of the window displays the *directory contents list* for the directory you've selected on the directory tree.

Directory windows for versions other than Windows for Workgroups 3.11 include a row of disk icons in each directory window. In Windows for Workgroups, only one row of disk icons appears below the menu bar. When you view the contents of a different disk drive, File Manager changes what's displayed in the current directory window. Once you've displayed the disk you want, select a specific directory to display that directory's contents (files and folders it holds) in the directory contents list.

Directory window   Directory contents list

Directory tree

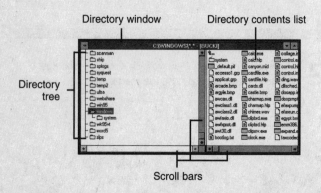

Scroll bars

Guided Tour   View a Disk's Contents with the Menu

1 Open the File Manager's **Disk** menu and choose **Select Drive**. The Select Drive dialog box appears.

2 In the **Drives** list, click the drive holding the disk you want to view.

3 Click **OK** or press **Enter** to close the Select Drive dialog box and display the contents of the drive you selected in the current directory window.

Guided Tour View a Disk's Contents with the Mouse or Keyboard

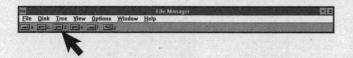

To display another disk in the current directory window, click a different disk icon at the top of the File Manager or directory window.

To do the same thing using the keyboard, press **Tab** or **F6** to move to the disk icons, use the **arrow** keys to move the dotted outline to another disk icon, and then press the **Spacebar**.

To open another directory window for any disk in File Manager, double-click the disk's icon. You can then use the Window menu to move between the open drive windows and display different directories and files in each window.

Guided Tour Select Directories in the Directory Tree

1 Use the scroll bar to display the directory you want in the directory tree.

2 Click a directory to select it. To select with the keyboard, press **Tab** to move the highlight to the directory tree, and then use the **up** and **down arrow** keys to select a directory.

3 To display (or hide) a directory's subdirectories in the tree, double-click the directory name. With the keyboard: Select the directory with the **arrow keys**, and then press **Enter**.

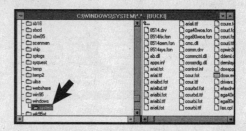

4 To move to the first subdirectory in a directory, click it or press the **right arrow** key.

5 Use the **up** and **down arrow** keys or click to move among the subdirectories.

6 Use the **left arrow** key or click to move up one directory level.

7 To return to the root directory, scroll up to display it, and then click its icon. From the keyboard, simply press \ (backslash).

Guided Tour Select Directories in the Directory Contents List

1 Use the directory list scroll bar to display the directory whose contents you want to view. With the keyboard, press **Tab** to move to the directory list, and then use the **up** or **down arrow** to highlight the directory you want to view.

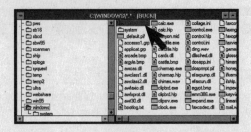

3 To move back up one directory level, double-click the icon with an up arrow and two dots. With the keyboard: Use the **up arrow** to highlight that choice, and then press **Enter**.

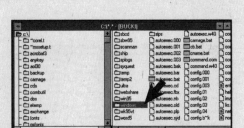

2 Double-click the directory to list its contents. With the keyboard, if you've highlighted the file name, press **Enter** to display its contents. Repeat this step to display a subdirectory's contents.

Select Files and Directories

To copy, delete, rename, or perform another operation on a file or directory in File Manager, you have to select the file or directory. Selecting a file or directory highlights it in the directory contents list.

It's easiest to select files with the mouse. Just display the file or directory you want in the directory contents list and click its icon to highlight it. If you click a directory, all of the subdirectories and files in that directory are selected. If you click a file, only that file is selected.

With the keyboard, press **Tab** to move the highlight to the directory contents list, and then use the **arrow** keys to move the highlight to the file you want. To undo any selection, press **Ctrl+** (or open the **File** menu, choose **Select Files**, and click **Deselect**).

To learn how to select more than one file or directory at a time, see the *Guided Tour* for this task.

There's a shortcut for selecting all the files in the current directory of the directory window. Click in the directory contents list or **Tab** to it, and then press **Ctrl+/** (the forward slash).

Open or Start Files

You highlight a file when you select it in the directory contents list. Then you can move it, copy it, and so on. Opening (starting) a file in File Manager runs a program file or opens a data file. As in Windows 95, opening an executable file with an .EXE, .COM., .PIF, or .BAT extension runs the program that the file is supposed to start. If you open a file called **msworks.exe**, for example, File Manager runs Microsoft Works for Windows. Opening a document file associated with an application starts the application on-screen and then loads the document file. To open a file in the directory contents list of a directory window, simply double-click the file name.

Guided Tour Select Adjacent Files and Directories

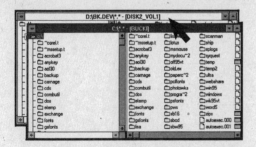

1 Select the directory window holding the files or directories you want to select; doing so makes it the *active* window.

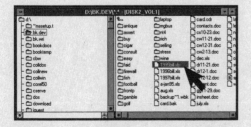

2 Click the first (top) file or directory in the group you want to select.

3 Press and hold **Shift**, and then click the last file or directory in the group you want to select.

Guided Tour Select Nonadjacent Files and Directories

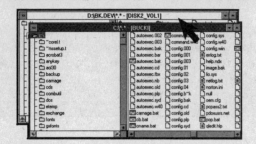

1 Select the directory window holding the files and directories you want to select; doing so makes it the active window.

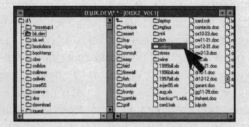

2 Click the first file or directory in the group you want to select.

3 Press and hold.**Ctrl**, and then click the next file or directory you want to select. With the keyboard, press **Shift+F8**, move to the next file or directory, and press the **Spacebar**.

4 **Ctrl+click** to select any additional files or directories (or highlight each one and press the **Spacebar**). If you used the keyboard to select the files, press **Shift+F8** again to finish making the selection.

Copy and Move Files and Directories

Copying a file creates an exact copy of the file's contents and places it in the directory on the disk you specify, leaving the original intact. If you copy a directory, File Manager copies all of the directories contents, including both files or subdirectories.

When you move a selected file or directory, File Manager removes the selection from its original location and places it in the new location you specify. Moving helps keep your hard disk lean and mean—you can place items where you want them without the clutter of multiple copies all over the place.

File Manager offers some easy mouse methods for copying and moving files and directories. It's definitely faster and easier to copy and move items with the mouse in File Manager than to remember exact path names (as you have to in order to move items under DOS).

The steps for both moving and copying differ depending on whether you want to copy or move items to another disk or to a directory on the same disk as the original selection. The *Guided Tour* here leads you through the details.

Guided Tour   Drag to Copy or Move to a Directory on Another Disk

1 Open the directory window for the disk that holds the item(s) you want to copy or move. Select the directory that holds the files and directories so they appear in the directory contents list.

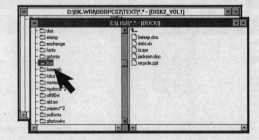

2 Open a directory window for the directory to which you want to copy or move the item(s). Then select that directory.

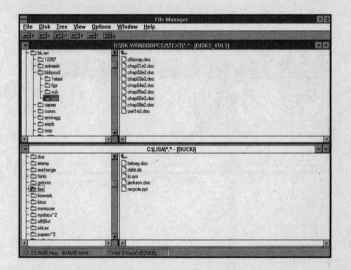

3 Arrange the two windows. You must be able to see the directory contents list of the directory you want to copy or move from, and at least the directory tree of the destination window. A good choice is to open the **Window** menu and select one of the **Tile** choices. Or you can drag the windows by their title bars, and then drag their borders to resize them.

(continues)

Guided Tour   Drag to Copy or Move to a Directory on Another Disk   *(continued)*

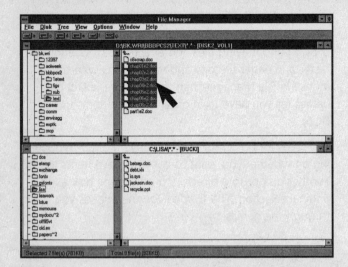

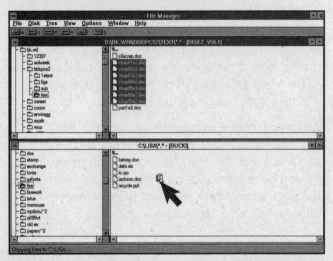

4 In the directory contents list of the first window, select the files and directories you want to copy or move.

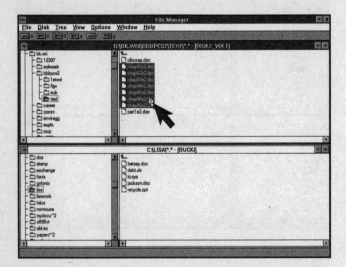

5 Point to the selected items. To copy the selection, press and hold the left mouse button; to move it, press and hold **Shift** and press and hold the left mouse button. Begin dragging. The pointer becomes a stack of papers with a **+** (plus sign) if you're copying, or it becomes just a stack of papers if you're moving.

6 Drag the selection to the window for the directory to which you're copying or moving. (Or you can drag them over that directory's icon in the tree or in the directory contents list.) Release the mouse button.

7 A dialog box appears, asking you to confirm the operation. Click **Yes** or press **Enter**.

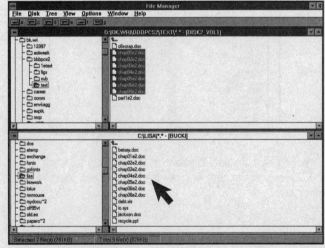

8 When File Manager finishes copying or moving the selection, the file(s) and directories appear in the directory contents list for the directory to which you copied them.

Guided Tour Drag to Copy or Move to a Directory on the Same Disk

1 Open the directory window for the disk that holds the item(s) you want to copy or move.

2 Open the **Tree** menu and select **Expand All Tree** to ensure that the directory to which you want to copy or move will be visible in the directory tree.

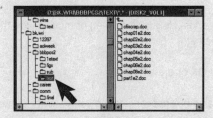

3 Select the directory that holds the item(s) you want to copy or move so those files and directories appear in the directory contents list.

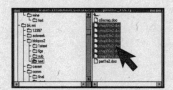

4 In the directory contents list, select the files and directories you want to copy or move.

5 Use the scroll bar beside the directory tree to display the file icon for the directory to which you want to copy or move the selection.

6 Point to the selected item(s). To copy, press and hold **Ctrl** and press and hold the left mouse button. To move, just press and hold the left mouse button. Begin dragging. The pointer becomes a stack of papers with a **+** (plus sign) if you're copying; it becomes just a stack of papers if you're moving.

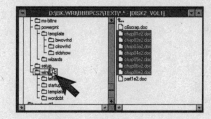

7 In the directory tree, drag the selection to the file icon for the directory to which you're copying or moving. Release the mouse button.

8 A dialog box appears, asking you to confirm the operation. Click **Yes** or press **Enter**.

Guided Tour Copy or Move Using the File Menu

1 Open the directory window for the disk that holds the item(s) you want to copy or move. Select the directory so its contents appear in the directory contents list.

3 To copy, open the **File** menu and click **Copy**, or press **F8**. The Copy dialog box appears. To move, open the **File** menu and click **Move**, or press **F7**.

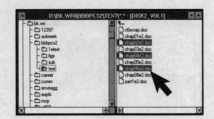

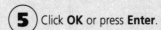

2 In the directory contents list, select the files and directories you want to copy or move.

4 In the **To** text box of the dialog box that appears, type the path for the directory to which you want to copy or move; include a drive letter, a colon, and a final backslash if you're copying or moving to another disk. If you want to specify a new name for a single file you're copying or moving, add the new name to the path.

5 Click **OK** or press **Enter**.

6 A dialog box appears, asking you to confirm the copy or move. Click **Yes** or press **Enter**.

Delete Files and Directories

Deleting an unneeded file or directory helps free up disk space for other purposes. None of us really needs a copy of every To Do we've ever written. By default, File Manager warns you when you're about to delete a file or directory. When you delete a file, File Manager doesn't let you undo the action. So be sure you want to delete a file or directory, and read the deletion message carefully to confirm that you're deleting the right item.

> ➤For a clearer picture of what happens on disk when you delete files or directories, see "Understand How the Computer Stores Files" on page 51.◄

There are a number of safety guidelines to keep in mind when you're deleting files and directories. ➤The task "Delete and Restore Files and Folders" on page 130 earlier in this book◄ covered those rules with regard to Windows 95. The same safety guidelines apply to deleting files and directories under Windows 3.11.

Guided Tour   Delete Files in File Manager

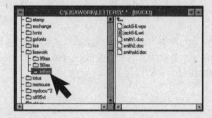

1 Open the directory window for the disk that holds the files you want to delete. Select the directory that holds the files, and then scroll (if necessary) until they appear in the directory contents list.

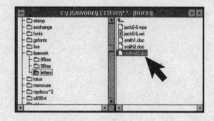

2 Select the file(s) you want to delete in the directory contents list of the directory window.

3 Open the **File** menu and click **Delete**. With the keyboard, press the **Del** key.

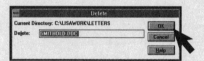

4 The Delete dialog box appears, listing the names of the file(s) you selected for deletion. Click **OK** to continue the deletion.

5 The Confirm File Delete dialog box appears. To delete a single file (or delete only the first file of a group), click **Yes** or press **Enter**. To continue deleting a group of files, click **Yes to All** (if that command button is enabled).

Guided Tour Get Rid of Directories

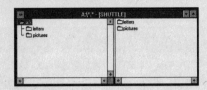

1 Open the directory window for the disk from which you want to delete a directory.

2 In the directory tree, select the (sub)directory you want to delete. Check the directory contents list quickly to make sure that it doesn't contain any files you want to keep intact.

3 Open the **File** menu and click **Delete**, or press the **Delete** key.

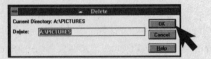

4 In the Delete dialog box, check the **Delete** text box to ensure that it's displaying the correct (sub)directory to delete. Click **OK** or press **Enter**.

5 Click **Yes** to close the Confirm Directory Delete dialog box and continue the deletion.

6 At the Confirm File Delete dialog box, click **Yes to All** to delete all the directory's files. (Use **Yes** if you want to confirm the deletion for each file.)

Rename Files and Directories

Windows 3.11 file names need to conform to DOS 8.3 file naming conventions. That is, a file name can consist of eight characters (no spaces or special characters), a period, and a three-letter extension indicating the file type. (By the way, it's a little-known secret that you can add a period plus an extension of up to three letters to any directory name.)

These limitations do make it difficult to come up with unique, yet descriptive, file names. If you find that you've named several files with similar names and can't recall how to tell them apart, take the time to do some renaming. Use the upcoming *Guided Tour* to learn how.

As a rule, when you rename a file, you should change the base name only and keep the extension intact; doing so makes it easier to open the file in your application (or keep its File Manager association, which is based on the extension). In addition, avoid renaming system or hidden files and the names of directories that hold program files. Doing so could (at best) mess up the way a program works or (at worst) keep it from working at all.

Note that you can rename only one directory or subdirectory at a time (because, coincidentally, you can select only one at a time). You can rename multiple files, but special rules apply.

> When you rename a file at the DOS prompt, DOS lets you move the file to a new drive or directory if you type the path, too. File Manager doesn't let you do this. You can only rename the file, not move it while you're renaming.

Rename a Group of Files Using Wild Cards

If you have several files with similar names and want to rename them all at once, you can do so, provided that the new names are also similar. For example, if you selected files named smith1.doc and smith2.doc, you could simultaneously rename them jacks1.doc and jacks2.doc, but not janes1.doc and jacks2.doc.

As when you perform other file operations, File Manager lets you use wild-card characters to rename groups of files with similar names. The * (asterisk) wild card takes the place of a group of contiguous characters, such as the three-letter file name extension. The **?** (question mark) wild card stands for a single character.

To rename a group of similarly named files in File Manager, start by selecting the files with similar names. Then select the **Rename** command as explained in the *Guided Tour*. Instead of entering a single new file name, you use wild cards to specify the new naming pattern for files. Here are a few examples:

Original Names	Naming Pattern You Type in the "To" Text Box	New Names
1992.xls	*.wks	1992.wks
1993.xls		1993.wks
1994.xls		1994.wks
1982.xls	??9?.*	1992.xls
1983.xls		1993.xls
1984.xls		1994.xls
smith1.doc	jones?.doc	jones1.doc
smith2.doc		jones2.doc

In the last example, you need to use a matching number of replacement characters leading up to the **?** wild card. If you use too few (as in j?.doc), the command won't work. If you try to avoid this by using the j*.doc pattern, the command will work, but the new file names will be jmith1.doc and jmith2.doc. File Manager will overwrite only the first character and keep the rest of the characters from the original file name intact.

Guided Tour   How to Rename

1 Open the directory window for the disk that holds the file or directory you want to rename. If you're renaming a directory, display it in the tree. If you're renaming a file, select the directory that holds the file; the file should appear in the contents list.

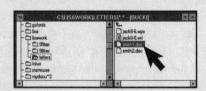

2 Select the file (in the contents list of the directory window) or the directory (in the tree) that you want to rename.

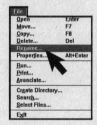

3 Open the **File** menu and click **Rename**.

4 The Rename dialog box appears, listing the name of the file or directory to be renamed. Type a new name in the **To** text box. You can use wild cards if you want. Make sure you type an appropriate file name extension.

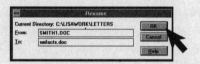

5 Click **OK** or press **Enter** to finish the renaming process.

Create New Directories

An empty directory is like a blank canvas: You name it and fill it with what you want. Directories and subdirectories are the equivalent of file folders on a disk. You use them to organize your documents. For example, you might want to keep all the data files related to home repair, your mortgage, and home maintenance in a directory called \HOME.

The File Manager directory tree uses a file folder icon along with a name to represent each directory. File Manager lets you create a new directory anywhere on the directory tree. You can create a brand new directory off the root directory of a disk (\), or you can create a subdirectory within any existing directory or subdirectory. You can even create directories and subdirectories on floppy disks (although most users aren't aware of this capability).

When you create a new directory, you not only specify where on the disk it should be located, but you also assign it a name of up to eight characters. You can even include a period and an extension of up to three letters in a directory name.

As when you name files, make sure you give your new directories descriptive names. Also, don't hesitate to use subdirectories to create a "deep" directory tree. A common beginner's mistake is to just add directory after directory under the root directory. For example, someone might create three directories named "carpymt," "carins," and "carrep" from the root to track information for a single car. A better strategy would be to create a directory off the root called "car." Then add three subdirectories within that directory called "payments," "insure," and "repairs." This strategy streamlines your root directory and lets you assign descriptive subdirectory names.

Guided Tour   Make Directories

1 Open the directory window for the disk on which you want to create a directory.

2 (Optional) Open the **Tree** menu and select **Expand All**. This ensures that you see all subdirectories, in case you want to create a subdirectory within an existing subdirectory.

3 If necessary, use the scroll bar beside the directory tree to display the directory in which you want to create a subdirectory.

4 Click the directory to select it.

(continues)

Guided Tour Make Directories   *(continued)*

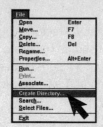

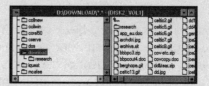

7 File Manager creates the new directory and adds a branch for it to the directory tree in the current directory window.

5 Open the **File** menu and select **Create Directory**.

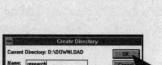

6 In the Create Directory dialog box, type a name for the new (sub)directory in the **Name** text box. Then click **OK**.

HOW TO...
Work with DOS

E ven though DOS has taken a bad rap over time as being "user-unfriendly"—and you may prefer to avoid it like the plague—it pays to know basic DOS survival skills. You never know when you may need them. After all, you may encounter a DOS application program (most likely a game program) that may be so cool you'll even brave the world of DOS to try it out.

This section teaches you the least you need to know about DOS. Here, you'll learn how to enter DOS commands, navigate through directories from the DOS prompt, start DOS programs, and more.

What You Will Find in This Section

Go to the DOS Prompt from Windows 95

If you still have a soft spot in your heart for DOS, or if you just prefer running your DOS programs from the prompt, you can visit the *DOS prompt*. DOS (which rhymes with "gloss" and stands for *Disk Operating System*) is a set of computer instructions that works in the background to help your computer do its job.

The DOS prompt is a symbol (or what techies call a command prompt) on the screen that tells you that you can type a command to run a program or do some work in DOS. In Windows 95, you should be able to avoid the DOS prompt altogether. If you need to run a DOS program, you can use Windows Explorer or My

Computer (▶see **"Manage Disks, Folders, and Files" on page 102◀**) to display the program's icon, and then double-click it. If you don't want to visit the DOS prompt, you can safely skip this *Guided Tour* and the next task.

However, if you must go to the DOS prompt for any reason, the *Guided Tour* shows you how—and how to get back to Windows 95. A plain vanilla DOS prompt looks like **C:\>**. However, when you display the DOS prompt in a window from the Windows 95 desktop, the prompt includes the name of the Windows folder or directory (the *current* folder), as in **C:\WINDOWS>**.

Guided Tour Display the DOS Prompt from the Windows 95 Desktop

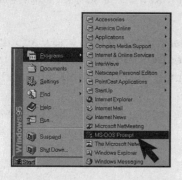

1 You can display the DOS screen in its own window at any time. Click the **Start** button, point to **Programs** to display its submenu, and click **MS-DOS Prompt** (the MS stands for Microsoft).

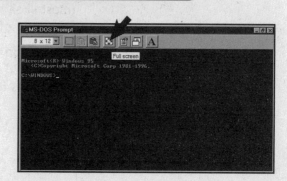

3 You can't resize the DOS window by dragging its borders. To resize it, pick a size from the drop-down list at the left end of the toolbar, or click the **Full Screen** button. (If the toolbar is not displayed, right-click inside the title bar and select **Toolbar**.) When the DOS prompt is in a window, you can switch between applications using the taskbar.

2 You now see the DOS prompt. To make the window bigger, click the **Maximize** button. Enter your commands at the DOS prompt as you normally would (see the later task in this section called "Enter Commands in DOS").

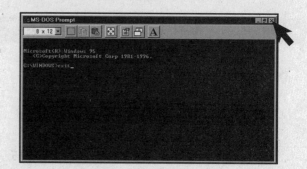

4 You can exit the DOS window at any time by clicking the **Close** button, or by typing **exit** at the DOS prompt and pressing **Enter**. Be sure to exit any DOS programs before you shut the DOS prompt window. If you don't, you may see a warning message telling you to exit the running DOS program.

Go to the DOS Prompt in Windows 3.11

In the heyday of Windows 3.11, it was even more common to have to work at the DOS prompt. Certain functions that are now built into Windows 95, such as certain disk management features, could only be handled at the DOS prompt. Also, DOS-based games were much more common because it was more difficult to create graphics-intensive programs that ran effectively under Windows 3.11.

If you're still using Windows 3.11, you may need to jump to the DOS prompt from time to time without

shutting down Windows or your Windows applications. For example, you may need to access information from a DOS-based database program on the company network and copy that information into a Windows 3.11 document. The following *Guided Tour* explains how to display the DOS prompt from the Windows 3.11 Program Manager. Again, when you display the DOS prompt in a window from the Windows 3.11 Program Manager, the prompt will include the name of the Windows folder or directory (the *current* folder), as in **C:\WINDOWS>**.

Guided Tour Display the DOS Prompt from the Program Manager

1 You can display the DOS prompt at any time. In the Windows 3.11 Program Manager, double-click the **Main** program group icon.

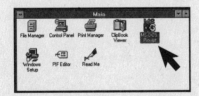

2 In the Main window, double-click the **MS-DOS Prompt** icon. The DOS prompt appears, filling the whole screen to use less memory.

3 Press **Alt+Enter** to display the DOS prompt in a window, as shown above. Use Alt+Tab to switch between the DOS prompt (whether it appears at full-screen size or in a window) and other running Windows applications, including the Program Manager.

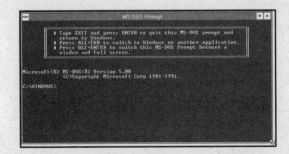

4 Enter commands at the prompt (see the later task in this section called "Enter Commands in DOS"). Under Windows 3.11, you can resize the DOS prompt window. Point to any border or corner of the window until you see a two-headed mouse pointer, and then press and hold the left mouse button while dragging. When the window reaches the new size you want, release the mouse button.

(continues)

Guided Tour Display the DOS Prompt from the Program Manager *(continued)*

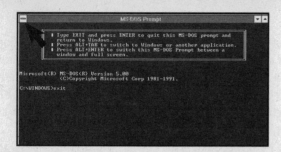

5 You can close the DOS window at any time by double-clicking the **Control-menu** box, or by typing **exit** at the DOS prompt and pressing **Enter**. Be sure to exit any DOS programs before you close the DOS prompt window. If you don't, you may see a warning message telling you to exit the running DOS program.

Enter Commands in DOS

Computers have to be told exactly what to do. They're smart, but they're ultra-obedient, and they lack initiative. For example, when you start your computer, it boots up and then sits there waiting for your instructions. The DOS prompt, which usually looks like **C:\>**, is DOS' way of letting you know it's ready and waiting for your command. DOS runs your computer (even the DOS that's part of Windows 95) and lets you communicate with your computer by giving it specific commands.

> When you display the DOS prompt in a window from the Windows 95 desktop or Windows 3.11 Program Manager, the prompt will include the name of the Windows folder or directory (the *current* folder), as in **C:\WINDOWS>**.

You type a command at the DOS prompt, and then press **Enter** to run the command. This sounds simple enough, but DOS speaks a unique, highly specialized language. The commands you type have to be entered absolutely correctly, and when you use a file name in a command, you generally need to include the full *path* (disk drive letter, folder or directory, and name) for a file. Otherwise, DOS won't understand what you mean and will flash the message **Bad command or file name**.

Decode DOS Command Rules

DOS calls the rules for entering commands its command *syntax*. There are specific parts to a DOS command, and they must be entered in the right order and typed correctly. All the parts of a DOS command you enter make up a *command line*. Here are the parts:

First type **the command** itself. It must be spelled correctly. For example, you use the COPY command to copy files. Some commands, like copy, consist of an entire word. Other commands are abbreviations (*mem*) or acronyms (*md*).

Add **parameters**. *Parameters* tell DOS which file or other object to perform the command on (some commands require them, some don't). To delete a file, for example, you have to type the exact file name, including the folder (directory) path and three-letter file name extension.

Add **delimiters**, if they're needed. *Delimiters* include special characters you add, like the backslash (\), forward slash (/), and colon (:). These "punctuate" the command line for DOS. For example, you need to use the \ and : characters correctly in the path statement for a file, as in **c:\work\file1.txt**. Delimiters usually appear within parameters.

Add **switches** to the end of command lines. *Switches* fine-tune how the command works (some commands let you use switches, others don't). You can add a **/p** switch to a DOS **del** (delete) command, for example, so that DOS will prompt you to verify that you want to delete the file. Available switches vary, and you can use more than one switch at a time. Some switches even can be fine-tuned by adding a colon and a parameter. For example, to display a list of files in a directory and sort the files by their three-letter extension, you would use the **dir** command and add the **:e** parameter to the **/o** switch. The full command with switch and parameter would be **dir /o:e**.

> You can type commands in uppercase or lowercase letters in DOS. The one thing DOS doesn't care about is which case you use.

You don't have to have a photographic memory to use DOS commands and remember all the parameters and switches. You can ask DOS for help with commands, their switches, and their parameters. This is useful if you can't remember an exact command name or what to type with it. There are two different ways to get this help:

- You can get help with a single command (such as finding out what switches you can use with it). At the DOS prompt, type the name of a command, press the **Spacebar**, and then type either **/?** or **/help** (as shown in the accompanying figure).

Press **Enter**, and DOS displays a description of the command and information about the parameters and switches you can or should use with the command.

- At the DOS prompt for a pre-Windows 95 DOS version, type **help** and press **Enter**. This displays a list of available commands, along with a brief description of what each does.

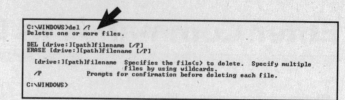

```
C:\WINDOWS>del /?
Deletes one or more files.

DEL [drive:][path]filename [/P]
ERASE [drive:][path]filename [/P]

  [drive:][path]filename  Specifies the file(s) to delete.  Specify multiple
                          files by using wildcards.
  /P                      Prompts for confirmation before deleting each file.

C:\WINDOWS>
```

Be careful when you type your DOS commands, though, because DOS doesn't offer an "undo" feature. The *Guided Tour* that follows shows you how to enter a command (in this case, the one that copies a file from the hard disk to a floppy disk).

> If you need further information about DOS commands, consider buying a book about your version of DOS. Que published a *Using* book about almost every version of DOS that was released. You can find *Using* books at your local bookstore, or you can visit **http://www.mcp.com/que/** and click the **Bookstore** link to see what DOS titles are available.

Guided Tour   Enter DOS Commands

```
C:\WINDOWS>copy
```

1 At the DOS prompt, type **copy** (the command). Then press the **Spacebar**.

```
C:\WINDOWS>copy c:\work\letter.doc
```

2 Type the name of the file you want to copy, including the drive, folder, and full file name with three-letter extension. This is a parameter required for the command, and it includes delimiters. In this case, you would type **c:\work\letter.doc**. Then press the **Spacebar**.

```
C:\WINDOWS>copy c:\work\letter.doc a:
```

3 This particular command requires a second parameter: the drive letter of the disk you want to copy to, followed by the folder you want to copy to (if any). To copy to drive A, for example, type **a:** and press the **Spacebar**. (Make sure you have a formatted floppy disk in the drive you want to copy to.)

```
C:\WINDOWS>copy c:\work\letter.doc a: /v
```

4 After you've entered the command and its parameters, you enter any switches you want to use with the command. In this case, type **/v** so DOS will prompt you to verify the copy operation.

5 Press **Enter** to run the command.

6 If a prompt appears, asking you for additional information before it can run a command (such as verifying the file copy in this case), respond to the prompt to finish the operation.

> To cancel a DOS command that's already running, press and hold the **Ctrl** key, press **C**, and then release both keys. Many DOS commands execute very quickly, though, so you may not have time to cancel them.

Change Which Drive Is Active

To perform work with the files on the disk in a particular drive, you need to *change* to that drive or *log on* to it. (This is also called activating the disk drive.) If you don't log on to the appropriate disk drive before trying to perform a DOS command on a file on that disk, DOS displays a **File not found** error message after you press Enter to execute the command.

These are just a few examples of when you would need to log on to another disk drive:

- You want to copy a file from a floppy disk to your hard disk. In this case, you could start the process by logging on to the floppy drive that contains the disk with the file you want to copy.

- You want to see which files are saved on a floppy disk or stored on a CD-ROM. In this case, you could start the process by logging on to the floppy disk drive or CD-ROM drive that contains the disk or disc whose contents you want to view.

- You've finished working with the files on a floppy disk, and you want to work with files on the hard disk. In this case, you would log back on to the hard disk.

▶**As you learned in the task called "Understand Disks and Drives" on page 52 of this book◀,** most computers have two disk drives. The floppy drive is named *A*, and the hard disk drive is usually named *C*. If your computer has a CD-ROM drive or a second hard disk drive, it will be named *D* or *E*. You can log on to any drive that's connected to your system.

It doesn't matter which folder is current when you log on to another drive. As you learned in the last three tasks, when you go to the DOS prompt from Windows (either 95 or 3.11), the prompt looks like C:\WINDOWS>, because the Windows folder is the current folder.

Do This in Case of Error

When you log on to a disk drive, it must contain a disk, and the disk must be formatted. Logging on to a hard disk drive isn't a problem because the drive always contains a disk and that disk is formatted when you buy your computer. (In fact, you should never try to format your hard disk; doing so will wipe out all the data and programs on the drive.)

You can encounter problems, however, when you try to log on to a floppy drive or CD-ROM drive. Let's say you try to log on to drive A, and you get an error message like this one:

```
Not ready reading drive A
Abort, Retry, Fail?
```

This message usually means that you can't log on because there is no disk in the drive. In this case, you can insert a disk in the drive and press **R** for Retry or **F** for Fail. To quit, you can press **F** for Fail twice, or you can press **A** for Abort as shown in this figure, which gives you a message telling you the drive isn't active. Then type the name of another drive plus a colon, and press **Enter**.

```
C:\WINDOWS>a:

Not ready reading drive A
Abort, Retry, Fail?a

Current drive is no longer valid>c:

C:\WINDOWS>_
```

You'll also get an error message if you put a floppy disk that isn't formatted in the drive and try to log on to it. (You can pay a little more to buy *preformatted* disks at any computer store.) You'll get the same error message if the floppy disk or CD-ROM you've put in the drive is formatted for Macintosh computers (a PC can't read it). Let's say you try to log on to drive A: and get an error message like this:

```
General failure error reading drive A
Abort, Retry, Fail?
```

```
C:\WINDOWS>a:

General failure reading drive A
Abort, Retry, Fail?a

Current drive is no longer valid>c:

C:\WINDOWS>
```

This message means the disk in the drive you're trying to log on to isn't formatted or is in Macintosh format. In this case, you can insert a disk with the correct format in the drive and press **R** for Retry. To quit, you can press **A** for Abort, as shown in this figure, which gives you a message telling you that drive isn't active. Then type the name of another drive plus a colon, and press **Enter**.

▶ To find out how to format a floppy disk with Windows 95, see "Format Disks" on page [p1s6 TBD].◀

When You Don't Need to Log On to a Drive

Suppose you want to work with a file on a disk in some drive other than the one DOS is currently logged on to. You would simply specify the full path name, including the drive letter. For example, let's say you have a floppy disk that you insert in drive A, and the disk holds a file called MEMO.TXT that you want to delete. You can use this shortcut method to delete the file:

- At the DOS prompt, type **del a:\memo.txt** and press **Enter**. DOS removes the file from the disk in drive A. You don't need to log back on to drive C, though, because you never logged off it and logged on to drive A.

You can use this faster technique with other DOS commands like COPY and DIR. Don't worry if this confuses you. As you become comfortable working in DOS, it'll all become second nature. If not, you can work in the Windows 95 Explorer or Windows 3.11 File Manager if that's more comfortable.

Guided Tour   Change Drives

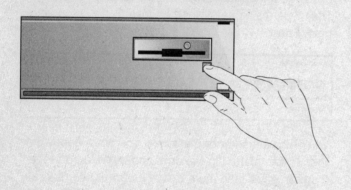

1 If you want to log on to a floppy disk drive or CD-ROM drive, insert a floppy disk or CD-ROM in that drive with the files you want to work with.

```
C:\WINDOWS>a:
```

2 At the DOS prompt, type the drive letter, followed by a colon. For example, to log on to floppy drive A:, type **a:**.

```
C:\WINDOWS>a:
A:\>
```

3 Press **Enter**. The computer logs on to that drive and redisplays the prompt, which now shows the new drive letter, indicating that it has logged on to the new drive.

Change Which Folder (Directory) Is Active

▶**In "Understand Folders (Directories)" on page 62 earlier in this book◀**, you learned that the folder structure of your hard disk resembles a tree. The main folder or root directory (signified by a backslash, \) contains your system's startup files and other folders (directories).

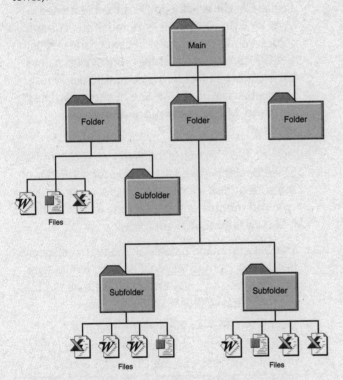

All *folders* (*directories*) branch from the main folder (*root directory*) and hold files or other folders. You can create folders with the names you want, such as an **\ALLWORK** folder to hold work-related files you create. The Install or Setup programs for applications create folders to hold the files for the programs. For example, the directory that holds the Windows program files is called **\WINDOWS**.

Folders (directories) can hold *subfolders* (*subdirectories*), which are also called child folders. These help group specialized files. For example, within the **\ALLWORK** folder you create, you might want to add subfolders to organize various types of work, such as **\ALLWORK\MEMOS**, **\ALLWORK\LETTERS**, and **\ALLWORK\BUDGETS**.

Just as you need to log on to the drive with the disk holding the files you want to work with, you also need to change to the folder where your files are located before you can work with them in DOS.

When you work with files, you usually need to specify the *path* or *path name* of the file. The full path includes the drive letter for the disk holding the file plus a colon, a backslash for the main folder (root directory), any folder and subfolder names (separated by backslashes), the file name, a period, and the extension. For example, C:\ALLWORK\MEMOS\4-14.DOC might be the full path name for a memo file named 4-14.DOC that you've stored in your \ALLWORK\MEMOS subfolder.

Moving Among Folder (Directory) Levels

Let's say you've just jumped to the DOS prompt, and the current folder is C:\WINDOWS (the prompt being C:\WINDOWS>). If you want to change to a folder on your system called C:\ALLWORK, how do you get there?

The main folder (root directory) is the top level. The folders within the root directory are sometimes called *first-level* folders; they're one level "below" the main. (Subfolders are one level "below" the folders that contain them.)

Why do you care? Because you can move up and down through the folder tree, but you can't really move "sideways" from one branch to another. To get to another branch (directory), you'd have to tell DOS to go back up a level, move over, then go down a level.

If you type **cd..** and press **Enter**, DOS moves up one level in the folder tree. (CD was an acronym for Change Directory under older DOS versions.) If you type **cd ** and press **Enter**, DOS returns you all the way to the main folder (root), even if you're starting from a sub-folder two or more levels down the tree.

So there are two ways to move between folders in different branches of the folder tree, as in the example mentioned above:

- Starting from the C:\WINDOWS> prompt, you could type **cd..** and press **Enter** to move back to the main folder. Then you could type **cd allwork** and press **Enter**. You'd change to the \ALLWORK folder, and the prompt would look like this: C:\ALLWORK>.

- Starting from the C:\WINDOWS> prompt, you could type **cd \allwork** and press **Enter**. The \ preceding **allwork** tells DOS to move back to the main folder before trying to change to the ALLWORK folder. The prompt would look like this: C:\ALLWORK>.

Perform Other Folder Tasks

There are just a few other commands for dealing with folders (directories) that you may need to know at some time.

- The DIR command lists the contents of a folder or subfolder. For example, from C:\ALLWORK>:, you could type **dir** and press **Enter** to list all the files in the C:\ALLWORK folder. The DIR command offers numerous switches, so use **dir /?** to see what options DOS offers with this command. For example, **dir /o** lists all the files and subfolders in a folder, sorting them in alphabetical order. To have DOS pause after listing each screen full of files, use **dir /p**. Another switch, **dir /w**, lists the files in a wide multicolumn display. Use a file name with the DIR command to search for a particular file: **dir wacky.doc** lists the file named WACKY.DOC, if that file is stored in the current folder. You also can use wild-card characters with the DIR command to list files with similar names: **dir s*.*** lists all files in the current folder whose names begin with "S." ▶**See "Search for Files" on page 147 to learn more about wild cards.**◀

- Use the MD command (originally an acronym for Make Directory) to create a folder or subfolder on the current disk. From C:\ALLWORK>, you could type **md memos** and press **Enter** to create the C:\ALLWORK\MEMOS subfolder.

- The DEL command deletes all the files in a specified folder. From C:\ALLWORK>, you would type **del memos** and press **Enter** to delete all the files in the C:\ALLWORK\MEMOS subfolder.

- The RD command (originally for Remove Directory) enables you to delete an empty folder or subfolder. First, use the DEL command to delete the folder's files. Then, from C:\ALLWORK, you could type **rd memos** and press **Enter** to remove the empty C:\ALLWORK\MEMOS subfolder.

Guided Tour Change Folders (Directories)

```
C:\WINDOWS>cd..
C:\>
```

1 To move up to the main folder (root directory) from the C:\WINDOWS folder, which is the current folder when you display the DOS prompt from Windows 95 or 3.11, type **cd..**, and then press **Enter**. The prompt for the main folder (root directory), C:\>, appears. (Remember, CD.. always moves up one folder level.)

```
C:\WINDOWS>cd..
C:\>cd
```

2 Type the name of the folder to change to, such as **windows**. (If you pressed **Enter** now, you would change to the C:\WINDOWS folder.)

```
C:\>cd windows
```

3 From the main folder, you usually need to move back down to a folder where your files are located. So, at the C:\> prompt, type **cd**. Then press the **Spacebar**.

```
C:\>cd windows\system
```

4 (Optional) If you're changing to a subfolder as well, type a backslash (\) followed by the name of the subfolder. For example, you could add **\system** to your command line.

```
C:\>cd windows\system
C:\WINDOWS\SYSTEM>
```

5 Press **Enter**, and DOS displays a new prompt indicating the folder (and subfolder) you've changed to. In this case, it's C:\WINDOWS\SYSTEM>.

```
C:\WINDOWS>cd system
C:\WINDOWS\SYSTEM>
```

6 Use a similar process to move from a folder to one of its subfolders. Type **cd**, press the **Spacebar**, and type the name of the subfolder (for example **cd system**). Then press **Enter**.

Start a DOS Program from the DOS Prompt

Earlier tasks in this book explained how to start Windows applications by using the Start button on the taskbar or by double-clicking icons. DOS is more mysterious: Instead of using icons to start DOS applications, you need to know the right startup command and enter it at the DOS prompt.

If you have installed a DOS application on your hard disk, you need to start it to load it into RAM (your computer's random-access memory). You can run some DOS programs directly from a floppy disk or a CD-ROM; you would start them from the disk in a drive.

To start a DOS application, you log on to the drive that contains the program files. Then you type the startup command and press **Enter**. The following table lists some common startup commands for DOS applications (most of which are much older versions than their Windows-based counterparts).

Common DOS Startup Commands

To Run a DOS Version of This Program...	Use This Command...
America Online	aol
Carmen Sandiego	carmen
DBASE	dbase
DOS 4.1 or 5.0 Shell	dosshell
Harvard Graphics	hg
Lotus 1-2-3	123
Microsoft Word	word
Microsoft Works	works
The Norton Utilities	norton
Paradox	paradox
PC Tools	pctools
PFS: First Choice	first
PFS: First Publisher	fp
PRODIGY	prodigy
Q&A	qa
Quattro Pro	qp
Quicken	q
TurboTax	ttax
WordPerfect	wp
WordStar	ws

Find the Startup Command

The startup command for most DOS programs really is the name of a program file called an *executable file*. Executable files contain instructions that your computer can read, such as program instructions. Executable files have the .EXE, .BAT, or .COM file name extensions. Find that executable file in a program's directory, and bingo! You've found your startup file.

The name for the executable file usually resembles the program's name, and so does the name of the folder that holds the program's files. Sometimes these names are abbreviations of the program's name. The following list provides a few examples:

Program Name	Directory Name	Startup File Name
Quicken	\quicken	quicken.exe or q.bat
The Norton Utilities	\nu	norton.exe
QuickLink Fax	\ql	qlmain.exe
Word 5.0	\word5	word.exe
Doom	\doom	doom.exe

When you have identified the folder holding your program files and have changed to that folder, use **dir *.exe** (or ***.bat** or ***.com**) to list files that might be the startup file. Then try running the file with the name that most resembles the program name.

Find the Switches

As with regular DOS commands, the startup commands for some applications offer switches you can use to customize the way the program runs. You find the available switches by typing the startup command followed by a space and **/?**, and then pressing **Enter**. For The Norton Utilities 6.0, for example, typing **norton /?** and pressing **Enter** displays the list of switches shown in this figure.

```
C:\NU>norton /?
Norton Utilities, Norton Utilities 6.0, Copyright 1991 by Symantec Corporation

Run the Norton Utilities (and other programs) from a menu.

NORTON [/BW|/LCD] [/G0|/G1|/G2] [/NOZOOM]

  /BW       Forces the use of the Black and White color set.
  /LCD      For laptop displays.  Forces the use of the LCD color set.
  /G0       Disable font redefinitions and graphic mouse.
  /G1       Disable the graphic mouse (EGA/VGA only).
  /G2       Disable graphic dialogs (EGA/VGA only).
  /NOZOOM   Disables dialog box zooming.

C:\NU>
```

Guided Tour   Start a DOS Program

```
C:\>cd word5
C:\WORD5>
```

1 Log on to the disk drive that has the files for the program you want to run. Change to the folder that holds the files for the program (if you need to). For example, if you have Microsoft Word 5.5 for DOS in a folder called WORD5, you change to the folder holding the program by typing **cd word5** and pressing **Enter**.

```
C:\>cd word5
C:\WORD5>word
```

2 Type the startup command for the application, and then press **Enter**. To start Word for DOS, for example, you would type **word** and press **Enter**.

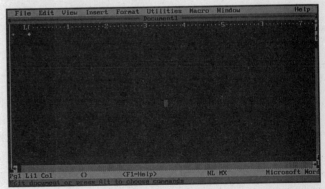

3 The application appears on-screen, usually with a brand new document open (as shown here).

Work with DOS Menus and Dialog Boxes

For the most part, menus and dialog boxes in DOS-based programs work like those for Windows-based programs and even offer many of the same commands (▶see **"Enter Commands in Windows 95" on page 72 and "Use a Dialog Box" on page 76**◀). However, because many DOS programs aren't as well-suited to work with the mouse as are their Windows counterparts or don't let you use a mouse at all, getting around with the keyboard can be as important as navigating with the mouse in DOS applications.

Many DOS applications (like Windows applications) have *menu bars* near the top of the screen that list the names of available pull-down menus. To tell your application what to do, open a pull-down menu and choose a command. Generally, you can press the **Alt** key or the **F10** key, or you can click a menu name to activate the menu bar. Then you can use the arrow keys or mouse clicks to move among menus and commands.

To close a menu without selecting a command from it, press **Esc** or click outside the menu. (If selecting a menu command displays a pop-up menu or submenu, use the same techniques presented in the *Guided Tour* to choose a command from it.)

Other applications, like Quicken, also offer a Main menu that looks like a dialog box with a list of commands, each of which has a selection number or letter beside it. This type of menu lets you jump to different modules of the program (usually these modules offer their own pull-down menus) or exit the program. Click the command you want, or press its selection number/letter.

When you choose a command, you may need to provide further information in order for the application to perform the specific action you want. When it needs more information, the program displays a *dialog box*, a special window that lets you tell the program exactly what to do. The program then carries out all the instructions you gave in the dialog box.

Dialog boxes offer different *controls* for choosing options, which work like those in Windows dialog boxes (as described earlier in the book). To move to a dialog box control with the keyboard, you can either press **Tab** repeatedly, press an **arrow key** repeatedly, or press **Alt** plus the highlighted selection letter in the control's name. In some cases, you then need to press the **Spacebar** to select or deselect a control (to check a check box, for example). You also may need to use an arrow key to scroll down through a list box-type control. After you've finished making all your choices in the dialog box, press **Enter** to close the dialog box and execute the command.

Guided Tour Choose a Command with the Keyboard

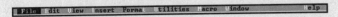

1 Activate the menu bar by pressing **Alt** or **F10**. This usually highlights the far left menu name on the menu bar.

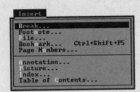

2 To display the pull-down menu of your choice, press the highlighted selection letter in its name (or use the **left** and **right arrow** keys to move the highlight to the name of the menu you want, and then press **Enter**).

3 To choose a command, press the highlighted selection letter in its name (or use the **down arrow** key to move the highlight to the name of the command you want, and then press **Enter**). If the command has a shortcut key combination beside it, you can press that key combination to bypass all of these steps.

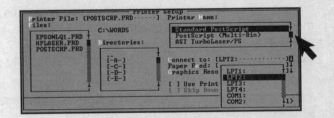

4 If a dialog box appears and you need to move to a control, press **Tab** repeatedly, press an **arrow key** repeatedly, or press **Alt** plus the highlighted selection letter in the control's name. Press the **Spacebar** or an **arrow key** to make a selection from a control, when needed. When you've finished making all your control choices, press **Enter** to close the dialog box and execute the command.

Exit a DOS Program

*E*xiting a DOS application closes any open files in the program and removes them from RAM (random access memory). Then the program itself closes (is removed from RAM), and you're returned to the DOS prompt. You can then generally return to Windows (if you displayed the DOS prompt from Windows) by typing **exit** and pressing **Enter**.

Before you exit from any program, you should save your work. This prevents data loss and gets you out faster. If you haven't saved your work, the program will prompt you to do so. Click **Yes** to save if you've saved the open file before. If you haven't saved the open file, the Save As dialog box will appear; name the file and specify a location for it.

If you're working in a DOS program and need to perform one or two simple DOS operations (like deleting a file or two), you can temporarily "shell out" to DOS instead of exiting the program. To do so, open the application's **File** menu. Look for a command like **Shell to DOS** or **DOS Commands**, and click it. Then perform the DOS operations you want. When you're finished, type **exit** and press **Enter** to return to your DOS application.

Guided Tour   Exit a Program

Open the program's **File** menu and click **Quit** or **Exit**. Or, press the exit shortcut key combination, usually found beside the Exit or Quit command on the File menu. This combination is often **Alt+Q**, **Alt+X**, or **Alt+F4**.

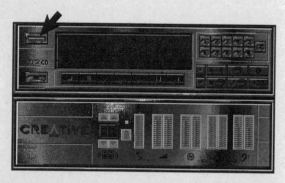

Some DOS applications have a *Close box* or a special icon you can double-click to exit. Close boxes are usually found in the upper-left corner of the application.

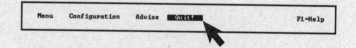

Some programs (like this one) offer a **Quit!** option on the menu bar. Simply click it to exit the program.

Other DOS programs offer a Main menu screen, which generally offers an Exit command. Select it to exit the program.

HOW TO...

Connect with the Outside World

No person is an island. Although you can use your computer in isolation if you prefer, adding a modem to your system enables you to connect with other users. In the last few years, millions of people have jumped online for the first time to search for information and graphics, get up-to-date reports on the news and stocks, buy and sell things, and chat or exchange messages with other users. This section introduces you to the Internet, bulletin board systems (BBSs), and two popular online services: America Online and CompuServe.

The tasks in this section are akin to dipping your toe into water (a *large* body of water). You're not going to learn everything you'll need to know to be proficient online. The Internet, BBSs, and individual online services are such large topics that an entire *Big Basics Book* could be devoted to each alone. What you will find in this section, however, are the basics of getting connected and moving around.

What You Will Find in This Section

Go Online: An Overview

You may have heard a lot of buzz lately about "going online" or "the Information Superhighway." If your computer has a modem (and you have a telephone line you can connect it to), the amazing world of electronic online communication is wide open to you. You can browse the Internet or join an online service or a bulletin board system (BBS) to share files and messages with other users.

Think of each online service, BBS, or Internet site as a "library" of information from various sources. Not every library offers the same selection of books and magazines. For example, while your neighborhood library may offer a lot to you, it may not have the Standard & Poor's stock information you need. You may have to go to another larger library to find that information.

Similarly, each Internet site, online service, or BBS offers a unique set of information. Joining only the service or BBS gives you access to its unique collection of information. Each online service also offers its own unique connection software (this isn't always true of BBSs and the Internet).

How to Join or Log On

New computer systems or modems purchased today generally come with software and offers for joining the major online services. You can join an online service for free for a while (America Online recently offered 50 free hours) to test it out. You also may receive software and instructions for finding an Internet service provider (ISP) so you can sign up for an Internet account. ISPs generally charge a flat monthly fee for Internet access. Often, new computer systems already have online service software and the Windows 95 Internet software installed.

To join an online service, you install the software (if it isn't already installed), and then start the software. When you do so, the software walks you through the process of joining. Have a credit card handy—you need to give that number for billing purposes.

If your modem or PC didn't come with a kit for setting up an Internet account, another option for getting connected is to buy an Internet startup kit from your local computer store. You can install the software and dial in with your modem to set up your account with a particular service provider.

To find an ISP on your own, you can ask a computer store salesperson or your friends who are already wired about Internet providers. You may find local providers in the Yellow Pages under "Computers" or "Internet." Another way is to visit your local bookstore and check out books that offer Internet sign-up kits or Internet magazines (which are littered with ads and offers from companies that want to get you connected). Finally, major long distance companies like MCI (Network MCI) and AT&T (AT&T WorldNet) offer Internet access. These can be convenient, as your Internet account will be billed with your long distance. ▶**You also can let Windows help you find an ISP; see the later task "Get Wired with the Internet Connection Wizard" on page 231.**◀ Make sure you ask for a PPP account. (The ISP will know what you mean.) This kind of account works more smoothly under Windows 95 and is the standard today.

When you get an account with an ISP, be sure to ask for a PPP (Point-to-Point Protocol) connection. Make sure the access phone number you get for dialing in to your account is a local call. If you travel a lot, you'll want a provider that has a toll-free access number, too.

There are several different ways to find BBSs to join. One computer magazine, *BoardWatch*, focuses specifically on BBSs and publishes a list each month of ones you can join. When you're using an online service, you can keep your eye out for descriptions of BBSs, and you can call a service called User Group Locator at 914-876-6678 to find out whether there's a computer user group near you that offers a BBS. The Yellow Pages in some areas even have entries for local BBSs. Look for these under "Computer Bulletin Boards."

When you join a BBS, usually you have to answer a list of questions to register. If there's a fee for joining the BBS (no, they're not all free), you may need to give a credit card number as well. The costs for joining BBSs vary wildly. Some are free. Some charge an annual fee. Some, like the one called ECHO (East Coast Hang Out), charge a monthly fee. Monthly fees generally range from $10 to $20. If possible, try to pay with check instead of a credit card, or check the BBS operator out thoroughly before you give your credit card number.

Guided Tour Things to Do Online

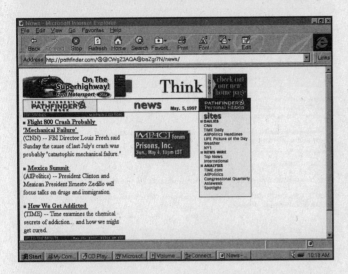

Read news. Most services offer hourly updates about current events, as well as specialized areas for business, weather, sports, and other information. On the Internet, you can subscribe to electronic magazines and various news services.

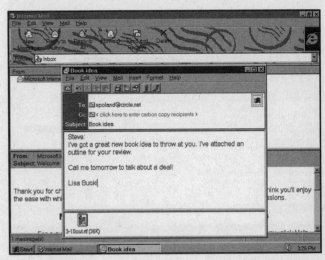

Exchange private electronic mail. Send a private letter to one or more users—without licking a single stamp.

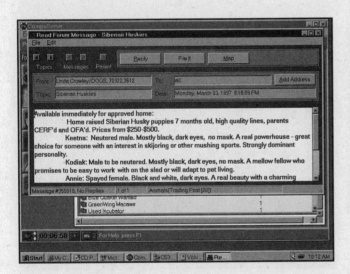

Read and post general messages. You can find these in *forums*, *departments*, or *newsgroups* (Internet) online areas where users go to share information about special topics like having a home business. You can read or post messages.

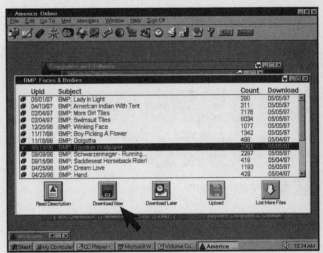

Exchange files. You can *upload* files (send them to another computer) for other users, or *download* files (get them from another computer) that you want. You may swap original documents, shareware or freeware programs, graphic files, sound files, and more in this way.

(continues)

Guided Tour Things to Do Online *(continued)*

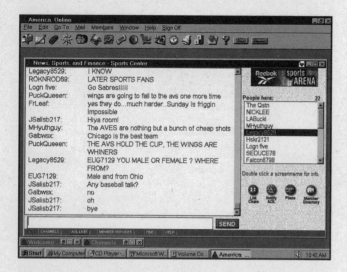

Talk live online with other users. Most services offer live chat areas where users can go to meet others from around the world to talk about a specific topic. On the Internet, you'll increasingly find chat areas, but you may need to install special software to join. When you're chatting, type your message, and it appears instantly for all the other users in the chat area, who can reply immediately.

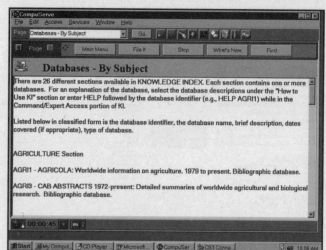

Work smarter, not harder. You can find a variety of databases and reference books online so you can find facts when you need them—whether for a school project, a client proposal, or to settle a bet.

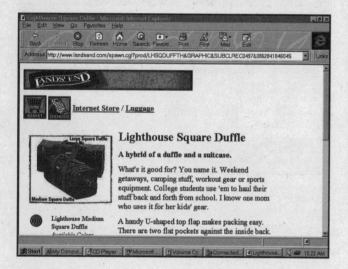

Buy stuff, and more. Visit a variety of online stores and spend, spend, spend. You can also make your travel reservations or purchase other services online.

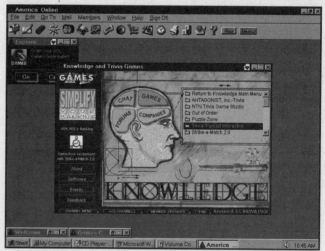

Play a little. Most online services offer game areas where you can play online by yourself or against online opponents, win contests, and download games for your personal use.

Get Wired with the Internet Connection Wizard

You've signed up for an account with an ISP, but you're not sure how to connect to it. One option is to use the setup software that your ISP provided. ISP setup software usually works fine, but it's not bulletproof. And, it doesn't always take advantage of Internet capabilities that are already available in Windows 95.

Windows 95 can help you establish a TCP/IP connection for connecting to the Internet. What you need to know about TCP/IP is that it connects you to your ISP in such a way that you can then run Windows-based graphical software like an e-mail program to work with the Internet by pointing and clicking.

In the initial release of Windows 95, setting up a TCP/IP connection was usually a manual process. Later, Microsoft introduced the Internet Connection Wizard, which walks you through the setup process step by step. The Internet Connection Wizard is installed by default on new systems with the latest Windows 95 OEM Service Release 2 (OSR 2) version, along with other TCP/IP and connection software. The *Guided Tour* in this task shows you how to use the Internet Connection Wizard to establish your connection and how to connect when you need to. (The Internet Connection Wizard also can help you find an ISP if you don't already have one.)

You will need a few pieces of information from your Internet service provider to set up the connection. Before you begin the *Guided Tour*, gather the following information.

- *ISP phone number.* This is the number you dial to connect.

- *User name and password.* Your ISP provides these when you create your account.

- *IP (Internet Protocol) addresses.* These are special numbers used to identify your ISP's servers on the Internet. IP addresses always have four sets of 1–3 numbers each, separated by periods. For example, 207.79.160.1 is an IP address. You need to know whether your ISP automatically (dynamically) assigns an ISP to your system when you log in. You also need to know the IP address for your ISP's Domain Name Service (DNS) server.

- *Login method.* If your ISP offers the PAP or CHAP protocols for logging in (you don't really need to know what these acronyms mean), you can set up your connection so it remembers your user name and password and provides them automatically when you connect.

If you don't have the Internet Connection Wizard on your system or it doesn't appear the first time you double-click the desktop's Internet icon, you'll need to install the latest version of Internet Explorer, version 3.02. You can have a friend download it for you from http://www.microsoft.com/msdownload/ieplat-form/iewin95.htm. Then install it ▶**as described in "Install a Program in Windows 95" (on page 312).**◀

Guided Tour Set Up Your Internet Connection

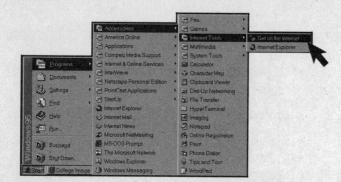

1 Click **Start**, point to **Programs**, and point to **Accessories** On the Accessories menu, point to **Internet Tools**, and click **Get on the Internet** (or **Internet Setup Wizard**). Alternatively, you can double-click the **Internet** icon on the desktop if you haven't previously used the Internet Connection Wizard (if you have, this icon launches Internet Explorer instead).

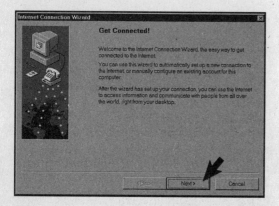

2 The first Internet Connection Wizard (ICW) dialog box appears. Click **Next**. In the next ICW dialog box, select how to set up your computer.

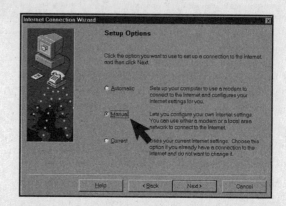

3 If you don't already have an account with an ISP, click **Automatic** and follow the rest of the wizard, which installs connection software and then logs you on to the Internet Referral Service (it gives information about ISPs you can sign up with). If you already have an account, click **Manual**, and then click **Next**. The rest of these steps assume you have an account with an ISP and that you clicked Manual here.

4 In the ICW Welcome dialog box, click **Next**.

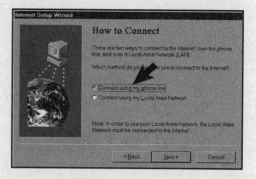

5 Assuming you're a home user and will be connecting to the Internet with a modem, leave **Connect Using My Phone Line** selected in the next ICW dialog box and click **Next**.

Guided Tour Set Up Your Internet Connection

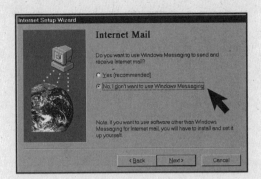

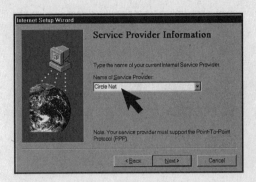

6 In the next ICW dialog box, click **No, I Don't Want to Use Windows Messaging**. This is because you're going to use Internet Mail, which comes with Windows 95 OSR 2, instead. Click **Next**.

8 ICW begins prompting you for information about your ISP. The first screen asks you for the **Name of Service Provider**. Enter it and click **Next**.

After step 6, the Internet Connection Wizard may prompt you to select your modem. If it does so, choose your modem and click **Next** to continue with the Internet Connection Wizard.

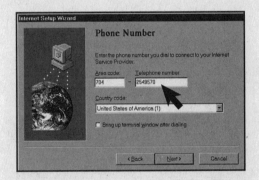

9 In the next ICW dialog box, enter the phone number for your ISP, including the area code. If your ISP doesn't offer PAP or CHAP login, click to check the **Bring Up Terminal Window after Dialing** check box. (This displays a window when you connect so you can enter your user name and password.) Click **Next**.

7 ICW tells you it's going to begin installing files. Click **Next**. If Windows 95 prompts you to insert your installation CD or disks, do so.

10 Enter your **User Name** and **Password**. Click **Next**.

(continues)

Guided Tour   Set Up Your Internet Connection   *(continued)*

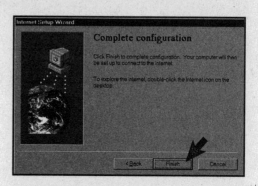

11 Most users can normally just click **Next** at this ICW dialog box. However, if your ISP doesn't dynamically assign IP addresses, click the **Always Use the Following** option button and enter an IP address before clicking **Next**.

12 Enter the **DNS Server** IP addresses for your ISP. Click **Next**.

13 An ICW dialog box appears, telling you that the connection is complete. Click **Finish**.

14 At the dialog box that prompts you to restart your computer, click **Yes**. The computer restarts and updates your system's settings.

Guided Tour Launch and Close Your Internet Connection

1 If you see an Internet icon on the desktop (meaning that Internet Explorer is installed), you can simply double-click that icon to display the Connect To dialog box. Then skip to step 4. After you connect, Internet Explorer launches.

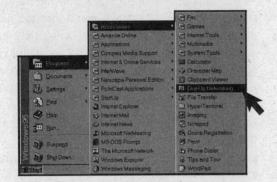

2 If you don't want to launch Explorer but do want to connect, click **Start**, point to **Programs**, and point to **Accessories**. On the Accessories menu, click **Dial-Up Networking**.

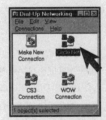

3 In the Dial-Up Networking window, double-click the icon for your Internet connection. (It has the name you entered in the Internet Connection Wizard.)

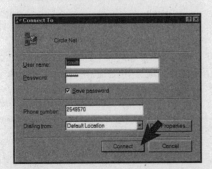

4 Click **Connect**. The modem dials, and Windows sends your logon information to the ISP. (If specified by your connection, a terminal window appears. When you're prompted, enter your user name and press **Enter.** Then enter your password and click **Continue**.)

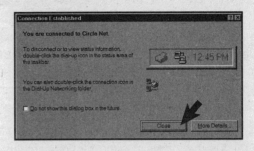

5 The Connection Established dialog box appears, providing information about your connection. Click **Close**.

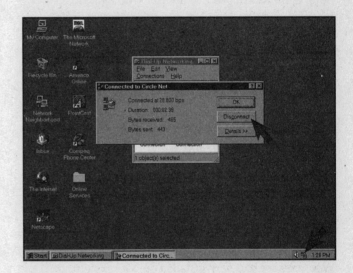

6 To close your connection, double-click the connection icon at the right end of the taskbar, and then click the **Disconnect** button. Windows logs off from your ISP and hangs up the modem.

Drag the icon for your Internet connection from the Dial-Up Networking window to the desktop to create a shortcut for it. Then you can simply double-click the shortcut to connect.

Launch Your Internet Tools

The Internet consists of a collection of networks operating together so that you can send or access information nearly anywhere on the globe. Thousands of academic, government, business, nonprofit, and public systems are connected to the Internet (simply *the Net* to real surfers).

While the Internet offers an almost infinite amount of information, it's been difficult to organize and use that information because of the differences among the computer systems attached to the Net. The individual systems connected to the Net are called *servers* or *sites*, because these computers are actually servers for local networks. Over time, several different server types and services have evolved as standards on the Internet.

E-mail, Internet Relay Chat (IRC), and newsgroups are services users can access to exchange private, instant, and public messages, respectively. Archie, Gopher, File Transfer Protocol (FTP), and World Wide Web (WWW) are different sites (servers) on the Internet that are repositories for many different kinds of information (files and resources), and each uses a different method for storage, organization, and access of that information. For example, to access information on a Web server, you need to have Internet access and have Web browser software installed on your system.

Most beginners and home users are primarily interested in three kinds of services: the Web, e-mail, and newsgroups. Recognizing user interest in these types of information, Microsoft has included applications for accessing them in the OSR 2 version of Windows 95 that's installed on new systems. These programs are called Internet Explorer (Web), Internet Mail (e-mail), and Internet News (newsgroups), and they're usually already installed for you.

▶**A later section in this book, "Work on the Internet" (page 423), provides details about working with these programs.**◀ The *Guided Tour* here shows you how to set up and launch each program on your system. You will need to gather some information (provided by your ISP) to get going.

- Once you've run the Internet Connection Wizard as described in the previous task, Internet Explorer will be ready to go.

- To set up your e-mail software (Internet Mail), you'll need your ISP's mail server addresses. There are usually two servers: the POP server that manages incoming mail and the SMTP server for outgoing mail. The address for each of these servers is usually something like mailhost.bubba.net. You also need to know what your e-mail ID is; usually, you combine your user name, an **@** symbol, and the *domain name* (address) for the service provider. For example, an e-mail address might look like jblow@bubba.net.

- To read newsgroups with Internet Mail, you'll need your ISP's news server address, which is usually something like newshost.bubba.net. This server computer holds the newsgroup information. Also verify whether your ISP requires that you use your user name and password to log on to the mail server.

One last issue: You can set up your Internet software to automatically dial the Internet when you start the software. This saves you the trouble of launching the Internet connection (which you created with the Internet Connection Wizard) before launching the software. The following *Guided Tour* assumes this is what you want. However, once you're connected (even if you launched the connection before starting a program), you can start one or all of the Internet software programs simultaneously. Each can then work with information on the Internet.

▶**For more on using any of the software covered in the *Guided Tour*, see the section "Work on the Internet" on page 423.**◀

Before you can connect with any of the programs described here, you have to use the Internet Connection Wizard to set up a connection for dialing the Internet. See the previous task, "Get Wired with the Internet Connection Wizard" for instructions.

Guided Tour Launch and Exit Internet Explorer

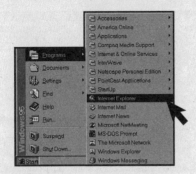

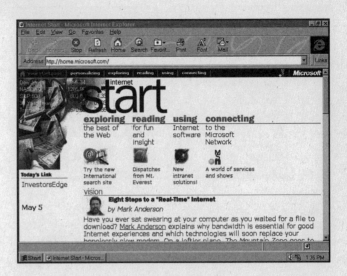

1 Click **Start**, point to **Programs**, and click **Internet Explorer**. Or, double-click the **Internet** icon on the desktop.

3 After the logon finishes, Internet Explorer opens automatically and takes you to the Microsoft Web site. When you finish using Explorer, open the **File** menu and select **Close**.

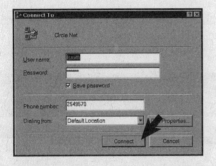

2 In the Connect To dialog box, click **Connect**. The modem dials, and Windows sends your logon information to the ISP. (Enter your logon information in the terminal window if it appears.)

4 At the dialog box asking whether to close your Internet connection, click **Yes**. Windows logs you off and hangs up the modem.

Guided Tour Launch and Exit Internet Mail

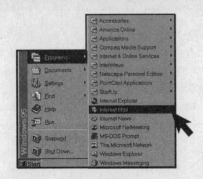

1 Click **Start**, point to **Programs**, and click **Internet Mail**. (This is the command you'll use in the future to launch Mail. However, you'll need to connect to the Internet first, because Mail does not automatically launch the Internet connection you created with the Internet Connection Wizard. This is because you may want to work with mail offline.)

2 Click **Next** at the first Internet Mail Configuration dialog box.

(continues)

Guided Tour Launch and Exit Internet Mail   (continued)

3 In the next dialog box, enter the sender **Name** that you want to use for your e-mail. (This can be a name or nickname.) Fill in the **Email Address** text box with your address. Then click **Next**.

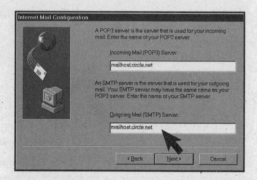

4 Enter the addresses for your mail servers in the text boxes of the next dialog box. Click **Next**.

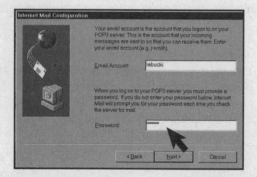

5 In the **Email Account** text box, enter your user name. (If you only have a mailbox attached to another user's Internet account, such as your spouse's or a small business account, enter the user name for that person or account.) Then enter the **Password** (it appears as asterisks). Click **Next**.

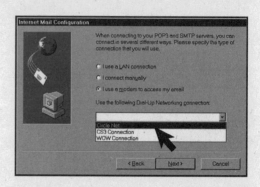

6 Unless you're connecting to the Internet via a network, in the next dialog box, click **I Use a Modem to Access My Email**, and then choose your ISP connection from the drop-down list. Click **Next**.

7 Another dialog box appears to tell you the setup is finished. Click **Finish**.

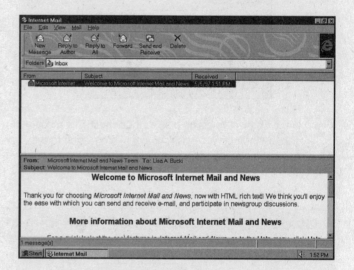

8 You're taken to the Internet Mail screen. To exit Internet Mail, open the **File** menu and choose **Close**.

Guided Tour   Launch and Exit Internet News

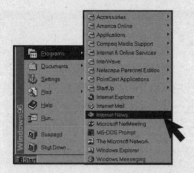

1 Click **Start**, point to **Programs**, and click **Internet News**. (This is the command you'll use in the future to start News and automatically display the Connect To dialog box to dial your Internet Connection.)

2 Click **Next** at the first Internet News Configuration dialog box.

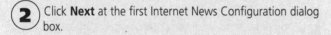
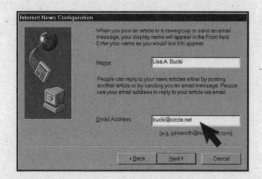

3 In the next dialog box, enter the sender **Name** that you want to identify you in any messages you post in a newsgroup. (This can be a name or nickname.) Fill in the **Email Address** text box with your address. Click **Next**.

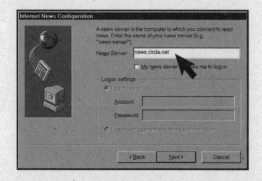

4 Enter your ISP's **News Server** address. If your ISP's news server requires you to log on with your user name and password, click to check **My News Server Requires Me to Logon**, and then fill in the **Account** (user name) and **Password** text boxes. Click **Next**.

5 Unless you're connecting to the Internet via a network, in the next dialog box, click **I Use a Modem to Access My Newsgroups**, and then choose your ISP connection from the drop-down list. Click **Next**.

6 Another dialog box appears to tell you the setup is finished. Click **Finish**.

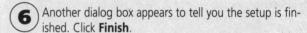
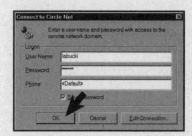

7 When the Connect To dialog box appears, click **OK** to dial your Internet connection and log on.

8 Internet News downloads the newsgroup listing from the news server.

(continues)

Guided Tour   Launch and Exit Internet News   *(continued)*

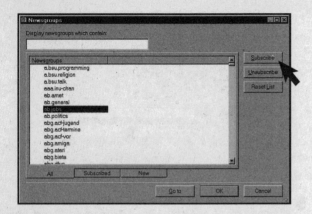

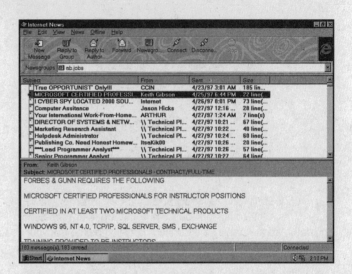

9 When it's finished, you'll see the Newsgroups window. You can click a group in the **Newsgroups** list, and then click **Subscribe** to subscribe to it. When you finish, click **OK**.

10 You're taken to the Internet News screen, where you can read the groups you've subscribed to. To exit Internet News, open the **File** menu and choose **Close**. At the dialog box asking whether to close your Internet connection, click **Yes**. Windows logs you off and hangs up the modem.

Connect to America Online

America Online (AOL) provides its information to millions of users in a very friendly way. On its plus side, it offers a clear graphical user interface, making it easy to get where you need to go by clicking. On the downside, the first time you visit a particular department, you have to wait while AOL downloads the graphics files for display on your system.

AOL presently offers 21 different channels: Computers & Software, Digital City, Entertainment, Games, Health & Fitness, The Hub, International, Internet Connection, Kids Only, Learning & Culture, Lifestyles & Interests, Marketplace, MusicSpace, Newstand, Today's News, People Connection, Personal Finance, Reference, Sports, Style Channel, and Travel. The Channels screen in AOL lets you enter any of the channels by clicking an icon.

The window for each channel offers listings of the various topics or services found in that channel. Click the button beside the name of a topic or service to go to it. Other graphic hot spots identify highly popular "newsy" topics or services; simply click a graphic to jump to that topic or service. The Channels button at the bottom of the window lets you jump back to the Channels screen to switch to another department. If you need help, click the **Member Services** button from any window; to get an alphabetical list of that channel's contents, click the **Find** button.

What you can do depends on the channel you're in. You can read and leave messages in *forums*, browse to find information, download files from *libraries*, and even chat with other users.

The icons along the top of the AOL Windows 95 software let you jump to specific services or perform specificactions. Here's a rundown of what each icon does.

AOL's Icons

Click the Icon...	To...	Click the Icon...	To...
	Read new mail.		Visit the Marketplace for online shopping.
	Compose a mail message.		Change your My AOL settings.
	Display the Channels window.		Display how long you've been connected to AOL.
	Display the What's Hot highlights window.		Print the displayed text or graphic.
	Enter the Chat area.		View the messages and files you've stored in your Personal Filing Cabinet.
	Search for files.		Display your list of Favorite Places to visit on AOL.
	Enter the Stocks & Portfolios stock service.		View the Member Services list.
	Read Today's News.		Find information and files.
	Browse the World Wide Web (Internet).		Display the Keyword dialog box, so you can enter a keyword to jump to an AOL location.

If the AOL software didn't come installed on your computer or come with your modem, you can get it by calling 1-800-827-6364. If you need to install the software, follow the instructions on the disk label to start the installation process, and then respond to the on-screen prompts.

Use a Keyword to Move Around

You can jump directly to a topic or service instead of moving to it by choosing a channel. To go directly to a location on AOL, you use its *keyword*. Here's how to go to a location using a keyword, whether you know the keyword or not:

1. Open the **Go To** menu and click **Keyword** (or press **Ctrl+K** or click the **Keyword** icon at the top of the screen).

2. If you know the keyword for the service you want to go to, type it in the **Enter Word(s)** text box, and then click **Go** or press **Enter**. If you don't know the keyword, proceed with the rest of the steps.

3. Type a topic to search for in the **Enter Word(s)** text box, and click the **Search** button.

4. The Search Results window appears, listing areas dealing with the topic you searched for. Double-click one of the matching entries to jump to that service or topic.

Guided Tour Sign On

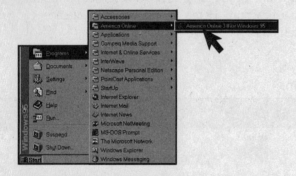

1 Click **Start**, point to **Programs**, point to **America Online**, and click **America Online 3.0 for Windows 95**. Or, double-click the **America Online** shortcut on the desktop.

2 In the Welcome dialog box, open the **Select Screen Name** list and choose your screen name if necessary.

3 Type your password in the **Enter Password** text box, and then click the **Sign On** button. Your computer dials into AOL, and you see the AOL Welcome screen.

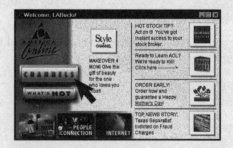

4 Click an icon to go to an area of AOL, or click the **Channels** button to start using AOL.

Guided Tour Sign On

⑤ From the Channels window, you can click a button to start using a channel.

Guided Tour Sign Off

① Open the **Sign Off** menu and click **Sign Off**.

② At the Goodbye dialog box, another user can sign on, or you can press **Alt+F4** to leave AOL.

Send Mail on America Online

To have semiprivate contact with another AOL user, you use the mail services to send e-mail. (While e-mail messages generally only travel between you and your recipient, AOL's staff members can review message contents. Remember, no information that's transmitted electronically is ever completely private.) AOL takes your e-mail messages, routes them along according to the address you give, and delivers them to your recipient's mailbox. E-mail exists only electronically; it is transported via phone lines and computer networks.

You can exchange mail with any other AOL user, as well as with users of many other online services and the Internet. All you need to know is the recipient's electronic address. (More on this next in this task.) You can work online to compose, send, read, and manage your mail in AOL. Of course, when you do, you'll be charged for your online time. As an alternative, AOL also lets you create mail offline and send it later. To learn more about this, see the **FlashSessions** choice on the **Mail** menu.

E-Mail Recipient Names

To send e-mail to another AOL user, you address it to that user's screen name. If a person's screen name were **LABucki**, that would also be her e-mail address. Use the correct capitalization when you type another person's screen name to address mail; you must capitalize all the right letters and use spaces when they're called for.

AOL connects to all other users via the Internet, so it treats all other e-mail addresses as Internet addresses. An *Internet address* is generally a combination of the recipient's user name or ID and a suffix that's specific to the service provider; you need to know both parts of the puzzle.

Note that the Internet is picky about capitalization and punctuation. You need to type everything in lowercase characters and correctly position all periods and @ symbols. Here's how to address e-mail when you're sending it to users of other online services:

- CompuServe addresses consist of the user ID number with a period instead of a comma, followed by @compuserve.com. To send e-mail from AOL to the CompuServe user whose ID is 12345,123, you would address the mail to **12345.123@compuserve.com**. This is changing, however. CompuServe is helping users pick more personal e-mail addresses. You can use either a user's new address or the older numeric address.

- Prodigy addresses consist of the user's ID in all lowercase characters, followed by @prodigy.com. So, the e-mail address for a Prodigy user with the ID of FDEP94B would be **fdep94b@prodigy.com**.

- Addresses for people with accounts directly on the Internet are even more unique. These consist of a user name, followed by the @ symbol and the name of the Internet site where that person's account is located. The catch is that there are thousands, if not millions, of Internet sites. Let's say you're addressing e-mail to someone whose user name is sjones, and that person's account is located at indiana.cica.edu. The user's full e-mail address would be **sjones@indiana.cica.edu**, and you'd have to type it exactly.

Bet you didn't know that you have an Internet address! It consists of your screen name typed in lowercase letters with no spaces, followed by @aol.com. For example, the Internet address for the screen name bj poland would be **bjpoland@aol.com**.

Guided Tour Create and Send Mail

1 Open the **Mail** menu and select **Compose Mail**. Alternatively, you can press **Ctrl+M**, or you can click the **Compose Mail** icon (the second from the left at the top of the screen).

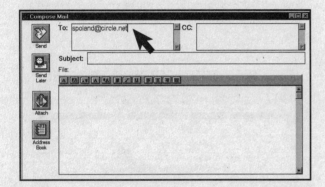

2 In the **To** list, type one or more e-mail addresses of the person(s) you want to send the message to. These addresses may include AOL addresses and addresses for other services.

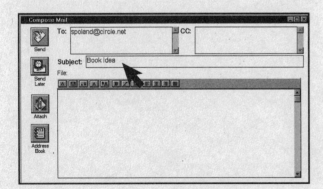

3 Click in the **Subject** line and type the subject for your message. Then click in the blank text area of the Compose Mail window and type the text of your message. Notice that you can also select some text and click a button to format it. Whether or not your recipient sees this formatting, however, depends on the recipient's e-mail program.

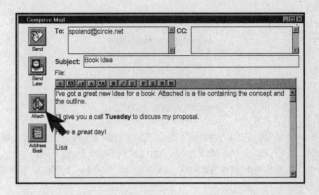

4 (Optional) If you want to send a file along with your message, click the **Attach** button.

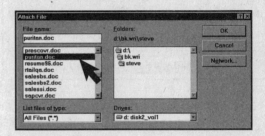

5 (Optional) In the Attach File dialog box, select the file to send with the message, and then click **OK** or press **Enter**.

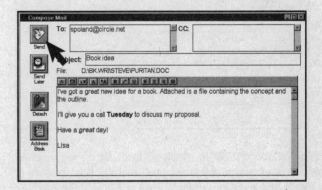

6 Click the **Send** button to send your message immediately. A window appears, informing you your mail has been sent. Click **OK** or press **Enter**.

Guided Tour   Read Mail

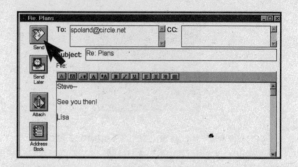

1 In the initial Welcome dialog box, click **You Have Mail**. Or, open the **Mail** menu and select **Read New Mail**, or click the **Read New Mail** icon (the far left one at the top of the screen).

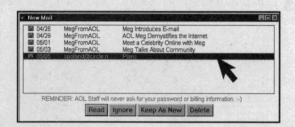

4 (Optional) Type your reply text, and then click the **Send** button. Click the **Close** button to close your message window and the Reply window. (If you're prompted to save a message as a file, make your choice by clicking the appropriate button.)

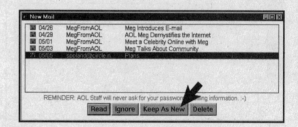

2 Either double-click the message you want to read, or use the **down arrow** key to highlight it and then click **Read**.

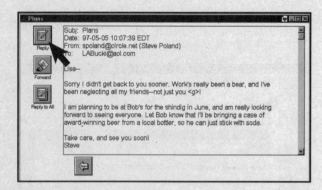

5 Select the **Keep As New** or the **Delete** button to determine what you want to do with the message you just read.

6 Read other messages, or close the mail windows to work elsewhere in AOL.

3 (Optional) Click the **Reply** button if you want to respond to a message. If you want part of the original message to appear as a quote in your reply, select or highlight the information you want to quote before clicking the Reply button.

Read Articles on America Online

AOL has articles all over the place. As you move around through various areas, windows will frequently include lists you can choose items from. Some of those items display additional choices, but others contain an article that you can open and read. You click colorful icons to move around from service to service and list to list.

When you're viewing a list of choices in AOL, look for items that have a document icon beside them. The document icon indicates that choosing that item displays an article. Double-clicking any list entry that has a file folder icon beside it reveals a list of additional choices, which may include more folders or individual documents.

Some articles may simply be text files; some may be graphic files, such as a maps of travel destinations. Others may combine graphics with text that you can scroll through, as shown in the *Guided Tour*.

▶See "Connect to America Online" on page 241 to learn how to move to the different areas on AOL.◀

Print or Save the Current Article

Once you display an article or a graphic image, you may save it to disk by using one of the icons toward the right side of the toolbar on-screen:

 Click to send the currently displayed article or graphic directly to your printer.

 Click to save the currently displayed article or graphic to disk; you have to specify a disk, directory, and name for the file in the dialog box that appears.

Guided Tour   Browse and Read Articles

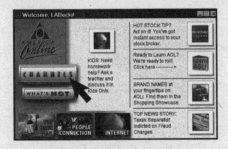

1 At the opening Spotlight screen, click the **Channels** button.

2 In the Channels window, click a channel to select it. For example, you can click the icon for the **Travel** area.

3 In the channel window that opens, you can click an icon for a particular topic or service. For example, you could click **Fantasize** and then click the **Ideas** button in the window that appears to display a list of folders holding articles.

(continues)

Guided Tour Browse and Read Articles   *(continued)*

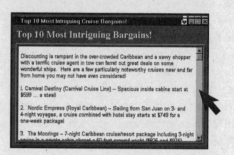

4 In the list of choices for the window, double-click a folder to open it and see its contents. If necessary, double-click folders in the subsequent windows that appear until you see a document listed that you want to read.

6 If the article holds more text than you can see at one time, use the scroll bar that appears to view more of the article. Save or print the article as desired. (You can start these processes using the **File** menu's **Print** and **Save** commands.)

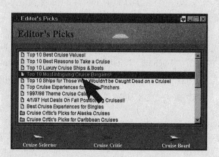

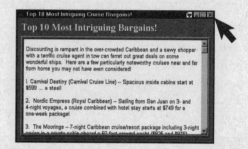

5 To open an article to read it, double-click it in the list.

7 Click the **Close** button for an article window to close it.

8 Continue browsing for articles by moving to new lists and selecting additional folders.

Guided Tour Search for a Topic

1 Open the **Go To** menu and select **Find**, or click the **Find** button near the right end of the toolbar.

2 In the AOL Find window, type the topic you want to search for, and then click the **Search** button.

Guided Tour   Search for a Topic

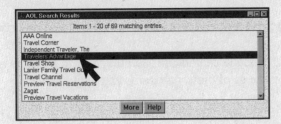

3 To go to one of the areas in the list that appears, double-click your choice.

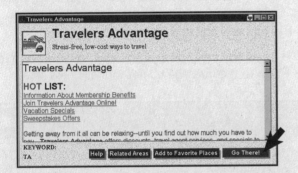

4 In the description window that appears, click **Go There!**.

5 In the topic window, click a button to select a particular kind of information.

6 To display a particular article, double-click it.

7 Read and save the article. You can then browse for other articles.

> Some topic windows have a Search button at the bottom. Click it to review all the information in the topic or to see a list of similar topics you can go to.

Post in America Online Message Centers

Despite the fact that most online service users never meet, most of them love to extend a helping hand or a little chitchat to other users whenever possible (thus the term "online community"). If you need a problem solved or want to look for advice or ideas from other users, check out the *message centers or message boards* in various AOL channels and topics. In a message center, users post questions or comments, and other users may post public replies.

To find a message center in a window, look for a button with a picture of a push pin and piece of paper (the button may even be in a list of articles). The button title will usually include "message center," "message board," "messaging," or "talk." Click a button like this to enter the message center.

Each message center offers numerous *categories* (sometimes called *folders*) and topics of discussion. While the AOL message centers are too numerous to list, here are a few types of message boards you might visit:

- If you want to ask questions about mutual funds you're considering buying, go to the Investor's Network and jump on its Mutual Fund message boards.

- When you have a home business question, visit the Home Business message boards in the Business Strategies Forum.

- If you're losing sleep about your exercise program, go to the message boards in the Fitness area.

In AOL, message boards are also sometimes called *forums*. No matter which it's called, you can read or post messages in one of these online areas.

Guided Tour   Read a Message

1 Go to the topic in which you want to search for a message board. Click the **Message Center** or **Message Board** icon in the service (or in the list of articles for the service).

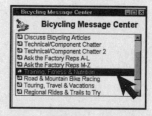

2 If you see another list of different message centers, select the one you want by double-clicking it.

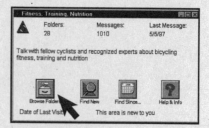

3 Click the **Browse Folders** button.

Guided Tour Read a Message

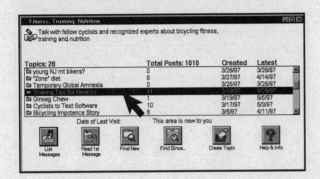

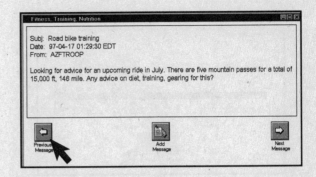

4 Use the **down arrow** key or the scroll bar to move down through the list of folders (categories). When you want to read the messages in one of them, double-click it.

5 Use the **down arrow** key or the scroll bar to move down through the list of messages. Note that the messages are listed from oldest to newest, so you need to scroll down through the list to get to the newer postings.

7 Use the **Next Message** and **Previous Message** buttons to view other messages in the folder.

6 When you find a message you want to read, double-click it.

Guided Tour   Post a Message

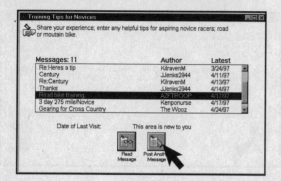

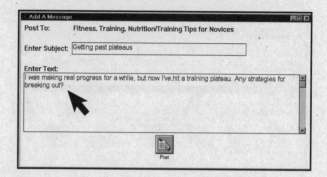

1 Go to a message board. Choose a category and, if you want, display a message you want to reply to. From the message list, click the **Post Another Message** button.

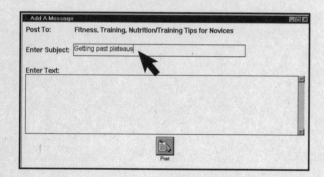

2 If necessary, type a topic for the message in the **Enter Subject** text box.

3 Type the text of your message. Include your user name and a specific request if you want other users to send replies via e-mail.

4 Click the **Post** button to select it.

5 AOL displays a dialog box telling you your message has been added to the folder. Click **OK**. Your newly posted message appears at the bottom of the list of messages in the folder.

Download Files from America Online

Online services offer fantastic resources: material you can view on-screen *and* material you can transfer to your own computer over the phone lines. The process of transferring the files to your computer is called *downloading*.

AOL offers document files, graphic files, program files, and more for download. Although there's no extra charge for downloading, you need to observe all copyright rules and other special rules when you reuse information. Generally, you can't reprint downloaded material for profit or plagiarize it; you need to get permission from the person who uploaded the information to reprint it. Most of the software programs you down-

load will be *shareware* (as opposed to *freeware*). Although you're welcome to test the shareware, if you plan to use it regularly, you need to register it with its online publisher, which usually requires a fee.

AOL uses icons to clue you in about areas where you can find downloadable files, and to identify which files you can download. A button with a stack of floppy disks on it identifies an area where you can find files to download, as does any button labeled "software." In lists of files and folders, look for stacked *floppy disk icons*, which identify both areas with files to download, and individual files to download.

Guided Tour Download a File

1 Display a file list that contains a file you want to download. You may have to go through several lists (or *layers*) by double-clicking different categories or topics in lists to get a list with a file you want.

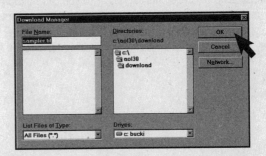

3 In the Download Manager dialog box, use the **Drives**, **Directories**, and **File Name** settings if you want to indicate where you want to store the downloaded file. Then click **OK** or press **Enter**.

(continues)

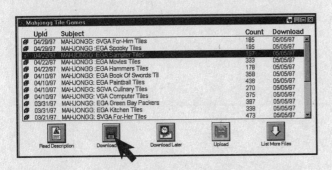

2 Scroll through the list. When you find a file you want to download, highlight it and click the **Download Now** button.

Guided Tour   Download a File *(continued)*

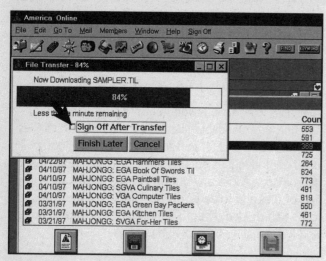

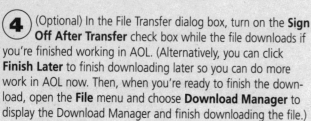

5 When the Download Manager finishes transferring the file, it displays a dialog box, saying so. Click **OK** to continue.

4 (Optional) In the File Transfer dialog box, turn on the **Sign Off After Transfer** check box while the file downloads if you're finished working in AOL. (Alternatively, you can click **Finish Later** to finish downloading later so you can do more work in AOL now. Then, when you're ready to finish the download, open the **File** menu and choose **Download Manager** to display the Download Manager and finish downloading the file.)

Browse the Web with America Online

One of the primary reasons folks join online services these days is to gain access to the World Wide Web. In fact, AOL has an entire channel devoted to the Internet to make it easy for you to jump on and find the information you need.

AOL actually offers access to a few different types of Web information. I'll just cover the Web here, as that's what most users are interested in.

The following *Guided Tour* shows how to connect to the Web via AOL. In article and file lists throughout AOL, be on the lookout for icons that look like a small spherical grid. Selecting any one of those choices also connects you to the Internet.

Guided Tour   Access the Web from AOL

1 Click the **Internet Connection** button in the Channels window.

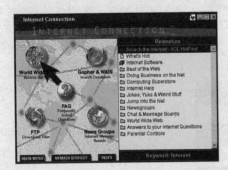

2 In the Internet Connection window, click the **World Wide Web** icon. AOL displays its Web site home page.

3 To view another page, type its URL (address) near the top of the window, and then press **Enter**.

4 The new site appears. You can click the **Back** button to go to the previous page, or you can click the window's **Close** button to resume working in AOL channels.

Connect to CompuServe

CompuServe is one of the oldest and best-known online services. It has traditionally catered to business users, offering extensive online data resources like the IQuest information databases, stock and company information, and Associated Press news (updated hourly). To use CompuServe, you can dial in with any communications software and navigate via text-based menus.

As of a couple of years ago, you could navigate with CompuServe Information Manager for Windows (WinCIM), graphical software from CompuServe. The current version of CompuServe's software, 3.0.2, is called CompuServe Interactive (CSi). This reflects a move by CompuServe to make its content look and work more seamlessly, like regular Internet World Wide Web content.

CompuServe offers a wide variety of services (where you can browse for articles and files), databases (where you can search for articles and abstracts), and forums (where you can exchange messages and files with other users). CSi gives you access to them all. The Services screen in CSi enables you to jump to some of the most popular areas in CSi.

To move around, generally you click icons (or double-click a choice in a list) to display related choices. Depending on the service you're in, you can perform different activities. You can read and leave messages in forums, browse to find information, download files from libraries, and even chat with other users.

Clicking an icon in the CSi window performs a specific action. Here's a rundown of what each icon (or list) does.

CSi Icons

Click the Icon...	To...	Click the Icon...	To...
Animals (dropdown)	Select a CSi page or Web page to visit.		Open your personal To-Do list.
Go	Go to a service.		Connect to CompuServe. (when you're online, this changes to an icon with which you can disconnect from CompuServe without closing CSi.)
	Add the current service to your list of Favorite Places.		
	Display your list of Favorite Places to choose a place to go.	Go...	Go to a recently visited service.
	Perform a search to find a service or forum.	Find	Search either CompuServe or the Internet.
	Access the Internet.	Mail Center	Manage your current mail.
CS$_\$$	Display current quotes for stocks you select.	My Information	Access both your Filing Cabinet and To-Do list.
	Get the current weather.	Learn About	Learn what's available in CompuServe, by category.
	Open your personal filing cabinet to manage messages and articles stored there.		Get new mail.

CSi really makes it easy to log on, as you'll see in the *Guided Tour*. Once you set up your system settings and account (including your password), all you have to do is start up CSi and choose where to go. CSi issues all the right commands to log on, including your password. The downside is that anyone can walk up to your computer and log on to your account.

Another nice feature of CSi is that it lets you do a lot of work offline. You can create and read mail messages, read and print stuff stored in your filing cabinet, and more.

Use a Go Command to Move Around

You can jump directly to a service or forum instead of moving to it by browsing around. To go directly to a service, you use its *Go command*. Here's how to go to a service using its Go command:

1. Open the **Access** menu and click **Go**. Alternatively, you can press **Ctrl+G**, or you can click the **Go** button at the top of the screen.

2. In the **Service** text box, type the **Go** command. Then click **OK** or press **Enter**.

To find a list of Go commands, click a Go Directory button when one appears on-screen.

Guided Tour Log On and Go to a Service

1 Click **Start** and click **CompuServe 3.0.2**, which has been added to the top of the Start menu. (You can also double-click the **CompuServe 3.0.2** icon on the desktop, or you can click **Start**, point to **Programs**, point to **CompuServe**, and click **CompuServe 3.0.2**.) Your system loads the CompuServe software and displays the Home Desktop.

2 You can click any icon or select a menu command (such as **Get New Mail** on the **Mail** menu) to perform an online activity. Making one of these choices starts the logon procedure.

(continues)

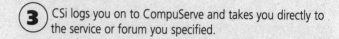

Guided Tour Log On and Go to a Service *(continued)*

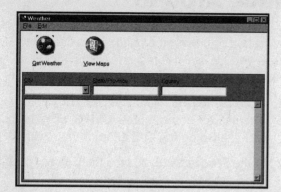

 CSi logs you on to CompuServe and takes you directly to the service or forum you specified.

Anytime you see a Main Menu button, you can click it to return to the Home Desktop.

Guided Tour Log Off

To log off, but leave CSi open on-screen so you can work offline, click the **Disconnect** icon, or open the **Access** menu and select **Disconnect** (or press **Ctrl+D**).

To log off and close the CSi window, click the **Terminate Connection** icon, or open the **File** menu and select **Exit** (or press **Alt+F4**).

Send CompuServe Mail

E-mail between CompuServe users is private, as on other online services. CompuServe takes your private electronic mail messages, routes them along according to the address you give, and delivers them to your recipient's mailbox.

You can exchange mail with any other CompuServe user, as well as with users of many other online services and the Internet. You can work online to compose, send, read, and manage your mail in CompuServe. With the Basic membership, you can send up to $9 worth of e-mail messages each month—roughly equivalent to 90 three-page, text-only messages.

You can find e-mail addresses for other users while you're working in forums. CompuServe also enables you to search for addresses if you know the name of the person you want to find an address for. Having that person's city, state, and country helps, too.

E-Mail to Other Services

To send e-mail to another CompuServe user, you address it to that user's CompuServe ID number. If a person's ID number is **12345,0000**, that's also his e-mail address. CompuServe connects to all other users via the Internet, so it treats all other e-mail addresses as Internet addresses. An Internet address is generally a combination of the recipient's user name or ID and a suffix that's specific to the service provider; you need to know both parts of the puzzle.

You also need to include **INTERNET:** before the address of any Internet user to send him or her a message from CompuServe. So, to send e-mail to a person whose address is joe.blow@any.school.edu, you would type **INTERNET:joe.blow@any.school.edu** in the message's **Address** text box, and you would enter that full phrase as the address in your address book.

Note that the Internet is picky about capitalization and punctuation. You need to type everything in lowercase characters and correctly position all periods and @ symbols. Here's how to address e-mail when you're sending it to users of other online services:

- America Online addresses consist of the user name followed by @aol.com. So to send e-mail

from CompuServe to the AOL user whose user name is JBlow, you would address the mail to **INTERNET:jblow@aol.com**.

- Prodigy addresses consist of the user's ID in all lowercase characters, followed by @prodigy.com. So the e-mail address for a Prodigy user with the ID of FDEP94B would be **INTERNET:fdep94b@prodigy.com**.

- Addresses for people with accounts directly on the Internet are even more unique. These consist of a user name, followed by the @ symbol and the name of the Internet site where that person's account is located. The catch is that there are thousands, if not millions, of Internet sites. Let's say you're addressing e-mail to someone whose user name is sjones, and that person's account is located at indiana.cica.edu. The user's full e-mail address would be **INTERNET:sjones@indiana.cica.edu**, and you'd have to type it exactly.

> You can create a more user-friendly alphanumeric CompuServe ID (and e-mail address) by using the Go command **Register.**

> Bet you didn't know that you have an Internet address! It consists of your CompuServe ID with a period in place of the comma, followed by @compuserve.com, as in **12345.0000@aol.com.**

Work Offline

CSi lets you compose and read mail offline, though there's no room to cover this in-depth here. As a brief example, open CSi but don't log on. Use the **Create Mail** command on the **Mail** menu. Compose a message, and then click the **Send Later** button. Create other messages this way as well. Then open the **Mail** menu and select the **Send/Retrieve All Mail** command. CSi logs you on to CompuServe and sends all your messages at once.

Use the Filing Cabinet

When you have a new mail message open in a window, you'll notice a button that reads "File It." Clicking this button enables you to save the message in your personal Filing Cabinet so you can read it and print it offline, saving your precious online time for more urgent work like searching for information. Similarly, you can store articles you find in your Filing Cabinet. You can even create custom *folders* in the Filing Cabinet to group messages and articles about a particular topic or client, for example. Here are some basics for using the Filing Cabinet:

- Click the **File It** button from a message or article window to display the Filing Cabinet. Click the folder you want to save to, and then click **Store**.

- To create a new folder, click the **New** button, type a name for the folder, and then click **OK**. You can then store messages and articles in it.

- To read files offline or delete or change folders, open the **File** menu and select **Filing Cabinet** (**Ctrl+F**), or click the icon at the top of the screen that looks like a filing cabinet. Double-click a folder to open it, and double-click a file or article to view it.

Guided Tour   Create and Send Mail

1 Open the **Mail** menu and select **Create New Mail**.

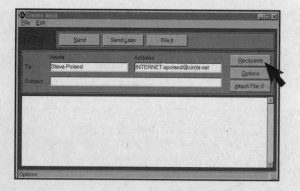

2 Type a name, press **Tab**, and then type an address. Click **Recipients** to place it in the recipient list. (If you haven't mailed to that user before, you'll be prompted to add the name to your Address Book.) If you have mailed to the user before, you can double-click an entry from the Address Book list instead of typing the name and address.

3 (Optional) To add more recipients to the recipient list, select the **TO:**, **CC:**, and **BCC:** option buttons as desired and enter the names and addresses as you did in step 2.

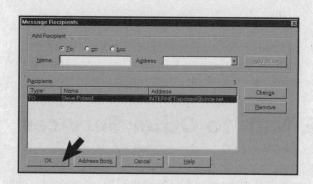

4 Click **OK** to finish the addressing and close the Recipient List dialog box.

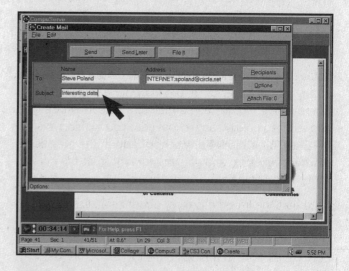

5 Type a subject for the message in the **Subject** line.

Guided Tour Create and Send Mail

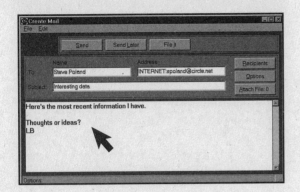

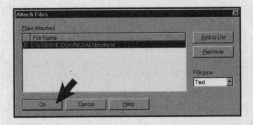

9 (Optional) In the Attach Files dialog box, click the **OK** button to return to the Create Mail window, or use the **Add to List** button to select another file.

6 Click in the blank text area of the Create Mail window, and type the text of your message.

7 (Optional) If you want to send a file along with your message, click the **Attach File** button.

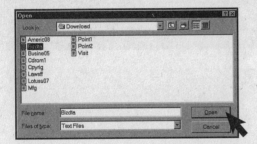

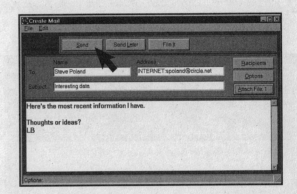

10 Click the **Send** button to send your message immediately. CompuServe closes the Create Mail window, sends the message, and displays a message in the status bar at the bottom of the CSi screen to tell you the message has been sent. If a message box appears, click **OK** to acknowledge it.

8 (Optional) In the Open dialog box, select the file to send with the message. If you're sending to an Internet address, you can only send a text file. Click **Open**.

Guided Tour Read Mail

1 If the Mail icon on the status bar has a number beside it (for the number of messages), click it. Or you can open the **Mail** menu and select **Send/Receive All Mail**.

(continues)

Guided Tour   Read Mail   (continued)

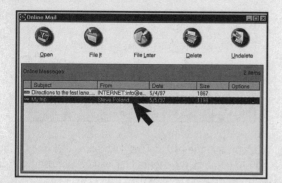

2 In the Online Mail window, double-click the message you want to read, or click it once and click **Open**.

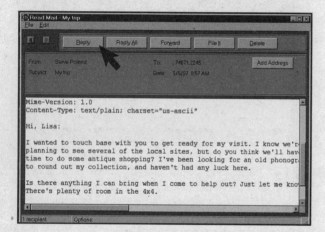

3 (Optional) Click the **Reply** button if you want to respond to a message.

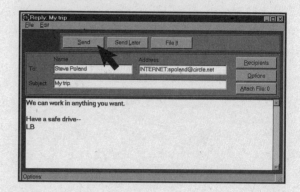

4 (Optional) Type your reply text, and then click the **Send Now** button.

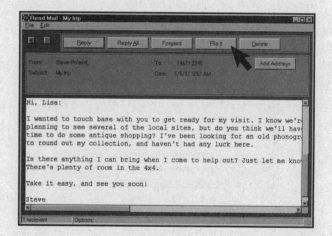

5 Select either the **File It** or **Delete** button to determine what you want to do with the message you just read. The first choice stores the message in the Filing Cabinet for later reading.

6 Read other messages, or click **Close** to close the Get New Mail window so you can work elsewhere in CompuServe.

Browse CompuServe and the Web

CompuServe currently offers more than 100 services, plus access to various areas of the Internet. You can simply move around by clicking your choices in the screens that appear. As you move around through the windows within different services, you'll frequently encounter lists you can choose items from. Some of those items display additional choices, but others (which sometimes have a document icon beside them) denote an article that you can open and read. You double-click list choices to move around from list to list or to display the text of an article.

When you're browsing around in CompuServe, there may be times when you go out to the Internet without actually knowing it. Keep your eye on the Page text box near the top of the CompuServe screen. It tells you your present location and identifies pages by their Web addresses (URLs).

The *Guided Tour* gives you a better idea of how to navigate in CSi and jump out to the Web.

Guided Tour   Browse CompuServe and the Web

1 Click an icon at the Home Desktop to jump to its subject matter.

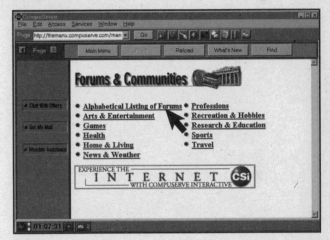

2 Anytime a list appears, you can double-click a topic to jump to the information it's linked to. Or, click the left pointing arrow beside the page label to go back.

(continues)

Guided Tour   Browse CompuServe and the Web   *(continued)*

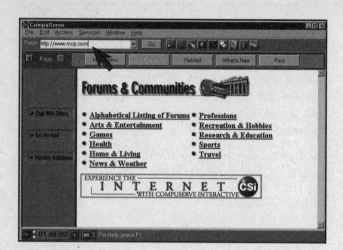

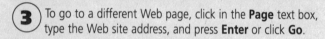

3 To go to a different Web page, click in the **Page** text box, type the Web site address, and press **Enter** or click **Go**.

4 You also can click the **Internet** button from the Home Desktop (Main menu), and CompuServe's main Web page appears.

Connect to a BBS with Windows HyperTerminal

Using your general communications software or the Windows HyperTerminal Accessory program, you can join and take advantage of any one of thousands of public BBSs in the world. Individuals and organizations run BBSs to provide electronic gathering places for users with common interests, or to provide information and support about products and services. For example, NASA has a BBS with information about space missions and the like. The people who run and maintain BBSs are called *sysops*—short for system operators.

If you find a BBS you want to dial in to, you have to start Windows HyperTerminal and set up a connection. You create an icon, enter the phone number, and dial in as explained in the *Guided Tour*.

If the phone number is a long distance call for you, don't forget that you'll have to pay long distance charges for the time you're logged on to the BBS or Internet, and you'll have to include **1** and the area code when you specify the phone number in Terminal.

When you establish the connection, you may need to provide certain information to access the BBS. Some BBSs ask you to provide a password or user information (if it's a BBS you have to join), and some present a questionnaire. Once you've provided your user information, you usually get an opening menu system from which you choose commands by typing a *hot key* (a highlighted letter in a menu command) and pressing **Enter**.

If you get a bunch of garbled gobbledygook when you dial in, you may need to change the modem settings for communicating with the BBS. (This can be a trial and error thing; different BBSs and ISPs may use different communications settings.) You'll need to know the appropriate communications settings to use. Common choices are 8 data bits, None for Parity, and 1 for Stop Bits (this is *8-N-1* in shorthand). This is the default setup for most modems. Normally, your modem will already be set up with its default speed—28,800 bps or better. (Choose the next higher number if your modem's speed isn't listed.) If these settings don't work for a BBS and you get garbled screens while you're in it, try a slower modem speed and change the other settings to **7-E-2**, another common combination. The *Guided Tour* will walk you through these settings, as well.

Some BBSs require special software to run (especially if it's a Windows-based BBS). When you try to sign on, the BBS will tell you that you need the software, and it may ask whether you want to download it to your system. To learn to download files in HyperTerminal, consult Help in HyperTerminal.

You also can use HyperTerminal to log on to some Internet accounts with an ISP. You might need to do this for certain maintenance functions like changing your password; you wouldn't want to do it much otherwise. The interface you get depends on your service provider and on the type of connection you have. Avoid doing this if possible. ▶**Instead, set up your Internet connection as described in the task "Get Wired with the Internet Connection Wizard" on page 231.**◀

Guided Tour Connect with HyperTerminal

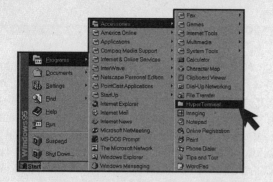

① Click the **Start** menu, point to **Programs**, point to **Accessories**, and click **HyperTerminal**. The HyperTerminal window opens.

④ In the Phone Number window, enter an **Area Code** and **Phone Number**. Change any other settings, if needed, and then click **OK**.

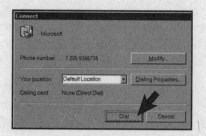

② Double-click the **Hypertrm** icon. HyperTerminal loads, and the Connection Description window for a new connection appears.

⑤ The Connect dialog box appears so you can dial the new connection. Click **Dial**, and HyperTerminal dials the BBS and connects.

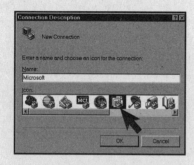

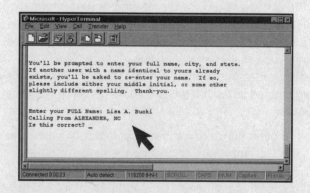

③ Type a **Name** for your BBS or ISP connection, and then select an icon for it. Click **OK**.

⑥ If it's your first time using the BBS, you'll probably have to fill out an online questionnaire or review some legal information. Otherwise, you'll be asked for your user name and password. Respond to each question and press **Enter** after each response. You may need to go through several screens.

Guided Tour Connect with HyperTerminal

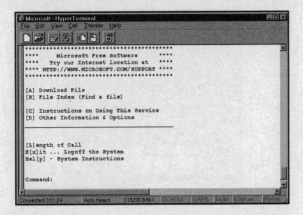

7 The main menu for the BBS appears. Do your work as needed, and then use the command for returning to the Main menu. (This is usually **S** for Stop or **M** for Menu.)

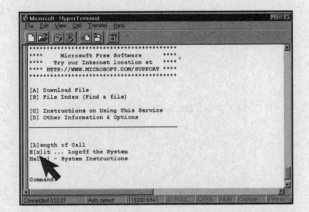

8 On the Main menu, look for the command that logs you off. It may be Quit, Goodbye, Logoff, Bye, Exit, or something similar. Type the command or the first letter of the command to select it. If you're asked to verify the logoff, do so.

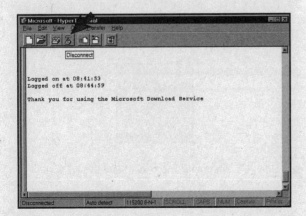

9 To ensure that you've disconnected the call, click the **Disconnect** button on the HyperTerminal toolbar.

10 Open the **File** menu and choose **Save** to save the connection. Then open the **File** menu again and choose **Exit** to close the HyperTerminal window for the connection.

11 In the main HyperTerminal window, you'll see an icon for your new connection. Double-click it at any time, and then click **Dial** to dial the BBS.

Guided Tour Change Communications Settings in HyperTerminal

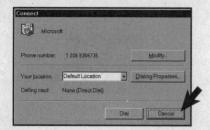

1 In the main HyperTerminal window, double-click the connection icon to open it, and then click **Cancel** in the Connect dialog box that appears.

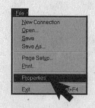

2 In the HyperTerminal window for the connection, open the **File** menu and select **Properties**.

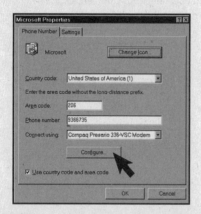

3 In the Properties dialog box for the connection, click the **Configure** button below the name of your modem.

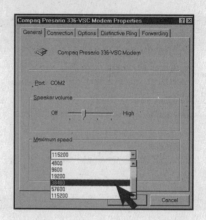

4 In the Properties dialog box for your modem, use the **Maximum Speed** drop-down list on the General tab to change the speed your modem uses for the connection, if necessary.

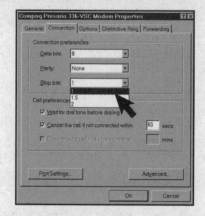

5 Click the **Connection** tab to display its options, and then make your choices there.

6 Click **OK** to close the modem Properties dialog box, and click **OK** again to close the Properties dialog box for the connection.

7 Open the **File** menu and select **Save** to save your changes.

Guided Tour Change Communications Settings in HyperTerminal

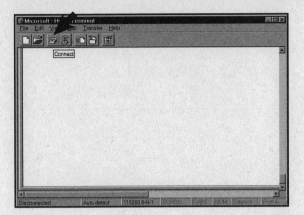

8 Click the **Connect** button on the toolbar to redisplay the Connect dialog box (see step 1), but click **Dial** to dial the BBS and test the new connection settings.

HyperTerminal may have trouble displaying the graphical screens in some BBSs. If you log on to a BBS and have some trouble with it, display the Properties dialog box for the connection, click the **Settings** tab, and try a different **Emulation** choice.

PART 2

Do It Yourself...

S ay you've had your PC for a few months. You're familiar with Windows now, and you're feeling comfortable behind the keyboard. You've written a few letters, played a few games, maybe even used an online service to connect to the outside world. However, until now, you've relied on someone with a little more computer savvy to help you with the advanced stuff. You haven't felt confident enough to try installing new hardware, cleaning the insides of your computer, defragmenting your hard drive, connecting directly to the Internet, or performing some of the other advanced tasks PC owners should be familiar with.

You don't have to rely on someone else anymore. In this part, you expand your PC knowledge by learning how to do some fundamental (but sometimes scary) PC tasks. By the end of this section, you'll realize that some of those things you were asking friends to do for you really aren't hard at all, and you can do them yourself.

What You Will Find in This Part

DO IT YOURSELF

Keep Your Computer Clean and Healthy

One of the basic requirements of owning a PC is that you keep it clean so it functions properly. If your PC's fan is full of lint, your keyboard is sticky from soda spills and chocolate-smudged fingers, and your monitor is coated with dust, you won't be able to get maximum performance from your PC.

How often you clean your computer depends on where you use it and how much you use it. A PC used eighteen hours a day in an un-air-conditioned construction office will need lots more regular cleaning than a computer used part-time in a fancy climate-controlled high-rise or your air-conditioned home. Of course, some parts of your PC will need to be cleaned more often than others. For example, your keyboard and monitor will probably need to be cleaned more often than the inside of your system unit. When it's time to clean a part of your PC, check the appropriate task in this section.

In addition to cleaning your computer, you will need to perform other tasks to keep it healthy and ready to run. For example, you need to change the toner or cartridges in your printer regularly, and you might have to install a surge protector.

What You Will Find in This Section

Clean Outside Your Computer

Computers are a lot like cars: Keep your PC in good shape, and it'll last a long, long time. Okay, so you don't need to change the oil in your computer or rotate its tires. But it's still a good idea to keep your computer free of dirt and grime by giving it a bath every so often.

This task talks about general computer cleaning. See the other parts of this section for specifics on cleaning the monitor, keyboard, mouse, disk drives, and other important parts of your computer.

Why bother keeping your computer clean?

- A build-up of dust around the computer can choke off air circulation inside the machine. That makes the PC run hotter, and it won't last as long.

- The same dust can get inside the PC and cover its delicate parts (like the disk drives). This dust can result in lost data, or it can cause premature failure; your computer may just stop working someday.

- Dust and dirt around the drive slots can muck up the disks as you insert and remove them. This might cause you to lose valuable data.

- Dirty connections on the back of your computer can make the accessories you've connected to it (like a printer) malfunction.

- A clean computer is just nicer to use and look at—and safer to use for your valuable data.

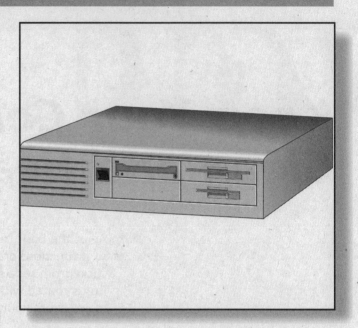

You don't need special tools or cleaners to give your computer a good wash. All you need is a regular mild household cleaner (Fantastik and Formula 409 work well) and some paper towels or soft cotton cloths. If you use cloths, be sure they're white; otherwise, the color can bleed from the cloth onto your computer!

For a professional, top-notch job, you also need a vacuum cleaner with a soft-brush hose attachment. (You can use your regular home vacuum cleaner for this purpose.) Change the bag before you start to ensure that the vacuum has good suction. The better the suction, the more thorough the cleaning. By the way, forget those miniature battery-powered vacuums they advertise for cleaning computers. They aren't strong enough.

Do It Yourself Clean Your Computer's Case

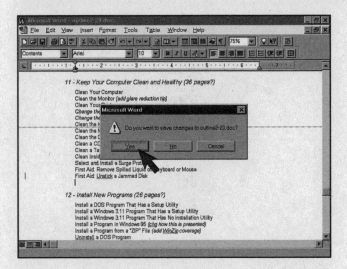

1 If the computer is on, save your work (if necessary), exit any programs that are running, and remove any disks in the disk drives. If necessary, exit Windows. Turn the PC off (very important). For added protection, unplug the computer.

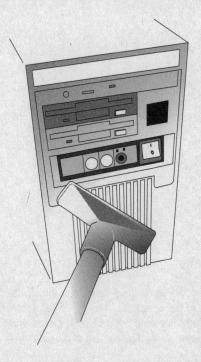

3 Again, using the soft-brush attachment of the vacuum, remove all loose dust inside the ventilation slots, the disk drive openings, and other nooks and crannies.

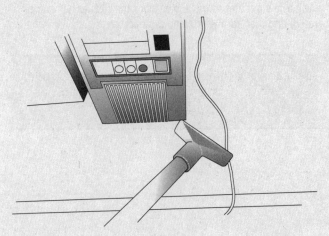

2 Use the soft-brush attachment of your vacuum to clean around the computer. If the PC is a floor-standing model, it's really important to clean the carpet or floor around the computer thoroughly, as this is a primary source of dust. Your computer is no cleaner than the bed it lies in!

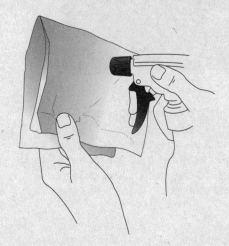

4 Moisten a paper towel or soft cloth with a regular household cleaner such as Formula 409 or Fantastik (don't use harsh soaps or detergents; they leave a residue). Never spray the cleaner directly on the computer! Especially don't spray on or in any openings. Also, don't overwet the towel or cloth.

(continues)

Do It Yourself   Clean Your Computer's Case   *(continued)*

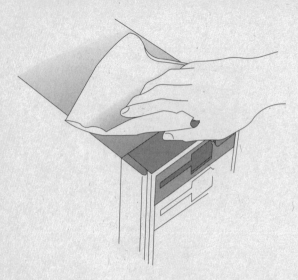

5 Using the damp towel or cloth, wipe off the outside surface of the computer. Then dry the surface with another towel or cloth. Remember: Don't spray cleaner right on your computer because the liquid could drip inside.

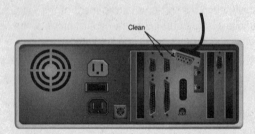

Clean

6 At the back of the computer, remove each cable and clean the mating parts (called connectors) with the vacuum cleaner. Do not use a wet cleaner for cleaning the connectors; they conduct electricity. Do just one cable at a time. When you finish cleaning one, reattach it and go to the next one. Clean the power cord, too.

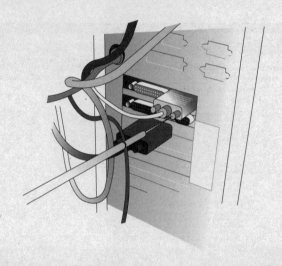

7 If any of the connectors are screwed on, you will need a small flat-head screwdriver to unscrew them. These screwdrivers are available at any hardware store.

8 When you finish cleaning the outside of your computer, make sure all the cables and power cords are reattached. Wait a few minutes to make sure all of the cleaner has evaporated, and then turn your computer back on.

Clean your computer once every week or two, or whenever you notice a buildup of dust and dirt.

Clean Inside Your Computer

Maybe you do this at you own house: Once a year, usually around springtime when the weather is clear, you go through the joint and give it a thorough cleaning. Upstairs, downstairs, attic, basement—you name it, it gets cleaned. This so-called "spring cleaning" is designed to give a much-needed facelift to your house, which has been closed up and collecting dust all winter.

Now imagine a spring cleaning for your PC. Don't laugh. Every once in a while, your computer can really use a thorough inside-out cleaning. Not only do you give the computer a bath on the outside (▶see **"Clean Outside Your Computer" on page 274**◀), but you also open her up and get all the accumulated dust and other junk out of the inside.

Why clean the inside of your computer? You'd be surprised at how much dust can collect inside that beast, even if you use your computer in a relatively clean environment like an air-conditioned office. PCs use fans to suck in air so the innards of the computer stay cool. Along with the air comes—you guessed it—dust.

There's no effective way to keep this dust out of your computer. It's a fact of life that after a year or two, most computers (assuming they are used daily) collect a thick layer of muck that can impede the operation of the machine.

Dust is like a blanket: The more dust, the hotter the components get. And hot electronics is something you want to avoid. Heat damages electronic equipment. More than once dust has been the reason for a computer "meltdown," in which one or more parts inside the computer fail under the heat, and the PC gives out. This can be expensive to fix.

In order to clean inside your computer, you have to remove its cover or case. This is not dangerous, and as long as you are careful, there is little risk of damaging anything. If you are comfortable with a screwdriver, you can safely clean the inside of your computer.

What you need for the job:

- A #1 Phillips-head screwdriver. This screwdriver fits the screws used to fasten down the cases of most computers. A few brands of computers (like certain models made by Compaq) use "Torx" screws that require a special tool, which is available at most hardware stores.

- A small flat-head screwdriver for removing cables screwed onto the back of the computer.

- An artist's brush (about one-inch wide will do it).

- A can of compressed air. You can buy this at most any photographic, automotive, or computer-supply store.

- A bunch of cotton-tipped swabs.

Clean the inside of the computer about once every year or two, or more if the PC shows signs of heavy dust buildup.

Do It Yourself   Clean Your Computer's Insides

1 Turn your computer off and unplug it.

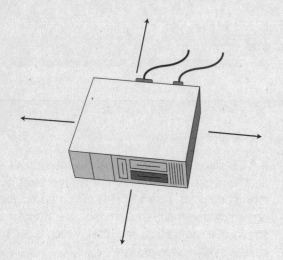

2 If your computer is a desktop model, remove the monitor (if it's sitting on top) and clear off your desk so you can access the top, sides, and back. If your computer is a floor-standing model, clear out an area so you can work on the computer.

3 For now, leave all cables attached to your computer unless they interfere with opening it up. If you must remove a cable from the front or back of the computer, note the connector to which the cable attaches. Use the small flat-head screwdriver to loosen the connector, if necessary.

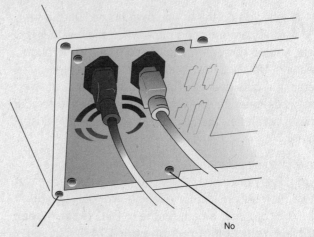

No

4 Locate the screws used to secure the top or case to the computer. (You may need to refer to the manual that came with your computer to locate all the screws). Whatever you do, don't just loosen any screw you see. This is especially true of screws on the back of the computer, away from the perimeter of the case. These screws are often used to secure parts (like the power supply and hard disk drive) inside the computer, and there is no reason to remove them. In fact, doing so may damage your computer.

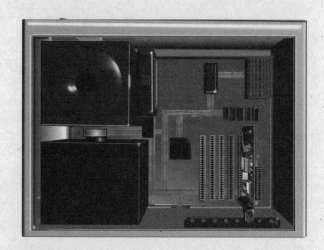

5 With all the appropriate screws removed, carefully lift the top or case and pull it away from the computer. The inside of your computer should now be visible.

6 As a precaution, touch a metal object like a doorknob. This discharges excess static from your body. Do not touch the computer case itself; you don't want to discharge static into the computer. Static electricity can damage your computer's electronics.

Do It Yourself Clean Your Computer's Insides

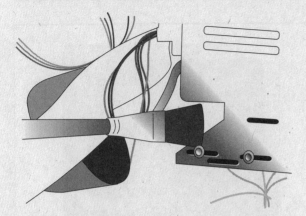

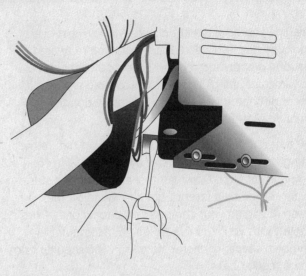

7 Use the artist's brush to whisk out the sediment of dust that has collected inside the computer. If the dust is heavy, you may want to wear a dust mask during this step, especially if you are sensitive to dust.

9 For out-of-the-way areas that are too dirty for the compressed air, use the cotton-tipped swabs to wipe off excess dust. Don't be miserly with the swabs. When the tip gets dirty, use the other end. When both ends get dirty, throw it away and use another swab. For the average computer, you may use one or two dozen swabs.

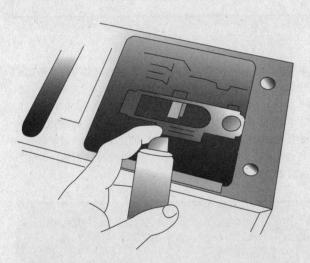

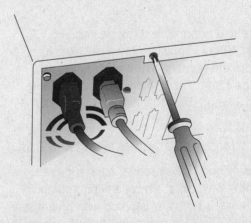

8 For hard-to-reach spots, use the can of compressed air to blast dust out of the crevices inside the computer. Try to aim the nozzle of the air can so that the dust is blown out of the computer, not further inside.

10 When all is clean inside, replace the cover, making sure that it fits snugly, the way it did before you removed it. Replace the screws, but don't overtighten them.

Never, ever use a cleaning fluid inside your computer. You could short out the electrical system and your PC.

Clean the Monitor

Imagine you have a giant picture window that over-looks the Pacific Ocean. Every night you're treated to beautiful orange-and-red sunsets over a cool blue sea. Now imagine the picture window covered with a thick film of dirt and grease. Hardly the inspiration for romantic sunset dinners.

You'd never think of marring the beauty of nature by letting the picture window stay dirty. Same with your computer monitor. Don't let its sharp, colorful pictures be diminished by a layer of dirt and grime on the screen. Cleaning your computer monitor is one of the simplest jobs you'll do in keeping your computer in top-notch shape, so there's no reason you shouldn't do it on a regular basis.

While keeping your monitor clean is no difficult task, you have to exercise some degree of care to prevent damage. Certain kinds of cleaners can be hazardous to the surfaces of your monitor. Here's what you need in your monitor-cleaning toolkit:

- A soft, white cotton cloth or a good-quality paper towel.

- A household nonresidue spray cleaner, like Formula 409 or Fantastik. Stay away from harsh soaps or detergents, which leave residue, and don't use furniture polish because many brands contain an ingredient that can actually attract dust.

- Some cotton swabs (otherwise known as Q-Tips).

- For a really good job, a special antistatic cloth. This cloth, available at almost any photographic supply store, is specially prepared with an antistatic "coating." Wiping something with the cloth helps reduce static that can attract dust.

Because your computer's monitor is your porthole into what your PC is doing, you ought to clean it every week or so, or whenever you notice buildup of dust. You'll notice that the more you use your computer, the more the screen will attract dust. Why? When the monitor is on, the screen creates an electrostatic field, which attracts dust.

After cleaning your monitor's screen, you may want to install a glare-reducing screen to improve visibility.

Do It Yourself   Clean Your Screen

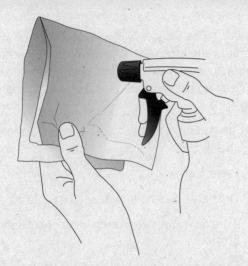

1 First, turn the monitor off. Spray some household cleaner onto a cloth. Don't spray too much; you want the cloth damp, not soaked.

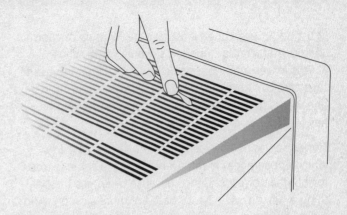

3 If there's any dust or dirt caught in the ventilation slots or other nooks-and-crannies of the monitor, dampen some cotton-tipped swabs with cleaner, and then use the swabs to clean the hard-to-reach places. Remember: Not too much cleaner. Use a dry cloth to wipe off any remaining cleaner.

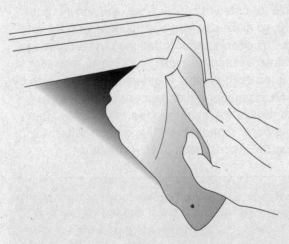

2 Use the cloth to wipe clean the cabinet of the monitor (but not the screen itself). If the monitor hasn't been cleaned for a while, it will probably have caked-on grime that will need some extra cleaner. Do not be tempted to spray the cleaner directly on the monitor cabinet; the excess cleaner may seep inside the monitor. Instead, simply go over the same area a few more times.

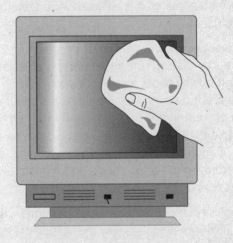

4 Wet another cloth with plain water and use it to clean off the monitor screen. Window cleaner is generally not recommended unless it is specifically designed for both glass and plastic surfaces. Regular window cleaner might harm the plastic coating used on some antiglare screens.

5 If you opted for the antistatic cloth, let the screen dry. Then use the cloth to wipe off the surface. Keep the cloth handy and use it on a weekly (or even daily) basis to keep dust off the monitor screen.

Clean Your Printer

Just about everyone's least favorite Peanuts cartoon strip character is Pigpen, a slovenly youth who always leaves a trail of grit behind him. Pigpen doesn't take care of himself, and his appearance shows it. No one wants to be around Pigpen's dust cloud, and he has few friends because of it.

Pigpen serves as an excellent example of a case in which appearances mean everything. The same is true for printed correspondence because often, it's the only thing a person will have to base an impression on. And a dirty printer makes for dirty documents. Because no one sees your fancy Armani suit when they read a letter you've sent them, their opinion of you is formed almost completely from the document they hold in their hands. Though the logic is sometimes strange, it's true: A dirty or smudged document must mean the person who prepared it is a Pigpen. And therefore, he has no friends.

If you want your work to impress people, a great way to start is by making sure your printer is producing the fine high-quality pages it's designed to produce. A minute spent cleaning the outside (and sometimes the inside) of your printer every now and then can help guarantee that your documents come out crisp and sharp. In addition, regular cleaning helps keep your printer running in tip-top shape, and it might even help prevent premature failure.

Most folks have one of three types of printers: laser, inkjet, or dot-matrix. Cleaning the outside of these three types is generally the same; cleaning the innards differs, though, because they all use different printing technologies. In the "Do It Yourself" section that follows, we provide instructions for general printer cleaning. (For deep-down inside cleaning, you will want to refer to the manual that came with the printer; the manufacturer may want you to perform some very specific cleaning steps required for the exact model you are using.)

What do you need to clean your printer? Not much. Here's a short list:

- Paper towels
- Ordinary household cleaner, like Fantastik or 409
- A medium-sized (half-inch-wide or so) soft artist's brush
- Some cotton-tipped swabs (Q-Tips)
- Printer cleaner paper

The printer cleaner paper described here is available at most any computer store. Different versions are available for different printer types (and some printer models), so make sure you buy the right kind for your printer. The cleaner paper is designed to feed through your printer like regular paper; in doing so, however, it picks up excess gunk that is otherwise hard to reach by hand. Most printer cleaner paper can be reused, though usually not more than five to ten times. The cleaning paper represents the easiest and safest way of cleaning the internal parts of your computer.

> For heavy deposits of grime, put the cleaner paper through the printer several times, and then throw away the gross thing when you're done.

Do It Yourself Clean the Printer, Inside and Out

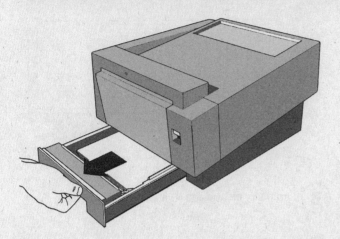

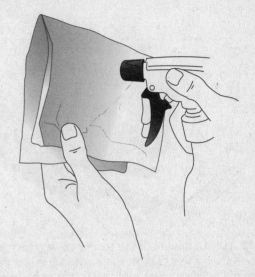

1 Turn the printer off and unplug it. Then remove all paper from the printer, and remove the paper trays.

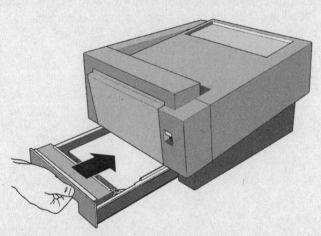

3 With the printer turned off, clean the outside of it using the household spray and paper towels. Lightly spray the household cleaner onto a towel, and use the damp towel to remove any dust and dirt from the printer.

2 If your printer uses a paper tray, clean it out by wiping it with a dry paper towel. Be sure to get all the dirt and paper dust out. Put the paper back in the tray, and then reinsert the tray into the printer when you're finished.

4 For laser printers, press the Release button (shown here) to open the printer so you can access the inside. Use the soft artist's brush to gently wipe away any dirt and paper dust that may have accumulated. Close the printer when you're done.

5 For inkjet printers, remove the ink cartridge (or cartridges). Use the brush to clean in and around the cartridge area. Replace the cartridge(s) when you're done.

6 For dot-matrix printers, use the brush to clean out any loose dirt or paper dust that has accumulated around the paper platen or the print head.

(continues)

Do It Yourself   Clean the Printer, Inside and Out   *(continued)*

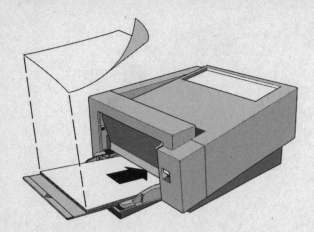

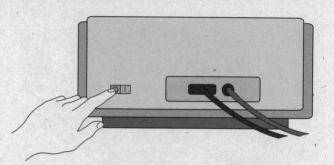

8 Turn the printer on and let it warm up if necessary.

7 Load a sheet of cleaner paper into the printer. (When using a laser or inkjet printer, load the cleaner paper on top of the regular paper; when using a dot-matrix printer, simply load the paper into the platen.) Be sure to observe proper orientation, as the cleaner paper is usually designed to go in a particular way. The paper may become jammed in the printer if you put it in backwards or upside-down.

9 Print a blank page using a word processor or text editor. (When using Windows, for example, start the Windows Notepad program.) In the empty blank document screen of Notepad (or whatever program), choose File, Print. Printing starts immediately. After the cleaning paper is pushed through the printer, remove it completely and store it for future use.

Change the Toner in Your Laser Printer

Of the three basic printer types: dot-matrix, inkjet, and laser, the laser printer produces the best quality printout. However, in order to maintain this high quality, you will need to change the toner in your laser printer from time to time. Before you attempt to change the toner, you might need to understand a bit about how your laser printer produces a printed page.

First of all, after a page description is sent to the printer from your software program, the entire page is composed within your printer's memory. That's why there's a bit of a delay before each page is printed. The images on the page (both text and graphics) are composed of tiny dots. If you imagine placing tiny checkers on a large checkerboard, you'll get the basic idea of how laser images are formed.

Once the page is composed in memory, the page is ready to be printed. Using its laser, the printer transfers the series of dots onto a drum, producing a reverse image of the entire page. The process works like this: When hit by the laser, a dot appears on the electrostatically charged drum. The dots hold a negative charge of electricity. As the drum rolls past the toner cartridge, its magnetic ink adheres to the drum at these negatively charged points. Meanwhile, the paper is passed by a charged wire (called the corona wire), which causes it to pick up a slight static charge. As the statically

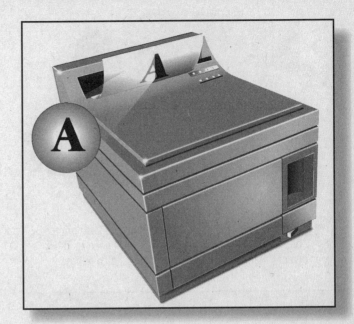

charged paper passes by the inked drum, the image of the page is transferred.

This whole process is remarkably similar to that used by a standard office copier. And like a copier, the toner cartridge in a laser printer must be changed from time to time. You'll know that you need to change the toner when your printouts are no longer dark and crisp.

Do It Yourself   Insert a New Toner Cartridge

1 Turn off your laser printer. Then open the laser printer by pressing its hatch release button. (You'll need to check your owner's manual for the location of the hatch release.)

> Changing the toner cartridge is a messy business. Before you begin, line the space around the printer with some old newspaper to catch any ink particles that may fall off the toner. Roll up your sleeves, and flip your tie out of harm's way

2 Grab the old cartridge by its tab and lift up and out to remove. Dump the cartridge into a bag or a box to contain its ink, and then place it in the trash.

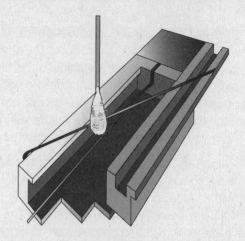

3 Remove any loose toner dust from the inside of your printer using a clean cloth and rubbing alcohol. You may want to clean the corona wire as well, using the special brush most manufacturer's supply just for this purpose, or a cotton swap dipped in rubbing alcohol.

> Your manufacturer may recommend that when you change the toner, you also change other things as well, such as a felt filter. Check the owner's manual for additional instructions.

4 Remove your new toner cartridge from its foil wrapper. Gently rock the cartridge back and forth a few times to distribute its ink. Then remove the seal that holds the toner in place.

5 Holding the new cartridge by its tab, slide it into the printer until it snaps into place. Close the laser door.

6 Turn the printer on and print out a few test pages before you print anything you want to keep. These first few pages will usually come out streaked with tiny ink particles that came loose from the toner during the changing process.

Change the Cartridge in Your Inkjet Printer

Although they don't offer the incredible quality of laser printers, inkjet printers are becoming more popular, for several reasons. For one, their print quality is greatly improved from earlier models, so that now it comes close to laser quality, at least for most purposes. Secondly, inkjet printers offer a feature that laser printers cannot (at least, not at an affordable price), and that's color. So if you're willing to lose some print quality, you can get an inkjet printer with the benefit of color for about the same price as most laser printers.

An inkjet printer, like a laser printer, creates text and graphics by applying ink to a page in a series of small dots. The way in which the dots of ink are applied to the paper varies a bit because there are actually two different types of inkjet printers: bubble jet and drop-on-demand. Although there are some mechanical differences, both printers work by heating ink and pushing a bubble or jet of it toward the paper to form a small dot.

The printhead of an inkjet printer contains a series of small vertical holes (nozzles) through which the ink is sprayed. The print head moves back and forth across the page and then down one line at a time, until the entire page is printed. This process is similar to the manner in which a typewriter head moves across a piece of paper as you type.

Most inkjet printers sold today are color printers. The printhead of color inkjet printers contain many ink cartridges, each of a different primary color. Additional colors are formed on the page by blending these single primary colors.

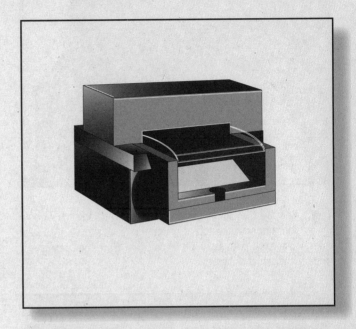

You'll probably find that the black ink cartridge runs out faster than the other colors, as text is usually printed in black. You can easily change one or all of the cartridges when needed, so this is not a problem.

Inkjet cartridges can be a bit pricey. One way to reduce the cost is to refill the cartridges yourself using a special refill kit. One warning, however: The process can be quite a messy one. Basically, you refill the cartridge through a hole in its top, using a small ink bottle with a long nozzle.

Do It Yourself Insert a New InkJet Cartridge

1 Remove the old ink cartridge by pulling backwards with your finger at the top of the cartridge, as shown. It should snap loose easily with just a bit of pressure. Place the used cartridge in a bag and discard.

If you have a color inkjet, pop the top of the printing unit to reveal its individual ink cartridges.

2 Unpack the new cartridge and remove the seal from its printhead. Hold the cartridge so that the pointed notch on its top points toward the green dot on the cartridge holder.

3 Holding the cartridge as before, slide it gently into place. Apply a bit of pressure with your thumb, and you should hear the cartridge snap into place.

Clean the Keyboard

No other part of your computer gets as grimy and yucky as the keyboard. And no wonder: You spend the day pounding on the keys and getting them all dirty. The little slots and openings between the keys seem to trap airborne dust willies, not to mention crumbs from those Cheetos you've been eating. Even your hair can fall into the keyboard and scuz up the works.

Okay, so now you know the bad news. The good news is that cleaning your keyboard is a simple job you can do any time. However, if you're cleaning your keyboard now because you just spilled something on it, ▶**see the task "Remove Liquid Spilled on Keyboard or Mouse" (page 294) for additional help.◀**

Here are the things you need to clean a keyboard:

- Some high-quality paper towels.

- Household nonresidue spray cleaner, like Formula 409 or Fantastik. Don't use harsh soaps, detergents, or furniture cleaner.

- A soft artist's brush, about one-half to three-quarters of an inch wide.

Do It Yourself Give Your Keyboard a General Cleaning

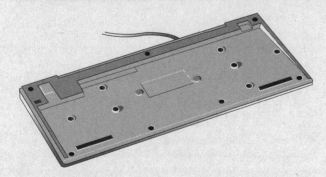

1 Turn the computer off. Lay several paper towels on the desk, and then turn the keyboard over and gently shake out any excess gunk. If there's an accumulation of dirt inside, gently tap on the back side of the keyboard to dislodge the excess.

2 Turn the keyboard back over. Use the brush to whisk out any remaining dirt, fur balls, and other foreign matter from between the keys.

(continues)

Do It Yourself Give Your Keyboard a General Cleaning   *(continued)*

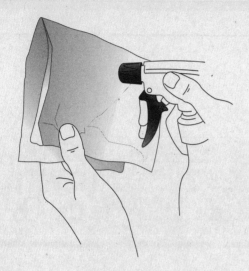

4 Use the cloth to wipe clean the tops of the keys. If the keyboard hasn't been cleaned for a while, it will probably have caked on grime that will need some extra work. Do not be tempted to spray cleaner directly on the keys; it may seep inside the keyboard. Instead, simply repeat the cleaning with a new cloth and some elbow grease.

5 Dry the keys with a new, dry cloth. Wait ten minutes for all the cleaner to evaporate before you turn the computer back on.

3 Spray some household cleaner onto the cloth. Don't spray too much; you just want the cloth damp, not soaked.

You will get best results if you clean the keyboard often. A buildup of muck can cause the keyboard to malfunction, requiring that it be replaced. Most computer keyboards are fairly inexpensive and can be replaced for under $50. But there's no sense in spending that money if you don't need to. Keep your keyboard clean, and it'll last longer.

Clean the Mouse

Thanks to Microsoft Windows, most computers—whether they are used in the office or at home—have a mouse. This little contraption lets you move an on-screen pointer by pushing a small soap-like device around the desk. The mouse works by rolling action: As you push the mouse, a ball underneath the thing turns, which in turn pushes an on-screen pointer in a similar direction.

No matter how good a housekeeper you are, in time the ball (and the delicate insides of the mouse) will get gritty and dirty. Periodic cleaning keeps the mouse in top shape and prevents premature wear. It also helps prevent these annoying side effects:

- The pointer "skips" and drags when you push the mouse. That is, instead of moving in a smooth motion, the pointer freezes then zooms whenever you push the mouse.

- The pointer doesn't move at all when you push the mouse. Although this problem can also be caused by such things as the mouse not being plugged in, it's also a sign that the mouse is dirty, especially if the pointer moves in one direction (like up and down) but not in the other direction (left and right).

- You hear crunching noises when you roll the mouse.

All of these are good indications that the mouse is dirty and should be cleaned. You're better off, however, if you don't wait for signs like these before you clean your mouse. It can be very difficult to remove months and months (or years and years) of dirty buildup inside the mouse. And dirty insides can wear down the rubber ball in the underbelly of the mouse. If the ball gets pitted and worn because of dirt, the mouse has to be replaced. They don't often sell replacement mouse balls, so you have to fork out for a whole new mouse, not just the ball.

You don't need anything special to clean the mouse. Often, a facial tissue is all that's required. But if the

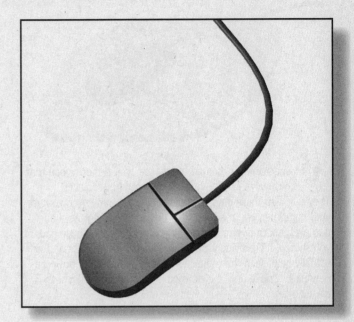

mouse suffers from a severe case of the grungies, you should add the following items to your cleaning repertoire:

- A pencil with an eraser. Just an ordinary eraser on an ordinary pencil will do. But the eraser should be clean.

- A couple of round toothpicks. Better yet, an "orange stick" from a manicure set.

- A small (quarter-inch-wide) artist's brush.

You can also purchase a mouse cleaner kit from most computer stores. About the only ingredient of the kit that's really worth the purchase price is the special cleaner engineered for use on the rubber mouse ball. This is the only cleaner you should use with the mouse ball. Do not use household cleaners, soaps, detergents, alcohol, or anything else. (In a pinch, you can use a little bit of water to remove excess crud from the ball.)

> Remember: Don't use cleaning fluid on the mouse ball. The fluid might dry out the rubber.

Do It Yourself Clean Your Mouse's Insides

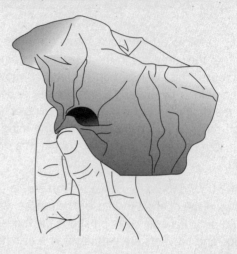

1 Inspect the mouse pad, if you use one. A mouse pad that is old, worn out, or visibly dirty should be replaced. They're cheap these days, and depending on how often you use your computer, you may want to consider replacing the mouse pad every six to twelve months. If you don't use a mouse pad, you should. It'll provide a better surface for your mouse and will actually help clean the mouse while you use it. When buying a new pad, choose only the cloth-covered ones, not the cheap plastic ones.

4 Use the facial tissue to wipe off the ball. If the mouse is extra dirty, use a small amount of water to help clean it off. If you're using a mouse cleaning kit, you can use the special cleaner that comes with the kit. Do not use any other kind of cleaner, especially cleaners containing alcohol. The alcohol can dry out the rubber of the ball and ruin it.

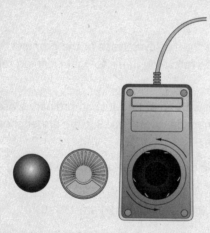

2 With the computer off, turn the mouse over and carefully remove the ball. On many brands of mice, this is done by twisting a plastic retaining ring a quarter or a half turn. If you're not sure how to remove the retaining ring and find no instructions printed on the bottom of the mouse, consult the manual that came with the mouse. Forcing the ring can break it, and you'll end up having to replace the entire mouse.

3 After you've removed the ring, empty the ball into your hand. Be careful not to drop it. The mouse ball is made of a special kind of rubber that can be permanently deformed if it's dropped on a hard surface.

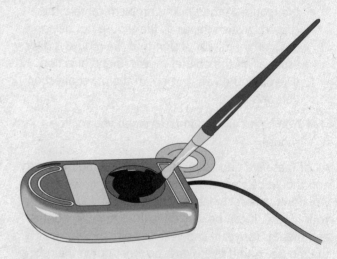

5 Use the brush to clean out excess dirt, lint, and other junk from the inside of the mouse. Avoid trying to blow out the gunk, with either your own breath or a can of compressed air. All this usually does is force the dirt deeper into the mouse.

Do It Yourself Clean Your Mouse's Insides

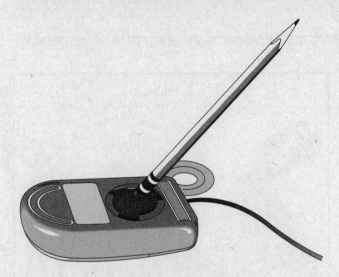

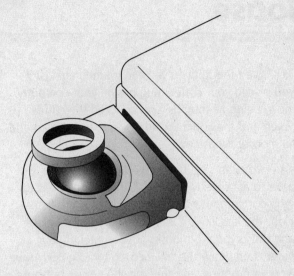

6 Rollers inside the mouse transmit the direction of the rolling ball to the computer; often dirt gets caked on these. This dirt is best removed with toothpicks and a pencil eraser. If you use the eraser, be sure errant eraser bits don't get trapped inside the mouse. Wipe out the insides of the mouse frequently when you are cleaning the rollers. For best results, the rollers should be completely free of caked-on grime. Any foreign matter will interfere with the smooth operation of the mouse.

8 Replace the retaining ring by placing it over the ball, and turning it to lock it back into position.

9 If your computer is equipped with a trackball instead of a mouse, the same cleaning steps apply. Trackballs should be cleaned more frequently, however, to remove dirt and the residue of skin oils. Note that most trackballs use a hard plastic ball instead of the semisoft rubber ball used in a mouse. This plastic ball can be cleaned with an ordinary household cleaner, such as Formula 409 or Fantastik.

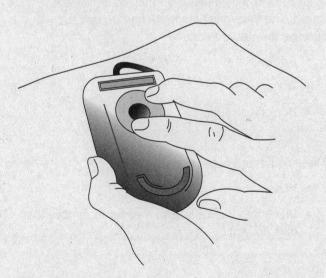

7 When you finish cleaning all the components (be sure all dirt, dust, eraser bits, and so forth are out), drop the ball back into the mouse.

Remove Liquid Spilled on Keyboard or Mouse

Yikes! Even though you've been warned against it, you placed your coffee mug beside your computer. And now, being all thumbs, you knocked the coffee mug over, and the liquid spilled inside the keyboard and on the mouse. What now?

Odds are, you can save both keyboard and mouse, but you have to act quickly. The most important step is to turn off your computer. The faster you turn the computer off, the less likely it is that a short circuit will damage the keyboard, mouse, or computer. If your computer is on when the spill occurs, try to quickly save any work in progress, and then hit the power button. With the computer safely turned off, you can go about trying to undo the damage you did.

The steps that follow involve disassembling the mouse or keyboard. There's a certain risk in damaging the mouse or keyboard even further by taking them apart, but consider this: Most mice and keyboards cost under $50. You don't risk much by trying to fix things yourself. And, if a new mouse or keyboard doesn't cost very much, there's no sense taking either one to the repair shop. The average repair bill there runs $75 for labor alone.

Of course, all this doesn't apply to laptop computers or specialty keyboards or mice—which may cost much more than $40. Use your own discretion in trying to fix those items yourself.

Although these first-aid directions are generic, they apply to the majority of keyboard and mouse designs now available. Some designs are different, and you'll have to accommodate them.

Your success at reviving a keyboard or mouse that's suffered a liquid spill depends on the liquid that was spilled. The following liquids are hard to get out because they leave a residue:

- Coffee
- Tea
- Drinks with sugar
- Juice

These liquids are easier to get out:

- Water
- Diet sodas (the clear kind is easier to remove than dark liquids)

Do It Yourself   Remove Liquid Spilled on the Keyboard

1 Unplug the keyboard from the computer. This is a precautionary measure to prevent further damage to your computer.

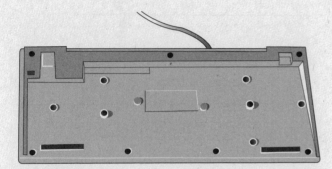

2 Spread out some paper towels on your desk. Then turn the keyboard over and let the excess fluid drip out.

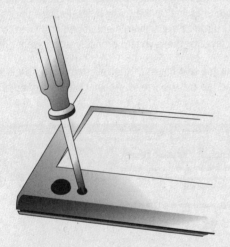

3 Using a small Phillips-head screwdriver, remove the screws on the bottom of the keyboard. Save the screws in a small cup. Note: On some keyboards, the screws are hidden (such as under stickers). Peel back the stickers to reveal all the screws, and then remove them.

4 Carefully separate the two halves of the keyboard casing.

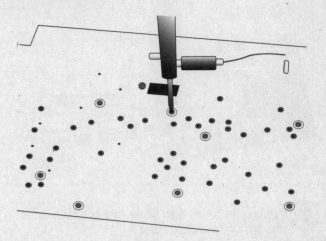

5 Using a jeweler's Phillips-head screwdriver (available at Radio Shack and many hobby stores), remove all the screws you see on the back side of the main printed circuit board inside the keyboard. Be sure to save all of these screws, too. The keyboard may not work right if you are missing just one of these screws when you put the thing back together.

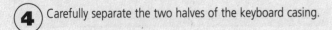

6 Carefully lift off the printed circuit board. Inside are the foam "cushions" attached to the back side of the keys. (Not all keyboards use this design, but many do. Your keyboard may use a rubber membrane, but the cleaning steps are generally the same.) These foam cushions are made with a piece of metalized plastic, so that when you press down on a key, electrical contact is made on the circuit board. Carefully inspect the foam cushions. If any are loose, use Super Glue to glue them back. If any are soaked with liquid, the keyboard is most likely totaled, and you should get a new one.

(continues)

Do It Yourself　Remove Liquid Spilled on the Keyboard　*(continued)*

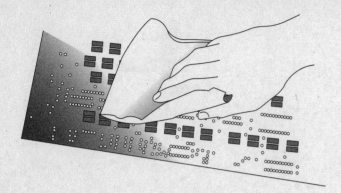

7 With a paper towel, clean off the contact surface of the keyboard's printed circuit board.

8 With another paper towel or with a cotton-tipped swab, gently clean off the metalized foil on the back side of the key contacts. You may want to wet the towel slightly with distilled water to help get the residue off. Don't wipe too vigorously, or you'll pull the cushion off the key.

9 Let the keyboard dry as long as you can. Overnight would be best.

10 When it's dry, replace the keyboard circuit board, being careful to line up the screw holes. Replace the screws and tighten, but don't overtighten. Remember: You need to replace all the screws, or the keyboard probably won't work right.

11 Put the two halves of the keyboard casing back together and replace the screws. Again, do not overtighten.

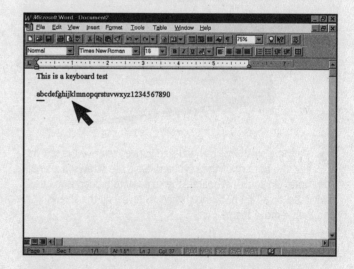

12 Test the keyboard by plugging it back into the computer. Turn the computer on. If the computer doesn't indicate a "stuck key failure" or other error message, try pressing each key to make sure it works. Be sure you test all the keys, including editing keys and function keys. Use one of your application programs, like a word processor, to test the full operation of the keyboard.

Do It Yourself Remove Liquid Spilled on a Mouse

1 Unplug the mouse from the computer. This is a pre-cautionary measure to prevent further damage to your computer.

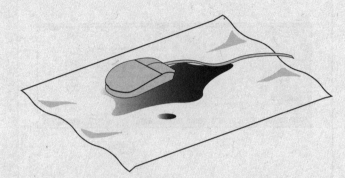

2 Spread out some paper towels on your desk. Place the mouse on it to let the excess liquid ooze out.

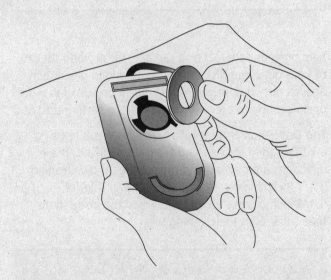

3 Open the mouse by twisting the plastic retaining ring on the bottom a quarter or a half turn. If you're not sure how to remove the retaining ring and no instructions are printed on the bottom of the mouse, consult the manual that came with the mouse. Forcing the ring can break it, and you'll end up having to replace the entire mouse.

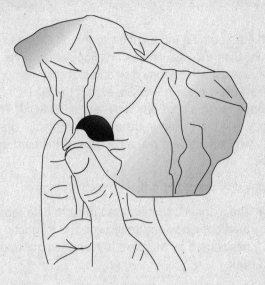

4 Remove the roller ball and clean it with plain water and a facial tissue. You can use distilled water if you want; it may work better for removing residue.

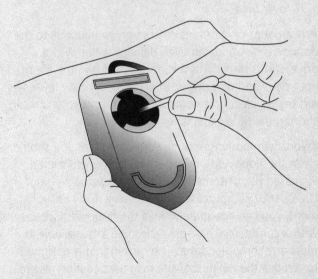

5 Use a cotton-tipped swab to remove the liquid inside the mouse. Let the mouse dry as long as you can. Overnight would be best.

6 When the mouse is dry, replace the ball and retaining ring.

7 Test the mouse by plugging it back into the computer. Turn the computer on. If the computer doesn't indicate an error message, try using the mouse by moving it on your table. Click all the buttons on the mouse to determine whether they work.

Clean the Disk Drives

There's nothing more critical to the operation of your PC than the cleanliness of its floppy disk drives. Everyone uses the floppy disk drives of their computer at least every once in a while, even if the PC is equipped with a hard disk drive and a CD-ROM. The floppy drives are used to install new programs, share data with others, and make backups of the hard disk drive.

Floppy disk drives get dirty in three ways:

- The magnetic coating used to store data rubs off the floppy disk and collects on the magnetic heads used by the drive to read the data from the disk.

- Dust and grime from the outside gets inside the drive when you insert a dirty disk.

- Dust naturally settles inside the floppy disk drive over time.

Any amount of dust and dirt can prove injurious to the data on a disk and can even damage a floppy disk drive. Dirt is gritty, and this grit can shorten the life of your disks and disk drives. In addition, a heavy layer of dirt makes electronic components run hotter, which can shorten their life expectancy.

If you clean nothing else on your computer, you should clean the floppy disk drives. If you don't, you run an increased risk of someday losing some valuable data. Unless your computer is used in a very dusty environment, you can adequately clean the floppy disk drives with a commercial disk-drive-cleaning kit, available at most any computer store. The cleaning kit is designed to remove the buildup of the magnetic coating (as well as dirt) that can collect on the magnetic heads inside the drive. Using the kit every couple of months can

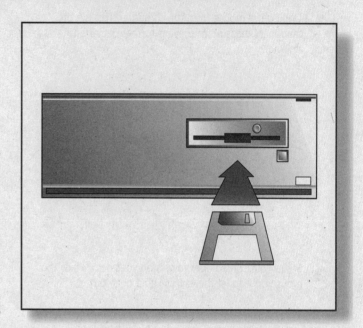

help prevent data loss and can actually prolong the life of your disks and disk drives. As an added precaution against dirty disk drives, store your floppy disks in a box or disk caddy to prevent the disks from getting dusty.

The *Do It Yourself* that follows assumes you're using a kit designed for cleaning floppy disk drives. These directions are generic and the pictures show cleaning 3 1/2-inch disk drives (kits are also available for 5 1/4-inch drives); for specifics, read the instructions that come with the cleaning kit.

Are your disk drives really dirty inside? You should remove the cover of the PC and clean inside, including the disk drives, ▶as explained in "Clean Inside Your Computer" on page 277.◀

Do It Yourself   Clean the Floppy Drives

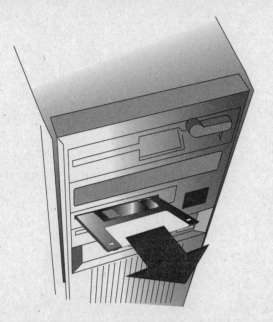

1 Leaving the computer turned on, remove any disks from the disk drives. (Removing the disk may seem pretty obvious, but you'd be surprised how many times people have tried to clean the floppy drives with a disk still inside!)

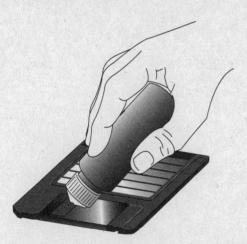

2 Using the cleaning spray included with the cleaning kit, liberally coat the cleaning-pad disk. Spray both sides of the disk. There are two magnetic heads inside the floppy disk drive: one for the top of the disk and one for the bottom.

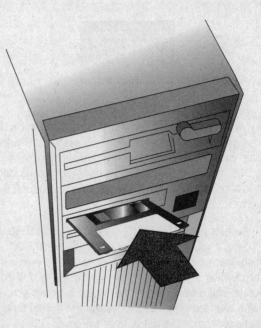

3 Insert the cleaning-pad disk into the floppy disk drive, just as if it were a regular floppy disk; make sure the opening of the carrier goes in first.

4 If you are using Windows, activate the disk drive by starting File Manager or Explorer. Click the icon for the disk drive containing the cleaning pad disk—either A: or B:. File Manager/Explorer will indicate an error. Click Retry several times to reactivate the drive. (Activation turns the pad, which cleans the magnetic heads in the disk drive.) If your cleaning kit comes with a program disk, use that program to activate the disk drives.

5 If you are using DOS, at the DOS prompt type the letter of the drive that contains the cleaning disk, followed by a colon, such as A: or B:. Then press Enter to activate the disk drive. After a moment, an error message appears, telling you the disk could not be read. Press R (to choose Retry) a few times to reactivate the drive.

(continues)

Do It Yourself Clean the Floppy Drives *(continued)*

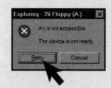

6 When you are done cleaning, remove the cleaning disk. If you're using the Windows File Manager or Windows Explorer, choose Cancel to stop reading the floppy disk. If you're using DOS, type F (for Fail) to tell the computer you no longer want to access the disk drive (you may have to choose Fail more than once).

7 Repeats steps 3 through 7 to clean the other floppy disk drive, if your computer is so equipped. IMPORTANT: After cleaning, wait at least five minutes (ten minutes is even better) for the cleaning solution that remains in the floppy disk drives to evaporate. This is an important step; trying to access a regular disk with wet read/write heads may cause even more buildup of magnetic coating on the heads inside the drive.

Unstick a Jammed Disk

It happens to most people eventually. You insert a disk, but it doesn't come back out. The disk is jammed, and no matter how hard you tug, the disk just won't come out.

The most common reason for a jammed disk is that the disk was inserted incorrectly. This is especially true of 3.5-inch disks, which contain a metal slide that can get jammed inside the works of the drive. Another common reason for jammed disks, especially the 3.5-inch variety, is a disk label that's come off. The label catches on the inside of the drive, and prevents you from pulling the disk out.

If you are the victim of a stuck disk, follow these steps to extract it from your computer disk drive. Warning: Even if you are very careful, there is the possible risk of damaging the disk.

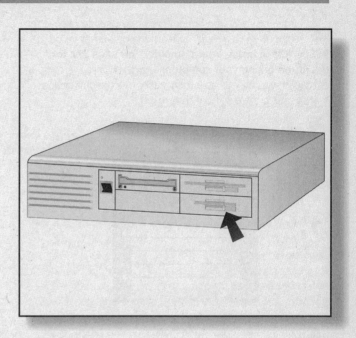

For a really stuck disk, you may need to take your computer into the repair shop.

Do It Yourself   Remove a Stuck Disk

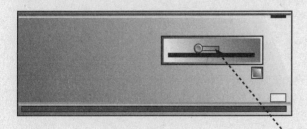

1 If the drive is the 5.25-inch variety, open the latch and try to wiggle the disk free. Sometimes, you can help extricate the disk by repeatedly opening and closing the latch.

2 If the drive is the 3.5-inch variety, push the release button all the way in and try to grab the disk with your fingers. If the disk doesn't come out far enough, try gently grasping it with a small pair of pliers. Don't pull so hard that you damage the drive or disk.

(continues)

Do It Yourself Remove a Stuck Disk (continued)

3 If the disk still won't budge, you may need to remove the computer's lid in order to reach the disk drives inside. ▶**(See "Clean Inside Your Computer" on page 277 for details on taking your computer apart.)**◀ Once the computer is apart, you may be able to manually free the obstruction that's keeping the disk from coming out.

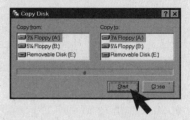

4 On 3.5-inch disks: If the metal slide was caught in the drive, more than likely it is now bent or damaged. Do not reinsert this disk into the drive, or it will get stuck again. The disk is not totally ruined, however. Carefully pry the metal slide from the disk. It is only there to protect the disk and is not absolutely required. Be careful not to touch the exposed disk or you may lose your data.

5 Once the slide is off the disk, insert the disk and copy its contents to a new undamaged disk. Verify that the copy is good, and then throw away the damaged disk.

Clean a CD-ROM Drive

CD-ROMs have been around for more than ten years, but only recently have they become really popular. These days, all new computers come with a CD-ROM drive already installed.

CD-ROM drives are used to read data stored on five-inch plastic discs. The discs look just like audio CDs. In fact, they are pretty much the same, except that a CD-ROM is designed to hold computer data instead of music. The big advantage of a CD-ROM is that one disc can store at least 600 million bytes of information. That's equivalent to roughly 500 high-density floppy disks!

Just like everything else in your computer, CD-ROM drives are prone to get dirty—especially the optical lens through which the disc is read. And when they get dirty, they don't work as well. The most common symptom of a dirty CD-ROM drive is something called random read errors. This simply means that the drive fails to read data on a more-or-less random basis. The software that controls the CD-ROM in your computer compensates for a few of these random read errors (the disk just re-reads the bad part), but it can't compensate for lots of errors. The result is a cryptic error message that says something like Drive X not ready or, worse yet, a malfunctioning program.

Fortunately, CD-ROM drives don't often get as dirty as other parts of your computer, and cleaning them is a rather straightforward task. For best results, use a commercial CD cleaning kit to keep your CD-ROM drive in tip-top shape. Because the basic mechanism of a

CD-ROM is identical to that of a home audio CD player, you can use a regular audio CD cleaning kit, which is essentially designed to clean the lens. (You should not attempt to clean the lens manually, as this could damage the fragile mounting of the lens.) There's no need to spend extra for an overpriced "CD-ROM cleaning kit."

The *Do It Yourself* that follows assumes you're using a CD cleaning kit, most of which consists of a cleaning disk and cleaning solution. These directions are generic; read the instructions that come with the particular cleaning kit you use for specifics.

Do It Yourself Clean Your PC's CD-ROM Drive

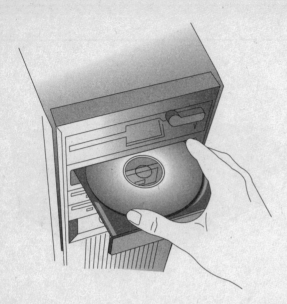

1 With your computer on, remove any disc from your CD-ROM drive. If your CD-ROM drive is the kind that uses disc caddies, have an empty caddy ready.

3 Insert the cleaning disk into the CD-ROM drive. (Put the cleaning disk in a caddy and then insert it, if your drive requires a caddy.)

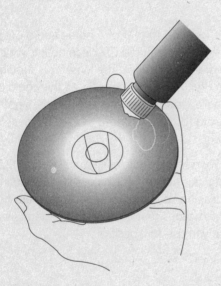

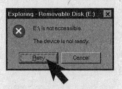

4 If you are using Windows, activate the CD-ROM drive by starting the File Manager or Explorer. Click the icon for the CD-ROM, such as D: or E:. File Manager/Explorer will indicate an error. Click Retry several times to reactivate the drive. (Activation turns the pad, which cleans the CD-ROM drive.) If your cleaning kit comes with a program disk, use that program to activate the disk drives.

2 Use the cleaner that comes with the kit to coat the cleaning disk. Don't apply too much cleaner. You need only apply the cleaner to the top of the disk, as a CD-ROM drive has only one read head (and not two, as in a floppy disk drive).

5 If you are using DOS, at the DOS prompt type the letter of the CD-ROM, followed by a colon, such as D: or E:. Then press Enter. Type DIR, and press Enter, to activate the drive. After a moment, an error message appears telling you the disc could not be read. Press R (to choose Retry) a few times to reactivate the drive.

Do It Yourself Clean Your PC's CD-ROM Drive

6 When you are done cleaning, remove the cleaning disc from the CD-ROM drive. If you're using the Windows Program Manager or Explorer, choose Cancel to stop reading the floppy disk. If you're using DOS, press F (to choose Fail) to tell the computer you no longer want to access the drive (you may have to choose Fail more than once).

7 After cleaning, wait at least five minutes (ten minutes is even better) for all the cleaning solution that remains in the CD-ROM drive to evaporate.

8 CD-ROMs can get dirty, too, and these should be cleaned if you notice any dirt and smudges on them. CD-ROM discs can be cleaned with a CD disc cleaner, available at most any music or record store. The cleaner comes with a cleaning mechanism and a bottle of cleaning liquid. Avoid the use of household cleaners (like Formula 409 or Fantastik) or glass cleaner, as not all glass cleaners are designed for use with plastic.

Clean a Tape Backup Drive

If you're serious about the data on your computer's hard disk drive, you probably have a tape backup drive installed on your PC. The tape drive stores data on a special high-quality cassette. Each cassette can hold several hundred megabytes of data from your hard disk drive. If something should happen to the hard disk drive, you have the copy of the data on the tape as a backup. Hence the name.

Tape backup drives are little more than fancy audio cassette players—well, at least the general idea is the same. The drive uses a magnetic head to read and write pieces of information on a long length of tape. The tape is shuttled back and forth past the head, the way it is in an audio cassette player.

The magnetic heads used in a tape backup drive get dirty over time. They also pick up residual magnetic coating from the tape. This dirt and magnetic coating can interfere with the proper operation of the tape backup drive and can conceivably cause data loss. Obviously, the purpose of a tape backup drive is to prevent data loss; therefore, anything that jeopardizes your data should be avoided.

You know the tape backup drive needs to be cleaned if you get errors when trying to back up or restore data. You should not wait until you get these errors to clean the drive. Depending on how often you use the tape backup drive, you may want to make cleaning it a regular job. For example, you might clean the drive twice a year (or pick any other dates you think you'll remember). If you think you'll forget, write it down on a calendar.

As with floppy disk drives, you can purchase a cleaning kit especially designed for tape backup drives. Such a

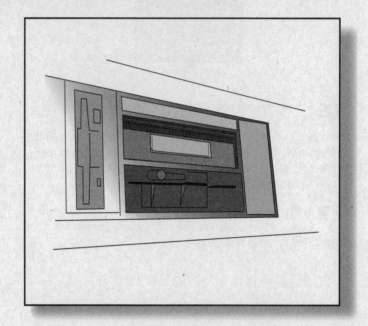

kit may even have been included with the drive when you bought it. You may also want to use a small artist's brush to aid in the cleaning.

The *Do It Yourself* steps that follow assume you're using a commercially available cleaning kit for tape backup drives; most of these consist of a cleaning tape and cleaning solution. These directions are generic. For specifics, read the instructions that come with the cleaning kit.

Tape backup drives use tapes of several different sizes. Be sure to get the cleaning kit for your particular kind of drive.

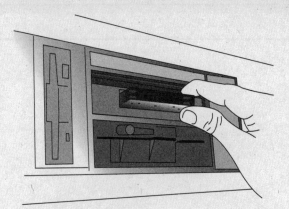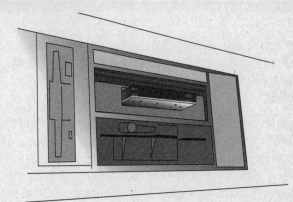

Do It Yourself   Clean a Tape Drive with a Cleaning Kit

1 With the computer on, remove any tapes from your tape backup drive.

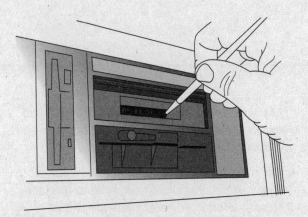

2 Use a small (quarter-inch-wide) artist's brush to whisk out any excess dust from the inside of the drive slot. To access this slot you will need to use your finger to open the protective door on the front of the drive.

3 Use the cleaner that comes with the cleaning tape to dampen it. Don't apply too much cleaner.

4 Insert the cleaning tape into the tape drive. Make sure you insert the cleaning tape the right way!

5 Use the software that comes with the cleaning kit to activate the tape backup drive. If no software is included, activate the drive by running your regular tape backup software. When you are done cleaning, exit the cleaning program that came with the cleaning kit. Remove the cleaning tape from the backup drive.

6 IMPORTANT: After cleaning, wait at least five minutes (ten minutes is even better) for all the cleaning solution that remains in the tape backup drive to evaporate. This is an important step; trying to use a backup tape with wet read/write heads may cause even more buildup of magnetic coating on the heads inside the drive.

Select and Install a Surge Protector

Snap! Crackle! Pop!! No, it's not breakfast cereal talking to you, it's the sound of various electrical demons that lurk inside the wiring at your home or office.

A little background: The juice at the electrical outlet is far from pure. The outlets in your home or office are supposed to deliver about 117 volts of electricity. But along with this 117 volts of regular electricity are short-lived jolts of much higher voltage—sometimes exceeding several hundred volts! The power supply inside your computer is designed to handle minor variations in excessive electricity, but it can't handle them all.

The problem is worse when there's an electrical storm. A nearby charge of lightning can get into the high tension lines, and some of that voltage can enter your computer by way of the power cord. A large enough bolt can permanently damage your computer, even if it's not turned on when the lightning strikes.

When there's a jolt of too much electricity in the power lines, it's called a spike or a surge. You can (and should) protect your computer investment by purchasing a surge protector, available at most any computer store. They're also available—usually for less money—at Radio Shack and many home-improvement or hardware stores. Just make sure you don't buy a simple power strip; check to be sure that it offers surge protection.

The typical surge suppressor looks like an electrical outlet strip. There are sockets for plugging in five or six electrical devices, like your computer, monitor, printer, external modem, and other goodies you have connected to your PC. Each outlet on the strip is protected against surges—those instantaneous spikes of too-high voltages. The strip is designed to filter out these surges and, in some cases, self-destruct if the voltage is way too high. It's cheaper to replace the surge protector than to replace all your computer gear.

Keep these points in mind when selecting a surge protector:

- Some power systems are inherently "dirtier" than others. In this case, "dirt" means lots of surges that can disrupt the operation of the computer.

Many modern high-rise buildings have big and expensive power conditioners that help filter out most of the surges.

- The most powerful surges come from lightning strikes. If you live in an area prone to thunderstorms—Florida, for example—you should definitely consider a surge protector for every electronic device in your house or office, such as your T.V. and your answering machine.

- Not all surges come from the outside like a lightning strike. Some are caused by appliances inside, such as a refrigerator or an air conditioner. In fact, surges like these are generally the most common.

- Many surges are not strong enough to do actual damage to your computer, but they can be troublesome just the same. For example, the surge from an electrical appliance (like a refrigerator) may not be strong enough to cause damage, but the spike could cause your computer to suffer momentary power overload. This can cause your computer to "freeze" in mid-track, which means you lose any data you were working on.

- Surges also occur over telephone lines; invest in a suppressor that contains a phone line surge suppressor. Then run your phone line through the surge suppressor before connecting it to your modem.

- Not all surge protectors are the same. Some do a better job at eliminating or reducing surges. You can gauge the quality of a surge suppressor by its specifications.

- Your best bet is to buy a quality name-brand surge protector from a reputable dealer. You can certainly pay too much for a surge protector, but for the most part, the ones that retail for under $10 generally don't provide enough protection. Watch magazines like Consumer Reports for

objective tests of surge suppressors. The better ones even offer insurance against computer damage.

- For best results, purchase a surge protector with a built-in circuit breaker. A circuit breaker rated at 15 to 20 amps is sufficient for computer use. You need the higher amperage if you use a laser printer.

- Surge suppressors can wear out. If your surge suppressor lacks an indicator that shows you it is no longer effectively blocking voltage spikes, you should replace the suppressor as a matter of course every 24 to 36 months (replace more often if you live in an area prone to lots of lightning strikes).

Do It Yourself Connect a Surge Suppressor

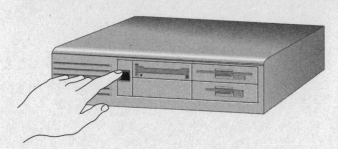

1 Turn off your computer and all other equipment connected to it (such as the printer, monitor, and external modem).

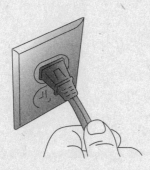

2 Unplug the power cords for your computer and peripherals from the wall.

3 Plug in the surge protector. Then plug all the power cords into the surge protector. If your surge suppressor offers phone line protection, insert your telephone line into the proper jack. Then run an additional phone line from the suppressor to your modem.

> If you have more power cords than surge-protector outlets, purchase a second surge protector. Do not plug extension cords into the surge suppressor. Plugging in too many electrical devices diminishes the effectiveness of the surge protector.

DO IT YOURSELF

Install New Programs

nstalling new programs isn't as hard as it sounds. Most programs nowadays come with special setup utilities that install the program for you. However, every program's setup utility is different, so you need to know how to handle the different types. In this section, you learn how to install programs in DOS, Windows 3.11, and Windows 95. You also learn how to uninstall (remove) programs when you no longer need them on your system.

Install a Program in Windows 95

With Windows 95's Install New Program Wizard, installing new programs is a breeze. You click an icon to add a new program to Windows, and then you follow the on-screen instructions. The Wizard leads you step-by-step through the installation process, telling you to insert the necessary disks (or disc), giving you a list of install commands to choose from, and starting the installation program for you.

Whether you're installing a DOS program, an old Windows 3.11 program, or a program designed especially for Windows 95, you can use the New Program Wizard to set it up under Windows 95.

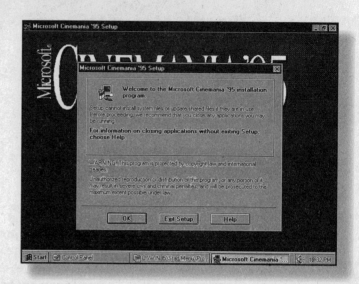

Do It Yourself   Add a Program to Windows 95

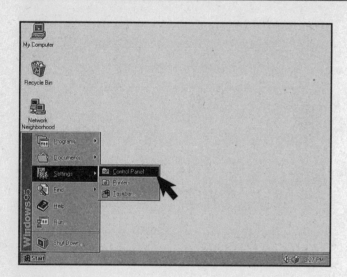

1 You use the Add/Remove Program icon, located in the Windows 95 Control Panel, to install new programs. Click the **Start** button, click **Settings**, and click **Control Panel**.

2 The Control Panel has icons that enable you to set up your system and enter your preferences. Double-click the **Add/Remove Programs** icon to install a new program.

Do It Yourself   Add a Program to Windows 95

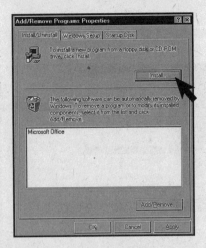

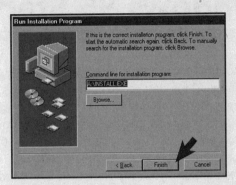

3 The Add/Remove Programs Properties dialog box is your key to installing programs. Click the **Install** button to begin. The Install New Program Wizard begins.

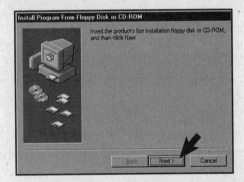

4 Insert the first floppy disk or the CD-ROM that stores the program into one of the drives. Then click the **Next** button.

5 The wizard searches your drives for a disk that contains a setup file. When it finds the file, it displays the file's name. If that is the correct file name, click the **Finish** button to start the program installation. If the file name is incorrect, click **Browse** and select the proper file name from the list. For example, some programs offer you several installation options, one for Windows 3.1 (otherwise known as 16-bit) and one for Windows 95 (32-bit), so you may need to use Browse to select the proper setup utility from the disk.

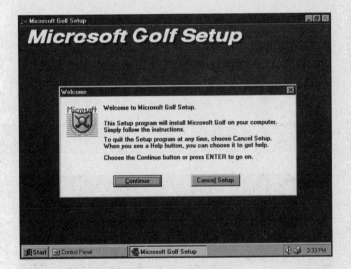

6 At this point, the setup utility will lead you step-by-step through the installation. Follow the on-screen instructions, choosing from any options you are given and inserting new disks as you are instructed.

Add a New Program to the Windows 95 Start Menu

Although a lot of programs will automatically add a command for starting them to the Windows 95 Start menu, some will not. Most often, those that do not are DOS programs, but they might be Windows 3.11 programs as well. In any case, it is an easy task to add a program to the Windows 95 Start menu. Then to open the program, you simply select its command from the Start menu, and Windows 95 starts it for you.

You should note that Start menu commands simply point to the startup files for the associated programs. This means that you can easily remove an unwanted command from the Start menu without harming the actual program itself. You might want to remove a command for a program you no longer use, for example. Or you might want to delete a command from one part of the Start menu and then add it somewhere else.

In order to add a program to the Start menu, you need to know the name of the directory in which the program's files are kept. In addition, you need to know the name of the file that starts the program. Typically, this file ends in .EXE and contains the name of the program

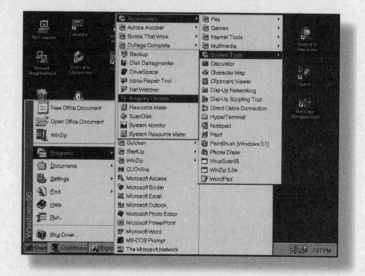

itself, such as GOLF.EXE. However, the startup file may end in .BAT or .COM, as in GOLF.BAT. Check the program's manual for help locating the name of the startup file.

Do It Yourself   Add Programs to the Start Menu

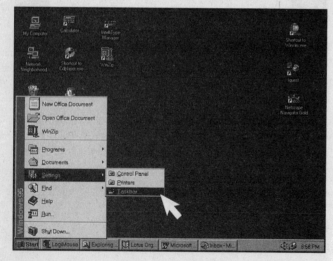

1 Click the **Start** button, select **Settings**, and then select **Taskbar**.

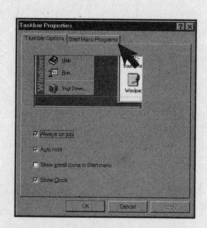

2 In the Taskbar Properties dialog box, click the **Start Menu Programs** tab.

Do It Yourself Add Programs to the Start Menu

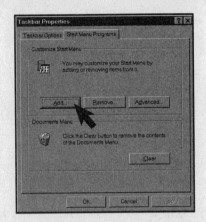

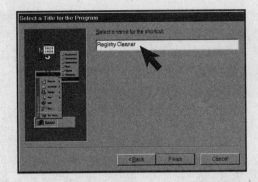

6 Type a name for the startup command as you'd like it to appear on the Start menu. Then click **Finish**.

3 Click **Add**, and the Create Shortcut dialog box appears.

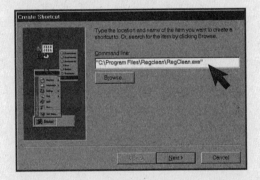

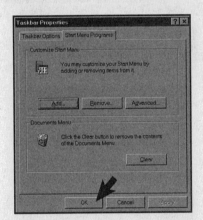

4 Enter the location of the startup file in the **Command Line** text box, or click **Browse** to select it from the list. (If you enter the command yourself, be sure to enclose it in quotation marks, as shown here.) Then click **Next**.

7 You're returned to the Taskbar Properties dialog box. Click **OK** to return to the Windows 95 desktop.

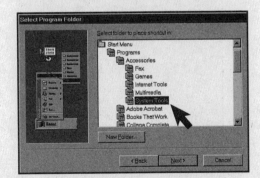

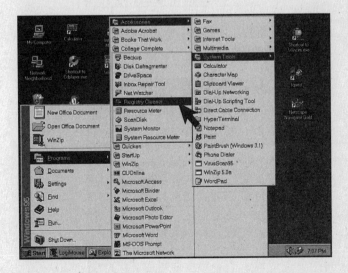

5 Click the folder in which you want to place the command for your new program. You can add it to the main Programs menu or to another folder. To create a new folder for the program, click **New Folder**, type a folder name, and click **OK**. With the desired folder selected, click **Next**.

8 To start your new program, click the **Start** button and select the program's command from the appropriate menu.

Do It Yourself Remove Programs from the Start Menu

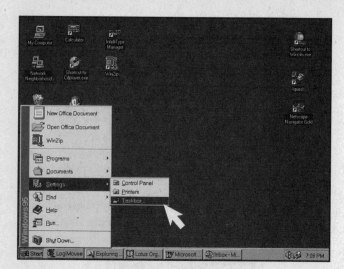

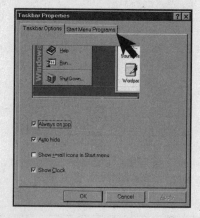

1 Click the **Start** button, select **Settings**, and then select **Taskbar**.

2 In the Taskbar Properties dialog box, click the **Start Menu Programs** tab.

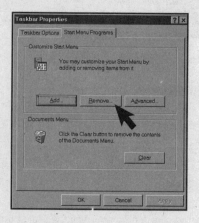

3 Click **Remove**, and the Remove Shortcuts/Folders dialog box appears.

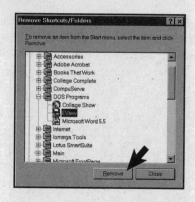

4 Click the command you want to remove, and then click **Remove**.

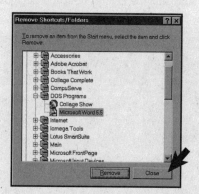

5 The command is removed from the displayed menu. Repeat step 4 to remove additional commands. When you finish, click **Close**.

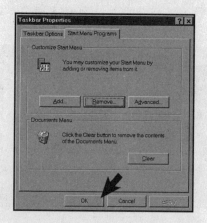

6 You're returned to the Taskbar Properties dialog box. Click **OK** to return to the Windows 95 desktop.

Install a Windows 3.11 Program

Included with your Windows 3.11 program is an installation (setup) utility. This program makes it easier to install the software on your computer's hard disk drive.

For the most part, this installation program—we'll call it a "SETUP utility"—is automatic. After you start the SETUP utility, the installation process more or less runs by itself. All the program files are copied to your hard drive, and an icon is automatically added to Windows. To start your new program after it is installed, all you have to do is double-click its icon in the Windows 3.11 Program Manager.

Depending on the software, the setup utility may need you to answer some questions about how you want the program installed. For example, you may need to tell the SETUP utility the name of the directory on your computer's hard disk drive into which you want the program files copied. You may also need to indicate the options of the software you want to use. The SETUP utility uses this information to copy only the needed files from the program disks to your computer's hard drive.

As it was in the task on installing a program from the DOS prompt, the name "SETUP utility" is generic here. The name of the actual program that does the installation may not be called SETUP. Although SETUP is by far the most common, the installation utility may be named INSTALL or something else. If you're not sure of the program's name, check the documentation.

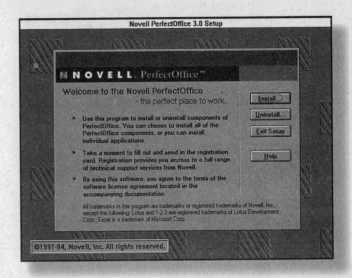

Don't be afraid to read the manual that comes with the Windows 3.11 software you are installing. It may provide useful tips and hints for installing the program on your computer.

Before installing any new software, you should make copies of your important system configuration files (AUTOEXEC.BAT, CONFIG.SYS, WIN.INI, and SYSTEM.INI). ▶**Refer to "Make a Backup of Important System Files" on page 400 for details on how to do this.**◀

Do It Yourself   Add a Program to Windows 3.11

Setup

1 After opening the software package, find the disk that contains the SETUP utility. This disk is often marked SETUP or INSTALL (or with some other descriptive name).

(continues)

Do It Yourself Add a Program to Windows 3.11 *(continued)*

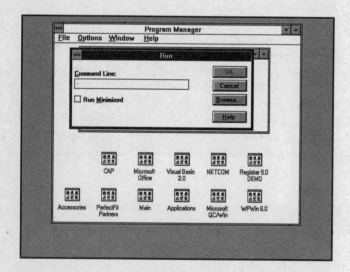

2 Start your computer if it's not already on. To run Windows 3.11 (if it's not already running), type **WIN** at the DOS prompt. Then put the setup disk in your computer's disk drive.

3 From the Windows Program Manager, select **File**, **Run**. The Run dialog box appears.

4 In the **Command Line** text box, type **A:\SETUP** or **B:\SETUP**, depending on the floppy disk drive that contains the SETUP disk, and then click **OK**. (If you are installing the software from a CD-ROM, use instead the drive letter that corresponds to the CD-ROM drive, such as **D:** or **E:**.) The SETUP utility starts (the one shown in the picture is just an example).

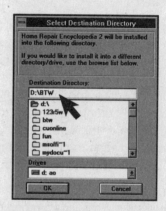

5 Most SETUP utilities are *prompt-based*: A series of prompts will ask how you want the program installed on your computer. What you are asked depends entirely on the specific program you are installing, but typically you can choose the directory into which the files are to be copied, along with other options. During the installation process, you may be asked to remove the current installation disk and replace it with another. At that point, you'll need to click **OK** or press **Enter** to continue with the next disk.

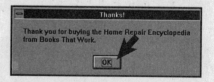

6 When you finish answering the prompts, the SETUP utility copies the appropriate files until the installation process is complete. Click **OK** to return to Program Manager.

Do It Yourself Add a Program to Windows 3.11

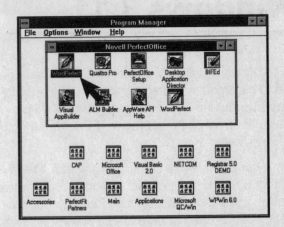

7 If your newly installed program requires that you restart the computer before you run the software (most do), restart your computer by first exiting Windows 3.11 (select **File**, **Exit Windows**, and then click **OK**). At the DOS prompt, press the **Ctrl**, **Alt**, and **Del** keys simultaneously.

8 With almost all Windows SETUP utilities, the installation software adds one or more icons for the newly added program to Program Manager. With Windows running, double-click the icon for your program in the Program Manager to run your new program.

Add an Icon for a New Program to Windows 3.11

Not all setup utilities will automatically add an icon to the Program Manager that you can use to start the new program. This is especially true of DOS programs, but it may be true of some Windows 3.11 programs as well.

This is not a problem; it is a fairly simple task to add an icon for a program to Program Manager. You may even want to add a program icon into more than one program group in order to provide several ways in which you can start your new application.

It's important to remember that in Windows, an icon is a picture that represents a program—it is not the program itself. So you can delete an icon and still run a program under Windows 3.11 if you like (although the process is more difficult). An icon makes it easy to start your program, because all you have to do is to double-click the program's icon in order to start the associated application.

In order to create a program icon, you need to know the name of the directory in which the program's files are kept. In addition, you need to know the name of

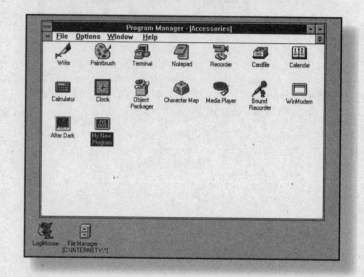

the file that starts the program. Typically, this file ends in .EXE and contains the name of the program itself, such as WP5.EXE. However, the startup file might end in .BAT or .COM, as in WP5.BAT. Check the program's manual for help locating the name of this startup file.

Do It Yourself   Create a Program Icon for Windows 3.11

3 In the New Program Object dialog box, make sure the **Program Item** option is selected and click **OK**. The Program Item Properties dialog box appears.

1 To add your new program icon to Windows 3.11, open a program group you already have (like **Accessories**) by double-clicking it.

2 Select Program Manager's **File**, **New** command. The New Program Object dialog box appears.

Do It Yourself   Create a Program Icon for Windows 3.11

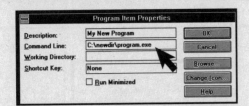

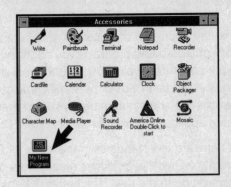

4 In the Program Item Properties dialog box, type a description of the file in the **Description** text box. In the **Command Line** text box, type the drive, directory, and file name for the program you just installed. Click **OK** when you're done. Windows adds an icon for the program to your desktop; it appears in the selected (open) program group.

5 To start the program, double-click its newly created icon in Program Manager.

Install a DOS Program

Despite the popularity of Windows, there are still plenty of DOS-based programs you might buy and use on your computer. Typical DOS-based programs include games, certain kinds of personal enhancement software (like diet and eating programs), and even mainstream applications like WordPerfect for DOS.

Because there are few standards in the world of DOS-based programs, installation differs greatly from one software package to the next. The better DOS-based software comes with a separate program just for installing it on your computer. This installation program helps you copy the program files to your computer's hard disk drive and sets up the software automatically so you can use it right away.

For this task, we'll refer to the program that helps you install a DOS-based program on your computer as a *SETUP utility*. This is just a generic name. The name of the actual program that does the installation might not be SETUP. It might be INSTALL, or SBINST, QSETUP, or another such name. If you're not sure of the name of the program's setup utility (common names are SETUP and INSTALL), check the documentation that came with the program to find out.

SETUP utilities are most often executable programs with .EXE file name extensions (such as SETUP.EXE)—but not always. Other possibilities include .COM and .BAT. The file name extension doesn't really matter, though, because you refer to the SETUP utility just by the main part of the name. So don't worry if you have a SETUP.BAT instead of a SETUP.EXE.

> Be sure to read the manual that came with the software you are installing. It may provide useful tips or important information for installing the program on your computer.

Some DOS programs do not use a setup utility. You might obtain this kind of software through an online service such as CompuServe or America Online, or even from the Internet. Programs that lack an installation program are generally easy to install, but you have to do all the work (such as creating a program directory and manually copying the files to your PC's hard disk) yourself. Follow these steps:

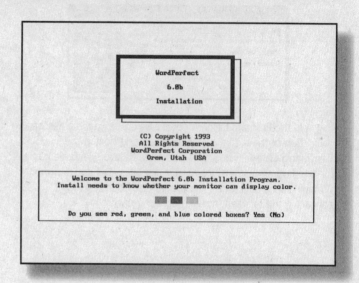

1. If you're in Windows, exit to DOS. Then create a new directory by typing **MD*programname*** and pressing **Enter**. (Replace the word *programname* with the actual name of the directory you want to create; for example, you might type MD\ COOLGAME and press Enter.)

2. Change to your new directory by typing **CD*programname*** and pressing **Enter**. (Again, replace the word *programname* with the actual name of the directory you created; for example, type CD\COOLGAME and press Enter.)

3. Insert the program's disk into drive A or B. To copy its files to the new directory, type **COPY A:*.* C:** and press **Enter**. (If you inserted the disk into drive B, type **COPY B:*.* C:** instead.)

4. Repeat step 3 for additional program disk.

> Before installing any new software, you should make copies of your important system configuration files, including AUTOEXEC.BAT and CONFIG.SYS, and if you use Windows, WIN.INI, SYSTEM.INI, and the System Registry (under Windows 95). ▶The task "Make a Backup of Important System Files" on page 400 tells you how to do this.◀

Tips for Installing a DOS Program to Run Under Windows

First, after installing your DOS program using the Do It Yourself steps, you can make it easy to start by adding an icon for your DOS program to Windows 3.11. **▶For help, see the task "Add an Icon for a New Program to Windows 3.11" on page 320. To add the program to the Windows 95 Start menu, see "Add a New Program to the Windows 95 Start Menu" on page 314.◀**

If your DOS program is a game, you may prefer to run it at the DOS prompt. This enables your computer to place all its resources at the program's command, which—because most games are pretty resource-hungry—will enable the game to run more quickly and easily. To run your game at the DOS prompt under Windows 3.11, simply exit Windows. To run it at the DOS prompt under Windows 95, click the **Start** button, select **Shut Down**, and select **Restart the Computer in MS-DOS Mode**.

Most games require a lot of memory, but to enable your game to use the memory that your PC has, you must make some modifications to your configuration files (AUTOEXEC.BAT and CONFIG.SYS). **▶For detailed instructions on how to edit these files, see the task "Modify Your Startup Files" on page 357.◀** Make sure that the following lines are included in your CONFIG.SYS file. They should be the *first three lines in the file*, appearing *in this order*:

```
DEVICE=C:\DOS\HIMEM.SYS
DOS=HIGH,UMB
DEVICE=C:\DOS\EMM386.EXE
```

You may want to modify that last line to fit your situation. For example, if your DOS games do not require any *expanded* memory (don't ask, just look on the box), you might want to use the following version of the EMM386 command:

```
DEVICE=C:\DOS\EMM386.EXE NOEMS
```

If your game does require expanded memory, specify how much you want in kilobytes (remember that 1M of memory equals 1,024 kilobytes). To specify 2M of expanded memory, for example, use this command:

```
DEVICE=C:\DOS\EMM386 2048 RAM
```

After making changes to your configuration files, be sure to restart your PC.

Do It Yourself Set Up a DOS Program on Your PC

① Open the software package and find the disk that contains the SETUP utility. This disk is often marked SETUP or INSTALL (or some other descriptive name). Start your computer if it's not on already, and then put the disk in your computer's disk drive.

② At the DOS prompt, type **A:** or **B:**, depending on the floppy disk drive that contains the SETUP disk, and press the **Enter** key. (If you are installing the software from a CD-ROM, type the drive letter that corresponds to the CD-ROM drive, such as **D:** or **E:**.) **▶If you use Windows, see the task "Go to the DOS Prompt from Windows 95" on page 212 for help.◀**

③ Type **SETUP** (or the unique name of the installation program if it's not SETUP) and press the **Enter** key. The SETUP utility starts.

(continues)

Do It Yourself   Set Up a DOS Program on Your PC   *(continued)*

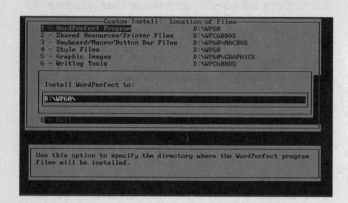

4 Most SETUP utilities are *prompt-based*: A series of prompts will ask you how you want the program installed on your computer. For example, you might be asked the directory into which you want the program's files copied. You will also be prompted to change installation disks when needed. When you are done answering the prompts, the SETUP utility copies the appropriate files until the installation process is complete.

5 If the program you just installed requires that you restart the computer before you run the software (most do), restart your computer now by pressing the **Ctrl**, **Alt**, and **Del** keys simultaneously. *If you are using Windows, return to Windows and exit properly. Then restart the PC.*

6 With the computer running, working at the DOS prompt, change to the drive/directory that contains the program you just installed (if the program is in the WP60 directory, for example, type **CD \WP60**) and press **Enter**.

7 Start the program by typing its name (such as **WP** for WordPerfect) and pressing **Enter**.

Install a Program from a ZIP File

Many shareware and free programs you might download from the Internet, CompuServe, America Online, and related sources are stored in a single large file called a Zip file. A Zip file is actually a "container" for a lot of other files.

The individual files in a Zip file are *compressed* (reduced in size), so that the Zip file itself takes up less disk space than the total of all its individual files. For example, even though a program's files may take up a total of several megabytes of hard disk space, they might take up only one megabyte when "compressed" into a Zip file. The Zip technique is not the only one used to compress files into a single chunk, but it is by far the most common.

One advantage of the smaller Zip file is this: A one megabyte Zip file can easily fit on a standard floppy disk, whereas the individual files for a larger program might not. In addition, it takes less time to download a Zip file from the Internet (or wherever) than it does to download all the individual files for a particular program. Using Zip files, you also can archive your older documents so that they take up less room on your hard disk—yet are easily accessible.

Zip files are generally easy to identify; their names have .ZIP extensions. If you see a file named PROGRAM.ZIP, for example, you can be pretty sure it is a Zip file.

The generic term for a Zip file is an *archive*. Before you can use the files in a Zip archive, you must *decompress* (or "unshrink") them. This requires a decompression program. The best program to use for zipping and unzipping files is a shareware program called WinZip. Shareware ("try-before-you-buy") software is available on most online services (such as CompuServe and America Online) and on the Internet. The idea behind shareware programs is that you can try them for awhile, and if you like them and want to keep them, you pay only a small registration fee. (**▶See "Connect with the Outside World" on page 227 and "Work on the Internet" on page 423 for help obtaining a copy of WinZip.◀)**

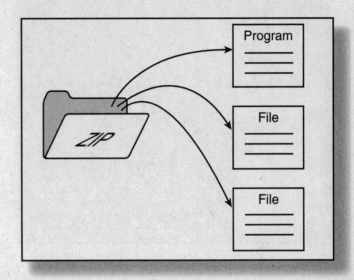

Zip files can be made to be *self-extracting*, which means that the recipient of such a file does not need to have WinZip (or any other Zip utility) to decompress the files in it. A self-extracting Zip file ends in .EXE, so it looks like a program file. But when you double-click the file in Windows Explorer or File Manager (or when you type its name at a DOS prompt), the individual files contained in it are automatically decompressed and copied to the current directory. If you download a copy of WinZip, you'll find that it is self-extracting. To install it, simply place the file in a new directory and double-click it. After WinZip has decompressed, a setup program automatically starts. Follow the on-screen instructions to complete your WinZip installation.

The following *Do It Yourself* tasks show you how to decompress the files in a Zip archive and create your own Zip files, using the "classic" WinZip interface. If you prefer, you can use the Wizard interface instead. The Wizard walks you step by step through the process of unzipping your files with a series of dialog boxes. The Wizard, however, cannot be used to create Zip files. To start the Wizard, click the Wizard button on the WinZip toolbar.

Do It Yourself Decompress a Zip File with WinZip

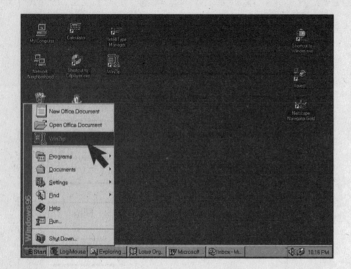

1 Start WinZip by clicking the **Start** button and selecting **WinZip**. (If you have not yet registered your copy of WinZip, you'll need to click **I Agree** to continue.)

When installing WinZip, you can set up an association so Windows knows that files ending in .ZIP are associated with WinZip. If you do that, all you need to do to open an archive is double-click the name of the Zip file within Windows Explorer or File Manager.

4 WinZip lists the contents of the Zip file. To extract (decompress) the files it contains, click **Extract**.

2 To open a Zip file you want to decompress, click the **Open** button.

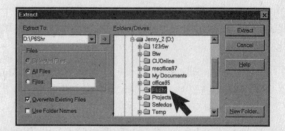

5 The Extract To drop-down list contains the names of folders to which you've extracted files before. Choose one of the folders from the **Extract To** list, or select any folder you want to use from the **Folders/Drives** list. Then click **Extract**.

3 The Open Archive dialog box appears. Select the file you want to open and click **Open**.

Do It Yourself Decompress a Zip File with WinZip

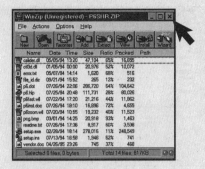

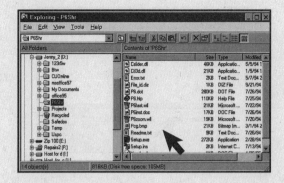

6 The extracting process may take some time, especially if you're decompressing a long list of files. Meanwhile, you can watch the progress bar at the bottom of the window. The red light lets you know that WinZip is still working; you can start a new task after you see the green light. When you're ready to leave WinZip, click its **Close** (X) button, or open the **File** menu and select **Exit** to return to the Windows desktop.

7 If you switch back to Explorer (or File Manager), you can see that the files in your Zip file were decompressed and placed in the folder you selected.

Do It Yourself Create a Zip File with WinZip

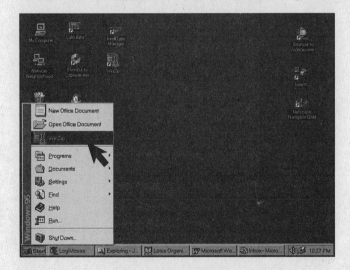

2 To create a new archive, click **New**.

When you install WinZip, you can have it add a command to the Windows 95 shortcut menu. Then, to create a new archive, you simply start Explorer, select the files you want to archive, and right-click. From the shortcut menu, select **Add to Zip**.

1 Start WinZip by clicking the **Start** button and selecting **Winzip**. (If you have not yet registered your copy of WinZip, you'll need to click **I Agree** to continue.)

(continues)

Do It Yourself Create a Zip File with WinZip *(continued)*

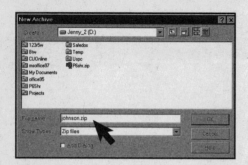

3 Change to the folder in which you want to create your Zip file, type a name in the **File Name** text box, and click **OK**.

You can skip step 4 by selecting the **Add** dialog box option before you click OK.

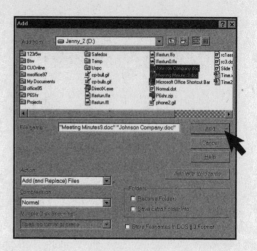

5 Press and hold the **Ctrl** key, and then click each file you want to add. When all the files are selected, click **Add**.

4 To select files you want to compress and place in your new archive, click **Add**. The Add dialog box appears.

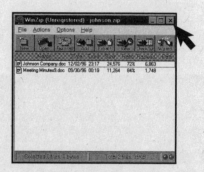

6 The files you selected are added to the archive. Repeat steps 4 and 5 to add files from other directories to the archive. When you finish, click the **Close** (X) button, or open the **File** menu and select **Exit**.

Uninstall a Windows 95 Program

Windows 95 comes with its own uninstall utility that enables you to uninstall Windows 95 programs simply and easily. You just select the program from a list of installed Windows 95 programs, and then click a button. Windows runs the program's setup utility, which enables you to remove some or all of the program's components.

Windows 95 itself does not uninstall the programs. It simply runs the program's setup utility, which contains an option for uninstalling the program. Most Windows 95 programs will come with such a utility, but older Windows programs and DOS programs do not. To uninstall programs that do not have an uninstall utility, you'll have to use My Computer or the Windows Explorer to manually delete the program's files. ▶**See the previous task, "Uninstall a Windows 3.11 Program" on page 332 for help.**◀

You can also use the Windows 95 uninstaller to add or remove Windows 95 components on your system. When you installed Windows 95, the installation program installed most of the commonly used components for you; however, to save disk space, it may not have

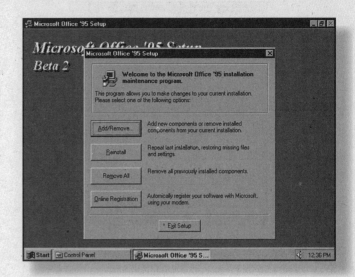

installed some of the more advanced features or features that would consume a lot of disk space. You can remove components that you don't plan to use or install components that you do want to use (assuming you have sufficient disk space).

Do It Yourself Remove Windows 95 Programs

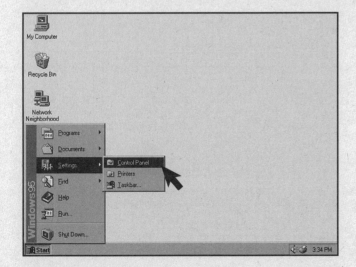

1 Windows lets you uninstall some Windows 95 programs, but not old Windows or DOS programs. Click the **Start** button, point to **Settings**, and then click **Control Panel**.

2 Double-click the **Add/Remove Programs** icon to uninstall Windows 95 programs.

(continues)

Do It Yourself Remove Windows 95 Programs *(continued)*

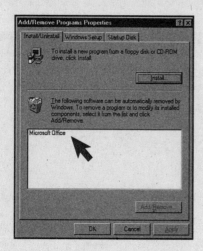

3 At the bottom of the Add/Remove Programs Properties dialog box is a list of all the programs you can remove from your system. If you don't see the program you want to remove, you can't use this procedure to remove it.

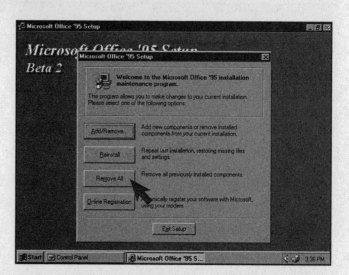

5 Windows runs the program's setup utility, which varies from program to program. In this case, you can click the **Remove All** button to remove all files that pertain to this program. Follow the on-screen instructions to complete the task for whatever program you're removing.

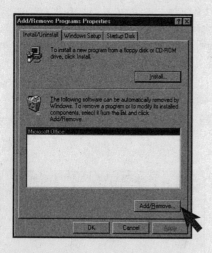

4 If you see the program you want to remove in the list, click it, and then click the **Add/Remove** button.

Do It Yourself Remove Windows 95 Components

1 When you installed Windows 95, it may have installed components you never use or failed to install components you want. To remedy this, click the **Start** button, point to **Settings**, and click **Control Panel**.

2 Make sure you have your Windows installation disks handy, and then double-click the **Add/Remove Programs** icon.

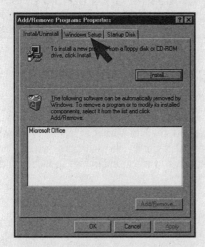

3 Click the **Windows Setup** tab to see a list of the Windows components installed on your computer. A white box with no check mark means the component is not installed. A gray box indicates that some parts of the component are installed. A white box with a check means all parts are installed.

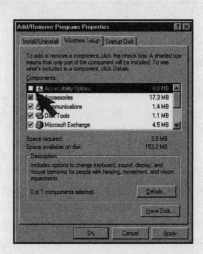

4 To *install* all elements of a component, click its check box until the check box appears white with a check mark in it. Continue to step 6.

To *uninstall* all parts of a component, remove the check mark and continue to step 6.

To *install selected elements* of a component, click the component's name and click the **Details** button and continue to step 5.

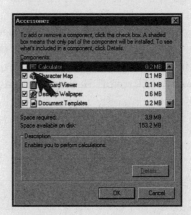

5 You see a list of the parts that make up the selected component. For each part, click the check box to add or remove the check mark. When you finish selecting the parts, click **OK**, and you're returned to the Add/Remove Programs Properties dialog box.

Repeat steps 4–6 for each component on the list (selecting individual parts of components as necessary). Then click the **OK** button.

Uninstall a Windows 3.11 Program

Have a Windows 3.11 program you no longer need? Odds are it's taking up a lot of space on your computer's hard disk, and you should delete it to clear room for another program. This process is called *uninstalling*—removing a program you no longer need (or want) from your computer system.

A number of the latest top-notch Windows software programs come with an "uninstaller" utility that makes this process easy. Typically, you access this utility through the program's setup routine. When you choose uninstall from the setup menu, the program removes all the files that were originally installed on your system. Just as importantly, it undoes all changes that were made to the Windows 3.11 environment by that program when it was installed. If your program came with an uninstall program, use it; it is by far the safest way to remove an old program you no longer need.

Uninstalling Windows 3.11 programs that do not come with these uninstall programs does have some risks. Attempting to delete files and alter Windows configuration settings in order to remove a program can render your computer unusable. Therefore, you should always, *always* make a backup of your computer's hard disk drive before uninstalling Windows software (▶**as explained in "Back Up the Contents of Your Hard Disk Drive with Microsoft Backup" on page 411◀)**. This will ensure the integrity of your system in case you accidentally remove a file the computer needs.

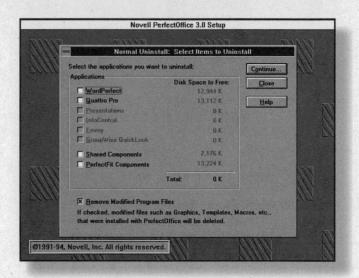

In addition, you should make "protection" copies of the computer's AUTOEXEC.BAT, CONFIG.SYS, WIN.INI, and SYSTEM.INI files by copying them to a blank disk. The AUTOEXEC.BAT and CONFIG.SYS files are located in the root directory of the computer's hard disk drive. The WIN.INI and SYSTEM.INI files are typically located in the \WINDOWS directory.

A simple way to remove unwanted Windows 3.1 or 3.11 programs is to use one of the new installation/deinstallation utilities such as Uninstaller.

Do It Yourself Remove a Windows 3.11 Program

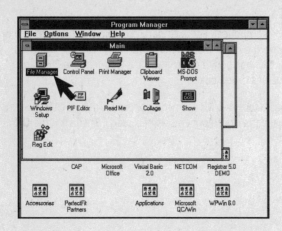

1 Double-click the **File Manager** icon in Windows 3.11 Program Manager. In File Manager's directory list, click the directory that contains the program files you want to delete.

Do It Yourself Remove a Windows 3.11 Program

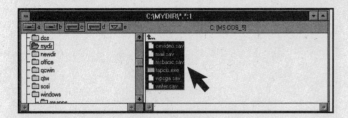

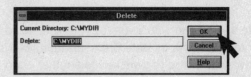

2 To select all the files in the folder, in the file list, click the first file in the directory, hold down the **Shift** key, and click the last file in the directory. Press **Delete**.

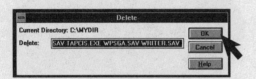

3 When the Delete dialog box appears, click **OK** to continue.

4 If the Confirm File Delete dialog box appears (it might not, depending on the options you've selected for File Manager), select **Yes to All**.

5 You are returned to File Manager. To delete the directory itself, click the empty directory, press the **Delete** key, and click **OK**.

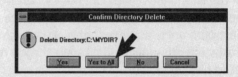

6 If the Confirm Directory Delete dialog box appears, select **Yes to All**. This will delete the directory and all subdirectories.

Many programs alter the WIN.INI and SYSTEM.INI files when they are installed. You can use the Notepad program to edit these files, removing unwanted references to the deleted file. You should only do so, however, if you know precisely what you are doing. Refer to the manual that came with your program, or consult a knowledgeable friend.

Uninstall a DOS Program

A few years ago, you swore by your ABC word processor with its state-of-the-art features. Now, you swear at it. You've switched to another word processing program, and the ABC word processor is just eating up space on your computer's hard disk drive.

Uninstalling is the act of removing a program you no longer need (or want) from your computer system. Many of the latest software programs—especially those designed for use with Microsoft Windows—come with an "uninstaller" utility that makes this process easy. Not all programs offer this utility; some leave the job of uninstalling files up to you.

Uninstalling software manually is easiest if the program is designed to be used under DOS, instead of Microsoft Windows. The reason: When they are installed, DOS programs typically make fewer changes to your system, and often program files are added to just one or two directories on your computer's hard disk drive. So to remove a DOS program, all you typically need to do is delete its directory (or directories).

Prior to uninstalling any software, make a backup of your entire computer's hard disk drive ▶**as explained in "Back Up the Contents of Your Hard Disk Drive with Microsoft Backup" on page 411**◀. This will ensure the integrity of your system in case you accidentally remove a file that the computer needs. You should also make "protection" copies of the computer's

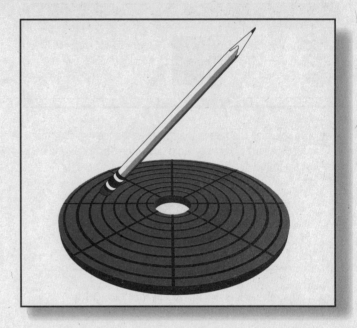

AUTOEXEC.BAT and CONFIG.SYS files by copying them to a blank disk.

If the program you want to delete consists of just one file, you can simply delete it from the computer's hard disk drive by typing **DEL *PROGRAM.EXE*,** where *PROGRAM.EXE* is the name of the program file you want to remove.

Do It Yourself Remove a DOS Program

1 If you use Windows, exit to the DOS prompt. Then identify the directory (or directories) that contain the files for the program you want to delete. To remove the directory and its files, type **DELTREE \MYDIR** and press **Enter**, where *MYDIR* is the name of the directory that contains the program files.

If you use an older version of DOS, it will not recognize the DELTREE command. In that case, type **DEL \MYDIR** to delete the files in the directory, and then type **RD \MYDIR** to remove the directory itself.

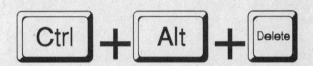

2 DOS asks whether you're sure you want to delete the directory. To delete, type **Y** at the prompt.

If DOS was unable to remove your directory, it might be because one or more files it contains have been "locked" against deletion (someone has turned on the "read-only" attribute of the file). See your DOS manual for more information on using the DOS ATTRIB command to remove the read-only attribute so you can delete the stubborn file.

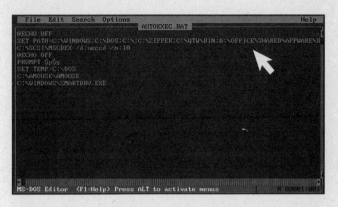

3 Some DOS programs modify the AUTOEXEC.BAT and CONFIG.SYS files. When installed, a program may (for example) add its directory path to the PATH= statement in the AUTOEXEC.BAT file. The program may have added information to the CONFIG.SYS as well. (▶**See "Modify Your Startup Files" on page 357 for details on removing such information.**◀)

Ctrl + **Alt** + **Delete**

4 After making changes to AUTOEXEC.BAT or CONFIG.SYS, restart your computer by pressing **Ctrl+Alt+Del**. Note any discrepancies if your computer does not start normally. Use your computer and other software for several minutes to ensure that everything is working correctly.

If all is NOT working satisfactorily, you might have accidentally deleted a file you should have kept. You can use the Undelete command in DOS 5.0 or later to restore files you previously deleted. ▶**See "Restore an Accidentally Deleted File" on page 404 for more information.**◀ If you edited the computer's CONFIG.SYS and AUTOEXEC.BAT files, you can restore them to their original condition by copying the versions you saved on the disk back to your computer's hard disk.

DO IT YOURSELF

Make Your Computer Work Faster and Better

No one likes to wait in line. You hate it at the grocery store, and you hate it sitting behind your computer, waiting for it to finish the job you gave it. But don't blame your computer. As software becomes more and more complex, your computer has more work to do. What used to take just a few computational steps using yesterday's software may now take dozens.

This doesn't mean you have to sit twiddling your thumbs as your computer grinds away at your letter to Aunt Martha. There are a number of simple steps you can do to increase the performance of your computer, and this section describes the most important ones. Even if your computer is reasonably fast and has sufficient memory, you may want to try one or two of the techniques in the following pages because, in reality, no computer is "too fast."

What You Will Find in This Section

Delete Old Files to Make More Room

With the large hard disks available today, it's hard to imagine ever running out of room—but believe me, it happens all the time. It seems that old adage applies here as well: No matter how much storage space you have in a new house, your "stuff" will quickly grow to fill it. So just as you eventually must rummage through closets, the garage, and your attic to throw away the junk you've accumulated over the years, you must eventually remove old, junky files from your hard disk to make room for new ones.

You'll find two general types of files on a computer: program files and data files. *Program files* are the files that came with the programs installed on your computer. If you are no longer using a certain program, you should consider removing its files. This will give you more space for programs you like. ▶**(See "Uninstall a Windows 95 Program" on page 329, "Uninstall a Windows 3.11 Program" on page 332, or "Uninstall a DOS Program" on page 334 for more information on removing programs you no longer use.)◀**

Data files are the files you create by using the programs on your computer. A typical data file is a document you write (like a letter or a school report) with a word processor such as Microsoft Word or WordPerfect. You might also have data files on your system that you didn't create, but that you downloaded from the Internet or an online service such as America Online. These files might include graphics, sound files, documents, and the like. Files you download can add up quickly.

On most computer systems, data files don't take up as much room as program files (especially if the programs are designed to be used with Microsoft Windows). However, you should still be in the habit of removing unnecessary data files from time to time. After a typical pruning of outdated data files, you may find you have 10–20 percent more hard disk space.

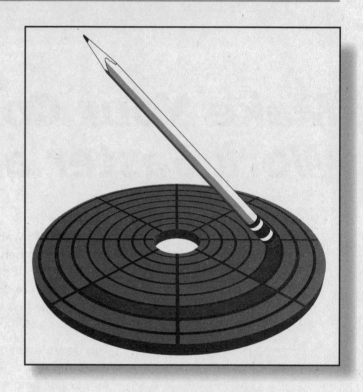

Now, before you jump in and start deleting files, you may want to copy them to a disk for safekeeping in case you should ever need them again. ▶**If you use Windows 95, see the task "Copy Files and Folders to Different Locations" on page 121 for help. If you use Windows 3.11, see the task "Copy and Move Files and Directories" on page 201 instead.◀**

After removing unwanted files from your hard disk, you can improve the disk's efficiency by rearranging how the files are stored. This process is called *defragmenting*, and you can learn more about it ▶in the task "Optimize a Hard Disk with Defrag" on page 345.◀

Do It Yourself Delete Old Files Using Windows 95

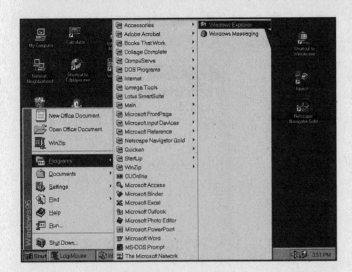

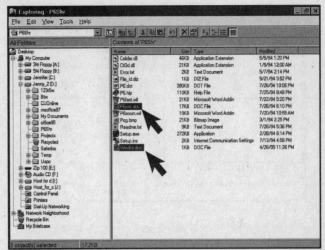

1 Click the **Start** menu, select **Programs**, and then select **Windows Explorer**. (You can also complete this task using My Computer if you prefer.)

3 In the file list, locate the file you want to delete and click it. To select several adjacent files, press and hold the **Shift** key and click the first and last files in the group. To select nonadjacent files, press and hold the **Ctrl** key and click each one.

4 With the file(s) you want to delete selected, press the **Delete** key.

> If you want to delete a directory and all the files it contains, select the directory and press **Delete**. Click **Yes** to confirm the deletion.

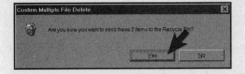

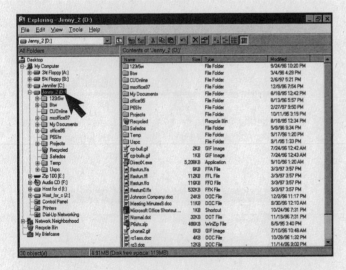

2 Click the directory that contains the file(s) you want to delete. The contents of the selected directory appears.

5 If the Confirm File Delete dialog box appears, click **Yes** to complete the deletion process.

Do It Yourself   Delete Old Files Using Windows 3.11

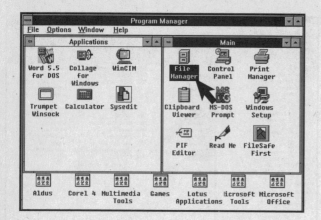

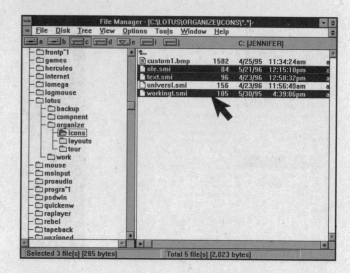

1 Double-click the **File Manager** icon in the Main program group.

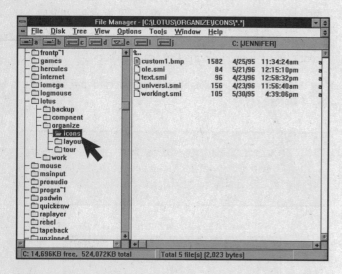

2 In File Manager, click the directory that contains the file(s) you want to delete.

3 In the file list, locate the file you want to delete and click it. To select several adjacent files, press and hold the **Shift** key and click the first and last files in the group. To select nonadjacent files, press and hold the **Ctrl** key and click each one.

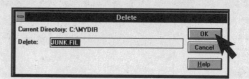

4 With the file(s) to delete still selected, press the **Delete** key. To continue, click **OK** in the Delete dialog box that appears.

5 If the Confirm File Delete dialog box appears, click **Yes** or **Yes to All** to complete the deletion process.

After all the files have been removed from a directory, you can remove the directory as well. Just select it in File Manager and press **Delete**. Then click **OK** to confirm. If the Confirm Directory Delete dialog box appears, click **Yes**.

Make a "Startup" Disk

When you turn on your computer, it goes through a number of steps before it's ready for use. At start up, your PC refers to several important files on the hard disk drive for instructions on how it should start. If something should happen to these files, your computer might be rendered completely unusable until the files on the hard drive could be replaced or repaired. An ugly catch-22 situation can occur, however: You need to access the hard drive to replace the system files, but you *can't* access the hard drive because the computer won't start without the system files!

Nine times out of ten, you will still be able to access your computer's hard disk drive even if the system files on it are damaged—or have somehow been erased. To work this magic, you create something called a *startup* or *boot disk*. The idea is simple: The disk contains the basic system files your computer needs to start. You start the computer with this disk, and then you can usually access the computer's hard disk drive and copy an undamaged version of your configuration files to it. Typically, this is all you have to do to fix the problem, provided the copies of your configuration files are fairly current.

Why create a startup disk in the first place? As you develop schemes and methods for improving the speed and efficiency of your computer, there is a greater chance of accidentally damaging or erasing an important file. Creating a startup disk just in case something happens to the system files is simply good (and cheap) insurance. You should create (or update) your startup disk before performing any type of "optimization" procedures outlined in the remaining tasks of this section.

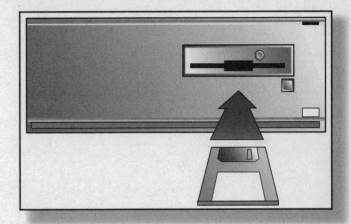

To create a startup disk you need a new blank disk for the A: drive of your computer. If the A: drive is a 5.25-inch disk drive, that should be the size you use to create the startup disk. If the A: drive is a 3.5-inch disk drive, that should be the size you use.

From time to time, update your startup disk to ensure that the operating system files are the latest versions. It is especially important to do this before beginning any of the maintenance tasks in this section. You should also update your startup disk before you install any new software. To do that, simply recopy your configuration files to the disk, as explained in the last steps of the *Do It Yourself*.

Do It Yourself Create a Startup Disk in Windows 95

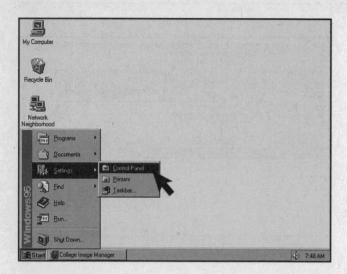

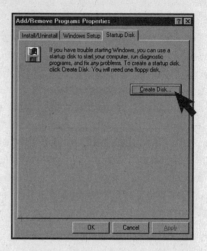

1 You use the Control Panel to create a startup disk. To display it, click the **Start** button, point to **Settings**, and click **Control Panel**.

3 Click the **Startup Disk** tab, and then click **Create Disk**.

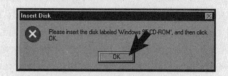

4 Windows copies the startup files from the installation disks. Insert your Windows 95 CD or floppy Disk 1 into the drive, and then click **OK**.

2 The Control Panel window appears. Double-click the **Add/Remove Programs** icon.

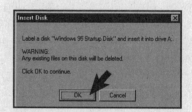

5 Windows copies the required files and then prompts you to insert a labeled disk into drive A. Label a blank floppy disk "Windows Startup" and stick it in floppy drive A. Click **OK**.

6 Windows formats the floppy disk and copies the startup files to it.

Do It Yourself Create a Startup Disk in Windows 95

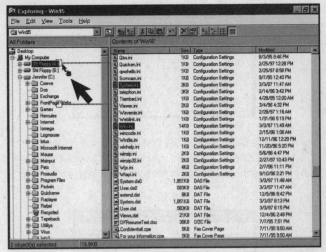

7 In addition to the files that Windows copies to your disk, you might want to copy certain configuration files. Start Windows Explorer and change to the **\WIN95** directory.

8 Press and hold the **Ctrl** key and click both the **WIN.INI** and **SYSTEM.INI** files.

9 Drag the files to drive A to copy them to the startup disk. When the copy procedure is complete, remove the new startup disk from your floppy disk drive and store it in a secure place.

You'll want to back up your system Registry as well. However, that file is too large to fit on one disk. ▶**See the task, "Make a Backup of Important System Files" (page 400) for help backing up the file.**◀

Do It Yourself Create a Startup Disk in Windows 3.11

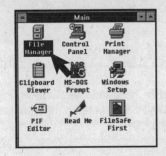

1 Even if the disk you use for the startup disk is formatted, you need to format it again before you create a startup disk. This is most easily done using the Windows File Manager. Start the **File Manager** by double-clicking its icon in Program Manager.

2 Insert the disk you want to format in drive A, and then (in File Manager) choose **Disk, Format Disk**.

(continues)

Do It Yourself Create a Startup Disk in Windows 3.11 *(continued)*

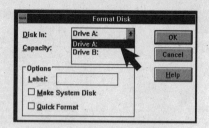

3 Choose **Drive A** from the **Disk In** list box if it is not already selected. Choose the capacity of the disk you are using (either standard or high-density; high-density is preferred).

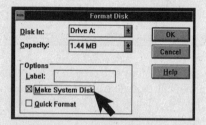

4 Click to select the **Make System Disk** option, and then click **OK**. This adds the special system files to the disk so that the computer can start when using that disk.

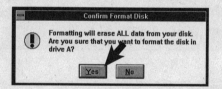

5 In the Confirm Format Disk dialog box that appears, click **Yes**. Formatting commences. When it is done, answer **No** to the prompt that asks if you want to format another disk.

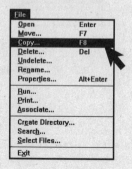

6 Keep your startup disk in its drive. To copy your first configuration file, go to File Manager and choose **File**, **Copy**. The Copy dialog box appears.

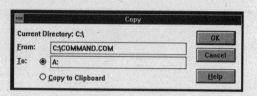

7 Type **C:\COMMAND.COM** in the **From** box, type **A:** in the **To** box, and then click **OK**.

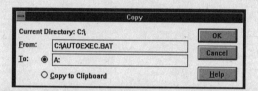

8 To copy the other configuration file, open the **File** menu and select **Copy** again. Then type **C:\AUTOEXEC.BAT** in the **From** box, type **A:** in the **To** box, and click **OK**.

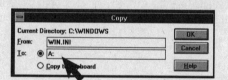

9 Although you don't need the configuration files in order to start your PC, Windows may not start if you don't have a valid copy of these files. Open the **File** menu, select **Copy**, type **C:\WINDOWS\WIN.INI** in the **From** box, type **A:** in the **To** box, and click **OK**.

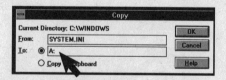

10 Open the **File** menu and select **Copy** again. Then type **C:\WINDOWS\SYSTEM.INI** in the **From** box, type **A:** in the **To** box, and click **OK**.

Optimize a Disk with Defrag

Your computer's hard disk is a lot like a record (remember those?). Your programs and files are recorded in concentric circles on the surface of the hard drive. When you copy or save files, it is the disk operating system (DOS) that determines where on your PC's hard disk to place them. Basically, DOS finds the first empty space on the hard drive and tries to place the file there. In many cases, large files are broken up and saved in several sections, often in places that are not adjacent.

Now suppose you delete files from the computer's hard disk drive. This process leaves "holes" (empty spaces where the files used to be). When you save a new file to the disk drive, DOS tries to use up these empty places. If one of the "holes" isn't big enough to hold the file, the file is chopped up and separated among lots of holes.

You can imagine what can happen to the files on your computer's hard disk drive after a while. Large files can be strewn over the surface of the disk. To read the file, your computer has to jump all over the hard disk drive to assemble all of its pieces.

When a file is chopped up and stored in different areas of your computer's hard disk drive, the file is said to be *fragmented*. One or two fragmented files are usually no problem. But a lot of fragmented files can seriously degrade the performance of your computer. Each time the file is chopped apart, the computer must work that much harder to read the file from the hard drive. In many cases, all this jumping around slows down the computer and decreases performance.

DOS (version 6.0 and later) and Windows 95 come with a handy utility program called Defrag (in DOS) and Disk Defragmenter (in Windows 95). Windows 3.1 does not come with such a program; if you use Windows 3.1, you simply exit to a DOS prompt and use the Defrag command. The name "Defrag" comes from the job it does: The utility *defragments* fragmented files. In other words, it reassembles your files and places them in adjacent sections on the hard disk. Despite their complex-sounding names, these utilities are actually easy to use. They guide you step-by-step through the

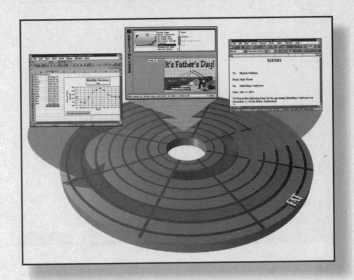

entire defragmenting process (which is often called "optimization"). They will even suggest the level of optimization your hard drive needs in order to be more efficient.

> Defrag your hard disk once every month or so to keep your computer in tip-top shape.

A Note About Compressed Drives

If your hard disk is compressed (**▶see the task, "Compress a Drive with DriveSpace" on page 353◀**), you can still defragment it. In fact, you should defragment a compressed drive about as often as you might a noncompressed drive—if not *more often*. Because your compressed drive is really just one big file, defragging it will allow the computer to access the information in this large file more efficiently. You should also defrag the uncompressed portion of your hard disk (typically known as drive H or I), in order not to compound the problem. Luckily, a defragging pass over the noncompressed portion of your hard disk is done automatically.

Do It Yourself Defrag Your Hard Disk in Windows 95

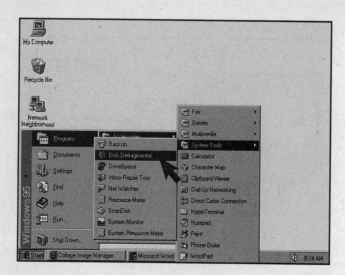

1 Windows 95 comes with a disk defragmenter that you can safely run from within Windows 95 (even when other programs are running). Click the **Start** button, select **Programs**, and select **Accessories**. Select **System Tools**, and then click **Disk Defragmenter**.

4 Click the **Start** button, and Defragmenter starts to defragment the files on the disk. You can continue to use your programs, but they will run more slowly. If you need to temporarily stop Defragmenter (in order to run a program at full speed), you can by clicking **Pause**. When you're done, click **Resume** to start Defragmenter again.

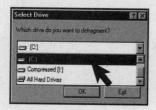

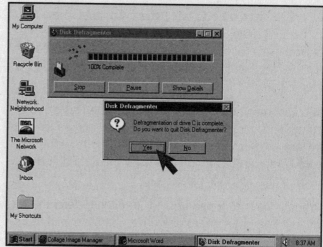

2 A dialog box appears, asking which disk drive you want to defragment. Open the **Which Drive Do You Want to Defragment?** drop-down list and click the desired drive. You can defragment all your disk drives by clicking **All Hard Drives**.

5 When you get the message saying that defragmentation is complete, click **Yes** to quit Defragmenter.

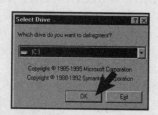

3 Click **OK**. Another dialog box appears, indicating the percent of file fragmentation on the disk and telling you whether or not you need to defragment the disk now.

Do It Yourself Defrag Your Hard Disk in Windows 3.11 or DOS

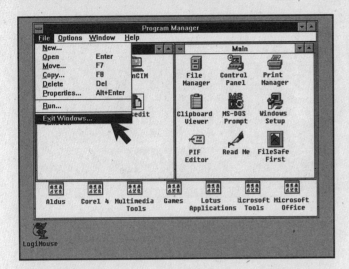

1 Exit all programs, including Windows 3.11. The Defrag utility will not run if you're in Windows 3.11.

Prior to running DEFRAG, run ScanDisk to check the disk for errors. ▶See "Check a Disk for Errors with ScanDisk" on page 407 for help.◀

2 Change to the DOS directory by typing **CD\DOS** and pressing **Enter**.

3 While still in the DOS directory, type **DEFRAG** and press **Enter**. The Defrag utility starts and does some preliminary testing.

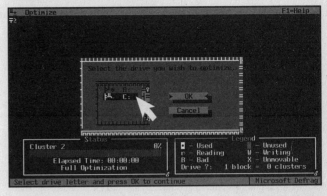

4 Defrag detects the disk drives you have installed in your computer, including the ones for floppy disks. To optimize the hard disk drive, choose **C:** (or whatever letter represents the hard disk drive you want to optimize). Choose **OK**.

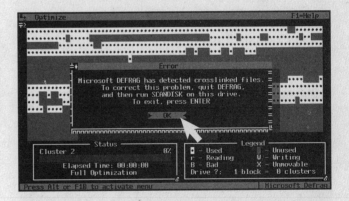

5 If the Defrag utility detects an error in the files, it displays a message indicating a problem, and asks you to run the ScanDisk utility. Choose **OK** to hide the message, and you are returned to the DOS prompt. Run ScanDisk, and then rerun Defrag.

(continues)

Do It Yourself Defrag Your Hard Disk in Windows 3.11 or DOS *(continued)*

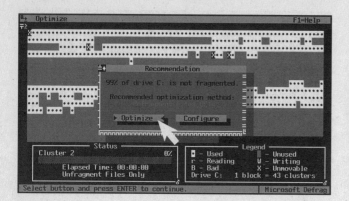

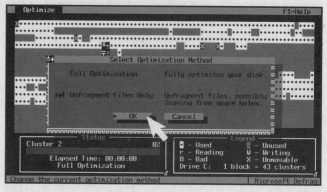

6 If it finds no errors, the Defrag utility indicates the percentage of the drive that is fragmented and recommends one of two optimization methods: files or full disk. The *file* method is faster and is usually recommended when the disk is not heavily fragmented. The *full disk* method is slower and is recommended when the disk is heavily fragmented. Choose **Optimize** to proceed with the recommended optimization process and then skip to step 10, or choose **Configure** to select a different optimization method and proceed to step 7.

8 Select the optimization scheme you want in the dialog box (either **Full Optimization** or **Unfragment Files Only**) and click **OK**. Optimization begins.

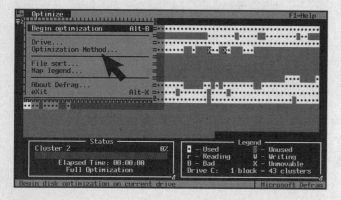

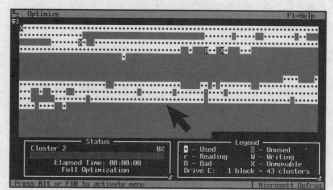

9 While the disk is being optimized, you can press the **Esc** key to safely cancel optimization. Do *not* turn off your computer during optimization, or data loss could result. If you need to stop the optimization process, press **Esc**. Then select **Cancel** to cancel optimization or **Resume** to keep going.

7 If you chose Configure, the Optimize menu appears. Select **Optimization Method** to select a different optimization method.

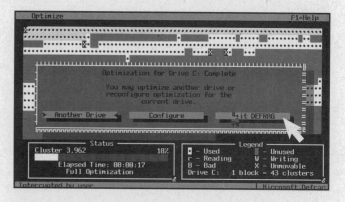

10 The Defrag utility displays a message when the process is complete. To exit the Defrag utility, click **Exit Defrag**.

Increase Available Memory

Memory (*random-access memory* or *RAM)* within your computer is a precious thing because it's in memory that your computer performs its work. Information stored in memory is temporary; it's placed there long enough for the computer to do something with it, and then the data is copied back to the hard disk for permanent storage. In this way, the memory in your computer is like your office desk: You place documents, magazines, or books on your desktop to work with them, and when you're through, you put them back where they belong.

In addition to the documents you may be working on, programs you start (such as Microsoft Word or Lotus 1-2-3) are also placed in memory so the computer can process their commands. It's always a good idea to use your computer's memory efficiently so you can get your computer to do all the things you need it to do. For example, suppose you attempt to run a program (particularly a DOS-based program such as a game), and it refuses to run. You'll probably see a message that says **Insufficient memory**. In reality, you actually have enough RAM installed in your computer to run the program, but your computer may not be using that memory very efficiently.

If you have Windows 3.11 (and at least DOS 6.0), you can run a utility called MemMaker to improve the way in which your PC uses memory. In addition, if your PC does not have a lot of memory (8M or less, for example), you can tell Windows 3.11 to use part of your

hard disk as a kind of fake memory called *virtual memory.* Then when RAM becomes full and Windows needs to place some information in memory, it simply copies it out to virtual memory (on the hard disk). Although using your hard disk for temporary storage is not terribly fast, it'll work in a pinch.

Windows calls your virtual memory a *swap file.* When creating a swap file under Windows 3.1, you can make it temporary, which means that Windows will only use the hard disk as memory when it has to. This enables you to use more of your hard disk for the purpose it was intended: as a permanent storage medium. You can also create a permanent swap file, staking out an area on the hard disk that's reserved for use as memory for Windows. Although this prevents you from storing data on that part of the hard disk, having a permanent swap file enables Windows to work more quickly.

If you have Windows 95, it will create virtual memory (a temporary swap file) for you. However, you can adjust the minimum and maximum size and the location of the swap file as needed. For example, you may want to move your swap file from a compressed drive to a noncompressed drive because it will make Windows faster.

By the way, if you're wondering, you won't need to run MemMaker if you have Windows 95. When you install Windows 95, it automatically sets up your computer so that it can make the best use of the memory (RAM) that your PC has.

Do It Yourself   Change the Location of a Windows 95 Swap File

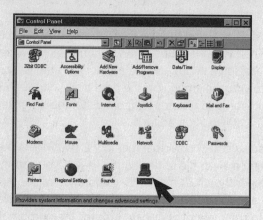

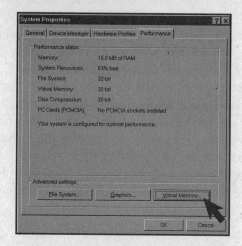

1 Click **Start**, select **Settings**, and then select **Control Panel**.

2 Double-click the **System** icon.

4 Click the **Virtual Memory** button, and the Virtual Memory dialog box appears.

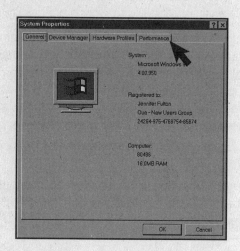

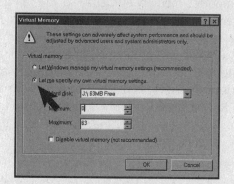

3 In the System Properties dialog box, click the **Performance** tab.

5 To move the swap file to a different drive (such as a non-compressed drive), select the **Let Me Specify My Own Virtual Memory Settings** option, and then select the drive you want to use from the **Hard Disk** drop-down list. Let Windows specify the Minimum and Maximum size for the swap file, and click **OK**.

Do It Yourself   Run MemMaker

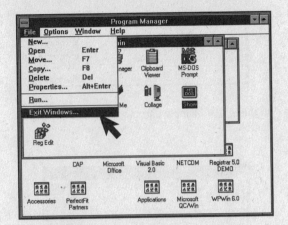

1 Exit all programs, including Windows 3.11. The MemMaker utility will not work if you're in Windows. (Do not run MemMaker if you have Windows 95.) Remove all disks from your computer's floppy disk drives.

2 At the DOS prompt, type **CD\DOS** and press **Enter** to change to the DOS directory.

3 Then type **MEMMAKER** and press **Enter** to run the MemMaker utility. The MemMaker utility starts and displays the opening screen. Press **Enter** to continue. If you want to quit instead, press **F3** to return to the DOS prompt.

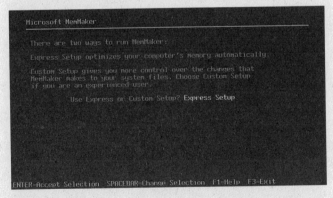

4 MemMaker has two modes: Custom Setup and Express Setup. Unless you are an experienced computer user, you should choose **Express Setup** by pressing the **Enter** key. The remaining steps assume you're using Express Setup.

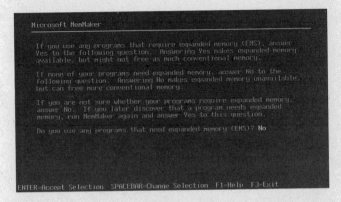

5 Indicate whether any of your DOS programs use *expanded memory* (*EMS*). Not many DOS programs (especially those that are less than four or five years old) use EMS memory so you are usually safe answering **No** (by pressing **Enter**). If you're not sure whether any of your DOS programs use EMS memory, answer **No** and then test the program. If you later discover that a program needs expanded memory, you can run the MemMaker utility again and answer Yes to this question.

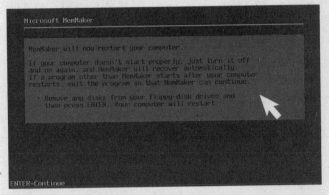

6 MemMaker analyzes your computer and makes tentative changes to its setup files. When prompted, restart your computer by pressing the **Enter** key. This process repeats twice. While your computer is restarting the second time, note any error messages or unusual behavior.

7 After the computer starts, MemMaker runs automatically. Eventually, it asks you if there was a problem. If you answer **Yes** to the question **Does your system appear to be working properly?**, Windows keeps the changes MemMaker made. If you answer **No,** it undoes the changes and returns your computer's old configuration. When you finish using MemMaker, press **F3** to return to the DOS prompt.

Do It Yourself Create a Permanent Swap File Under Windows 3.1

1 Open the **Control Panel** and double-click the **386 Enhanced** icon.

Before creating a permanent swap file, take the time to defragment your hard disk. ▶See "Optimize a Disk with Defrag" on page 345 for help.◀

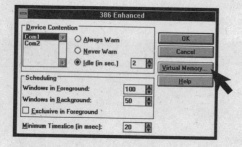

2 Click the **Virtual Memory** button.

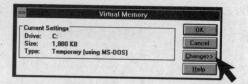

3 In the Virtual Memory dialog box, click the **Change** button.

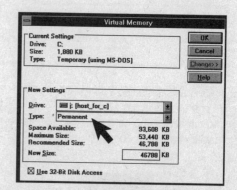

4 The Virtual Memory dialog box expands. From the **Drive** drop-down list, select the drive on which you want the swap file placed. Then select **Permanent** from the **Type** list and enter a size for the swap file in kilobytes (or just accept the size that Windows suggests). Click **OK**.

Compress a Drive with DriveSpace

ard disk space is just like closet space—you never seem to have quite enough. This isn't surprising, what with all the disk-hogging programs out there. That 230M hard disk that seemed so huge a few years back is now brimming with files, leaving you no extra room. Fortunately, DOS and Windows 95 have built-in utilities to solve your storage problems.

If you use Windows 3.1 (and you have at least DOS version 6.0), you can use a utility called DriveSpace (or DoubleSpace in versions 6.0 through 6.2 of MS-DOS) to store more data on your hard disk. If you use Windows 95, you can use its DriveSpace utility.

> Versions of DOS earlier than 6.0 do not include DriveSpace or any other compression utilities.

With DriveSpace/DoubleSpace, you can effectively double the capacity of your hard disk. Obviously, the disk doesn't physically change—rather, the method used to store files changes. Here's how it works.

A specific portion of your hard disk is set aside as a huge hidden file. Assuming you compress a 230M hard disk, this hidden file might consume 225M of that as a *compressed drive*. Your operating system (DOS or Windows 95) performs some acrobatics and renames the few remaining megabytes—5M in this example—as drive H: (or something similar), while referring to the newly compressed drive (the big hidden file) as drive C:. As far as you and your programs are concerned, everything works just as before; however, you now have approximately 555M of disk space (225M × 2 + 5M).

Of course, some files compress more than others, so the size of your existing hard disk may not exactly double. For example, word processing or database files

compress more (take up less space on a compressed drive) than do program files. DOS or Windows 95 takes care of storing files on a compressed drive in a shrunken format; they also uncompress (unshrink) your files "on-the-fly" as you need them.

> Before you compress a hard disk, you might want to back it up. ▶See "Back Up the Contents of Your Hard Disk Drive with Microsoft Backup" on page 411.◀

Do It Yourself   Compress a Drive for Windows 95

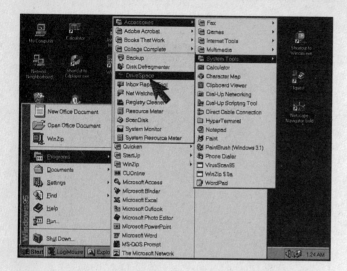

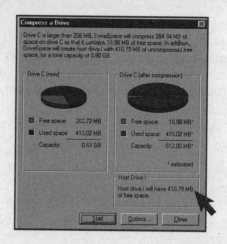

1 Click the **Start** button, select **Programs**, and select **Accessories**. Choose **System Tools**, and then click **DriveSpace**.

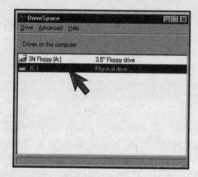

2 The DriveSpace dialog box appears, showing you a list of the drives you can compress. Click the letter of the drive you want to compress.

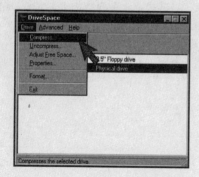

3 Open the **Drive** menu and select **Compress**.

4 These graphs show you how much free space the drive currently has and how much space it will have after compression. If you are compressing a large hard disk, the graphs are confusing (like the ones shown here). From the graphs, you'd think you're going to lose disk space; however, if you look in the lower-right corner of the dialog box, you'll see that after compression you will gain a new uncompressed drive that more than makes up for the free space you're about to lose.

5 Click the **Start** button. A dialog box appears, cautioning you to back up your files before compressing them. Assuming you already did this (or you're feeling very lucky), move on to step 6.

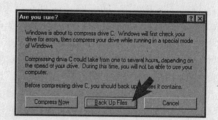

6 Click the **Compress Now** button, and wait until the compression is complete. Depending on the size of the compressed drive and the amount of data to be compressed, this can take from several minutes to several hours.

Never run an old version of DriveSpace after installing Windows 95. Older versions of DriveSpace can't handle the long file names that Windows 95 allows. You'll end up losing your data.

Do It Yourself Compress a Drive for DOS or Windows 3.11

1 Exit all programs, including Windows. Type **CD\DOS** and press **Enter** to change to the DOS directory. Then type **DRVSPACE** and press **Enter**. (If you have DOS 6.0 to 6.2, type **DBLSPACE** instead of DRVSPACE.)

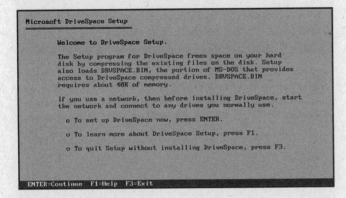

2 Read the instructions on the screen about DriveSpace, and then press **Enter**.

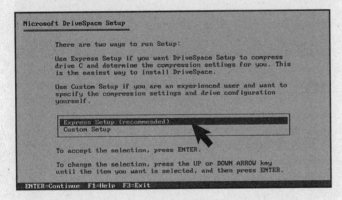

3 The easiest way to compress your drive is to choose **Express Setup**. Press **Enter** to accept this option (which is already highlighted). If you want to set aside some already-empty space on your disk as a compressed drive, choose **Custom Setup**. (These steps assume you've selected Express Setup.)

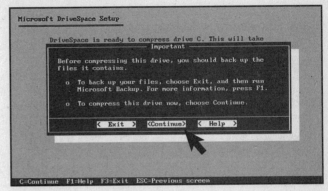

4 A warning appears, reminding you to back up your files (which you should have done already). Press **Tab** to select **Continue**, and then press **Enter**.

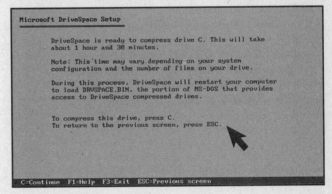

5 DriveSpace Setup estimates and displays the time it will take to compress your drive. Depending on your hard disk's size and the present number of files, drive compression can take anywhere from 30 minutes to more than 3 hours. Press **C** to compress the drive.

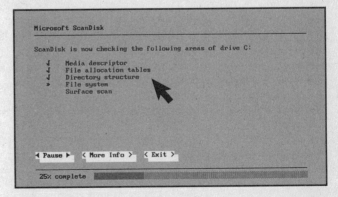

6 To begin the compression process, ScanDisk checks your disk for any potential problems and corrects them.

(continues)

Do It Yourself Compress a Drive for DOS or Windows 3.11 *(continued)*

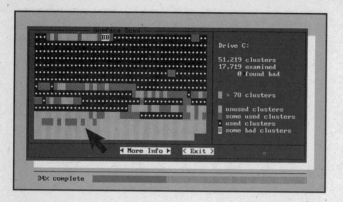

7 ScanDisk also double-checks your drive's reliability by performing a surface scan.

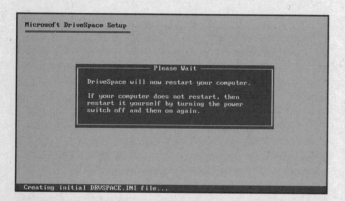

8 When the surface scan is complete, DriveSpace restarts your computer to enable its new settings.

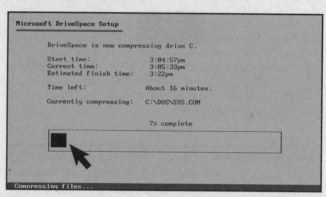

9 After restarting, DriveSpace proceeds to compress and defragment the files on your hard disk.

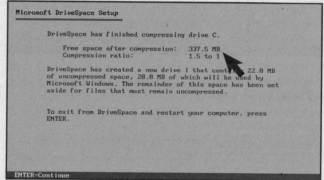

10 Finally, DriveSpace displays the results of the drive compression, showing approximately how much free space is available and the compression ratio. Press **Enter** to restart your computer.

Modify Your Startup Files

Out of the hundreds, possibly thousands, of files on your computer, only a handful specifically instruct it on how to operate. Two files in particular, CONFIG.SYS and AUTOEXEC.BAT, are loaded after you turn on your computer. These contain commands to load drivers, define settings, and generally prepare your computer for everyday use. Sometimes you may need to modify these *startup files* to make your system run more efficiently.

When properly configured, these files tell your computer how to operate at peak performance. If you notice that your system runs more slowly than usual, your startup files may be due for a tune-up. Under Windows 95, you may need to make modifications to the startup files in order to run certain DOS programs.

Properly configuring these files can be like tuning up your car—overwhelming unless you know exactly what to look for. Editing the files is the easy part, but knowing the correct settings is where things get tricky. So unless you really need to change them, don't modify your startup files.

There is no hard-and-fast rule to dictate what should be in these files. Individual users have different needs, and the files will vary accordingly. The contents of sample CONFIG.SYS and AUTOEXEC.BAT files are shown in this section. These samples give you a good idea of the basic items in your startup files, but you can modify them to suit your own needs. Also, depending on the version of DOS you use, some commands may not be available.

As you can see, these are simple text files; you can use Sysedit in Windows 3.11 or Windows 95 to modify (edit) these files. This task explains how to open, modify, and save changes to the configuration files, should it ever be necessary.

```
DEVICE=C:\DOS\HIMEM.SYS
DEVICE=C:\DOS\EMM386.EXE
DOS=UMB
DOS=HIGH
DEVICE=C:\DOS\SETVER.EXE
DEVICE=C:\DOS\ANSI.SYS
SHELL=C:\DOS\COMMAND.COM C:\DOS\ /E:256 /p

echo off
prompt $p$g
C:\DOS\SMARTDRV.EXE
PATH C:\WINDOWS;C:\DOS
```

The CONFIG.SYS and AUTOEXEC.BAT files reside in the root directory of drive C. Two additional configuration files, WIN.INI and SYSTEM.INI, are stored in the \WINDOWS directory. These files are used exclusively by Windows 3.11 and Windows 95; their contents are typically set by Windows and Windows applications. However, you can manually edit these files if necessary. ▶See the task "Manage Your Windows INI Files" on page 361 for more information.◀

Before you make any changes to a configuration file, be sure to make copies of it on a separate floppy disk. ▶See "Copy Files and Folders to Different Locations" page 121 or "Copy and Move Files and Directories" page 201 for help. You might also want to create a startup disk; see "Make a 'Startup' Disk" on page 341.◀

Do It Yourself Use SysEdit to Modify Your Startup Files

1 In Windows 95, click the **Start** button and select **Run**. In Windows 3.1, open the **File** menu and choose **Run**.

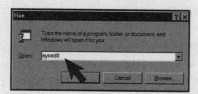

2 Type **SYSEDIT** in the Run dialog box and click **OK**.

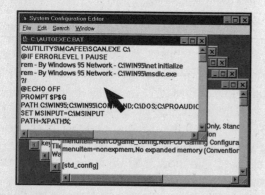

3 Immediately, the System Configuration Editor loads and displays several files: SYSTEM.INI, WIN.INI, CONFIG.SYS, and AUTOEXEC.BAT. In addition, under Windows 95, the MAIL.INI and PROTOCOL.INI files are opened.

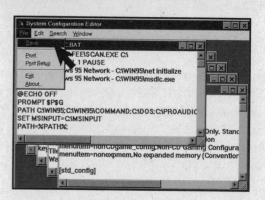

4 Although four or more files are displayed, you don't need to edit each one. Simply edit the file(s) you want. When you finish editing, save the file by choosing the **File**, **Save** command.

5 To exit SYSEDIT, open the **File** menu and choose **Exit**. Any changes you made to the startup files won't take effect until you restart your PC. If you changed a Windows configuration file, you must restart Windows for your changes to take effect.

Manage Windows 95 System Registry File

Microsoft got tired of the mess some programs were making of the WIN.INI, so in Windows 95, it was decided that all program registrations would go into one file called the *Registry*.

The Registry existed under Windows 3.1, but its purpose was greatly expanded under Windows 95. The Windows 95 Registry contains all system configuration information: hardware components and their settings, system settings such as the appearance of the Windows 95 environment, application notes, and so on.

Under Windows 95, removing (uninstalling) an unwanted program is relatively easy. Simply follow these steps:

1. Click the **Start** button on the taskbar.

2. Select **Settings**, and then click **Control Panel**.

3. Double-click the **Add/Remove Programs** icon.

4. Select the program you want to uninstall from the list and click the **Add/Remove** button.

5. Follow the on-screen prompts, which vary from program to program.

You must be very careful when changing the information in the Registry. Because it is used by Windows for so many things, you could accidentally render your system inoperable if you delete important information. So the safest way to keep the Registry under control is with a nifty little program called RegClean, created by Microsoft.

To get a copy, connect to the Internet, jump to Microsoft's home page (at **www.microsoft.com**), and then follow the link to free downloads. You'll find RegClean listed there. ▶**See the task "Download Files from the Internet" on page 440 for help.**◀

Do It Yourself Use RegClean to Clean Up the Registry

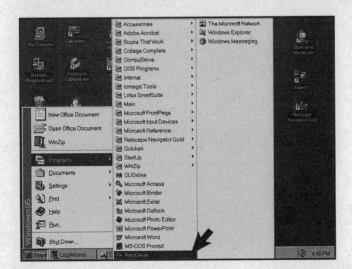

1 After installing RegClean, start the utility by clicking the **Start** button, selecting **Programs**, and selecting **RegClean**.

(continues)

Do It Yourself Use RegClean to Clean Up the Registry (continued)

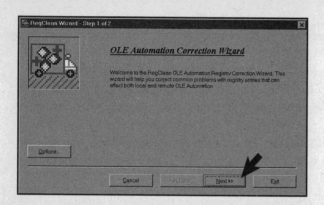

2 After RegClean scans the Registry, it displays the OLE Automation Correction Wizard. Click **Next>>** to begin.

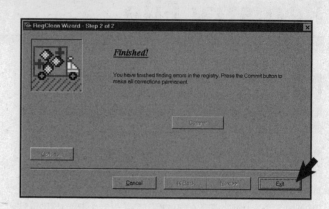

4 Click **Exit** to return to Windows.

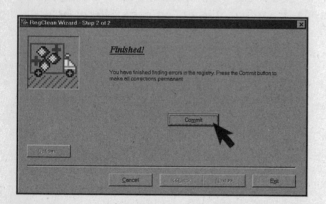

3 To save the changes RegClean wants to make, click **Commit**.

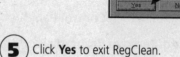

5 Click **Yes** to exit RegClean.

Your old Registry is saved to a separate file, so if something goes wrong with the changes RegClean makes, you can always undo them.

Manage Your Windows INI Files

Windows has several configuration files, called INI files because they're read when Windows *initializes* itself (starts). Their file names end with .INI. The two most important INI files are WIN.INI and SYSTEM.INI.

For the most part, you can ignore the existence of these files. These files contain "notes" that Windows makes from time to time so it can remember your exact configuration: the programs that should open automatically when you start Windows, the size of each window and its position on-screen, the color of your Windows background, and so on.

In addition to Windows, your programs can add their own notes to the WIN.INI file as well. For example, a program may make a note of its startup directory or any files you want it to open automatically. By contrast, the SYSTEM.INI file deals specifically with Windows and its associated drivers, not with applications like Word or 1-2-3. Therefore, you probably won't need to make any manual changes to SYSTEM.INI.

The problem with WIN.INI is that, even though programs are good about adding information to it, they're not very good about removing that information. So when you remove (uninstall) a program from Windows, it leaves a bit of itself behind. Therefore, it's up to you to manually edit your .INI files from time to time to remove unneeded junk and reduce their size.

Under Windows 95, programs do not add their notes to WIN.INI, but to the *system Registry* instead. This change allows Windows 95 to keep its notes separate from your programs' notes. So although WIN.INI still exists under Windows 95, you won't need to make changes to it very often. Instead, you will need to look at the system Registry after you uninstall a program. ▶**See the task "Manage Windows 95 System Registry File" on page 359 for more information.**◀

In addition to removing notes placed in WIN.INI by programs you have long since deleted, you might want to remove their font references as well. You see, quite a lot of programs come with their own built-in fonts, which they add to the [Fonts] list in the WIN.INI. By reducing the size of your INI files to their bare minimum, you can speed up Windows itself, because it often loads these files into memory to make changes to them.

The WIN.INI, like the other INI files, consists of sections which look something like this:

```
[SectionTitle]
;There may be a comment or two at the top of the
   section.
;Comments begin with a semi-colon.
;Windows ignores such comments
Keyword=somevalue
Keyword=somevalue
```

Each section is usually separated from the one in front of it by several blank lines, making it easier for you to locate sections you want to remove.

Do It Yourself   Remove a Program's Notes from WIN.INI

1 Open **File Manager** and change to the **Windows** directory.

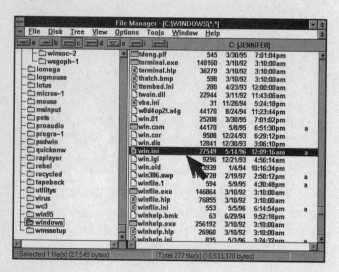

2 Double-click the **WIN.INI** file.

You can also use SysEdit (as explained in the previous task) to make changes to the WIN.INI file.

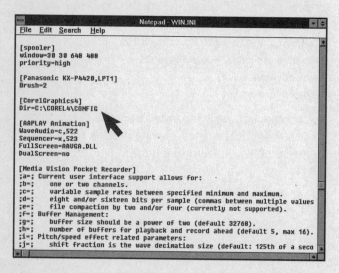

3 The WIN.INI file opens in Notepad. Scroll through the file until you find a section whose title is similar to the program you recently deleted. For example, if you recently uninstalled CorelDRAW!, you might scroll down until you came to the [CorelGraphics4] section of the WIN.INI file.

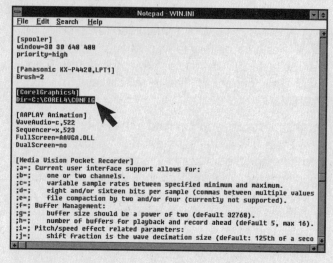

4 Select the text you want to remove by clicking at the beginning of the section title and dragging to the end of the section text. The text you select appears highlighted (white text on a black background).

5 Press **Delete** to remove the selected text.

6 Continue to scroll through the WIN.INI file. Many programs add several sections to the WIN.INI (for example, there may be some fonts listed in the [Fonts] section), and you need to find them all to successfully remove all references to the program you deleted.

7 When you finish deleting old notes, open the **File** menu and select **Save**.

Do It Yourself   Remove a Program's Notes from WIN.INI

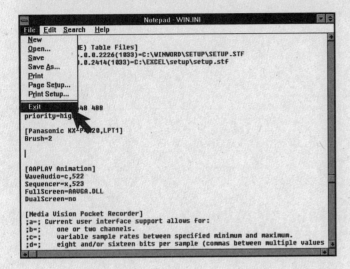

8 Open the **File** menu and select **Exit** to return to Windows.

DO IT YOURSELF

Install New Hardware

A computer is a sort of "work in progress": It's never really complete because you can continue to add stuff to it as your needs change. You might be satisfied with your computer today, but tomorrow you may want to add a new printer or install a modem so you can join all your friends on the Internet.

This section discusses things you can add to your computer. We've limited it to general accessories, such as a printer, a joystick, more memory, or a modem. Other accessories may be available for your specific computer and, although your specific accessory may not be covered in this section, you'll still find enough general information here that you should be able to install the accessory with ease.

While reading this section, bear in mind that of all things related to your computer, hardware differs the most. For example, a sound card from one manufacturer may look and act different from the sound card made by someone else. So use this section as a guide only—to help you understand the basic procedures of installing accessories. When you install any hardware, always have the instruction manual for both your computer and the accessory available, and refer to it often.

What You Will Find in This Section

Install Hardware in Windows 95

When you installed Windows 95, the setup program searched for hardware devices (sound card, modem, printer, mouse, and so on) already installed in your computer and set up these devices to work in Windows. However, if later on you add a sound card, game card, or other device to your system, you must run through the hardware setup again.

Fortunately, Windows 95 offers a wizard that leads you through the process of installing new devices and helps you resolve any problems that might occur. Just follow the steps to run the Add New Hardware Wizard, and then follow the on-screen instructions.

Plug-and-Play Hardware in Windows 95

If you purchase a plug and play device, you can ignore the Add New Hardware Wizard altogether. That's because plug-and-play devices are semi-intelligent, meaning that Windows 95 can "ask" the device what it is and basically take care of the setup process without any intervention on your part. You simply turn off the computer, connect the device, and turn on your computer, and you're ready to roll.

But in order for plug-and-play to work, your computer (and the device you want to install) must meet the following requirements:

- Your computer must have PCI or VLB expansion slots (or some other type of expansion slot that is capable of handling plug-and-play expansion boards).

- Your computer must have a BIOS (a chip that contains a set of instructions that tells the various computer components how to work together) that supports plug-and-play.

- Your operating system (Windows 95, in this case) must support plug-and-play standards, which it does.

- The device you are connecting to your computer must be plug-and-play compatible.

If your system (or new device) does not meet all of the requirements on the Plug and Play list, you won't be able to simply plug it in and relax. If you install the device and turn on your PC, and Windows 95 still does not recognize it, simply run the Add New Hardware Wizard to install the new device on your computer.

Do It Yourself Install a New Device in Windows 95

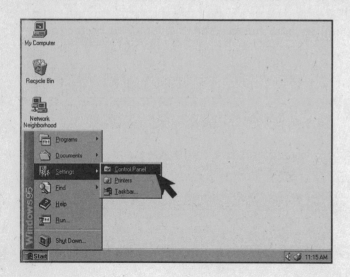

1 Exit all running programs. This prevents you from losing any data in case Windows locks up during the process. Click the **Start** button, select **Settings**, and then click **Control Panel**.

Do It Yourself Install a New Device in Windows 95

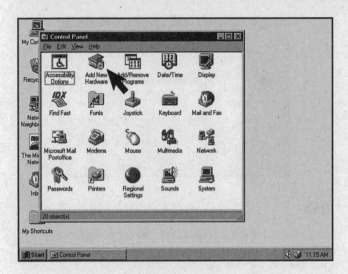

2 Double-click the **Add New Hardware** icon.

3 The Add New Hardware Wizard appears, telling you what the wizard will do. Click the **Next>** button.

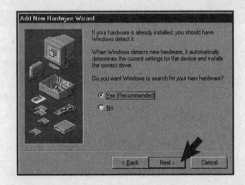

4 The wizard asks if you want it to search for new hardware on your system. Make sure **Yes (Recommended)** is selected, and then click the **Next>** button.

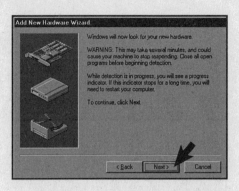

5 The wizard indicates that it is about to search your system for any new devices. Click the **Next>** button.

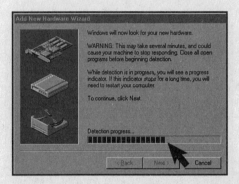

6 The wizard displays a progress meter as it searches your computer for any new hardware that's installed. This can take several minutes.

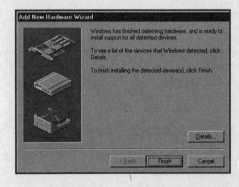

7 Wait until the detection process is complete (several minutes), and then click the **Finish** button. The wizard installs the new device.

(continues)

Do It Yourself   Install a New Device in Windows 95   *(continued)*

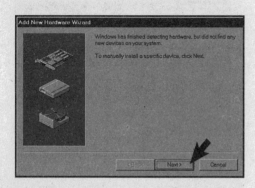

8 If the wizard is unable to detect your new device, you'll see this message. Click **Next>**.

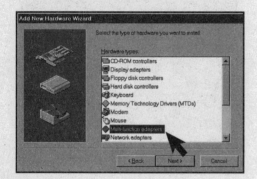

9 Select the type of device you want to install from those listed. Click **Next>**.

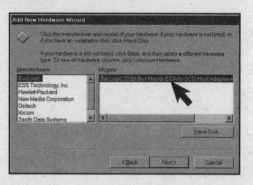

10 Select the manufacturer and model number of the device you want to install. If your device is not listed and you have an Install disk, click **Have Disk**, select the install program, and click **OK**. You're returned to the Add New Hardware Wizard. Click **Next>**. You may see additional setup screens for particular devices; if so, select the appropriate on-screen options and click **Next>** to move to the next screen. Eventually, the wizard will install your new device.

11 Click the **Start** button, click **Shut Down**, and follow the on-screen instructions to shut down and restart your computer.

Install a Printer

Printers come in all sorts of shapes and sizes, and they use different technologies to produce a finished page. The most popular printer types are dot-matrix, inkjet, and laser. *Dot-matrix* printers are all but extinct. They produce text in a manner similar to a typewriter: by pressing the character to be printed against an inked ribbon, which in turn, leaves its image on a piece of paper. Dot-matrix printers produce the fuzziest results. *Laser* printers use a pencil-point laser beam to create a reproduction of the entire page, in a manner similar to a Xerox machine. Laser printers are the most expensive printers, but their print quality is unrivaled. As you might have guessed, the output quality of *inkjet* printers (which produce text by spurting a jet of ink onto a piece of paper) is somewhere between that of dot-matrix and laser printers. You can purchase a color inkjet printer for about the same price as a non-color laser printer. However, to get color-capability, you'll give up some of the print quality you'd get with a laser printer.

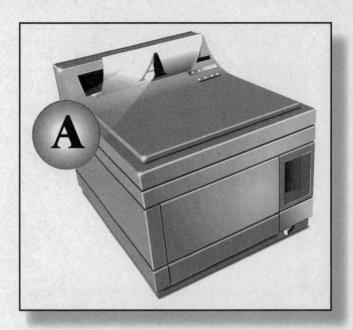

Fortunately, the type of printer—and whether or not it prints in color—doesn't matter at all when you're connecting the thing to your computer. All printers hook up to computers with a single cable, and the installation is typically simple and straightforward. You plug one end of the cable into the printer and the other end into the computer.

That said, you may run into complications when you try to get your computer to communicate with your printer. Different printers respond to different instructions. In fact, printers use a unique language, and they require your computer to speak that language as well.

Differences in language are handled not by your applications (the word processor, electronic spreadsheet, and so forth), but by a small program known as a *printer driver*. There is a printer driver for every model of printer on the market. When you install a new printer, hooking the thing up to your computer is only one part of the job; the other part is installing the printer driver and getting your software to recognize the new printer you have installed.

If you use DOS, you'll need to setup your new printer within each of your applications (check each program's manual for how-to's). During setup, the program will install the appropriate printer driver for use with that program only. You'll then repeat this process for each DOS application in which you want to print. If you use Windows, you'll only need to set up the printer once—the setup in Windows 95 is automatic; for Windows 3.1, you'll need to follow the steps in the Do It Yourself task. When you print in Windows, your program sends its data to the Windows printer driver you install, which handles things from there. However, if you want to print from a DOS program (even if you're running the program from within Windows), you'll still need to set up a printer for that program using its installation disks, just as you would if you were not using Windows at all. In this task, you'll learn how to install a new printer in Windows. To install a printer for a DOS program, follow that program's installation instructions.

We'll look at connecting a printer using one of your computer's *parallel* connections, which is by far the most common way (and on many printers, the only way) to attach a printer to a computer. If your printer uses a *serial* connection, the task of attaching the printer to the computer is considerably more difficult. You will need to consult the manual that comes with the printer to find out what kind of connection you need. You may also need to ask a knowledgeable friend or associate for help.

You will need your original Windows 3.1 disks to complete this task.

Do It Yourself Connect a Printer

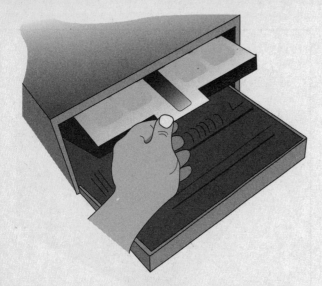

1 Unpack the printer from the box and remove all shipping materials. Insert the ribbon, ink cartridge, or toner cartridge (depending on the type of printer you have), according to the instructions packed with the printer.

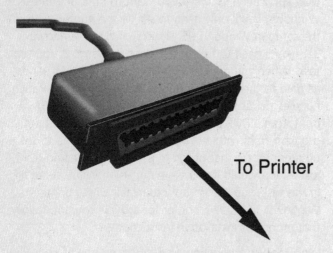

To Printer

2 Find the printer cable and connect one end to the printer. The printer cable uses different connectors on each end; only one of these will attach to the printer.

To Computer

3 With your computer off, connect the other end of the printer cable to the computer. Most likely, your computer will have only one connector of the correct size and shape to accept the printer cable. Use this connector.

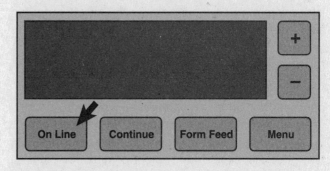

| On Line | Continue | Form Feed | Menu |

4 Most printers have a built-in self-test, often activated by pressing and holding one of the control buttons on the front panel of the printer (usually the **On Line** button) while turning the printer on; check the manual that came with your printer for more information. Insert some paper into the printer and perform the self-test now.

Do It Yourself Set Up a Printer in Windows 3.1

```
C:\>WIN
```

1 Turn on your computer and start Windows by typing **win** at the DOS prompt (if Windows doesn't start automatically).

▶To install a printer under Windows 95, see the task, "Install Hardware in Windows 95" on page 366.◀

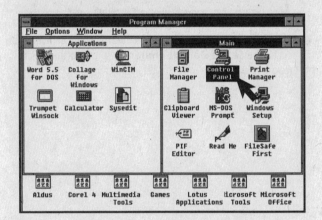

2 In Windows Program Manager, open the **Main** program-group. Then double-click the **Control Panel** icon.

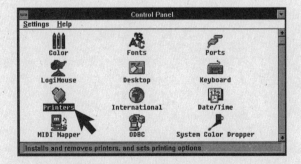

3 In the **Control Panel** window, find and double-click the **Printers** icon to open the Printers window. The Printers dialog box appears.

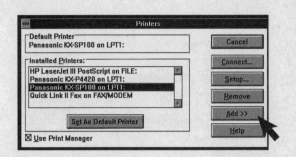

4 Click the **Add>>** button to add a new printer.

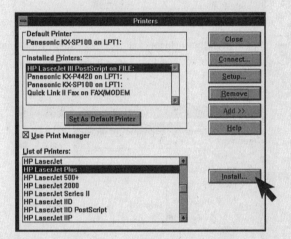

5 Locate your printer in the **List of Printers** list and click it. Then click the **Install** button.

If your printer is not listed, select a compatible printer instead (a printer type that your printer emulates or mimics).

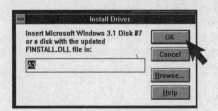

6 Insert the requested Windows disk (that came with your package of Windows) into the appropriate disk drive as instructed, and then click **OK**.

(continues)

Do It Yourself Set Up a Printer in Windows 3.1   *(continued)*

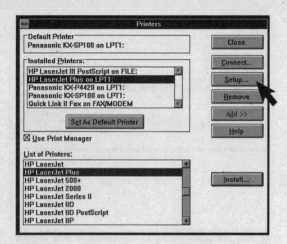

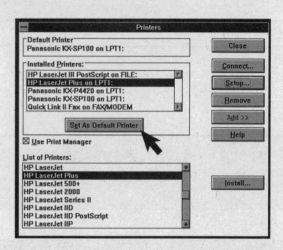

7 In the **Installed Printers** list, click the name of the printer you just installed, and then click the **Setup** button.

9 With the printer still selected in the **Installed Printers** list, click the **Set As Default Printer** button, and then click the **Close** button to close the Printers window.

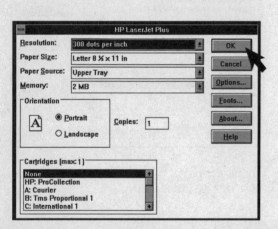

8 In the Setup dialog box, select the setup options for your printer. The dialog box might look different from the one shown here depending on the specific printer you use. You probably won't need to make any changes (in which case, just click **Cancel**). But if you do make changes, select the options you want and click **OK** when you're done.

Install a Joystick

Many computer games—especially the "shoot 'em up" action types—require (or at least heavily recommend) that you use a joystick for controlling the on-screen action. A *joystick* is a small, flat box with a handle-like stick stuck into the center of it. To control your on-screen tank, gun, airplane, or whatever, you merely move the stick around. It's called a "joystick" after the name given by early fighter pilots to the control yoke in airplanes. Although all joysticks work the same, some are fancier than others.

Installing a joystick is easy, but it requires that your computer already be equipped with an adapter card that has a *game port* on it. If your computer lacks an adapter card with a game port, you will need to add one. ▶**See "Install an Adapter Card Inside Your Computer" on page 385 for more information.**◀

Many sound cards come with a game port. If your computer has a sound card, look on it to see if you can find the distinctive game port. If you're lucky, it will be labeled for you.

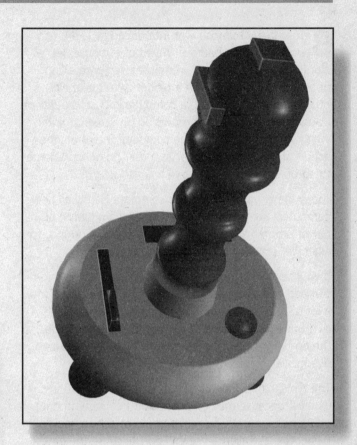

Do It Yourself Plug In a Joystick

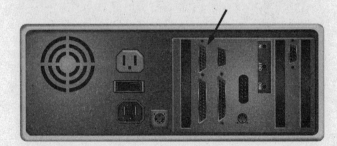

1 With your computer turned off, locate the game port on the back of your computer. It is shaped like a "D" and has 15 pins on it.

You can calibrate a joystick in Windows 95 by double-clicking the **Joystick** icon in the **Control Panel**. (To display the Control Panel, click the **Start** button, point to **Settings**, and click **Control Panel**.)

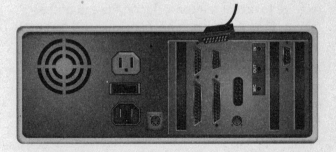

2 Plug the end of the joystick cable into the game port. Then turn on your computer and run your game software.

3 When using your game software, you will likely be asked to "calibrate" the joystick. This is easy and usually entails moving the stick to the upper-left and then to the lower-right. Once it's calibrated, you can start playing!

Install a Mouse

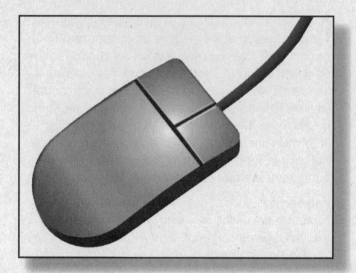

Before the Macintosh was introduced in 1984, few computer users had ever heard of a *mouse*, let alone seen one. The kind of mouse used with a computer doesn't have ears or a tendency to make elephants scramble. Instead, a computer mouse is a device (roughly palm-sized) that moves an on-screen pointer when you roll it around. The computer interprets the action of the mouse pointer as a user pointing at something on-screen and saying "*I want this.*"

Today the computer mouse is common. Nearly all new computers are sold with a mouse, and a growing number of programs require them. (Microsoft Windows, for example, is nearly useless without a mouse.)

If your computer is not yet equipped with a mouse, you can add one with relative ease. Though you can spend a lot of money on a mouse, typical no-name models cost under $20. For the most part, and for most jobs, the no-names function just as well as the more expensive models.

The typical *after-market* mouse (one you have to install yourself because the computer didn't come with one) uses one of your PC's serial ports to attach to your computer. It's called a "serial" port because the data goes in and out of the connector one bit at a time in series (one after the other). Because the mouse hooks up to your computer by way of a serial port, your computer must have one available, and it must be the correct size to accept the connector on the end of the mouse cable. A serial port has pins; a parallel port (usually used for printers) has holes instead.

More than likely, unless you have attached an external modem to your computer, the serial port on your PC is available and waiting to be hooked up to a mouse. In the event that a serial port is not available, you'll have

to add one. This entails opening your computer and installing an adapter card that has one or more serial ports on it. ▶**See the task "Install an Adapter Card Inside Your Computer" (page 385).**◀

In addition to connecting the mouse to your PC, you will need to install a *mouse driver*. This special program enables your PC to "talk" to your mouse. (The driver program comes on a disk included with your mouse.)

The cable of the typical serial mouse is equipped with a 9-pin "D" connector. If the serial port on your PC is a 25-pin "D" connector, you will need an adapter, available from your dealer. If you have a BUS mouse, it has a round plug that you insert into a special mouse port on your computer. The outlet should be clearly marked; if it's not marked, look for it near the port for your keyboard.

Do It Yourself Install a Mouse in Windows 95

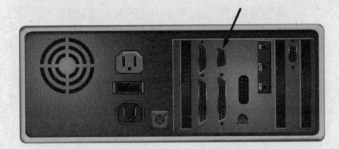

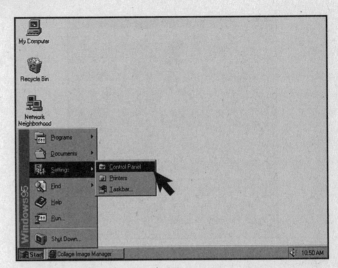

1 With your computer turned off, locate the 9-pin "D" connector or circular mouse port on the back of your computer. (Some computers have the mouse and keyboard ports on the front of the system unit.)

3 Turn on your computer. Windows 95 starts. If the Welcome dialog box appears, click the **Close** button. Click the **Start** button, point to **Settings**, and click **Control Panel**.

To Computer

2 Plug the end of the mouse cable into the serial or mouse port on the back of the computer.

4 Double-click the **Mouse** icon to view the current mouse settings.

(continues)

Do It Yourself Install a Mouse in Windows 95 *(continued)*

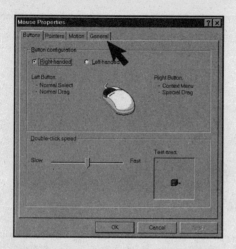

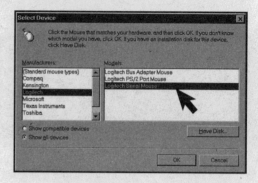

5 The Mouse Properties dialog box shows the current settings for the mouse. Click the **General** tab to specify the type of mouse you have.

7 The Select Device dialog box lets you pick a mouse type. If needed, click the **Show All Devices** option. Click the manufacturer's name and the model. (If the mouse came with a disk that has its own Windows 95 driver, click the **Have Disk** button and follow the on-screen instructions.) Click **OK**.

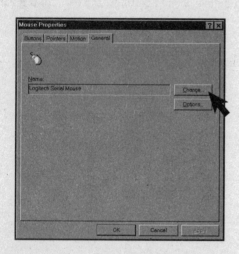

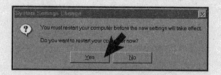

8 The required mouse driver may not be on the hard drive. Windows might need to copy it from one of the Windows installation disks. If prompted for a disk, insert the specified disk and click **OK**. After installing the mouse driver, Windows will ask if you want to restart the PC. Click **Yes**.

6 The Name text box displays the type of mouse Windows thinks is installed. Click the **Change** button to pick a different mouse type if the suggested name is wrong.

Do It Yourself Install a Mouse in Windows 3.11

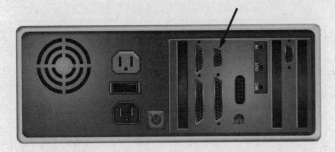

1 With your computer turned off, locate the 9-pin "D" connector or circular mouse port on the back of your computer. (Some computers have the mouse and keyboard ports on the front of the system unit.)

To Computer

2 Plug the end of the mouse cable into the serial or mouse port on the back of the computer.

3 Turn on your computer. If Windows loads automatically, leave Windows by choosing **File**, **Exit** in the Program Manager.

```
C:\>A:
```

4 Insert the driver disk that came with the mouse in your computer's floppy disk drive. Type **A:** (or **B:** if the disk is in drive B) and press **Enter**.

```
A:\>A:
A:\>INSTALL
```

5 Type the name of the mouse software installation program (such as **INSTALL** or **SETUP**) and press **Enter**. Follow the on-screen prompts (if any) to complete the installation of the mouse.

6 When the software installation is complete, restart your computer by pressing the **Ctrl**, **Alt**, and **Del** keys at the same time. When your computer restarts, you will be able to use your mouse.

Install an External Modem

Modems allow your computer to talk to other computers over the telephone. Computers "talk" in a strange high-pitched squeal that's unintelligible to us. But modems understand this gibberish, and that's all that matters.

Talking to other computers has its benefits. For example, you might call up the computers at one of the online services such as CompuServe, America Online, or PRODIGY (▶see **"Connect with the Outside World" on page 227 for help**◀). Or, you might call up your service provider's computer to connect to the Internet. Once connected, you could browse for a particular program and then download it (receive it) on your computer. Or, you might search for the information you need for a report, or locate the current prices of your favorite stocks. You might even send some e-mail messages or chat with other computer users from around the world.

Modems come in two general flavors: internal and external. The *internal* kind fits inside your computer. To install an internal modem, you need to open the computer, plug the modem into an empty expansion slot, and maybe set a few switches on it in order to get it to work. An *external* modem sits in its own case outside your computer and connects to your PC by a cable. Therefore, external modems are generally easier to install; however, they also tend to be a little more expensive.

These days, most modems include fax capability, which enables you to send and receive faxes. Software that runs on your computer controls the modem so it sends out the right kind of squeals (they are different for other modems and for fax machines).

This task describes installing an external modem to your computer. ▶**(For instructions on installing an internal modem, see "Install an Adapter Card Inside Your Computer" on page 385.)**◀ In order for you to

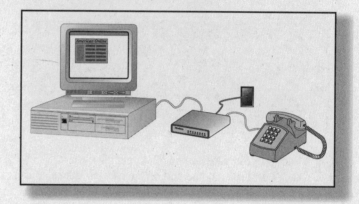

connect the external modem, your computer must have a serial port available (a serial port has either 9 or 25 pins). If there is no such serial port, you'll need to add one. This entails opening your computer and installing an additional adapter card that has one or more serial ports on it. Adding more serial ports can be a highly complicated issue. If you need to install an additional serial port, have your dealer do it or get help from a knowledgeable friend.

In addition to installing the modem itself, you'll need to install the software that runs it; this software comes with the modem. If your modem serves double duty—as a modem and a fax—it will have two programs: one for using it as a modem and one for using it as a fax.

You don't have to use the software that comes with the modem, if your online service provides its own software for example. Also, Windows 3.11 comes with a simple telecommunications program called Terminal (in Windows 95, it's called HyperTerminal) that you can use to connect to a BBS or to your Internet service provider the first time (in order to download your Internet software).

Do It Yourself Connect an External Modem

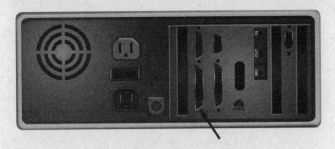

1 With your computer turned off, locate the serial 9-pin or 25-pin connector on the back of your computer. It is shaped like a "D" and has pins on it.

3 Plug the other end of the modem cable into the 9- (or 25-) pin connector on back of the modem.

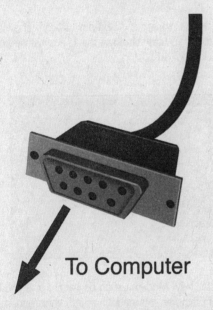

To Computer

2 Plug one end of the modem cable into the serial port. If the cable doesn't match your connector, you'll need to get an adapter (9-pin-to-25-pin, or vice versa), available at your computer dealer.

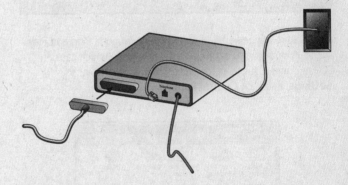

4 Plug one end of the phone wire into the modem's Phone or Telco jack and the other end into a nearby telephone outlet. If you have only one phone line in your office, connect the phone line coming from your telephone into the modem's Wall or Line jack. This will allow you to use your phone whenever you're not using your modem, and vice-versa.

Do It Yourself Set Up a Modem for Windows 95

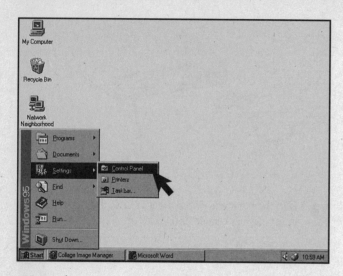

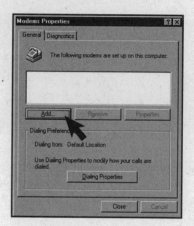

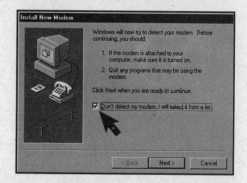

1 Start Windows 95. If your modem supports Plug and Play, Windows may set it up automatically (in which case, you're done). Otherwise, click the **Start** button, point to **Settings**, and click **Control Panel**.

2 Double-click the **Modems** icon.

3 The Modems Properties dialog box appears, showing a list of the modems that Windows thinks are installed on your computer. Click the **Add** button.

4 The Install New Modem dialog box appears. If you know the manufacturer and model name of your modem, you can select it from a list by choosing the **Don't Detect My Modem** option. Alternatively, you can let Windows attempt to determine your modem's type itself by *not* selecting this option. Click the **Next>** button.

Do It Yourself Set Up a Modem for Windows 95

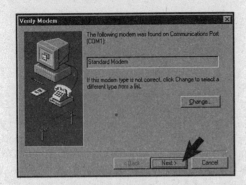

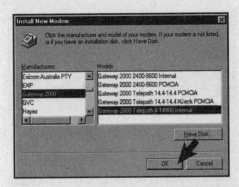

5 Take one of the following steps:

If Windows picked a modem type and you agree with it, click the **Next** button, and then click the **Finish** button. You're done.

If Windows picked a modem type that does not match your modem (or if it picked Standard), click the **Change** button and proceed to step 6.

If you select the **Don't Detect My Modem** option so you can pick your modem type from a list, proceed to step 6.

7 Click **OK**.

8 You're returned to the Verify Modem dialog box, where the name of the selected modem is displayed. Click the **Next** button.

9 If your modem has any special setup requirements, you may see additional screens. Eventually, Windows will indicate that the installation is over. Click the **Finish** button, and you're returned to the Modem Properties dialog box. Click the **Close** button to save your change.

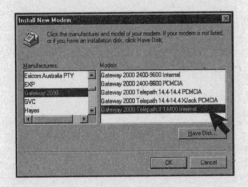

6 Click the brand name of the modem in the **Manufacturers** list, and then click the model in the **Models** list. (If the precise model is not listed, pick a model that looks close. If the modem came with a disk, insert the disk, click **Have Disk**, and follow the instructions.)

Do It Yourself Set Up a Modem for DOS or Windows 3.11

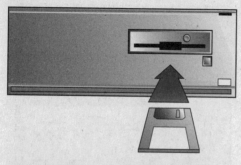

3 If you're using Windows, start Windows (by typing **WIN** at the DOS prompt), and then open Program Manager's **File** menu and select **Run**. In the Run dialog box, type **A:INSTALL** or **B:INSTALL**, depending on the drive and the name of the installation program. Click **OK**. Follow the on-screen prompts to complete the modem software installation.

1 Insert the disk that came with the modem in your computer's floppy disk drive.

```
C:\>A:
A:\>INSTALL
```

2 Determine whether the installation software that comes with your modem is supposed to be used under DOS or Windows. If you're using DOS, type **A**: at the prompt (or **B**: if the disk is in drive B) and press **Enter**. Type the name of the modem software's installation program (such as **INSTALL** or **SETUP**) and press **Enter**. Then follow the on-screen prompts to complete the installation.

Attach Speakers and a Microphone to a Sound Card

More and more computers are coming with sound capability. The sounds your computer makes are up to you. You can make it chirp like a *Star Trek* communicator whenever you start Windows. You can have it groan if you make a mistake or generate exciting sound effects and background music when you're playing a game.

This sound capability comes from a *sound card* installed in the computer ➤**(if you don't have one installed, see "Install an Adapter Card Inside Your Computer" on page 385 for help installing one).**◄ Most sound cards play back digitized sound effects and music. They can also record sound, so you can make your own effects (or share voice-annotated documents with friends and associates).

For a sound card to make sound, you have to attach some speakers to it. This is a simple job: Just insert the plug for the speakers into the appropriate jack on back of the sound card. If you want to record sound, you'll need a microphone, too. Simply plug the microphone into its jack on the sound card. Then, using the Sound Recorder program that comes with Windows (or a similar program), you're ready to go!

Before continuing, however, let's pause to consider the speakers you'll need for computer sound. The speakers that come with many sound-card-equipped computers don't provide amplification of their own. The strength of the sound depends entirely on the sound card, and some cards put out louder sound than others.

If you find the sound isn't loud enough for your tastes, first try to turn up the volume on the sound card (many sound cards have volume controls) or the "master volume" control on the sound software running on your computer. In Windows 95, this master volume control is often found on the taskbar in the form of a horn icon. If these steps don't improve the sound volume, you

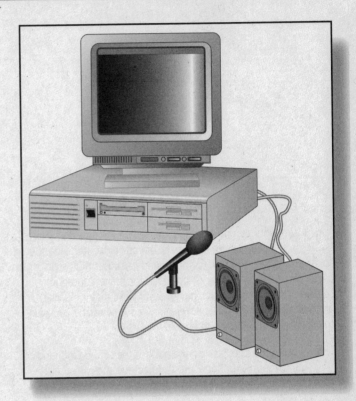

may want to consider replacing the speakers with better amplified types. Amplified speakers come with (surprise!) their own amplifiers. Their sound tends to be much louder (and of better quality) than what you get from unamplified speakers.

Be sure to buy "shielded" speakers designed specifically for computer use. Don't use just any old speakers (like the ones on your stereo) unless your sound card uses RCA style plugs and specifies that stereo speakers are okay to use.

Do It Yourself Connect Speakers and a Microphone to a Sound Card

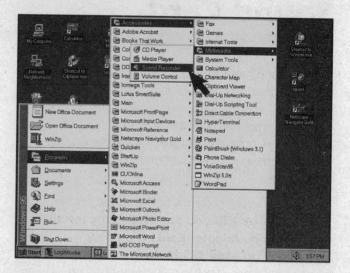

1 With your computer turned off, locate the **Speaker** jack on the sound card in the back of your computer. Plug the speaker plug into this jack (if your sound card uses RCA style plugs, there will be two jacks, one each for the left and right speakers.) Most sound cards have several jacks that look alike, and you can damage the speakers and/or sound card if you plug the speakers into the wrong jacks.

2 Locate the Micr jack on the back of the sound card, and plug your microphone into it. Again, be sure you use the correct jack in order to avoid damaging your sound card.

4 You can now test your new speakers by starting any program that uses sound. While listening, adjust the volume control (if applicable) on the sound card.

5 To record sound (for a test, for use as an annotation, or within Windows), start **Sound Recorder**. In Windows 95, click **Start**, select **Programs**, select **Accessories**, and then select **Multimedia**. Click **Sound Recorder**. In Windows 3.1, you'll find the Sound Recorder icon in the Accessories group. Double-click it to start the program.

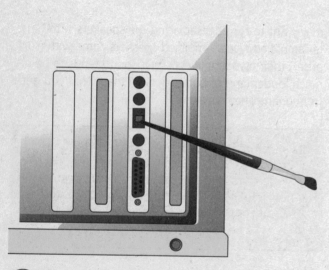

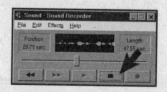

6 Click the **Record** button (its the last one on the right). Speak or play music into the microphone. When you're done recording, click **Stop** (it's the fourth button).

7 Click **Play** (the middle button) to play your recording. To save it, open the **File** menu and select **Save**. Then enter a file name for the recording and click **OK**. The file is saved in .WAV format, which all Windows programs support.

3 If your sound card has a volume control on it, set the control initially to about half to three quarters (if the control is numbered, set it between 5 and 7).

Install an Adapter Card Inside Your Computer

The original IBM PC revolutionized the computer industry because it was the first PC you could add extra junk to. These accessories were attached inside the computer in special connectors known as *expansion slots*, and they were commonly referred to as *expansion cards* or *adapter cards*. Modern day computers continue this tradition by allowing you to expand the capability of your PC with adapter cards.

When you buy your computer, one or more expansion slots are probably already taken up by adapter cards. So-called *base unit* adapter cards typically control the disk drives in your computer, as well as the hard disk, the monitor, and the parallel and serial ports.

Although there are hundreds of different kinds of adapter cards, most computer users are involved with only a handful. These include sound cards, CD-ROM interface cards, and internal modems.

Adapter cards can be easy to install, or they can be extremely difficult. The level of complexity varies depending on the card and the computer. Your computer may be set up in such a way that a card most people have no trouble installing causes you splitting headaches.

In addition, to install most adapter cards you need to know some technical details about computers—such as how to tell a serial port from a parallel port, how ports are named, and what is meant by *interrupts*, *port addresses*, and a strange thing known as *DMA channels*. If these subjects are alien to you, you're better off having someone who knows computers install your adapter cards for you.

This task only summarizes the technical setup of adapter cards. Because each card is different, you *must* have the manual for your card by your side when installing it. If you don't have a manual handy or if you don't understand it, don't even think about installing the card. Get help instead.

Keep these things in mind when installing adapter cards:

- Be careful not to short out your computer with excess static electricity. To discharge any static you may be harboring, touch something metal before touching the computer.

- When you're installing a sound card, you will need to specify the *interrupt* (also called an "IRQ") and *address* for the card. The address and interrupt you use cannot be shared with any other device in your computer. You may also need to specify the DMA channel.

- When you're installing a mouse card (for a so-called "port" mouse rather than for a serial mouse), you will need to specify the interrupt. The interrupt you use cannot be shared with any other device in your computer.

- When installing an internal modem (with or without a fax capability), you will need to specify the interrupt and serial port designator (such as COM1 or COM2) used for the card. Normally the interrupt and serial port designator you use cannot be shared with any other device in your computer.

Read This If You Use Windows

In order to get your new adapter card to work with your computer, you may need to install a driver program. A driver enables your computer to talk to particular devices such as a mouse, a sound card, etc.

▶**If you use Windows 95, see "Install Hardware in Windows 95" on page 366 for help in getting Windows to communicate with your new toy.**◀

If you use Windows 3.11, you can add a mouse driver by opening the **Main** program group, double-clicking the **Windows Setup** icon, and selecting your mouse brand from the **Mouse** drop-down list.

To add drivers for other toys to Windows 3.11, open the **Main** program group and double-click the **Control Panel** icon. Double-click the **Drivers** icon, and then click **Add**. Select the appropriate driver from the list and click **OK**, or select **Unlisted** to add an unlisted driver program.

Do It Yourself Install an Adapter Card

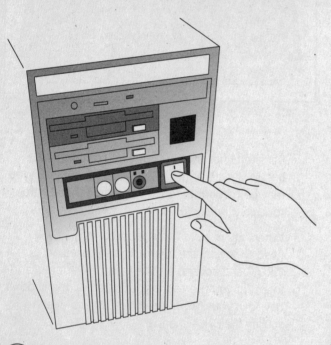

1 Turn your computer off, and then unplug it.

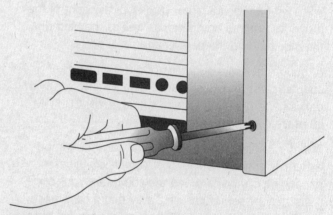

2 Open the computer by removing the cabinet screws.
▶**(You can find specifics on how this is done in "Clean Inside Your Computer" on page 277.)**◀

Windows 95 comes with a special hardware installation tool that can help you set up new adapter cards. It even includes a utility for tracking down and resolving any conflicts that may render an adapter card unusable. ▶**For details, refer to "Install Hardware in Windows 95" on page 366.**◀

Do It Yourself Install an Adapter Card

3 Locate an empty expansion slot inside your computer. On most PCs, some slots have two connectors, and others have one. In addition, the connectors may vary in length. Look at the bottom of the adapter card, and use an expansion slot that matches the connector on the card. (In a pinch, you can install an adapter card that needs only one connector in an expansion slot with two connectors.)

5 Before installing the adapter card, set any DIP or jumper switches on the card that are required to use the card with your computer. (This is where the technical mumbo-jumbo, like interrupts and address ports, comes in. Be sure to refer to the manual that comes with the card for specific details.)

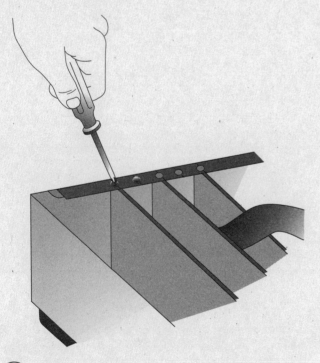

6 Insert the adapter card into the slot by gently sliding the card into the connector. A little bit of resistance is normal, but don't apply too much pressure, or you may break something.

(continues)

4 Using a #1 Phillips screwdriver, remove the back plate for the expansion slot you want to use. Store the removed plate in a safe place. Keep the screw handy because you'll need it in a bit.

Do It Yourself Install an Adapter Card *(continued)*

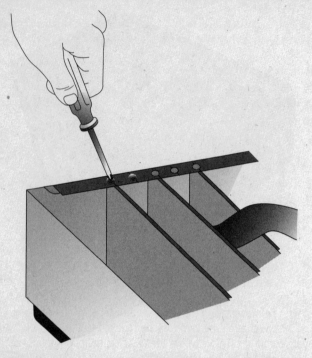

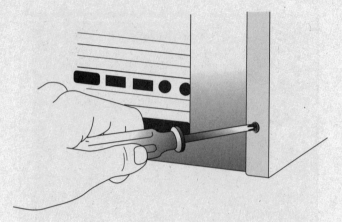

9 If the operation of the adapter card checks out, turn your computer back off. Put the computer back together by replacing the cabinet and cabinet screws. Your computer is now ready for regular use.

7 Using the screw you removed in step 4, secure the adapter card to the computer's case. Don't over-tighten. Before replacing the cabinet and closing the computer, you should test the operation of the adapter card. If the card connects to some external accessories (like a mouse, modem, or speakers), attach them now.

8 Plug your computer back in and turn it on. If the adapter card requires special software, install that software now (the software usually comes with the adapter card).

Install a CD-ROM Drive

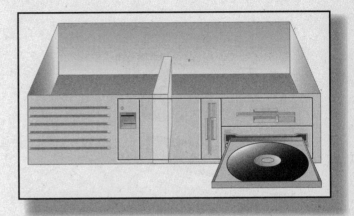

CD-ROM (Compact Disc Read-Only Memory) is the trendy thing in computers these days. A CD-ROM looks identical to an audio compact disc, but is designed to hold computer data—over 600 megabytes of it—instead of music. Because of the vast amounts of data that can be economically stored on a single disc, CD-ROMs are fast becoming a popular way to distribute large amounts of information. This information might be an encyclopedia, or it might be the complete works of William Shakespeare.

Installing a CD-ROM drive takes two steps: installing the drive itself (if it's an internal model; external models are also available but are generally more expensive), and installing the *interface (adapter) card* used as the actual link between the CD-ROM drive and your computer.

There is nothing particularly difficult about installing a CD-ROM drive in your computer, but complications can and do occur. The problem is the interaction between the CD-ROM interface card and your computer. If the card is not set up just right, your computer may balk and refuse to let you use the CD-ROM. Worse, your computer may refuse to work altogether. Though not common, it's not unheard of to install a CD-ROM only to have a computer "play dead" when you turn it on! Should your CD-ROM installation prove challenging, your best bet is to enlist the help of your dealer or a knowledgeable friend.

This task describes installing an internal CD-ROM and briefly discusses the technical issues you may have to resolve to get the drive to work. To be successful, you need to know some of the technical details about computers, including interrupts and port addresses. If you are unfamiliar with these subjects, have your dealer or a knowledgeable friend install the CD-ROM drive for you.

You'll need an empty disk drive bay (the "bay" is the opening where the floppy disk drive mechanism fits in your computer) into which to install an internal CD-ROM. If you don't have a free disk drive bay, you won't be able to install an internal CD-ROM without removing a floppy disk drive. If you decide to do this, your best bet is to take your computer to a dealer. This could get complicated.

Do It Yourself Install an Internal CD-ROM Drive

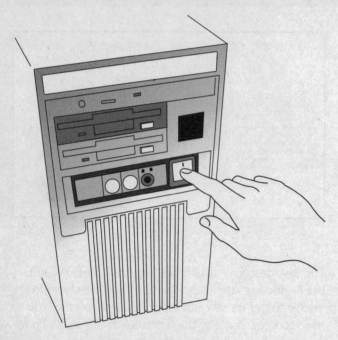

1 Turn your computer off and unplug it.

3 Locate an empty expansion slot inside your computer. On most PCs, slots have two connectors; some have one. In addition, the connectors may vary in length. Look at the bottom of the adapter card and use an expansion slot that matches the connector on the card. (In a pinch, you can install an adapter card that needs only one connector in an expansion slot that has two connectors.)

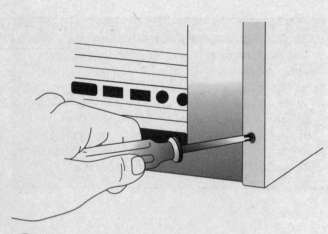

2 Open the computer by removing the cabinet screws.
▶**You can find specifics on how this is done in "Clean Inside Your Computer" on page 277.**◀

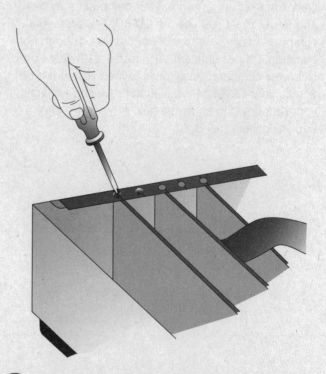

4 Using a #1 Phillips screwdriver, remove the back plate for the expansion slot you want to use. Store the removed plate in a safe place. Keep the screw handy.

Do It Yourself Install an Internal CD-ROM Drive

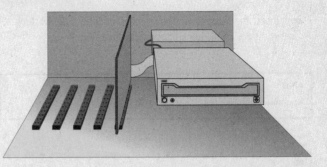

5 Before installing the CD-ROM interface adapter, set any DIP or jumper switches on the card that are required to use the card with your computer. Most cards come factory set for the most common installations, but you may need to reset the card to accommodate your specific computer. Be sure to refer to the manual that comes with the card for specific details.

6 Insert the CD-ROM interface card into the slot by gently sliding the card into the connector. A little bit of resistance is normal, but don't apply too much pressure or you may break something.

7 Using the screw you removed in step 4, secure the adapter card to the computer's case. Don't over-tighten.

8 Remove the plastic cover for the disk drive bay you want to use. Set any jumper or DIP switches as needed. If you're installing a SCSI CD-ROM, you may need to remove its terminating resistor (look for a jumper or chip marked T-RES).

9 Insert the CD-ROM drive into the bay and attach it to your computer using the screws supplied with the CD-ROM drive. (You may need to attach special drive rails to the CD-ROM drive in order to accomplish this.) Connect the CD-ROM drive to the interface card you installed in step 6, making sure you orient the cable properly. Connect the power cable (included with the drive) between the CD-ROM drive and the computer's power supply. Then connect the audio cable (if any) to your sound card or to the adapter card.

10 Plug in your computer and turn it on. Before you can use your CD-ROM drive, you must set up your CD-ROM, as described in the next *Do It Yourself* steps.

Do It Yourself   Set Up a CD-ROM

1 Insert the floppy disk that came with the CD-ROM drive into your computer's floppy disk drive.

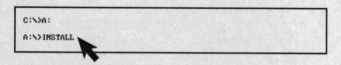

```
C:\>A:
A:\>INSTALL
```

2 Determine if the installation software that comes with your CD-ROM drive is supposed to be used under DOS or Windows. If you're using DOS, type **A:** (or **B:** if the disk is in drive B) and press **Enter**. Type the name of the CD-ROM software installation program (such as **INSTALL** or **SETUP**) and press **Enter**. Follow the on-screen prompts to complete the installation.

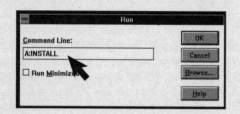

3 If you're using Windows 3.11, start Windows and then open Program Manager's **File** menu and select **Run**. In the Run dialog box, type **A:INSTALL** or **B:INSTALL** (depending on which drive contains the installation disk) and click **OK**. Follow the on-screen prompts to complete the installation. (If you're using Windows 95, skip ahead to the next section, "Install Hardware in Windows 95.")

4 After installation is complete, test the operation of the CD-ROM drive by inserting a disc into the drive and trying to access its data.

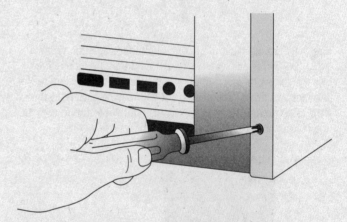

5 If the operation of the CD-ROM drive checks out, turn your computer off again. Put the computer back together by replacing the cabinet and cabinet screws. Your computer is now ready for regular use.

Install a Zip Drive

With today's larger hard disks, it's becoming more and more difficult for the average user to back up important data to floppy disks. Some users opt for a good tape backup system, but more and more users are choosing Zip drives.

Zip drives (and their larger capacity cousins, Jaz drives) are operated like floppy disk drives: You insert a formatted disk and then copy onto the disk in the usual manner. The main advantage here is storage capacity. A Zip disk can store up to 100M of data, and a Jaz disk can store about 1G.

Their large capacities make Zip drives a good choice for a backup system because you won't need to change your disks as often (if at all) in order to back up your important data. In addition, a Zip drive can act as a removable hard disk: A program can be installed on a disk, along with the documents you might create while using the program. Storing programs that you don't use very often on removable disks is convenient because the programs won't be taking up valuable space on your hard disk.

> Keep in mind that a program stored on a Zip disk (as opposed to the hard disk) will run a bit slower, but probably not enough to be very noticeable.

Zip disks are useful for many purposes as well, With a Zip drive, you can do any of the following things:

- Copy large amounts of data from one computer to another (provided the second computer also has a Zip drive)

- Store large multimedia files, such as scanned photos and sound files

- Transport data between home and work much more easily

- Store financial and other confidential data on a Zip disk that you can keep in a safe overnight

Of course, you can do all of these things with a Jaz drive as well.

Installing a Zip (or a Jaz) drive is relatively simple. First, you connect the drive to your PC, and then you run a Setup program to tell your PC that the drive exists. Zip drives come in two flavors: SCSI and parallel. By far, the easiest type of drive to install is the parallel one, which kind of piggybacks onto the same port your printer uses. Installing a SCSI drive is best left to advanced users because it involves setting switches and things. If you choose a SCSI drive, get someone technical to help you with its installation.

Do It Yourself Connect a Zip Drive

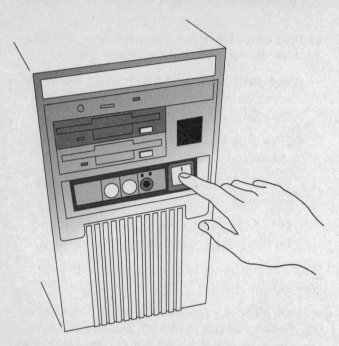

1 Turn your computer off. Turn your printer off as well.

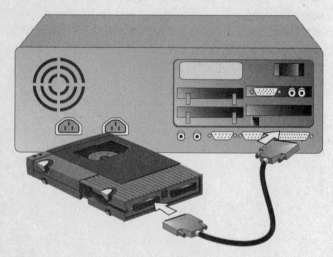

2 Using the cable that came with your drive, connect the end marked "ZIP" to the back of the Zip drive.

3 Connect the other end of the cable to a parallel port on the back of your PC. (If your PC has only one parallel port, disconnect your printer so you can plug in the Zip drive. You'll reconnect the printer in step 4.)

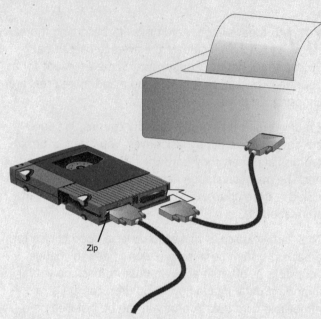

Zip

4 If you disconnected your printer in step 3, connect your printer cable to the second port on the back of the Zip drive.

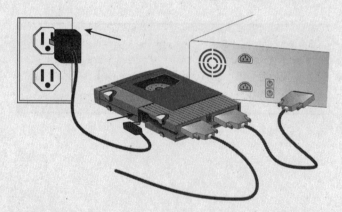

5 Connect the Zip drive to a power supply. A green light on the front of the drive indicates that it is ON and receiving power.

Do It Yourself Connect a Zip Drive

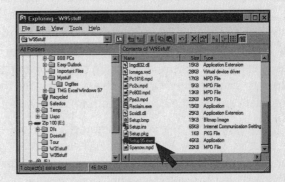

8 Install the Zip tools software by clicking the **Zip drive** in Explorer, opening the **W95stuff** folder, and double-clicking **Setup95**. The Zip driver program is installed in Windows 95, and your drive is now ready to use.

6 Insert the Zip tools disk into the drive, and insert the Install disk into your floppy disk drive.

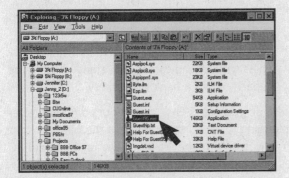

7 If you use Windows 95, open Explorer, click the drive containing the Install disk, and then double-click **Guest95.exe**. Install runs automatically. Your Zip drive is operational, albeit temporarily. To make the drive permanently operational, you still have one more step to complete.

If you use Windows 3.1, open Program Manager's **File** menu, select **Run**, and type **A:SETUP** in the **Command Line** text box. Click **OK** to install your Zip drive. Your Zip drive is now ready to use.

If you use DOS only, type **A:GUEST** and press **Enter**. When the Guest program is complete, type **D:\DOSSTUFF\RECLAIM** and press **Enter** (this assumes that the letter D has been assigned to your Zip drive by Guest). When the Reclaim program is done, your Zip drive is ready to use.

Install Memory

Memory is one of the most important components of your computer. In order to run a program or make changes to a file, that program or file must first be placed into memory. Once the file is in memory, the computer can read the data and perform tasks with it.

In this way, memory acts as the computer's desktop—the place in which work gets done. When you run many programs at one time (which is easy to do with Windows), you can quickly use up your computer's available memory. Sometimes running only one complex program with a large file can use up all your available memory. When Windows runs out of memory, it starts copying the oldest data out of memory to a temporary holding area on the hard drive. From there, if the data is later needed back in memory, Windows copies the data back. As you can imagine, this whole process of copying data in and out of memory slows down your computer a considerable amount. The only solution is to run fewer programs at the same time, to use smaller data files, or to add more memory.

When installing memory, you need to consider many things. For example, memory comes in several flavors: DIP, SIMM, and DIMM. DIP memory chips are inserted individually, making them more difficult to install. SIMM and DIMM memory chips are installed on a separate board, making them simple to install. So if your PC uses DIP chips, you may want a computer technician to install them for you.

Some other things to think about:

- Every PC has a limit to the amount of memory you can install. Check your owner's manual to determine the amount of memory you can add, if any.

- Memory comes in different speeds, such as 100 nanoseconds (100 ns). You have to match the speed of the memory chips your PC already has (unless you opt to replace the existing memory chips).

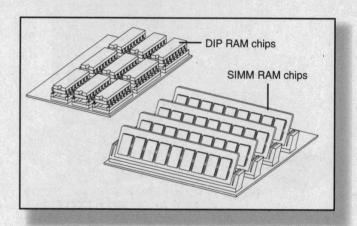

DIP RAM chips

SIMM RAM chips

- Memory also comes in various capacities, such as 16M or 32M. All the memory chips in the same bank of memory must have the same capacity. With SIMMs, this isn't a problem because all the chips on a SIMM memory board automatically have the same capacity. But when installing DIP chips, you'll need to get nine chips of the same capacity to fill a bank of memory.

Where do you start? First, open your computer (after unplugging it of course) and locate the memory chips currently installed. They're in rows of nine (if your PC uses DIP chips) or on a card with nine small chips on it (if your PC uses SIMMs). Write down the number that appears on the top of the chips and make a note of the number of blank memory rows still available. Take this information to your local computer store, and they should be able to help you purchase compatible memory chips for your PC.

Do It Yourself Install DIP Chips

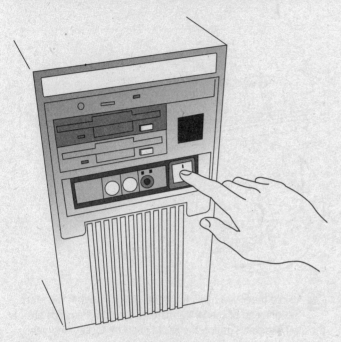

1 First, turn off your PC and unplug it.

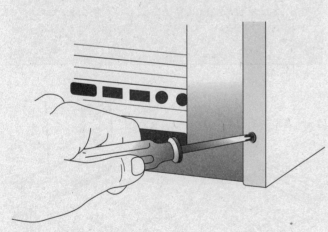

2 Unscrew the PC's cover and remove it.

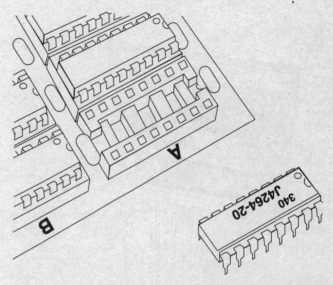

3 Match up the notch at one end of the chip with the same notch on the empty socket.

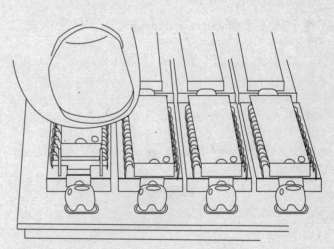

4 Match up the legs on the chip with the holes in the socket and gently press the chip in place. Repeat steps 3 and 4 to insert each additional memory chip into its socket.

5 Put your PC back together and turn it on. Most PCs will automatically recognize the new memory. If yours does not, you will need to update the CMOS (an internal chip that contains details about your PC's configuration). Have someone who is technical help you.

Do It Yourself Install SIMM Chips

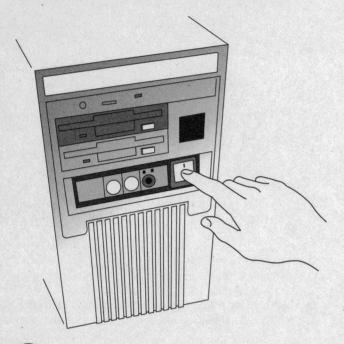

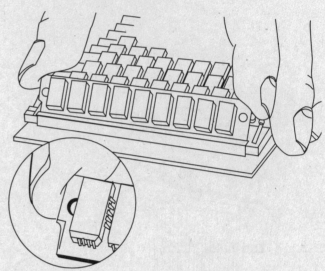

1 First, turn off your PC and unplug it.

3 Hold the SIMM by its top edge. Make sure that the notch at one end of the SIMM matches up with the notch on the SIMM socket. Position the SIMM over the socket, and gently insert it at an angle, as shown in the figure.

Some SIMMs are inserted at a 90 degree angle and then pressed forward into the 10 o'clock position.

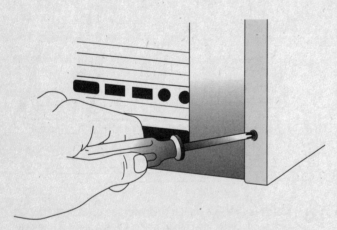

2 Unscrew the PC's cover and remove it.

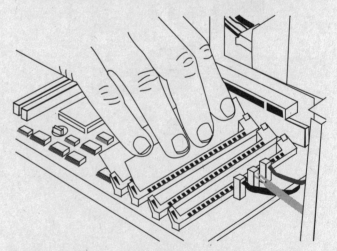

4 After inserting the SIMM, press it gently backwards until the tabs on either side pop up to lock it in place.

5 Put your PC back together and turn it on. Most PCs will automatically recognize the new memory. If yours does not, you will need to update the CMOS (an internal chip that contains details about your PC's configuration). Have someone who is technical help you.

DO IT YOURSELF

Keep Your Data Safe

Many people are too trusting of their computers. It's not uncommon for someone to spend hours—even days—working on a large document, only to lose the document somewhere in the bowels of the computer. How the data is lost is not important (often it's some momentary glitch that no one can explain); what is important is that the work is gone forever. History. Deep-sixed.

Most computer users, especially novice users, are simply unaware of the potential for losing important work. They think computers are the wonder of the twentieth century and, therefore, must be infallible.

Don't be lulled into a false sense of security when using your computer. While catastrophes don't happen every day, you should remember that bad things can and do happen to the precious data you toil and sweat over. Fortunately, there are a number of simple techniques you can use to help prevent the loss of that data, which you'll learn about in this section. You'll also read about ways to check the integrity of your disk drive and files, how to make protection copies of important system files in case something happens to the originals, and more.

What You Will Find in This Section

Make a Backup of Important System Files

Before you install any new software, the first order of business is to make "protection" copies of the critical files that customize the way your computer works. These system files go by such cryptic names as CONFIG.SYS, AUTOEXEC.BAT, WIN.INI, SYSTEM.INI, and SYSTEM.DAT. Note that not all computers have these four files. Which of these *customization files* you have depends on whether you have Windows installed on your PC and which version of Windows you are using. You'll learn more about this later.

The system files tell your computer exactly how you want it to behave. They contain settings that are unique to your computer. Often when you install a new application, its setup program makes changes to your system files. Sometimes your computer doesn't take well to these changes and refuses to operate properly—if at all. So if something should happen to your system after you install a new program, you can use your copies of the original system files to put your system back to the way it was, where you can better determine what to do next.

No, contrary to what you may be thinking, you can't just copy the same files from a friend's computer and expect your computer to work properly. You have to use copies of your own system files. You can see why it makes sense to make copies of these files *before* you install any new software. You keep a copy in case anything happens to the original file—and believe me, many unexpected things can happen. Often the problem has nothing to do with what you do day-to-day on your computer. But the loss of these important files can render your computer useless. So in this task, you'll learn how to copy your system files to a disk that you can use to boot your system if it should fail to do so on its own.

What exactly do the system files do?

- **CONFIG.SYS** tells your computer you want to run special programs called *drivers* whenever the PC is started. Most drivers enable you to use special hardware like a CD-ROM drive or a sound card with your computer.

- **AUTOEXEC.BAT** is a collection of commands your computer runs every time it starts. You

might (for example) include commands in the AUTOEXEC.BAT file that tell your computer to load a memory manager program when it starts up and then to run Windows automatically.

- **WIN.INI** contains basic Windows system settings. In addition, under Windows 3.1, programs often add their own settings to this file.

- **SYSTEM.INI** contains important system information that tells Windows how to interact with your computer.

- **SYSTEM.DAT** is used with Windows 95, and it's called the *system registry*. The system registry is supposed to track the type of files you use and the programs that create them. As a result, when they are installed, Windows 95 programs typically make changes to the registry instead of to WIN.INI (at least, that's how it's supposed to work). However, you should still back up the WIN.INI and SYSTEM.INI files in order to be safe. Windows 95 also makes changes to the system registry.

- **USER.DAT** is another registry file used by Windows 95. The USER.DAT file keeps track of user preferences. Although it's not affected by program installations, you should back up the file from time to time because it is important.

The CONFIG.SYS and AUTOEXEC.BAT files are typically located in the "root" directory of your hard disk drive (for example, C:\). The root directory is the main directory, and all other directories—like the DOS directory or the WINDOWS directory—branch from it. Therefore, to copy these files, look for them in the root directory.

The WIN.INI, SYSTEM.INI, USER.DAT, and SYSTEM.DAT files are typically located in the WINDOWS directory of your hard disk drive (for example, C:\WINDOWS\). Look there for these files.

If you find your computer does not work properly following the installation of a new program, use the copies of the system files on the disk to return your system configuration choices to the way they were. If possible, you may first want to make a copy of the altered system files on a separate disk so you can compare the old and new versions of the files.

Do It Yourself Update Your Startup Disk Using Windows 95

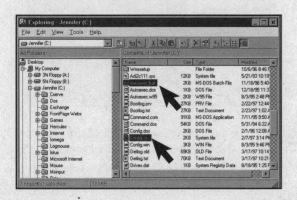

1 Insert your startup disk into the A: drive. ▶**If you don't have a startup disk, see the task "Make a 'Startup' Disk" on page 341.**◀ Then open Explorer and click the drive **C:** icon. The files in the root directory appear listed on the right.

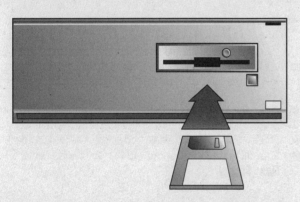

2 Press and hold the **Ctrl** key and click the **AUTOEXEC.BAT** and **CONFIG.SYS** files.

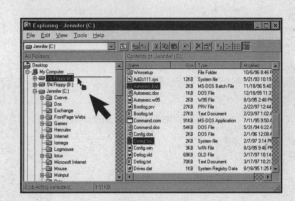

3 Drag the files onto the drive **A:** icon.

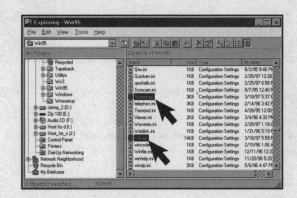

4 Click the **Windows** folder to display the files in the Windows directory. Then press and hold the **Ctrl** key and click the **WIN.INI** and **SYSTEM.INI** files.

(continues)

Do It Yourself   Update Your Startup Disk Using Windows 95   *(continued)*

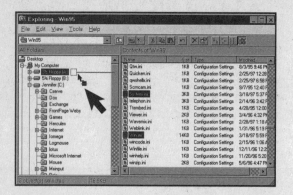

5 Drag the files onto the drive **A:** icon. Then remove the startup disk from the drive, label it, and store it in a safe place.

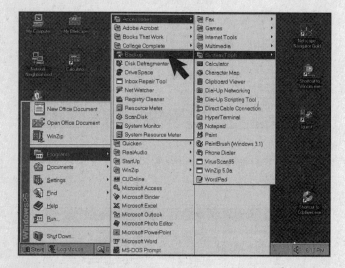

6 The system and the user registries are typically too large to fit on a single disk, so you'll need to back them up onto a separate set of disks. Insert a new disk into drive A, and then click **Start**, select **Programs**, select **Accessories**, select **System Tools**, and click **Backup**.

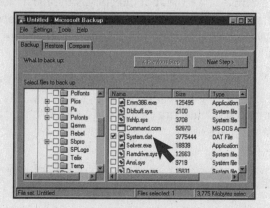

7 If the opening screen appears, click **OK** to bypass it. You may also see a warning telling you that Windows did not detect a tape backup. Click **OK** to bypass the warning. Next, you see the Microsoft Backup screen. Click the plus sign (+) in front of drive C to see a list of folders on that drive.

8 Click the **Windows** folder to open it. Then scroll down and click the box in front of the **SYSTEM.DAT** file to select it. Locate the USER.DAT file and select it as well. A check mark appears in the box to show you that the file is selected. Click **Next Step >**.

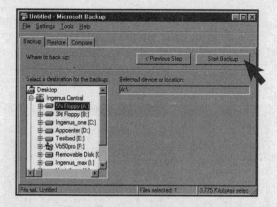

9 Click the drive **A:** icon, and then click **Start Backup**. You may be asked to insert an additional disk when the first disk becomes full.

10 When the backup is complete, you'll see a message telling you so. Click **OK**. Then click **OK** again, and you're returned to the Backup window.

11 Open the **File** menu and select **Exit** to exit the program.

Do It Yourself Update Your Startup Disk Using Windows 3.11

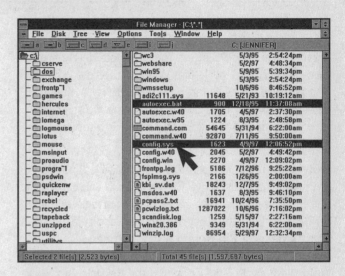

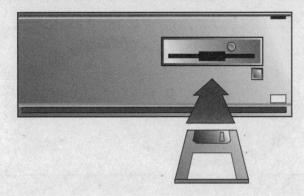

1 Insert your startup disk into the A: drive. ▶**If you don't have a startup disk, see the task "Make a 'Startup' Disk" on page 341.**◀

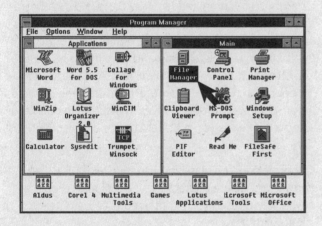

2 Open the **Main** program group and double-click the **File Manager** icon.

3 Display the files in the root directory. Then press and hold **Ctrl** and click both the **AUTOEXEC.BAT** and the **CONFIG.SYS** files to select them.

4 Drag the files to the A icon to copy them to the disk.

5 Display the files in the Windows directory. Then press and hold **Ctrl** and click both the **SYSTEM.INI** and the **WIN.INI** files to select them.

6 Drag the files to the A icon to copy them to the disk.

Restore an Accidentally Deleted File

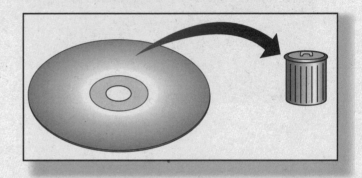

If you accidentally delete a file, there's no need to panic. Windows 95 offers you complete delete protection through its Recycle Bin. When you delete a file, it is moved to the Recycle Bin, which is actually a hidden directory on your hard disk drive. So the file still exists and will continue to exist until the file is removed from the Recycle Bin.

How does a file disappear from the Recycle Bin (and from your hard disk drive forever)? Well, you can empty the Bin completely—removing *all* of your deleted files—by right-clicking the **Recycle Bin** icon and selecting **Empty Recycle Bin** from the shortcut menu. Alternatively, you can remove one or more specific files from the Recycle Bin by opening the **Recycle Bin**, clicking the file names, and pressing **Delete**.

If you don't empty the Recycle Bin occasionally, it starts to fill up. When the Recycle Bin becomes full of deleted files, the oldest files in the Bin are removed (deleted from the hard disk drive) to make room for more recently deleted files. You can increase the size of the Recycle Bin by right-clicking the **Recycle Bin** icon, selecting **Properties**, and dragging the **Maximum Size of Recycle Bin** slider to the right. Click **OK** to save your change.

Under Windows 3.1 and DOS (versions 5.0 and later), the process of restoring an accidentally deleted file (using a program called Undelete) is different. When you delete a file, its name is removed from your PC's master index, but the data in the file remains intact. The operating system also marks the space previously taken by the file as available, so that another file can eventually be stored in its place. As long as you reclaim the file quickly—before doing much more work on your computer—there is a very good chance that you will be completely successful raising your deleted file from the "dead." The longer you wait, however, the greater the chance that the data from another file will overwrite the spot occupied by the deleted file. Once that

happens, you may be able to revive only part of the file, or you may not be able to get back any at all.

The Undelete command has two basic levels of operation. The first level, called *standard*, does its magic by using the quirk of MS-DOS just described. It's the method the Undelete command uses if you have not directly specified that you want to use the second level of operation: Delete Tracking. Delete Tracking stores information about deleted files in a special hidden registry, which gives you a better chance of reclaiming lost files.

Important note: Unless you use the Delete Tracking system, if you delete a directory, you will not be able to revive any of the files it contained that were deleted along with it.

> MS-DOS (versions 6.x and above) offers an additional delete-protection system called Delete Sentry. It provides an even higher level of protection than Delete Tracking.

To set up Delete Tracking or Delete Sentry in Windows 3.1, open the **Options** menu in Windows Undelete (located in the Microsoft Tools program group) and select **Configure Delete Protection**. Select the type of protection you want and click **OK**.

Do It Yourself Restore a File Using Windows 95

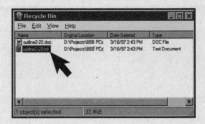

2 Press the **Ctrl** key and click the names of the files you want to undelete.

1 Double-click the **Recycle Bin** icon, and a list of recently deleted files appears.

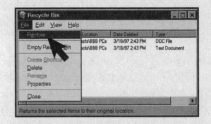

3 Open the **File** menu and select **Restore**. The files you selected are restored to their original directories.

Do It Yourself Restore a File Using Windows 3.11

1 As soon as you realize you've deleted a file by mistake, run the Windows Undelete program. Double-click the **Undelete** icon, which is typically located in the **Microsoft Tools** group.

3 Select the directory that contains the erased file, and then click **OK**.

(continues)

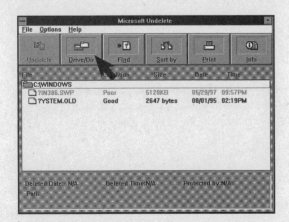

2 In the Microsoft Undelete window, click the **Drive/Dir** button.

Do It Yourself Restore a File Using Windows 3.11 *(continued)*

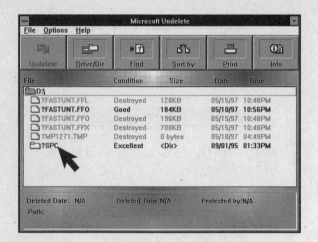

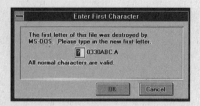

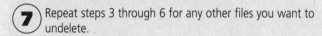

6 If you are undeleting a file that was not tracked with Delete Tracker, you are asked to provide a first letter for the file name. Type the letter and click **OK**.

7 Repeat steps 3 through 6 for any other files you want to undelete.

8 When you finish undeleting, select **File**, **Exit** to close the Microsoft Undelete window.

4 The Microsoft Undelete window displays the recently deleted files in the selected directory, along with their names and the condition they're in. Click the file or files you want to undelete. (If a file name starts with a question mark, MS-DOS didn't track it with Delete Tracker and doesn't know the full file name; files with complete names were tracked.)

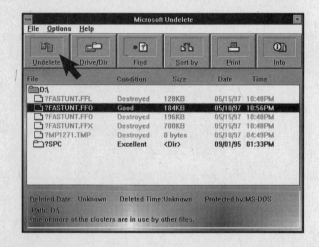

5 Click the **Undelete** button, and the Undelete program attempts to undelete the file.

Check a Disk for Errors with ScanDisk

If you are using Windows 3.11 (with MS-DOS 6.x or later) or Windows 95 on your computer, you have a powerful ally available: the ScanDisk program. This program checks the integrity of your hard disk drive (and floppy disks too, though that isn't done as often), as well as all the files on it. For example, if the computer is having trouble reading the contents of a file, sometimes ScanDisk can locate the problem and fix it.

In addition, ScanDisk can survey the entire surface of your computer's hard disk drive, looking for trouble spots. If there's a glitch on the surface of the hard disk drive—whether or not data is there—ScanDisk can spot it. The ScanDisk program can then "mark" the bad spot so that it will never be used to store data. And if the bad spot already contains data, ScanDisk can often recover it and move it to an undamaged area, preventing data loss.

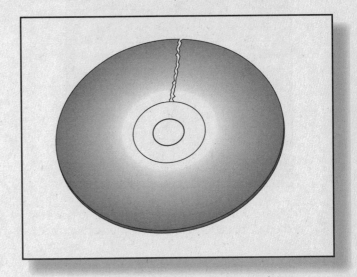

You should use the ScanDisk program at least once a week to check the integrity of your computer's hard disk drive. Perform ScanDisk's thorough scan once a month.

Do It Yourself   Check a Disk in Windows 95

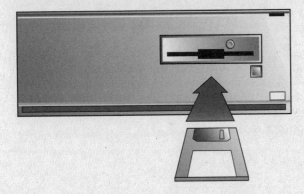

1 To fix a floppy disk, insert the disk into one of the floppy disk drives and close the door (if necessary). To scan your hard disk, skip this step.

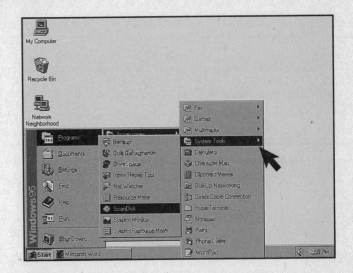

2 Click the **Start** button, point to **Programs**, select **Accessories**, select **System Tools**, and then click **ScanDisk**.

(continues)

Do It Yourself Check a Disk in Windows 95   *(continued)*

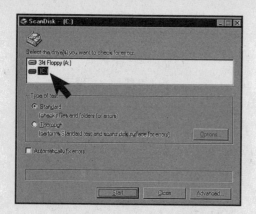

3 The ScanDisk dialog box appears, asking you to pick a disk to check. Click the letter of the drive you want to check.

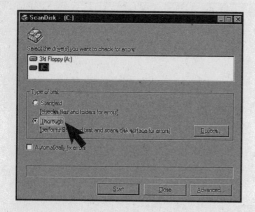

4 To have ScanDisk check for and repair only file and folder problems, click **Standard**. If you want ScanDisk to also check for bad places on the disk, click **Thorough**.

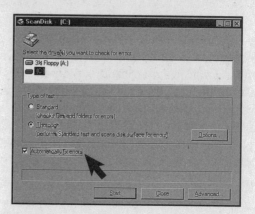

5 To have ScanDisk repair errors without asking for confirmation, check the **Automatically Fix Errors** check box. (If you leave this unchecked, ScanDisk will let you choose how to repair the error. For example, if ScanDisk finds a lost file cluster, it lets you decide whether to delete the cluster or save it.) In most cases, you can select the **Automatically Fix Errors** option without any problem.

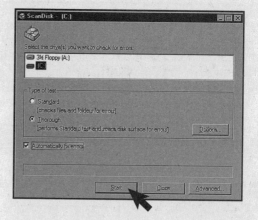

6 Click the **Start** button, and ScanDisk starts checking the disk. If ScanDisk finds a problem, it either corrects the problem or displays a prompt asking you how you want to correct the problem. Follow the on-screen instructions until the operation is complete.

Do It Yourself Check a Disk in Windows 95

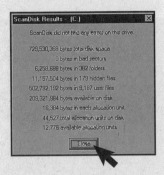

7 When ScanDisk is done, it displays a log of all the problems it found and corrections it made. Click the **Close** button, and then click **Close** again to quit.

Do It Yourself Check a Disk with Windows 3.11

1 Exit all programs, including Windows. At the DOS prompt, change to the DOS directory by typing **CD\DOS** and pressing **Enter.**

2 Type **SCANDISK** and press **Enter**. The ScanDisk utility program starts and immediately reviews your computer's hard disk drive.

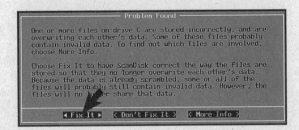

3 If ScanDisk finds a problem, it displays a message and asks whether or not you want to fix it. Usually, you'll want to select **Fix It** to correct the problem.

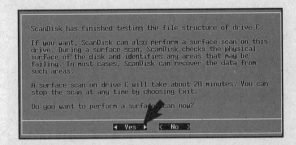

4 After scanning the disk drive and fixing problems (if necessary), ScanDisk offers to scan the entire surface of the hard disk drive. Choose **Yes** to start the scan (which can take from five minutes to over an hour, depending on the size of the hard disk drive). Or, choose **No** to bypass the surface scan test.

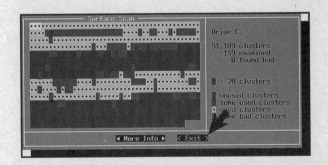

5 (Optional) If you do elect to perform a surface scan, you can stop the process any time by choosing **Exit**.

(continues)

Do It Yourself Check a Disk with Windows 3.11   *(continued)*

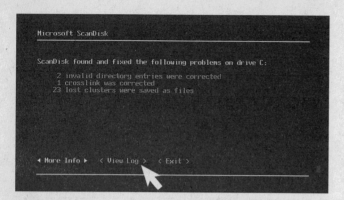

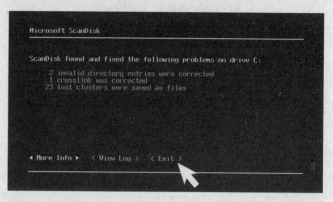

6 When the surface scan is complete, ScanDisk displays a report indicating what, if any, problems were found and the remedies taken. You can choose to view the complete log by selecting **View Log**.

8 Select **Exit** when you finish using ScanDisk.

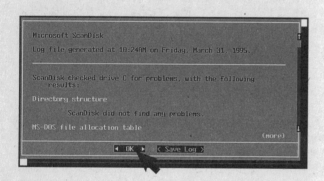

7 The View Log screen displays a categorized report of the scanning process. When you finish reading the log, click **OK**, or select **Save Log** to save the log in a text file (the file is named SCANDISK.LOG).

Back Up the Contents of Your Hard Disk Drive with Microsoft Backup

Computers can be finicky. Though a finicky personality suits most cats, it's not an endearing trait in a computer. Because you use your computer to keep track of important information, you want to be able to trust that the data you feed into your computer will be there when you need it.

Unfortunately, there are no guarantees in life. Murphy is alive and well and living inside your computer, and he has a whole set of laws just for PCs. One goes something like this: "The odds of losing a file are directly proportional to the importance of the data it contains." It always seems that the more you need some scrap of data stored on your computer, the more likely it is that the computer gremlins just had that scrap for lunch.

To ward off such a catastrophe, you should make regular *backup copies* of the data stored on your computer's hard disk drive. You can back up your program files as well, but because you have copies of them already (on the program's original installation disks), you don't usually need to back them up. If anything happens to the files you back up, you can repair the damage using the copies you made. Of course, you only use the backup copy if something awful happens to the original file; if nothing ever happens to the original, the backup is never used. It's just there for your peace of mind.

You don't have to make copies of all the files on your entire hard drive every time you want to create a backup. You have these backup options to choose from:

> **Full** backs up all files, even if they haven't been altered since the last backup.

> **Incremental** backs up only those files that have been altered since the last backup (whether it was full or incremental).

> **Differential** backs up only those files that have been altered since the last full backup.

If your computer has a *tape backup* drive that is compatible with Windows 95, you can use it to make regular backups of your PC's hard disk. If you have a Zip or a Jaz drive, that will work just as well as a tape backup drive. However, if your computer does not have a tape backup, a Zip, or a Jaz drive, you will need to use the

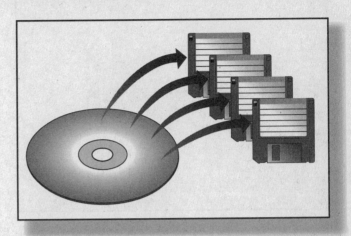

floppy disk drives to create your backup files. Backing up on floppy disks is harder and more time-consuming, but such is the cost of doing business with a cold-blooded and finicky computer. Also, note that the more data on your computer's hard disk drive, the more floppy disks it takes to back it up. It is not uncommon to need 30 or 40 disks to store the complete contents of a 250 megabyte hard drive. For today's 1 gigabyte drive, expect to use four times as many disks or more. Because so many floppy disks are needed for a full backup of the entire hard drive, you might want to back up only certain files (such as data files) or folders.

If you use Microsoft Windows 3.1, it comes with a utility called Backup that helps you make that all-important copy of your computer's hard disk drive—all of it or just parts of it. Unfortunately, the version of Microsoft Backup that comes with Windows 3.1 does not support the use of tape backups. However, both Zip and Jaz drives *do* come with software that will work with Windows 3.1. Windows 95 comes with an updated version of Microsoft Backup that supports compatible tape drives, along with Zip and Jaz drives.

The following tasks discuss the various Windows versions of Backup. MS-DOS also comes with a backup program; check the MS-DOS manual for more information.

Do It Yourself   Back Up in Windows 95

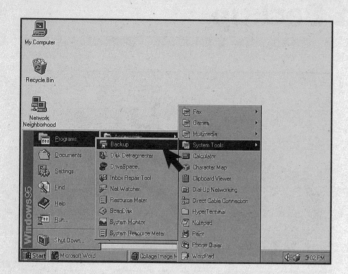

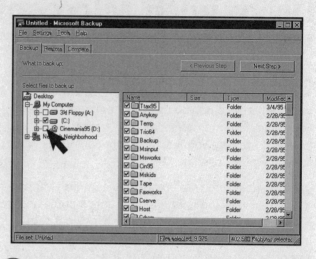

(1) Click the **Start** button, select **Programs**, select **Accessories**, select **System Tools**, and then click **Backup**.

(4) The Backup screen appears, allowing you to start backing up files. To back up all the files on a drive, click the check box next to the drive letter, and then skip to step 8. To back up only selected files and folders, proceed with step 5.

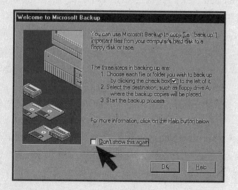

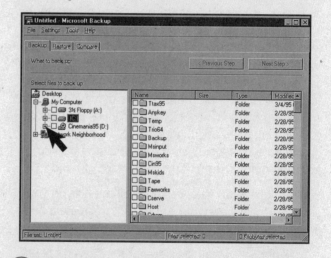

(2) The first time you run Backup, a dialog box appears, providing an overview of the process. Read the information, and then click the **Don't Show This Again** check box (so it won't come up next time). Click **OK**.

(5) Click the plus sign (+) next to the icon for the drive that contains the folders and files you want to back up. The tree expands to show the first layer of folders on the selected drive.

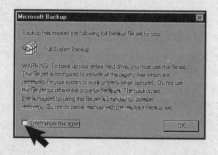

(3) Another dialog box appears, indicating that Backup created a file set for backing up all your system files. Read the message, click the **Don't Show This Again** check box, and click **OK**.

Do It Yourself Back Up in Windows 95

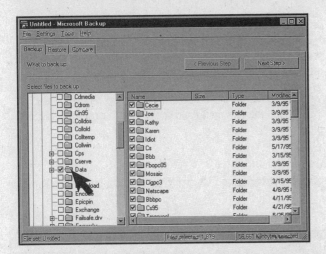

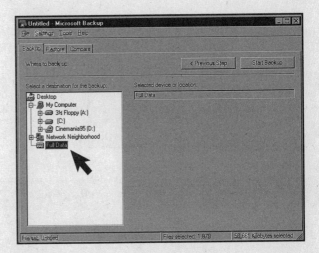

6 To back up an entire folder, click the check box next to its icon. If you click the check box next to a folder that has subfolders, all its subfolders and files are selected.

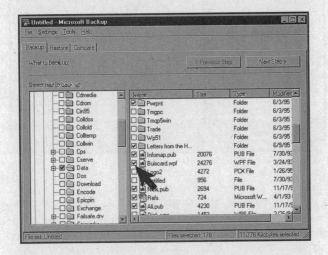

7 To back up only some files in a folder, click the folder's icon in the tree list (on the left), and then click the check box next to each file and subfolder you want to back up in the file list (on the right).

8 Click the **Next Step** button.

9 Backup asks which drive you want to use to store the backup files. Click the icon for the drive you want to use to store the backup files. This can be a floppy disk drive, a tape backup drive, a Zip or Jaz drive, a network drive, or another hard disk drive.

10 If you're backing up to a floppy disk drive, a Zip or Jaz drive, or a tape backup unit, make sure you have a disk or tape in the drive. Then click the **Start Backup** button.

> You can continue to work as Windows 95 performs its backup; however, your programs may work a bit more slowly.

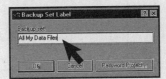

11 A dialog box appears, prompting you to type a name for the backup set. A record of the backup will be stored under this name, which enables you to quickly restore files later. Type a name for the backup set, and then click **OK**.

(continues)

Do It Yourself   Back Up in Windows 95   (continued)

12 Backup starts the backup operation and displays on-screen instructions to help you complete the process. When you see a message telling when the backup is done, click **OK.** You're returned to the Backup dialog box.

13 Click **OK** to return to the main Backup window. Then open the **File** menu and select **Exit** to close the Backup program.

Do It Yourself   Back Up in Windows 3.11

1 Open the **Microsoft Tools** program group and double-click the **Backup** program icon to start the Backup program.

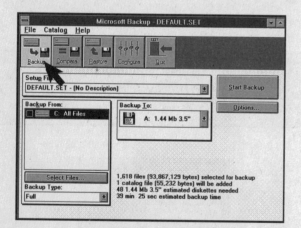

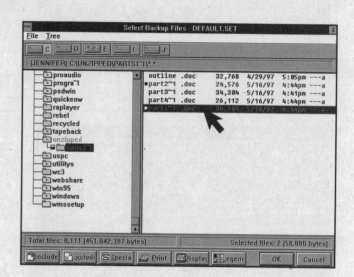

2 In the Microsoft Backup window, click the **Backup** button. If the words "All Files" appear next to a drive, all the files on that drive are currently selected for backup. (Even if you select "All Files," you can *prevent* certain files from being backed up; see step 3.) To remove the "All Files" message, double-click the drive icon. Double-click the drive icon again to make the words, "All Files" reappear. If you decide to back up all the files on a drive, skip to step 7.

3 If you want to specify files to back up (or if you want to prevent selected files from being backed up), click **Select Files**.

4 To specify the files you want to back up, click their directory in the list on the left. The files then appear in a list on the right. Double-click the files you want to select. To select adjacent files, press and hold the **Shift** key as you drag over the file names. To select all the files in a particular directory, double-click the directory in the list on the left. When a file is selected, it appears with a black box. To deselect a file (in order to prevent it from being backed up), double-click the file.

Do It Yourself Back Up in Windows 3.11

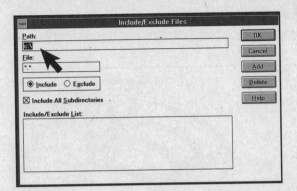

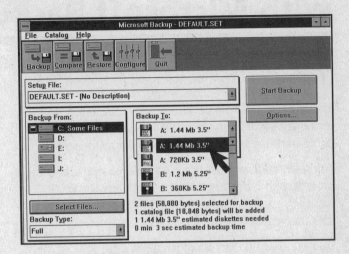

5 (Optional) If you want to specify a particular group of files to include or exclude from the backup (such as all the files that end in *.DOC), click either the **Include** or **Exclude** button at the bottom of the window. The Include/Exclude Files dialog box appears. In the **Path** text box, type the directory path for the series of files you want to include or exclude. In the **File** text box, type a file spec such as *.DOC (or leave it at *.* to select all the files in the specified path). Specify whether or not you want to **Include All Subdirectories**. Then click **Add** and click **OK**. You're returned to the Select Backup Files dialog box.

6 When you finish selecting files, click **OK** to return to the main Microsoft Backup dialog box.

8 From the **Backup To** drop-down list, select the floppy drive you want to back up to.

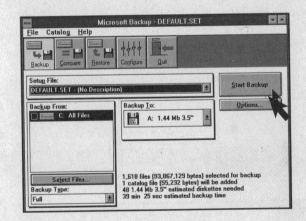

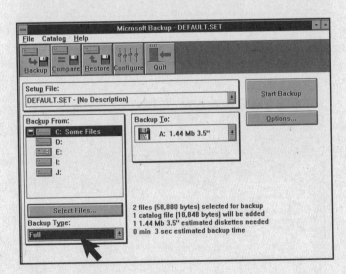

9 Click **Start Backup** to start the backup process. You'll see a warning telling you not to try to access the drive while it's doing a backup. Click **OK**. While the backup's going on, have your disks ready; insert them one by one into the floppy disk drive as prompted. *Number the disks as you use them.*

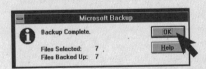

10 Microsoft Backup shows this message when the backup is complete. Click **OK**, and you're returned to the main Microsoft Backup dialog box.

7 In the **Backup Type** drop-down list, select the backup type you want: **Full**, **Incremental**, or **Differential** (each was described earlier in this task).

11 Click the **Quit** button to leave the Backup program. If you're asked to save any changes you've made to the backup settings, choose to save the settings in **DEFAULT.SET**, and then click **OK**.

Restore the Contents of Your Hard Disk with Microsoft Backup

The inverse of backing up the files on your computer's hard disk drive is restoring files that have been lost or damaged. The Backup program, described in the previous task, is useful not only for backing up your computer's hard disk drive, but also for restoring files.

The restoration process is a bit simpler than the backup process, and it doesn't take as long. Normally, you'll want to restore only one or two files that were erased (or otherwise met an untimely end).

Do note that the success of restoring a file to your computer's hard disk drive depends entirely on how "fresh" the file is. If you've deleted a file that you alter from time to time—it's the text of the book you're writing, for example—you will only be able to restore the file to the way it was the last time you backed it up. If you haven't backed up the file in two months, the restored copy will be two months old—and you will have lost two months' work. This is why making regular backups is so important.

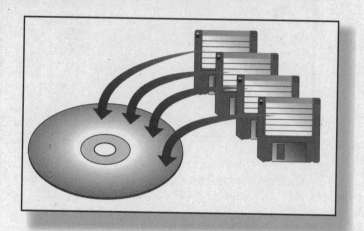

Before you start to restore a file, make sure you have all your backup disks handy. During the restoration process, you will be prompted to insert specific numbered disks into the computer.

Do It Yourself   Restore in Windows 95

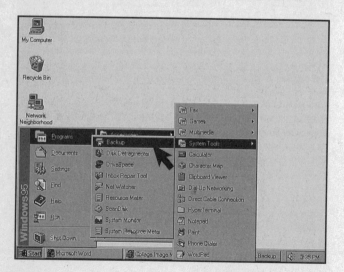

1 With Windows 95 running, click the **Start** button, select **Programs**, select **Accessories**, select **System Tools**, and then click **Backup**.

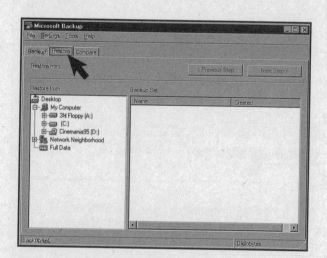

2 Microsoft Backup starts, and you see the main window. Click the **Restore** tab.

Do It Yourself Restore in Windows 95

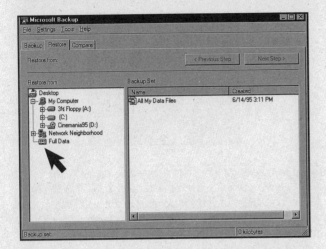

3 A list of the drives you might have used for the backup appears on the left side. Insert your backup tape or the last floppy disk of the backup set into the drive. In the **Restore From** list, click the drive that contains the backup disk or tape.

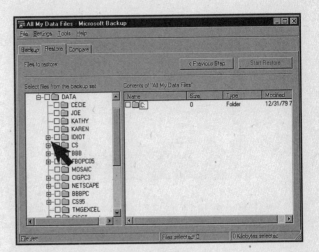

6 The list on the left changes to show all the folders and files that are on the backup tape or disks. Under **Select Files from the Backup Set**, click the plus sign (**+**) to display the files in a particular folder.

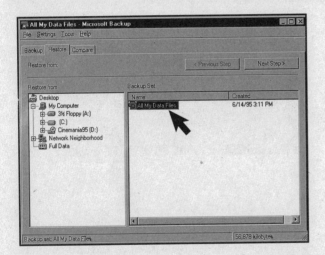

4 If there is more than one backup set name in the Backup Set list, click the name of the backup set you want to restore. (You entered a backup set name when you performed the backup.)

5 Click the **Next Step** button.

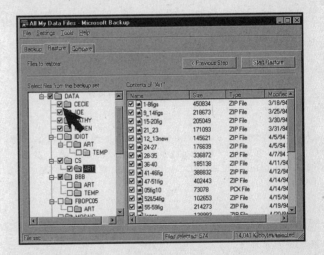

7 To restore the contents of an entire folder, click the folder's check box in the **Select Files from the Backup Set** list (as shown here). To restore only selected files in a folder, click the folder icon in the **Select Files from the Backup Set** list, and then click the check box next to each file you want to restore in the **Contents Of** list (on the right side of the screen).

8 Click the **Start Restore** button.

(continues)

Do It Yourself Restore in Windows 95 *(continued)*

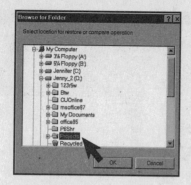

9 Select the drive or folder to which you want to restore your files, and then click **OK**.

10 If you are restoring from floppy disks, a dialog box appears, telling you which disk to insert. Follow the on-screen instructions until the restoration is complete. When you see a message telling you the restoration is finished, click **OK**. You're returned to the Restore dialog box.

11 Click **OK**, and you're returned to the main Restore window. Then open the **File** menu and select **Exit** to exit the program.

Do It Yourself Restore in Windows 3.11

1 In Windows, locate the **Backup** program icon and double-click it to start the Backup program. The normal location for the Backup program icon is the **Microsoft Tools** group in Program Manager.

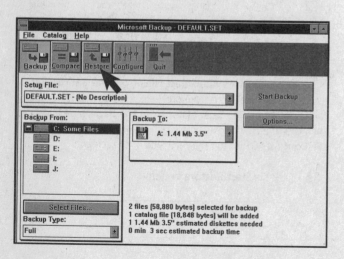

2 In the Microsoft Backup window, click the **Restore** button.

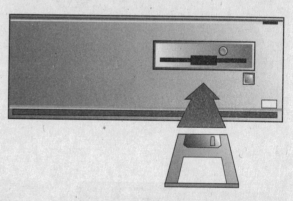

3 Put the first disk from your set of backup disks into the drive.

Do It Yourself Restore in Windows 3.11

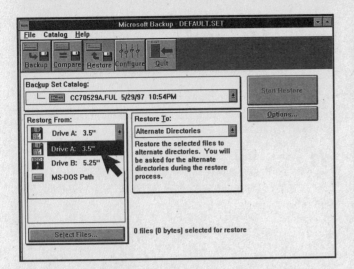

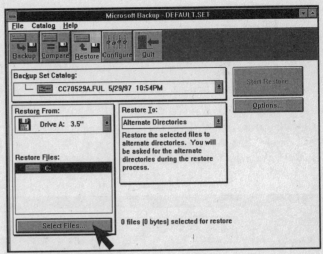

4 In the **Restore From** drop-down list, select the disk drive you want to restore files from.

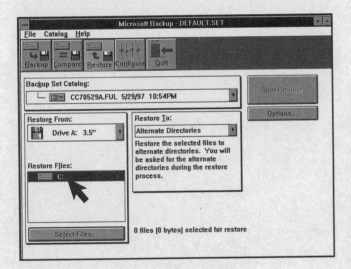

5 To restore all the files backed up from a particular drive, double-click the hard disk drive's letter in the **Restore Files** list and skip to step 7. To select only certain files to restore, click the drive's letter once instead and proceed with step 6.

6 If you want to select certain files to restore, click the **Select Files** button. In the Select Restore Files dialog box, double-click those files you want to restore. (If you want to select adjacent files, press and hold the **Shift** key and drag the mouse pointer over those files you want to select.) When you finish selecting files, click **OK**.

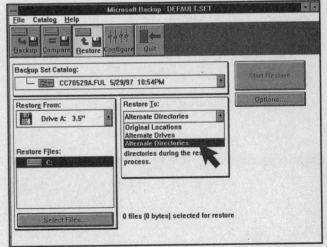

7 In the **Restore To** list, select where you want the files restored to. Your available options are **Original Locations** (the usual choice), **Alternate Drives**, and **Alternate Directories**.

(continues)

Do It Yourself   Restore in Windows 3.11   *(continued)*

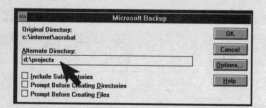

8 If you selected Alternate Drives or Alternate Directories in step 7, this dialog box appears. Select the drive or folder to which you want to restore the files, and then click **OK**.

10 Microsoft Backup displays this message when the restoration is complete. Click **OK**, and you're returned to the Microsoft Backup dialog box.

11 Click the **Quit** button to return to Windows. If you're asked to save any changes you made to the Restore settings, choose to save the settings in **DEFAULT.SET**, and then click **OK**.

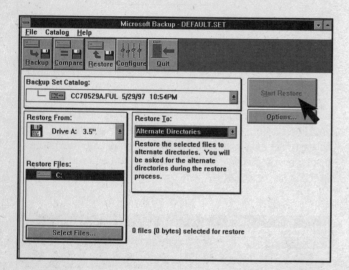

9 Click **Start Restore** to begin the restoration process. You'll see a warning telling you not to access the drive while the restoration is in progress; click **OK**.

Check for Viruses with Microsoft AntiVirus

We live in strange times. Not only can people get sick with a virus, computers can, too. With computers, however, a virus is not a living microbe, but a program specifically designed by some bored programmer to cause damage to the data in your computer. No one really knows why people make the effort to create a computer virus (few ever admit doing so), but we computer users have to live with the fact that there are now several hundred known computer viruses out there—and any one of them could cause trouble for you.

Viruses can invade a personal computer in a number of ways. The most common happens when you use an "infected" program. You might obtain this program from a friend, or you might download it from an online service like CompuServe or from the Internet. It can even come from a commercial program you bought and installed on your computer, although that's unlikely.

Realistically (and fortunately), commercial software is seldom infected by a computer virus, and the same is true of programs available through online services like CompuServe, America Online, and PRODIGY (but not the Internet). Programs that might affect the reputation of a service or a company are checked before they are made available to the public. It is far more likely your computer will become infected by a program you get from a friend or associate.

If your system becomes infected, you may find it acting quite strange. It may not even start!

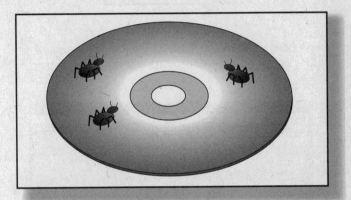

▶(In such a case, you'll need to boot your system with your startup disk, which you created in the task "Make a 'Startup' Disk" on page 341.◀) Once you can start up your system, you can use an antivirus program to ferret out your viruses—and if possible, destroy them. One such program, Microsoft AntiVirus, comes with Windows 3.1. Windows 95 does not provide its own antivirus program, but there are many such programs available commercially and on the Internet. ▶See the "Software Buyer's Guide" (page 521) for more information.◀

You should get into the habit of running an antivirus program at least once a month—more often if you regularly install new software on your computer or share disks with others. Some antivirus programs can be set up to run in the background while you work on other programs, thereby providing you with 24-hour protection.

Do It Yourself Check for Viruses in Windows 3.11

1 Open the **Microsoft Tools** program group and double-click the **Anti-Virus** icon to start the Anti-Virus program.

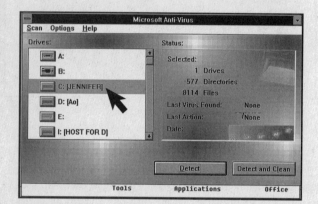

2 The Anti-Virus program starts and does some preliminary testing. When you're ready to scan for viruses, select the drive you want to check, such as drive **C:** for your computer's hard disk drive.

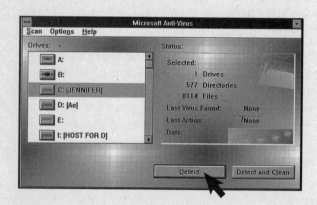

3 Click **Detect** if you only want the program to look for viruses; click **Detect and Clean** if you want the program to not only look for viruses, but to attempt to get rid of them.

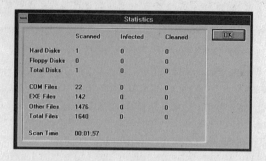

4 After scanning your computer's disk drive, the program displays a Statistics report, which indicates the number and type of files it checked and whether any files were infected and/or cleaned. Review the report, and then click **OK**.

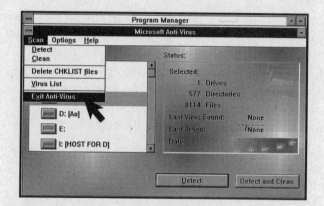

5 Select **Scan**, **Exit Anti-Virus** to leave the Anti-Virus program.

DO IT YOURSELF

Work on the Internet

I n the section "Connect with the Outside World" (page 227)◄, you learned how to get onto the Internet "on-ramp" using your Web browser; in this section, you'll learn how to find your way around one particular part of the Internet: the World Wide Web.

The WWW (World Wide Web, or simply Web for short) is made up of special sites along the Internet that support a technology known as Web browsing. On the Web, you can navigate from one place to another by selecting a link that appears on a Web page. A link might be a picture or some highlighted text that appears on-screen. You just click the picture or text, and your Web browser links (or jumps) you to the requested spot on the Internet. With a Web browser such as Netscape Navigator (which is part of the larger package of Netscape Communicator) or Internet Explorer, surfing the Web is as simple and easy as using Windows.

Also, with Netscape Navigator or Internet Explorer, you can easily access the other parts of the Web, such as FTP (File Transfer Protocol) sites, UseNet (newsgroup) sites, and Gopher sites. You can even send electronic messages (e-mail) using your Web browser.

What You Will Find in This Section

Jump from Web Page to Web Page Using Links

When you start your Web browser, it displays your home page. Typically, this home page is the "home" of the browser itself: For example, if you use Netscape Navigator (or the larger program, Netscape Communicator), you'll start out on Netscape's home page. From there, you can go to other pages on the Web in one of several ways:

- By clicking a *link*
- By entering the *Web address* of the page you want to view
- By selecting a previously saved address from a list
- By backing up to the last Web page you viewed

Links are by far the easiest way to explore the World Wide Web. Links are graphic pictures or specially highlighted text that automatically jump you to a different Web page when you click them. In this task, you'll learn how to use links to explore the World Wide Web. In upcoming tasks, you'll learn more about entering Web addresses, selecting previously saved addresses, and backing up to a previously viewed Web page to explore the Web.

Typically, text links are marked in blue by default. When you visit a particular link, your Web browser changes the link's text color to purple so you can easily tell which links you've already explored. Of course, like many things on the Web, even this small convention is changing. So you might run into colors other than blue and purple, but you get the idea. In addition to text links, you'll find graphical pictures that are links. However, when you click one of these graphic links, the picture doesn't change so it is harder to tell which ones you've used.

When you move the mouse pointer over a link, the address of the Web page to which it will connect you appears at the bottom of your Web browser screen. This gives you some idea of where you'll be going if you decide to click the link at some point.

In the *Do It Yourself* task, you'll use Netscape Navigator to learn how to use links to navigate the Web. However, You can follow these same basic steps for using links no matter which Web browser you're using.

What to Do When a Link Fails

You need to know one important thing before you start exploring the Web. Sometimes when you try to connect to a Web page, it isn't displayed completely (it fails to load). Here's how to tell when you're in trouble. Normally, when you click a link or enter an address to jump to, meteors flash across the Netscape icon (the big "N" in the upper-right corner). In Internet Explorer, a comet spins around the big E. This is good. If the meteors stop flashing (or the comet stops spinning), it means that Netscape Navigator or Internet Explorer has hung—meaning you're getting nowhere quickly.

If that happens, click the **Reload** button at the top of the Navigator window. If you use Internet Explorer, click the **Refresh** button instead. If the meteors (or comets) move again but then stop and nothing happens for a minute or two, something's hung up again. Click **Stop** to discontinue loading the Web page. Then try clicking the link again.

Do It Yourself Using Links

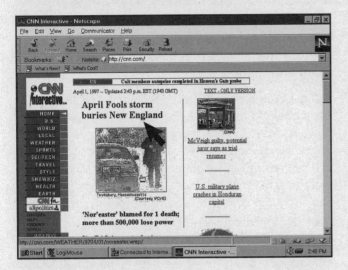

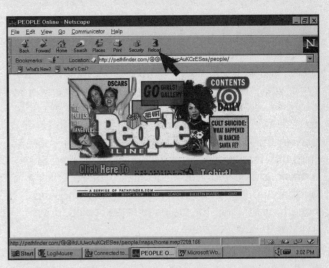

1 Connect to the Internet and start your Web browser. If you need help connecting to the Internet or starting your Web browser, ▶**see the section "Connect with the Outside World" on page 227.**◀

2 When you move the mouse over a link, the address of the Web page it links to appears at the bottom of the Web browser's window. To connect to a linked Web page, click the link.

After you visit a linked site, the text link typically changes color from blue to purple.

3 Some links are graphic images instead of text. To connect to the linked Web page, just click the graphic.

4 If a link fails, you can click **Reload** (or **Refresh**, if you use Internet Explorer) to reload the page. You might have to do this, for example, if a page contains a lot of complex graphics; graphics often cause loading problems.

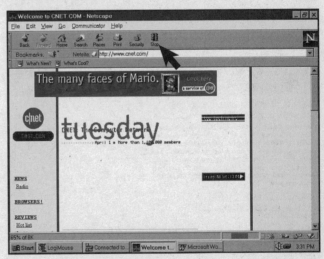

5 If you fail to connect to a page, click **Stop**. This tells your Web browser to stop trying to load the page. You can click the link again to retry.

Visit a Previously Viewed Web Page

As you change from one page to another on the Web, you create a kind of working history of where you've been. Your Web browser saves this history for you, making it easy for you to return to any previously viewed page. Because it can take a few seconds to copy Web pages to your PC so that they can be displayed, the Web pages you view are stored on your hard disk temporarily. That way if you ever need to see a previously viewed Web page again, you can click a button, and it pops back up in about a second—no need to wait again for the page to be copied (downloaded) to your computer.

Sounds great? It is, except that the history your Web browser tracks is for the current session only; it is erased when you exit the program. However, if you find a Web page that you like, you can save its address

permanently so you can return to it at any time. ▶**See "Return to a Favorite Web Page" on page 431 for more information.**◀

Using a Web browser's history feature is a lot like reading a book. To return to a previously viewed page, you move backward in the "book." You can move as many pages backward as you like. After moving backward, you can return to your starting point by moving forward through your previously viewed Web pages. You can also jump directly to a particular previously viewed page by selecting it from the history list.

Although Netscape Navigator is featured in the following task, you can follow these steps to navigate history within Internet Explorer as well.

Do It Yourself Navigate Through History

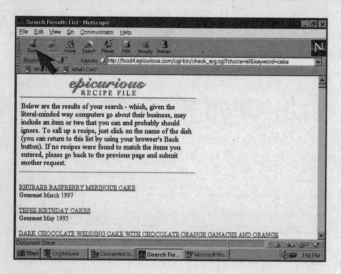

1 To return to the Web page you just viewed, click the **Back** button.

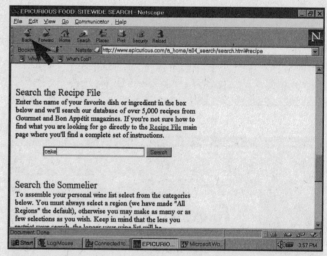

2 Move backward one more page by clicking the **Back** button again. You can repeat this as many times as you need to return to a previously viewed page. If you use Netscape Communicator, you can click and hold the **Back** button and select a previously viewed page to jump directly to that page.

Do It Yourself   Navigate Through History

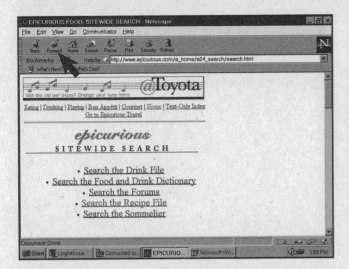

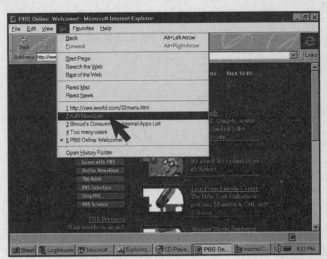

3 To return to the page you were just on, click the **Forward** button. As with the Back button, you can click the Forward button as many times as necessary to return to your starting position. If you use Netscape Communicator, you can return to any previously viewed page by clicking and holding the **Forward** button and selecting a page from the list.

5 If you use Internet Explorer, you can jump directly to a previously viewed page by opening the **Go** menu and selecting the page you want to visit from those listed at the bottom of the menu.

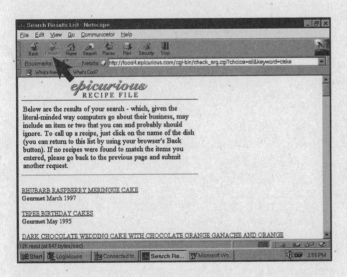

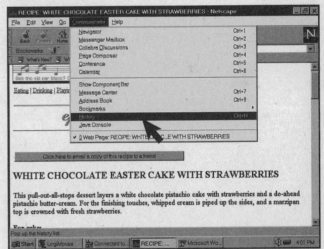

4 If the Forward (or Backward) button is gray, you have moved to the end (or the beginning) of the history. You can't select the gray button because you've moved as far forward or backward in history as you can.

6 If you use Netscape Navigator, open the **Communicator** menu and select **History** instead. The History dialog box appears. Internet Explorer has a History dialog box too; to make it appear, open the **Go** menu and select **Open History Folder**.

(continues)

Do It Yourself Navigate Through History *(continued)*

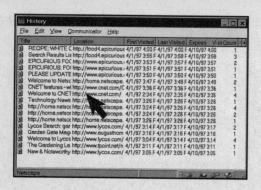

7 In the History dialog box, double-click the page you want to view. Netscape Navigator or Internet Explorer displays the page you selected.

8 Click the **Close** button to remove the History dialog box.

View a Specific Web Page

Each Web page has its own address or URL (Uniform Resource Locator). A typical URL looks like this:

> http://pages.nyu.edu/~liaos/indigo.html

If you know its address, you can jump directly to the Web page you want by simply typing that address into your Web browser. Every address or URL (pronounced "earl") has two parts: a content identifier and a location.

> If you don't know the address of a particular Web page or even which pages you might want to view, you can search for applicable pages using a Web search tool such as Yahoo!. ▶See "Search for Information" on page 437 for more information.◀ You can also get addresses for hot Web sites from any of several magazines such as *The Net*, *Websight*, and *Internet World*.

The first part, the content identifier (or content-id for short), tells you what protocol or language was used to create the page being displayed. For Web pages, the content-id is http:// because Web pages are written using HyperText Transfer Protocol (HTTP). This means that most of the addresses you'll enter into your Web browser will begin with the letters http.

Web browsers also support other protocols such as ftp://, gopher://, telnet://, and news://. These protocols connect you to other parts of the Internet besides the Web. For example, you might connect to an ftp site to download (receive) a file, or you might connect to a gopher site to research a topic in some university's archives.

The second part of every URL identifies the location of the page. This part of the address looks suspiciously like a directory path—which is exactly what it is. Every Web page is actually a file that exists on some Internet computer. These directory paths follow the UNIX format, using forward slashes (/) in place of the backslashes (\) you're used to seeing in DOS and Windows. The paths can also contain periods (.). Take a look at this address:

> http://www.conline.com/txmall/garden.html

The address indicates that the file garden.html is located on the Internet computer known as www.conline.com in the txmall directory.

Once you enter an address into your Web browser, you can save it so that you can revisit it later. ▶See "Return to a Favorite Web Page" on page 431 for details.◀

Do It Yourself Enter an Address (URL) into Netscape Navigator

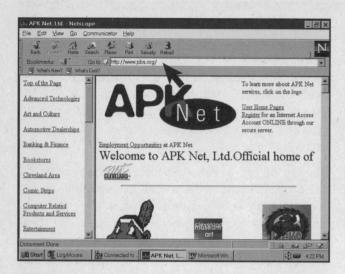

1 Type the address of the page you want to go to in the **Go to/Location** text box. Make sure that you use forward slashes (/) to separate the parts of the address. Press **Enter**.

2 After you enter an address, your Web browser keeps it in a list of recently typed addresses. To return to a previously entered address (even one from an earlier session), click the **Netsite/Location** drop-down arrow and select an address from the list.

Do It Yourself Enter an Address (URL) into Internet Explorer

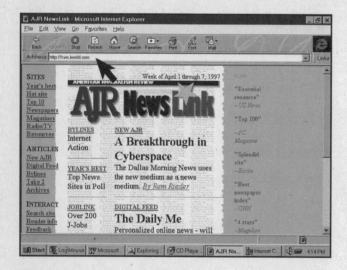

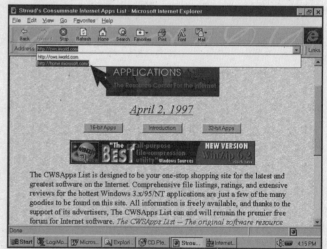

1 Type the address of the page you want to go to in the **Address** text box. Make sure that you use forward slashes (/) to separate the parts of the address. Press **Enter**.

2 After you enter an address, your Web browser keeps it in a list of recently typed addresses. To return to a previously entered address (even one from an earlier session), click the **Address** drop-down arrow and select an address from the list.

Return to a Favorite Web Page

Web addresses (URLs) are often long and complex, which makes it difficult to enter them correctly. When you finish typing an address into your Web browser, you may not want to lose it. But there's no need to worry about that because every Web browser provides a means of saving the addresses of Web pages you like to visit.

Browsing the Web is like browsing through the pages of a large book. When you find a particular passage in a book that you want to be able to find again quickly, you insert a bookmark. You can do the same thing with your Web browser. Then, to return to a page you've marked, you select the proper bookmark (favorite page) from a list.

Occasionally, the address of a Web page changes. Many companies that produce Web pages rent computer storage space from a type of computer called an Internet Service Provider. And because there's a big market in Web space rental these days, some companies tend to move from one provider to another. When that happens, their addresses change (just as their U.S. postal addresses would if they moved their real office). So a bookmark that you can count on one week to take you to a favorite site may not be valid the next week. When that happens, you might need to use one of the Internet's many search tools to find the new address; then you can use your Web browser's bookmark editor to correct the old address.

It's easy to collect a lot of bookmarks, which might leave you confused as to what some of the bookmarks lead to. For that reason, a lot of Web browsers allow you to organize your bookmarks in folders and add comments that help you identify them.

Do It Yourself Set a Bookmark in Netscape Navigator

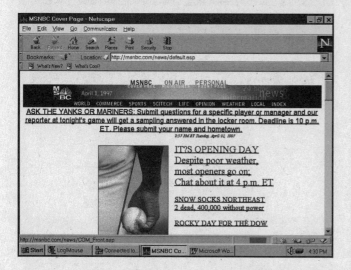

1 First, jump to a page whose address you want to save.

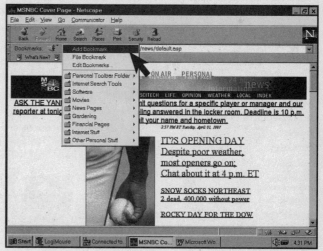

2 Click the **Bookmarks** button and select **Add Bookmark**. Netscape Navigator saves the address of the current Web page, adding it to the main Bookmarks list.

(continues)

Do It Yourself Set a Bookmark in Netscape Navigator *(continued)*

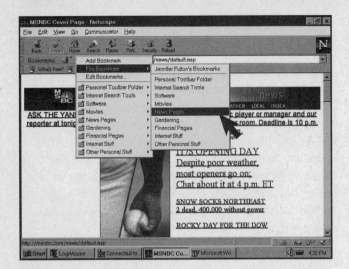

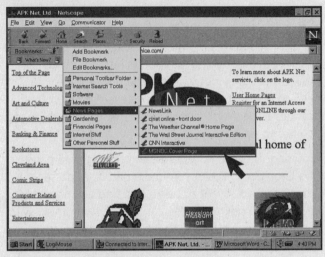

3 If you use folders to organize your bookmarks, you can place your new bookmark directly into a folder. Click the **Bookmarks** button and select **File Bookmark**. Then click the folder to which you want to save your bookmark from the list that appears. If you select Personal Toolbar Folder from this list, a button for that page is added to the Personal toolbar.

5 To return to a page you've stored in a bookmark folder, click the **Bookmarks** button and select the folder from the Bookmarks menu.

6 Select the page you want to jump to from the cascading menu that appears.

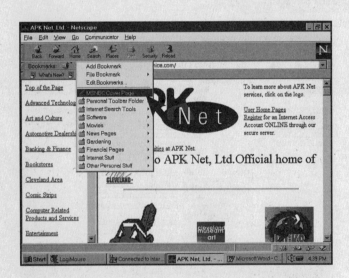

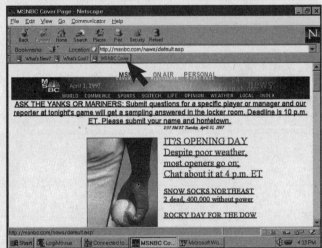

4 To return to a page whose address you've saved, click the **Bookmarks** button and select the page from the list that appears.

7 If you added the page to the Personal Toolbar Folder, a button appears on the Personal toolbar. Simply click the button to jump to that page.

Do It Yourself Set a Bookmark in Internet Explorer

(1) First, jump to a page whose address you want to save.

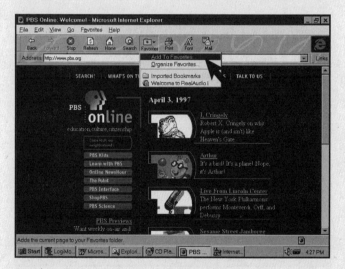

(2) Click the **Favorites** button and select **Add To Favorites**.

(3) (Optional) Change the name of the Web page by typing the new name in the **Name** text box.

(4) To save the page to the main Favorites list, click **OK** and you're done.

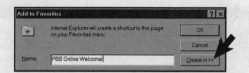

(5) If you use folders to organize your favorite Web pages, click **Create In** to place your new bookmark directly into a folder.

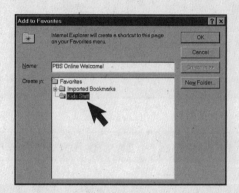

(6) The Add to Favorites dialog box expands. Click the folder in which you want to save your bookmark, and then click **OK**.

(7) To return to a page whose address you've saved, click the **Favorites** button and select the page from the list that appears.

(continues)

Do It Yourself Set a Bookmark in Internet Explorer   *(continued)*

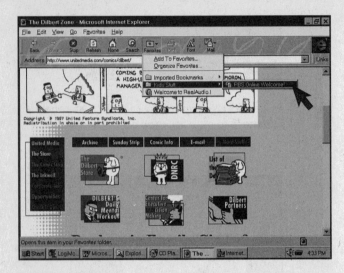

8 To return to a page you've stored in a folder, click the **Favorites** button, select the folder from the Favorites list, and then select the page to which you want to jump from the cascading menu that appears.

Do It Yourself Create Bookmark Folders in Netscape Navigator

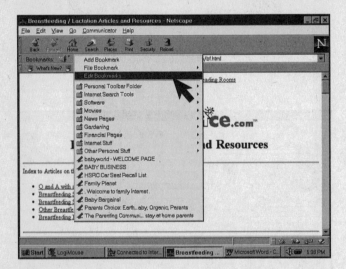

1 Click the **Bookmarks** button and select **Edit Bookmarks**.

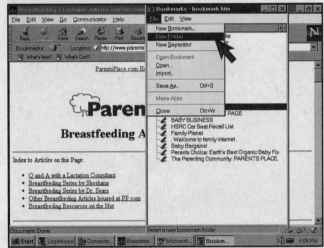

2 In the list of folders, click in the location where you want the new folder to appear. Then open the **File** menu and select **New Folder**.

Do It Yourself Create Bookmark Folders in Netscape Navigator

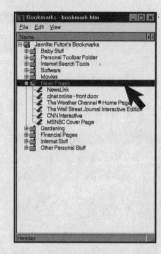

3 In the Bookmark Properties dialog box, fill in the **Name** and **Description** text boxes for the new folder, and then click **OK**. The folder now appears in the Bookmarks list.

5 To display the bookmarks in a folder, click the plus sign next to the folder's name. You can hide the bookmarks in a folder by clicking its minus sign.

6 When you're through, close the Bookmarks window by clicking its **Close** (X) button.

4 To add an existing bookmark to a folder, click the bookmark and drag it into the folder.

Do It Yourself Create Bookmark Folders in Internet Explorer

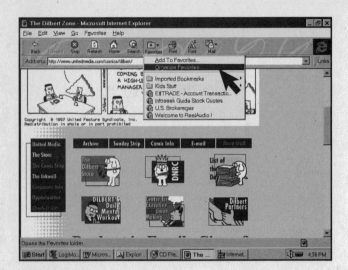

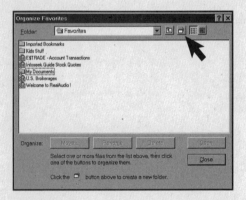

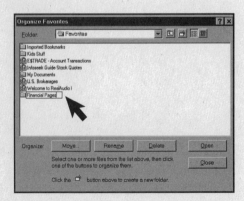

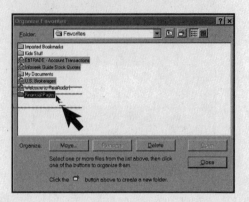

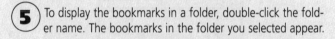

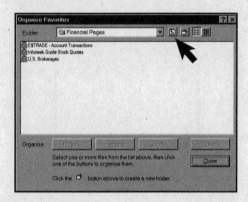

1 Click the **Favorites** button and select **Organize Favorites**.

2 In the Organize Favorites dialog box, click the **Create New Folder** button.

3 Type a name for the folder and press **Enter**.

4 To add an existing bookmark to a folder, click the bookmark and drag it into the folder. You can select multiple bookmarks at one time by pressing **Ctrl** and clicking each one. Then drag the group to the folder in which you want to place the bookmarks.

5 To display the bookmarks in a folder, double-click the folder name. The bookmarks in the folder you selected appear.

6 To move one level up the Favorites list, click the **Up One Level** button.

7 When you're through, click the **Close** (X) button to close the Organize Favorites dialog box.

Search for Information

The World Wide Web is a big place. Sometimes it's almost impossible to find the information you want. Web search tools can help you narrow your search by providing you with a list of pages that might contain the information you're searching for.

Common search tools (and their addresses) include:

InfoSeek http://infoseek.com/

Yahoo! http://yahoo.com/

Lycos http://lycos.com/

Alta Vista http://altavista.digital.com/

Excite http://www.excite.com/

When you jump to a Web search page, you're typically presented with a *form*. A form looks like a dialog box; you enter the subject you want to search for into a text box, select additional options by clicking them, and then start the search by clicking a Search or Submit button. Sometimes you can narrow your search by selecting a category such as news or recreation first. When the search is complete, you're presented with a list of Web pages that match your search criteria. To jump to a page, you click its link.

How Web Search Tools Work

When you use a Web search tool to locate a particular Web page, you're not actually searching the Web—that would take too long. Instead, you're searching through a list of Web pages collected and organized by the Web search tool you're using. To compile their lists, each Web search tool regularly explores the Web in search of new Web pages. When it finds a new page, the search tool scans its contents and adds the page's location to its master list.

When you enter your search criteria, the Web search tool simply scans its master list and produces the addresses of the Web pages whose contents match what you're looking for. The Web pages are listed in order of probability. Therefore, the pages whose contents most closely match your search criteria are displayed at the top of the list.

Each Web search tool has a different method for searching the Web, so each one produces its own unique listing of Web pages. If you don't find what you want by using one Web search tool, you should try your search again using one of the other tools.

How to Get Better Results

Some Web search tools, such as Yahoo!, allow you to narrow your search by selecting the category in which your topic belongs. For example, you might select Arts if you were searching for a Web page containing information on the hottest new Jazz artists.

You can narrow your search further by using unique search criteria. For example, if you're looking for information on how to fertilize your lawn and you type **gardening**, you'll get quite a list. However, if you enter **organic fertilizers** or **organic lawn care** instead, you'll narrow your list considerably. To increase your chances of finding the page you want as quickly as possible, try to use search words that are unique and specific.

One problem with entering more than one search word is that most Web search tools are set up to look for pages that contain *any* of the search words. So entering something like **deep sea fish** will produce a list of pages that contain the word "deep," or "sea," or "fish." Pages that contain two or more of the search words will be displayed at the top, but you'll still end up with a long list of Web pages to search through.

Fortunately, you can usually tell the Web search tool to include only those pages that contain all of your search words instead of pages that contain any of them by simply typing quotation marks around your search words like this: "**deep sea fish**." You can also use plus signs or the word AND to indicate that you want to locate only those pages that contain your search words, as in **infant AND car AND seat** or **+infant+car+seat**. You can use a minus sign or the word NOT to exclude pages that contain certain words, as in **pets NOT cats** or **pets – cats**. Finally, the word OR tells the search tool to display pages that contain either of your search words, as in **Indiana OR Ohio**.

Do It Yourself   Search the WWW

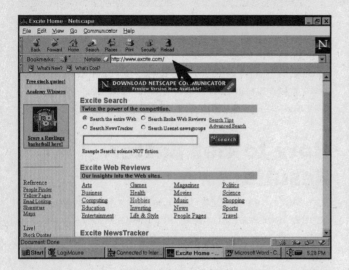

1 Excite is one of the more popular Web search tools. To jump to Excite, enter its address into your Web browser: **http://www.excite.com**.

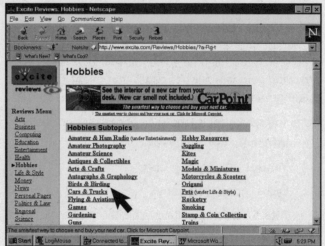

3 A list of subcategories is displayed. From here, you might click **Birds and Birding**.

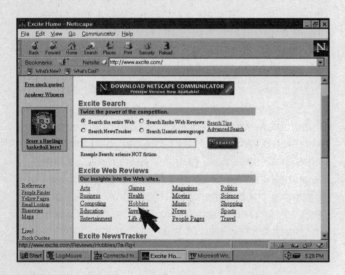

2 Excite, like a lot of Web search tools, provides a list of categories that enable you to narrow down the search list to a likely area. For example, you might click **Hobbies** to select it from the categories listed.

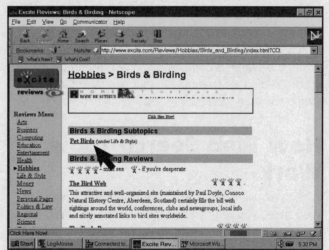

4 Eventually, a list of Web pages that fit the category you selected appears. To jump to a particular Web page, click its link.

Do It Yourself   Search the WWW

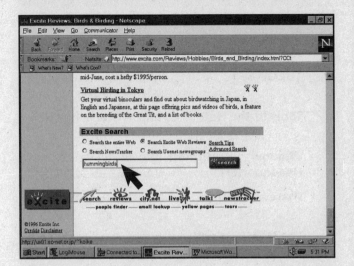

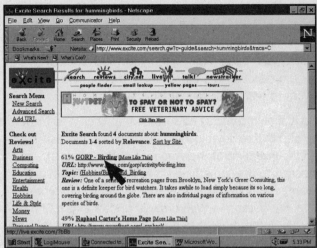

5 Another way to search for a Web page is to enter a series of search words. Excite allows you to begin a search on its main page or on one of the subcategory pages. Simply type your search words into the appropriate text box, and then press **Enter** or click the **Search** button.

6 A list of Web pages that match the search criteria appears. The pages that most closely match what you're looking for appear at the top of the list. To jump to a Web page, click its link.

Download Files from the Internet

A Web browser makes the Internet easy to use and understand. Just click a link, and you jump to the associated Web page. Want to go back? No problem. Want to jump directly to a particular Web page? No sweat. Want to search for something? Easy.

So it should come as no surprise that your Web browser also makes downloading files a simple process. Prior to the invention of the Web (and Web browsers), you needed to use something called an FTP program if you wanted to download (receive) a file from an Internet site. But because a Web browser understands FTP protocols, you can use it to download files instead. A Web browser makes downloading files as simple as point and click: Just point to a link that's connected to a file on an FTP site, and then click to begin the downloading process. Select an existing folder into which you want the file placed or create a new folder, and the downloading begins.

> You may want to create a single folder on your hard disk for all the files you get off the Internet. That way, you can keep all your downloaded files in a safe place until you've had a chance to use an antivirus program to verify that the files you've received are virus-free before you attempt to install and use them on your system.

In order to download a file from the Internet, you have to find its location first. The best place to start is at a Web site that specializes in the type of file you're looking for. The following is a list of popular software sites.

Stroud's	http://cws.iworld.com/ Internet software
TUCOWS	http://www.tucows.com/ Internet software
Tools of the Net	http://TOOLS.ofthe.NET Internet software
Windows 95 Internet Headquarters	http://windows95.com Windows 95 software
shareware.com	http://shareware.com/ PC software
The WinSite Archive	http://www.winsite.com/ Windows software

Once you find a Web page with a direct link to a file, all you have to do is click the link to begin downloading it. If you happen to know the address of the ftp site that contains the file you're looking for, you can connect to the ftp site directly, locate your file, and then download it.

> A Web browser can only link to "open" systems—ftp sites that allow anonymous logins. If you need to access an FTP site that allows only restricted access, you're going to need an actual ftp program.

Most software sites work in a similar manner: Typically, you select the category of software in which you're interested, and then you select the software program you want from those listed. The file you select is then downloaded to your system. In the following task, you'll learn how to download a file from a Web site called Stroud's. You'll also learn how to download a file directly from an ftp site.

Do It Yourself   Download a File from Stroud's

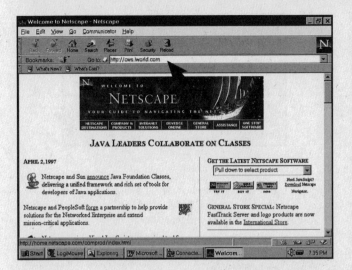

1 A good source of Internet-related files is Stroud's. To jump to the Stroud's site, type **http://cws.iworld.com** in your Web browser and press **Enter.**

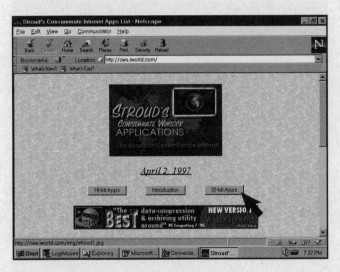

2 For our example, let's look for a good compression utility for Windows 95. Click **32-bit Apps**.

3 First, you select the file category you want to search. Scroll down to the list and click **Compression Utilities**.

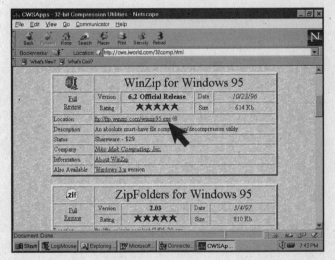

4 Each program includes a rating, a brief description, a full review, and a link to the file. Click the link to begin the download.

(continues)

Do It Yourself Download a File from Stroud's *(continued)*

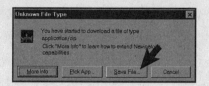

5 If the file you're downloading is compressed (zipped), you may see the Unknown File Type dialog box. Click **Save File**. Because the file in our example is self-extracting (it ends in .EXE), you can skip this step.

6 In the Save As dialog box, select a directory in which to save the file and click **Save**. After the file is downloaded to your PC, you're returned to your Web browser.

Do It Yourself Download a File Directly from an FTP Site

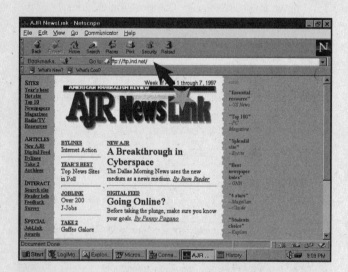

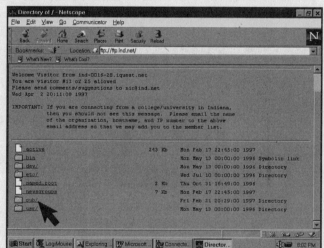

1 If you know the FTP site that a particular file is on, you can go directly to that site. For example, type **ftp://ftp.ind.net** in the **Location/Go to** text box and press **Enter**.

2 You're currently in the root directory of this FTP server. To move from directory to directory, simply click the folder you want to open. For example, click the **pub** directory.

Do It Yourself Download a File Directly from an FTP Site

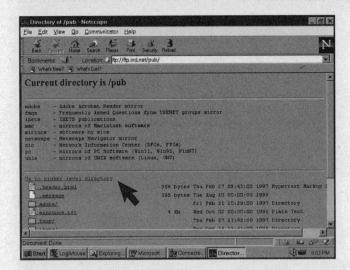

3 At the top of the page, you'll see a brief description of each folder in the pub directory. To display the files in one of those directories, click it. To move back up the directory tree, click the **Up to Higher Level Directory** link.

5 If the file you're trying to download is compressed (zipped), you may see the Unknown File Type dialog box. If so, click **Save File**.

6 Select the folder in which you want to save the file, and then click **Save**. You can change the name of the file before saving it by typing a new name in the **File Name** text box. When the file has been downloaded to your PC, you're returned to your Web browser.

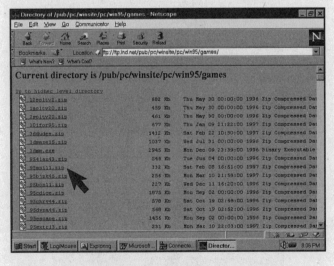

4 Continue to browse directories until you find the file you want. To download the file, just click its name.

Configure Your E-Mail Program

Before you can use either Netscape Communicator or Internet Explorer to send or receive e-mail, you must first configure it. This process is fairly painless; however, you may need to obtain certain information from your Internet service provider (or your network service administrator) before you attempt to complete this task.

Here's a list of the information you'll need to obtain before you begin:

Your e-mail address and password

The address of your service provider's outgoing mail (SMTP) server

The address of your service provider's incoming mail (POP3 or IMAP) server

Your e-mail user name—the name you use to log onto the e-mail servers

You might also want to get the name of your service provider's news (NNTP) server, so you can enter it as well. This is the server to which you connect in order to read and view newsgroup messages.

The following tasks explain how to configure both Netscape Messenger and Internet Explorer. If you use a different e-mail program, the steps may vary a bit.

Do It Yourself Configure Netscape Communicator for E-Mail

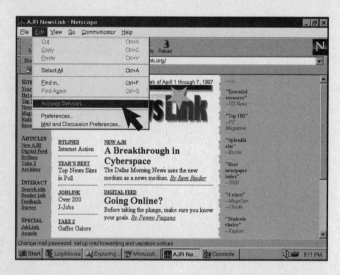

1 Open the **Edit** menu and select **Account Services**.

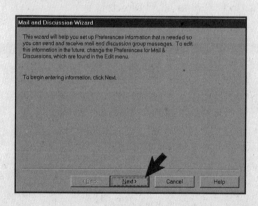

2 The Main and Discussion Wizard appears. Click **Next >**.

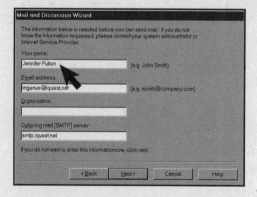

3 Fill in the **Your Name** text box. This is not your user name, but simply your real name. You can also enter the name of the organization or company to which you belong.

Do It Yourself   Configure Netscape Communicator for E-Mail

4 Enter your e-mail address in the **E-Mail Address** text box. Finally, fill in the address of your **Outgoing Mail Server (SMTP) Server**. Click **Next >**.

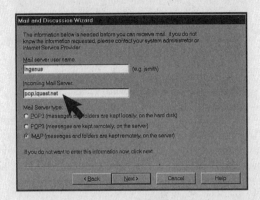

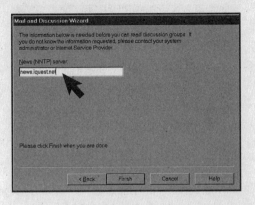

7 If you want, enter the address of your service provider's news server in the **News (NNTP) Server** text box. When you're through, click **Finish**.

5 Enter your user name in the **Mail Server User Name** text box. This is the name you use to log onto your service provider's mail server.

6 Enter the address of the **Incoming Mail Server** (POP3 or IMAP server). Make sure that the correct mail server type is selected. Click **Next >**.

Do It Yourself   Configure Internet Explorer for E-Mail

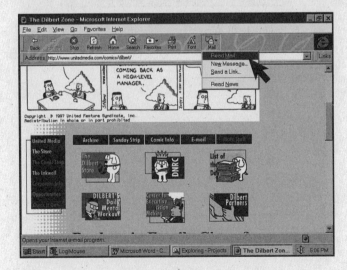

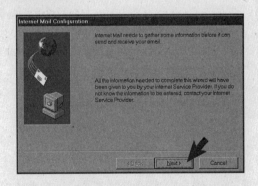

2 The Internet Mail Configuration Wizard appears. Click **Next >**.

(continues)

1 Click the **Mail** button and select **Read Mail**.

Do It Yourself Configure Internet Explorer for E-Mail *(continued)*

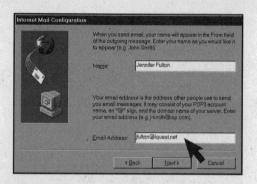

3 Enter your name in the **Name** text box. This is not your user name, but simply your real name.

4 Enter your **E-Mail Address** and click **Next >**.

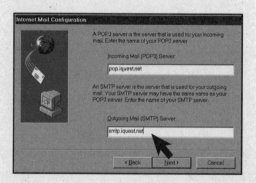

5 Enter the address of the **Incoming Mail (POP3) Server**.

6 Enter the address of **Outgoing Mail (SMTP) Server** as well. Then click **Next >**.

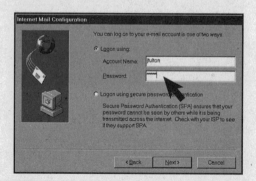

7 Select the logon option you want to use. If you choose **Logon using**, then enter your logon name and password. When you're through, click **Next >**.

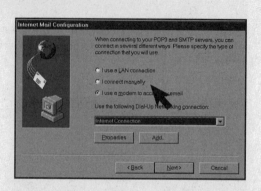

8 Select the option that best describes your logon method: a LAN (network) connection, a modem (dial-up) connection through Windows 95, or a manual (Winsock) connection through Windows 3.1. If you connect through your modem and Windows 95, select the name of your Dial Up Networking connection from the drop-down list. Click **Next >**.

9 Click **Finish**. (If necessary, you can click **< Back** to return to any of the previous dialog boxes in order to change information.)

Send E-Mail over the Internet

Using a Web browser such as Netscape Navigator or Internet Explorer, you can send e-mail to anyone who's connected to the Internet—even if that person is connected to the Internet indirectly (such as through CompuServe or America Online). All you need to know is his or her e-mail address. An Internet address looks something like this:

jnoname@que.mcp.com

The first part of the address is the person's user name (the name by which he is known to his home system). Most user names consist of the person's first initial and last name run together, although the user name can be anything, including a nickname or a code name. An at symbol (@) always comes after the user name. The part of the e-mail address that follows the @ sign is a location on the Internet. In this case, it's the address of Que, which is a part of Macmillan Computer Publishing—hence the location name que.mcp. The .com part of the location tells you that que.mcp is a commercial (business) venture. Other endings you'll see include .edu (educational), .net (an Internet server), and .mil (military).

> When addressing e-mail, be careful to use upper- and lowercase letters *exactly* as they are given to you. If someone tells you that his address is SAMBeldon@imagineTHAT.com, you must type the address exactly that way. He will not receive his mail if you send it to sam-beldon@imaginethat.com because that is a completely different address.

If you're sending e-mail to a person who connects to the Internet through an online service such as CompuServe, you will need to adjust the address itself for use on the Internet. For example, when sending e-mail from one member to another through CompuServe, you might enter an address such as 71520,3121. To send a message to that same person through the Internet, you must change the address to 71520.3121@compuserve.com. The following list shows you the format of e-mail addresses for the most popular online services.

Online Service	Sample Address
CompuServe	71354.1234@compuserve.com
America Online	joeblow@aol.com
Prodigy	joeblow@prodigy.com
The Microsoft Network	joeblow@msn.com

Most e-mail programs include an address book in which you can save the e-mail addresses of the people to whom you most often send messages. That way, you don't have to worry about making a typing mistake when addressing a message to one of your friends or colleagues.

If you have several e-mail messages to send at one time, you can create each one while you're offline (that is, not connected to the Internet) and save them to send later. When you're ready to send the messages, you connect to the Internet and send all the messages in your Outbox at once.

In addition to being able to send multiple messages at one time, you can also include files with your e-mail messages. Although you can include any file, you may want to "shrink" or compress the file first, in order to make it as small as possible for transmission. Doing so reduces the chance of the file not arriving intact. ▶**See "Install a Program from a Zip File" on page 325 for help.**◀

> The Internet Explorer tasks in this section assume that you use Microsoft Internet Mail (the e-mail program that comes with Internet Explorer) to send and receive e-mail. However, you can use Outlook or Windows Messaging (formally known as Exchange) as your e-mail program instead. Just open the **View** menu and select **Options**. Then click the **Programs** tab, select the e-mail program you want to use from the **Mail** list, and click **OK**.

Do It Yourself Send an E-Mail Message with Netscape Messenger

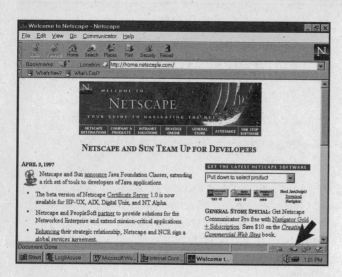

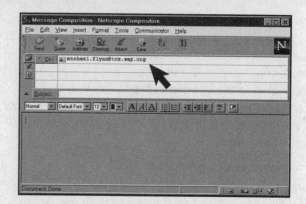

3 Enter the recipient's address in the **To:** text box. If you're sending to more than one person, separate additional addresses with semicolons as in joenoname@BigCo.com;jdpower@sales.DMB.com.

1 Click the **Mailbox** button at the bottom of the Navigator window. Netscape Messenger opens.

You do not have to connect to the Internet in order to use Messenger to create an e-mail message. In fact, it's less expensive to create your e-mail messages offline and then connect to the Internet and send all your messages at the same time.

To send a message to someone whose address you've saved, click the **Address** button and select the address to which you want to send your message. Click **To**, and then click **OK**.

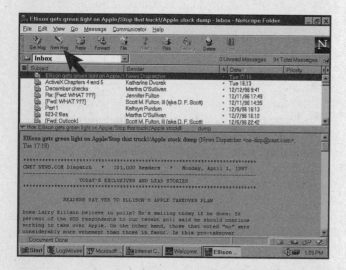

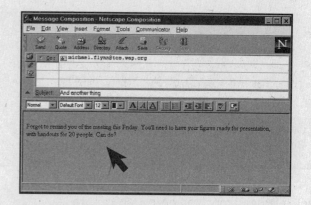

4 Enter a subject in the **Subject:** text box, and then type your message. Messages, by default, are sent as HTML. You can convert your message to text only (for those users who do not use a Web browser-based e-mail program) by clicking the **Message Sending Options** tab and selecting **Plain Text Only** from the **Format** list.

 Click the **New Msg** button.

Do It Yourself Send an E-Mail Message with Netscape Messenger

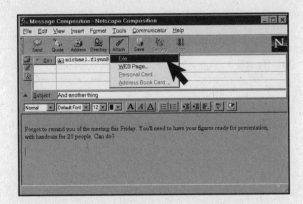

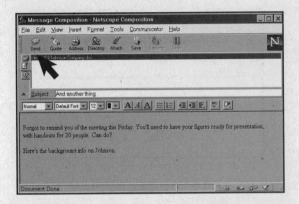

5 To attach a file to send with your message, click the **Attach** button, select **File**, select your file, and then click **Open**. To attach a Web page, click the **Attach** button, click **WEB Page**, type the address of the page you want to include (the address of the current Web page is automatically displayed for your convenience), and click **OK**.

6 Click the **Send** button to send your message. If you're working offline and you want to send your message later, open the **File** menu and select **Send Later** instead. To send these messages later, either check your e-mail (using the **Get Msg** button), or open the **File** menu in the Composer window and select **Send Messages in Outbox**.

Do It Yourself Send an E-Mail Message with Internet Explorer

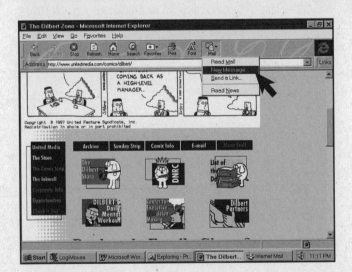

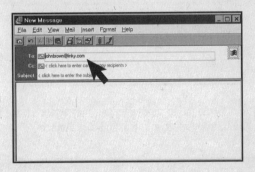

1 In Internet Explorer, click the **Mail** button and select **New Message**. From within Internet Mail, click the **New Message** button instead.

2 The New Message window appears. Enter the recipient's address in the **To:** text box. If you're sending to more than one person, separate additional addresses with semicolons as in joenoname@BigCo.com;jdpower@sales.DMB.com.

You don't have to connect to the Internet in order to create an e-mail message. In fact, it's less expensive to create your e-mail messages offline and then connect to the Internet and send all your messages at the same time.

To send a message to someone whose address you've saved, click the **Address Card** icon that appears in the To text box. Select the name of the person to whom you want to send your message, click **To ->**, and click **OK**.

(continues)

Do It Yourself Send an E-Mail Message with Internet Explorer *(continued)*

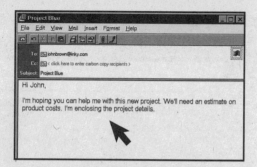

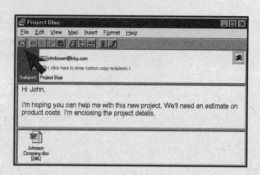

3 Enter a subject in the **Subject:** text box, and then type your message in the large text area at the bottom of the window. Messages, by default, are sent as text only. You can convert your message to HTML (so you can enhance it with text formatting) if you're sending your message to a person who uses a Web browser-based e-mail program by opening the **Format** menu and selecting **HTML**.

5 The attached file appears as an icon at the bottom of the message window. Click the **Send** button to send your message.

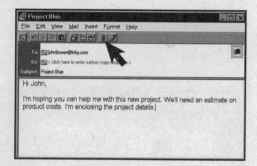

4 To attach a file to send with your message, click the **Insert File** button, select your file, and click **Attach**.

6 If you see a warning telling you that the message will be placed in your Outbox (to be sent later), click **OK**. To subsequently send the message, click the **Send and Receive** button.

You can insert the contents of a text file directly into the e-mail message by opening the **Insert** menu and selecting **Text File**. Select the file and click **OK**.

Retrieve and View E-Mail Messages

The e-mail program included with Netscape Communicator and Internet Explorer is capable of both sending and receiving your e-mail messages over the Internet. The process of retrieving an e-mail message is like going to your mailbox and checking for mail. If there's mail in your mailbox, you take it out, open it, and read it. The e-mail program does the same thing: It goes to your electronic mailbox (which is located on your Internet provider's computer), checks for mail, and brings back anything it finds.

Both Netscape Communicator and Internet Explorer can be made to check for mail periodically, but you can also initiate the checking process whenever you want. Once you retrieve your mail, you "open" it to read it. You can print an open message if you want and save it in your files. You can also reply to the message by sending a new message back to the originator (➤see **"Reply to an E-Mail Message" on page 455**◄). Also, if the message contains an attached file, you can save that file to your PC's hard disk for use in the appropriate program.

Do It Yourself Check New Mail with Netscape Messenger

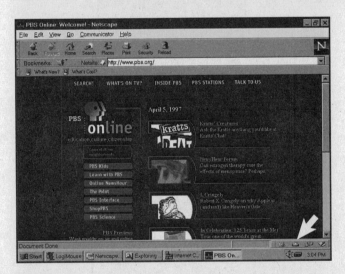

1 If you're connected to the Internet, Netscape can check for new mail periodically. It displays a green arrow on the Mailbox button of the Component bar when new mail arrives. To manually check for new mail at any time, click the **Mailbox** button to display Netscape Messenger.

2 Click Messenger's **Get Msg** button (if necessary) to check for new mail.

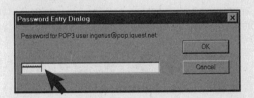

3 If the Password Entry Dialog dialog box appears, enter your password and click **OK**.

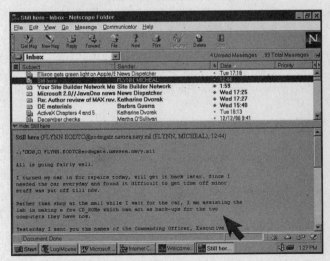

4 After messages are received, they are listed at the top of the window in bold text. When you click a message header, the contents of the message appear in the Message Pane. If necessary, scroll down to read the complete message. After you've viewed a message, its header changes from bold to regular text.

(continues)

Do It Yourself   Check New Mail with Netscape Messenger   (continued)

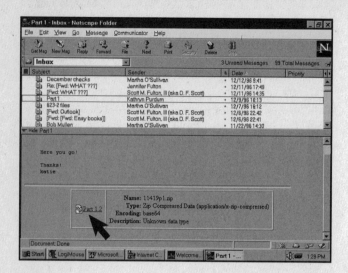

(5) If the message contains an attached file, its file name appears as a hyperlink. To save this file to your PC's hard disk, press and hold the **Shift** key and click the link.

(6) Select a directory into which to save the file, and then click **Save**. (You can rename the file prior to saving it by typing a new name in the **File Name** text box.)

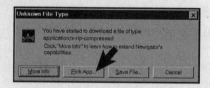

(7) If you clicked the file link in step 5 (instead of holding down the Shift key as you click), Messenger attempts to open the appropriate program so you can view the file's contents. If Messenger doesn't know which program to use, you'll see this dialog box. Click **Pick App**.

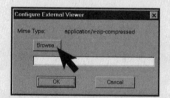

(8) In the Configure External Viewer dialog box, click **Browse**. Then select the program you want to use when viewing files of this type and click **Open**.

(9) You're returned to the Configure External Viewer dialog box, and the name of the program you selected appears in the text box. Click **OK**.

(10) When the proper program associated with this file type has been identified, the file's contents are displayed.

Do It Yourself Check for New Mail with Internet Explorer

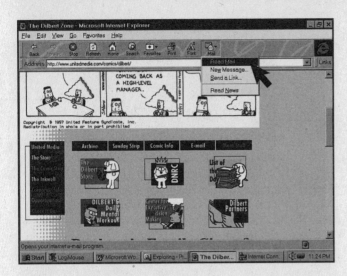

1 If needed, click the **Mail** button and select **Read Mail** to open the Internet Mail window.

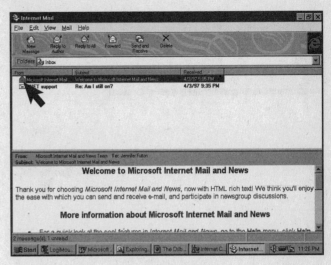

3 Messages you have received are listed at the top of the window in bold text. To view the contents of a message, click its header.

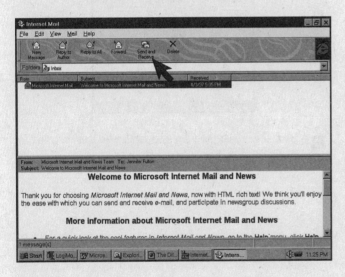

2 Click the **Send and Receive** button to check for new mail.

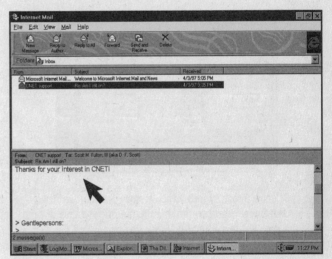

4 The e-mail message appears in the Preview Pane. (If the Preview Pane is not currently displayed, open the **View** menu, select **Preview Pane**, and select **Split Horizontally** or **Split Vertically**.) If necessary, scroll down to read the complete message. After you've viewed a message, its header changes from bold to regular text.

(continues)

Do It Yourself Check for New Mail with Internet Explorer *(continued)*

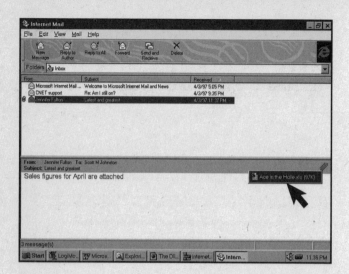

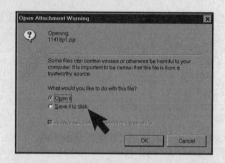

7 If you clicked the file icon in step 5 (instead of holding down the Ctrl key and clicking), Internet Mail attempts to open the appropriate program so you can view its contents. First, however, you'll see the warning shown here. Click **Open It**, and then click **OK** to continue.

5 If the message contains an attached file, a paper clip icon appears at the left end of the message header. To save this file to your PC's hard disk, press and hold the **Ctrl** key as you click the icon, and then select the file name from the list that appears.

8 Once the proper program associated with this file type has been identified, the file's contents are displayed.

6 Select a directory into which to save the file, and then click **Save**. (You can rename the file prior to saving it by typing a new name in the **File Name** text box.)

Reply to an E-Mail Message

You can reply to or forward any message you receive. When you reply to a message, the e-mail program automatically fills in the address of the originator as the recipient address for your new message. You can also send your reply to anyone who received the original message. In any case, all you have to do is type your message reply, and it will be sent to either the originator or the originator and all its recipients—whichever option you select.

When you reply to a message, the text of the original message is included for reference. You can customize your e-mail program so that the original text is never included, or you can simply delete the original message text if you don't want to include it in a particular reply.

When you forward a message, your e-mail program sends a copy of the original message to the person you indicate. You can forward a message to more than one person if you want. When you forward a message, the original message is treated as an attachment. You can add a message of explanation about the attachment to a forwarded message if necessary.

Do It Yourself   Reply to a Message with Netscape Messenger

---

1 Click the message to which you want to reply.

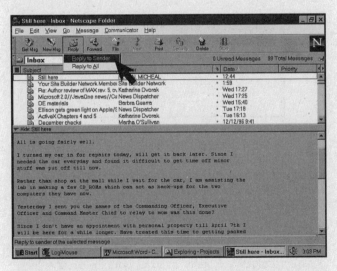

2 Click the **Reply** button and select either **Reply to Sender** or **Reply to All**.

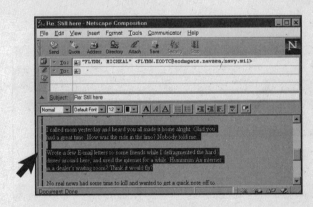

3 Messenger updates the header information, filling in the To: and Subject: lines. In the message area, the text from the original message appears. Each line of the original message is marked with a blue vertical bar. If you want to delete any of these original lines, just select them and press **Delete**.

4 Type your message under the copy of the original message. Or you can type your reply between the lines of the original message if you prefer; to do so, place the cursor at the end of an original line and press **Enter** to create a blank line on which you can type.

(continues)

Do It Yourself Reply to a Message with Netscape Messenger *(continued)*

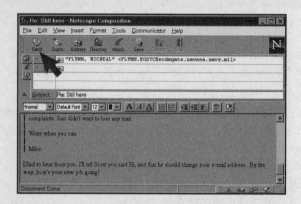

5 Click **Send** to send your reply.

Do It Yourself Reply to a Message with Internet Mail

1 Click the message to which you want to reply.

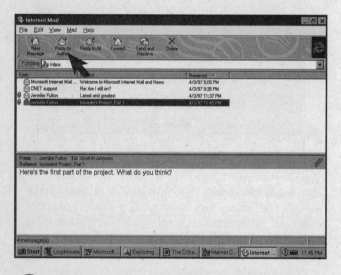

2 Click either the **Reply to Author** or the **Reply to All** button.

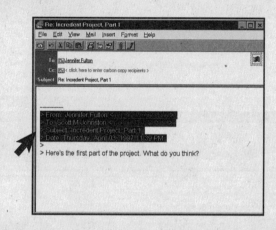

3 Internet Mail updates the header information, filling in the To: and Subject: lines. In the message area, the text from the original message appears, preceded by arrows (>). If you want to delete any of these original lines, just select them and press **Delete**.

4 Type your message above the copy of the original message. Or you can type your reply between the lines of the original message if you prefer; to do so, place the cursor at the end of an original line and press **Enter** to create a blank line on which you can type.

Do It Yourself Reply to a Message with Internet Mail

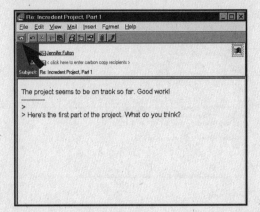

5 Click the **Send** button to send your reply. If you see a warning telling you that the message will be placed in your Outbox (to be sent later), click **OK**. To subsequently send the message, click the **Send and Receive** button.

Do It Yourself Forward a Message with Netscape Messenger

1 Click the message you want to forward.

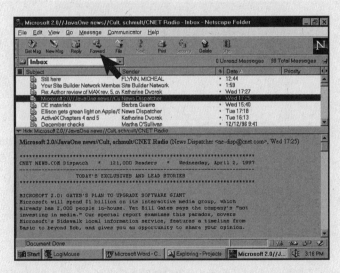

2 Click the **Forward** button.

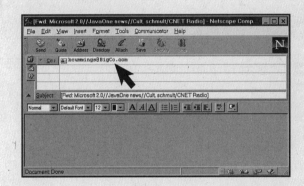

3 The original message is attached to this new message as a file. In the **To:** text box, type the address(es) of the person(s) to whom you want to forward this message.

4 Type an explanation for the forwarded message in the large gray box at the bottom of the window.

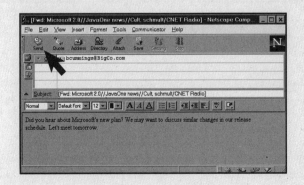

5 Click the **Send** button to forward the message.

Do It Yourself   Forward a Message with Internet Mail

1 Click the message you want to forward.

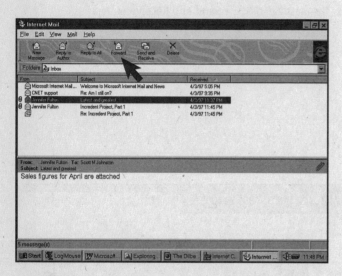

2 Click the **Forward** button.

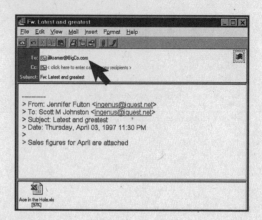

3 The original message appears in the text window, preceded by arrows (>). In the **To:** text box, type the address(es) of the person(s) to whom you want to forward this message.

4 Type any additional message above the text for the forwarded message.

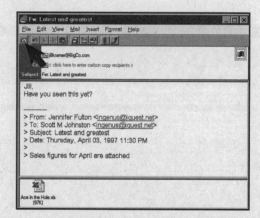

5 Click the **Send** button to forward the message. If you see a warning telling you that the message will be placed in your Outbox (to be sent later), click **OK**. To subsequently send the message, click the **Send and Receive** button.

PART 3

101 Quick Fixes

I f you're lucky, you'll be able to run your computer and programs without encountering a single problem. However, most people are not so fortunate. One day, you'll turn on your computer and encounter a blank screen, or your printer won't print, or you'll get an error message telling you that a file you've worked on for a month has gone south.

Whatever the problem is, you'll need help, and you'll want that help quick. In this section, 101 of the most common problems and their solutions are listed. In this basket of solutions, you'll find answers to hardware problems, software problems, and problems with DOS, Windows (versions 3.1 and 3.11), and Windows 95, intermixed—because it's not always clear which particular part of your computer is causing the problem. In each solution, however, you'll find out just where to look to find the root cause.

If you're completely lost, turn to the Quick Finder table at the beginning of each section for help. There, you'll find a statement of the problem and some places in the section where you can locate the answer.

101 QUICK FIXES

Startup Problems

(continues)

(continued)

Problem	Quick Fix Number	Page
Power on—strange computer beeps	3	462
Reboot to Windows 95 doesn't work	9	464
Startup commands run too fast	7,8	464
Startup commands in Windows 95	8	464
Step through the startup commands	7,8	464
Tracing a startup problem	7,8	464
Windows 95 startup options	8	464
Windows 95 won't start	9	464

1: I have no lights, no sounds, nothing.

If you flip the power switch or press the button on your computer and you don't hear some grinding or see any lights come on, the PC isn't getting juice. Make sure the power cord is securely plugged into a wall outlet and into the back of the PC. If you plug your PC into a power strip, make sure the power strip is plugged in and turned on.

If all the connections are okay, unplug your computer from the wall outlet and plug in a device (such as a lamp) that you know works. If the lamp doesn't work in that outlet, you may have tripped a circuit breaker or blown a fuse; fix that problem, and your computer should start. If the lamp works but the computer doesn't, your computer may have a faulty power cord or power supply; seek professional help.

2: I see the lights and hear the sounds, but there's still no display.

Your computer is probably starting all right, but something is wrong with the monitor or one of its connections. Try the following solutions:

- Make sure the monitor is plugged into a wall outlet or power strip, and that it is on (see the previous solution for more information). Your monitor should have a power indicator that lights when the power is on.

- If the power is on but you still have no picture, crank up the brightness control on your monitor. Then readjust the brightness once you get a picture.

- Turn everything off and check the connection between the monitor and the system unit. (This connection wiggles free at times.)

- If your computer beeps at startup, see the next question.

3: Why is my computer beeping?

If you hear a series of loud beeps when you start up the computer, several things might be wrong:

- There might be a problem with the motherboard (system board) or the power supply.

- There might be a problem with a memory (RAM) chip going out, or you may not have upgraded some new RAM properly.

- The keyboard may not be connected properly, or you accidentally pressed several keys during startup.

- The monitor may not be connected properly, or your graphics adapter card may be going out.

- You may have left a disk in one of the floppy drives, or the drive itself may not be responding.

Typically, some type of error message accompanies the beeping noise. Start with the simple things first: Check your connections and then reboot. If you just installed something, check its installation. Restart the PC. If you get the same beeping noise, something may be critically wrong, in which case you should have your PC checked out by a professional.

4: My monitor displays "Non-system disk or disk error."

You usually get this message if you happened to leave a non-bootable floppy disk in drive A. Take the disk out of drive A and press any key to boot from your hard disk. If you have an old computer and you boot it from a floppy disk, this message is telling you to insert a bootable floppy disk into drive A and press any key.

If you don't have a bootable disk handy, you'll have to get one from a friend or colleague unless you followed the instructions ▶**outlined in "Make a 'Startup' Disk" on page 341 in Part 2 to create one of your own.◄** (You should do that, by the way, after you get your PC up and running, so that you'll always have a startup disk handy for emergencies like this one.)

5: My monitor displays "CMOS RAM error."

Something's wrong with your computer setup. At this point, you can usually perform one of the following to display your PC's setup options:

- Watch the computer screen during startup to see which key to press—most likely, it's the F1, F2, or Delete key. Press the appropriate key to access your computer's setup options.

- Try restarting your PC by pressing **Ctrl+Alt+S** or **Ctrl+Alt+Enter**. On older PCs, this should bring up the setup display.

- If your PC is a 286, you'll need to restart it using its setup disk.

Check the options and change any settings you know are wrong; don't mess with any you are unsure of. Basically, you press **Tab** or the **down arrow key** to move from item to item. Typically, you use the left or right arrow key to change the value of a particular setting. When you're finished, press **Esc** or select **Yes** to save the settings, and then try to reboot. In most newer computers (manufactured in the last three years), you can simply access the setup options and then save (without changing anything). This makes the computer recheck its memory and fix any memory problems automatically.

If you keep getting this message, it may be a sign that the battery that keeps your CMOS alive is losing its charge. Seek professional help at this point to replace the CMOS battery. (CMOS, pronounced "SEA-moss," is a battery-powered device that stores important information—including the date and time, the number of disk drives the computer has, the type of hard disk it's using, and how much memory is installed.)

6: What is a bad or missing command interpreter?

If you start your computer and you get a message that says you have a **Bad or missing command interpreter**, your DOS *command interpreter* (a file called COMMAND.COM) is either missing or messed up. The command interpreter is your PC's captain; it loads when you boot your computer, and it interprets commands sent to the central processor or CPU. If COMMAND.COM doesn't load on startup, you can't use your computer. Even Windows 3.11 and Windows 95 need the command interpreter to "translate" what they want the computer to do.

To fix the problem, first you have to boot your computer from your startup disk. ▶**If you don't have a bootable floppy disk (startup disk), get one from a friend or colleague or create one on another computer, as explained in "Make a 'Startup' Disk" on page 341.**◀ Once you have your computer running, you should be able to copy the COMMAND.COM file from the start-up disk to the root directory of drive C (C:\); COMMAND.COM must be in the root directory, or it won't load on startup.

7: Can I slow down the DOS startup to see what's happening?

Whenever you boot your computer, the startup commands often scroll by too fast for you to read them. If you have DOS 6.0 or later, you can slow down and step through the commands. When you turn on the computer, wait until you see the **Starting MS-DOS...** message; when you see it, press and release the **F8** key. DOS runs the startup commands one at a time, asking you to confirm each line by pressing **Y** (you can skip the commands you think are causing problems).

To bypass all the startup commands, wait for the **Starting MS-DOS...** message, and then hold down the **F5** or the **Shift** key. If the computer starts okay, you know that one of the commands in CONFIG.SYS or AUTOEXEC.BAT is causing the problem. ▶**For details on how to edit these files, see "Modify Your Startup Files" on page 357.**◀

If you have an older version of DOS (5.0 or earlier), you can't step through the commands. You can bypass all the commands in AUTOEXEC.BAT and CONFIG.SYS by renaming those files (try AUTOEXEC.OLD and CONFIG.OLD) and rebooting. To isolate a problem command line in one of the startup files, you have to engage in some serious trial and error. Copy CONFIG.SYS and AUTOEXEC.BAT to another disk or directory (so you can safely edit the original files); then try preventing any problem command lines from running. You do this by typing **REM** and a space before the command line you want your computer to ignore.

8: Can I slow down Windows 95 startup so I can see what's happening?

In Windows 95, you can also step through the startup commands. When you see the message **Starting Windows 95**, press the **F8** key. You'll see a menu of startup options. Type the number next to the desired option.

9: After booting to DOS in Windows 95, I can't get back.

If you choose the **Restart the Computer in MS-DOS Mode** option from the Shut Down Windows dialog box, your computer will restart, and you'll be left at the DOS prompt. From there, you can perform any regular DOS function, such as running a DOS-based game.

To return to Windows 95, all you need to do is reboot by pressing **Ctrl+Alt+Delete**. Sometimes this does not return you to Windows; instead, you may appear to be stuck in DOS. To solve the problem, you need to remove the line DOS=SINGLE from your CONFIG.SYS. ▶**See "Modify Your Startup Files" on page 357 for help.**◀

How did the line get there? Well, that's anyone's guess. But typically, when installing a DOS utility, game, or other program, Windows 95 inserts the line on behalf of the setup program, intending to take it out again when the installation is through. That, however, does not always happen, so you have to do it yourself to return your system to normal. After editing the CONFIG.SYS and removing the line, restart your PC, and you should see Windows 95.

Disk Problems

Problem	Quick Fix Number	Page
Bad disk	11,14	466-467
Cannot write to disk message	10	465
Can't save a file to a floppy disk	10,11,13,14	465-467
Can't save a file; disk is full	13	466
Computer is slower than normal	15	467
Disk full message	13	466
Drive is invalid or not ready message	12	466
Error writing to or reading from disk message	11	466
File opens slowly	15	467
Floppy drive grinds unnaturally	11,14	466-467
Floppy drive is invalid or not ready	12	466
Floppy drive won't read the disk	11,12,14	466-467
Insufficient disk space message	13	466
Invalid drive message	12	466
Lost area on a disk	11,14	466-467
Making a bad disk usable again	11,14	466-467
More disk space needed	13	466
Not ready drive message	12	466
Saving files doesn't work	10,11,13,14	465-467
Sector not found message	14	467
Speeding up a computer	15	467
Write-protecting disks	10	465

10: My computer says it cannot write to the disk.

The disk you're trying to save to is probably *write-protected*. Don't remove the write-protection just yet; most disks are write-protected for a reason. For example, most application disks come write-protected so that you can't hurt the disk when installing the application. In addition, sometimes you might write-protect a disk that contains important files.

When you're sure you want to write to this disk, go ahead and remove the write-protection. For 3.5-inch disks, slide the write-protect tab so you can no longer see through the hole in the disk. For 5.25-inch disks, remove the sticker that covers the notch on the side of the disk. Then retry the copy or save operation.

11: I get error messages saying "Error writing to or reading from disk in drive."

This error message usually pops up after you hear your floppy disk drive grinding unnaturally. The drive is trying its best to use the floppy disk, but it's not having any luck. The disk is probably bad, and you'll have to throw it away. Before you fling the disk in the nearest trash can, try to recover any files it may have:

- Try copying the files from the damaged floppy disk to your hard disk or to another floppy disk.

- If you have Windows 95, click the **Start** button; point to **Programs**, **Accessories**, and **System Tools**; and then click **ScanDisk**. ▶**For details on how to use ScanDisk, see "Check a Disk for Errors with ScanDisk" on page 407.**◀

- If you have DOS 6.2 or later, go to the DOS prompt, type **scandisk a:** or **scandisk b:**, and press **Enter**. Follow the on-screen instructions to recover your files.

- If you have a version of DOS that's earlier than 6.2, go to the DOS prompt, type **chkdsk a: /f** or **chkdsk b: /f**, and press **Enter**.

If you use Windows 95, you will get an error when trying to format a disk if you have a window open that's displaying the disk's contents. Simply close the window and continue with the formatting process.

12: What does it mean when it says the drive's not ready or is invalid?

You activated drive A before inserting a disk (or, if the drive has a door, you forgot to close the door). Insert a disk, close the door if there is one, and press **R** or click **Retry**. If that doesn't work, try another disk that you know for sure is formatted (such as a disk with data already on it). If the problem persists, turn your computer off and check under the hood (inside the system unit) for a disconnected or damaged floppy drive cable. If the cable's disconnected, plug it back in. If it's damaged, get help from a qualified service technician.

If you get a **General failure reading drive A** message, you inserted a disk but the disk was not formatted (or it has a flaw). Type **A** for Abort or **F** for Fail. If the disk is new, change back to drive C, and then enter the **format a:** or **format b:** command to format the floppy disk. If the floppy disk has data on it, *don't* format it. Instead, use ScanDisk to check the floppy for problems. ▶**See "Check a Disk for Errors with ScanDisk" on page 407.**◀

13: I get an error message saying that my disk is full.

Your disk is probably full. Use a different disk, or delete files from the disk before you try to save additional files. On a hard disk, it is good practice to use no more than 90 percent of the total space. Your computer needs some space for temporary files, and if you don't provide this space, you might encounter serious problems.

If you use Windows 95, your hard disk may not be full; it could be that the Recycle Bin is filled with deleted files. If so, you can empty it to free up more room on the hard disk.

If you get this message while trying to save a file to your hard disk (and your Recycle Bin is already empty), you might have to save the file to a formatted floppy disk for the time being. Then move some data files (files you create) off the hard disk to floppy disks to free up some space. ▶**See "Make Your Computer Work Faster and Better" on page 337 for details.**◀

For a permanent solution to an overcrowded hard drive, consider having a newer, bigger hard drive installed. Most applications nowadays gobble up hard drive space; there never seems to be enough. Or you might add a Zip drive ▶(see **"Install a Zip Drive" on page 393 for help**).◀ Another option is to run a *disk compression* utility. If you have Windows 95, use DriveSpace, which you'll find on the System Tools menu off the Accessories menu. If you use Windows 3.11, use the DOS utility known as DoubleSpace or DriveSpace (which comes with DOS 6.0 and later), or use Stacker. These utilities compress the files on your disk so they take up less space when not in use. When you run or open the file, the utility automatically decompresses the file. Although this slows down your computer a little, it is much less costly than installing a new hard drive.

▶**For instructions on how to use DriveSpace or DoubleSpace to double the size of your hard disk, see "Compress a Drive with DriveSpace" on page 353.◀**

> Caution! If you have Windows 95, be sure to use its DriveSpace program and not the one that comes with DOS. The DOS DriveSpace utility does not handle the long file names that Windows 95 allows. Also, do not use DriveSpace on the drive in which Windows 95's virtual memory is installed.

14: What does "Sector not found" mean?

The disk has a bad spot on it. (Hey, it happens.) The bad sector isn't a big problem unless there's some data saved to that sector, in which case you might lose the data. You may be able to recover the data using ScanDisk; ▶**for help, see "Check a Disk for Errors with ScanDisk" (page 407).◀**

If the error occurred on a floppy disk, try to recover any data from the disk (using ScanDisk), and then throw the disk away. On floppy disks, if one sector goes bad, it's likely that additional neighboring sectors will follow suit sometime soon. Rather than risk losing data, discard the disk.

Hard disks are too expensive to throw away (and bad sectors usually are not a sign of the demise of neighboring sectors), so the best thing to do is use ScanDisk to scan the hard disk. It locks out any bad sectors so your computer won't try to use them again.

15: My disk seems slower than usual.

Run a defragmentation program. Both Windows 95 and DOS 6.0 or later have a utility called Defrag (or Disk Defragmenter) that will solve your problem. ▶**See "Optimize a Hard Disk with Defrag" on page 345 for help.◀**

How does Defrag (Disk Defragmenter) help when your disk is running slow? Well, after using your computer for a while, space on the hard disk becomes fragmented, meaning that files have been broken up and placed in pieces at various points on the hard disk. Obviously, having parts of a file scattered willy-nilly over your hard disk is not the most efficient method of storage. And it makes it more difficult (and time-consuming) for your computer to retrieve such a file when needed.

So why do it in the first place? Well, your computer doesn't have much of a choice, because its file saving program is designed to place a file in the first available space on the hard disk. When a file is deleted, its space becomes available. But if that space isn't big enough for the next file, the file is broken up and placed in several sections, in the first two or three available spots. Eventually, every file is broken up all over the hard disk, stored in random spots that happened to be available when the file was first created or saved to the hard disk. So over time, fragmentation simply gets worse—until you finally notice a real difference in speed.

A defragmenter such as Defrag or the Disk Defragmenter pulls all the pieces of each file together, placing them on neighboring areas of the disk. This makes it easier (and faster) for your computer to read the files.

File Problems

Problem	Quick Fix Number	Page
Accidentally deleted a file	16	468
Can't insert a picture in a document	19	470
Can't use file copied from another computer	20	470
Deleted a file accidentally	16	468
Document has disappeared	18	470
Downloaded files, using	20	470
File has disappeared	18	470
File created in another program, using	19	470
File format problems	19	470
Files, using downloaded files	20	470
Finding lost files	17,18	469-470
Forgot to save a file	18	470
Graphics, can't use in a document	19	470
Inserting pictures	19	470
Internet files, how to use	20	470
Lost files, finding	17,18	469-470
Power outage before saving a file	18	470
Recover accidentally deleted file	16	468
Recycle Bin, how to use	16	468
Searching for a lost file	17,18	469-470
Unzipping compressed files	20	470
Using copied files	20	470
Where is my file?	17,18	469-470

16: Oops! I deleted a file; can I get it back?

Maybe. If you use Windows 95, you can restore the deleted file from the Recycle Bin, provided you haven't emptied the Bin already. ▶**See the task "Delete and Restore Files and Folders" on page 130 for help.**◀

> If you delete a file accidentally, don't copy any files to the disk that contains the deleted file—and don't install any applications on the disk. If you write anything to the disk, you might destroy parts of the deleted file, making it unrecoverable.

If you use Windows 3.11 and you have DOS 6.0 or higher, you can use a program called Undelete to help you recover deleted files.

If you use DOS only, change to the C:\DOS directory and enter **undelete c:*dirname*** (where c:*dirname* is the drive and directory that contain the deleted file).

If you don't have DOS 6.0 or later, run out to the store and buy it, but don't install it. Installing the program can destroy the deleted file completely. You can run Undelete from one of the DOS disks. Another option is to invest in a utility program, such as The Norton Utilities or PC Tools (that is, if you can find an old copy lying around somewhere). Don't install these programs right now; run the program's Undelete utility from one of the floppy disks. After undeleting the file, you can safely install your new program.

17: I know the file's here, but where is it?

If you misplace a file in Windows 95, follow these steps to locate it. First, click the **Start** button, point to **Find**, and click **Files or Folders**. A dialog box appears, asking you to type the name of the lost file or folder. Type a name in the **Named** text box, pick the disk you want to search from the **Look In** drop-down list, and then click the **Find Now** button. Windows searches the selected drive for the specified file or folder and displays a list of items that match your search instructions.

If you're looking for a document file in Windows 95, you can find recently opened documents on the Documents menu. Click the **Start** button and point to **Documents**. Windows shows a list of files you've recently worked on. Click the file to run the program used to edit the file, and then open the file in that program.

If the file you're looking for has no extension (or you can't remember it), insert an asterisk at the end of the search file name. For example, type **myfile.*** to search for all files that start with MYFILE and end in any extension. You can also use the question mark (**?**) wild-card character to search for files. For example, **M????.*** finds all files whose name starts with M, has five or fewer characters, and ends in any extension.

If you use Windows 3.1 (or 3.11), the File Manager can help you find misplaced files. Just follow these steps. Open the **Main** group and double-click the **File Manager** icon. Open the **File** menu and select **Search**. The Search dialog box appears. Type the name of the file you're looking for. In the **Start From** text box, type the letter of the drive you want to search, followed by a colon and backslash (for example, type **c:**). To search all the directories on the drive, make sure there is an X in the **Search All Subdirectories** check box and click **OK**. File Manager searches the disk and then displays a list of all the files that match your search entry. You can now select files from this list.

If all you have is DOS, you can search for files at the DOS prompt. Type **dir *filename.ext* /s** (where *filename.ext* is the name of the file you're looking for) and press **Enter**.

One trick I often use to find misplaced files is to run the application I used when I created or saved the file. Then I open the **File** menu. Sometimes, the file is listed at the bottom of the menu. If I don't see it, I select **Save**. The application usually displays a dialog box showing the name of the directory where the application saves its files. Nine times out of ten, my lost file is in that directory.

18: The file I was working on is gone!

Often people "lose" files by closing (or minimizing) the window that the file is in or by opening another window on top of it. If the program you're working in has a Window menu, open it; chances are the file's name will appear at the bottom of the menu. You can display the file by clicking its name.

If you turned off your computer without exiting the program first—or if your computer crashed or suffered a power outage—the file probably *is* gone. You may be able to salvage the file (or parts of it) by running SCANDISK (or, if you use only DOS, **CHKDSK /F**) and telling the program to save the parts of the files it finds. You can then open those files in a text editor (such as Windows Notepad) to see what they contain. Look for these files in the root directory of the drive you checked. Recovered files are named *FILEnnnn*.CHK (where *nnnn* is a number from 0001 to 9999).

Some applications back up your documents automatically as you work. When you run the application after a system crash, the application gives you the option of recovering your lost file. But even if your application doesn't offer this valuable feature, most applications create backup files for each file you save. You may be able to recover your work by opening the backup file. (Backup files commonly have the same name as the original file, but they use the .BAK extension.)

To avoid losing files, always exit a program before shutting down your computer. Most programs have a safety feature that asks if you want to save your work before exiting. If you shut down your computer when your program is running, you bypass this important safety net. Also, get into the habit of saving your files periodically as you work (that is, if your program doesn't automatically do that for you).

19: Why can't I insert this graphic in my document?

Your document might not like that particular graphic. Most applications allow you to use graphics that are saved in a specific *format* (or file type). For example, an application may be able to handle only those graphics that were created with PC Paintbrush (files that end in .PCX). If the file is saved as a Windows Metafile (.WMF), the application may not accept it (or be able to read it).

If you're having trouble with a particular graphic, open it in the program you used to create it, and then try to save the graphic in a different format. (Simply changing the file's extension doesn't change the file type; you must select a file type, usually from the Save As list in the Save As dialog box.) If you did not create the graphic (for example, if it is a piece of clip art), you may be out of luck, unless you happen to have a graphics program that can open the file and allow you to save it in a different format. You can find such a program on the Internet without too much trouble.

20: I just downloaded a file—how do I use it?

Downloading consists of copying a file (usually from an online service or the Internet) to your computer. Many files are in a form you can use as-is. Other files might be *compressed* so they'll take up less disk space and travel faster over phone lines or a network connection. So the answer to the question of what to do with a downloaded file depends on what kind of file you downloaded.

If you obtained a graphic image or movie clip, you need a *viewer application* that can display the image or clip. Usually, you can find the viewer in the same place you downloaded the other files (assuming you got it on the Internet or through an online service, such as CompuServe or America Online).

If you downloaded a text file (one that ends in .TXT), you can open the file in any word processing or text-editing application (such as Notepad) and read it.

Most other downloaded files are compressed; you can't use the file until you decompress it. If you're lucky, you got hold of a *self-extracting* file (the file's name ends in .EXE). Move the file to a separate directory and then expand the file into its usable form by double-clicking it in File Manager or Windows Explorer. Once the file's been expanded into its component files, you can delete the .EXE file you downloaded to free up some disk space.

Most other compressed files end in .ZIP. To decompress a ZIP file, you need a program called PKZIP (if you use DOS) or WinZip (if you use Windows). Download one of these programs from your online service or from the Internet site where you downloaded the ZIP file. ▶**Then follow the instructions in the task "Install a Program from a Zip File" on page 325.◀**

Memory Problems

Problem	Quick Fix Number	Page
Creating memory	22	472
Conventional memory too low	21	471
DOS out of memory	21	471
Free up memory	21	471
Insufficient memory message in Windows	22	472
MemMaker, how to run	21	471
Memory problems in Windows	22	472
Memory, how much do I have?	21	471
Memory, freeing up more memory	21	471
Memory, using disk space in Windows to create	22	472
More memory, DOS	21	471
More memory, Windows	22	472
Out of memory message	21	471
Programs run slow in Windows	22	472
Programs won't run	21	471
Running more applications in Windows	22	472
Virtual memory in Windows	22	472
Windows needs more memory	22	472

21: I keep getting "Out of memory" messages when I try to run my DOS programs.

Although you can run your DOS application in Windows, you'll usually have better luck running the program from a DOS prompt. In Windows 95, click the **Start** button, select **Shut Down**, select **Restart in DOS Mode**, and click **OK**. In Windows 3.11, simply open Program Manager's **File** menu and select **Exit** to return to DOS.

If you get an **Out of memory** error message when trying to run your program from the DOS prompt, the next step is to find out how much memory the program you are trying to run needs— and what type. Check the program manual for details.

Once you know what you need, find out what your PC has by typing **MEM** at the DOS prompt and pressing **Enter**. Look at the conventional memory figure and (if your program needs it) extended memory. Some very old programs may need expanded memory as well. If your system is lacking in extended (or expanded) memory and your DOS program needs it, your system may be able to provide what you need with a few simple changes to the CONFIG.SYS. You see, conventional memory is memory below 640K. Extended memory is memory above 1M. However, your PC can't access this memory without the help of a special program, which you can load through the CONFIG.SYS. So even if your PC has 16M of RAM, DOS won't be able to use it without help.

In Windows, open the CONFIG.SYS file using Notepad or another text editor and add the following lines (at the very top of the file) if needed:

DOS=HIGH,UMB

DEVICE=C:\DOS\HIMEM.SYS

DEVICE=C:\DOS\EMM386.EXE NOEMS

If your DOS program needs expanded memory, change the last line above to read something like this:

DEVICE=C:\DOS\EMM386.EXE 1024 RAM

The 1024 RAM part will provide 1M of expanded memory. Adjust the figure as needed to fit with your requirements.

22: Can I make the "Insufficient memory" messages in Windows go away?

If your computer has 4M or less of RAM, you're probably going to encounter the **Insufficient memory** message on a regular basis. (If you use Windows 95, you'll get this message even if your PC has 8M of RAM.) The good news is that you can do something about it. Try the following suggestions:

- Install more RAM. If you use Windows 3.11, consider 8M the *absolute* minimum amount of RAM you should have on your system. If you use Windows 95, upgrade to at least 16M.

- Quit all the applications except the one you want to use. (Don't just minimize the windows; exit the applications.)

- Run Windows 3.1 or 3.11 in Enhanced mode. To do that, exit windows and then start it again by typing **WIN /3** and pressing **Enter**. If you have Windows for Workgroups or Windows 95, you have no choice; it always runs in Enhanced mode, so don't worry about it.

- Turn off any fancy options, such as screen savers, wallpaper, or Windows color schemes.

- In Windows 3.1 or 3.11, increase the size of the swap file used as virtual memory (disk space that acts like RAM). A *swap file* is a temporary file that Windows uses to transfer data back and forth between RAM and the disk. To increase the swap file size, open the **Main** group window, double-click the **Control Panel** icon, double-click the **386 Enhanced** icon, and click the **Virtual Memory** button. The following dialog box appears. Click the **Change** button and type a bigger number in the **New Size** text box. Enter a number that's close to the number given in the **Recommended Size** box and click **OK.**

- In Windows 95, low-memory messages usually indicate that the combined total of RAM and virtual memory (disk space) is insufficient. Try to upgrade to at least 16M of RAM. Also, try clearing some hard disk space, so Windows can use the free space as virtual memory. Windows 95 does a good job of grabbing as much free disk space as it can for use as virtual memory, so you should not have to change any settings.

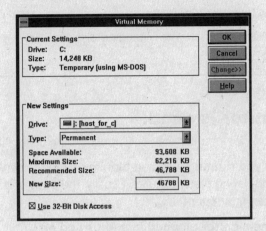

Video Problems

Problem	Quick Fix Number	Page
Bad-looking graphics	25	474
Blank screen, Windows	23,26	474-475
Blank screen, DOS	23	474
Dead monitor	23	474
Flickering monitor	27,30	476-477
Fuzzy pictures	25	474
Game looks bad	25	474
Garbage on-screen	28	476
Graphics and movies look bad	25	474
Headaches	27,30	476-477
Icons too small	29	477
Installed new display card, monitor whining	24	474
Monitor blank	23	474
Monitor whine	24	474
Nothing on monitor	23	474
Screen fuzzy	25	474
Screen saver problems	23	474
Small pictures	29	477

(continues)

(continued)

Problem	Quick Fix Number	Page
Strange patterns on-screen	28	476
Windows won't start after changing display driver	26	475
Whining noise	29	477

23: My monitor is dead!

Don't panic. The monitor may only appear to be dead. First, check the obvious:

- **Are you running a screen blanker?** Some screen saver programs blank the screen instead of displaying pretty pictures. Usually, the press of a key or a mouse move will snap your screen right out of it.

- **Is the monitor plugged in and turned on?** Your monitor should have a power indicator that lights when the power is on. Could the outlet be bad? If so, test the monitor in an outlet that you know is good.

- **Crank up the brightness control.** The brightness control is usually on the front or side of the monitor, making it easy to turn it way down by mistake.

- **Maybe it's the connection between the monitor and the system unit.** Turn everything off and check the connection between the monitor and the system unit (sometimes it wiggles free).

- **Is the video card loose?** Turn off the computer, open the case, and make sure the video card is seated firmly in its slot. If the card is loose, gently rock it back into place.

If nothing seems to work, maybe your monitor is dead. If you have a friend or colleague who has a similar computer system, try connecting his or her monitor to your computer. If your friend's monitor works on your computer, you know that the monitor is the problem. Call the manufacturer (or a computer technician).

24: Can I stop the high-pitched whining noise?

If you just installed a new video card, and your monitor starts to cry out in an unusually high-pitched whine, turn everything off *immediately*. The card may be set to a higher resolution than the monitor can handle. Check the manual that came with the video card and the one that came with your monitor. Make sure the card is set to display at the same resolution as the monitor. If you can't stop the whining, turn the computer off and call a qualified computer technician.

If the monitor has always whined, maybe you just purchased a whiny monitor. Earplugs may be the only solution.

25: Why are the pictures so fuzzy?

Either you have a low-resolution monitor, or your monitor is using a low-resolution video driver. If you have a VGA monitor (640×480 dpi, 16 colors) you can expect any pictures or movie clips to look pretty fuzzy. If you have an SVGA monitor capable of displaying at least 256 colors, pictures should look pretty clear, even at the lower resolution (640×480 dpi).

If you use Windows 3.11, you can change to a different resolution (provided your monitor supports it). Open the **Main** program group and double-click the **Windows Setup** icon. Open the **Options** menu and select **Change System Settings**. In the Change System Settings dialog box (shown here), open the **Display** drop-down list box and select the resolution you'd like to use. If you don't see the one you want, you may be able to add it to your system using the disk that came with your monitor. In that case, choose **Other Display** from this list. Click **OK**. Depending on the option you selected from the Display list, you may be prompted to insert a Windows installation disk or the disk that came with your monitor. Do that and click **OK**. Eventually, you'll be prompted to restart Windows, which you have to do in order to change resolutions. If you run into a problem, see the next quick fix for help.

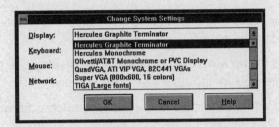

Windows 95 makes it easy to change resolutions as well. Simply right-click a blank area of the Windows desktop, click **Properties**, and click the **Settings** tab. You'll see the options shown in the next figure. Drag the **Desktop Area** slider to increase or decrease your resolution. You may want to change the **Font Size** and the **Color Palette** settings as well. Settings of 256 colors and 640×480 are usually sufficient for displaying images clearly. If you need to change the monitor type, click **Change Display Type**, and then click **Change** in the Monitor Type area. Click the **Show All Devices** option and select the monitor type you need. If yours is not listed, click **Have Disk** and insert the disk that came with your new monitor. Click **OK** and then **Close**. Click **OK** again to return to the desktop. ▶**For more details, see "Take Control of Your Keyboard and Mouse" on page 173.◀**

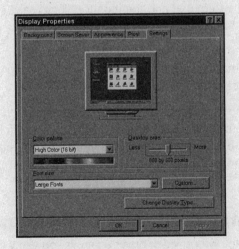

26: I changed my Windows display driver, and now Windows won't display anything!

You picked the wrong Windows video driver for your display adapter. Trouble is, you can't see anything in order to fix the problem.

If you have Windows 3.1 or 3.11 on your computer, the first step is to reboot. If your computer is set up to start Windows automatically (and you have DOS 6.0 or later), wait for the **Starting**

MS-DOS... message to appear, and then press and release the **F8** key. Step through the commands one by one, and answer **No** to the WIN command. While you're at it, watch for a command line that runs the video driver; you might need this information when you select a video driver for Windows. (If you don't have DOS 6.0 or later, start your computer with a bootable floppy disk.) Now you're ready to pick a Windows video driver.

Here's what you do to pick a video driver in Windows 3.1 or 3.11:

1. Change to the **WINDOWS** directory. For example, at the **C:\>** prompt, type **cd \windows**, and press **Enter**.

2. Type **setup** and press **Enter**. The Setup screen appears, allowing you to change video drivers and other options.

3. Use the **up arrow** key to move to the **Display** option, and press **Enter**. At the bottom of the screen, Setup displays a list of video drivers.

4. Highlight your monitor's video driver and press **Enter**, or select **VGA** (this sets the display back to the Windows-standard VGA, which works for all VGA and SVGA monitors).

5. Restart Windows, and it should come up.

In Windows 95, turn off your computer, wait a minute, and then turn it back on. When you see the message **Starting Windows 95**, press the **F8** key. A menu appears, showing a list of startup options. Select the **Safe Mode** option by typing the number next to it. In safe mode, Windows uses a basic video driver. You can repeat the steps in the previous quick fix to pick a different video driver or continue working with the basic driver.

27: That flickering is driving me crazy!

Either the cord that connects your monitor to the system unit is loose, your monitor is too close to a source of electrical interference, or you have an old interlaced monitor. To check the connection, turn off the system unit and the monitor. Then make sure the monitor cord is securely plugged into the back of the system unit; tighten the screws (if the cord has them).

If you still see a flicker, try moving the monitor a couple feet away from the wall or from another device that may be causing interference—a TV set, for example. Sometimes another electrical energy source can make the screen flicker.

If the screen still flickers, you probably have an old *interlaced* monitor. These monitors have an almost imperceptible flicker (like that of fluorescent lights). As the monitor ages, the flicker may become more noticeable. Sometimes you can solve the problem by selecting a lower resolution setting, but then your graphics will look lousy. Your best bet is a new monitor and a graphics adapter card.

28: My screen has all sorts of weird patterns.

You picked the wrong video driver again. If you use Windows, see Quick Fix 26 for help. If the problem happened in a DOS application, run the application's setup program again and pick a different video driver.

If you can't find a video driver that works, contact the manufacturer of the video card and find out if you have the most up-to-date driver. The *driver* (the program that tells the video card how to display text and pictures) commonly undergoes revisions to fix any bugs; new versions keep coming out. By installing the latest driver, you reduce the likelihood that you'll encounter display problems with new applications.

While you're talking to the manufacturer, ask if anyone else has experienced similar problems with the video card, video driver, or monitor. In some cases, a poorly designed video card or monitor might be the cause of the problem.

29: Why are the pictures so tiny?

When you hear all the hype about multimedia, you expect your monitor to display full-screen pictures like a TV set. In the real world, however, this rarely happens. Instead, you get these dinky pictures surrounded by a sea of black; you expect to see a disclaimer that reads, "This picture has been formatted to fit your screen."

The trouble is that the technology of graphic files hasn't quite caught up with display technology. A full-screen graphic image or movie clip takes up an enormous amount of storage space and would require Herculean computer power to display. What you end up with are dinky pictures. Don't worry—it's normal.

If the picture is way too small, you might try changing to a lower resolution display setting. For example, if you selected 1024×768, try changing to 640×480, 256 colors. Although your pictures won't look as sharp, you will be able to see them full-size.

30: My monitor gives me headaches.

Mine does, too. I'm going to get complaints from ergonomics specialists for saying this, but I've found that if I look up slightly at my monitor (about 10 degrees), I get fewer headaches than if I look straight ahead or down slightly. I also do neck rolls every 15 to 20 minutes to make sure I still have a neck.

Then again, it might not be all the monitor's fault. Sometimes headaches result from working in an area with poor lighting or that's lighted with fluorescent lights. In addition, some light sources (a lamp or window) can bounce light off your monitor, creating screen glare. Try positioning the monitor at a 90-degree angle to any light source. If you have an old interlaced monitor, it might have an imperceptible flicker that may be causing the problem. Go out and buy a non-interlaced monitor; the additional expense will pay off in health benefits.

Also, take frequent breaks—walk, talk, live a little. Although the news is ripe with stories about the computer age, don't forget that you are a person. You can't stare at a monitor all day and expect to feel limber and energized when you go home.

Sound Card Problems

Problem	Quick Fix Number	Page
CD-ROM drive, no sound	35,43	481,484
Conflict with another device	31,33,35	478,480-481
Control the volume	32	479
Device conflict	31,33,35	478,480-481
Drivers for sound card	31,36	478,481
Installed sound card, but it doesn't work	31	478
Installing drivers	31	478

(continues)

(continued)

Problem	Quick Fix Number	Page
IRQ conflict	31,33,35	478,480-481
Loading sound card drivers in Windows	31,36	478,481
Microphone doesn't work	38	481
MIDI port settings in Windows	36	481
Missing command lines in Windows startup files	36	481
Mouse and sound card problems	33,35	480-481
No sound after returning to Windows from DOS	34	480
Only one speaker works	37	481
Out of environment space message	31	478
Recording sounds, can't record	38	481
Sound card doesn't work in Windows	34,36	480-481
Sound card never worked	31	478
Sound card stops working	33,34	480
Sound too loud	32	479
Speaker problems	31,37	478,481
Stereo sound doesn't work	37	481
Turn volume up or down	32	479
Upgraded sound card; mouse or other device doesn't work	35	481
Volume control	32	479
Windows stops playing sounds	34,36	480-481

31: I just installed the sound card, and it doesn't work.

This is a tough one, because the solution can range from something simple (like cranking up the volume) to something complex (like fooling around with switches on the card). Here are some solutions to try.

- **Look for simple solutions.** Are your speakers plugged into the right jack: the output jack? (It's easy to plug the speakers into the microphone or the input jack by mistake.) If you have amplified speakers, are they plugged into the power supply and turned on (or do they need batteries)? Is the volume cranked up (most sound cards have a volume control like on a radio)? Are you running a program that plays sounds and that is compatible with your sound card? Is sound turned on (and turned up) in the program?

- **Did you install the drivers?** The sound card should come with one or more disks containing the sound card drivers. You must run the installation program to set up your computer to use the sound card.

- **Did you get the "Out of environmental space" message?** Try adding the following line to the end of your CONFIG.SYS file:

      shell=c:\command.com /e:512 /p

  ▶**For details on how to edit CONFIG.SYS, see "Modify Your Startup Files" on page 357.**◀ Reboot your computer after making the change.

- **Is the sound card in conflict with another device?** Each device has its own *input/output address* and *interrupt* settings (IRQs). (The address tells the computer where the device is, and the interrupt provides a way for the device to demand attention.) If two devices try to use the same settings, one or both devices won't work.

  Check the documentation that came with each card that's installed in your computer. If you find a setting that matches a setting on your sound card, change the setting on the sound card (usually by using jumpers or flipping tiny DIP switches). You'll also have to run the sound card's setup program again. (Resolving hardware conflicts is usually a very tedious process.) Common interrupts are 7, 9, 10, and 11.

- **To resolve a device conflict in Windows 95, you can use the Hardware Conflict Troubleshooter.** To run it, click the **Start** button, click **Help**, click the **Contents** tab and double-click **Troubleshooting**. Double-click **If You Have a Hardware Conflict**, and then follow the on-screen instructions. The Hardware Conflict Troubleshooter asks a series of questions to help you determine the cause of the problem and correct it.

  ▶**For more details about installing sound cards and other hardware, see "Install New Hardware" on page 365.**◀

32: How do I turn the sound down (or up)?

You'd think there would be one master volume control, but there are usually at least three. Most sound cards have a volume control (on the back of the card) that allows you to adjust the strength of the signal coming out of the card. The speakers also have a volume control. In addition, if you're playing a CD-ROM, you may have to adjust the volume knob on the CD player itself. And finally, there's usually some kind of software control built into whatever program you're using to play the sound. For example, most games have a sound command with which you can adjust the volume (or turn it completely off).

To get the right loudness, I usually set each control at midrange and then adjust from there. You'll have to experiment with the controls to get the right combination.

In Windows 95, you can quickly display the volume controls by double-clicking the speaker icon in the taskbar (just to the left of the time display). This displays volume and balance controls for the sound card, CD-ROM drive, microphone, and other devices (see the following figure).

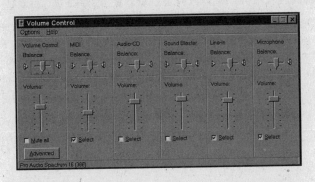

33: The sound card worked before, but then I installed XXXXX.

If you installed a new hardware device, chances are the device is using the same input/output address or interrupt setting as your sound card. You'll have to change the conflicting setting on one of the cards and then run its installation or configuration program again. ▶**For details, see "Install New Hardware" on page 365.**◀

If you installed a new application or game that's messing up your sound card, check your CONFIG.SYS and AUTOEXEC.BAT files to make sure the application installation didn't change your sound card settings. ▶**See "Modify Your Startup Files" on page 357 for details on how to view and change CONFIG.SYS and AUTOEXEC.BAT.**◀

If you have Windows 95, you can view the current settings for your sound card by using the Device Manager. Open the Control Panel (**Start**, **Settings**, **Control Panel**), and then double-click the **System** icon. Click the **Device Manager** tab. Click the sound card in the list of hardware, and then click **Properties**. Click the **Resources** tab to view the interrupt, DMA channel, and I/O settings for the card (shown here). At the bottom of this dialog box is a list showing any devices with which your sound card may be in conflict.

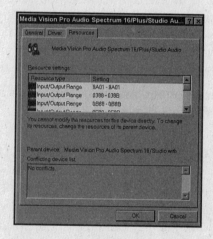

To resolve a device conflict in Windows 95, you can use the Hardware Conflict Troubleshooter. To run it, click the **Start** button, click **Help**, click the **Contents** tab and double-click **Troubleshooting**. Double-click **If You Have a Hardware Conflict**, and then follow the on-screen instructions. The Hardware Conflict Troubleshooter asks a series of questions to help you determine the cause of the problem and correct it.

34: I run a DOS application from Windows, and when I return, my Windows applications won't play sounds.

When you go from Windows 95 to DOS, the DOS sound drivers take control of the sound card. They don't relinquish control when you return to Windows. And in some cases, Windows 95 will attempt to "reinstall" your sound card, even when you're still in DOS playing your game! If you installed Windows 95 with the dual boot option, boot to your old DOS and play your game. Otherwise, give up playing the game or install the game on another PC.

With Windows 3.1, you don't have this problem as long as you completely exit Windows before playing your game (do not attempt to run the game while in Windows).

35: The sound card upgrade *degraded* my system.

If you install a sound card and lose your mouse or CD-ROM drive in the process, you can usually trace the problem back to a hardware conflict. The sound card is using the same input/output address or interrupt setting as the device you lost. You'll have to change the address or interrupt on the sound card and then run the sound card's installation or configuration program again. ▶**For details, see "Install New Hardware" on page 365.**◀

36: I can't get my sound card to work in Windows.

If you're working in Windows 3.1 or 3.11, you probably need to manually enter some command lines in WIN.INI and SYSTEM.INI. (These files contain important commands that Windows carries out on startup.) Usually, when you install the sound card drivers, the installation program edits these files for you—but sometimes the installation program fails.

Check the documentation that came with your sound card. It should include a list of the commands you need to add to your Windows system files and directions on where you need to add them. ▶**For information on how to edit WIN.INI and SYSTEM.INI, see "Modify Your Startup Files" on page 357.**◀

One more thing: If you get a message about the MIDI Port Setting in Windows 3.1 or 3.11, there's probably nothing wrong with the MIDI Port Setting. To solve the problem, exit Windows, turn off your computer, wait about 30 seconds, and restart your computer.

If you have problems with your sound card in Windows 95, try reinstalling the sound card using the Add New Hardware Wizard. ▶**For details, see "Install Hardware in Windows 95" on page 366.**◀

37: It's supposed to be in stereo!

If this problem just cropped up, chances are you turned off one of the speakers by mistake or one speaker became disconnected from the power source. (I had a pair of cheap speakers that constantly disconnected from the power source.)

If the problem has been present from day one, you probably selected the wrong output setting for the card. Run the sound card's setup or configuration utility again; make sure you've selected **stereo** (rather than mono) output. Also, if the sound card program (device driver) has a balance control, make sure it is set in the middle.

38: My microphone doesn't work.

If you have a Soundblaster (or compatible) card and you're working in Windows, run the **SB16Mixer** utility (it's in the Soundblaster 16 group window). Crank up the **Mic** setting. Open the **Options** menu and make sure **Save Settings on Exit** has a check mark next to it. Then exit the SB16 Mixer utility.

If you have a different type of card, or if adjusting the Mic setting doesn't help, check for hardware problems. Make sure the microphone is plugged into the Mic jack on the sound card, and make sure the microphone is turned on.

If you use Windows 95, you may need to turn on the microphone output. Double-click the sound (speaker) icon on the taskbar, and the Volume Control dialog box appears. Open the **Options** menu and select **Properties**. Click the **Recording** option, make sure that the microphone control is checked, and click **OK**. Then, in the Recording Control dialog box (shown in the next figure), make sure that the **Select** check box is checked. This turns on the microphone control. Adjust the volume and balance as needed, and click **OK**.

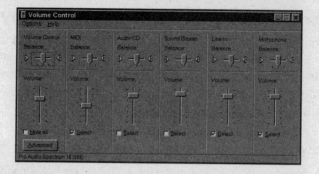

CD-ROM Problems

39: The CD-ROM drive doesn't work.

Whenever something doesn't work (no lights, no sound, no sign of life), check the obvious first:

- Do you have an external CD-ROM drive? If so, make sure it is plugged in, connected to your system unit, and turned on.

- Make sure the drive has a *computer* CD-ROM in it (not an audio CD) and that the disc is inserted properly in the drive (label-side up).

- Did you install the drivers that came with the CD-ROM drive? Without a driver (instructions that tell your computer how to use a device), your CD-ROM drive won't respond.

- If you just installed the CD-ROM drive, check for hardware conflicts. Each device has a specific input/output address and interrupt assigned to it. If the address and interrupt conflict with another device, your CD-ROM drive won't work. Check the documentation that came with your CD-ROM drive and the other drives that are installed on your system.

- If you're having trouble in Windows 95, try running the Add New Hardware Wizard. ▶**For details, see "Install Hardware in Windows 95" on page 366.**◀ You can also run the Hardware Conflict Troubleshooter: Click the **Start** button, click **Help**, click the **Contents** tab, and double-click **Troubleshooting**. Double-click **If You Have a Hardware Conflict**, and then follow the on-screen instructions. The Hardware Conflict Troubleshooter asks a series of questions to help you determine the cause of the problem and correct it.

40: The drive seems to work all right, but I can't get at the files on the disc.

If you know that the CD-ROM drive has power—and that it's spinning the disc all right—you probably did not install the driver for the CD-ROM drive or you installed the wrong driver. Try the following fixes:

- Make sure the correct driver is loading. There should be a command in your CONFIG.SYS file that loads the driver. You should see a command something like this:

    DEVICEHIGH=C:\CDROM\MTMCDAI.SYS /D:MTMIDE01 /P:170,15

    Check your CD-ROM documentation to find out the exact command to type. Also, make sure the driver specified in CONFIG.SYS is on your disk in the specified directory.

- Check AUTOEXEC.BAT for a line that has **MSCDEX.EXE** in it. Without this line, your computer won't recognize the CD-ROM drive. If the line is missing, add a line like **C:\DOS\MSCDEX.EXE /D:MTMIDE01 /M:10** to your AUTOEXEC.BAT file. Again, check your documentation to find out the exact command to enter.

- If the driver or MSCDEX.EXE is set up to load into the high memory area (with commands like LOADHIGH or DEVICEHIGH), remove the LOADHIGH (or LH) command and change DEVICEHIGH to **DEVICE**. This loads the drivers into conventional memory instead. ▶**For details on how to edit CONFIG.SYS and AUTOEXEC.BAT, see "Modify Your Startup Files" on page 357.**◀

- If you're having trouble in Windows 95, try running the Add New Hardware Wizard. ▶**For details, see "Install Hardware in Windows 95" on page 366.**◀

41: The CD-ROM drive locks up my system.

Don't jump to conclusions. Is it the CD-ROM drive or the application you're running from the disc? If your computer freezes up when you run a particular application, it's the application's fault. Check the documentation that came with the application to determine whether there's a fix for the problem. If you can't find anything, call the developer's technical support line.

If every CD-ROM application you try to run freezes your system, you probably have a hardware conflict. One of your other devices (maybe a sound board or the mouse) is in conflict with your CD-ROM drive. You'll have to check the documentation to find out which settings are conflicting, and then change the settings on one of the devices. ▶**Refer to "Install New Hardware" on page 365 for more information on how to resolve hardware conflicts.◀**

42: Where's the sound supposed to come from?

Most CD-ROM drives have two sound output jacks: one on the front and one (or two for stereo output) on the back. The front jack is for a set of earphones. Plug the earphones in, and you can jam while you're playing DOOM.

The jack on the back allows you to connect your CD-ROM drive to a set of amplified speakers or to a sound card. If you have a sound card, you'll probably want to connect the CD-ROM sound output jacks to the sound card's input jacks. Then connect the sound card's output jacks to your speakers. You end up with a ball of tangled wire behind your computer, but the sound quality will be pretty good.

43: What about music CDs?

Most newer CD-ROM players can play audio CDs, but you need a special program to play them. If you have Windows 95, playing audio CDs is a no-brainer. You simply load the audio CD into the CD-ROM drive and close the drawer. Windows 95 starts playing the CD automatically, using the CD Player program.

If you use Windows 3.1 or just DOS, don't fret: Most sound cards and CD-ROM players come with the program you need. For example, Soundblaster 16 comes with a program called QuickCD that enables you to play audio CDs in DOS or Windows.

Windows 3.1 requires a special driver, as well. It's called the MCI Audio driver. To activate this driver, open the **Main** group window, double-click the **Control Panel** icon, double-click the **Drivers** icon, and click the **Add** button. Select **[MCI] CD Audio** from the list of drivers, click the **OK** button, and follow the on-screen instructions to complete the installation.

If [MCI] CD Audio is not on the list of drivers, look for a file on your Windows installation disks named **MCICDA.DR_**. Insert the disk in the floppy drive (A or B). Then go to the DOS prompt, change to the WINDOWS directory, and type

```
expand a:mcicda.dr_ c:\windows\system\mcicda.drv
```

or

```
expand b:mcicda.dr_ c:\windows\system\mcicda.drv
```

depending on which drive contains the disk. Press **Enter**. You can now perform the steps given in the previous paragraph to activate the driver.

44: The movie clips are s-l-o-w.

Buy a computer with at least a 100MHz Pentium chip and a 4X ("quad-speed") CD-ROM drive. My point is that movie clips require a pretty fast computer. If you have a 486SX 25MHz computer with 4 megabytes of RAM, you can expect the movies to crawl.

In Windows 95, you can increase the speed of the CD-ROM drive simply by telling Windows the speed of your CD-ROM drive. To do this, double-click the **System** icon in the Control Panel. Click the **Performance** tab, and then click the **File System** button. Click the **CD-ROM** tab to see the options shown in the following figure. From the **Optimize Access Pattern For** drop-down list, click the speed of your CD-ROM drive (the speed is usually etched into the front of the drive). You can drag the **Supplemental Cache Size** slider to the right to increase the cache size for the drive, but this uses additional memory. Increase the cache size only if you use the CD-ROM drive frequently.

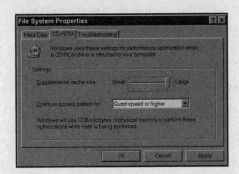

If you use Windows 3.1 or DOS, the only way you can really speed up a CD-ROM drive is to use a *disk caching* program (such as SmartDrive). Check your CONFIG.SYS and AUTOEXEC.BAT files to make sure one of the files has a command line that loads SmartDrive. If neither file has the command, add the following command to AUTOEXEC.BAT (add the command before the command that loads MSCDEX):

c:\dos\smartdrv.exe

45: I stood my system unit on end, and now the CD-ROM drive is slow.

Never set a system unit that's equipped with a CD-ROM drive on its side. Besides the fact that you'll have a hard time inserting the disc, CD-ROM drives aren't built to spin vertically.

Printing Problems

Problem	Quick Fix Number	Page
Drivers, installing	48	488
Entered multiple print commands, still no printing	46,47	487
Feed adjustment knob on form-feed printers	50	489
Garbage printout	48	488
Half-page printouts	49	489
Laser printer won't print	46,47,49,53	487-490
Light printout	48	488
Memory problems, laser printers	49,53	489-490

(continues)

(continued)

46: My printer won't print.

Make sure the printer has paper, that it's plugged in and turned on, and that the Online light is lit (not blinking). Check that the printer has paper as well.

If everything checks out and the printer still won't print, look for the following:

- If you're printing to a laser printer, it typically won't eject the page until it's full. Press the **Load/Eject/Form Feed** button to eject the page.

- If you have a tractor-feed mechanism on the printer, make sure the sheet feeder switch is in the proper position (for single-sheets or continuous forms).

- Check your printer setup in the application you're printing from to make sure it's sending the data to the right printer. In Windows 3.1, do the following to check the printer port (which is usually set to **LPT1**): Open the **Main** group window, double-click the **Control Panel** icon, double-click **Printers**, and click the **Connect** button. Pick the correct printer port, and then click the **OK** button. In Windows 95, double-click the **Printers** icon in the **Control Panel**. Right-click the printer icon, select **Properties**, and click the **Details** tab to check the printer port (see the following figure).

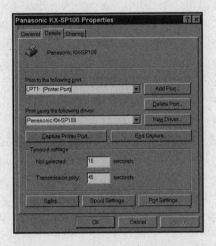

- Are you having problems in only one application? If you can print from other applications, the problem is with the printer setup in the problem application.

- Is it a printer problem? To determine whether the printer has a problem, type **dir > lpt1** at the DOS prompt and press **Enter**. This prints the current directory list. If it prints okay, the problem is in the Windows printer setup—or the application's setup. If the directory does not print (or prints incorrectly), the problem is probably with the printer. Most printers have a self-test; check the documentation to figure out how to run the test for your printer.

If you've tried everything and the printer still isn't responding, your printed documents might be "stuck in traffic" in the print queue. Skip to the next quick fix to learn how to proceed.

47: I tried three times to print this thing, and I haven't gotten even one copy!

Your printed documents are in the *print queue*—a waiting line. Applications commonly send print-ed documents to a temporary waiting area and then feed them from there to the printer. If something goes wrong, the document has to stand in line until the printer is ready. If you keep entering the print command over and over, you end up with a long line of documents.

In Windows 95, you can quickly view the print queue by double-clicking the printer icon on the taskbar. The following figure shows the print queue window. You don't typically have to do anything to get Windows 95 to retry printing a document that it might have paused on; it'll do that on its own after a few seconds. To change the print order of the waiting documents (so one prints before some other one), just drag one up to the top of the list. To remove a document from the queue, click it and press **Delete**. (Doing that may cause the printer to stop if part of a printed page gets stuck in it. If that happens, press the printer's **Load/Eject/Form Feed** button to eject the page.)

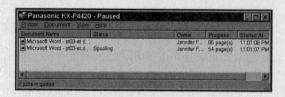

In Microsoft Windows 3.1 and 3.11, a program called Print Manager handles the printing for all your applications. To view the Print Manager's queue, press **Ctrl+Esc** to display the Task List. If documents are waiting in the queue, Print Manager should appear in the list. Select **Print Manager** and click **Switch To**. The Print Manager window appears, showing a list of files waiting in the print queue. Click the printer you're using. It should be marked **[Stalled]**. Click the **Resume** button, and printing should start again. You can also click an individual print job and click **Retry**.

If you're working with a DOS application, it probably has its own print queue (or *spooler*) that handles background printing. Check the documentation to find out what the application calls its queue and where it stores the command to get to it.

48: It prints all right, but the print looks like garbage.

If you get a bunch of foreign-looking symbols, you selected the wrong printer driver for your printer. In Windows 95, you can view the installed printer drivers by double-clicking the **My Computer** icon and then double-clicking the **Printers** icon. Right-click the printer driver you want to use as the default and click **Set As Default**. If the correct printer driver is not displayed, double-click the **Add Printer** icon and follow the on-screen instructions. ▶See **"Install Hardware in Windows 95" on page 365 if you need help.**◀

In Windows 3.1 or 3.11, open the **Main** group window and double-click the **Control Panel** icon. Double-click **Printers**. The Installed Printers list appears, showing the names of the printers that Windows is set up to use. Click the printer you're using, and then click the **Set As Default Printer** button. Click the **Close** button to save your changes.

> In DOS applications, you usually have to run the application's setup utility again to select a different printer driver.

If you have an off-brand printer, you can probably set it up to *emulate* (act like) a brand-name printer. In most cases, you have to pry open a panel on the printer and flip some DIP switches to turn on the emulation. The printer documentation tells you how to get to the switches, which ones you need to flip, and what position each one has to be in. You then select the printer driver for the brand-name printer.

If by "the print looks like garbage" you mean that the print is too light or streaky, you may have to change the print cartridge or ribbon (or clean it). Before cleaning an inkjet cartridge, read the instructions. I once destroyed a $20 cartridge by swabbing the wrong area with alcohol.

49: It prints only half of a page!

Laser printers (and some inkjets) print an entire page at one time, storing the entire page in memory. If the page has a big, complex graphic image (or lots of fonts), the printer may be able to store only a portion of the page. The best fix is to get more memory for your printer.

The quickest fix is to use fewer fonts on the page and try using a less complex graphic image. You can also try resizing a graphic so that it's smaller.

You might also try printing the document at a lower resolution. In most applications (and in Windows), you can choose a lower resolution through the printer setup. For example, in Windows 95, click **Start**, select **Settings**, and then select **Printers**. Right-click the printer icon and select **Properties**. Then click the **Graphics** tab and select the **Resolution** you want (see the following figure). Click **OK** when you're through.

50: I can't get the type lined up right.

If the print is too close to the top or bottom of the page, you can usually make adjustments using the printer's controls. Most dot-matrix printers have a *feed adjustment button* that allows you to move the page up or down a short distance for minor problems. With inkjet and laser printers, the feed is controlled internally, so you usually don't have a problem with aligning text at the top or bottom of the page.

If the print is too close to the left or right edge of the page, you might be able to adjust how the paper feeds into the printer. If you can't make adjustments on the printer itself, try changing your margins in your document. If the entire document is out of whack, be sure to select the entire document before changing margins.

Most inkjet and laser printers have a *non-printable* region around the page. If you set the margins too narrow, you might end up having text chopped off the left or right side of the page. Try increasing (widening) the margins to move the text back into the printable region of the paper.

51: The print on-screen doesn't match the page.

Fonts typically come in pairs—one font for the printer and one for the screen. If the *printer font* has no matching *screen font*, the application takes liberties and selects a screen font it thinks looks like the printer font.

To correct this problem, make sure you install both the screen and printer font for every font you use. If you're using fonts in Windows, keep in mind that TrueType fonts (displayed with a **TT** on

Windows menus) consist of one font that controls both the screen and the printer. By using TrueType fonts only, you're sure to get in print what you see on the screen.

52: I hate these paper jams.

You can prevent most paper jams by loading the paper properly into the printer. With laser and inkjet printers, be sure not to fill the paper trays too full. Also, use the recommended weight and type of paper suitable for your kind of printer.

53: Is it always this slow?

Yes. Printing is one of the slowest operations a computer performs, especially if you're printing complex color graphics. There are, however, a few things you can do to speed up printing:

- Don't do anything else while you're printing. If you work in another application while you're printing, you use computer resources that might otherwise be used solely for printing.

- Add memory to your printer. This shifts the work load from your computer to your printer.

- In Windows 3.1 or 3.11, run the Print Manager (from the Main window), open the **Options** menu, and select **High Priority**. Windows allocates more computing power to your print jobs and less to any other tasks you're trying to perform.

- Use the latest printer driver. New and improved printer drivers usually print faster. Contact the printer manufacturer to find out whether they've created any new drivers for your printer. (A driver is a program that tells Windows or an application how to communicate with the printer.)

- In both Windows 3.1 and Windows 95, use TrueType fonts (fonts marked **TT**).

- Use only the built-in printer fonts. Most printers have about a dozen built-in fonts that aren't very fancy, but they do print fast. (In Windows applications, printer fonts have a printer icon next to them.)

Mouse Problems

Problem	Quick Fix Number	Page
Application can't use a mouse	54	491
Com port problems	54,56,57	491-493
Device driver problems	54,55,57	491-493
Dirty mouse	55	492
Double-click doesn't work	59	495
DOS applications run from Windows, no mouse pointer	58	493
Fast mouse pointer	59	495
Installing mouse driver	54,55	491-492
Jumpy mouse pointer	55	492
Modem works, mouse doesn't	54,56	491-492

Problem	Quick Fix Number	Page
Mouse doesn't work	54	491
Mouse driver in Windows, selecting	57	493
Mouse disappears from DOS programs in Windows	58	493
Mouse pointer disappears	54,58	491,493
Mouse set up on wrong COM port	54,56,57	491-493
No mouse	54	491
Skipping mouse pointer	55	492
Slow mouse	59	495
Slowing down the mouse	59	495
Speeding up the mouse	59	495
Windows mouse problems	54,55,57,58	491-493
Wrong Windows mouse driver	57	493

54: My mouse doesn't work, period.

If you don't even get a mouse pointer, make sure your mouse is plugged securely into the correct port, and then check the following:

- **When you connected the mouse, did you install a mouse driver?** Connecting a mouse to your computer is not enough. You must install a *mouse driver* that tells the computer how to use the mouse. ▸**See "Install a Mouse" on page 374 for help.**◂

- **Have you recently installed a Disney game?** Unlike most Windows programs, some Disney games install their own screen drivers, causing problems within Windows, including a disappearing mouse. So check your display driver setup and verify that you have the correct driver installed for your monitor.

- **Do you have the mouse problem in Windows 95?** To change a mouse setting, press **Alt+F4** to close any windows that are in your way. Then press **Tab** until **My Computer** is highlighted and press **Enter**. Use the arrow keys to highlight the **Mouse** icon, and then press **Enter**. If you can't even get the mouse pointer to appear, press **Ctrl+PgDn** to select the **General** tab, and then press **Alt+C** to select the **Change** button. Use the down arrow key to select the mouse manufacturer. Press **Tab** and use the down arrow key to select the mouse model you have. Press **Enter** to save your change.

- **When you installed the mouse driver, did you specify a COM port?** When you install a mouse driver, you might need to specify which port the mouse is plugged into: COM1, COM2, COM3, or a special mouse port. If you pick the wrong port, your computer won't be able to find your mouse. Run the installation or setup program again and select a different COM port. You must reboot your computer after selecting a new COM port.

- **Make sure the mouse driver is loading.** Reboot your computer, wait until you see the message **Starting MS-DOS...**, and then press and release the **F8** key. Step through the startup commands. You should see a message like **Mouse Driver Loaded**. If you see something like **Mouse Not Found**, you probably have the mouse connected to the wrong port (or the driver is set up to use the wrong mouse port).

- **Look for a README file in the MOUSE directory.** Some mice have strange quirks that are documented in a README.TXT file. Look for such a file in your MOUSE directory, open it, and read it. In Windows, use Notepad to read the file. Then go to the DOS prompt, type **CD*MOUSEDIR*** to change to the mouse directory (substitute the real name of the directory for *mousedir*), and type the command **type readme.txt |more**. The **|more** switch tells DOS to display one screen at a time.

- **Is the mouse pointer hidden?** Mouse pointers like to hide in the corners or edges of your screen. Roll the mouse on your desktop to see if you can bring the pointer into view.

- **Are you in a program that uses a mouse?** Some programs don't *support* (aren't designed to run with) a mouse; you won't see the mouse pointer in these programs. For example, you won't see a mouse pointer at the DOS prompt, but you should see it in most other programs. Run a program that you know uses a mouse to see whether it works there.

55: My mouse pointer is jumping all over the screen.

Turn off your computer and clean your mouse. ▶**(See "Clean the Mouse" on page 292 for details.)**◀ If the problem occurs in a DOS program running under Windows, skip ahead to Quick Fix #57: "My mouse won't do Windows."

If you clean the mouse and you're still having trouble, open your CONFIG.SYS and AUTOEXEC.BAT files; make sure you have only one mouse driver loading. If you find a mouse command line in both files, add **REM** plus a space before *one* of the commands. ▶**For details on how to edit CONFIG.SYS and AUTOEXEC.BAT, see "Modify Your Startup Files" on page 357.**◀

If you're having trouble with MOUSE.SYS and you have a MOUSE.EXE (or MOUSE.COM) file, remove the MOUSE.SYS command from CONFIG.SYS, add the MOUSE.EXE (or MOUSE.COM) command to AUTOEXEC.BAT, and then reboot your computer.

If that doesn't work, call the mouse manufacturer and make sure you have the latest mouse driver (the program that tells your computer how to use the mouse). Microsoft, Logitech, and other mouse manufacturers constantly improve their mouse drivers to correct for bugs that crop up in the latest programs.

56: I installed a modem, and now the mouse doesn't work!

Mice and modems both use COM ports. Normally the mouse uses COM1 and the modem uses COM2. If your mouse and modem don't seem to get along, they're probably set to use the same COM port. Leave the mouse port setting as is, and try changing the setting for the modem. Here's what you do:

1. If you have an internal modem, look at the back of it for a set of tiny switches. These switches let you change the COM port setting for the card itself.

2. If you find the switches, write down their original positions, and then flip the switches to select a different COM port (try **COM2** or **COM4**). (If you don't see switches, you might have to go inside your computer to change jumpers on the modem card; consult the documentation.)

3. Once you've changed the COM port on the hardware, you must change it in the telecommunications program you're using. This can be a fax program, online service, Internet program, Windows Terminal or HyperTerminal, or whatever program you use with your modem. In America Online, for example, you click the **Setup** button, select **Setup Modem**, and then click the COM port setting.

In Windows 95, you can change the modem's COM port setting by selecting the **Modems** icon in the Control Panel and selecting the **Diagnostics** tab (you can change tabs by pressing **Ctrl+PgDn**). Press **Alt+H** or click the **Help** button to run the Modem Troubleshooter. The Troubleshooter will ask you a series of questions to help you identify the problem and fix it.

57: My mouse won't do Windows.

First, make sure the mouse is set up on COM1 or COM2 (in Windows, the mouse won't work on COM3 or COM4). Then, make sure you have the correct mouse driver loaded.

In Windows 95, you can change your mouse port by double-clicking the **Mouse** icon in the Control Panel. But, if you can't use your mouse, you can't click. So, to pick a different mouse driver with your keyboard, press **Ctrl+Esc**, press **Esc**, and then press the **Tab** key until **My Computer** is highlighted. Press **Enter**. Use the arrow keys to highlight the **Mouse** icon, and then press **Enter**. If you can't even get the mouse pointer to appear, press **Ctrl+PgDn** to select the **General** tab, and then press **Alt+C** to select the **Change** button. Press **Alt+A** to display all available drivers. Use the down arrow key to select the mouse manufacturer. Then press **Tab** and use the down arrow key to select the mouse model you have (as shown here). Press **Enter** to save your changes.

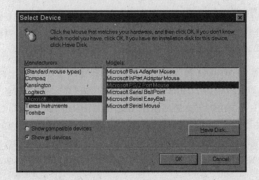

In Windows 3.1 or 3.11, open the **Main** group window, and double-click the **Windows Setup** icon. Open the **Options** menu and select **Change System Settings**. The Change System Settings dialog box appears. Open the **Mouse** drop-down list and click the driver for your mouse. If you're unsure, select a **Microsoft** mouse driver (most mice are Microsoft-compatible).

If you're still having trouble in Windows 3.1 or 3.11, look in your mouse driver directory for a README file. Open it and read its contents. You may need to edit some of the mouse commands in the SYSTEM.INI file. The README file should tell you which commands you need to edit. ▶**To learn how to edit the SYSTEM.INI file, see "Modify Your Startup Files" on page 357.**◀

58: My mouse won't do DOS applications from Windows.

If your mouse works fine in Windows applications, but freaks out when you try to run a DOS application from Windows, try the following fixes:

- **If the DOS application is in a window, press Alt+Enter to run it in full-screen mode.** If you can use the mouse in full-screen mode (in Windows 3.1 or 3.11), try adding the following command to the [NonWindowsApp] section of your SYSTEM.INI file:

  MouseInDosBox=1

  The 1 means Yes (you do want the mouse pointer to appear in a DOS window).

In Windows 95, you can make a DOS application run in full-screen mode by right-clicking the program's icon and selecting **Properties**. Click the **Screen** tab and click **Full-screen**. Click **OK** to save your change.

- **Make sure the correct mouse is selected in Windows.** In Windows 3.1 or 3.11, open the **Main** group window, double-click the **Windows Setup** icon, open the **Options** menu, and select **Change System Settings**. Open the **Mouse** drop-down list and select the mouse you're using.

  In Windows 95, double-click **My Computer**, double-click **Control Panel**, and then double-click the **Mouse** icon. Click the **General** tab. If the correct mouse driver is not displayed, click the **Change** button, and then select the correct manufacturer and model.

- **In Windows 95, you may have trouble using your mouse in a DOS application if you have QuickEdit mode turned on.** To turn it off within a particular DOS program, right-click the program's icon and select **Properties**. Click the **Misc** tab. Click the **QuickEdit** option to turn it off, and then click **OK**.

- **If your problem is selecting text while running a DOS application in Windows 95,** make sure that the program is running in a *window*. If it's running full screen, press **Alt+Enter** to put it in a window. Then open the **Control** menu, select **Edit**, and select **Mark**. Drag over the text you want to select and press **Enter** to copy it to the Clipboard. To paste the copied text, use the **Edit, Paste** command.

- **If the problem is an invisible mouse pointer on a laptop running Windows 95,** you can turn on pointer trails to make it easier to see the mouse pointer. Double-click the **Mouse** icon in the Control Panel. Click the **Motion** tab and click the **Show Pointer Trails** option. You can also increase the size of the pointer by clicking the **Pointers** tab and selecting **Windows Standard (Extra Large)** from the **Scheme** list box. (The following figure shows the available mouse pointer options.) Click **OK** when you're done selecting options.

- **Make sure only one mouse driver is running.** If both AUTOEXEC.BAT and CONFIG.SYS contain a mouse command, use the **REM** command to disable the **DEVICE=MOUSE.SYS** command in CONFIG.SYS. Usually, MOUSE.COM (or MOUSE.EXE) works better.

- **Use the latest version of the mouse driver.** If you have an old mouse driver (pre-version 8.20), contact the mouse manufacturer and ask for an updated driver.

- **Make sure there is only one MOUSE.INI file on your hard drive.** In Windows 3.1 or 3.11, use the File Manager's Search feature (select **File**, **Search**) to find the MOUSE.INI files. Delete all the MOUSE.INI files except the one in the \WINDOWS directory. Windows 95 doesn't use a MOUSE.INI file to control your mouse, so you don't have to worry about it.

- **Use the VGA driver that came with Windows.** You can change video drivers in Windows 95 by right-clicking a blank area of the Windows desktop and selecting **Properties**. Click the **Settings** tab, and then click **Change Display Type** to view the current video driver and change it, if desired.

  In Windows 3.1 or 3.11, open the **Main** group window, double-click the **Windows Setup** icon, open the **Options** menu, and select **Change System Settings**. Open the **Display** drop-down list and select **VGA**. This tells Windows to use its standard VGA driver. (This might solve your DOS problem, but it might also reduce the quality of the display in Windows applications. Check with the manufacturer of the display card you're using to see about a permanent fix.)

59: My mouse pointer moves too fast or too slow.

You can usually change the mouse speed by running a mouse setup program at the DOS prompt or in Windows. Setup programs usually let you change the mouse speed, flip the mouse buttons (for left-hand use), and change the double-click interval (the speed at which you have to click twice when you enter a "double-click").

In Windows 95, double-click the **Mouse** icon in the Control Panel (**Start**, **Settings**, **Control Panel**) to change your mouse settings. Click the **Motion** tab and adjust the **Pointer Speed** setting (as shown here).

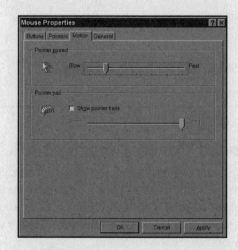

In Windows 3.1 or 3.11, open the **Main** group window and double-click the **Control Panel** icon. Double-click the **Mouse** icon. The Mouse dialog box appears. Drag the box in the **Mouse Tracking Speed** control bar to the left to slow down the mouse pointer or to the right to speed it up. Click the **OK** button to save your changes.

In DOS, find the directory that contains the mouse files, and then look for a SETUP or MSETUP program file. Then run the program to change the mouse settings.

Keyboard Problems

Problem	Quick Fix Number	Page
Beeping when typing	65	498
Computer beeps when I type	65	498
Computer locked	60	496
Keys messed up	64	497
Keyboard cable disconnected	60	496
Keyboard doesn't work	60,64,65	496-498
Keyboard locked	60	496
Keyboard not found message	60,61	496-497
Keyboard stopped working after using MemMaker	60	496
Mapping keys	64	497
MemMaker wrecked my keyboard	60	496
New text replaces old text	63	497
Pressing keys causes beeping	65	498
Pressing one key gets something else	64	497
Type is all CAPS	62	497
Typing replaces existing text	63	497
UPPERCASE LETTERS for everything I type	62	497
Wrong keys	64	497

60: My keyboard doesn't work at all.

Turn your computer off and make sure your keyboard is plugged securely into the keyboard port (usually at the back of the system unit). Also make sure the cord is connected securely to the keyboard; you might have to flip the keyboard over to do this. Then turn on your computer. (Never connect or disconnect a keyboard or any other device when the computer is on.) If the keyboard still doesn't work, check the following:

- Is the computer locked? Many computers come with a lock and key most people never use. If you keep the keys in the lock, however, someone might have turned the key for fun. After unlocking the computer, you usually have to press a special key to proceed with the boot operation.

- Turn off your computer, unplug the keyboard from the computer, and check to see whether any pins in the keyboard plug are bent or pushed in. (When my son was six, he tried plugging in the keyboard—and ended up jamming three of the pins.) You can usually repair the plug with a pair of long-nose pliers and a gentle touch. Be careful when plugging it back in.

- If the keyboard doesn't work in Windows 95, double-click the **Keyboard** icon in the Control Panel (you can display the Control Panel by double-clicking **My Computer** and then **Control Panel**). Click the **General** tab to see which keyboard Windows is set up to use. Click the **Change** button to change the keyboard type.

  In Windows 3.1 or 3.11, open the **Main** group window, and then double-click the **Windows Setup** icon. Open the **Options** menu and select **Change System Settings**. From the **Keyboard** drop-down list, select the keyboard that matches yours. If you're not sure, select the **Enhanced** option.

- Did the keyboard stop working after you ran MemMaker? You probably ran MemMaker with the option to scan the upper memory area aggressively. MemMaker may have taken the memory area used by the keyboard. Enter **memmaker /undo** at the DOS prompt, and follow the on-screen instructions. If you choose to run MemMaker again, set the **Scan the Upper Memory Area Aggressively?** option to **No**.

If you can't bring your keyboard back to life, maybe it's fried (or maybe the keyboard cord is damaged). If you have access to another keyboard, plug it into your computer and see if it works. If the other keyboard works, your keyboard is dead. If you're personally attached to your keyboard, you can take it to a repair shop, but it's probably cheaper to just buy a new one.

61: I get a "Keyboard not found" message.

Either your keyboard plug popped out of its socket, or your computer is locked. Check the lock first. If that doesn't solve your problem, turn off your computer and make sure the keyboard is plugged in. Some keyboards have a connector on the keyboard, too (the connector looks like a phone connector); check this connection while you're at it.

62: When I type, everything is in UPPERCASE LETTERS.

You pressed the Caps Lock key by mistake. Press it again to return your keyboard to normal. By the way, if you're "talking" to someone on an online service (conversing by typing), it's considered bad manners to type in all uppercase letters—it's the equivalent of shouting.

63: Everything I type replaces existing text.

You changed from Insert mode to Overtype mode. In Insert mode, all text is inserted at the cursor position, and surrounding text is adjusted to make room for the new text. In Overtype mode, everything you type replaces existing text. In most applications, you can switch back to Insert mode by pressing the **Ins** key. If that doesn't work, check the documentation or the application's Help system to determine how to change modes.

64: I press one key, but it acts like a different one.

If you have a Gateway computer, you inadvertently remapped your keyboard. Some keyboards have a Remap feature that allows you to make one key act like another. Advanced users like to remap keys to customize the keyboard and make it a real time-saver. The rest of us dream about replacing our keyboard with one that has no Remap key.

If you happen to remap a few keys, you can bring them back to normal. Press the **Remap** key, and then press the key you remapped twice. This essentially maps the key to itself. On a Gateway AnyKey keyboard, you can return the entire keyboard to normal by pressing **Ctrl+Alt+Suspnd Macro**.

65: Each key I press beeps at me.

It could be that the *keyboard buffer* is full (the buffer holds approximately 15–20 keystrokes). Maybe the computer is busy performing some other task and can't give the keyboard its full attention yet. Wait until the computer is finished with whatever task it's performing, and then try typing again.

If you wait a sufficient amount of time and you're still getting beeps, maybe you're pressing the wrong keys. Some applications beep if you click an option or press a key that's not currently available. If you know you're pressing the right keys, exit the application, and reboot your computer.

If the problem persists, turn off your computer and check your keyboard connections. If the keyboard is securely connected, maybe the wiring inside the cable is damaged, or maybe your keyboard is on the blink.

Modem Problems

Problem	Quick Fix Number	Page
Baud rate problems	70	500
Busy signal	68	500
Call waiting, problems with	67,71	500-501
COM port wrong	66	499
Communications settings, entering	70	500
Dial 9 for an outside line	67	500
Dialing, modem won't dial	66	499
Disable call waiting	67,71	500-501
Disable modem speaker	72	502
Disconnect, modem disconnects when someone calls	67,71	500-501
Disconnect, modem disconnects prematurely	67,70,71	500-501
Hearing voices	69	500
Local echo, turning off	74	502
Local echo, turning on	73	502
Loud modem	72	502
Modem dials, doesn't connect	67,70	500
Modem disconnects when someone calls	67,71	500-501
Modem doesn't work at all	66	499
Modem initialization string, entering	70	500
Modem jacks, wrong jack in use	67	500
Modem lights don't come on	66	499
Modem setup in a program	70	500

Problem	Quick Fix Number	Page
Muting the modem	72	502
No carrier message	70	500
No sound from modem	66,72	499-502
Premature disconnect	67,70,71	500-501
Screen doesn't respond during typing	73	502
Terminal emulation, picking the right one	70	500
Text doesn't appear	73	502
Turning off modem speaker	72	502
Typing appears double	74	502
Typing doesn't appear	73	502
Use phone with modem	66,67	499-500
Voices from modem	69	500
Wrong baud rate	70	500
Wrong number	67,69	500

66: There's no sign of life—no dialing, no lights, no modem.

If nothing happens or if your communications program displays a distress signal saying that it cannot find the modem, try the following to determine the cause:

- In Windows 95, you can use the Modem Troubleshooter to fix any modem problems. First, display the Control Panel (click **Start**, point to **Settings**, and click **Control Panel**). Double-click the **Modems** icon, and then click the **Diagnostics** tab. Click the **Help** button. The Modem Troubleshooter screen appears. Answer the questions to determine the cause of the problem and to fix it.

- If you have an external modem, make sure the power is turned on and the modem is plugged into the serial (COM) port on your computer. Most internal modems have tiny switches on the back that you can flip to give the modem a different COM port setting. After setting the COM port, make sure the correct COM port is selected in Windows.

- In most cases, your mouse is set up to use COM1, and your modem is on COM2. If your modem is set up to use COM3, the mouse on COM1 might conflict with it. Try changing the modem to **COM2** or **COM4**.

- To test your modem, run **Windows Terminal** or **HyperTerminal** (located in the **Accessories** group). Type **AT** and press **Enter**. If you get an **OK** message, your modem and COM port settings are okay. As a further test, type **ATDT** followed by your phone number and press **Enter**. The modem should dial, and you should get a message that says **Busy**. This tells you that your modem is capable of dialing out, and that the problem is probably with the modem setup in the application you're using. Check the settings in the communications program you're using to determine whether they're correct for your modem.

- To test the phone line, plug a regular phone into the phone jack and make sure you get a dial tone. Also, check the phone plug connection on the modem and phone jack. (I once encountered a brand-new modem that was missing one of the copper contacts inside the modem jack.) Make sure all the contacts are there, and that the cable you're using is in good shape.

67: My modem dials, but it never connects.

Well, your modem is working, but you may have a problem with the number you're dialing or with the phone line. Check the following:

- Is the Line jack connected to the phone jack on the wall? Most modems have two jacks: one marked Phone and one marked Line. Make sure you connect the Line jack to the wall jack. (The Phone jack is often connected to your telephone, in cases where the modem and the phone are sharing the same telephone line.)

- Did you set up your application correctly for *pulse* or *tone dialing*? Pick up your phone and dial a couple of numbers. If you hear tones of various pitches, you have tone service. If you hear clicks, you have rotary (or pulse) service. Select the type of service in your application's Modem Setup dialog box, or use the command **ATDT** to make a tone call or **ATDP** for rotary (pulse) service.

- Do you need to dial a special number to get an outside line? If you work in an office, you may have to dial a 9 or some other number to get an outside line. Add this number, followed by a comma, before the phone number you want to dial. The comma tells the modem to pause and wait for a dial tone before dialing the rest of the number.

- Is your communications program set up with the same settings as the modem to which you're trying to connect? Every communication session has three settings: data, parity, and stop bits. Typically, you'll use 8-none-1, but if you encounter problems connecting to a particular service, call them to check on their settings. You may also want to reduce the baud rate used in your communications program (or in your Windows 95 setup) and see if that helps.

- Disable call waiting if your phone line has that feature. In Windows 95, double-click the **Modem** icon in the **Control Panel**. Click the **General** tab and then click **Dialing Properties**. Select the **This Location Has Call Waiting** check box and type the sequence needed to disable call waiting (such as *70,). Click **OK**.

68: I keep getting a busy signal.

You may not hear it, but if a message appears on-screen saying the line is busy, the computer you're calling is all tied up with incoming calls. Enter the **Hangup** command and try again later. Also, check the number you're dialing.

69: I hear voices from the modem.

You dialed the wrong number. If your phone is plugged into your modem, lift the receiver and apologize for dialing the wrong number. (If your phone isn't connected, you'll notice that the voice keeps getting more and more angry, and then the person hangs up.) Check the phone number you entered, and pray that this guy doesn't have Caller ID.

70: My modem dials and then immediately disconnects or displays a "NO CARRIER" message.

Look at the bright side: At least your modem is working. You probably have a problem with your telecommunications settings or with your login entries.

- If you're trying to call a bulletin board or online service that requires you to enter a name and password, maybe your name and password entries are wrong (or you didn't pay your bills).

- Make sure you have the correct modem selected. In most applications, you can select the type of modem from a list. If your modem isn't listed, check the documentation to find out its *modem initialization string*, and then enter it manually. (The modem initialization string sets preferences for how the modem operates. For example, **ATM0** mutes the modem so that it makes no sound as it dials.)

- Try setting the baud rate (the speed at which modems transfer data) to a slower speed. Maybe the service or BBS you're calling can handle only 2400 bps. (Most newer modems have an *automatic fallback* feature that enables the modem to drop to a slower baud rate automatically if necessary.)

- Check the *terminal emulation*. The terminal emulation setting tells your computer how to act when connecting to another computer. This is usually DEC VT-100, but if that doesn't work, try a different emulation.

- Check the following communications settings: data bits, parity, and stop bits. Most computers are set up to use 8 data bits, No parity, and 1 stop bit. Try to reconnect using these standard settings.

71: I have call waiting, and whenever I get a call, I lose my modem.

Any interference on the phone line can disconnect the modem. To disable call waiting, pick up the receiver and dial ***70** (or ***1170** if you have pulse or rotary service). This disables call waiting for your next call. When you disconnect, call waiting is re-enabled automatically.

Windows 95 comes with a special option that can disable call waiting for you. Display the Modems Properties dialog box (by double-clicking the **Modems** icon in the Control Panel) and click the **Dialing Properties** button. The Dialing Properties dialog box (shown here) appears. Click **This Location Has Call Waiting.** Then from the **To disable it, dial** drop-down list, pick the number you would have to dial to disable it. Click **OK** to save your change.

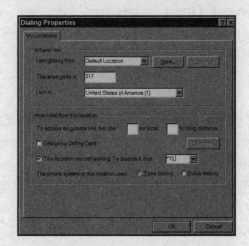

72: Do I have to listen while my modem dials?

No. You can silence your modem speaker by entering the command **ATM0** (that's "A-T-M-Zero") in your telecommunications program (or by adding it to your modem initialization screen). This tells your modem to set the speaker volume at zero. To turn the speaker volume back on, type **ATM1**.

Some online services (CompuServe, for example) allow you to turn the modem speaker off in the modem setup dialog box. In other services, you have to add the **ATM0** code to the modem initialization string.

In Windows 95, you can set the modem speaker volume through the Modems Properties dialog box. To display the dialog box, double-click the **Modems** icon in the Control Panel. Click the **Properties** button. Under **Speaker Volume**, drag the slider to the left to lower the volume or to the right to crank it up (see the following figure). Click **OK** to save your change.

73: I'm typing, but I don't see anything.

Try turning on **Local Echo**. You can do this manually in a telecommunications program by entering the command **ATE1**.

74: Everything I type appears twice.

Change the **Duplex** setting to **Full** and the **Local Echo** setting to **Off**. Full Duplex means the computer can send and receive data at the same time. Local Echo makes everything you type appear on your screen. If the remote computer is also echoing everything you type, you get a double echo.

Problems with DOS Applications

Problem	Quick Fix Number	Page
Antivirus program conflict	77,78	504
CD-ROM doesn't work	80	505
Computer freezes when running applications	78	504
Full-screen mode doesn't work	81	505
Game problem	75,78,80,82	503-505

Problem	Quick Fix Number	Page
Installation problem	77	504
Installed new device, program frozen	78	504
Marking text	83	506
Maximize button doesn't work	81	505
Monitor blanks out	79	505
PIF files	75	503
Program conflicts with another program	77,78	504
Screen doesn't look right	78,79	504-505
Selecting text	83	506
Slow program	76,80	503,505
Switching between programs	84	507
Windows won't run my DOS program	75,76,78,80,81,84	503-505,507

75: Can I run a DOS application from Windows?

Usually, yes. A quick way to run a DOS application in Windows 3.1 or 3.11 is to open Program Manager's **File** menu, select **Run**, and then enter the command required to run the application from the DOS prompt. (You may have to specify the drive letter and directory name, or use the Browse button to select it from a list.) In Windows 95, click the **Start** button and select **Run** to display the Run dialog box.

However, using the File, Run command isn't the best way to run a DOS application in Windows. It's better to create an icon for the application. In Windows 95, simply drag the program's file from Explorer onto the desktop to create an icon. Then right-click the icon, select **Properties**, and change the settings as appropriate for your program. To learn what the options in this dialog box do, right-click the option and click **What's This?** If you have trouble running the application in Windows 95, you may want to restart in MS-DOS mode and run it from a prompt.

Windows 3.1 uses a *program information file* (*PIF*) for each DOS application to tell it the best way to run the program. To create a PIF file, open the **Main** window and double-click the **Windows Setup** icon. Open the **Options** menu and select **Set Up Applications**. Click **Ask You to Specify an Application** and click **OK**. Click the **Browse** button, and then select the drive, directory, and name of the file that runs the program. If you see a file whose name ends in .PIF, that's the file you want; otherwise, pick one of the files that ends in .BAT, .COM, or .EXE. Click **OK**. From the **Add to Program Group** drop-down list, click the program group in which you want the icon to appear. Click the **OK** button. If all goes as planned, Windows creates a program information file for the application, assigns it an icon, and places the icon in the Applications group. If you get a message indicating that Setup cannot set up this application, you can create an icon using the Program Manager's File, New command.

76: Why is my program running so s-l-o-w-l-y?

Windows allows you to *shell out* to DOS (return to the DOS prompt without exiting Windows), in order to type in some DOS command or to run a DOS program. However, because your computer is still running Windows in the background, the commands you type or the programs you run may respond a bit more slowly. Your best bet is to exit Windows 3.1 or to restart Windows 95 with DOS, and then run your DOS application.

77: When I install DOS applications, my computer tells me to close any antivirus programs that are running.

Some installation programs edit your AUTOEXEC.BAT and CONFIG.SYS files to make sure your system can run the application. But antivirus programs don't like changes. As soon as the installation program starts to meddle with your system files, the antivirus program kicks in and says, "Whoa, bud, this is my computer," and it refuses to let the installation program continue. You will have to disable the antivirus program if you hope to get anywhere.

If you use Windows 3.1, you should exit to DOS to install your DOS program. But when you do, you may run into a problem if your antivirus program is still running. Antivirus programs are commonly loaded on startup by a command in the AUTOEXEC.BAT file. You can open this file, add **REM** before the antivirus command line, save the file, and reboot. Another way is to reboot the computer, and then press and release the **F8** key when you see the **Starting MS-DOS...** message. Step through the startup commands, but skip the command that runs the antivirus program. If you used REM to skip the antivirus command, you can remove the REM after you install the application to have antivirus run on startup again.

If you use Windows 95, you can install your DOS program without rebooting to DOS. You may still see this message, but you'll be able to continue with the installation of your program.

78: My DOS program runs and then crashes.

The causes of system crashes are difficult to track because any conflict between two applications or devices can cause the problem. Try the following fixes:

- If the program doesn't even show its face, you probably selected the wrong video driver when you installed the program. Run the setup program again and try a different video driver.

- Do you have other applications running? If you do, try closing them and then running your application. Also, check your AUTOEXEC.BAT file to see if it is running any applications on startup (such as a screen saver or antivirus program). These *memory-resident programs* often cause problems. Add the REM command before these commands to prevent them from running, and then reboot your computer.

- If you're trying to run this program from within Windows, you may have better luck exiting Windows and booting to DOS.

- You could possibly run your program within Windows 95, provided you optimize it. To do that, right-click the program's icon and select **Properties**. You can change a lot of settings with this dialog box; however, most problems can be cleared up by changing the settings on the Memory, Screen, and Misc tabs. See the Windows Help system for additional information.

- If the program freezes when you move the mouse, the mouse driver is usually at fault. Try reinstalling the mouse driver that came with your mouse.

  If you just installed another device (such as a sound card), it may have an interrupt setting (IRQ) that conflicts with the mouse interrupt. Try running the sound card's setup program again and choosing a different IRQ setting. For more information, see Quick Fix # 31: "I just installed the sound card, and it doesn't work."

If that doesn't fix the problem, call the mouse manufacturer and ask for an updated mouse driver.

- As a precaution and to free up disk space, delete any unused files from the Windows TEMP directory.

- Try reinstalling the application. Sometimes a corrupted file can make an application crash. By replacing the corrupted file with a fresh copy, you might be able to prevent future crashes.

- Run ScanDisk. Sometimes *lost file clusters* (parts of files that get scattered over a disk) can cause strange problems. ScanDisk sweeps these clusters off the disk.

79: The display doesn't look quite right.

When you installed the program, you probably selected the wrong video driver. If the display is clear enough to allow you to work, you may be able to select a video display driver. Look for an **Options** menu or command; this should provide you with a list of video drivers. Select the driver that matches your monitor and driver type.

If you can't make out the screen, run the program's Install or Setup utility again. With most applications, you can change an installation setting without having to go through the entire installation process again. However, with other applications, you may not be so lucky.

80: My game runs too slowly.

Your best bet is to exit Windows and reboot to DOS, and then run your game. Running your game within Windows makes it share processor time with other Windows functions. If you run the game under DOS only, all of your computer's resources can be allocated to the game program, and it will run faster.

If you want to run the game within Windows 95, try adjusting its property settings: Right-click the program's icon and select **Properties**. Click the **Program** tab, and then click **Advanced**. Select **MS-DOS Mode**, which tells Windows to give the game its exclusive attention (you'll have to shut down other Windows programs before running the game). You may also want to select the **Fast ROM Emulation** option on the **Screen** tab to speed up the screen display. Or, you could just bag the whole idea and simply run your game from MS-DOS (after restarting the computer in MS-DOS mode).

81: I clicked the Maximize button, but my DOS window isn't maximized.

In Windows 95, the size of the window in which your DOS program runs depends on its screen resolution. For this reason, you may not be able to completely maximize a DOS window (to fill the screen) when you click the Maximize button.

To run a DOS program full-screen, right-click the program's icon and select **Properties**. Click the **Screen** tab and select the **Full-screen** option. Click **OK** to save your changes.

82: I can use my CD-ROM in Windows, but when I try to run a DOS game, my computer won't recognize the drive.

This problem occurs in Windows 95 because it loads a *virtual device driver* to control your CD-ROM drive. The advantage of a virtual device driver is that it doesn't take up any conventional memory, so that leaves more room for your DOS program to run. However, virtual device drivers don't work when you try to run a program in MS-DOS mode (by either selecting that option from the Properties dialog box, or by rebooting to DOS itself).

To solve this problem, when you plan to run the game from within Windows, you need to change its Properties settings. Right-click the program's icon and select **Properties**. Click the **Program** tab, and then click **Advanced**. Make sure that the **MD-DOS Mode** option is selected (see the following figure), and then click **Specify a New MS-DOS Configuration**. In the CONFIG.SYS box, add the line to load your CD-ROM driver (consult with the driver's manual for details). It might look something like this.

> **DEVICE=C:\CDSYS\SLCD.SYS /D:MSCD001 /B:340**

In the AUTOEXEC.BAT box, add the line:

> **C:\WINDOWS\COMMAND\MSCDEX /D:MSCD001 /M:4**

What follows the /D: and the /M: may be different for your particular CD-ROM drive. Again, check the manual. Make your changes and click **OK**. Your game should now run within Windows 95.

If you want to reboot to DOS and run your game, follow these steps to "turn on" a CD-ROM drive. First, make sure that your CONFIG.SYS file contains the command to load your CD-ROM device driver. Again, the command may look something like this (but consult your manual for exact specifications):

> **DEVICE=C:\CDSYS\SLCD.SYS /D:MSCD001 /B:340**

Then add the following to the DOSSTART.BAT file you'll find in the Windows directory (if it's not there, create one using Notepad):

> **C:\WINDOWS\COMMAND\MSCDEX /D:MSCD001 /M:4**

Again, the values that follow the /D: and the /M: may be different for your particular CD-ROM drive. Be sure to check the manual for your CD-ROM drive for details. ▶**If you need help making changes to your CONFIG.SYS, see "Modify Your Startup Files" on page 357 for help.**◀

83: I can't select any text in my DOS program.

If you want to select text in order to copy it to another document, you won't be able to do that unless your DOS program is running in a window. If you're currently running the program full-screen, press **Alt+Enter** to switch to a window.

To select the text you want, open the **Control** menu, select **Edit**, and then select **Mark**. Drag over the text you want to select, and then press **Enter** to copy it to the Clipboard. You cannot cut or move text, only copy. To move text, copy it to your other document and then return to your DOS program and delete the copied text.

84: I can't switch to other programs in Windows.

When running a DOS program full-screen in Windows 95, you may encounter a problem when you want to switch from it to another program, because the taskbar is not visible. So how do you switch programs without exiting your DOS program?

Easy. Press **Alt+Esc**, and you'll see the taskbar. Click the program to which you want to switch.

Microsoft Windows Woes

Problem	Quick Fix Number	Page
Accidentally deleted a program group	90	512
Application freezes Windows	86,92	509,512
Application slow in Windows	87,88	510
Associating files	91	512
Bad command or filename message when starting Windows	85	508
Can't print	89	511
Can't run Windows	85,95	508,515
Deleting unused fonts and files	94	514
Disk space, out of	88,94	510,514
DOS is okay, but Windows 95 won't start	95	515
Entered WIN command, but Windows won't start	85	508
Exit Windows, can't	86	509
Explorer won't open file	91	512
Fax application, printing problems	89	511
File associations, creating	91	512
File Manager won't open file	91	512
Fonts, deleting	88,94	510,514
General Protection Fault message	92	512
Long file names, problems with	93	514
Lost files	93	514
Memory problems	87	510
MemMaker caused Windows not to start	85	508
Modes, running Windows 3.1 in different modes	85	508

(continues)

(continued)

Problem	Quick Fix Number	Page
Permanent swap file, creating	88	510
Out of disk space	88,94	510,514
Out of Memory message	87	510
Printer won't work after installing fax program	89	511
Program group accidentally deleted	90	512
Program won't start	91	512
Quitting Windows, can't	86	509
Recovering deleted program groups	90	512
Rebooting from Windows	86	509
Speeding up Windows	88	510
Startup, Windows won't	85,95	508,515
Swap file, creating	87,88	510
System locked up	86,92	509,512
Too many fonts	88,94	510,514
Too many Windows applications running	87,88	510
Unused fonts and files, deleting	88,94	510,514
Windows freezes	86,92	509,512
Windows won't start	85,95	508,515

85: I entered the WIN command, but Windows won't start.

You don't have to enter a command to start Windows 95, but you might have trouble when you enter the WIN command to start Windows 3.1 or 3.11. Try changing to the drive and directory that contains the Windows files (usually C:\WINDOWS). Then type **win** and press **Enter**. If that doesn't work, check the following:

- Is your system powerful enough to run Windows? You must have a 286 or better computer (386, 486, Pentium), and it must have at least 2 megabytes of RAM before Windows will even say hello.

- If you're running any other programs (such as a DOS screen saver, an antivirus program, or a menu program), exit those programs and unload them from memory before running Windows. You may have to remove the commands that start these programs from your AUTOEXEC.BAT file (or add the **REM** command before their command lines) and then reboot your computer.

- Try starting Windows in a different mode. Windows 3.1 can run in one of three modes: Enhanced, Standard, or Real. Windows starts in Enhanced mode on a 386 or better computer with 2 or more megabytes of RAM. In Enhanced mode, Windows allows you to multitask (perform operations in two applications at the same time) and use disk space as memory. On a 286 computer (or a 386 with less than 2 megabytes of RAM), Windows starts in Standard mode (which does not allow multitasking and cannot use disk space as RAM). Real mode is for old computers that can't run Windows in Standard or Enhanced mode.

If you have trouble running Windows 3.1, try starting it with the **WIN /S** or **WIN /R** command. If you have an older computer, it may not be able to run Windows in Enhanced mode. The **/S** switch starts Windows in Standard mode, and the **/R** switch starts it in Real mode.

Windows for Workgroups starts in Enhanced mode. Although you can't use the /R switch to run it in Real mode, you can use WIN /S to run it in Standard mode.

- Make sure your CONFIG.SYS file has one of the following commands:

    DEVICE=C:\WINDOWS\HIMEM.SYS

    or

    DEVICE=C:\DOS\HIMEM.SYS

  Add the line if it is missing. This loads a memory-management driver that gives Windows access to additional memory. If your computer has a 286 processor—or less than 1 megabyte (1,024K) of RAM—don't use HIMEM.SYS.

- Make sure the CONFIG.SYS file has a **BUFFERS=20** (or 30) command and **FILES=20** (or more) command. After editing and saving CONFIG.SYS, reboot your computer. Then try running Windows again. Your computer uses the buffers when reading and writing to disk.

- If you could run Windows in the past, but you couldn't run it after you installed MemMaker, you probably ran MemMaker with the aggressive memory option on. Type **memmaker /undo** and press **Enter** to return your system to normal. You can run MemMaker again, but stick with the default (safe) configuration.

If you have trouble running Windows 95, try using the startup disk you created during the installation process. Once you get Windows up and running from the floppy drive, try running ScanDisk on your hard drive (the drive that contains Windows 95). A crash may have damaged some of the Windows files. ▶**If you created an emergency boot disk following the steps in the task "Make a 'Startup' Disk" (page 341), use it to get your system up and running again.**◀

If you have trouble starting Windows 95 after having booted to DOS, see Quick Fix #95: "When I exit to DOS from Windows 95, I can't get back" for help.

86: I can't get out of Windows.

You probably have a DOS application running. Switch to that application by pressing **Ctrl+Esc** to view the Task List (in Windows 3.1 or 3.11). Or, in Windows 95, click the program's name in the taskbar. Exit the application as you normally would (usually by selecting **File** and then **Exit**). Then try to exit Windows.

If one of your applications froze Windows, giving you no access to your mouse or keyboard, wait a while. Sometimes Windows is busy printing or playing around with files in the background. It needs a few minutes to put its toys away before it will shift its attention back to your mouse or keyboard.

If you've waited long enough, press **Ctrl+Alt+Del**. If all goes as planned, you get a screen telling you which application is causing the problem and giving you some options. For example, in Windows 95, you can select the program from the list and click **End Task** to shut it down. If your computer is still locked up, press **Ctrl+Alt+Del**, and then press that key combination again to reboot. It's not a good idea to reboot your computer when Windows is running, but sometimes it's the only option. If Ctrl+Alt+Delete produces no response, you may have to cold boot (turn the PC off and then back on).

87: Windows 95 keeps telling me that I'm out of memory.

You should really have at least 16M of memory (RAM) to run Windows 95 effectively (although it will run with only 8M). In any case, your lack of RAM may not be the reason you're getting this error message. More than likely, Windows 95 is trying to tell you that it's running out of *virtual memory*, which is formed from free space on your hard disk.

You see, when Windows 95 runs out of RAM, it temporarily stores active programs and files on the hard disk until they are needed. When you run short of hard disk space, Windows 95 cannot create the amount of virtual memory it needs, hence the error message. To solve the problem, try to delete all files you no longer need from your hard disk. Store seldom used files on floppies instead of the hard disk to save even more space.

After deleting files, be sure to empty the Recycle Bin. Until you do, the space allocated to those files is not really freed up.

Finally, run Defragmenter to organize free space on the hard disk. ▶**See "Optimize a Hard Disk with Defrag" on page 345 for help.◀** You may also want to run DriveSpace to increase the amount of hard disk space you have. DriveSpace compresses your files so that they take up less room, giving you more free space on the drive. ▶**See "Compress a Drive with DriveSpace" on page 353 for more information.◀**

88: Is Windows always this s-l-o-w?

Yes, Windows is slow. The good news is that you can improve your system's performance without upgrading.

- **Bypass the advertising screen in Windows 3.1 or 3.11.** To start Windows this way, type **win :** and press **Enter**. The colon tells Windows not to display the Windows advertising screen at startup.

- **Run fewer applications.** The more applications you have running at once, the slower Windows performs. To find out which applications are running, press **Ctrl+Esc**. To quit an application, select it from the Task List and click the **End Task** button. In Windows 95, you can quickly close down an application by right-clicking its name in the taskbar and clicking **Close**.

- **Clean up your INI files in Windows 3.1 or 3.11.** When Windows starts, it reads each and every line in WIN.INI and SYSTEM.INI. By removing blank lines, you give Windows less to read. ▶**See "Make Your Computer Work Faster and Better" on page 337 to learn how to edit your system files.◀** Windows 95 uses INI file commands sparingly, so editing these files in Windows 95 won't help much.

- **Create a permanent swap file in Windows 3.1 or 3.11.** Windows 95 creates it own size swap file on-the-fly. So you don't typically need to make any adjustments there. Windows 3.1 and 3.11 are a different matter, however. By default, Windows 3.1x uses a temporary swap file, but a permanent swap file works faster. To create a permanent swap file, first run DOS's Defragment utility (enter **defrag** at the DOS prompt). Then open the **Main** group window, double-click the **Control Panel** icon, and double-click the **386 Enhanced** icon. Click the **Virtual Memory** button and click **Change**. Open the **Type** drop-down list and select **Permanent**. Keep clicking **OK** until you're back in the Control Panel. When asked if you want to restart Windows, click the **Restart Windows** button.

- **Reduce available fonts.** In Windows 3.1 and 3.11, each font has a line in the WIN.INI file, which Windows must read at startup. To remove fonts, open the **Main** group window, double-click the **Control Panel** icon, and double-click the **Fonts** icon. Select the fonts you want to remove and click the **Remove** button. This removes the instructions from WIN.INI, but keeps the font files on disk so you can add them back in later. Do *not* remove the font called MS Sans Serif; Windows uses this easy-to-read font to display text in its menus, dialog boxes, and windows.

You can also remove fonts in Windows 95, although they don't slow down the startup process as much. Double-click the **Fonts** icon in the Control Panel, select the fonts you want to remove, and then open the **File** menu and select **Delete**.

- **Defragment your hard drive.** The temporary swap files that Windows uses require disk space. By *defragmenting* your hard disk, you free up sections of the disk to use for these temporary swap files. Windows 95 comes with its own Disk Defragmenter that you can safely run from Windows. To run it, click the **Start** button; point to **Programs**, **Accessories**, and **System Tools**; and then click **Disk Defragmenter**.

  In Windows 3.1, exit Windows and run Defrag from the DOS prompt. To use DOS 6 Defrag, exit Windows, and then enter **defrag** at the DOS prompt. Then follow the on-screen instructions. If you don't have DOS 6.x, you can use a third-party program such as Norton Utilities (assuming you can still find one that's compatible with Windows 3.1).

- **Use solid colors as your background.** In Windows 95, right-click the desktop and select **Properties**. On the **Background** tab, select **None** from the **Pattern** and **Wallpaper** lists. Click the **Appearance** tab and select one of the colors in the **Color** drop-down list (do not select Other). Click **OK**.

  In Windows 3.1 and 3.11, open the **Main** group window and double-click the **Control Panel** icon. If you're currently using a fancy color scheme, double-click the **Colors** icon and use the dialog box that appears to select a simple color scheme for Windows. If you're using a screen saver or fancy wallpaper, double-click the **Desktop** icon in the Control Panel and turn off the screen saver and fancy wallpaper.

- **Change your video driver to a lower resolution and fewer colors.** Although high-resolution graphics look good, they also slow down your computer. In Windows 95, right-click the desktop and select **Properties**. Click the **Settings** tab and change the resolution by sliding the **Desktop Area** tab. Adjust the number of colors used by selecting a different value from the **Color Palette** list box.

  In Windows 3.1, if you have an icon for your video adapter, double-click it and use the dialog box that appears to select a 640×480 resolution, 16-color driver. If you don't have an icon, open the **Main** group window, double-click the **Windows Setup** icon, open the **Options** menu, and select **Change System Settings**. Open the **Display** drop-down list and select **VGA**. Click **OK**. Click **Restart Windows** to put your changes into effect.

89: I installed a fax program, and now I can't print.

Fax programs typically disguise themselves as printers. Whenever you enter the Print command in an application, the fax program kicks in, transforms your document into a graphic image that can be transmitted as a fax, and starts dialing your modem.

In Windows 95, fax programs are treated as printers. Double-click the **My Computer** icon, and then double-click the **Printers** icon. Right-click the printer you want to use, and click **Set As Default**. Now when you print, the information will be sent to the selected printer instead of to the fax program.

To prevent this from happening again in Windows 3.1 or 3.11, you must set up your printer to act as the *default printer*. Open the **Control Panel** and double-click the **Printers** icon. Click your printer in the **Installed Printers** list, and then click the **Set As Default Printer** button. Click the **Close** button to save your changes.

90: I just deleted a program group, and I want it back!

If you wiped out one of Windows 3.1's standard program groups (StartUp, Main, Accessories, or Games), you can re-create the groups with the Windows Setup command. Open the File Manager's **File** menu and select **Run**. Type **setup /p** and press **Enter**. (This won't work in Windows for Workgroups.)

If you wiped out a program-group window that was created when you installed a Windows application, you have to rebuild the window. Open the Program Manager's **File** menu, select **New**, select **Program Group**, and click **OK**. Type a name for the group window and click **OK**. You can then use the **File**, **New**, **Program Item** command to create program-item icon(s) for running the application(s). Use the dialog box that appears to name the icon and to select a name and location for the executable program file.

If you deleted the program group in Windows 95, it might still be residing in the **Recycle Bin** (if you didn't empty it). Double-click the **Recycle Bin** icon and select all the files that were in the program group. Open the **File** menu and select **Restore**.

91: I double-clicked a file icon in Windows, but it won't run.

You haven't *associated* the selected file with an application. File Manager (in Windows 3.1 and 3.11) and My Computer or Windows Explorer (in Windows 95) use *file associations* to figure out which program to run for each file type. If you double-click a file that ends in .PCX, for example, Windows runs Paintbrush or Paint and opens the selected .PCX file. If the file you selected is not associated with an application, Windows doesn't know which application to run.

In Windows 95, whenever you double-click an unassociated file, a dialog box appears asking you to specify which program you want to run to open the file. If the program is listed, click it. If the program is not listed, click the **Other** button, and then use the dialog box that appears to select the desired program file. To create a permanent file association (so Windows will always run the selected program when you double-click this file type), make sure **Always Use This Program to Open This File** has a check mark next to it. Then click **OK**.

To associate a file type with an application in Windows 3.1 or 3.11, click the document file you want to associate. Open the **File** menu and select **Associate**. From the **Associate With** list, select the application to which you want to associate this file type. If the application does not appear in the list, click the **Browse** button and select the drive, directory, and name of the file that executes the program. Click the **OK** button. (Don't associate a file type with a DOS application unless you can run the application successfully from Windows.)

92: I got a "General Protection Fault" error—what does it mean?

This type of error appears in Windows 3.1 more often than Microsoft would like to admit. (It was basically eliminated from Windows 95; however, some Windows 3.1 programs, when run under Windows 95, will cause this error.) The problem is this: If an application attempts to store some data in a place in memory that's already being used, the application will lock up and Windows will usually display a message indicating that a *general protection fault* (GPF) has occurred, or your system may simply lock up. If this happens to you, take the following steps:

1. Write down the GPF message (if there is one). This message usually indicates the name of the application that caused the fault and the memory address where the fault occurred.

2. Write down exactly what you were doing when the fault occurred. Were you saving a file, printing, or moving the mouse? Write down the names of the other applications you were running.

3. If no message is displayed, wait about a minute to see if your system will unlock itself. Sometimes (especially on slower computers), the system may just be busy, not locked, and it will return control to you if you just wait.

4. If no message appears and Windows is still locked, press **Ctrl+Alt+Del**. A message appears, indicating the name of the application that's causing problems and asking you to make a decision. This message may also indicate that the system is simply busy and you should wait longer.

5. Perform one of the following steps:

    Press **Esc** to cancel the reboot.

    Press **Enter** to quit the current application and return to Windows.

    Press **Ctrl+Alt+Del** to reboot. Avoid taking this option whenever possible. When you reboot Windows, you risk losing anything you were working on, and you may end up with lots of .TMP files scattered all over your hard disk.

If you consistently encounter the same GPF in an application, try the following fixes:

- **Exit and restart Windows.** Sometimes one GPF will cause additional GPFs in the current work session. Exiting and restarting resets Windows and may prevent additional GPFs.

- **Upgrade to the latest version of DOS.** If you have a version of DOS written for a specific computer (say Compaq), run that DOS version only on the Compaq computer for which it was designed. If you run it on a different make or model of computer, you may encounter problems. Also, try using DOS 5 or DOS 6.x. Both versions of DOS come with advanced memory-management tools that may help eliminate problems.

- **Disable any memory-resident applications.** If you have any memory-resident applications that run from your AUTOEXEC.BAT file, use the **REM** command to disable them. Memory-resident programs include DOS screen savers and screen-capture programs. If you're not sure, copy CONFIG.SYS and AUTOEXEC.BAT (naming them CONFIG.OLD and AUTOEXEC.OLD), and then create the following "plain vanilla" versions to boot your computer.

    For AUTOEXEC.BAT:

    ```
    C:\WINDOWS\SMARTDRV.EXE
    PROMPT $P$G
    PATH C:\DOS;C:\;C:\WINDOWS
    SET TEMP=C:\TMP
    ```

    For CONFIG.SYS:

    ```
    DEVICE=C:\DOS\SETVER.EXE
    DEVICE=C:\WINDOWS\HIMEM.SYS
    DOS=HIGH
    BUFFERS=50
    FILES=30
    STACKS=9,256
    ```

- **Use SMARTDrive as your disk-caching program.** If you have a disk-caching program, such as QEMM or 386MAX, use the **REM** command in CONFIG.SYS and AUTOEXEC.BAT to remove any of its command lines, and then add the SMARTDrive command line to AUTOEXEC.BAT:

        C:\WINDOWS\SMARTDRV.EXE

- **Reinstall the application.** Sometimes reinstalling the application or device driver that is causing problems will correct the problem.

- **Call the manufacturer for an updated driver.** Sooner or later, manufacturers hear of problems that occur with their products. They may have the fix you need.

93: I renamed my file to First Quarter Sales, and now I can't find it.

If you use Windows 95 to rename a file using more than the old eight characters, you may encounter a problem when you try to open that file in a Windows 3.1 based program. The reason is that a Windows 3.1 program isn't capable of reading the long file names. So Windows 95 accommodates the program by shortening the file names to something the old Windows program can read and use. So your long file name of "First Quarter Sales" becomes something like this:

        FIRSTQ~1.XLS

You can still open the file in a Windows 3.1 program, make changes to it, and save it again, but the file name will appear in its shortened format in the program's File Open and File Save dialog boxes.

94: I don't use many of my fonts and some of my Windows files; can I get rid of them?

The best way to get rid of unneeded fonts and Windows files is to work through Windows. Don't just fire up File Manager or Explorer and hack away; you might delete something important.

You can add and remove fonts in Windows 95 by double-clicking the **My Computer** icon, double-clicking **Control Panel**, and double-clicking the **Fonts** icon. The window that appears shows icons for all the fonts installed on your computer. To remove a font, simply drag it over the **Recycle Bin** icon. To install new fonts, open the **File** menu and select **Install New Font**.

To get rid of fonts you don't use in Windows 3.1 and 3.11, open the **Main** group window, double-click the **Control Panel** icon, and double-click the **Fonts** icon. Select the fonts you want to remove (hold down the **Ctrl** key while clicking each font). Do *not* select any of the System fonts; Windows needs these for the display. Click the **Remove** button. A dialog box appears, asking for confirmation. To remove the font files from disk, click the **Delete Font File from Disk** option, and then click the **OK** button. (If you don't delete the file from the disk, Windows merely removes the font reference from the WIN.INI file.)

▸**For help in removing Windows 95 components that you don't use, see the task "Uninstall a Windows 95 Program" on page [p2s11 TBD].◂**

The easiest and safest way to delete nonessential Windows 3.1 and 3.11 files is to use Windows Setup. Open the **Main** program group and double-click the **Windows Setup** icon. Open the **Options** menu and select **Add/Remove Windows Components**. The Windows Setup dialog box appears, showing the groups of nonessential Windows files. To delete an entire group of Windows files, click the group to remove the **X** from its check box. To delete individual files, click the **Files** (or **Select Files**) button for the group that contains the file(s) you want to delete, and then click each file you want to delete. Click the **Remove** button. Click **OK**. You are returned to the Windows Setup dialog box, where you can choose to delete more files. Click **OK** when you're through. Click **Yes** or **Yes to All** to confirm the deletions.

95: When I exit to DOS from Windows 95, I can't get back.

Sometimes after booting to DOS from Windows 95, when you attempt to return to Windows by restarting the computer, you're returned to the DOS prompt instead. This process can go on forever: Everytime you restart the PC, it loads DOS instead of Windows 95.

Well don't panic. All you need to do is to remove the line **DOS=SINGLE** from your CONFIG.SYS. ▶**See "Modify Your Startup Files" on page 357 for more information.**◄

How exactly did the line end up in your CONFIG.SYS? Well, usually when installing a DOS program, Windows 95 will insert the line on behalf of the setup program, intending to take it back out when the installation is through. That doesn't always happen, though, so you sometimes have to do it yourself to return your system to normal. After editing the CONFIG.SYS and removing the line, restart your PC, and it should load Windows 95.

Problems with Windows Applications

Problem	Quick Fix Number	Page
Application freezes	97	516
Application won't run	98	516
Can't run DOS utilities	99	516
Defrag won't run in Windows	99	516
DOS utilities won't run	99	516
Group window, where did it go?	96	515
Lost application	96	515
Missing application file	98	516
Program won't run	98,99	516
ScanDisk won't run	99	516
Windows freezes	97	516

96: I installed the application, now where is it?

In Windows 3.1 and 3.11, most Windows applications plop a big group window on your screen, complete with one or two icons for running the application. Just double-click the icon to run the application.

Some applications, however, minimize the group window and hide it somewhere in the Program Manager. Maximize the Program Manager window. If you see a scroll bar at the bottom edge or right side of the Program Manager window, use it to bring additional icons into view. Double-click the group icon for the application, and you'll find the program-item icons you use to run the application.

In Windows 95, programs are typically added to the Start menu. Click the **Start** button, move the mouse pointer over **Programs**, and look for your new program. Some items on the Programs sub-menu display additional submenus; try pointing to these items. If you can't find the program there, try using My Computer to look in various folders for the program. You can also use the Find command on the Start menu to search for programs.

97: My application locks up Windows.

Join the club. Applications commonly lock up Windows for one reason or another. Wait a minute or two to see if Windows snaps out of it; sometimes Windows is busy doing other things like printing or putting files away.

If Windows remains frozen, press **Ctrl+Alt+Del**, select the program that is not responding from those listed, and press **Enter** or click **End Task** to quit the application. You might want to restart Windows before restarting your program. This will "clear out any junk" in memory that might have caused the program to lock up in the first place. If Windows is hung up too, you'll have to press **Ctrl+Alt+Del** twice to restart. And if that doesn't work, press your computer's **Reset** button.

If the same application repeatedly locks up Windows, refer to Quick Fix #92: "I got a "General Protection Fault" error—what does it mean?" for help. The application may have a bug that prevents it from running smoothly on your system or with other applications.

98: When I try to run the application, it says I'm missing a file.

One of the files the application needs in order to run is missing, or the application doesn't know where to look for it. If you use Windows 3.1, make sure your AUTOEXEC.BAT file has the **C:\WIN-DOWS** directory somewhere in the PATH statement. (The PATH statement tells DOS where to look for files.) If C:\WINDOWS is not in the PATH statement, go to the end of the PATH statement and type **;C:\WINDOWS**. Save the AUTOEXEC.BAT file, exit Windows, and reboot your computer. ►**If you need help making changes to the AUTOEXEC.BAT, see the task "Modify Your Startup Files" on page 357 for more information.◄**

In Windows 95, right-click the program's icon and select **Properties**. Click the **Shortcut** tab, and make sure that the correct directory path appears in the **Start In** text box.

If that doesn't solve the problem, try reinstalling the application. Sometimes essential files can get deleted when Windows crashes (or if you turn off your computer before exiting Windows). If the problem persists, call the technical support number for your program; you can usually find it in the documentation.

99: Why can't I run DOS utilities from Windows?

Some DOS utilities, such as ScanDisk and MemMaker, fiddle with your hardware and configuration settings—really important, complicated stuff. If Windows is running, it makes matters even more complicated. If one of the DOS utilities happens to conflict with Windows while doing its job, your system might crash and mess itself up. For example, if your system crashes while ScanDisk is rear-ranging all your data, you might lose a chunk or two, or it might make your entire hard drive inac-cessible. To stay on the safe side, exit Windows 3.1, and then start the DOS utility from the prompt. Do *not* attempt to use either DOS or Windows 3.1 utilities with Windows 95. Doing so could cor-rupt your files because Windows 95 uses a different filing system (which allows you to use long file names).

Fortunately, Windows 95 comes with its own set of utilities, making it unnecessary to purchase a lot of new ones. You can find most of these utilities by clicking the **Start** button and then pointing to **Programs**, **Accessories**, and **System Tools**. Click the desired utility to run it.

Miscellaneous Problems

Problem	Quick Fix Number	Page
Battery going out	100	517
Date wrong	100,101	517
Setting date and time	101	517
Time wrong	100,101	517
Wrong date and time	100,101	517

100: My computer loses time.

If your computer is losing 15 seconds a day or more, you may have a cheap clock, or your computer's internal battery is going bad (a much more serious problem). This battery keeps juice flowing to the computer's CMOS (Complementary Metal-Oxide Semiconductor, pronounced *SEA-moss*), which stores some pretty important information, such as how much memory the computer has, where the hard drive is, and so on. If the CMOS "forgets" everything, you won't be able to use your computer.

Your computer uses the internal battery only when the power is turned off. So the more you use your computer (or keep it on), the longer the battery lasts. Batteries typically last two to five years.

If your computer starts to lose time, don't panic. You may have a rechargeable battery. Leave your computer on for an entire day, and see if that corrects the problem. If the problem persists, replace the battery before it dies. (This usually requires opening the system unit, disconnecting the old battery, and plugging in the new one. You might want to have a service technician do this for you. If you're a do-it-yourselfer, call Ray-O-Vac for a booklet on how to choose and replace CMOS batteries: 1-800-CCB-CLOCK.)

To be on the safe side, you should get a utility program such as PC Tools or The Norton Utilities. These programs can help you create a *recovery disk* that stores a copy of the CMOS information. If your battery dies, you can have it replaced and then use the recovery disk to rebuild the CMOS. These utility programs also allow you to check the CMOS battery—something that MSD (Microsoft Diagnostics) does not let you do. A less expensive way to copy this information is to run your computer's setup program and copy down all the settings. (You don't have to know what all these settings mean; just make sure you log them all.)

101: The date and time are incorrect; how do I change them?

In Windows 95, double-click the time display on the taskbar. Then on the Date/Time tab, adjust the date or the time as needed. You can change time zones with the Time Zone tab, if needed. Click **OK** when you're done.

In Windows 3.1, the date and time is set through DOS. Exit Windows and return to a DOS prompt. Then type the command **DATE** and press **Enter**. Type the new date in the format mm-dd-yy (as in 4-8-97) and press **Enter**. To adjust the time, type the command **TIME** and press **Enter**. Enter the time in military format (hh:mm) and press **Enter**. For example, to enter 11:14 AM, type 11:14. To enter 11:14 PM, type 23:14.

PART 4

Buyers Guide...

T his section contains a software and hardware buyer's guide. It will give you the basic information you need to go out and purchase software and hardware for your computer. You will find information on each piece of software/hardware covered here, as well as ratings in popularity and ease of use.

The Software Buyer's guide contains information on the most popular programs on the market at the time of this writing. You will find a few choices in each category to compare. Remember, new software is released daily, so don't eliminate a particular program just because it isn't included in the list. The Hardware Buyer's guide contains basic information on the most common hardware you might want to upgrade. In each category there are several brands listed along with information about each one. Which item you will buy is a tradeoff between price and performance. Decide how much you want to spend, and get the best item you can afford.

This list is far from exhaustive, but a few of the most popular items are covered for each category. When you decide to buy a particular category, these lists will give you a good starting point for your research.

What You Will Find in This Part

Software Buyer's Guide

By themselves, computers are merely big, dumb brutes that are only too happy to just sit there mindlessly, fans a-whirring, clocks a-ticking, hard drives a-spinning. Your hardware is, in fact, totally useless without some kind of software to bring the computer to life. Whether you want to write letters, keep track of your money, store addresses, or paint some digital masterpiece, you'll need to install the appropriate programs on your machine.

For most people, though, the hard part is choosing which software to buy. Whatever you're looking to do with your computer, there are probably several different software packages available, each with varying features and prices. How's a body to choose? Well, that's what this section is all about. I'll take you on a guided tour of dozens of software programs in all the most popular categories. You'll get basic data such as the manufacturer's name and address and the price of the program, and I'll also rate each program in terms of features, ease of use, and popularity.

What Software Categories Are Covered?

The Buyer's Guide is divided into sections that cover the following categories:

Communications	Home finance and accounting
Databases	Integrated packages
Desktop publishing	Internet browsers
Education	Personal organizers
Entertainment	Presentation graphics
E-mail	Spreadsheets
Graphics and drawing	Word processing
HTML Editors	Antivirus/Utility

Just so you know what's what, the next few sections give you a brief description of each category.

Antivirus/Utility

Antivirus programs are one of the most important programs you can have on your computer (especially if you download files from the Internet). Unfortunately, there are a lot of sick people out there who think it's funny to write programs specifically designed to destroy your data. With an antivirus program running in the background, you will be able to detect and destroy many viruses before they can do damage.

Utility programs are also an important addition. These programs can be used to keep your PC running at an optimum level.

Communications

Communications programs (▶**see page 526**◀) enable you to connect to the outside world using a modem. You can use them to dial in to commercial online services such as CompuServe, America Online, The Microsoft Network, bulletin board systems, or computers linked to the Internet. If you have a fax/modem, some programs even let you send faxes directly from your computer (and receive incoming faxes, as well).

Databases

A *database* is a collection of information that's organized so that retrieving and manipulating the information is relatively painless. A database can store information on anything from the CDs in your CD library to recipes to addresses to beer bottle collections. You use database software (▶**see page 528**◀) to create the various databases you need, input and edit the data, and perform tasks such as sorting, searching, and printing reports.

Most database programs come in one of two flavors:

- A *flat-file* database program uses independent databases to store information. Each entry is separated into multiple *fields*, where each field contains a specific piece of information. In an address database, for example, you'd likely have fields for first name, last name, street address, city, state, ZIP code, and so on. Each of these entries is called a *record*. Because flat-file database programs are simple to use and inexpensive, they're a good choice for home use.

- In a *relational* database program, each database is also organized by record, with each record having multiple fields. The difference is that two or more databases can be related by data in a common field. For example, a database of customer information and a database of orders placed by customers could be related by a common "customer account number" field. Relational database programs are powerful, complex, and more expensive than their flat-file cousins, so they're mostly used in businesses.

Desktop Publishing

Desktop publishing (DTP, for short; ▶**see page 530**◀) involves using your computer to create and print documents that combine text and graphics. Typical DTP projects include newsletters, pamphlets, ads, leaflets, brochures, and even books. Many high-end word processors include some powerful DTP features, but major DTP jobs require the specialized page layout and organization features that are found only in dedicated DTP programs. There are also programs that, while not strictly a part of the DTP family, perform a similar function by enabling you to create greeting cards, banners, and the like.

Education

Educational software is designed to teach some kind of skill or subject. Adult educational programs (▶**see page 530**◀) might teach you how to type, how to speak a foreign language, or how to play the piano. Educational programs for kids (▶**see page 532**◀) run the gamut from math and reading skills to adventure stories and animal facts. This guide also includes a separate table for reference software such as encyclopedias and dictionaries (▶**see page 536**◀).

E-Mail

E-mail is short for *electronic mail* (▶**see page 538**◀). E-mail is becoming so popular that virtually everyone with a computer and a modem has some way to receive e-mail. You use e-mail programs to send and receive messages, as well as to organize the messages you receive.

Games

If, as they say, all work and no play creates dull boys (and, presumably, dull girls), then help is just around the corner in the form of the myriad of games available for PCs (▶**see page 538**◀). There are fast-paced arcade games, shoot-em-up games with an emphasis on blood and gore, simulation games, adventure games, and lots more.

Graphics and Drawing

Artistic stumblebums who wouldn't dream of slapping around oils or watercolors on a real canvas usually find they have no trouble getting up to speed on the virtual canvas of a graphics or drawing program (▶**see page 540**◀). That's because most of these programs make drawing basic shapes and adding cool effects as easy as wiggling a mouse.

HTML Editors

The Internet is growing so quickly that it is hard to find anyone who doesn't have his or her own Web page. If you want to create your own, you'll need an HTML (short for Hypertext Markup Language) editor to create your page. All Web pages are created in HTML, so you'll want an editor that's easy to use.

Integrated Packages

If you think you'll only be using the basic features of your software, it's a waste to plunk down the big bucks for a fancy-schmancy program that has all the bells and whistles. Instead, you might want to consider an integrated package (▶**see page 544**◀) that combines multiple programs (usually at least a word processor, spreadsheet, and database) into a single program. Sure, the individual modules lack many of the features found in dedicated programs, but you pay a fraction of the cost for them.

Internet Browsers

The Internet is the computer buzzword for the '90s. Everyone seems to be talking about the Internet and the World Wide Web (Web for short). There is a wealth of information out there, but you can't get to it without an Internet browser. This section (▶**see page 544**◀) outlines the features of the most popular Internet browsers.

Personal Finance and Accounting

This category (▶**see page 544**◀) includes low-end programs that are sophisticated checkbook substitutes for home use and high-end packages that offer full-blown accounting features for small- and medium-sized businesses.

Personal Organizers

Personal organizers (or personal information managers, as they're often called; ▶**see page 546**◀) are like the electronic version of a secretary or assistant. You can use them to store addresses and phone numbers, create to-do lists, schedule meetings and appointments, and more (everything except fetching you coffee).

Spreadsheets

Spreadsheet programs (▶**see page 548**◀) are the software that took the "crunch" out of that familiar business pastime, "number-crunching." Use a spreadsheet to figure up your car payments or your financial future. These programs can do nearly anything from simple arithmetic to complex math and can help you get a handle on loan payments, mortgages, or paying for your kids' college educations.

Software Suites

Software suites (▶**see page 548**◀) are the latest trend in program packaging. A "suite" is a collection of applications bundled together and sold for a fraction of what the applications would cost separately. Unlike an integrated package (one big application that works like several small ones), the various programs in a suite can be run as stand-alone applications; they work fine by themselves and have full features. Usually the manufacturers of a suite design the applications so you can transfer your work easily from one component of the suite to another.

Word Processing

Word processing is the most popular of all the software categories. That's because writing—whether it's a letter to a loved one, a memo, or a book—is something most of us do every day either at work or at home. You can use a word processing program (▶**see page 550**◀) not only to type your prose, but also to edit it, format it, print it, and (in some cases) check the spelling and grammar of your work.

What's in the Table?

In the table that makes up the rest of this section, you'll find these fields to help you make informed decisions when you buy software:

Program   The name of the software program.

Manufacturer   The name, address, Internet address, and phone number of the company that manufactures the program.

Price   The list price of the program and the upgrade price, if applicable. Note, however, that you'll rarely have to pay list price for a program these days. Most software stores should be selling programs at anywhere from 25% to 50% off the list price.

Platforms   The types of operating systems the program needs: DOS by itself or Windows 3.1x (that is, DOS-plus-Windows, which means you'll need a version of DOS that can run Windows), Windows 95, or Windows NT.

System Requirements   The equipment and features needed on your computer to run the program. For both PC platforms (Windows and DOS), I've created a "Minimum System" that you need for basic tasks. The System Requirements field tells you what you need over and above these minimums (if anything). Here are the Minimum Systems for each platform:

- **Minimum Windows 95 System:** 386 25MHz processor; VGA graphics adapter; 4M RAM; 30M hard disk space; mouse; 1.2M or 1.44M floppy disk drive.

- **Minimum Windows 3.1x System:** 286 processor; EGA graphics adapter; 2M RAM; DOS 3.1; mouse; hard disk.

- **Minimum DOS System:** 8088 processor; CGA graphics adapter; 640K RAM; hard disk.

➤If you need help reading and understanding the system requirements on a software package, refer to "Look at Software Requirements" on page 7 in Part 1 of this book.◄

Hard Disk Usage   The number of kilobytes or megabytes the program takes up on your hard disk. For programs that enable you to install subsets, I'll give both the minimum and maximum amounts of space the program will use.

Full-Featured   Rates the program on whether it has enough features to do a good job for you. I use these ratings:

   ★★★★ Excellent

    ★★★ Very good

     ★★ Adequate

      ★ Caution when buying

Ease of Use   Rates the program on how easy it is to use. "Ease of use" encompasses whether the program is easy to install and well organized, has a well-designed interface, offers a useful help system, and makes everyday tasks easier to do. I use the same rating scale.

Popularity   Rates the program on recent sales and the total number of users. In the software industry, the cream usually rises to the top, so you're pretty safe correlating strong sales with good quality. (The popular stuff is also easier to find.)

Features   A summary of the program's main features.

With the onslaught of new programs designed especially for Windows 95, read the software packages carefully. If you have Windows 3.1x applications, they will run under Windows 95, but Windows 95 programs will not run under Windows 3.1x. Also, programs designed especially for Windows 95 will naturally run better under Windows 95 than will older programs designed for Windows 3.1x. Most Windows 95 programs will also run under Windows NT. Just make sure you purchase the right program for the operating system you have by reading the system requirements on the software box carefully.

Antivirus and Utility Programs

Program	Manufacturer	Price	Platforms	System Requirements
First Aid 97	CyberMedia Inc. Santa Monica, CA (800) 721-7824 (310) 581-4700 **www.cybermedia.com**	List price: $40	Windows 95	8M RAM
IBM AntiVirus	IBM Corp. Sterling Forest, NY (800) 742-2493 (512) 434-1554 **www.av.ibm.com**	List price: $49	Windows 3.1, Windows 95	386 processor, 4M RAM
PC-cillin II	TouchStone Software Corp. Huntington Beach, CA (800) 531-0450 (714) 969-7746 **www.checkit.com**	List price: $49.95	Windows 95	
Norton Antivirus	Symantec Corporation 10201 Torre Avenue Cupertino, CA 95014 (800) 554-4403 (541)-984-2490 **www.symantec.com**	List price: $69.95	Windows 3.1, Windows 95, Windows NT	386 processor for Win 95/NT
Norton Utilities	Symantec Corporation 10201 Torre Avenue Cupertino, CA 95014 (800) 554-4403 (541) 984-2490 **www.symantec.com**	List price: $80	Windows 95	8M RAM
ViruSafe 95	EliaShim Inc.Pembroke Pines, FL (800) 477-5177 (954) 450-9611 **www.eliashim.com**	List price: $79	Windows 95	486 processor, 8M RAM
WINProbe 95	Quarterdeck Corp. 13160 Mindanao Way Marina del Rey, CA (800) 354-3222 (310) 309-3700 **www.quarterdeck.com**	List price: $50	Windows 95	8M RAM

Communications Programs

Program	Manufacturer	Price	Platforms	System Requirements
Crosstalk inter.comm Suite	Attachmate Corporation 3617 131st Ave. S.E. Bellevue, WA 98006 (800) 426-6283 (206) 644-4010 **www.attachmate.com**	List price: $179	Windows 3.1, Windows 95	Windows 3.1: 4M RAM Windows 95: 8M RAM
Focal Point	Global Village Communication 1144 E. Arques Ave. Sunnyvale, CA (800) 736-4821 (408) 523-1000 **www.globalvillage.com**	List price: $129	Windows 3.1, Windows 95	8M RAM

Hard Disk Usage	Full-Featured	Ease of Use	Popularity	Features
40M	★★★★	★★★	★★★	Troubleshooting and tune-up utility; warns of impending hard drive failure; crash protection module; can be updated over the Internet.
4M	★★★	★★	★★★	Full-featured virus detection; Internet protection; automatic virus detection; free downloadable updates.
6M	★★★★	★★★	★★★	Full-featured virus detection; Internet protection; automatic virus detection; free downloadable updates.
12M	★★★★	★★★★	★★★★	Full-featured antivirus utility; can detect viruses in the background; Internet download protection; scans compressed files; free downloadable updates.
31M	★★★★	★★★★	★★★★	Diagnostic and repair utility; supports FAT32 partitions; Registry Tracker; Registry Editor; Norton Disk Doctor can repair many hard disk problems; can be updated over the Internet.
3M	★★★	★★★★	★★★	Full-featured virus utility; background virus detection; Internet download protection; scans compressed files; free downloadable updates.
14M	★★★	★★★★	★★★	PC diagnostic utility; reports and repairs common problems; includes a crash-protection module; Registry Editor.
5M–20M	★★★	★★★	★★★	Scripting and automation; e-mail; FTP client; includes Netscape 2.0.
17MB	★★★	★★★★	★★★★	Single address book; message management; fax; fax on demand; e-mail; voice mail.

Communications Programs   Continued

Program	Manufacturer	Price	Platforms	System Requirements
HyperAccess	Hilgraeve, Inc. Genesis Centre 111 Conant Ave., Suite A Monroe, MI 48161 (800) 826-2760 (313) 243-0576 **www.hilgraeve.com**	List price: $129	Windows 3.1, Windows 95	8M RAM
Procomm Plus	Quarterdeck Corp. 13160 Mindanao Way Marina del Rey, CA 90292 (800) 354-3222 (573) 443-3282 **www.quarterdeck.com**	List price: $139	Windows 95	8M RAM (16M recommended)
WinFax Pro	Symantec Corporation 10201 Torre Avenue Cupertino, CA 95014 (800) 554-4403 (541)-984-2490 **www.symantec.com**	List price: $99	Windows 95, Windows NT	486 processor (Pentium recommended) 8M RAM (16M recommended)
ZOC	BMT Micro 5019 Carolina Beach Rd. Suite 202 Wilmington, NC 28412 (800) 414-4268 (910) 791-7052 **www.emtec.com**	List price: $69	Windows 95	Minimum system

Database Programs

Program	Manufacturer	Price	Platforms	System Requirements
Access	Microsoft Corp. One Microsoft Way Redmond, WA 98052 (800) 426-9400 (206) 882-8080 **www.microsoft.com**	List price: $495 Upgrade price: $129	Windows 95, Windows NT	12M RAM
Approach	Lotus Development Corp. 55 Cambridge Parkway Cambridge, MA 02142 (800) 343-5414 (617) 577-8500 **www.lotus.com**	List price: $105	Windows 95, Windows NT	8M RAM
FileMaker Pro	Claris Corp. Santa Clara, CA (800) 544-8554 (408) 727-8227 **www.claris.com**	List price: $199	Windows 95	8M RAM
Paradox	Borland International 100 Borland Way Scotts Valley, CA 95066 (800) 233-2444 (408) 431-1000 **www.borland.com**	List price: $299	Windows 95, Windows NT, Windows 3.1	8M RAM

Hard Disk Usage	Full-Featured	Ease of Use	Popularity	Features
6M	★★★	★★★★	★★★★	Includes Netscape 3.0 and Microsoft Internet Explorer; graphics viewer; host program; weather report service; automatic file uncompression; detects common viruses in downloaded files.
45M	★★★	★★★	★★★★	Fax; integrated Web browser; e-mail; Internet newsreader; FTP; Procomm Remote to link home and office PC.
25M–40M	★★★	★★★	★★★★	Full-featured fax program including cover page designer, Optical Character Recognition, scheduling, voice messaging, and fax on demand.
2M	★★	★★	★★	Simple, inexpensive program that includes everything you need for basic communications.
14M	★★★★	★★★★	★★★★	Relational; Wizards for automating table creation, queries, and more; Cue Cards; automatic form and report generation; Quick Sort; OLE support; Visual Basic programming language; Internet features.
15M	★★★★	★★★★	★★★	Relational; Assistants for automating table creation, queries, and more; data dictionary; OLE support; report editor; Action Bar for keeping commonly used menu items.
4M	★★★	★★★	★★★	Relational; unlimited file size; OLE support; auto-enter fields; sample templates and files; capability to share files with Macintosh workstations.
13M	★★★★	★★★	★★★★	Relational; Experts for automating table creation, queries, and more; query-by-example; Visual Form Designer; Report Designer; ObjectPAL programming language.

Desktop Publishing Programs

Program	Manufacturer	Price	Platforms	System Requirements
Corel Ventura	Corel Corp. 1600 Carling Avenue Ottawa, ON K1Z 8R7 (800) 722-6735 (613) 728-3733 **www.corel.com**	List price: $895 Competitive upgrade: $249	Windows 95, Windows NT	486 processor, 16M RAM, CD-ROM drive
FrameMaker	Adobe Systems 1585 Charleston Rd. Mountain View, CA 94039 (800) 833-6687 (415) 961-4400 **www.adobe.com**	List price: $895 Upgrade price: $225	Windows 95, Windows NT	8M RAM, CD-ROM drive
Interleaf 6	Interleaf, Inc. 62 Fourth Ave. Waltham, MA 02154 (800) 688-5151 (617) 290-4990 **www.ileaf.com**	List price: $1895	Windows 95, Windows NT	486 processor, 16M RAM (24M recommended)
Microsoft Publisher	Microsoft Corp. One Microsoft Way Redmond, WA 98052 (800) 426-9400 (206) 882-8080 **www.microsoft.com**	List price: $79.95	Windows 95, Windows NT	8M RAM
PageMaker	Adobe Systems 1585 Charleston Rd. Mountain View, CA 94039 (800) 833-6687 (415) 961-4400 **www.adobe.com**	List price: $895 Upgrade price: $95	Windows 95, Window NT 4.0	486 processor, 8M RAM (Windows 95), 16M RAM (Windows NT)
Print Shop Ensemble	Broderbund Software 500 Redwood Blvd. Novato, CA 94948 (800) 521-6263 (415) 382-4700 **http://www.broder.com**	List price: $49.95	Windows 95	486DX33, 8M RAM (16M recommended)
QuarkXPress	Quark, Inc. 1800 Grant Street Denver, CO 80203 (800) 676-4575 (303) 894-8888 **www.quark.com**	List price: $895	Windows 3.1	386 processor, 4M RAM, VGA graphics adapter

Educational Programs: Adult

Program	Manufacturer	Price	Platforms	System Requirements
American Medical Association Family Medical Guide	DK Multimedia (800) 356-6575 (212) 213-4800 **www.dk.com**	List price: 39.95	Windows 3.1	486DX33 processor, CD-ROM drive

Hard Disk Usage	Full-Featured	Ease of Use	Popularity	Features
90M–250M	★★★★	★★★★	★★★	Includes Corel WordPerfect, Database Publisher, DataBase Edit; automatic archiving and version control; includes PhotoPaint for image editing; screen capturing, CD creation.
10M–30M	★★★★	★★★	★★★	Support for headers, footers, and footnotes; Page Layout palette; global styles; text wraps, text and object rotation; automatic paragraph and figure numbering; cross-referencing; OLE support; capability to create HTML code for Web pages.
45M–100M	★★★★	★★★★	★★★	Word processing with spell-checking in 13 languages; multi-page tables; supports graphics and equations; powerful layout and formatting tools; OLE compatible; revision management.
10M	★★★	★★★★	★★★★	PageWizards for automating page layout; Cue Cards; WordArt; spell checker; drawing tools; OLE support; Print Troubleshooter; Layout Checker; Web-site wizard for creating HTML code.
26M	★★★★	★★★	★★★★	New tabbed palettes for organizing desktop; supports document and object layers; spell checker; multiple document interface; capability to create HTML for Web pages; automatically converts graphics into JPEG or GIF format.
13M	★★	★★★★	★★★★	Creates greeting cards, banners, signs, and calendars; large graphics library; hundreds of template designs; Photo Accessories for inserting personal photos; spell checker and thesaurus; Online Greetings for sending e-mail greeting cards.
10M	★★★	★★★	★★★	Style sheets; spell checker; thesaurus; four-color separation; support for all major color systems (Pantone, etc.); precise control of rotation and kerning; drag and drop text and pictures.
1M	★★★	★★★★	★★★	Flowcharts to help diagnose symptoms; detailed description of body symptoms; drug glossary.

(continues)

Educational Programs: Adult   Continued

Program	Manufacturer	Price	Platforms	System Requirements
Bodyworks	The Learning Company One Athenaeum St. Cambridge, MA 02142 (800) 227-5609 (617) 494-5898 **www.softkey.com**	List price: $49.95	Windows 3.1, Windows 95	Double-speed CD-ROM drive
Betty Crocker's Cookbook	Lifestyle Software Group 2155 Old Moultrie Road, Suite A St. Augustine, FL 32086 (800) 289-1157 (904) 794-7070 **www.lifeware.com**	List price: $29.95	Windows 3.1, Windows 95	8M RAM, CD-ROM drive
Cinemania	Microsoft Corp. One Microsoft Way Redmond, WA 98052 (800) 426-9400 (206) 882-8080 **www.microsoft.com**	List price: $34.95	Windows 95, Windows NT	486/33 processor, 8M RAM (Windows 95), 16M RAM (Windows NT)
French Assistant	MicroTac Software, Inc. 4375 Jutland Drive Suite 110 San Diego, CA 92117 (800) 366-4170	List price: $99.95	Windows 3.1	386 processor
Mavis Beacon Teaching Typing	Mindscape 60 Leveroni Court Novato, CA 94949 (415) 883-3000	List price: $49.95	Windows 95, Windows 3.1	486DX66 processor, 8M RAM, double-speed CD-ROM drive
Piano Discovery System	Jump Software 201 San Antonio Circle Suite 172 Mountain View, CA 94040 (800) 488-2221	List price: $249.99	Windows 3.1, Windows 95	486/33 processor, 8M RAM, sound card, double-speed CD-ROM drive
Pediatric HouseCall	Applied Medical Informatics 2681 Parley's Way Suite 101 Salt Lake City, UT 84109 (800) 584-3060 (801) 464-6200	List price: $29.95	Windows 3.1	Minimum system, CD-ROM drive
Reader's Digest Complete Do-It-Yourself Guide	Microsoft Corp. One Microsoft Way Redmond, WA 98052 (800) 426-9400 (206) 882-8080 **www.microsoft.com**	List price: $35	Windows 95, Windows NT	486/33 processor, 8M RAM, double-speed CD-ROM drive, Super VGA display

Educational Programs: Children

Program	Manufacturer	Price	Platforms	System Requirements
Dr. Seuss's ABC	Broderbund Software 500 Redwood Blvd. Novato, CA 94948 (800) 521-6263 (415) 382-4700 **www.broder.com**	List price: $29.95	Windows 95, Windows 3.1	486 processor (Win 95), 8M RAM (Win 95), CD-ROM drive

Hard Disk Usage	Full-Featured	Ease of Use	Popularity	Features
8M	★★★★	★★★★	★★★	Comprehensive anatomy reference; 170 color diagrams; 25 3-D models; 60 minutes of live-action video.
10M	★★★	★★★★	★★★	More than 1,000 recipes; includes gourmet recipes and photos of recipes; search feature; recipe management; how-to advice; shopping list creator.
1M	★★★	★★★★	★★★★	Movie reviews; biographies of film personalities; Academy Award winners; movie industry articles.
4M	★★★	★★★★	★★	100,000 word dictionary; automatic and interactive translating; more than 3,000 verb conjugations; grammar help.
1M	★★★★	★★★★	★★★★	Artificial intelligence simulates typing teacher; on-the-fly custom lessons; games.
10M–25M	★★★★	★★★★	★★★★	Comes with MIDI keyboard (plugs into sound card); interactive lessons; practice games; Performance Hall where you can play with orchestral accompaniment.
5M	★★★	★★★★	★★★	Includes medical records, drug interactions, symptom analysis, and an encyclopedia.
10M	★★★	★★★★	★★★	Complete reference on home repairs; includes 3-D animation and full-motion video; step-by-step illustrations.
1M	★★★	★★★★	★★★★	Ages 3–7; interactive storybook from the popular Living Books series.

(continues)

Educational Programs: Children   Continued

Program	Manufacturer	Price	Platforms	System Requirements
JumpStart Kindergarten	Knowledge Adventure 4502 Dyer St. La Crescenta, CA 91214 (800) 542-4240 (818) 542-4200 **www.adventure.com**	List price: $29	Windows 95, Windows 3.1	486SX25 processor, double-speed CD-ROM drive
Magic Schoolbus Explores Inside the Earth	Microsoft Corp. One Microsoft Way Redmond, WA 98052 (800) 426-9400 (206) 882-8080 **www.microsoft.com**	List price: $39.95	Windows 95, Windows 3.1	486SX25 processor, double-speed CD-ROM drive
Math Blaster Episode I: In Search of Spot	Davidson & Associates P.O. Box 2961 Torrance, CA 90509 (800) 556-6141 **www.davd.com**	List price: $35	Windows 95, Windows 3.1	486/33 processor, 8M RAM, double-speed CD-ROM drive
Millie's Math House	Edmark Corporation P.O. Box 97021 Redmond, WA 98073 (800) 691-2986 (206) 556-8400 **www.edmark.com**	List price: $29.95	Windows 95, Windows 3.1	Double-speed CD-ROM
Reader Rabbit 1	The Learning Company 6493 Kaiser Drive Fremont, CA 94555 (800) 852-2255 **www.learningco.com**	List price: $50	Windows 95, Windows 3.1	486DX66 processor, 8M RAM, double-speed CD-ROM drive
Richard Scarry's Best Reading Program Ever	Simon & Schuster Interactive (800) 910-0099 (212) 698-7000 **www.scarry.com**	List price: $29.95	Windows 95, Windows 3.1	486/33 processor, 8M RAM (Win 3.1), 16M RAM (Win 95), double-speed CD-ROM drive
Toy Story Animated StoryBook	Disney Interactive 500 S. Buena Vista St. Burbank, CA 91521 (800) 900-9234 (818) 841-3326 **www.disney.com**	List price: $39.95	Windows 95, Windows 3.1	486/50 processor, 8M RAM, double-speed CD-ROM drive
Word Munchers Deluxe	MECC 9715 Parkside Drive Knoxville, TN 37922 (800) 227-5609 (617) 494-5898 **www.mecc.com**	List price: $29.95	Windows 3.1	486/50 processor, double-speed CD-ROM drive

Hard Disk Usage	Full-Featured	Ease of Use	Popularity	Features
5M	★★★	★★★★	★★★★	Covers a full year of early math, pre-reading, language, and creative arts; tracks up to 99 children.
5M	★★★★	★★★	★★★★	Ages 6–10; six geologic settings with more than 200 objects to click; eight games; similar to Magic School Bus television series on PBS.
1M	★★★	★★★	★★★★	Ages 6–12; four math teaching games: Math Blaster, Trash Zapper, Number Recycler, and Cave Runner; six difficulty levels.
3M	★★★★	★★★★	★★★★	Ages 2–10; seven independent learning activities; prompts for correct answer when incorrect answer is given.
10M	★★★	★★★★	★★★★	Ages 4–7; early reading program; basic reading skills; stresses phonics, vocabulary building, spelling, letter recognition, and memory.
8M	★★★	★★★	★★★	Ages 3–6; features the stars of Richard Scarry's books and television series; focuses on letter recognition, rhyming, phonics, and sight word development; includes mini word-processor.
20M	★★★	★★★★	★★★	Interactive story allows children to have the story read to them or to explore scenes in the story; includes activities throughout the story.
5M	★★★	★★★	★★★	Ages 6–11; focuses on grammar, phonics, verbs, nouns, general vocabulary, and sentence completion.

(continues)

Educational Programs: Children   Continued

Program	Manufacturer	Price	Platforms	System Requirements
Where in the World is Carmen Sandiego	Broderbund Software 500 Redwood Blvd. Novato, CA 94948 (800) 521-6263 (415) 382-4700 **www.broder.com**	List price: $39.95	Windows 95, Windows 3.1	486/33 processor, 8M RAM, double-speed CD-ROM drive

Educational Programs: Reference

Program	Manufacturer	Price	Platforms	System Requirements
ABC World Reference 3D Atlas	Creative Wonders P.O. Box 9017 Redwood City, CA 94063 (800) 543-9788 (415) 482-2400 **www.cwonders.com**	List price: $29.95	Windows 95, Windows 3.1	486 processor
American Heritage Talking Dictionary	SoftKey International 201 Broadway Cambridge, MA 01239 (800) 227-5609 (617) 494-1200	List price: $49.95	Windows 95, Windows 3.1	486 processor (Win 95), 386/25 processor (Win 3.11), 8M RAM
Bookshelf	Microsoft Corp. One Microsoft Way Redmond, WA 98052 (800) 426-9400 (206) 882-8080 **www.microsoft.com**	List price: $54.95	Windows 95, Windows 3.1	486SX33 processor, 4M RAM, double- speed CD-ROM drive
Britannica CD	Encyclopedia Britannica Chicago, IL (800) 323-1229 (312) 347-7005 **www.eb.com**	List price: $299	Windows 3.1	386 processor, 4M RAM (8M recommended), CD-ROM drive
Compton's Interactive Encyclopedia	Softkey International Compton's NewMedia, Inc. 9715 Parkside Dr. Knoxville, TN 37922 (800) 622-3390 **www.comptons.com**	List price: $49.95	Windows 95, Windows 3.1	486/66 processor, 8M RAM, double- speed CD-ROM drive
Encarta, Deluxe Edition	Microsoft Corp. One Microsoft Way Redmond, WA 98052 (800) 426-9400 (206) 882-8080 **www.microsoft.com**	List price: $60	Windows 95, Windows NT, Windows 3.1	486DX33 processor, 8M RAM, double- speed CD-ROM drive
Grolier Multimedia Encyclopedia	Grolier Interactive Inc. 90 Sherman Turnpike Danbury, CT 06816 (203) 797-3530 **www.grolier.com**	List price: $50	Windows 95, Windows 3.1	8M RAM, CD-ROM drive
World Book Multimedia Encyclopedia, Deluxe Edition	IBM Corp. Atlanta, GA (800) 426-7235 (770) 644-4881 **www.worldbook.com**	List price: $60	Windows 95, Windows 3.1	486SX25 processor, 16M RAM, double- speed CD-ROM drive, 16-bit sound card

Hard Disk Usage	Full-Featured	Ease of Use	Popularity	Features
2M	★★★	★★★★	★★★★	Ages 8 and up; geography and social studies lessons via photos, video, and sound.
5M	★★★	★★★★	★★★	Multiple 3-D pictures viewable from space at levels; thousands of satellite images; 3-D climate globes; thousands of statistics on every country; global effects of ozone depletion, pollution, and deforestation.
22M	★★★★	★★★	★★★	200,000 definitions; 72,000 audio pronunciations; 500,000 synonyms; WordHunter for help finding words; anagram feature.
5M	★★★★	★★★★	★★★★	American Heritage Dictionary; Columbia Dictionary of Quotations; Concise Columbia Encyclopedia; People's Chronology; Roget's Thesaurus; World Almanac and Book of Facts; Internet Directory; Encarta World Atlas; Year in Review.
10M	★★★	★★	★★★	Contains full text of printed version (67,000 articles); includes electronic version of Merriam-Webster's Collegiate Dictionary.
1M	★★★	★★★★	★★★	37,000 articles; 100 videos and animations; 600 sound clips; dictionary; free monthly updates; bookmark feature.
15M (Win 95), 13M (Win NT), 20M (Win 3.1)	★★★★	★★★★	★★★★	31,000 articles; 153 videos and animations; 14,000 photos and illustrations; 970 maps; 2,300 sound clips; 5,000 Web links; dictionary; free monthly updates.
10M	★★★	★★★★	★★★	35,000 articles; 10,000 photos and illustrations; 1,200 maps; 600 sound clips; 20,000 Web links; free monthly updates; bookmark feature.
18M	★★★	★★★	★★★	Contains full text of printed version (17,500 articles); 361 sound clips; 145 videos and animations; 700 maps; dictionary; free updates.

E-Mail Programs

Program	Manufacturer	Price	Platforms	System Requirements
Eudora Pro	QUALCOMM Inc. 6455 Lusk Boulevard San Diego, CA 92121 (619) 587-1121 **www.eudora.com**	List price: $60	Windows 95, Windows NT, Windows 3.1	4M RAM
Pronto Mail Professional Edition	CommTouch Software Inc. 298 S. Sunnyvale Ave. Suite 209 Sunnyvale, CA 94086 (408) 245-8982 **www.commtouch.com**	Free (Advertiser supported)	Windows 95, Windows NT	486 processor
Netscape Messenger	Netscape Communications 501 E. Middlefield Rd. Mountain View, CA 94043 (415) 937-3777 **www.netscape.com**	Netscape Communicator List price: $59 (free for educational and non-profit use)	Windows 95, Windows NT, Windows 3.1	486 processor, 8M
Outlook	Microsoft Corp. One Microsoft Way Redmond, WA 98052 (800) 426-9400 (206) 882-8080 **www.microsoft.com**	List price: $109	Windows 95, Windows NT	486 processor, 8M RAM (Win 95), 16M RAM (Win NT)
Outlook Express	Microsoft Corp. One Microsoft Way Redmond, WA 98052 (800) 426-9400 (206) 882-8080 **www.microsoft.com**	Free	Windows 95, Windows NT, Windows 3.1	386DX processor, 16M Ram
Z-Mail Pro	NetManage 10725 North De Anza Blvd. Cupertino, CA 95014 (408) 973-7171 **www.netmanage.com**	List price: $59	Windows 95, Windows NT	8M RAM

Games

Program	Manufacturer	Price	Platforms	System Requirements
The Beast Within: A Gabriel Knight Mystery	Sierra On-Line 3380 146th Place SE Suite 300 Bellevue, WA 98007 (800) 757-7707 (206) 649-9800 **www.sierra.com**	List price: $65	Windows 3.1	486/33 processor, 8M RAM, CD-ROM drive
Command & Conquer	Virgin Interactive Entertainment/ Westwood Studios (800) 874-4607 (714) 833-8710 **www.westwood.com**	List price: $49.99	DOS, Windows 3.1	486/66 processor, 8M RAM

Hard Disk Usage	Full-Featured	Ease of Use	Popularity	Features
4M	★★★★	★★★★	★★★★	Comprehensive filters to sort messages; supports multiple accounts and signature files; support for MIME rich-text format; spell checker.
8M	★★★★	★★★★	★★★	Intuitive interface; support for MIME; spell checker; advanced filtering controls; multiple address books; automatic mail management; multiple signature files; voice-mail messaging.
30M (complete install with Communicator)	★★★	★★★★	★★★★	Included with Netscape Communicator; HTML aware; spell checker; extensive filtering; address book with LDAP support.
26M–46M	★★★★	★★★	★★★	Full-featured personal information manager; HTML aware; spell checker; centralized address book with LDAP support; extensive filtering.
30M with Internet Explorer	★★★	★★★★	★★★	Included with full version of Internet Explorer (version 4.0 and above); HTML aware; spell checker; centralized address book LDAP with support; extensive filtering.
16M	★★★	★★	★★	HTML-aware; spell checker; address book with LDAP support; extensive filtering; IMAP support; built-in encryption.
20M	N/A	★★★	★★★★	Video-based adventure game; you're Gabriel Knight and you must find those responsible for attacks in Germany.
20M	N/A	★★★	★★★★	Battle simulation game; you can play as the good guys or the bad guys; you are the commander and must command your soldiers through a series of battles in a global conflict.

(continues)

Games   Continued

Program	Manufacturer	Price	Platforms	System Requirements
Duke Nukem 3D	3D Realms Entertainment P.O. Box 496419 Garland, TX 75049 (800) 337-3256 **www.3drealms.com**	List price: $49.95	DOS	486 processor, 8M RAM (486/66, 16M RAM recommended)
Flight Simulator	Microsoft Corp. One Microsoft Way Redmond, WA 98052 (800) 426-9400 (206) 882-8080 **www.microsoft.com**	List price: $59.95	Windows 95	Basic system
Mech Warrior 2	Activision, Inc. (800) 477-3650 **www.activision.com**	List price: $59.95	DOS, Windows 95	486/66 processor, 8M RAM, Pentium (Win 95), double- speed CD-ROM drive
Myst	Broderbund Software 500 Redwood Blvd. Novato, CA 94948 (800) 521-6263 (415) 382-4700 **www.broder.com**	List price: $39.95	Windows 3.1	386DX33 (486 recommended), 4M RAM (8M recommended), CD-ROM drive
NBA Live	Electronic Arts 1450 Fashion Island Blvd. San Mateo, CA 94403 (800) 245-4525 (415) 572-2787 **www.ea.com**	List price: $54.95	Windows 95, DOS	Pentium 75 processor, 16M RAM, high-color graphics card, double- speed CD-ROM drive
PGA Tour	Electronic Arts 1450 Fashion Island Blvd. San Mateo, CA 94403 (800) 245-4525 (415) 572-2787 **www.ea.com**	List price: $44.95	Windows 95	486/66 processor, 8M RAM, double- speed CD-ROM drive
Sid Meijer's Civilization II	MicroProse-Spectrum HoloByte USA 2490 Mariner Square Loop Alameda, CA 94501 (510) 522-1164 **www.microprose.com**	List price: $50	Windows 95, Windows 3.1	486/33 processor, 8M RAM, double- speed CD-ROM drive
Warcraft II	Blizzard Entertainment P.O. Box 18979 Irvine, CA 92623 (800) 953-7669 **www.blizzard.com**	List price: $44.95	DOS	486/33 processor, 8M RAM, double- speed CD-ROM drive

Graphics and Drawing

Program	Manufacturer	Price	Platforms	System Requirements
Adobe Photoshop	Adobe Systems, Inc. 1585 Charleston Rd. Mountain View, CA 94039 (800) 843-7263 (408) 536-6000 **www.adobe.com**	List price: $895	Windows 3.1	486 processor, 16M RAM

Hard Disk Usage	Full-Featured	Ease of Use	Popularity	Features
30M	N/A	★★★	★★★★	Action game; as Duke Nukem, you are responsible for saving the planet when aliens take over Los Angeles.
12M	★★★★	★★★★	★★★★	Full-featured flight simulator; contains realistic scenery and hundreds of airports; can fly a variety of airplanes; scenery add-ons available.
30M	N/A	★★★	★★★★	Action game; you choose from many body armor styles to fight as the MechWarrior; detailed battle scenarios heighten the challenge.
2M	N/A	★★★★	★★★★	Adventure game; save the underground Empire of Zork from the evil IT&L Corporation.
30M–40M	N/A	★★★★	★★★★	Arcade-style basketball game; supports up to four players; instant replay feature.
30M	N/A	★★★★	★★★★	Golf game; can be played head-to-head over a modem or LAN; Ball Cam feature; two Championship courses to play; can play as or against 14 PGA Tour pros.
1M	N/A	★★★★	★★★★	Strategy game; build an empire and make critical economic, political, and social decision; contains full-motion video of 28 Wonders of the World.
3M	N/A	★★★	★★★★	Action/strategy game; the humans have been invaded by the Orcs; you command the army to fight back; first you'll need to build farms, chop trees, and mine gold to prepare for the battle.
25M	★★★	★★★	★★★★	Complete image editing package; can use Adjustment Layers to change color and tone; rotate, skew, distort, and scale images; grids and guidelines help you draw.

(continues)

Graphics and Drawing   Continued

Program	Manufacturer	Price	Platforms	System Requirements
CorelDRAW!	Corel Corp. 1600 Carling Avenue Ottawa, ON K1Z 8R7 (800) 772-6735 (613) 728-8200 **www.corel.com**	List price: $695	Windows 95, Windows NT 4.0	Pentium processor, 16M RAM
Fractal Design Painter	Fractal Design Corp. P.O. Box 66959 Scotts Valley, CA 95066 (800) 846-0111 (408) 430-4000 **www.fractal.com**	List price: $549	Windows 3.1	486 processor, 8M RAM
Macromedia FreeHand	Macromedia Inc. 600 Townsend St. San Francisco, CA 94103 (800) 288-4797 (415) 252-2000 **www.macromedia.com**	List price: $400	Windows 95, Windows NT	486 processor, 12M RAM
Visio	Visio Corp. P.O. Box 1500 Fairport, NY 14450 (800) 446-3335 (206) 521-4500 **www.visio.com**	List price: $249	Windows 95, Windows NT, Windows 3.1	386 processor, 4M RAM (Win 3.1), 8M RAM (Win 95/NT)
Write Image	Write Technologies Ltd. 1200 Sheppard Ave. East Suite 301 North York, Ontario 2K2S5 (888) 261-2261 (416) 497-8388 **www.wrightna.com**	List price: $399	Windows 95, Windows NT	486 processor, 16M RAM (Win 95), 32M RAM (Win NT)

HTML Editors

Program	Manufacturer	Price	Platforms	System Requirements
AOLpress	America Online Vienna, VA (703) 448-8700 **www.aolpress.com**	List price: Free	Windows 3.1, Windows 95, Windows NT	386 processor; 8M RAM
FrontPage	Microsoft Corp. One Microsoft Way Redmond, WA 98052 (800) 426-9400 (206) 882-8080 **www.microsoft.com**	List price: $149	Windows 95, Windows NT 3.51 or greater	486 processor; 8M RAM (Win 95), 16M RAM (Win NT)
Home Page	Claris Corp. Santa Clara, CA (800) 544-8554 (408) 727-8227 **www.claris.com**	List price: $99	Windows 95, Windows NT	486 processor; 8M RAM (16M for Win NT)

Hard Disk Usage	Full-Featured	Ease of Use	Popularity	Features
40M	★★★	★★★★	★★★★	Drawing program; extensive toolset; extrude 2-D into 3-D drawings; excellent text-handling; cropped images; color filters; includes Photo-Paint.
20M	★★★	★★★	★★★	Drawing tools; brushes; special effects; natural paint tools and textures; Mosaic; Image Warp; Page Rotate; TWAIN support; macro recorder.
25M	★★★★	★★★★	★★★	Drawing program; expert print output; precise color matching; supports Pantone and Hexachrome; effects include reflect, skew, rotate, and scale; excellent text handling; Web export tools.
8M	★★★★	★★★★	★★★★	Drawing/diagramming program; Wizards for chart construction; supports Microsoft Office Binder; three-dimensional perspective; toolbars; multilevel undo; optional grid.
4M	★★★	★★	★★★	Image editing program; page layout allows you to place objects on page; fully editable gradient mask; special effects include sharpen, derivative, motion blur, noise, emboss, and smooth.
8M	★★★	★★	★★★	Full-featured HTML editor; editing screen doubles as Web browser; includes spelling checker.
15M	★★★★	★★★★	★★★★	Full-featured HTML editor; WebBot automates forms and discussion groups; contains a desktop Web server to test your pages; spelling checker.
8M	★★★	★★	★★★	Good for creating individual Web pages; automatic site publisher; spelling checker; creates frames.

(continues)

HTML Editors   Continued

Program	Manufacturer	Price	Platforms	System Requirements
Netscape Composer	Netscape Communications 501 E. Middlefield Rd. Mountain View, CA 94043 (415) 937-3777 **www.netscape.com**	Netscape Communicator List price: $59 (free for educational and nonprofit use)	Windows 95, Windows NT, Windows 3.1	486 processor, 8M

Integrated Packages

ClarisWorks	Claris Corp. 5201 Patrick Henry Dr. Santa Clara, CA 95052 (800) 325-2747 (408) 987-8227 **www.claris.com**	List price: $49	Windows 95	386 processor, 8M RAM
Microsoft Works	Microsoft Corp. One Microsoft Way Redmond, WA 98052 (800) 426-9400 (206) 882-8080 **www.microsoft.com**	List price: $54.95	Windows 95, Windows NT	386 processor, 6M RAM (Win 95), 12M RAM (Win NT)

Internet Browsers

Communicator	Netscape Communications 501 E. Middlefield Rd. Mountain View, CA 94043 (415) 937-3777 **www.netscape.com**	List price: $59 (free for educational and nonprofit use)	Windows 95, Windows NT, Windows 3.1	486 processor, 8M RAM
Internet Explorer	Microsoft Corp. One Microsoft Way Redmond, WA 98052 (800) 426-9400 (206) 882-8080 **www.microsoft.com**	Free	Windows 95, Windows NT, Windows 3.1	386DX processor, 16M RAM
NCSA Mosaic	National Center for Supercomputing Applications **www.ncsa.uiuc.edu**	Free	Windows 95, Windows NT, Windows 3.1	386 processor, 4M RAM

Personal Finance and Accounting

Managing Your Money	MECA Software, L.L.C. 115 Corporate Drive Trumbull, CT 06611 (800) 288-6332 (203) 268-2797 **www.mymnet.com**	List price: $79.95		
Money	Microsoft Corp. One Microsoft Way Redmond, WA 98052 (800) 426-9400 (206) 882-8080 **www.microsoft.com**	List price: $34.95	Windows 95, Windows NT	386DX processor, 8M RAM (Win 95), 12M RAM (Win NT)

Hard Disk Usage	Full-Featured	Ease of Use	Popularity	Features
30M (complete install with Communicator)	★★★	★★★★	★★★★	Great for creating individual Web pages; can drag and drop images from Netscape Navigator.
5M–20M	★★★★	★★★★	★★★	Word processor; spreadsheet; database; charting; presentation; drawing/painting; outlining
5M–20M	★★★★	★★★★	★★★★	Includes word processor, spreadsheet, database, communication; Wizards that automate routine tasks; Microsoft Draw; WordArt; clip art; spell checker; thesaurus; address book.
30M	★★★★	★★★★	★★★★	Includes Navigator, Messenger (e-mail), Collabra (a newsreader), Composer, and Conference; supports secure Web sites; Java support; ActiveX support.
30M	★★★★	★★★★	★★★★	Includes Web browser, Outlook Express (mail and newsreader), Netmeeting (conference/phone client); supports secure Web sites; Java support; ActiveX support.
	★★★	★★★★	★★★	The first Web browser; newsreader; FTP support; AutoSurf feature; Collaborate.
	★★★	★★★	★★★	SmartDesk natural interface; Financial SnapShot; tax management; Graph Gallery; link to CheckFree; QuoteLink for stock quotes; Portfolio management; Home Inventory Manager; Smart Planner.
11M	★★★	★★★★	★★★★	Account register; Payment Calendar; Home Banking; Chart of the Day; Account Manager; Investment Portfolio; Report and Chart Gallery; Payees and Categories; Planning Wizards; online banking.

(continues)

Personal Finance and Accounting Continued

Program	Manufacturer	Price	Platforms	System Requirements
Quicken Deluxe for Windows	Intuit Inc. 155 Linfield Ave. P.O. Box 3014 Menlo Park, CA 94026 (800) 446-8848 (415) 944-6000 **www.intuit.com**	List price $59.95	Windows 3.1, Windows 95	486 processor, 8M RAM, double-speed CD-ROM drive
Smart Home Manager	Surado Solutions Inc. 1960 Chicago Ave. Suite D9 Riverside, CA 92507 (800) 478-7236 (909) 682-4895 **www.surado.com**	List price: $59.95	Windows 95, Windows 3.1	486 processor, 8M RAM, VGA monitor

Personal Organizer Programs

Program	Manufacturer	Price	Platforms	System Requirements
ACT!	Symantec Corporation 10201 Torre Avenue Cupertino, CA 95014 (800) 554-4403 (541)-984-2490 **www.symantec.com**	List price: , $199 Upgrade price: $89.95	Windows 95, Windows NT	486 processor, 8M RAM
Day Runner Planner	Day Runner Inc. Fullerton, CA (800) 232-9786 (714) 680-3500 **www.dayrunner.com**	List price: $75	Windows 3.1	Minimum system
Day-Timer Organizer	Day-Timer Technologies San Mateo, CA (800) 225-5005 (415) 572-6260 **www.daytimer.com**	List price: $59.95	Windows 95, Windows NT, Windows 3.1	386 processor
Ecco Pro	NetManage Inc. ECCO Division 2340 130th Ave. NE Bellevue, WA 98005 (800) 457-4243 (206) 885-4272 **www.netmanage.com**	List price: $139	Windows 95, Windows NT, Windows 3.1	486 processor, 8M RAM (16M recommended), CD-ROM drive
Goldmine for Windows 95	Goldmine Software Corp. 17383 Sunset Boulevard Pacific Palisades, CA 90272 (800) 654-3526 (310) 454-6800 **www.goldminesw.com**	List price: $295	Windows 95, Windows NT 4.0	486 processor, 8M RAM
Organizer	Lotus Development Corp. 55 Cambridge Pkwy. Cambridge, MA 02142 (800) 635-6887 (617) 577-8500 **www.lotus.com**	List price: $149	Windows 3.1, Windows 95	386 processor, 4M RAM (6M recommended), VGA monitor

Hard Disk Usage	Full-Featured	Ease of Use	Popularity	Features
27M–39M	★★★★	★★★★	★★★★	Predefined accounts; predefined charting and reports; tax planner; online banking; Debt Reduction Planner; Mutual Fund Finder; Investor Insight; Home Inventory.
18M–25M	★★	★★★	★★	Basic finance program; budgeting; bank reconciliation; loan tracking; investment tracking; reports; includes databases to track home repairs, medical records, insurance policies, and more.
23M	★★★	★★★	★★★	Contact manager; customizable database and views; Internet and e-mail support; calendar and to-do list; report generation; project management; contact and calendar sharing; links to popular word processors.
4M	★★	★★★	★★	Resembles Day Runner printed calendar; printed output can be used in most organizers; address book; task list; expense report.
6M	★★★	★★★	★★★	Drag and drop scheduling; contact manager; printed output can be used in most organizers; automatically launches your Web browser or e-mail program; banners for multi-day events.
12M	★★★★	★★★	★★★★	Group scheduling; project management; contact management; integrated data exchange with laptops and popular Personal Digital Assistants; Internet Address Book; supports drag and drop; to-do lists; customizable holidays; alarms.
8M	★★★★	★★★	★★★★	Group scheduling; project management; contact management; Web import; Web page launcher; automatic e-mail addressing; report writer; spell checker; WordPad link; record tagging; Peg Board (tracks each user's possible whereabouts); time clock and userlog.
8M	★★★	★★★	★★★★	Group scheduling; calendar; to-do lists; address book; contact management; call manager; 12-month planner; anniversary reminders; printouts can be used in popular organizers; information can be exported to laptop.

(continues)

Personal Organizer Programs   Continued

Program	Manufacturer	Price	Platforms	System Requirements
Outlook	Microsoft Corp. One Microsoft Way Redmond, WA 98052 (800) 426-9400 (206) 882-8080 **www.microsoft.com**	List price: $109	Windows 95, Windows NT	486 processor, 8M RAM (Win 95), 16M RAM (Win NT)
Sharkware Pro	CogniTech Corp. 500 Sugar Mill Rd. #240-A Atlanta, GA 30350 (800) 947-5075 (770) 518-4577 **www.sharkware.com**	List price: $149.95	Windows 3.1	486DX processor, 8M RAM (16M recommended), VGA monitor
Sidekick Deluxe	Starfish Software 1700 Green Hills Rd. Scotts Valley, CA 95066 (800) 765-7839 (408) 439-0942 **www.starfishsoftware.com**	List price: $49.95 ($39.95 if downloaded from Web site)	Windows 95, Windows NT 4.0	486 processor, 8M RAM (Win 95), 16M RAM (Win NT), double-speed CD-ROM drive

Spreadsheet Programs

Program	Manufacturer	Price	Platforms	System Requirements
Excel	Microsoft Corp. One Microsoft Way Redmond, WA 98052 (800) 426-9400 (206) 882-8080 **www.microsoft.com**	List price: $339 Upgrade price: $109	Windows 95, Windows NT	486 processor, 8M RAM (Win 95), 16M RAM (Win NT)
Lotus 1-2-3	Lotus Development Corp. 55 Cambridge Pkwy. Cambridge, MA 02142 (800) 635-6887 (617) 577- 8500 **www.lotus.com**	List price: $289	Windows 95, Windows NT 4.0	486/50 processor, 8M RAM (Win 95), 16M RAM (Win NT)
Quattro Pro	Corel Corp. 1600 Carling Avenue Ottawa, ON K1Z 8R7 (800) 772-6735 (613) 728-8200 **www.corel.com**	List price: $69.99	Windows 95	486 processor; 8M RAM (16M recommended), double-speed CD-ROM drive

Software Suites

Program	Manufacturer	Price	Platforms	System Requirements
Lotus Smartsuite Professional Edition	Lotus Development Corp. 55 Cambridge Pkwy. Cambridge, MA 02142 (800) 635-6887 (617) 577- 8500 **www.lotus.com**	List price: $349	Windows 95, Windows NT 4.0	486/50 processor, 8M RAM (Win 95), 16M RAM (Win NT)
Microsoft Office Professional	Microsoft Corp. One Microsoft Way Redmond, WA 98052 (800) 426-9400 (206) 882-8080 **www.microsoft.com**	List price: $599 Upgrade price: $349	Windows 95, Windows NT	486 processor, 12M RAM (Win 95), 16M RAM (Win NT)

Hard Disk Usage	Full-Featured	Ease of Use	Popularity	Features
26M–46M	★★★★	★★★	★★★	Group scheduling; shared contact and task lists; to-do lists; calendar; contact manager; journal; Outlook notes; document explorer; full-featured e-mail client; spell checker; printouts can be used in popular organizers.
17M	★★★	★★★	★★	Contact management; activity management; automatic notification of scheduling conflicts; prioritize to-do lists; automatic dialing and call logging; dynamic data exchange with popular word processors; extensive searching and reporting; printouts can be used in popular organizers.
12M	★★★	★★★	★★★	Contact management; schedule group meetings via the Internet; receive reminders via pager; creates and tracks appointments, calls, and to-do lists; Write module for organizing random info; customizable interface; Auto Spell Check; printouts can be used in popular organizers.
22M–64M	★★★★	★★★★	★★★★	Wizards automate routine tasks (charting, functions, etc.); Office Assistant provides intelligent suggestions; formula AutoCorrect; in-cell editing; spell checker; Microsoft Query; pivot tables; Analysis Toolpack; Solver; Scenario Manager; charting; auditor; Web integration; Visual Basic for Applications macro language.
25M	★★★★	★★★	★★★	Asistants automate routine tasks; AutoTotal; InfoBox; Outlining; Lotus Chart; Lotus Assistant; in-cell editing; SmartMaster templates; mapping; links to Approach and Notes; Web integration; macro language.
30M	★★★★	★★★★	★★	Experts automate routine tasks; Interactive Tutors; Data Modeling Desktop; Toolbar Designer; QuickCorrect; PerfectExpert; mapping; QuickFill; scenario manager; charting; spell checker; Web integration; PerfectScript macro language.
75M	★★★★	★★★★	★★	Lotus 1-2-3 spreadsheet; Lotus Word Pro word processor; Lotus Approach database; Lotus Freelance Graphics presentation; Lotus Organizer time management; Lotus ScreenCam multimedia software.
73M–191M	★★★★	★★★★	★★★★	Microsoft Word; Microsoft Excel; Microsoft Access; Microsoft PowerPoint; Microsoft Outlook; Bookshelf Basics.

(continues)

Software Suites   Continued

Program	Manufacturer	Price	Platforms	System Requirements
Microsoft Office Small Business Edition	Microsoft Corp. One Microsoft Way Redmond, WA 98052 (800) 426-9400 (206) 882-8080 **www.microsoft.com**	List price: $499 Upgrade price: $249	Windows 95, Windows NT	486 processor, 8M RAM (Win 95), 16M RAM (Win NT)
WordPerfect Suite	Corel Corp. 1600 Carling Avenue Ottawa, ON K1Z 8R7 (800) 772-6735 (613) 728-8200 **www.corel.com**	List price: $695 Upgrade price: $249	Windows 95, Windows NT 4.0	486 processor, 8M RAM (16M recommended), double-speed CD-ROM drive

Word Processing

Program	Manufacturer	Price	Platforms	System Requirements
Microsoft Word	Microsoft Corp. One Microsoft Way Redmond, WA 98052 (800) 426-9400 (206) 882-8080 **www.microsoft.com**	List price: $339 Upgrade price: $84.95	Windows 95, Windows NT	486 processor, 8M RAM (Win 95), 16M RAM (Win NT)
WordPerfect	Corel Corp. 1600 Carling Avenue Ottawa, ON K1Z 8R7 (800) 772-6735 (613) 728-8200 **www.corel.com**	List price: $449	Windows 95, Windows NT 4.0	486 processor, 8M RAM (16M recommended), double-speed CD-ROM drive
WordPro	Lotus Development Corp. 55 Cambridge Pkwy. Cambridge, MA 02142 (800) 635-6887 (617) 577-8500 **www.lotus.com**	List price: $64.99	Windows 95, Windows 3.1	486 processor, 8M RAM

Hard Disk Usage	Full-Featured	Ease of Use	Popularity	Features
196M–246M	★★★★	★★★★	★★★	Microsoft Word; Microsoft Excel; Microsoft Outlook; Microsoft Publisher; Microsoft Small Business Financial Manager; Automap Streets Plus.
30M–220M	★★★★	★★★★	★★★	Corel WordPerfect; Corel Quattro Pro; Corel Presentations; Envoy;Corel Barista; DAD (Desktop Application Director); QuickTasks; CorelFlow; VisualDTD; IBM VoiceType Control; Corel Screen Saver; Sidekick; Dashboard.
20M–60M	★★★★	★★★★	★★★★	Spell checker; grammar checker; thesaurus; AutoCorrect; AutoText; multiple levels of Undo; Wizards automate routine tasks; Office Assistant automates simple tasks; tables; templates; Word Art; Microsoft Draw; Web integration; create basic HTML documents; Visual Basic for Applications macro language.
30M–220M	★★★★	★★★★	★★★	Spell-As-You-Go spell checker; Grammatik grammar checker; thesaurus; QuickCorrect; QuickFormat; QuickFinder; QuickList; QuickFonts; Web Integration; Corel Barista publishes documents to Java; tables; templates; TextArt; WordPerfect Draw; macro language.
33M	★★★	★★★★	★★	Team features allow multiple authors on the same document; SmartMasters templates; Spell Check; SmartCorrect; Format Check; Grammar Checker; Thesaurus; SmartFill; SmartControls; automatic table formatting; Lotus Assistants.

Hardware Buyer's Guide

Perhaps you've had your computer a while, and you're not quite happy with the performance anymore. When you first bought it, the programs it came with just flew. Now, with the latest and greatest software, your computer seems like a slug. A few of the upgrades described in this section can give your computer a little bit of a face lift.

About the Hardware Categories

Once again, you may be a little intimidated by the vast expanse of hardware available on the market. In this section, I'll take you through five of the most common upgrade items: hard drives, modems, monitors, printers, and video cards.

Hard Drives

A hard drive is the place in your computer where all of the information is stored to run your programs. Because hard drives are relatively inexpensive, software writers are creating programs that are larger and larger. It doesn't take long to fill up a hard drive, so upgrading is a common occurrence. Most computers come with one hard drive and have the room to add at least one more. Check your system documentation for information on adding a new hard drive.

Because IDE hard drives are the most common in home computers, they are the only ones covered in this section. While several sizes are available, only one size is listed in the table. For the most part, if a drive manufacturer produces a good drive in one size, the other sizes offered will be just as good.

Modems

A *modem* (short for modulator/demodulator) is your computer's link to the outside world. It enables you to connect to the Internet and online services such as CompuServe, America Online, and The Microsoft Network via an ordinary phone line. Most modems enable you to send and receive faxes, and some even let you use your computer as an answering machine. At the time of this writing, the standard for modem connections over an ordinary phone line was 33.6 kbps (kilobits per second), so most of the modems reviewed are of that speed. However, at the time of this writing, a standard is being developed for modem speeds as fast as 55.6 kbps. As a general rule, if a particular manufacturer makes a good modem now, they will make a good modem in the future.

Monitors

A monitor is a very important component of your computer. It is your interface to the brains of your computer. I'll review 15- and 17-inch monitors because they are the most popular sizes on the market. You could save a little money and buy a 14-inch monitor, but you may get eyestrain looking at the small print. On the other hand, if you're really ambitious, you can buy a 21-inch monitor, but you'll pay a hefty price for it.

One of the most important aspects of monitor selection is dot pitch (the size of the individual pixels on the screen). The smaller the dot pitch, the better. 0.28mm dot pitch is pretty good, but many monitors now are 0.26 or better. Another aspect to look for is viewable image size. Even though a monitor is labeled as 17-inch, it probably has a viewable image size around 15.7 inches diagonal. Manufacturers label their monitors on the size of the tube, not the size of the image. The Features column will list the viewable image size for the monitors reviewed here.

Printers

The printer takes your hard work and transforms it into printed form. Both laser and inkjet printers are reviewed here. The advantage of a laser printer is very high print quality at a low per page print cost. Unfortunately, if you want color, a laser printer is not for you. While black and white laser printers are very affordable, a color laser printer will cost you thousands of dollars. For color, an inkjet printer is the way to go. You can get good print quality from a modestly priced inkjet printer. The per page cost is higher than a laser printer, but the cost of the printer is usually lower.

Video Cards

The video card is probably one of the most economical upgrades you can get for your computer. Because Windows is a graphical interface, it is often the video card that slows down your system. The video cards today all have a video accelerator chip on board that speeds up the graphical processing of the system. A video card upgrade can often add new life to an old computer.

What's in the Table?

The table in this section is very similar to the one in the software buyer's guide. You will see the following fields:

Hardware   The name of the hardware device.

Manufacturer   The name, address, Internet address, and phone number of the company that manufactures the hardware.

Price   The list price of the program. As with software, you'll rarely have to pay list price for your hardware. Most computer stores should be selling hardware at anywhere from 10% to 30% off the list price.

Performance   Rates the hardware on how well it performs in your system. For modems and video cards, it relates to speed; for monitors and printers it relates to the image quality. I use these ratings:

★★★★ Excellent

★★★ Very good

★★ Adequate

★ Caution when buying

Ease of Use   Rates the hardware on how easy it is to install and use. "Ease of use" also includes any software that is included with the hardware.

Popularity   Rates the hardware on recent sales and the total number of users. As with software, the cream usually rises to the top, so you're pretty safe correlating strong sales with good quality. (The popular stuff is also easier to find.)

Features   A summary of the hardware's main features.

Hard Drives

Hardware	Manufacturer	Price
Fujitsu M1624TAU	Fujitsu Computer Products of America, Inc. 2904 Orchard Pkwy. San Jose, CA 95134 (800) 626-4686 (408) 432-6333 **www.fcpa.com**	List price: $245
IBM DeskStar 3	IBM Corporation Old Orchard Rd. Armonk, NY 10504 (800) 237-5511 (914) 765-1900 **www.pc.ibm.com**	List price: $375
Maxtor DiamonMax 85120A	Maxtor Corp. 211 River Oaks Pkwy. San Jose, CA 95134 (800) 262-9867 (408) 432-1700 **www.maxtor.com**	List price: $500
Quantum Bigfoot CY 6.4	Quantum Corp. 500 McCarthy Blvd. Milpitas, CA 95035 (800) 826-8022 (408) 894-4000 **www.quantum.com**	List price: $499
Seagate Medalist Pro 2520	Seagate Technology, Inc. 920 Disc Dr. Scotts Valley, CA 95067 (408) 438-8222 **www.seagate.com**	List price: $290
Western Digital Caviar 22100	Western Digital Corp. 8105 Irvine Center Dr Irvine, CA 92718 (714) 932-5000 **www.wdc.com**	List price: $250

Modems

Hardware	Manufacturer	Price
Cardinal MVPV34ISP	Cardinal Technologies, Inc. 1827 Freedom Rd. Lancaster, PA 17601 (800) 775-0899 **www.cardtech.com**	List price: $189
Megahertz XJ4336	U.S. Robotics Mobile Communications Corp. P.O. Box 16020 605 N. 5600 W Salt Lake City, UT 84116 (800) 527-8677 **www.usr.com/mobileusr**	List price: $299
Motorola VoiceSURFR	Motorola 50 E. Commerce Drive Schaumburg, IL 60173 (800) 426-6336 **www.mot.com/modems**	List price: $159

Performance	Ease of Use	Popularity	Features
★★★	★★★	★★	2.2G drive; face plate includes LED; installation software included.
★★★	★★★	★★★	3.2G drive; 24-hour technical support; installation software included.
★★★★	★★★	★★★★	5.0G drive; excellent performance for price; installation software included.
★★★	★★★	★★★	6.4G drive; great value for the price; installation software included.
★★★★	★★★★	★★★★	2.4G drive; step-by-step manual makes installation a snap; excellent technical support; installation software included.
★★★★	★★★★	★★★★	2.1G drive; step-by-step manual makes installation a snap; excellent technical support; software included.installation.
★★★	★★★★	★★★	Internal 33.6 kbps; speakerphone; voice mail; MNP-10EC error control; simultaneous Voice and Data; software upgradable; VoiceView; FaxWorks fax software; limited lifetime warranty.
★★★★	★★★★	★★★	PC Card 33.6 kbps; software upgradable; digital line voltage protection; MNP-10EC error control; stores multiple profiles; excellent documentation; 5-year warranty.
★★★	★★★★	★★★★	Internal 33.6 kbps (external available); speakerphone; voice mail; Caller ID; alphanumeric paging; fax on demand; Quicklink data/fax software; 5-year warranty.

(continues)

Modems   Continued

Hardware	Manufacturer	Price
Motorola Montana 33.6	Motorola Mobile Computing Products Division 50 E. Commerce Drive Schaumburg, IL 60173 (800) 427-2624 **www.mot.com/modems**	List price: $225
Practical Peripherals PC336LCD V.34	Practical Peripherals 5854 Peachtree Corners East Norcross, GA 30092 (770) 840-9966 **www.practinet.com**	List price: $299
U.S. Robotics Courier V.Everything/V.34	U.S. Robotics (800) 877-2677 **www.usr.com**	List price: $289
U.S. Robotics Sportster Voice	U.S. Robotics (800) 342-5877 **www.usr.com**	List price: $189
Zoom V.34X Plus	**Zoom Technologies, Inc.** 207 South St. Boston, MA 02111 (800) 631-3116 (617) 423-1072 **www.zoomtel.com**	List price: $129

Monitors: 15-inch

Hardware	Manufacturer	Price
MAG InnoVision DX15T	MAG InnoVision Co. Santa Ana, CA (800) 827-3998 (714) 751-2008 **www.maginnovision.com**	List price: $399
Panasonic PanaMedia PM 15	Panasonic Computer Peripheral Co. Secaucus, NJ (800) 742-8086 (201) 392-4812 **www.panasonic.com**	List price: $399
Samsung SyncMaster 15Gli	Samsung Electronics America Ridgefield Park, NJ (800) 933-4110 (201) 229-4000 **www.sosimple.com**	List price: $429
Sony CPD-100VS	Sony Electronics Inc. San Jose, CA (800) 476-6972 **www.sel.sony.com/sel/ccpg**	List price: $599
ViewSonic 15GS	ViewSonic Corp. Walnut, CA (800) 888-8583 (909) 869-7676 **www.viewsonic.com**	List price: $399

Performance	Ease of Use	Popularity	Features
★★★★	★★★★	★★★★	PC Card 33.6 kbps; software upgradable; digital line voltage protection; Quicklink Mobile fax/data software; 5-year warranty.
★★★★	★★★	★★★	External 28.8 kbps; LCD text display; 50 status messages; multiple profiles; distinctive ring; Quicklink II fax/data software; caller ID; manual volume control; . lifetime warranty.
★★★★	★★★	★★★★	External 33.6 kbps; software upgradable; distinctive ring; Quicklink II fax/data software; callback security; password protection; manual volume control; 5-year warranty.
★★★★	★★★★	★★★★	Internal 33.6 kbps; distinctive ring; multiple profiles; speakerphone; Caller ID; Quicklink Message Center data/fax/voice software plug-and-play; 5-year warranty.
★★★	★★★	★★★	External 33.6 kbps; distinctive ring; MNP-10EC error control; stores multiple profiles; DOS/WinFax Lite fax/data software; 7-year warranty.
★★★	★★★	★★★	13.9-inch viewable area; 0.25mm Trinitron tube; 85 Hz refresh rate; plug-and-play; on-screen menus; 3-year warranty.
★★★★	★★★★	★★★★	14-inch viewable area; 0.27mm dot pitch; 107 Hz refresh rate; plug-and-play; speakers and microphone integrated in monitor; on-screen menus; 3-year warranty.
★★★★	★★★★	★★★	13.8-inch viewable area; 0.28mm dot pitch; 100 Hz refresh rate; INVAR shadow mask; plug-and-play; on-screen menus; 3-year warranty.
★★★★	★★★★	★★★★	13.8-inch viewable area; 0.25mm Trinitron tube; 85 Hz refresh rate; plug-and-play; integrated speakers, sub-woofer, and microphone; 1-year warranty.
★★★	★★★	★★★	13.7-inch viewable area; 0.28mm dot pitch; 108 Hz refresh rate; plug-and-play; on-screen menus; 3-year parts, 1-year labor warranty.

Monitors: 17 inch

Hardware	Manufacturer	Price
Mitsubishi Diamond Pro 87TXM	Mitsubishi Electronics America Cypress, CA (800) 843-2515 **www.mitsubishi-display.com**	List price: $899
NEC MultiSync M700	NEC Technologies Inc. Boxborough, MA (800) 632-4636 **www.nec.com**	List price: $900
Panasonic PanaSync S17	Panasonic Computer Peripheral Co. Secaucus, NJ (800) 742-8086 (201) 392-4812 **www.panasonic.com**	List price: $799
Princeton Graphics Systems Ultra 17+	Princeton Graphics Systems Santa Ana, CA (800) 747-6249 (714) 751-8405 **www.prgr.com**	List price: $629
ViewSonic PT770	ViewSonic Corp. Walnut, CA (800) 888-8583 (909) 869-7676 **www.viewsonic.com**	List price: $895

Printers: Laser

Hardware	Manufacturer	Price
Brother HL-720	Brother International Corp. Somerset, NJ (800) 827-6843 (908) 356-8880 **www.brother.com**	List price: $350
Canon LBP-465	Canon Computer Systems Inc. Costa Mesa, CA (800) 848-4123 (714) 438-3000 **www.ccsi.canon.com**	List price: $379
HP LaserJet 5LXtra	Hewlett-Packard Co. Palo Alto, CA (800) 752-0900 (208) 323-2551 **www.hp.com**	List price: $589
NEC SuperScript 860	NEC Technologies Inc. Mountain View, CA (800) 632-4636 (415) 528-6000 **www.nec.com**	List price: $500
Panasonic KX-P6100	Panasonic Computer Peripheral Co. Secaucus, NJ (800)742-8086 (201) 348-7000 **www.panasonic.com**	List price: $499

Performance	Ease of Use	Popularity	Features
★★★	★★★★	★★★	16.0-inch viewable area; 0.25 Diamondtron tube; 107 Hz refresh rate; plug-and-play; on-screen menus; 3-year warranty.
★★★	★★★★	★★★★	15.6-inch viewable area; 0.25mm CromaClear tube; 86 Hz refresh rate; integrated speakers; plug-and-play; on-screen menus; 3-year warranty.
★★★★	★★★	★★★★	15.7-inch viewable area; 0.27mm dot pitch; 85 Hz refresh rate; plug-and-play; on-screen menus; 3-year warranty.
★★★	★★★	★★	15.8-inch viewable area; 0.28mm dot pitch, 85 Hz refresh rate; plug-and-play; on-screen menus; 3-year warranty.
★★★	★★★★	★★★★	15.9-inch viewable area; 0.25mm SonicTron tube; 107 Hz refresh rate; plug-and-play; on-screen menus; 3-year warranty.
★★★★	★★★★	★★★	600×600 dpi resolution; 6 ppm output; 200 sheet paper tray; plug-and-play.
★★★	★★★	★★★	600×600 dpi resolution; 4 ppm output; supports PCL 4; plug-and-play.
★★★★	★★★★	★★★★	600×600 dpi resolution; 4 ppm output; 100 sheet paper tray; plug-and-play; compact design.
★★★★	★★★★	★★★	600×600 dpi resolution; 8 ppm output; 200 sheet paper tray; plug-and-play.
★★★	★★★★	★★★	1200×300 dpi resolution; 6 ppm output; 100 sheet paper tray; tower design; plug-and-play.

Printers: Ink Jet

Hardware	Manufacturer	Price
Canon BJC-620	Canon Computer Systems Inc. Costa Mesa, CA (800) 848-4123 (714) 438-3000 **www.ccsi.canon.com**	List price: $399
Epson Stylus Color 500	Epson America Inc. Torrance, CA (800) 463-7766 (310) 782-0770 **www.epson.com**	List price: $329
HP DeskJet 820Cse	Hewlett-Packard Co. Palo Alto, CA (800) 752-0900 (208) 323-2551 **www.hp.com**	List price: $486
Lexmark Color Jetprinter 2050	Lexmark International Inc. Lexington, KY (800) 358-5835 (606) 232-2000 **www.lexmark.com**	List price: $299

Video Cards

Hardware	Manufacturer	Price
ATI 3D Xpression+ PC2TV	ATI Technologies Inc. Thornhill, Ontario (905) 882-2600 **www.atitech.com**	List price: $199
Diamond Stealth 3D 3000	Diamond Multimedia Systems San Jose, CA (800) 468-5846 (408) 325-7000 **www.diamondmm.com**	List price: $249.95
Hercules Terminator 3D	Hercules Computer Technology Inc. Fremont, CA (800) 532-0600 (510) 623-6030 **www.hercules.com**	List price: $159
Matrox Mystique	Matrox Graphics Inc. Dorval, Quebec (514) 685-2630 **www.matrox.com**	List price: $259
Orchid Fahrenheit Video 3D	Orchid Technology Fremont, CA (800) 577-0977 (510) 651-0230 **www.orchid.com**	List price: $199
STB Velocity 3D	STB Systems Inc. Richardson, TX (888) 234-8750 **www.stb.com**	List price: $199

Performance	Ease of Use	Popularity	Features
★★★★	★★★★	★★★★	720×720 dpi resolution; 6 ppm output (black-and-white); 2 ppm output (color); 100 sheet paper tray; plug-and-play; separate color cartridges.
★★★★	★★★★	★★★★	720×720 dpi resolution; 4 ppm output (black-and-white); 1 ppm output (color); 100 sheet paper tray; plug-and-play; manual feed tray; 2-year warranty.
★★★	★★★★	★★★★	600×600 dpi resolution; 5 ppm output (black-and-white); 1.5 ppm output (color); 150 sheet paper tray; plug-and-play.
★★★	★★★	★★★	600×600 dpi resolution; four-color; 4 ppm output (black-and-white); .5 ppm (color); 150 sheet paper tray.
★★★	★★★★	★★★★	4M SDRAM; 90 Hz refresh rate and 16.7 million colors at 1280×1024 resolution; 3-D acceleration; ATI Rage II graphics chip; ATI MPEG software included; can be connected to a standard television.
★★★★	★★★★	★★★★	4M VRAM; 75 Hz refresh rate and 16.7 million colors at 1280×1024 resolution; 3-D acceleration; S3 ViRGE-VX graphics chip; Mediamatics MPEG software included.
★★★	★★★★	★★★	2M EDO DRAM; 75 Hz refresh rate and 65,000 colors at 1280×1024 resolution; 3-D acceleration; S3 ViRGE chip; Xing MPEG software included.
★★★★	★★★	★★★★	4M SGRAM; 75 Hz refresh rate and 16.7 million colors at 1280×1024 resolution; 3-D acceleration; MGA-1064SG graphics chip; Compcore MPEG software included; plug-and-play.
★★★	★★★★	★★	2M EDO DRAM; 75 Hz refresh rate and 256 colors at 1280×1024 resolution; 3-D acceleration; S3 ViRGE graphics chip; Xing MPEG software included.
★★★	★★★★	★★★★	4M VRAM; 75Hz refresh rate and 16 million colors at 1280×1024 resolution; 3-D acceleration; S3 ViRGE-VX graphics chip; MPEG software included.

Cool Internet Sites

The Web is becoming a very popular place, and with millions of Web sites, it can be pretty overwhelming. This short list of sites will get you started exploring the World Wide Web.

Site Name	Site Address	Comment
Windows95.com	**http://windows95.com**	Tips, driver updates, free software, and more for the Windows 95 operating system.
Shareware.com	**http://www.shareware.com**	A comprehensive site containing links to thousands of shareware programs.
CNN Interactive	**http://www.cnn.com**	Find out what's in the news at CNN's Web site.
The Microsoft Network	**http://www.msn.com**	The Microsoft Network home page contains links to news, reviews, entertainment, and more.
ZD Net	**http://www.zdnet.com**	Ziff-Davis Web site. Includes links to popular online computer magazines.
ESPNet SportZone	**http://espnet.sportzone.com**	Find out the latest scores on ESPN's Web site.
The Weather Channel	**http://www.weather.com**	Check the weather from this page.
USA Today	**http://www.usatoday.com**	See the popular stories from the printed version.
Edmund's Automobile Buyer's Guides	**http://www.edmunds.com**	Get new and used car buying advice including new car pricing.
Microsoft Expedia	**http://www.expedia.msn.com**	Plan your next vacation with Microsoft's travel planning site.
Microsoft Investor	**http://www.investor.msn.com**	Keep track of your portfolio, and get company information and stock quotes with Microsoft Investor.
American Medical Association	**http://www.ama-assn.org**	Search through the Journal of the American Medical Association; keyword search of diseases.
MapQuest	**http://mapquest.com**	Provides maps of cities and countries. Street finder allows you to search for an address.
NASA	**http://www.nasa.gov**	Hundreds of pictures from space, shuttle launch schedules, and more.

Site Name	Site Address	Comment
Museum of Modern Art	**http://www.moma.org**	See paintings, drawings, and sculptures without leaving your den.
CNet	**http://www.cnet.com**	Excellent source of computer information; contains a wealth of product reviews.
Sandy Bay Software's PC Webopaedia	**http://sandybay.com/pc-web/ index.html**	Search the site to find the definitions of obscure computer terms.
Stroud's CWS Apps List	**www.stroud.com**	Stroud's Consummate Winsock Apps List contains up-to-date information on the hottest utilities and Internet tools.
Happy Puppy Game Site	**http://happypuppy.com**	Complete gaming site.
Kids' World	**http://www.kidsworld.com**	Great site for kids.
Internet Movie Database	**http://imdb.com**	Contains information on movies, actors, crew members, and more.
Microsoft Search Page	**http://home.microsoft.com/ access/allinone.asp**	Allows you to use popular Internet search engines to search the Web.

Index

MACMILLAN COMPUTER PUBLISHING USA

A VIACOM COMPANY

Technical Support:

If you need assistance with the information in this book or with a CD/Disk accompanying the book, please access the Knowledge Base on our Web site at **http://www.superlibrary.com/general/support**. Our most Frequently Asked Questions are answered there. If you do not find the answer to your questions on our Web site, you may contact Macmillan Technical Support **(317) 581-3833** or e-mail us at **support@mcp.com**.

Check out Que® Books on the World Wide Web
http://www.mcp.com/que

As the biggest software release in computer history, Windows 95 continues to redefine the computer industry. Click here for the latest info on our Windows 95 books

Make computing quick and easy with these products designed exclusively for new and casual users

Examine the latest releases in word processing, spreadsheets, operating systems, and suites

The Internet, The World Wide Web, CompuServe®, America Online®, Prodigy®—it's a world of ever-changing information. Don't get left behind!

Find out about new additions to our site, new bestsellers and hot topics

In-depth information on high-end topics: find the best reference books for databases, programming, networking, and client/server technologies

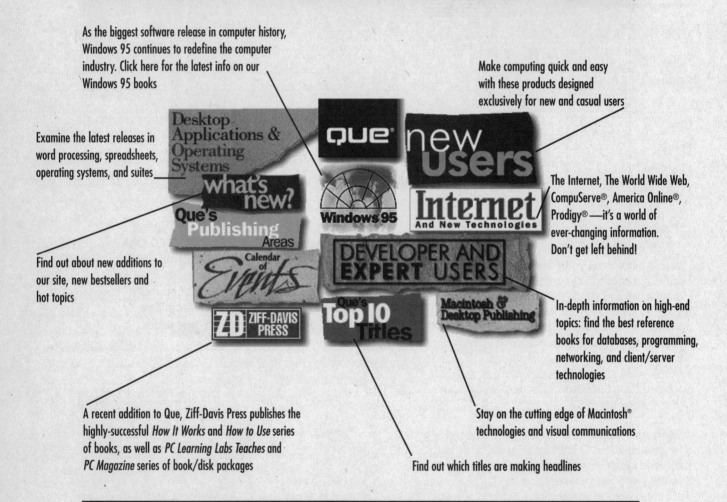

A recent addition to Que, Ziff-Davis Press publishes the highly-successful *How It Works* and *How to Use* series of books, as well as *PC Learning Labs Teaches* and *PC Magazine* series of book/disk packages

Stay on the cutting edge of Macintosh® technologies and visual communications

Find out which titles are making headlines

With 6 separate publishing groups, Que develops products for many specific market segments and areas of computer technology. Explore our Web Site and you'll find information on best-selling titles, newly published titles, upcoming products, authors, and much more.

- Stay informed on the latest industry trends and products available

- Visit our online bookstore for the latest information and editions

- Download software from Que's library of the best shareware and freeware

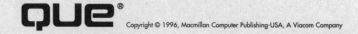

Copyright © 1996, Macmillan Computer Publishing-USA, A Viacom Company

7. Which of the following best describes your job title?

Administrative Assistant .... ☐
Coordinator .... ☐
Manager/Supervisor .... ☐
Director .... ☐
Vice President .... ☐
President/CEO/COO .... ☐
Lawyer/Doctor/Medical Professional .... ☐
Teacher/Educator/Trainer .... ☐
Engineer/Technician .... ☐
Consultant .... ☐
Not employed/Student/Retired .... ☐
Other (Please specify): _____ ☐

8. Which of the following best describes the area of the company your job title falls under?

Accounting .... ☐
Engineering .... ☐
Manufacturing .... ☐
Operations .... ☐
Marketing .... ☐
Sales .... ☐
Other (Please specify): _____ ☐

9. What is your age?

Under 20 .... ☐
21-29 .... ☐
30-39 .... ☐
40-49 .... ☐
50-59 .... ☐
60-over .... ☐

10. Are you:

Male .... ☐
Female .... ☐

11. Which computer publications do you read regularly? (Please list)

_____
_____
_____
_____
_____
_____
_____
_____
_____
_____

Comments: _____
_____
_____

Fold here and scotch-tape to mail.

NO POSTAGE
NECESSARY
IF MAILED
IN THE
UNITED STATES

BUSINESS REPLY MAIL
FIRST-CLASS MAIL PERMIT NO. 9918 INDIANAPOLIS IN

POSTAGE WILL BE PAID BY THE ADDRESSEE

ATTN MARKETING
MACMILLAN COMPUTER PUBLISHING
MACMILLAN PUBLISHING USA
201 W 103RD ST
INDIANAPOLIS IN 46290-9042

Complete and Return this Card
for a *FREE* Computer Book Catalog

Thank you for purchasing this book! You have purchased a superior computer book written expressly for your needs. To continue to provide the kind of up-to-date, pertinent coverage you've come to expect from us, we need to hear from you. Please take a minute to complete and return this self-addressed, postage-paid form. In return, we'll send you a free catalog of all our computer books on topics ranging from word processing to programming and the internet.

Mr. ☐   Mrs. ☐   Ms. ☐   Dr. ☐

Name (first) ☐☐☐☐☐☐☐☐☐☐☐☐   (M.I.) ☐   (last) ☐☐☐☐☐☐☐☐☐☐☐☐☐☐☐

Address ☐☐☐☐☐☐☐☐☐☐☐☐☐☐☐☐☐☐☐☐☐☐☐☐☐☐☐☐☐

☐☐☐☐☐☐☐☐☐☐☐☐☐☐☐☐☐☐☐☐☐☐☐☐☐☐☐☐☐

City ☐☐☐☐☐☐☐☐☐☐☐☐☐☐☐   State ☐☐   Zip ☐☐☐☐☐ ☐☐☐☐

Phone ☐☐☐ ☐☐☐ ☐☐☐☐   Fax ☐☐☐ ☐☐☐ ☐☐☐☐

Company Name ☐☐☐☐☐☐☐☐☐☐☐☐☐☐☐☐☐☐☐☐☐☐☐☐☐☐

E-mail address ☐☐☐☐☐☐☐☐☐☐☐☐☐☐☐☐☐☐☐☐☐☐☐☐☐☐

1. Please check at least (3) influencing factors for purchasing this book.

Front or back cover information on book .... ☐
Special approach to the content .... ☐
Completeness of content .... ☐
Author's reputation .... ☐
Publisher's reputation .... ☐
Book cover design or layout .... ☐
Index or table of contents of book .... ☐
Price of book .... ☐
Special effects, graphics, illustrations .... ☐
Other (Please specify): _____ ☐

2. How did you first learn about this book?

Saw in Macmillan Computer Publishing catalog .... ☐
Recommended by store personnel .... ☐
Saw the book on bookshelf at store .... ☐
Recommended by a friend .... ☐
Received advertisement in the mail .... ☐
Saw an advertisement in: _____ ☐
Read book review in: _____ ☐
Other (Please specify): _____ ☐

3. How many computer books have you purchased in the last six months?

This book only .... ☐   3 to 5 books .... ☐
2 books .... ☐   More than 5 .... ☐

4. Where did you purchase this book?

Bookstore .... ☐
Computer Store .... ☐
Consumer Electronics Store .... ☐
Department Store .... ☐
Office Club .... ☐
Warehouse Club .... ☐
Mail Order .... ☐
Direct from Publisher .... ☐
Internet site .... ☐
Other (Please specify): _____ ☐

5. How long have you been using a computer?

☐ Less than 6 months   ☐ 6 months to a year
☐ 1 to 3 years   ☐ More than 3 years

6. What is your level of experience with personal computers and with the subject of this book?

	With PCs	With subject of book
New	☐	☐
Casual	☐	☐
Accomplished	☐	☐
Expert	☐	☐

Source Code ISBN: 0-7897-1339-x